In Appreciation

Dining With Pioneers has been made possible by the efforts of a group of dedicated individuals who, in the true spirit of pioneering, felt the challenge and, with a little encouragement, took on the task of compiling this book. We are especially grateful to the many employees, both active and retired, who have shared their recipes with us.

Frank Biles

**Chairman - Chapter Fund
Raising Committee**

Dedication

This book is dedicated to Tennessee Life Members who are continually giving of themselves in this and many other worthwhile efforts. Their dedication to the principles of Pioneering - service, loyalty, and fellowship provide inspiration to all other Pioneers and employees on a continuing basis. By their example they provide a path for all others to follow leading to happy and satisfied lives with the added benefit of a great sense of accomplishment.

It would perhaps be appropriate to provide in this medium a recipe for a typical Life Member:

> To one retired employee, add a measure of wisdom, aged with experience. Blend in a full portion of loyalty to their business, an overflowing cup of love and a large measure of willingness to help others. Add a pinch of a smile. Combine this mixture over the warmth of leadership and a life member meeting. Use caution when heating as this mixture multiplies itself and serves untold numbers of others.

R. J. Sharp
President

D

Cookbook Committee

Editors

Publisher
Compilation
Fund Raising Chairman

Peggy Hunter
Barbara Stanfill
Jane York
Judy Gibson
Frank Giles

Judy Arnold
Barbara Ball
Marie Barnett
Judy Christopher
Bessie S. Crosby
Cheryl Enoch
Denise Gill
Barbara Harris

Marcia Jackson
Mary Lynn Johnson
Susan Joyner
Joyce Mattice
Marian Molteni
Tricia Owens
Kathy Pack
Bob Unkenholz

Artists

Liz Coleman
Virginia Kaderabek
Dinah Randolph

Sharon Rawlings
Janet Sexton
Leslie Stephens

Table Of Contents

APPETIZERS & BEVERAGES

QUANTITIES TO SERVE 100

Baked beans . . . . 5 gallons
Beef . . . . 40 pounds
Beets . . . . 30 pounds
Bread . . . . 10 loaves
Butter . . . . 3 pounds
Cabbage for slaw . . . . 20 pounds
Cakes . . . . 8 cakes
Carrots . . . . 33 pounds
Cauliflower . . . . 18 pounds
Cheese . . . . 18 pounds
Chicken for chicken pie . . . . 40 pounds
Coffee . . . . 3 pounds
Cream . . . . 3 quarts
Fruit cocktail . . . . 1 gallon
Fruit juice . . . . .4 (No. 10) cans
Fruit salad . . . . 20 quarts
Ground beef . . . . 30 to 36 pounds
Ham . . . . 40 pounds
Ice Cream . . . . 4 gallons
Lettuce . . . . 20 heads
Meat loaf . . . . 24 pounds
Milk . . . . 6 gallons
Nuts . . . . 3 pounds
Olives . . . . 1³/₄ pounds
Oysters . . . . 18 quarts
Pickles . . . . 2 quarts
Pies . . . . 18 pies
Potatoes . . . . 35 pounds
Roast pork . . . . 40 pounds
Rolls . . . . 200 rolls
Salad dressing . . . . 3 quarts
Scalloped potatoes . . . . 5 gallons
Soup . . . . 5 gallons
Sugar cubes . . . . 3 pounds
Tomato juice . . . . .4 (No. 10) cans
Vegetables . . . . .4 (No. 20) cans
Vegetable salad . . . . 20 quarts
Whipping cream . . . . 4 pints
Wieners . . . . 25 pounds

ASTRO-PIZZA SANDWICH

12 slices sandwich bread
1/2 c. pizza sauce
1/2 tsp. oregano
36 slices pepperoni

1 c. shredded Mozzarella
  cheese
Soft butter or margarine

Spread slices of bread on one side with pizza sauce. Sprinkle 6 of the slices with oregano; top each with 6 slices of pepperoni and sprinkle with cheese. Place remaining 6 slices of bread on top to form sandwich and spread outside slices of bread with butter. Broil 4 to 5 inches from flame until bread is browned. Turn and brown other side. Cheese should melt as sandwich toasts. Cut each into 4 squares. Serve hot. Makes 6 sandwiches.

Evelyn B. Bean
Harpeth Council

BACON AND CHESTNUT HORS D'OEUVRES

Mix:

2 Tbsp. brown sugar
2 Tbsp. catsup

2 Tbsp. butter, melted
4 Tbsp. bourbon

Roll bacon (1/2 strip) around chestnuts. If chestnut is large, cut in half. Hold together with a toothpick. Cook on a grill until all grease has dripped out. Put in a shallow pan and add sauce; heat well. Bacon should be crisp and sauce cooked enough to dip well. I use water chestnuts from Taiwan.

Peggy Burr
Harpeth Council

"BEA'S" BIG ORANGE SANDWICH

Spread both slices of rye bread with horseradish. Add lettuce leaf, 1 slice of salami, 1 slice ham, 1 slice Swiss cheese, tomato and onion. Serve with pickle and your favorite beverage. A good tailgate sandwich.

Bernice Curtis
Knoxville Council

ZESTY BEEF DIP

1 lb. ground beef	1/4 tsp. oregano
1 clove garlic	1 (8 oz.) can tomato sauce
1 medium onion	1 (8 oz.) pkg. cream cheese
1 tsp. sugar	1/4 c. Parmesan cheese

Brown ground beef. Add garlic and onion; cook till tender. Drain; add sugar and tomato sauce and cook, covered, for 15 minutes. Add cream cheese and Parmesan cheese, stirring until cheese is melted. Serve warm.

Reba Gray
Harpeth Council

BEER WIENERS

Large can of beer	1 1/2 lb. wieners
1/2 jar Tabasco sauce	

Slice wieners in serving size pieces. Mix beer and Tabasco sauce; pour over wieners. Boil until wieners are dry. Serve on toothpicks.

Mary Crabtree
Knoxville Council

CAVIAR SUPREME

1 pkg. unflavored gelatin	1/4 c. cold water

Egg Layer:

4 hard cooked eggs, chopped	1 large green onion, minced
1/2 c. mayonnaise	3/4 tsp. salt
1/4 c. parsley leaves, minced	Dash of hot pepper sauce
	Freshly ground white pepper

Avocado Layer:

1 medium (9 oz.) avocado, pureed just before adding	2 Tbsp. fresh lemon juice
1 medium (9 oz.) avocado, diced just before adding	2 Tbsp. mayonnaise
1 large shallot, minced	1/2 tsp. salt
	Dash of hot pepper sauce
	Freshly ground black pepper

Sour Cream and Onion Layer:

1 c. sour cream
1/4 c. minced onion
Fresh lemon juice

1 (3 1/2 or 4 oz.) jar black
   or red caviar
Thin sliced pumpernickel
   bread

Line bottom of 1 quart souffle dish with foil, extending 4 inches beyond rim of dish on 2 sides; oil lightly. Soften gelatin in cold water in measuring cup. Liquefy gelatin by setting cup in pan of hot water or in microwave oven for about 20 seconds at lowest setting. This gelatin will be divided among the 3 layers.

Egg Layer: Combine all ingredients with 1 tablespoon of gelatin. Taste and adjust seasoning. Neatly spread egg mixture into prepared dish with spatula, smoothing top. Wipe any egg mixture from foil with paper towel.

Avocado Layer: Combine all ingredients with 1 tablespoon dissolved gelatin. Taste and adjust seasoning. Gently spread mixture evenly over egg.

Sour Cream and Onion Layer: Mix sour cream, onion and remaining 2 tablespoons gelatin. Spread carefully over avocado layer. Cover dish tightly with plastic wrap and refrigerate overnight.

Just before serving, place caviar in fine sieve and rinse gently under cold water. Sprinkle with lemon juice; drain. Lift mold out of dish, using foil extensions as "handles". Transfer mold to serving dish using wide spatula. Spread caviar on the top. Serve with thin sliced pumpernickel bread.

Sherree Weisenberger
Harpeth Council

CHAMPION SANDWICH

6 hard cooked eggs,
   chopped
1/4 c. chopped celery
1/4 c. chopped stuffed
   green olives
Salad dressing or
   mayonnaise

Salt and pepper
16 rye bread slices
8 boiled or baked ham slices
8 Swiss cheese slices, cut in
   halves
Lettuce

Combine eggs, celery, olives and enough salad dressing to moisten; mix lightly. Season to taste. For each sandwich, spread 2 bread slices with salad dressing.

1489-81

Fill with egg salad, meat, cheese and lettuce. Cut diagonally in half. Fantastic for Sunday night supper.

Doris Binkley
Nashboro Council

BEEF CHEESE ROLL

3 (8 oz.) pkg. softened
  cream cheese
4 or 5 green onions,
  chopped

2 (2 1/2 oz.) jars Armour
  dried beef
1 Tbsp. Accent
2 Tbsp. Worcestershire sauce

Mix together; shape into 2 rolls. Sprinkle with paprika; chill. Serve with Wheat Thins.

Ann R. Wooten, Jewell Hall
Memphis Downtown Council

CHEESE BALLS

2 c. grated extra sharp
  or sharp cheese
2 c. self-rising flour

2 c. Rice Krispies
Pinch of garlic
Pinch of red pepper

Mix above ingredients. Melt 1 3/4 sticks margarine. Pour over and mix well. Roll in small balls about the size of walnuts. Bake at 350° for about 15 minutes. Do not over-brown. Can be frozen.

Sivalene Rouse
Morristown Council #12

CHEESE BALL

1 lb. Velveeta cheese
1 lb. sharp Cheddar
  cheese, grated
1 small pkg. Roquefort or
  Blue cheese, grated

2 large pkg. cream cheese
1/2 c. nuts
1 medium onion, minced
1 tsp. horseradish
1 tsp. Worcestershire sauce

Cream all cheeses together (may have to mix with hands). Add a few nuts and onion; mix well. Keep adding a few at a time (save some to roll in). Add horseradish and sauce; mix all well. Roll into ball and put in refrigerator.

6

When firm, roll in remainder of nuts. This makes 2 large balls or 5 "softball" sizes.

Mrs. Jim (Fern) Williams
Green Hills Council

CHEESE BALL

2 (8 oz.) pkg. cream cheese

1 (8 oz.) pkg. Cheddar
    cheese (any age)

When at room temperature, grate and mix together. Add and mix in:

1 tsp. lemon juice

2 Tbsp. chopped onion
1 Tbsp. Worcestershire sauce

Roll in ball and sprinkle crushed pecans all over. Let set overnight for flavor to blend and chill in refrigerator. Set out before serving, so it will spread. This will freeze also.

Johnnie Foster
Harpeth Council

CHEESE BALL

2 (8 oz.) pkg. cream
    cheese, softened
1 (8 1/2 oz.) can crushed
    pineapple, drained

1 c. pecans, chopped fine
1/2 c. green pepper,
    chopped fine
2 Tbsp. grated onion
1 Tbsp. seasoning salt

Save at least 1/2 cup pecans to roll ball in. Mix all ingredients together and chill slightly. Shape into ball and roll in chopped pecans.

Mary Cate
Knoxville Council

CHEESE BALL

2 (8 oz.) pkg. cream cheese
1 small can crushed pine-
    apple, drained

1/4 c. green pepper,
    chopped
2 tsp. minced onion

1489-81

7

1 tsp. seasoning salt   1 c. pecans, cut in small
                                        pieces

Mix above ingredients and roll in pecans.

Mary Brown
Harpeth Council

CHEESE BALL

2 (8 oz.) pkg. cream cheese   1 c. grated mild Cheddar
1/2 sq. Bleu cheese   cheese
1 small onion, grated   1 Tbsp. Worcestershire sauce

Combine cheeses, onion and flavoring. Roll in chopped walnuts.

Mary Brown
Harpeth Council

CHEESE BALL

1 1/4 lb. Philadelphia   Dash of paprika
  cream cheese   Sprinkle of garlic salt
1 lb. Old English cheese   1 c. pecans
1 small onion, chopped fine   1 c. parsley, chopped
1 tsp. Worcestershire sauce

Let soften, then mix with mixer and roll in 1/2 of parsley and pecans. Chill and make ball.

Claudia Davenport
Clarksville Council

CHEESE BALL

2 (8 oz.) pkg. cream cheese   2 tsp. Worcestershire sauce
1 (8 oz.) pkg. mild   1 tsp. lemon juice
  Cheddar cheese   1 dash of red pepper
1 Tbsp. chopped pimento   1 dash of salt
1 Tbsp. chopped onion   Garlic if you like

Mix and shape. Cover with pecans or parsley.

Carol McKinnon
Harpeth Council

BEVERLY'S CHEESE BALL

2 (8 oz.) pkg. cream cheese
1 (8 oz.) pkg. Kraft's Old
  English cheese
1 Tbsp. pimento, chopped
1 Tbsp. onion, chopped

1 Tbsp. green pepper,
  chopped
2 Tbsp. Worcestershire sauce
1 Tbsp. lemon juice
Garlic salt to taste

Grate Old English cheese and mix into cream cheese along with rest of ingredients. Form into ball and chill. Roll in chopped pecans.

Beverly Jones
Andrew Jackson Council

BLUE CHEESE BALL

8 oz. cream cheese, softened
4 oz. Blue cheese, softened

1 Tbsp. Worcestershire sauce
2 Tbsp. mayonnaise
2 tsp. garlic powder

Shape into ball and roll in nuts, chives or parsley. Chill well overnight.

Evelyn Carrico
Nashboro Council

CHARLIE'S CHEESE BALL

1 lb. sharp Cheddar cheese
1 (8 oz.) pkg. cream cheese
6 oz. garlic cheese roll
1 Tbsp. mayonnaise
1 Tbsp. sweet milk

1 tsp. lemon juice
Small grated onion (or to
  please taste)
2 or 3 dashes of
  Worcestershire sauce

Mix all ingredients together and roll into a ball or 2 long rolls (or more), then roll into chopped pecans. Can be frozen.

Anita Vardell
Green Hills Council

EMILY'S CHEESE BALL

1 (8 oz.) pkg. cream cheese
1 (3 oz.) pkg. sliced,
  chopped pressed, cooked
  corned beef, smoked beef
  or ham

1 small onion, chopped
1 Tbsp. Worcestershire sauce
Dash of garlic salt or powder

    Let cream cheese soften. Chop meat up fine; mix with chopped onion, Worcestershire sauce and garlic. Garnish with chopped nuts, parsley or olives. Bell pepper can be added, if desired.

Emily Townes
Harpeth Council

GARLIC CHEESE BALL

1/2 lb. Swiss cheese, grated
1/2 lb. creamed cheese
1 lb. Velveeta cheese

1 small clove crushed garlic
Nuts

    Bring cheese to room temperature and cream. Add garlic and nuts; mix well. Roll into logs on waxed paper. Sprinkle cheese with paprika. Chill.

Peggy Hunter
Harpeth Council

GOURMET CHEESE BALL

2 (8 oz.) pkg. cream cheese
1 (8 oz.) pkg. Cracker
  Barrel sharp cheese,
  shredded
1 Tbsp. chopped pimentos
1 tsp. finely chopped onion

1 Tbsp. chopped green
  pepper
1 tsp. lemon juice
2 tsp. Worcestershire sauce
Dash of cayenne pepper or
  Tabasco sauce
Dash of salt

    Cream the cream cheese until smooth. Add shredded cheese; mix well. Add other ingredients and stir well. Shape into ball and chill at least 24 hours. If eaten immediately, roll in chopped pecans. Makes 1 1/2 pounds.

M. Carolyn Hunter
Harpeth Council

HAM CHEESE BALL

1 small can Tender Chunk
  ham (by Hormel)
2 (8 oz.) pkg. cream cheese

2/3 c. finely chopped olives,
  without pimento
Dash or two of onion powder
1 tsp. prepared mustard

Combine all ingredients with softened cheese. Shape into ball or mold in small jello mold. Decorate with pimentos and olives, if desired. Chill well; can be kept for 2 or 3 days.

Betty Birdwell
Harpeth Council

HOT DOG CHEESE BALL

1 Tbsp. season salt
2 Tbsp. chopped onion
2 pkg. (6 oz.) cream cheese

1/4 c. bell peppers, chopped
2 c. chopped pecans
1 c. hot dogs, chopped fine

Mix all ingredients together, except 1 cup of pecans. After all ingredients are mixed well, roll into a ball and roll in remaining cup of pecans. Chill in refrigerator for 8 hours and serve.

Ann Gaines
Knoxville Council

PARTY CHEESE BALL

2 (8 oz.) pkg. Philadelphia
  brand cream cheese
2 c. (8 oz.) shredded
  Cracker Barrel sharp
  Cheddar cheese
1 Tbsp. chopped pimiento
2 tsp. Worcestershire sauce

1 Tbsp. chopped green
  pepper
1 Tbsp. finely chopped onion
1 tsp. lemon juice
Dash of cayenne pepper
Dash of salt
Finely chopped pecans

Combine softened cream cheese and Cheddar cheese, mixing until well blended. Add pimiento, green pepper, onion, Worcestershire sauce, lemon juice and seasonings; mix well. Chill; shape into ball. Roll in nuts. Serve with crackers. During the party season, leftover cheese ball can be reshaped and refrigerated until the next event.

David Lewis
Clarksville Council

1489-81

"PARTY CHEESE BALL"

1 (8 oz.) pkg. cream cheese
1 (10 oz.) cold pack sharp
  Cheddar cheese
1 (4 oz.) jar bacon flavor
  cheese spread
2 (4 oz.) jars Olde English
  cheese
1 medium onion, chopped
1 (4 oz.) jar pimento cheese
  spread
1 (4 oz.) jar garlic cheese
  spread
1 (4 oz.) pkg. French onion
  dip
1 tsp. garlic, minced
2 Tbsp. Worcestershire sauce

Allow cheeses to soften at room temperature. Mix all ingredients together and form into ball. Roll in chopped pecans or parsley.

Lisa Hearon
Knoxville Council

PINEAPPLE CHEESE BALL

2 (8 oz.) pkg. Philadelphia
  cream cheese, softened
1 small can Dole crushed
  pineapple, drained
2 (1/4 c.) pkg. pecan pieces
1 Tbsp. green pepper
1 tsp. onion
1 tsp. seasoned salt

Combine all of the above with just 1 package of nuts, then roll all of this in the other package of nuts. Best served with Ritz crackers.

June Smithson
Harpeth Council

PINEAPPLE CHEESE BALL

2 (8 oz.) pkg. cream
  cheese, softened
1 (8 1/2 oz.) can crushed
  pineapple, drained
2 c. chopped pecans
1/4 c. finely chopped green
  pepper
2 Tbsp. finely chopped onion
1 Tbsp. seasoned salt

Beat cream cheese with fork until smooth. Gradually stir in pineapple, 1 cup pecans, the green pepper, onion and salt; chill. Shape into ball; roll in remaining nuts. Refrigerate until well chilled. Garnish with pineapple slices, cherries and parsley. Makes about 40 appetizer servings.

Sheila Fleming
East Memphis Council

DEVILED CHEESE BITES

2 (3 oz.) pkg. cream cheese, softened
1 (4 oz.) pkg. Blue cheese, crumbled
2 (2 1/4 oz.) cans deviled ham
1/2 c. chopped pecans
Onion juice to taste
1/2 - 1 c. finely chopped parsley
1/2 c. commercial sour cream
Garlic salt to taste
Thin pretzel sticks

Combine cream cheese and Blue cheese; blend until smooth. Stir in deviled ham, pecans and onion juice; chill. Shape into balls the size of walnuts; roll them in parsley. Chill until serving time. Combine sour cream and garlic salt; chill. Serve as a dip and use pretzel sticks to spear cheese balls. Makes about 40 appetizers.

Judy Christopher
Harpeth Council

CHEESE KRISPIES

2 sticks oleo, softened
2 c. sharp cheese, grated
2 c. plain flour
2 c. Rice Krispies

Blend cheese into softened oleo; work in flour. Add Rice Krispies; roll into small balls and flatten with fork. Bake at 350° for 10 to 13 minutes on ungreased sheet. Yield: 10 to 12 dozen.

Ann R. Wooten
Memphis Downtown Council

CHEESE NACHOS

1 can bean dip
1 pkg. taco chips
Grated Cheddar cheese

Spread small amount of dip on each taco chip; place on paper plate. Sprinkle with grated cheese. Cook in microwave oven for 35 seconds or until cheese has melted.

Pat Ferguson
Harpeth Council

CHEESE PENNIES

1/3 c. butter
2 c. shredded Cheddar
   cheese

1 c. flour
3 Tbsp. dry onion soup mix

Combine butter and cheese. Add flour and soup mix; blend until dough forms. Divide in half and shape into 2 long rolls, about 1 1/2 inches in diameter. Wrap in waxed paper; chill until firm, about 1 hour. Cut in rounds, 1/4 inch thick. Bake on ungreased baking sheet at 400° for 8 to 10 minutes. Yield: 5 dozen.

Vickie Jones
Harpeth Council

CHEESE PUFFS

1 c. sifted self-rising flour
1 Tbsp. shortening

1/4 c. pimento cheese spread
1/2 c. milk

Cut shortening and cheese spread into flour until mixture is crumbly. Add milk; mix until a soft dough is formed. Drop by spoonfuls on tuna mixture. Bake about 25 minutes. Makes 6 generous servings.

Note: If using plain flour, add 1/4 teaspoon salt to flour.

Vickie Jones
Harpeth Council

CHEESE ROLL

1/2 lb. Roquefort cheese
2 pkg. Philadelphia cream
   cheese
1 small grated onion

1/2 c. olives, chopped and
   drained
2 pkg. Old English cheese
1 tsp. mustard
Tabasco sauce

Mix until smooth; chill overnight. Form into roll; chill again. Roll in ground nuts before serving.

Carolyn Mitchell
Memphis Downtown Council

CHEESE STRAWS

1 lb. New York sharp cheese	3 c. flour
1/2 lb. butter	Few drops of hot pepper sauce

Grate cheese and add to softened butter. Add pepper sauce; mix with electric mixer. Add flour gradually. Roll or press into shape and bake at 325° for 10-12 minutes. Add salt and paprika after removing from oven.

Louise Breeden
Nashboro Council

CHEESE WAFERS

1 stick butter, soft	1 c. Rice Krispies
1 c. sharp Cheddar cheese (or 1 pkg.)	Nutmeg to taste Tabasco sauce to taste
1 c. flour	

Blend butter and Cheddar cheese. Add to remaining ingredients and mix by hand. Put on cookie sheet by teaspoonfuls. Bake at 350° for 10 to 12 minutes.

Eugenia W. Smith
Chattanooga Council

CHINESE CHEESE WAFERS

2 c. unsifted flour	2 c. Rice Krispies cereal
2 c. grated sharp Cheddar cheese	1/4 tsp. salt
2 sticks margarine or butter, softened	1/4 tsp. red pepper 1/4 tsp. garlic powder

Mix all ingredients together by hand to form large ball of dough. Pinch off walnut sized pieces; roll into balls and place on greased cookie sheet. Press each ball with thumb to form wafers. Bake at 350° for 15-20 minutes.

Leslie Stephens
Harpeth Council

CHEESE AND SAUSAGE BALLS

8 oz. Cheddar cheese, 1 lb. sausage
  grated 3 c. Bisquick

Work together with hands. Roll into medium size balls and bake 20 minutes at 400°, until done.

Pat Carpenter
Nashville Council

CRABMEAT SLICES

1 (6 1/2 - 8 oz.) can 2 Tbsp. mayonnaise
  crabmeat (Hellmann's)
1 (5 oz.) jar Kraft sharp 1/2 stick butter (real)
  cheese 1/4 tsp. garlic powder
  5 English muffins, halved

Mix ingredients and spread on muffins; partially freeze. Cut each into 8 sections (pie shaped); freeze. To serve: Thaw slightly; toast under the broiler for 5 minutes.

M. Carolyn Hunter
Harpeth Council

HAM BALL

2 small cans deviled ham 1 Tbsp. mustard
3 Tbsp. chopped olives 4 or 5 drops Tabasco sauce

Mix together and mound; refrigerate. Spread 1 small package softened cream cheese plus 2 teaspoons of milk on ham ball. Sprinkle with paprika and parsley.

Peggy Burr
Harpeth Council

HAM AND CHEESE CHIP PINWHEELS

3 oz. pkg. cream cheese 1/3 c. chopped stuffed olives
2 Tbsp. mayonnaise 2/3 c. finely crushed potato
1 tsp. grated onion chips
2 tsp. horseradish 6 thin slices boiled ham

Combine and blend all ingredients, except ham. Spread

mixture on ham slices. Roll each edge lengthwise and fasten with toothpicks; chill. Cut rolled ham crosswise into thin slices.

Rosemary Catalani
Harpeth Council

NAOMI'S HAM CANAPES

6 slices boiled ham	1/2 tsp. lemon juice
1 large pkg. cream cheese	1 tsp. onion juice
1 small pkg. cream cheese	1 tsp. sugar
1 (4 oz.) pkg. Blue cheese	4 Tbsp. mayonnaise

Mix cheeses; add lemon, onion, sugar and mayonnaise. Put equal amounts on one end of ham. Roll up ham slice and wrap in aluminum foil; freeze. Remove 30 minutes before serving from freezer. Slice.

Judy Christopher
Harpeth Council

ITALIAN EGG BALLS

4 eggs, beaten	1 tsp. parsley flakes
3/4 c. white bread crumbs	1 tsp. salt
3/4 c. grated Parmesan	1/5 tsp. pepper
cheese	Vegetable oil for frying

Combine all ingredients, except oil; mix until smooth. Heat oil in fry pan until hot. Drop mixture by tablespoonfuls into oil and brown on both sides. Drain on paper towels. Yields 18 balls.

Peggy Burr
Harpeth Council

JALAPENO QUICHE

1 can jalapeno peppers	2 c. Cheddar cheese,
1 lb. bacon	shredded
	12 eggs

Fry bacon until crisp and crumble. Spray a 9x11 inch casserole dish with Pam or butter. Chop jalapeno peppers and spread on bottom of casserole dish. Spread bacon over peppers evenly; sprinkle shredded cheese over bacon. Beat the eggs until fluffy and pour over top of cheese. Bake at 350° for 20-25 minutes. Remove from oven; cut in squares. Serve upside down while hot.

Mary Crabtree
Knoxville Council

MIDGET PUFFS

1/2 c. butter
1 c. boiling water
1/2 tsp. salt

1 c. sifted all-purpose flour
(plain)
4 large eggs

Heat butter, salt and flour with boiling water in medium saucepan over high heat. When butter is melted, remove from heat and beat constantly until mixture leaves sides of pan and forms a ball. Remove from heat and quickly beat in eggs, one at a time, beating until smooth after each egg is added with spoon or electric beater. Continue beating hard until dough has satin like sheen and breaks away in strands. Dough will be stiff and hold its shape. Drop by scant tea-spoonfuls 2 inches apart on lightly greased baking sheet, shaping each into a mound with a peak in the center, or use a pastry tube. Bake in preheated 400° oven until puffed and golden, 20 to 25 minutes. Do not open oven until last few minutes of baking time. Cool on rack. (May be made in advance and frozen. Thaw at room temperature.)

Carolyn Mitchell
Memphis Downtown Council

MINIATURE CHEESE CAKES

1 lb. cream cheese, softened
   30 minutes
3/4 c. sugar

1 Tbsp. lemon juice
2 eggs
1 tsp. vanilla

Combine all ingredients in large bowl and beat at high mixer speed for 5 minutes. In miniature muffin tins put 2 inch paper baking cups, a vanilla wafer in bottom of each. Fill each cup with cream cheese mixture. Bake at 350° for 15 minutes or until cracks appear on each cake; cool. Top with cherry pie filling. Makes 36 cakes and can be frozen.

Helen Widick
Harpeth Council

CLAM STUFFED MUSHROOMS

1 lb. medium mushrooms
1/4 c. butter, melted
1 (8 oz.) can minced
   clams, drained
1 c. soft bread crumbs
2 eggs, lightly beaten

2 Tbsp. chopped scallions or
   onion
4 Tbsp. mayonnaise
2 tsp. lemon juice
1/8 tsp. ground white pepper
Parmesan cheese

Rinse, pat dry and remove stems from mushrooms (save stems for another use). Brush caps with melted butter; arrange in baking pan. In medium bowl, combine remaining ingredients, except Parmesan cheese. Fill each mushroom cap with some of the mixture; sprinkle with Parmesan cheese. Bake at 375° until hot, about 15 minutes.

Rosemary Grand
Harpeth Council

DEEP FRIED BREADED MUSHROOMS

1 lb. (fresh) mushrooms,
   cleaned and diced
1 c. complete pancake mix
   (just add water)
Very little lemon juice

1 box corn flakes, crushed
   fine
Dash of salt
Grated Parmesan cheese
   (optional)

Wash mushrooms; paper towel dry. Cut into bite size pieces; sprinkle with very little lemon juice. Add just enough water to pancake mix to reach desired consistency, not too thick. Dip bite size pieces in mixture, then dip in crushed cereal and deep fry at 375° for about 2 minutes or until golden brown. Sprinkle with salt and drain on paper towel. Sprinkle Parmesan cheese for extra flavor.

Note: One cup dry pancake mix makes enough batter to coat about 3/4 pound of mushrooms. If batter thickens, add small amount of water.

Margaret Greer
Harpeth Council

FRIED MUSHROOMS

1 (8 oz.) pkg. fresh mushrooms, washed, drained
1/2 c. corn meal (self-
   rising or plain)
1/2 tsp. garlic salt
1489-81

1/4 c. flour (self-rising or
   plain)
1 egg
1/2 c. milk
Shortening for deep frying

In a medium bowl, stir together flour, corn meal and garlic salt. Combine milk and egg; add to dry ingredients. Dip mushrooms in batter until coated. Fry, a few at a time, until golden brown, 3 to 4 minutes. Drain on paper toweling. Serves 4 to 6. Serve hot with dip as appetizer or party snack.

Dip:

1/2 c. barbecue sauce

1 Tbsp. horseradish (or more according to taste)

Mix together in serving bowl. Serve as dip for fried mushrooms.

Emily Townes
Harpeth Council

FRENCH FRIED MUSHROOMS

1 lb. mushrooms
1/4 c. flour
1 tsp. salt

2 eggs, beaten
3/4 c. fine dry bread crumbs
Dash of black pepper

Rinse, pat dry and trim mushrooms. Combine flour with salt and black pepper. Dredge mushrooms first in flour mixture, then dip in eggs. Roll in bread crumbs. Fry until golden brown in deep fat preheated to 350° about 3 minutes. Drain on paper towel. Serve as an hors d'oeuvre or meat accompaniment. Yield: 25 to 30 mushrooms.

Judy Gibson
Harpeth Council

MUSHROOMS DIVINE

1 pt. fresh whole mushrooms   1 lb. red hot pork sausage

Wash mushrooms and remove stems. Chop stems finely and mix with sausage. Stuff mushroom caps generously and bake at 375° for 30 minutes. These can be prepared in advance and served as soon as they are baked.

Cindy Martin
Harpeth Council

MUSHROOM TURNOVERS

9 oz. cream cheese, room
   temperature
1 stick butter, room
   temperature
1 1/2 c. flour
1 large onion, chopped

1 large can mushrooms,
   chopped, drained
3 Tbsp. butter
1/4 tsp. thyme
1/2 tsp. salt
2 Tbsp. flour
1/4 c. milk

Dough: Combine cream cheese, butter and flour; chill 1/2 hour. Roll 1/8 inch thick. Cut with 3 inch diameter circle. Put filling in center. Fold dough over and press edges together with a fork. Place on greased cookie sheet and bake at 375° for 15 minutes.

Filling: Saute onion and mushrooms in butter. Add rest of ingredients; heat until smooth. Yield: 2 dozen.

Janis G. Black
Green Hills Council

PICKLED MUSHROOMS
(Diabetics)

1/3 c. red wine vinegar
1/3 c. water
1 small onion, thinly sliced
   and separated in rings
1 tsp. salt
2 tsp. snipped parsley

1 tsp. prepared mustard
Non-caloric sweetener equal
   to 1 Tbsp. sugar
2 (6 oz.) cans mushroom
   crowns, drained

In small saucepan, combine vinegar, water, onion rings, salt, parsley, mustard and sweetener. Bring to a boil. Add mushrooms; simmer 5 to 6 minutes. Pour into a bowl; cover. Chill several hours or overnight, stirring occasionally. Drain; serve with cocktail picks. Recipe yields 2 cups. One serving is <u>free</u>.

NUTS AND BOLTS

1 box Corn Chex
1 box Cheerios

1 lb. pecans
1 box pretzels

Melt 1 pound margarine in saucepan; add 2 tablespoons Worcestershire sauce and 2 teaspoons garlic salt. Pour margarine mixture over ingredients, mixing thoroughly.

Heat oven to 200°; bake for 2 hours, stirring every 15 minutes, or until margarine is dissolved. You may also add peanuts, Wheat Chex or Rice Chex, just according to your taste.

Johnnie Foster
Harpeth Council

PARTY MIX

1 1/2 sticks margarine
8 tsp. Worcestershire sauce
3/4 tsp. garlic powder
1/4 tsp. salt
1/2 box Wheat Chex

1/2 box Rice Chex
1/2 box Corn Chex
1/2 box thin pretzels
1 can mixed nuts (assorted)

Melt margarine in saucepan. Add Worcestershire sauce, garlic powder and salt. Combine cereals, pretzels and nuts in baking pan. Drizzle liquid mixture over this and stir. Heat oven to 250°. Bake for 45 minutes, stirring every 15 minutes.

Joyce M. Crump
Knoxville Council

CUCUMBER SANDWICHES

1 cucumber, peeled and
   grated
1 small onion, grated
Salt and pepper to taste

1 (8 oz.) pkg. cream cheese
2-3 Tbsp. mayonnaise
Tabasco sauce to taste
Worcestershire sauce to taste

Peel and grate cucumber and onion. Combine cucumber and onion with salt and pepper; set aside to drain. Whip cream cheese until fluffy. Add mayonnaise and fold in well drained cucumber and onion into cream cheese. Add Tabasco sauce and Worcestershire sauce. Spread on white or dark bread.

Judy Christopher
Harpeth Council

FINGER SANDWICHES

8 oz. cream cheese
1 small onion, grated
1 small cucumber, grated

3 Tbsp. mayonnaise
Salt and pepper

Drain vegetables; add to cream cheese and mayonnaise. Spread bread lightly with mayonnaise or soft butter before filling sandwiches. This helps to prevent sogginess.

Variations: Substitute grated carrot or chopped asparagus for the grated cucumber.

Louise Breeden
Nashboro Council

PARTY MEAT BALLS

2 lb. ground beef
1 egg, beaten

1 medium onion, grated
Salt and pepper to taste

Mix and shape above into tiny balls (about 60).

Sauce:

1 bottle chili sauce
1 tsp. lemon juice

1 c. grape jelly

Drop balls into simmering sauce; cook until tender. Better when made the day before and reheated.

Robert and Terry Johnson
Harpeth Council

SHERRIED NUTS

1 1/2 c. sugar
1/4 tsp. salt
1/2 c. sherry

1/2 tsp. cinnamon
2 1/2 c. pecans

Boil sugar, salt and sherry to soft ball or 240° on candy thermometer. Remove from heat. Add cinnamon and nuts; stir until cloudy. Turn onto waxed paper and separate, using 2 forks.

Mary Beth McLaurine
Harpeth Council

ROASTED SALTED PECANS

1 egg white, stiffly beaten   1 tsp. sugar
2 c. pecan halves   1 tsp. milk
1 tsp. salt   1 tsp. water

Combine salt, sugar, milk and water; fold into the egg white. Add pecans; coat well. Pour on foil lined cookie sheet. Bake at 250° to 300° for 1 hour. Stir every 15 minutes.

Barbara S. Stanfill
Harpeth Council

SWEDISH NUTS

2 egg whites   1 c. sugar
Dash of salt   2 c. pecan halves
1/2 stick margarine

Beat egg whites; add sugar slowly and salt. Add nuts to sugar and egg whites; stir until nuts are coated. Melt margarine in 9x13 inch pan. Spread nut mixture and bake 30-35 minutes at 325°; stir every 10 minutes.

Jewell Mercer
Nashville Council

SUGAR-SPICED PECANS

1 c. sugar   1/2 c. water
3/4 tsp. salt   1/2 tsp. vanilla
2 tsp. cinnamon   1 lb. (2 or 2 1/2 c.) pecan
    halves

Combine all ingredients, except nuts and vanilla. Cook until syrup spins a thin thread, about 5 minutes. Remove from fire; add nuts and vanilla. Stir nuts quickly until syrup crystallizes. Pour on waxed paper and gently separate nuts.

Bettye Lou Nicely
Knoxville Council

SUGARED WALNUTS

2 c. sugar
1/2 c. water
1 tsp. vanilla

1 c. miniature marshmallows
5 Tbsp. Karo syrup
4 c. nuts (English walnuts; halves are better)

Mix together sugar, water and Karo syrup. Bring to a boil and boil for approximately 5 minutes. Blend in marshmallows and vanilla. When mixture begins to thicken, add nuts. Pour out of pan onto waxed paper and separate immediately into sections with fork.

Johnnie Foster
Harpeth Council

SMOKED OYSTER LOG

1 (8 oz.) pkg. cream
  cheese, softened
1 1/2 Tbsp. mayonnaise
1 tsp. Worcestershire sauce
Dash of garlic powder

Dash of onion powder
Dash of salt
1 (3.6 oz.) can smoked
  oysters, drained, chopped
Chopped chives

Combine cheese and mayonnaise; blend well. Stir in next 4 ingredients; spread 1/4 inch thick on waxed paper. Chill at least 30 minutes. Spread oysters on cream cheese mixture and roll up jelly roll fashion. Roll log in chopped chives. Chill overnight. Makes 2 dozen slices.

Bernice Curtis
Knoxville Council

PEPPER CHICKEN SATE

Have ready 2 large whole chicken breasts, skinned, boned and cut into 32 (3/4 inch) cubes.

Marinade:

1/2 c. oil (preferably
  safflower)
1 (4 oz.) jar pimentos,
  drained and pureed
2 Tbsp. red wine vinegar
2 large shallots, minced
1 large clove garlic, minced
1 1/2 tsp. salt

1/2 tsp. dried red pepper
  flakes
1/2 tsp. dried cumin
Freshly ground pepper
2 large green peppers, cut
  into 32 (3/4 inch) squares
16 (3 inch) wooden skewers,
  soaked in water

1489-81

Place chicken in plastic bag. Combine ingredients for marinade in mixing bowl, food processor or blender; mix thoroughly. Add to chicken. Tie bag airtight and marinate 1 to 2 days in refrigerator, turning bag several times to re-distribute marinade. Preheat broiler. Alternate 2 pieces of chicken with 2 pepper squares on each skewer. Place in shallow pan. Broil 4 inches from heat source for 8 minutes, turning once. Serve immediately with remaining sauce. Serves 16.

Sherree Weisenberger
Harpeth Council

PARTY PIZZETTES

1 (11 oz.) pkg. refrigerated biscuits
1 large can pizza sauce
1 large can mushrooms
1 (4 1/2 oz.) can deviled ham
1 1/2 c. (6 oz.) shredded Mozzarella cheese

Roll each biscuit into a 4 inch circle; place on greased baking sheet. Combine pizza sauce and deviled ham. Spread a small amount on each biscuit; top with mushrooms and cheese. Bake at 450° for about 10 minutes or until golden brown. Cool about 5 minutes.

Mary Crabtree
Knoxville Council

PIZZA RITZ

1 lb. hot sausage, cooked and drained
1 lb. Velveeta cheese
3 Tbsp. soy sauce
Sprinkle with garlic salt
1 pkg. party rye bread

Melt cheese; stir in sausage, soy sauce and salt. Spoon onto party rye bread. Bake at 375° until bubbly and brown around the edges. May be frozen before baking.

Sue Close
Harpeth Council

ROQUEFORT CHEESE LOG

8 oz. cream cheese   4 oz. Roquefort or Blue
                                cheese

Let stand at room temperature; blend with fork.
Scrape onion for juice; add to cheese with garlic, Worcestershire sauce and a dash of Tabasco sauce. Shape into 2
logs; chill. Roll in finely chopped pecans. Garnish with
parsley. Serve with crackers.

Virginia Q. Kaderabek
Harpeth Council

BARBECUE SAUSAGE BALLS

1/2 lb. bulk pork sausage   1/2 c. catsup
1/2 lb. ground chuck   2 Tbsp. brown sugar
1 egg, slightly beaten   1 Tbsp. vinegar
1/3 c. fine dry bread   1 Tbsp. soy sauce
   crumbs

Mix sausage, chuck, egg and bread crumbs; shape in
about two dozen 1/2 inch balls. In ungreased skillet, brown
balls slowly on all sides about 15 minutes. Pour off excess
fat. Combine remaining ingredients and pour over meat.
Cover and simmer 10 minutes, stirring occasionally to coat
meat balls. To use as appetizer, place in chafing dish.

M. Carolyn Hunter
Harpeth Council

ORIGINAL SAUSAGE BALLS

3 c. Bisquick   1 (8 oz.) pkg. Cheddar
1 lb. hot sausage   cheese
                              Dash of cayenne pepper

Have sausage and cheese at room temperature; mix together with cayenne pepper. Gradually add Bisquick.
Set in refrigerator till cool. Form into small balls and bake
at 350° for about 10 minutes or until brown. Makes about
70.

Martha Sherrod
Knoxville Council

SAUSAGE CHEESE BALLS

10 oz. sharp Cheddar cheese   1 lb. hot sausage
3 c. Bisquick mix

Grate cheese; mix Bisquick and sausage together. Add grated cheese and form into balls. Bake on greased cookie sheet at 350° until done, approximately 25-30 minutes.

Minnie McFarland
Harpeth Council

SAUSAGE-CHEESE BALLS

3 c. Bisquick baking mix
1 lb. bulk pork sausage
  (hot or mild)
4 c. (about 16 oz.) shredded
  Cheddar cheese

1/2 c. grated Parmesan
  cheese
1/2 tsp. dried rosemary
  leaves
1/2 tsp. parsley flakes

Heat oven to 350°. Mix all ingredients; shape mixture into 1 inch balls. Place in ungreased jelly roll pan, 15 1/2 x 10 1/2 x 1 inches. Bake until brown, 20 to 25 minutes. Makes about 8 1/2 dozen appetizers.

David Lewis
Clarksville Council

SAUSAGE BALLS

1/2 lb. sausage (Jimmy
  Dean mild)
1/2 lb. sausage (Jimmy
  Dean hot)

2 c. Bisquick mix
3 Tbsp. milk
1 stick (Coon cheese) extra
  sharp cheese

Grate cheese; mix all ingredients well. Roll in balls the size of a quarter and bake on large cookie sheet at 350° for 25 to 30 minutes.

Tip: Cut a paper bag the size of cookie sheet and put sausage balls on this to absorb grease. Do not substitute sausage or cheese.

Sivalene Rouse
Morristown Council

28

SAUSAGE PINWHEELS

2 c. flour
2 tsp. baking powder
1/4 tsp. soda
1 lb. fresh sausage

1 tsp. salt
1/2 c. shortening
3/4 c. milk

Mix dry ingredients; cut shortening into dry ingredients. Gradually add milk. Work into a smooth dough. Divide dough into 3 parts; roll to about 1/16 inch. Whip or mash sausage until it will spread easily. Spread 1/3 of the sausage over dough; roll like a jelly roll. Wrap in waxed paper. Repeat with the remaining dough and sausage. Chill for 1 hour or overnight. Slice about 1/8 or 1/4 inch thick. Bake at 400° for 12 to 15 minutes or until golden brown. Makes 6 dozen.

Dorothy Bryant
Clarksville Council

SAUSAGE RINGS

Make 1 cup biscuit dough. Roll thin and spread 1 pound sausage over flattened dough. Roll up dough in jelly roll fashion; refrigerate until firm. Slice into rings and bake at 400° until done.

Pat Carpenter
Nashville Council

SAUSAGE ROLLS

2 lb. sausage
4 c. plain flour
1 1/2 c. shortening

1 egg
1 c. water
Pinch of salt

To make pastry, put flour, salt and shortening in a bowl; blend together. Add water to make pliant consistency. Roll out pastry in oblong shape, approximately 12x3 inches. Shape sausage into a 12 inch roll and place down center of dough. Roll over sideways and cut into 2 inch lengths. Make horizontal cuts on top and brush with beaten egg. Bake at 350° for about 25 minutes.

Norma Ann Webb
Harpeth Council

SAUSAGE 'N CHEESE BRUNCH TARTS

1/2 lb. bulk pork sausage
1 1/4 c. Bisquick baking mix
1/4 c. margarine or butter, softened
2 Tbsp. boiling water
1/2 c. half & half
1 egg
2 Tbsp. thinly sliced green onions
1/4 tsp. salt
1/2 c. shredded Swiss cheese

Heat oven to 375°. Generously grease 12 muffin cups (2 1/2 x 1 1/4 inches). Cook and stir sausage until brown; drain. Mix baking mix and margarine. Add boiling water; stir vigorously until soft dough forms. Press 1 level tablespoonful of dough on bottom and up side of each cup. Divide sausage evenly among cups. Beat half & half and egg; stir in onions and salt. Spoon about 1 tablespoonful into each cup; sprinkle cheese over tops. Bake until edges are golden brown and centers are set, about 25 minutes. Refrigerate any remaining tarts. Makes 1 dozen tarts.

Frances Neuette
Harpeth Council

SHRIMP COCKTAIL

1 c. chili sauce
1 c. catsup
2 Tbsp. horseradish
1 Tbsp. Worcestershire sauce
2 tsp. lemon juice
2 Tbsp. vinegar
Dash of hot sauce
Fresh, cool shrimp

Combine all ingredients, mixing well. Chill sauce at least 1/2 hour before serving. Serve with shrimp and garnish with lemon wedges, if desired. Yield: About 2 cups.

Boil fresh shrimp in water with juice of 1 lemon and rind and 1 tablespoon butter or margarine until shrimp turns pink, approximately 5 minutes (hard boil).

Margaret Ann Marshall
Clarksville Council

WHITE CHEESE TART
(Food Processor Recipes)

1/2 lb. Swiss cheese, grated
1/2 c. Ricotta cheese
1 tsp. salt
1 1/2 sticks (3/4 c.) butter, softened
1/4 tsp. white pepper

3-4 Tbsp. cream   1/3 c. flour

3 egg yolks

Place all ingredients, except the egg yolks and flour, into the bowl of a food processor fitted with the steel blade; blend until mixture is well combined. Add 3 egg yolks, one at a time, and 1/3 cup flour, spinning machine until mixture is well combined. Spoon mixture into a prebaked pastry shell, which has been carefully placed on a baking sheet. Bake tart in the middle of a preheated, moderately hot oven, 375°, for 25 minutes, or until the top is puffed and browned. With a long metal spatula, transfer tart to a rack and let it cool for about 20 minutes. This recipe fits a 9 inch round tart pan.

Pate Brisee (for pie shell):

1 1/4 c. all-purpose flour,
   unsifted
1/4 tsp. salt
1/4 c. frozen butter

1/4 c. frozen shortening
   (remove from measuring
   cup before freezing)
3 Tbsp. ice water

Place flour and salt in processor bowl, fitted with metal blade. Cut shortening and butter in 1/2 inch chunks and distribute over flour. Process until fat particles look like small peas, 8 seconds. Measure water into a cup; turn motor on again and add water slowly through feed tube. Turn off motor; mixture will look crumbly. Do not allow mixture to form a ball or pastry will not be as flaky. Roll out on a lightly floured board to 1/8 inch thickness. Fit loosely into a 9 inch tart pan; trim to 1/2 inch from rim and fold edges in. Line shell with foil; fill with dried peas or beans and bake in a preheated 400° oven for 10 minutes. Remove foil and beans; prick shell and bake 10 more minutes. Remove shell from pan; cool on rack. Shell is now ready to be filled.

Sherree Weisenberger
Harpeth Council

ZUCCHINI FRITTERS

1 medium zucchini, sliced
   and cut lengthwise in
   strips
1/4 c. flour (self-rising
   or plain)

1/2 c. corn meal (self-rising
   or plain)
1 egg
1/2 c. milk
1/2 tsp. garlic salt
Shortening for deep frying

1489-81   31

In a medium bowl, stir together flour, corn meal and garlic salt. Combine milk and egg; add to dry ingredients. Dip zucchini strips in batter until coated. Fry, a few at a time, until golden brown, 3 to 4 minutes. Drain on paper toweling. Serve as appetizer or party snack. Serves 4 to 6. Serve hot with dip.

Dip:

1/2 c. barbecue sauce

1 Tbsp. horseradish (or more according to taste)

Mix together in serving bowl. Serve as dip for fritters.

Emily Townes
Harpeth Council

ARTICHOKE DIP

1 can artichoke hearts
1 c. Parmesan cheese

1/2 c. Hellmann's mayonnaise

Drain and mash artichokes; mix with cheese and mayonnaise. Broil in pie plate until bubbly. Serve hot on soda crackers.

Dot Crouch
Clarksville Council

BEER CHEESE SPREAD

1 lb. Cheddar cheese, shredded, at room temperature
2 Tbsp. catsup
1/2 c. beer

1/2 small onion, grated (2 Tbsp.)
2 Tbsp. Worcestershire sauce
Dash of hot pepper sauce
1 clove crushed garlic

Beat cheese until creamy. Add remaining ingredients and continue beating until light and fluffy. Chill in covered container. Can be stored in refrigerator for up to 2 weeks. Flavor improves with age.

Wendell Harmon
Nashville Council

BEER CHEESE SPREAD

1 lb. sharp Cheddar
  cheese, grated
4 oz. Bleu or Roquefort
  cheese
1 stick butter, room
  temperature
1 can beer

3 tsp. wine vinegar
1 Tbsp. Worcestershire sauce
1 tsp. Tabasco sauce or
  cayenne pepper
1 clove garlic, crushed
1 tsp. Dijon mustard

Combine all ingredients; mix thoroughly with food processor or electric beater. Serve as a dip for raw vegetables, chips or crackers.

M. Carolyn Hunter
Harpeth Council

BROCCOLI DIP

2 pkg. frozen chopped
  broccoli
1 can cream of mushroom
  soup
1 roll Kraft garlic cheese

1/2 stick butter or margarine
1 small onion, chopped fine
1 small can sliced mushrooms,
  drained
1 small pkg. slivered almonds

Melt butter in skillet; saute onion. Add broccoli; simmer until it falls apart. Cut cheese into small pieces and add to mixture; simmer until melted. Add soup, mushrooms and almonds. Pour mixture into fondue pot. Serve warm with chips or Ritz crackers.

Lila Grisham
Memphis Council

HOT BROCCOLI DIP

2 onions, chopped
1 stick butter
6 pkg. frozen broccoli
3 cans cream of mushroom
  soup
3 pkg. garlic cheese

1 can chili peppers, seeded
  and diced
1 large can mushrooms, sliced
1 c. blanched almonds,
  chopped
Dash of Worcestershire sauce
Few drops green food color

Cook broccoli; drain. Saute onions in butter. Mix

other ingredients and serve in chafing dish. Use chips or crackers for dip. Serves 100.

M. Carolyn Hunter
Harpeth Council

HOT BROCCOLI DIP

3 stalks celery, chopped fine
1/2 large onion, chopped
1 small can mushroom pieces

1 pkg. frozen chopped broccoli
1 can cream of mushroom soup
1 roll Kraft garlic cheese

Saute onion, celery and mushrooms in butter. Cook broccoli and drain. Add mushroom soup to first mixture. Melt cheese in double boiler; add to above. Mix in cooled broccoli last. Serve in chafing dish.

Marian Molteni
Harpeth Council

CHEESE DIP

1 lb. American cheese (blue box)
1 can Ro-Tel tomatoes
3/4 tsp. ground cumin

3/4 tsp. garlic powder
1/4 tsp. black pepper
3/4 c. water

Place cheese in blender (do not blend), all other ingredients in saucepan. Bring to a boil; pour over cheese. Blend 30 to 60 seconds.

Memphis Council

CHEESE DIP

8 oz. pkg. Philadelphia cream cheese, room temperature
2 Tbsp. mayonnaise

1 tsp. garlic salt
2 Tbsp. sweet pickle juice
1/4 c. tomato catsup
2 Tbsp. French dressing

Mix all ingredients thoroughly, so that all the cheese will be colored, rather than having little white dots in it; a hand mixer will be helpful. Serve with favorite dip chips.

Virginia Werrbach
Harpeth Council

CHEESE DIP

1 (8 oz.) pkg. Velveeta
  cheese
1 (10 oz.) can Ro-Tel with
  tomatoes and green chilies

1 chopped jalapeno pepper
  (optional)

Pour can of Ro-Tel into small saucepan. Add cheese and pepper, if desired. Cook over low heat until cheese is melted. Serve with Tostados or Doritos. (More cheese can be used to make thicker sauce.)

Donna Jo Miller
Green Hills Council

HOT CHEESE DIP

Melt 1 pound Velveeta cheese in a double boiler with 5 tablespoons milk; add more milk if needed. After cheese has melted, put in some crushed red peppers or jalapeno peppers to taste. Keep cheese dip warm in a fondue server. Serve with nacho chips, Doritos or corn chips.

Othelia Taylor
Harpeth Council

TASTY CHEESE DIP
(Low Fat - Low Cholesterol Diet)

Press through a fine sieve or blend in an electric blender for a smoother dip 2 cups skim milk cottage cheese or baker's cheese. Add:

1/2 c. skim milk yogurt
2 tsp. seasoning salt

2 tsp. chopped parsley
1 Tbsp. Worcestershire sauce

Refrigerate for an hour or more to blend the flavors. Serve in a bowl surrounded by chilled, crisped raw vegetables or suitable toast or crackers. Makes approximately 2 1/2 cups. Total recipe (vegetables not in calculations):

Oil: 0 teaspoons
Cholesterol: 36 milligrams
Saturated fat: 0 grams
Linoleic acid: 0 grams

Protein: 80 grams
Carbohydrate: 22 grams
Calories: 425

1489-81

EVERYONE'S FAVORITE CHEESE SPREAD

1 (8 oz.) pkg. cream cheese
Small onion, grated
1 tsp. parsley, chopped fine
  (dehydrated may be used)
2 tsp. chili sauce
1/8 tsp. curry powder

1 pkg. G. Washington beef
  broth
1/4 tsp. dry mustard
1/4 tsp. Worcestershire sauce
Few drops of Tabasco sauce

Mix all together well. Very good for stuffed celery.

Harriet Morgan
Knoxville Council

CLAM DIP

Large pkg. Philadelphia
  cream cheese

Minced clams
Seafood cocktail sauce

Spread softened cheese on platter. Pour on cocktail sauce; sprinkle drained clams on top.

Debbie Mays
Harpeth Council

CRAB DIP

1 c. mayonnaise
1/2 c. sour cream
1 Tbsp. chopped parsley
1 can crabmeat, drained

1 tsp. cooking sherry
1 tsp. lemon juice
Salt and pepper to taste

Mix together and refrigerate.

Peggy Burr
Harpeth Council

DIP BATTER

1/2 c. flour
1/3 c. cornstarch
2 tsp. baking powder

1 Tbsp. A.1. steak sauce or 1
  Tbsp. soy sauce
1/2 - 2/3 c. water

Mix flour, cornstarch, baking powder and steak sauce together in small bowl. Gradually add water to form a batter the consistency of pancake batter. Dip onion rings, shrimp, oysters or anything else.

Cheryl V. Alderson
Columbia Council

DIP FOR CAULIFLOWER

1 c. Hellmann's mayonnaise
1 tsp. grated onion
1 tsp. curry powder
1 Tbsp. horseradish
1 Tbsp. wine vinegar

Mix all ingredients in small bowl.

Lena Roberson
Andrew Jackson Council

VEGETABLE DIP

1 c. Hellmann's mayonnaise
1 c. sour cream
1 Tbsp. parsley flakes
1 Tbsp. dried onion
1 Tbsp. celery salt or celery seed
1 Tbsp. Beau Monde seasoning or poppy seed

Blend by hand in medium size bowl. Serve with raw vegetables.

Leslie Stephens
Harpeth Council

FESTIVE EGG DIP

1 (8 oz.) pkg. cream cheese, softened
3 Tbsp. milk
3 hard cooked eggs, finely chopped
2 Tbsp. mayonnaise
2 tsp. chopped chives
1 tsp. prepared mustard
1/4 tsp. salt
1/8 tsp. pepper

Combine cream cheese and milk in a small mixing bowl; beat until creamy. Add remaining ingredients, mixing until light and fluffy. Serve with fresh vegetables. Yield: 1 2/3 cups.

Mary S. Crabtree
Knoxville Council

HEAVENLY FRUIT DIP

1/2 c. sugar
2 Tbsp. all-purpose flour
1 c. pineapple juice

1 egg, beaten
1 Tbsp. butter or oleo
1 c. whipping cream, whipped

Combine first 5 ingredients in a heavy saucepan. Cook over medium heat, stirring constantly, until smooth and thickened. Let cool completely; fold in whipped cream. Serve with fresh fruit. Yield: About 2 cups.

Billie Fleming
Nashboro Council

HOT HAMBURGER DIP

1 lb. hamburger, crumbled
and browned
1 can Frito-Lay bean dip
2 or 3 green onions, chopped

1 lb. Velveeta cheese, cubed
1/2 green pepper, chopped
1 (8 oz.) can tomato sauce

Place all ingredients in a crock pot. Cook on low for 10 to 12 hours or on high for 5 hours. Watch for scorching at higher setting. Set on low to keep warm. Serve with cheese chips. May be used as topping on hot dogs or hamburgers.

Peggy Burr
Harpeth Council

HOT JALAPENO DIP

1 (2 lb.) box Velveeta
cheese
1 can Cheddar cheese soup

1 small can jalapeno (El Paso)
relish
Dash of salt and pepper

Using low heat, heat Velveeta cheese until melted. Add Cheddar cheese soup; stir in relish. Add salt and pepper. Serve warm with chips, Fritos, raw broccoli and cauliflower.

Margaret Greer
Harpeth Council

QUICKIE DIP

3 Tbsp. (1 1/2 oz. pkg.)   2 c. dairy sour cream
  spaghetti sauce mix

In a bowl, gently blend spaghetti sauce mix into sour cream. Cover and chill.

Judy Gibson
Harpeth Council

ROQUEFORT SPREAD OR DIP

Mix equal parts of Bleu cheese and Philadelphia cream cheese well. Add a little Worcestershire sauce. Thin with half & half cream until thin enough for spread or dip.

Mrs. Adelene Queenan
Harpeth Council

MEXICAN FONDUE

1/2 lb. ground chuck
1/2 lb. American cheese
1/4 oz. can green chiles,
  diced

1 (15 oz.) can special tomato
  sauce or tomato sauce with
  tomato tidbits
1 can refried beans

Brown beef; add cheese and beans. Stir until cheese melts. Add chiles and tomato sauce; heat. Use French bread cubes, tortilla chips or cocktail franks.

Peggy Burr
Harpeth Council

HOT SHRIMP DIP

2 cans frozen cream of
  shrimp soup
2 rolls garlic cheese (Kraft)
2 cans mushrooms, drained

Worcestershire sauce to taste
Lemon juice to taste
Hot sauce to taste

Put in top of double boiler until melted. Serve with garlic rounds.

Clara Rainey
Harpeth Council

SHRIMP DIP

1 c. sour cream
1 (8 oz.) pkg. cream cheese
1/2 c. mayonnaise
4 tsp. finely chopped onion
4 tsp. chopped pimento
1/4 tsp. garlic powder

1 tsp. Tabasco sauce
2 cans small shrimp, drained
Salt to taste
4 tsp. chopped frozen chives
1 tsp. parsley flakes

Mix together.

Ann R. Wooten
Memphis Downtown Council

CREAMY SHRIMP DIP

2 (8 oz.) pkg. cream cheese
3 oz. cream cheese with chives
1 can frozen cream of shrimp soup
1 1/2 c. cooked shrimp, chopped

1 tsp. dry mustard
1 tsp. Worcestershire sauce
1/4 tsp. garlic powder
3/4 tsp. paprika
Salt
Pepper

Thaw soup; combine with remaining ingredients. Chill at least 2 hours before serving.
Note: This also makes a delicious spread on tea sandwiches.

Patsy Carter
Harpeth Council

SHRIMP DIP

1 can shrimp, mashed with fork
1 small pkg. cream cheese

3 drops Tabasco sauce
1 tsp. minced onion
1/3 c. mayonnaise

Mix all ingredients, except shrimp, with an electric mixer until creamy. Fold in mashed shrimp. This is better if made a day ahead. Also, it is very good with raw celery, carrots, cauliflower, etc.

Dot Crouch
Clarksville Council

SHRIMP DIP

2 lb. boiled shrimp
1 (8 oz.) pkg. soft cream
  cheese
Juice of 1 lemon
10 green onions, minced

Mayonnaise
Tabasco sauce
Worcestershire sauce
Salt and pepper

Soften cream cheese with lemon juice. Add shrimp and green onions and enough mayonnaise to give a consistency for dipping chips or crackers. Season with Tabasco sauce, Worcestershire sauce, salt and pepper. Better if made 8 hours before serving.

Marcia Jackson
Harpeth Council

SHRIMP DIP

1 c. cooked, deveined
  shrimp
2 (3 oz.) pkg. cream cheese
1 Tbsp. Worcestershire
  sauce
1 Tbsp. grated onion
1 tsp. horseradish

1 tsp. dry mustard
1/2 tsp. salt
1/2 tsp. pepper
Dash of hot sauce
Dash of garlic salt
Mayonnaise to consistency
  desired

Cream together and serve with small crackers such as Wheat Thins. Serves 15.

Diane L. Cresswell
Chattanooga Council

SHRIMP SPREAD

2 cans shrimp, drained and
  chopped
3/4 c. onion, chopped
3/4 c. celery, chopped
1 large pkg. cream cheese

1 can undiluted tomato soup
1 c. mayonnaise
2 env. unflavored gelatin
1/3 c. boiling water

Blend cream cheese, soup and mayonnaise until smooth. Dissolve gelatin in boiling water and pour over celery and onion. Combine all ingredients; chill until firm.

Note: I use only 1/3 cup onion and celery. I have substituted celery salt.

C. Turner
Knoxville Council

SOMBRERO CHILI DIP

1 lb. ground beef
1/2 c. chopped onion
2 (8 oz.) cans red kidney
   beans
1/2 c. hot catsup
3 tsp. chili powder
1 tsp. salt
1 c. shredded sharp cheese

Brown the ground beef and onion in skillet. Mash the beans with a fork in the liquid. Add the beans, catsup, chili powder and salt to the beef mixture; blend well. Cook until bubbly. Pour into a 2 quart chafing dish and sprinkle the cheese over the top. Serve hot with corn chips.

Vangie Whitley
Harpeth Council

SOY DIP

1 pt. Hellmann's mayonnaise
4 Tbsp. soy sauce
4 Tbsp. onion flakes
2 Tbsp. milk

Mix all ingredients together and refrigerate at least 6 hours, preferably overnight, before serving.

Peggy Wilkins
East Memphis Council

SPINACH DIP

1 (10 oz.) pkg. frozen
   spinach
1/2 c. chopped parsley
1/2 c. chopped green onions
1/2 tsp. dill weed
Seasoned salt to taste
1 c. mayonnaise
1 c. sour cream
Juice of 1/2 lemon

Thaw spinach and squeeze to drain. Combine with other ingredients; mix well. Serve with raw vegetables.

Peggy Burr
Harpeth Council

TUNA DIP

1/2 c. sour cream
1 (7 oz.) can tuna
1 Tbsp. horseradish
1 tsp. Worcestershire sauce
1/2 tsp. salt
1 (8 oz.) pkg. cream cheese,
   broken in pieces
1/2 small onion, sliced
Dash of pepper
1 clove garlic

Place all ingredients in blender; blend only until smooth. Chill for several hours. Serve with crackers.

Lena Roberson
Andrew Jackson Council

AMARETTO ALEXANDER

12 oz. Amaretto liqueur
1 pt. half & half

6 oz. white creme de cacao
1 1/2 qt. vanilla ice cream

Combine Amaretto, creme de cacao and half & half in blender. Put a scoop of ice cream in each sherbet glass and the remainder in blender. Blend well. Pour in glass and serve. Serves 10.

Patsy Carter
Harpeth Council

BOILED CUSTARD

Whip 3 eggs in top of double boiler. Add 1 scant cup of sugar. Add 1 quart sweet milk and a pinch of salt. Cook (over boiling water) and stir until it's ready to boil, about 180° on candy thermometer. Add 1 teaspoon vanilla. Pour through a strainer and chill.

Reba Gray
Harpeth Council

BOILED CUSTARD

4 eggs
1/2 c. sugar
1/4 tsp. salt

1 qt. milk
2 tsp. vanilla

Beat eggs with salt and sugar in top of double boiler. Scald milk (in separate pan) and pour over egg mixture and cook in double boiler on medium, stirring constantly, until coats the spoon. Add vanilla.

Jean Hunt
Nashboro Council

BOILED CUSTARD

1 qt. sweet milk	9 Tbsp. sugar (a little more
2 eggs	more if you want it very
1 Tbsp. plain sifted flour	sweet)

Mix all ingredients together. Cook in a double boiler until the mixture will coat a spoon. Suggest a wooden spoon for cooking this. Set off of water and stir in a cup of small marshmallows or regular marshmallows, cut up in small pieces. You can use the marshmallow topping in a jar if you desire. Be careful not to beat, but to stir with consistency as not to cause this to be fluffy, but have a smooth creamy look. Can be poured into tall glasses topped with whipped cream and a cherry for serving. Makes better than a quart.

Nell Young
Harpeth Council

BOILED CUSTARD

4 qt. milk	1 1/2 c. (8) whole eggs
1 tsp. salt	2 c. sugar
4 tsp. vanilla extract	2 tsp. nutmeg, grated

For the whole eggs you may substitute either 1 cup (16) egg yolks or 1 1/4 cups yolks and whole eggs. Put milk in 1 1/2 gallon pan. Place over controlled low heat or set in larger pan filled to a depth of 1 inch with water and cook over medium heat. A double boiler may be used. Pour eggs into a large mixing bowl. Beat slightly; add salt and sugar. Mix well, then add 2 cups of the hot milk to the egg mixture while beating for smoothness. Pour egg mixture through a strainer into the larger container of hot milk. Stir often for 20 minutes or longer. Custard is done when it coats spoon well or reaches 190° on a candy thermometer. Covering with a lid between stirring helps develop an interesting texture and using a wooden spoon for stirring prevents discoloration of milk-egg mixture. Cool custard as quickly as possible by placing in a pan or sink of cold water; continue to stir at intervals. Add vanilla; chill thoroughly and top with a dash of grated nutmeg when served. Makes 18 cups; 36 (1/2 cup) servings. (This custard is cooked at a temperature below "boiling point". It is thin enough to drink and is very popular during the Christmas season, served for dessert with coconut cake or alone. A flavoring other than vanilla may be used.

Joyce Mattice
Harpeth Council

PEARL'S BOILED CUSTARD

1/2 gal. sweet milk	6 whole eggs, beaten well
1 1/2 c. sugar	1 small can evaporated milk

Have milk at room temperature (it can set out overnight). Combine all ingredients and cook in double boiler until mixture coats spoon. Strain custard. When custard is cool, add 1 tablespoon vanilla.

Pat Carpenter
Nashville Council

RAW BOILED CUSTARD

3 qt. sweet milk	3 boxes Jell-O instant vanilla
1 c. sugar	pudding mix
1 Tbsp. vanilla	1 pt. whipping cream

Mix pudding mix well with a small amount of milk. Stir in remainder of milk; beat 5 minutes. Add sugar and cream and beat 3 minutes. Chill 45 minutes to 1 hour.

Robi Akers
Harpeth Council

BOILED CUSTARD
(Easy)

Beat 5 eggs. Add 3/4 cup sugar and 1 quart milk (a pinch of salt to each quart). Cook in double boiler till it coats a wooden spoon; that is about 10 minutes after the water starts to boil in double boiler. Serves 6.

Johnnie Foster
Harpeth Council

UNCOOKED BOILED CUSTARD

1 can Eagle Brand milk	2 small pkg. vanilla instant
1/2 gal. milk	Jell-O pudding

Blend Eagle Brand milk and Jell-O pudding with mixer until well mixed. Gradually add 1/2 gallon milk, stirring well. Set aside until it thickens, then refrigerate.

Jean Bethel
Memphis Council

COCOA MIX

1 (6 oz.) jar Coffee-mate
1 lb. 9 oz. box instant milk

2 lb. Nestle's Quik
1 box confectioners sugar

Mix all ingredients together. To serve, use 3 teaspoons mix to 1 cup water.

Tricia Owens
Harpeth Council

COFFEE FRAPPE

1 gal. vanilla ice cream
1 pt. cream, whipped

1 qt. double strength coffee

Chill coffee and pour over ice cream, which has been broken into chunks. Stir in whipped cream and serve. It should be about the consistency of a milk shake. This can be made ahead and frozen. Serves 35.

Patsy Carter
Harpeth Council

DAIQUIRI

2 (12 oz.) cans pink
   lemonade
1 (12 oz.) can limeade
5 cans of water

Juice of 1 lemon
1/5 of Bacardi white rum
Cherries and juice

Mix and store in plastic container in freezer. Allow for expansion of mix as it freezes. Stir occasionally.

Peggy Hunter
Harpeth Council

HOLIDAY EGGNOG

6 eggs, separated
3/4 c. sugar
2 c. milk
2 c. heavy cream

1 1/2 c. bourbon (or brandy)
2 Tbsp. dark rum
Nutmeg

Beat egg yolks until very thick and lemon colored. Add 1/2 cup sugar and continue beating until sugar is dissolved. Add milk and cream, then slowly stir in liquors. Refrigerate about 4 hours to "cook" eggs. When ready to serve, beat egg whites until stiff. Gradually beat in remaining sugar and fold into mixture. Sprinkle lightly with nutmeg. Makes 12 servings.

Pat Prosser
Columbia Council

INSTANT HOT CHOCOLATE MIX

1 (11 oz.) jar Coffee-mate
1 (8 qt.) box powdered milk
  (Carnation nonfat)

1 (2 lb.) box Nestle's Quik
1 box powdered sugar

Sift and mix all ingredients. Serve by using 1/2 cup of mix and 1/2 cup hot water.

Dorothy Stanton
Knoxville Council

MOCK SANGRIA

3 c. grape juice
2 c. cranberry juice
2 c. lemon flavored soda
  (Sprite)
Rind of 1 orange, cut into
  strips

3 Tbsp. orange juice
2 Tbsp. lemon juice
2 Tbsp. lime juice
Orange, lemon and lime
  slices
Mint sprigs

Combine grape juice, cranberry juice, orange rind and juices in pitcher or punch bowl. Add ice. Garnish with fruit slices and mint. Yields 16 (1/2 cup) servings.

Doris Binkley
Nashboro Council

ORANGE BREAKFAST NOG

1/2 (6 oz.) can (1/3 c.)
  frozen orange juice
  concentrate, thawed
1 c. milk

1 c. vanilla ice cream,
  slightly softened
2 eggs
1 Tbsp. sugar

Place all ingredients in blender; cover and blend at low speed till combined, then at medium-high speed till foamy, about 30 seconds (or place ingredients in small bowl

1489-81

of electric mixer and beat). Pour into glasses; garnish with
mint leaves. Makes 3 or 4 servings.

M.E. Womble, Jr.
Memphis East Council

ORANGE JULIUS

1/2 (6 oz.) can frozen
   orange juice concentrate
1/2 c. milk

1/2 c. water
1/2 Tbsp. vanilla
5-6 ice cubes

Combine all ingredients in blender for 30 seconds.
Serve immediately. If you have some left over in blender,
blend a few seconds before serving again.

Frank Giles
Harpeth Council

ANNIVERSARY PUNCH

1 fifth champagne
1 fifth sherry
1/2 pt. cherry brandy

1 bottle soda water
1 small pkg. frozen
   strawberries

Mix all ingredients together. Chill and pour over a
chunk of dry ice in bottom of punch bowl. Makes 2 quarts.

Patsy Carter
Harpeth Council

CHAMPAGNE PUNCH

1 bottle sauterne
1/2 bottle peach brandy
1 qt. lemon sherbet

1 bottle soda water
1 bottle champagne
1 bottle ginger ale

Mix all ingredients together. Chill and pour over large
chunk of ice in punch bowl. Float fresh fruit on top.

Patsy Carter
Harpeth Council

CHAMPAGNE PUNCH

1 1/2 c. powdered sugar
1/2 c. curacao
1/2 c. cognac
1/2 c. maraschino cherry
   juice

1 qt. pineapple sherbet
3 bottles champagne
1 orange, sliced
1 lemon, sliced

Place in chilled punch bowl. Mix sugar and caracao thoroughly in a pitcher. Stir in cognac and cherry juice. Add sherbet, then <u>slowly</u> add champagne. Do not stir after adding champagne.

Zoerita Proctor
Nashboro Council

HOLIDAY CHAMPAGNE PUNCH

1 fifth Southern Comfort
1/2 c. light rum
1 c. pineapple juice
1 c. grapefruit juice

1/2 c. lemon juice
2 qt. champagne or soda
Water

Chill ingredients overnight. You may mix ahead, but add the champagne at the last minute. Pour over ice in punch bowl. Float thin slices of citrus on top.

Patsy Carter
Harpeth Council

CRANBERRY PUNCH

1 (12 oz.) can frozen
   orange juice concentrate
1 (46 oz.) can pineapple
   juice

1 (12 oz.) can frozen
   lemonade concentrate
1 (46 oz.) can cranberry
   juice cocktail

Add water to frozen concentrates as directed on cans and mix all together. Serve in punch bowl over custard ice or cubes, or freeze part of the punch in ring mold or as cubes, adding slices of lemon and orange, or maraschino cherries, if desired. Garnish with mint leaves. Serves 50.

Joyce Mattice
Harpeth Council

FRUIT PUNCH

2 (6 oz.) cans frozen orange juice
1 (6 oz.) can frozen lemonade

1 c. pineapple juice
1/4 c. cherry juice (optional)
2 qt. pale dry ginger ale

Mix fruit juices; cover and let stand 12 hours or more in refrigerator. Add cold ginger ale to juices just before serving. Serve over crushed ice or freeze half the ginger ale in refrigerator trays. Yield: 24 servings.

Lauraette Cheatham
Harpeth Council

FRUIT PUNCH SLUSH

6 ripe bananas
1 (6 oz.) can frozen lemonade, thawed, undiluted
1 (12 oz.) can frozen orange juice, thawed, undiluted

1 (46 oz.) can pineapple juice
3 c. water
2 c. sugar
2 (32 oz.) bottles lemon-lime carbonated beverage, chilled

Combine bananas and fruit juice concentrate in container of electric blender; blend until smooth. Combine banana mixture, pineapple juice, water and sugar in a large mixing bowl; mix well. Pour into plastic freezer containers. Freeze to serve. Thaw until mushy. Add carbonated beverages. Garnish with orange slices.

Sue Amburn
Knoxville Council

HOLIDAY PUNCH

1 (16 oz.) can sliced peaches, pineapple or fruit cocktail, drained (you may also use fresh fruits)
1/2 c. sugar

1/2 - 1 c. white wine or 1/2 - 1 c. brandy
1 or 2 bottles white wine
1 bottle champagne (optional)
1 large bottle 7-Up or something like it

Put peaches into punch bowl; mix with sugar. Add 1/2 to 1 cup of wine or brandy and let set overnight or all day in refrigerator. When serving, add white wine first, then the champagne, then the 7-Up. Add ice cubes and you can also add the frozen leftover fruit juice from the peaches, etc.

Elizabeth Lemonte
Clarksville Council

ICE CREAM PUNCH

2 1/2 gal. sherbet
4 c. pineapple juice
2 cans orange juice

1 gal. vanilla ice cream
2 bottles ginger ale

Put ice cream and sherbet in a large bowl; let soften. Mix with a potato masher. Add juices and ginger ale. Mix well and serve.

Minnie McFarland
Harpeth Council

MILK PUNCH

1 c. brandy (bourbon or
  rum is also good)
2 c. cold milk
6 Tbsp. powdered sugar

1/2 tsp. vanilla
6-8 ice cubes, coarsely
  crushed
Nutmeg

Pour spirits into blender with all ingredients, except nutmeg; blend well. Pour into glasses or cups and sprinkle with nutmeg. Makes about 5 1/2 cups punch.

Patsy Carter
Harpeth Council

MIMOSA PUNCH

4 bottles champagne, chilled   4 qt. orange juice, chilled

Just before serving, pour champagne and orange juice into large punch bowl; ladle into champagne glasses. Makes 58 four ounce servings, about 75 calories each.

Casandra Key
Harpeth Council

NASHVILLE'S HOT CRANBERRY MULL

1 gal. cranberry juice
2 (6 oz.) cans frozen
  lemonade

2 (6 oz.) cans frozen orange
  juice
1 c. sugar

Place above ingredients into a large kettle or saucepan. Make a spice bag of:

1 tsp. whole cloves
1/2 tsp. allspice
Peel from 1/2 orange, cut
  into strips

Peel from 1/2 lemon, cut into
  strips
1/4 stick butter

Place spices and peels in a square of cheesecloth. Tie securely and drop into juice mixture; bring to a boil. Reduce heat immediately to low. Keep burner turned on just enough to keep mull hot. Remove spice bag and add the butter; stir well. Great for the holidays!

Marian Molteni
Harpeth Council

PEPPERMINT PUNCH

2 qt. cold milk
2 qt. ginger ale

1 qt. peppermint ice cream
5 sticks peppermint candy,
  crushed

In punch bowl, mix together milk and ginger ale. Scoop ice cream on top. Garnish with crushed peppermint candy.

Shirley Robertson
Harpeth Council

PINK PUNCH

1 pkg. cherry jello
2 tea bags
3 cinnamon sticks
15 whole cloves

3 c. sugar
1 large can pineapple juice
1 (8 oz.) bottle ReaLemon
  juice
Water

Place tea bags in 1 pint of boiling water with cinnamon and cloves; let stand for 2 hours. Dissolve jello in 1 pint of boiling water; add sugar, pineapple juice, lemon juice and

3 quarts water. Strain tea mixture and combine with juice mixture; stir to blend. Makes 2 gallons.

Peggy Hunter
Harpeth Council

RUM PUNCH

2 qt. freshly squeezed
　orange juice
40 oz. frozen lemon juice
1 pt. Curacao

1 c. grenadine
1 fifth dark rum
2 fifths light rum

Mix all ingredients together. Serve over ice. Garnish with slices of orange and lemon and sprigs of mint. Serves 25.

Patsy Carter
Harpeth Council

SPRING TEA PUNCH

1 qt. boiling water
6 tea bags or 6 tsp. instant
　tea
1 (6 oz.) can frozen
　pineapple juice concen-
　trate, undiluted

1 (6 oz.) can frozen lemonade
　concentrate, undiluted
1/4 c. grenadine syrup
3 c. lemon-lime carbonated
　beverage
1 qt. cold water
1/4 c. sugar

Bring water to a full rolling boil. Pour over tea; cover and brew for 3 to 5 minutes. Remove tea bags. Add sugar; stir until dissolved. Add frozen concentrates; stir to dissolve. Add cold water and grenadine; chill. When ready to serve, pour over ice cubes in punch bowl. Add carbonated beverage and garnish with lemon slices and strawberries. If using instant tea, simply combine boiling water with tea and follow recipe. No need to brew. Yield: 3 quarts.

Carolyn Mitchell
Memphis Downtown Council

STRAWBERRY PUNCH

2 (10 oz.) pkg. frozen
strawberries, thawed

1 large can frozen lemonade,
thawed
3 large bottles 7-Up

Blend 2 packages frozen strawberries, thawed, in blender. Add lemonade to strawberry mixture; mix well. Add 3 bottles 7-Up; stir well. Makes approximately 25 servings.

Rosemary Catalani
Harpeth Council

TEA PUNCH

7 tea bags   2 c. water

Bring to boil. In a 1 gallon container, mix:

1 small can orange juice
1 small can lemonade

1 1/2 c. sugar or 1 Tbsp.
Sweeta

While tea is hot, pour over the sugar; mix well, then add juices. Mix well. Fill container to the top with water enough to make 1 gallon.

Marian Molteni
Harpeth Council

TEA PUNCH

4 tea bags
2 c. boiling water
3 large lemons
2 c. sugar

4 c. cold water
1 tsp. vanilla flavoring
1 tsp. almond flavoring
2 (28 oz.) bottles ginger ale

Make tea with tea bags and boiling water. Mix juice of 2 lemons with tea. Add sugar, cold water, vanilla and almond flavorings to tea mixture. Pour in ginger ale before serving and garnish with remaining lemon, sliced. Serve over ice.

Katrina Carter
Harpeth Council

TEA PUNCH

1 qt. boiling water
2 1/2 c. sugar
1 (12 oz.) can frozen
   orange juice

Fresh mint leaves
5 tea bags
2 (6 oz.) cans frozen
   lemonade
1 qt. ginger ale

In a gallon container, pour boiling water over tea bags. Cover and steep 5 minutes. Add sugar; stir until dissolved. Add orange juice and lemonade; mix. When ready to serve, add ginger ale and water to make 1 gallon. Serve over ice and garnish with mint leaves. Makes 1 gallon.

Joyce Mattice
Harpeth Council

TRADER'S PUNCH

2 c. bottled orange juice
2 c. bottled lemon juice
   (ReaLemon)

2 c. grenadine syrup
2 1/2 qt. ginger ale, chilled

Combine orange juice, lemon juice and grenadine syrup. Pour into punch bowl. Just before serving, pour ginger ale down the side; stir to blend. Makes 4 quarts.

Evalyn Morris
Harpeth Council

SANGRIA

1 bottle burgundy
4 oranges, squeezed
1/2 c. water

1/4 - 1/2 c. sugar
Maraschino cherries
1 orange, sliced

Mix burgundy, orange juice, water and sugar together. Garnish with orange slices and maraschino cherries. Add ice and serve cold.

Patsy Carter
Harpeth Council

HOT RUSSIAN TEA

Bring 2 quarts water to a boil on stove and remove. Add 1/2 cup loose tea leaves; steep exactly 5 minutes. Strain into a large enamel pot. Add:

1 qt. water
1 large can crushed
   pineapple and juice

1 (46 oz.) can pure orange
   juice
Juice of 2 lemons
2 c. sugar

Put into a muslin bag or your tea ball 20 whole cloves and three 3 inch sticks of cinnamon. Boil exactly 3 minutes. Remove bag of spices and serve hot with sliced oranges on top.

Marian Molteni
Harpeth Council

HOT SPICED TEA

2 c. Tang orange juice
1 c. sugar
1 (10 oz.) pkg. dry
   lemonade mix

1/2 c. instant tea
1 tsp. cinnamon
1 tsp. ground cloves

Mix all ingredients and keep covered in glass jar. Use about 2 teaspoons per cup of hot water.

Cindy Martin
Harpeth Council

INSTANT RUSSIAN TEA

Mix together:
1/2 c. instant tea
1 1/4 c. sugar
2 c. Tang
1 tsp. ground cinnamon

2 small pkg. Wyler's lemonade
   mix (3/4 c. if using from
   a large can)
1/2 tsp. ground cloves

Store in an airtight glass container. Pour 1 cup boiling water over 2 to 3 tablespoons dry mix for 1 cup of hot tea.

Marian Molteni
Harpeth Council

MORE TEA

2 Tbsp. or 4 tea bags
    Constant Comment tea
6 cloves
2 sticks cinnamon

Juice of 1 lemon and 1 lime
16 oz. can frozen orange
    juice
1 1/2 c. sugar
4 qt. water

Bring 1 quart water to boil; take off stove. Add tea bags, cloves and cinnamon to water and steep for 10 minutes. Add sugar, orange juice, lemon juice and lime juice and remainder of water. Store in refrigerator until ready to serve. Makes approximately 1 1/2 gallons.

Halliel Thomas
Nashville Council

SPICED TEA

1 small jar instant tea with
    lemon
1 small jar Tang

2 c. sugar
1/2 tsp. cinnamon
1/2 tsp. cloves

Mix all ingredients together well. Store in a tightly closed container. To mix with boiling water, use 2 teaspoons tea mixture per cup.

Tricia Owens
Harpeth Council

SPICED TEA

1/2 c. instant tea with lemon
2 c. Tang (powdered orange
    mix)

1 tsp. ground cinnamon
1 tsp. ground cloves
2 1/2 c. sugar

Mix and store in Tupperware sealed container. For 1 serving by the cup, add 2 teaspoons mix and fill with boiling water; 3/8 cup mix for 1 quart; 3/4 cup mix for 1/2 gallon; 1 1/2 cups for 1 gallon.

Carolyn North
Harpeth Council

TROPICAL ICE

2 c. orange juice
1 (No. 2) can crushed
  pineapple
2 Tbsp. lemon juice

2 c. (6 or 7) mashed bananas
1 c. sugar
10-12 maraschino cherries

Combine and freeze in ice cube trays. Pretty when served in your favorite holiday punch.

Carolyn Mitchell
Memphis Downtown Council

WASSAIL

2 lemons, juiced
2 oranges, juiced
3 c. water
1 c. sugar

1 cinnamon stick
1 Tbsp. whole cloves
2 gal. apple cider

Put sugar and spices in water; bring to a boil. Pour all ingredients together and mix; heat. Serve hot.

Peggy Hunter
Harpeth Council

WINE

4 1/2 lb. (9 c.) fruit

2 1/2 lb. (5 c.) sugar

Pick and wash fruit and place with sugar in a gallon jar. Fill with cold water. Cover with cheesecloth and keep in a warm place. Stir twice a week for 6 weeks. Strain and let stand 2 weeks longer. Strain again and bottle. Do not cork or seal tight for several more weeks.

Maxine Scott
East Memphis Council

SALADS, SOUPS, SAUCES

HERBS AND SPICES

Allspice — Pungent aromatic spice, whole or in powdered form. It is excellent in marinades, particularly in game marinade, or in curries.

Basil — Can be chopped and added to cold poultry salads. If the recipe calls for tomatoes or tomato sauce, add a touch of basil to bring out a rich flavor.

Bay leaf — The basis of many French seasonings. It is added to soups, stews, marinades and stuffings.

Bouquet garni — A must in many Creole cuisine recipes. It is a bundle of herbs, spices and bay leaf tied together and added to soups, stews or sauces.

Celery seed — From wild celery rather than domestic celery. It adds pleasant flavor to bouillon or a stock base.

Chervil — One of the traditional *fines herbes* used in French-derived cooking. (The others are tarragon, parsley and chives.) It is good in omelets or soups.

Chives — Available fresh, dried or frozen, it can be substituted for raw onion or shallot in any poultry recipe.

Cinnamon — Ground from the bark of the cinnamon tree, it is important in desserts as well as savory dishes.

Coriander — Adds an unusual flavor to soups, stews, chili dishes, curries and some desserts.

Cumin — A staple spice in Mexican cooking. To use, rub seeds together and let them fall into the dish just before serving. Cumin also comes in powdered form.

Garlic — One of the oldest herbs in the world, it must be carefully handled. For best results, press or crush garlic clove.

Marjoram — An aromatic herb of the mint family, it is good in soups, sauces, stuffings and stews.

Mustard (dry) — Brings a sharp bite to sauces. Sprinkle just a touch over roast chicken for a delightful flavor treat.

Oregano — A staple herb in Italian, Spanish and Mexican cuisines. It is very good in dishes with a tomato foundation; it adds an excellent savory taste.

APPLE SALAD

1 (3 oz.) pkg. lemon or
lime jello
1 (8 1/4 oz.) can crushed
pineapple

1 c. miniature marshmallows
1/2 (8 oz.) ctn. Cool Whip
1 c. chopped apples
3 oz. pkg. cream cheese

Put jello in saucepan. Drain pineapple; add water to pineapple juice to make 1 cup. Let come to a boil; add cream cheese and marshmallows. Let dissolve. Put in long Pyrex dish. Add pineapple and apples, then Cool Whip; mix well. Refrigerate.

Helen Widick
Harpeth Council

APPLE-MINT SALAD

3 1/2 c. water
1/3 c. mint flavored apple
jelly
1 c. chopped apple

1 (3 oz.) pkg. lime flavored
gelatin
1 (3 oz.) pkg. lemon
flavored gelatin

Combine 2 cups water and jelly; bring to boil, stirring until jelly melts. Add to combined gelatins; stir until gelatin dissolves. Add remaining water. Chill until partially set; fold in apples. Pour into lightly oiled 9 inch layer pan; chill until firm. Unmold on serving platter.

Topping:

1 c. heavy cream, whipped
1/2 c. mayonnaise

2 c. miniature marshmallows

Combine whipped cream and mayonnaise; fold in marshmallows. Spoon onto gelatin. Garnish with apple slices and mint, if desired. Makes 8-10 servings.

Rosemary Grand
Harpeth Council

APRICOT SALAD

1 medium size can crushed pineapple, undrained	2 c. buttermilk
	1 (8 oz.) ctn. Cool Whip
1 large box apricot jello	1 c. chopped pecans

Empty pineapple in saucepan (large pan). Add jello; heat until jello dissolves. Allow to cool. Add buttermilk, Cool Whip and pecans; mix well. Empty into dish and chill (I let it chill overnight).

Yvonne Eldridge
Knoxville Council

APRICOT SALAD

8 oz. Cool Whip	12 oz. ctn. cottage cheese
3 oz. apricot jello	1/2 c. slivered almonds

Mix jello in cottage cheese. Add Cool Whip, then almonds. (Ready to eat.)

Audrey T. Lancaster
Knoxville Council

ASPARAGUS SALAD

Heat together:
1 can asparagus soup	1/2 c. boiling water

Add 1 package lemon jello; cool mixture. Mash and blend together:

1 (8 oz.) pkg. cream cheese	1/4 c. sweet pickle relish
1/2 c. mayonnaise	1 small onion, scraped
3/4 c. chopped celery	Salt

Blend the two mixtures. Pour in mold and chill overnight. An 8 or 9 inch pan does nicely for cutting into squares. Serve on lettuce leaf. Serves 8 or 9.

Berry Marshall
Nashville Council

60

BLUEBERRY SALAD

2 pkg. grape jello
1 (No. 2) can crushed
  pineapple

2 c. boiling water
1 (No. 2) can blueberry pie
  filling

Mix together and chill.

Topping for Blueberry Salad:

8 oz. cream cheese,
  softened
8 oz. sour cream

1/2 c. sugar
1/2 tsp. vanilla
1/2 c. pecans

Mix topping ingredients together and spread over congealed jello mixture.

Katrina Carter
Harpeth Council

BLUEBERRY CONGEALED SALAD

1 can blueberry pie filling
2 regular boxes Concord
  grape jello
1 large can crushed pine-
  apple in heavy syrup

1 (8 oz.) pkg. Philadelphia
  cream cheese
1 (8 oz.) ctn. sour cream
2 Tbsp. sugar
1/2 c. crushed pecans
1 c. chopped pecans

Put dry jello in large bowl; add 2 cups boiling water. Stir in pie filling, pineapple with syrup and crushed pecans (optional). Pour in oblong dish; cover and let congeal overnight in refrigerator. Next day, blend cream cheese, sour cream and sugar until smooth. Spread this on top of salad, then sprinkle chopped pecans on top.

Nancy Peete
E. Memphis Council

BLUEBERRY JELLO SALAD

Salad:

2 (3 oz.) pkg. blackberry
  jello
2 c. boiling water

1 c. cold water
1 can blueberry pie filling
1 small can crushed pineapple

Topping:

1/2 pt. sour cream
1 (8 oz.) pkg. cream cheese
1/2 c. sugar

1/2 tsp. vanilla
1/2 c. nuts

Mix salad ingredients together; let congeal.
For topping: Cream cream cheese and mix with sour cream. Add vanilla, sugar and nuts. Spread on top of congealed salad. Serve on crisp lettuce.

Frances R. Lauderdale
Downtown Memphis Council

BROCCOLI SALAD

1 large bunch raw broccoli, cleaned and chopped

1 lb. mushrooms, sliced

Dressing:

5 hard boiled eggs
1 large onion, chopped

1 c. mayonnaise
1 Tbsp. lemon juice

Mix together and toss with broccoli and mushrooms. Let marinate in refrigerator 6 to 8 hours.

Mary Crabtree
Knoxville Council

RAW BROCCOLI SALAD

1 bunch broccoli, washed and cut
1/2 c. onion, chopped
1/2 c. ripe olives, sliced
3 hard cooked eggs, sliced

1 Tbsp. lemon juice
Salt and pepper
1 pkg. "Hidden Valley Ranch" buttermilk dressing

Combine all raw vegetables, except eggs. Mix dressing according to package directions and use enough to coat broccoli mixture well. Add sliced eggs last and stir as little as possible.

Sonya C. Fagan
Nashboro Council

62

BUTTERMILK SALAD

1 large can crushed
  pineapple
2 (3 oz.) pkg. peach jello

2 c. buttermilk
1 (9 oz.) ctn. Cool Whip

Heat undrained pineapple until boiling. Add jello and dissolve. Cool; add buttermilk. Let this mixture cool and fold in Cool Whip; mix thoroughly and congeal.

Eugenia W. Smith
Chattanooga Council

CHERRY SALAD

2 pkg. cherry jello
2 c. hot water
1 can (Comstock) cherry
  pie filling
1/2 c. chopped pecans

1 (No. 2) can crushed pineapple, juice and all
1 (8 oz.) pkg. cream cheese,
  room temperature
Milk

Mix jello and water together; let stand for about 10 minutes. Add pie filling and pineapple; stir until well blended. Pour half of mixture into 13x9x2 inch dish. Chill until firm. (Let other half of mixture stand at room temperature until needed.) After first part is chilled, mix cream cheese and just enough milk together so that it will spread easily. Spread over first portion and sprinkle with chopped nuts. Add last half of jello mixture; chill until firm.

Mrs. R.C. Burton
Knoxville Council

CHERRY SALAD

1 can pie cherries
2 1/2 c. water
1/2 c. sugar
1 c. Coca-Cola

1 large pkg. jello or 2 small
  pkg. (cherry)
1 (No. 2) can crushed
  pineapple
1/2 c. pecans, chopped

Combine cherries, 1/2 cup water and sugar in saucepan; boil for 5 minutes. Mix jello with 2 cups boiling water; add Coke. Cool until mixture begins to thicken slightly. Add cherry mixture, nuts and pineapple. Yield: 12 servings.

Dot Crouch
Clarksville Council

AUNT JENNY'S CHERRY SALAD

Mix together:

1 can cherry pie filling
1 can Eagle Brand milk
1 or 2 c. chopped pecans

1 can drained pineapple
   (crushed or chunk style)
1 large ctn. Cool Whip

Mix and chill before serving.

Kay Boswell
Andrew Jackson Council

FROZEN CHERRY SALAD

1 (16 oz.) can cherry pie
   filling
1 (14 oz.) can crushed
   pineapple

1 (14 oz.) can condensed milk
   (Eagle Brand)
1 (13 oz.) ctn. whipped
   topping

Mix all ingredients; freeze in 9x13 inch pan. Cut in squares and garnish with pecans.

Denise Gill
Harpeth Council
Sharon Rawlings
Harpeth Council

ENGLISH'S FROZEN CHERRY SALAD

1 can cherry pie filling
1 can Eagle Brand milk
1 c. small marshmallows
1 large container Cool Whip

1 c. pecans, broken
   (optional)
2 small cans crushed
   pineapple

Drain crushed pineapple well, then mix all ingredients together. Pour into a greased 9x13x2 inch pan; place in freezer. May be served frozen or slightly thawed.

Marian Molteni
Harpeth Council

CHEERY CHERRY SALAD

1 large can pineapple
   chunks
1 small can Mandarin
   oranges

1 large banana, sliced
1 can cherry pie filling
Marshmallows
Chopped pecans

Drain pineapple and oranges. Fold in cherry pie filling and sliced bananas. You may add marshmallows and chopped pecans, if desired.

Judy Ragan
Clarksville Council

BLACK CHERRY SALAD

Dissolve together:
2 (3 oz.) pkg. cherry jello   1 c. boiling water
(1 black cherry, 1
regular cherry)

Add to the dissolved gelatin:
1 (No. 2) can crushed pine-   1 (No. 2) can pitted, halved
apple, including juice   black cherries, including
1 c. sweet red wine   juice
                                 1/2 c. chopped pecans

Turn mixture into 1 1/2 quart mold and chill. Before well set, chip into mixture 2 (3 ounce) packages Philadelphia cream cheese. Chill until firm. Especially good with chicken or ham dinner.

Deenie Thornton
Nashville Council

CHICKEN SALAD

1 medium hen (about 4 lb.)   Mayonnaise
Chopped celery   Salt
1 lemon

Clean and salt hen. Boil gently until tender, then cool. Pull meat from bones; cut white meat in larger chunks than dark meat. Add 1 cup chopped celery to every 2 cups chicken. Add juice of 1 lemon and enough mayonnaise to make a moist salad. Salt to taste and add cayenne pepper, if desired.

Eugenia W. Smith
Chattanooga Council

CHICKEN SALAD

1 hen (about 4 lb.)
4 sweet pickles, diced (or
  sweet relish)
2 hard boiled eggs, diced
3 or 4 ribs celery, cut fine
1 Tbsp. vinegar

4 Tbsp. chicken broth
Salt and pepper to taste
Mayonnaise to moisten (salad
  dressing)
1/2 c. broken pecans
  (optional)

Simmer the hen until tender in water to which you have added salt and a bay leaf. Cool chicken in broth, then remove meat from the bones and cut into small pieces. Add all remaining ingredients, except nuts and mayonnaise. Refrigerate overnight. Add mayonnaise and nuts before serving.

Theresa Alexander
Harpeth Council

CHICKEN SALAD

6 c. chopped, cooked
  chicken
1 c. chopped celery
1 c. seedless grapes, sliced

1 small can chunk pineapple,
  drained
1/2 c. chopped nuts (pecans,
  etc.)

Mix lightly and add salad dressing to moisten.

Mary Grey Jenkins
Green Hills Council

BAKED CHICKEN SALAD

4-6 c. cubed chicken
2 c. chopped celery
1/3 c. almonds
6 boiled eggs
4 Tbsp. grated onion
2 Tbsp. lemon juice
1 c. salad dressing (Miracle
  Whip)

1 c. cracker crumbs
Dash of Worcestershire sauce
Salt and pepper to taste
3 cans cream of chicken soup
  and 1 small can mushrooms,
  drained, or 2 cans cream of
  chicken soup and 1 can
  mushroom soup

Combine all, except cracker crumbs, and place in greased baking dish. Top with cracker crumbs and cover. Bake 45 minutes at 400° or less. You may omit almonds and mushrooms.

Pattie Hoffman
Nashboro Council

BAKED CHICKEN SALAD

2 c. cubed, cooked chicken
2 c. chopped celery
1/2 c. chopped, toasted
almonds
1/2 tsp. salt
2 Tbsp. grated onion

1/2 c. chopped green pepper
1/2 c. mayonnaise
2 Tbsp. lemon juice
1/2 can creamed chicken soup
1/2 c. grated American
cheese
3 c. crushed potato chips

Combine all ingredients, except cheese and potato chips; toss lightly. Spoon into 1 1/2 quart casserole. Spread cheese and potato chips on top. Bake at 350° for 25 minutes or until heated through and browned. Garnish with paprika and parsley, if desired. Yield: 8 servings.

Annie H. Harper
Nashville Council

CALIFORNIA CHICKEN SALAD

1 stick butter
2 c. mayonnaise
1/4 c. minced parsley
1/2 tsp. curry powder

4 c. shredded, cooked
chicken breasts
2 c. seedless green grapes
1/2 c. toasted, slivered
almonds

Melt butter in saucepan; let cool. Stir in mayonnaise, parsley and curry powder. Pour mixture over chicken. Serve on lettuce leaves and top with grapes, almonds and paprika.

Tricia Owens
Harpeth Council

CHRISTMAS SALAD

1 small can crushed
pineapple
1 pkg. cherry jello
1 c. water

1/2 c. chopped nuts
1/2 pt. whipping cream
1 c. cottage cheese

Heat 1 cup water to boiling. Add 1 small can crushed pineapple and continue cooking for 3 minutes. Add 1 package cherry jello to pineapple and water; stir until well dissolved. Set aside and let cool to syrup stage. Add 1 cup

1489-81

cottage cheese and 1/2 cup nuts. Whip 1/2 pint whipping cream; stir into mixture. Let stand until chilled.

Helen Hardison
Columbia Council

CLASSIC RICE SALAD

3 c. cooked rice
1/4 c. diced pimento (also
  use olives, if desired)
1 tsp. salt
1/4 tsp. pepper

1 c. Hellmann's mayonnaise
1 tsp. prepared mustard
1/2 c. finely chopped onion
1/2 c. finely chopped sweet
  pickles

Blend thoroughly and chill. Yield: 6 generous servings.

Inda Adams
Andrew Jackson Council

COLE SLAW

1 medium head cabbage,
  shredded or grated
2 1/2 small carrots,
  scraped and grated
1 c. Hellmann's mayonnaise
1/4 c. light cream or milk

1/3 c. onion, finely minced
Salt and pepper to taste
  (black or white)
1/2 bell pepper, chopped
1 Tbsp. sugar
1 Tbsp. vinegar

Combine cabbage, carrots and bell pepper in large salad bowl. Add mayonnaise, onion and light cream or milk; mix well. Add salt, pepper, sugar and vinegar; mix well. Cover and refrigerate.

Ruth and Deborah Cole
Harpeth Council

COLE SLAW SOUFFLE

1 (8 oz.) can crushed
  pineapple
1 (3 oz.) pkg. orange
  flavored gelatin
3/4 c. boiling water
3/4 c. mayonnaise

1 c. shredded carrot
1/2 c. raisins (optional)
1/2 c. chopped walnuts or
  pecans (optional)
3 egg whites, stiffly beaten
1 c. finely shredded cabbage

Fold a 6x22 inch piece of aluminum foil in half

68

lengthwise. Tape firmly around top of 1 quart souffle dish, having about 2 inches of foil extending over top of dish. Drain pineapple; reserve liquid. Dissolve gelatin in boiling water; add reserved pineapple liquid. Beat in mayonnaise. Pour into loaf pan; freeze until firm 1 inch from edge, but soft in center, about 20 minutes. In large bowl, beat until fluffy. Fold in pineapple, cabbage, carrots, raisins and walnuts, then egg whites. Pour into prepared dish. Chill until set; remove foil. Serves 6.

Rosemary Grand
Harpeth Council

CREAMY COLE SLAW
(A creamy delight thanks to the richness of Pet.)

1 small can (2/3 c.) Pet
   the cream of evaporated
   milk
1/4 c. Musselman's apple
   cider vinegar
2 Tbsp. sugar
1 tsp. salt

1/4 tsp. celery seeds
1/8 tsp. pepper
1/2 c. mayonnaise
4 c. shredded cabbage
1 carrot, shredded
1 stalk celery, diced

1. Stir together Pet, vinegar, sugar, salt, celery seeds, pepper and mayonnaise; chill until ready to serve. 2. Combine cabbage, carrot and celery; chill. 3. To serve: Pour Pet mixture over cabbage mixture; toss to coat well. Serve immediately. Makes six servings, 1/2 cup each.

Cornelia L. Mangrum
Harpeth Council

GERMAN COLE SLAW

Chop:
1 medium head cabbage
1 medium onion

1 bell pepper

Sprinkle 1 cup of sugar over slaw; let stand while you bring to a boil:

1 c. Wesson oil
1 c. vinegar

1 1/2 tsp. salt
1 tsp. dry mustard
Celery seed

Pour over slaw while hot and let set overnight. Will keep several days in refrigerator.

Belinda Dorris
Nashboro Council

HOT SLAW

1 head cabbage, cut up fine
2 small onions, cut up fine
1 c. sugar
1/2 tsp. celery seed
1/2 c. oil
1/2 c. vinegar
1 tsp. salt
1/4 tsp. dry mustard

Combine sugar, celery seed, oil, vinegar, salt and dry mustard in saucepan; bring to a boil and pour over cabbage and onions. Carrots or green peppers can also be used in this recipe, if you wish. Good hot or cold.

Phyllis Whaley
Andrew Jackson Council

REFRIGERATOR SLAW

1 medium head cabbage
1 medium onion
3/4 c. sugar
1 c. vinegar
2/3 c. salad oil
1 tsp. celery seed
1 Tbsp. salt
1 Tbsp. prepared mustard
1/3 c. sugar

Shred cabbage and onion. Combine with 3/4 cup sugar mix well. Heat remaining ingredients to boiling and pour over cabbage mixture; mix. Cover and refrigerate overnight before serving. Keeps well for at least 1 week. This slaw is one of the few cabbage salads that improves with refrigerator storage.

Kay Lindsey
Nashboro Council

SLAW SUPREME

1 large head shredded
  cabbage
1 can onion flakes
1 can pepper flakes
1 can celery flakes
1/2 can parsley flakes
1 Tbsp. salad supreme
1 Tbsp. lemon pepper
2 Tbsp. sugar
1 regular bottle Wish-Bone
  Italian dressing

Add salt and pepper to taste. Let set overnight in refrigerator before serving.

Ginger Lewis
Harpeth Council

SWEDISH SLAW

1 head cabbage, grated   1 medium onion, chopped
1 bell pepper, chopped

Combine the following; boil 1 minute:

1 c. sugar   1 tsp. dry mustard
1 c. wine vinegar   1 tsp. turmeric

Pour over vegetables; chill overnight.

Clara Rainey
Harpeth Council

24 HOUR SLAW

1 head cabbage, chopped   1 bell pepper, chopped
1 onion, chopped

Mix together:
1 c. vinegar   1 Tbsp. turmeric
1 c. sugar   1 Tbsp. salt
1 Tbsp. mustard seed   1 Tbsp. celery seed

Bring to a boil; pour over chopped ingredients while still hot. Let set in refrigerator for 12 hours.

Claudia Davenport
Clarksville Council

MEXICAN CABBAGE SLAW

1 small head cabbage   1 medium onion
1 green pepper

Shred cabbage. Chop onion and bell pepper; set aside. Mix:

1 c. vinegar   1 tsp. dry mustard
1 c. sugar   1 tsp. salt
1/2 tsp. turmeric
1489-81   71

Heat vinegar, sugar, salt, turmeric and mustard mixture. Let cool about 5 minutes; pour over cabbage mixture. Cover in bowl; let stand 24 hours. Will keep in covered bowl 2 to 3 weeks.

Lena Roberson
Andrew Jackson Council

CONGEALED SALAD

1 small pkg. lemon jello
1 c. water (this includes juice from pineapple)
1 small ctn. Cool Whip
1 small can crushed pineapple, drained

1 can Eagle Brand milk
1 pkg. coconut (frozen)
1 c. nuts
1 banana
Miniature marshmallows (about 1/2 pkg.)

Heat water to boiling and pour over gelatin; dissolve. Cool and then put in other ingredients. Mix well and chill.

Maelene Haggard
Jackson Council

CONGEALED SALAD

1 small box orange jello
1 (3 oz.) pkg. cream cheese
1 c. whipped cream

1 small bottle maraschino cherries and juice
1 small can crushed pineapple

Combine softened cream cheese, cherries and juice, pineapple and whipped cream. Add jello, which has been dissolved in 1 cup water and allowed to cool. Chill until firm. To serve, cut into serving sized squares and lightly press a halved pecan into each square.

Pat Carpenter
Nashville Council

CRANBERRY SALAD

1 large or 2 small pkg. jello (cherry, strawberry or raspberry)
1 (20 oz.) can crushed pineapple, drained (reserve juice)

1 can Mandarin oranges, drained
1 can whole berry cranberry sauce
1 c. chopped pecans
2 apples, peeled and grated, plus 1/2 tsp. lemon juice

Mix jello with 2 cups boiling water. Use pineapple juice and enough water to make 2 cups liquid. Add pineapple, oranges, cranberry sauce, nuts and apples. Mix well and pour in pan or mold.

Ann R. Rickard
Memphis Downtown Council

CRANBERRY SALAD

1/2 box cranberries (or   1 c. water
   1 c. cranberries)

Cook until berries pop open. Add:

1 small box cherry jello (powdered, no water)	1 small can crushed pineapple
1 1/2 c. sugar	1/2 c. chopped nuts

Chill.

Topping:

1 ctn. whipping cream	1 (3 oz.) pkg. cream cheese, chopped
1/2 bag small marshmallows	

Mix above 3 ingredients together and let set in refrigerator 3 or 4 hours. Whip and spread on top of cranberry mix.

Dean Tidwell
Nashboro Council

CRANBERRY SALAD

3 c. raw cranberries, ground	1 c. sugar
1 small pkg. lemon jello	1 c. chopped celery
	1 c. chopped nuts

Dissolve jello in 1 pint of boiling water. Add sugar to jello while hot. When cool, add celery, nuts and cranberries. Pour into Pyrex dish or mold; refrigerate.

Mary Cate
Knoxville Council

CRANBERRY SALAD

1 (13 1/2 oz.) can crushed
  pineapple
2 (3 oz.) pkg. lemon jello
7 oz. ginger ale
1 lb. jellied cranberry sauce
1/2 c. chopped pecans

1 Tbsp. butter
1 env. Dream Whip
Milk
Vanilla
8 oz. cream cheese, softened

Drain pineapple well; reserve juice. Add water to make 1 cup; heat to boiling. Add to jello and cool. Gently stir in ginger ale. Chill until partially set. Blend cranberry sauce and pineapple well; chill. Fold into jello; turn into 9x9 inch dish. Toast pecans in butter in 350° oven for 10 minutes. Mix Dream Whip with milk and vanilla as directed on package. Whip cream cheese. Fold Dream Whip gradually into cream cheese. Spread on top of jello mixture. Sprinkle with cooled pecans; chill.

Judy Desendorf
Harpeth Council

FROZEN CRANBERRY SALAD

1 c. sugar
1 (No. 2) can crushed
  pineapple, drained

1 can cranberry sauce (with
  whole berries)
2 bananas, sliced
1 medium ctn. Cool Whip

Put cranberry sauce and sugar in a bowl; let stand 30 minutes. Slice bananas and add to bowl of sugar, cranberry sauce and pineapple. Fold in Cool Whip; freeze.

Katrina Carter
Harpeth Council

MOLDED CRANBERRY SALAD

2 small pkg. strawberry
  jello

3 c. water (2 boiling, 1 cold
  to cool down)

Let this thicken while preparing the following:

1 can whole cranberry sauce
4 medium apples, peeled and
  grated, folded into the
  cranberries to keep from
  turning dark

1 c. broken pecans
15 marshmallows, cut up, or
  2 c. miniature marshmallows

74

When jello has thickened, add the previous mixture to it and fold in 1/2 pint of whipped cream. Pour into mold to set. (This holds up well to take to a covered dish meal.) Makes 2 molds.

Marguerite Webb
Green Hills Council

CRANBERRY-CHICKEN SURPRISE
(A Two-Layer Treat)

Layer 1: 1. Dissolve 1 package lemon jello in 3/4 cup boiling water. 2. Add 1/2 cup orange juice and 1 (8-10 ounce) can cranberry sauce, without berries; mix well. 3. Pour into casserole dish, approximately 13x11 inches; refrigerate until jelled well. While the first layer is chilling you can make the second.

Layer 2:

2 c. diced, cooked chicken	1/2 c. diced celery
2 hard boiled eggs, chopped	1 tsp. onion, finely chopped
1/2 c. sliced olives	1 c. mayonnaise
1 pkg. unflavored gelatin	

1. Dissolve gelatin in 3/4 cup boiling water. Add mayonnaise and mix well. 2. Mix in all remaining ingredients, then pour this layer on top of the first jelled layer. 3. Refrigerate several hours; cut in squares and serve on lettuce.

Virginia Taylor
Nashville Council

CUCUMBER SALAD

1 pkg. lime jello	2 Tbsp. grated onion
3/4 c. hot water	3/4 c. shredded, unpeeled
1 c. sour cream	cucumber, drained
1 c. cottage cheese	

Combine jello and hot water. When cool, add sour cream, cottage cheese, cucumber and onion. Stir only until mixed; congeal. Great summer salad; refreshing!

Doris Binkley
Nashboro Council

DATE SALAD

2 (3 oz.) pkg. cream cheese
1 c. mayonnaise
2 Tbsp. gelatin
1/4 c. cold water
1 (20 oz.) can pineapple
chunks (reserve juice)
1/2 pkg. chopped dates
1 c. nuts, chopped

Mix cheese with mayonnaise. Soak gelatin in cold water. Heat pineapple juice and add to gelatin, stirring until dissolved. Cool and add first mixture. Add dates, nuts and pineapple; chill in mold.

Margaret Powers
Harpeth Council

5-CUP SALAD

1 c. pineapple chunks,
drained
1 c. Mandarin orange slices,
drained and halved
1 can Angel Flake coconut
1 c. miniature marshmallows
1 c. sour cream

Mix and refrigerate.

Deenie Thornton
Green Hills Council

FLUFFY PECAN SALAD MOLD

6 oz. lemon jello
1 c. very hot water
2 c. unsweetened pineapple
juice
2 Tbsp. lemon juice
1 c. chopped pecans or
walnuts
2 egg whites
1/4 c. sugar
1 c. Cool Whip

Pour hot water over jello; stir until dissolved. Stir in pineapple and lemon juices. Chill, stirring occasionally, until slightly thickened. Stir in nuts. Beat egg whites until frothy. Gradually add sugar while beating until peaks begin to form. Spread Cool Whip and egg whites over jello mixture and gently fold together. Turn into 1 1/2 quart mold and chill until firm. Unmold onto chilled dessert dish.

Judy Desendorf
Harpeth Council

4 BEAN SALAD (500)

1 1/2 c. sugar
1 c. salad oil
Salt
1 c. vinegar
1 c. diced green pepper
2 c. thin sliced onion rings

2 (No. 10) cans wax beans
2 (No. 10) cans kidney beans
2 (No. 10) cans French
   green beans
2 (No. 10) cans lima beans

Thoroughly mix all ingredients. Refrigerate several hours or overnight. Use three No. 10 cans of each.

FRESH BROCCOLI SALAD

2 c. broccoli florets and
   tender parts of stems,
   cut in small pieces
2/3 c. sliced salad olives
1 large onion, cut in small
   cubes
2 Tbsp. lemon juice

6 hard cooked eggs, cubed
1/2 c. mushrooms, cut in
   pieces
1 tsp. sugar
Dash of salt and pepper
Shredded cheese or paprika
1/2 c. mayonnaise

Combine all ingredients, except eggs and cheese. Add eggs; stir gently. Refrigerate 2 to 4 hours. Before serving, decorate with grated or shredded cheese and/or paprika. This keeps well.

Dorothy Sue Tipton
Jackson Council

FRESH VEGETABLE SALAD

Combine:
1 bunch broccoli flowerets
1 head cauliflowerets
   (2 1/2 c.)

1 onion, chopped
1 c. cherry tomatoes

Dressing:

1 c. mayonnaise
1/2 c. sour cream

1 tsp. vinegar
2 tsp. sugar

Combine and toss lightly with vegetables listed above. This recipe can be made several days ahead and refrigerated until needed.

Mrs. E. Catlin
Memphis Council

FROST PINK SALAD

1 (8 oz.) pkg. cream cheese
2 Tbsp. sugar
1 can whole cranberries
1/2 c. nuts

2 Tbsp. mayonnaise
1 c. Cool Whip
1 small can crushed
   pineapple, drained

Soften cream cheese and mix in mayonnaise and sugar; blend well. Stir in pineapple, cranberries and nuts. Fold in Cool Whip; freeze. Serve semi-frozen or thawed.

Kathy Pack
Harpeth Council

FROZEN FRUIT SALAD

Mix together:
8 oz. cream cheese
2 Tbsp. mayonnaise
1 1/2 c. sugar

1 c. whipping cream,
   whipped, or small ctn.
   Cool Whip

Add to the above:
1 (No. 2) can fruit cocktail
   with juice

1 (No. 2) can crushed pineapple with juice
1/2 c. chopped pecans

Pour into a mold and freeze until hard.

Billie Fleming
Nashboro Council

FROZEN FRUIT SALAD

1 can Eagle Brand milk
1 container Cool Whip
1 can crushed pineapple

1 can apricots, drained and
   sliced
1 jar maraschino cherries

Mix and pour in dish. Freeze until solid.

Tricia Owens
Harpeth Council

FROZEN FRUIT SALAD

8 oz. Cool Whip
8 oz. cream cheese, whipped
3/4 c. sugar
2 bananas, cut up

No. 2 can crushed pineapple,
  drained
1 pt. strawberries, sliced
1/2 c. chopped nuts

Combine Cool Whip and cream cheese; stir in sugar. Add fruit and nuts. Pour into 9x11 inch Pyrex dish and freeze.

Beverly Pettigrew
Harpeth Council

FROZEN SALAD

1 (20 oz.) can cherry pie
  filling
1 (14 oz.) can Eagle Brand
  milk
1 (16 oz.) can crushed
  pineapple

1 (16 oz.) can fruit cocktail
1 (8 oz.) can sliced pears
1 (8 oz.) can sliced peaches
4 ripe bananas
1/4 c. lemon juice
1 (12 oz.) box whipped
  topping

Combine all ingredients; mix well. Put in Pyrex pan and freeze.
Optional: Cut and serve on lettuce leaf. Top with whipped cream and green cherry.

Margaret Ann Marshall
Clarksville Council

FROZEN SALAD

1 can whole berries
  cranberry sauce
3 bananas, sliced

1 (15 1/2 oz.) can crushed
  pineapple
1 small ctn. Cool Whip

Mix all ingredients and put in freezer. Take out about 15 or 30 minutes before serving.

Betty J. Garrett
Downtown Memphis Council

1489-81

FROZEN STRAWBERRY SALAD

1 (8 oz.) pkg. cream cheese
3/4 c. sugar
Regular container Cool Whip

1 can crushed pineapple
1 pkg. frozen strawberries
1 c. nuts (optional)

Mix sugar, cream cheese and gently fold in pineapple, then Cool Whip. Add nuts; fold in strawberries and freeze. Serves 10.

Betty Campbell
Knoxville Council

FROZEN TOMATO SALAD

1 qt. tomato juice
1 (3 oz.) pkg. cream
 cheese, softened
1 1/2 c. mayonnaise
1/8 tsp. ginger
Few drops of hot pepper
 sauce

1 env. unflavored gelatin
1 c. cottage cheese
2 tsp. onion juice
1 (8 3/4 oz.) can crushed
 pineapple
Salt and pepper to taste

Soften gelatin in 1 cup of the tomato juice. Heat the remaining tomato juice. Dissolve gelatin/tomato juice mixture in heated juice. Mix the cream cheese, cottage cheese, mayonnaise, onion juice, crushed pineapple and spices. Add to the juice; blend well. Freeze in individual salad molds or sheet mold. Serves 16-20.

Joyce Mattice
Harpeth Council

MARTHA CARTER FRUIT SALAD

1 can peach pie filling
16 oz. strawberries
1 small can white grapes,
 drained

1 small can chunk pineapple,
 drained
3 bananas, sliced

Mix together.

Addie Downs
Green Hills Council

80

FRUIT AND CHICKEN SALAD

3 c. chopped, cooked
  chicken
1 c. chopped celery
1 c. seedless white grapes,
  halved
1/2 c. white raisins

1 (11 oz.) can Mandarin
  oranges, drained
1 c. salad dressing
1/2 tsp. salt
Pepper to taste

Mix together gently, but well. Serve on lettuce leaf with melons such as watermelon, cantaloupe and honey dew. Assorted fruits such as pineapple, strawberries, etc. can also be added. Great for luncheons or light supper. Delicious with bran muffins. Serves 4.

Katie Braden
Harpeth Council

FRUIT SALAD

1 pkg. instant vanilla
  pudding
1 can fruit cocktail, drained

1 can pineapple chunks,
3 medium bananas

Drain pineapple and add juice to vanilla pudding; mix well. Add pineapple chunks, fruit cocktail and bananas. If more liquid is needed, add fruit cocktail juice. Chill in refrigerator.

Wilma O. Kelly
Knoxville Council

FRUIT SALAD

1 can Mandarin oranges
1 can pineapple chunks
1 small bottle cherries
1/2 c. broken pecans

1/2 pkg. frozen coconut
1/2 pkg. small marshmallows
1 c. cream (sour or whipped
  or Cool Whip)

Combine all ingredients with sour cream or whipped cream or Cool Whip.

Linda Kitchens
Green Hills Council

FRUIT SALAD

1 can Mandarin oranges
1 can pineapple chunks
1 pt. frozen strawberries

1 can peach pie filling
2 or 3 large bananas
2 Tbsp. Cool Whip

Drain juice from oranges, pineapple and strawberries. Do not use juices in the salad. Mix together, except bananas; add them when ready to serve.

Helen DeWolfe
Nashville Council

FRUIT SALAD

Boil together:
1/2 c. lemon juice

1/2 c. pineapple juice

Stir together:
2/3 c. sugar

2 beaten eggs

Add sugar and eggs to boiling juice; cook and stir until thick. Sauce will keep well in refrigerator. Use sauce over pineapple chunks, sliced bananas, maraschino cherries and miniature marshmallows.

Belinda Dorris
Nashboro Council

FRUIT SALAD SUPREME

1 can peach pie filling
1 small can pineapple
   chunks, drained

1 small can Mandarin oranges,
   drained

Mix thoroughly and add any fresh fruits available (nectarine, banana, cherries, pears, seedless grapes, strawberries, etc.). Coconut or miniature marshmallows can also be added. The variety makes this a different salad everytime it's made. Chill at least 2 hours before serving.

Ron Stunda
Harpeth Council

GRAPE JELLO

2 small pkg. grape jello	2 c. boiling water
1 can (Comstock) blueberry pie filling	1 (No. 2) can crushed pineapple, undrained

Mix jello and water together; let stand for about 10 minutes. Add pineapple and pie filling; stir until well blended. Pour into 13x9x2 inch dish; chill until firm.

Topping:

1 small ctn. sour cream	1/2 c. sugar
1 (8 oz.) pkg. cream cheese	2 Tbsp. vanilla
	1/2 c. nuts

Mix all ingredients until light and fluffy. Spread like icing over first mixture.

Mrs. R.C. Burton
Knoxville Council

GREEN SALAD DELIGHT

1 (6 oz.) pkg. lime jello	1 c. salad dressing or mayonnaise
2 c. boiling water	
1 large (20 oz.) can crushed pineapple	1 can Eagle Brand sweetened milk
1 small ctn. cottage cheese	1 c. chopped pecans

Dissolve jello in boiling water. Add a little at a time to salad dressing until blended. Add pineapple, juice included. Add other ingredients; stir. Pour in 9x13x2 inch pan or Pyrex bowl and refrigerate overnight. Slice and serve. Delicious!

Mary Brown
Harpeth Council

GREEN WONDER SALAD

1 (No. 303) can French green beans	1 (No. 303) can fancy Chinese vegetables (without meat)
1 (No. 303) can small English peas	1 (6 oz.) can water chestnuts
1 1/2 c. celery, diced	3 medium onions, sliced

Drain all cans and place in large bowl, also celery and onions. Heat 1 cup sugar (I use 2/3 cup), 3/4 cup vinegar, 1 teaspoon salt and pepper to taste. Pour over vegetables; refrigerate 8 hours or more. Good for 3 weeks.

Martha Cannon·
Knoxville Council

GUACAMOLE

2 avocados, mashed	1/4 tsp. chili powder
1 Tbsp. lemon juice	Dash of cayenne pepper
2 Tbsp. lime juice	1/3 c. mayonnaise
1 Tbsp. onion, grated	1/4 c. ripe olives, chopped
1 tsp. salt	4 slices crisp bacon, crumbled

Blend all ingredients thoroughly. Serve with warmed corn chips or spoon over shredded lettuce as a salad.

Patsy Carter
Harpeth Council

GUACAMOLE SALAD

2 large ripe avocados	1/2 tsp. salt
1/4 tsp. garlic powder	2 Tbsp. finely chopped onion
2 Tbsp. chili sauce or hot tomato sauce	1 Tbsp. lemon juice
	1 Tbsp. salad dressing

Peel avocados; mash well. Mix well with remaining ingredients. Serve on lettuce leaf with tostadas. (May also be used as a dip. Cottage cheese may be added as extender for dip.) Serves 4.

Joyce Mattice
Harpeth Council

HOMINY SALAD

1 (1 lb. 13 oz.) can gold and white hominy, drained, or 1 (1 lb.) can gold hominy and 1 (1 lb.) can white hominy, drained	4 slices bacon, fried crisp, crumbled
	1/2 c. green bell pepper, chopped
	1/2 c. red bell pepper, chopped
1 c. celery, sliced thin	1/2 large sweet onion, peeled, cut in half, thinly sliced

Saute onion in bacon drippings until soft but not brown. Mix all ingredients together; salt and pepper to taste. For dressing, you can use 1/2 to 1 cup dairy sour cream or mayonnaise. Or, make the following dressing.

Dressing:

1/2 large sweet onion,
   minced
1/2 c. cider vinegar
1/2 c. water
1 tsp. salt

1/4 tsp. pepper
1 Tbsp. sugar
1 tsp. cornstarch
Dash of Worcestershire sauce
Minced parsley for garnish

Mix together vinegar, water, salt, pepper, sugar and cornstarch until blended. Stir into onion. Heat until boiling and sauce has thickened. Add Worcestershire sauce; mix well. Cool.

Betty J. Cowherd
Andrew Jackson Council

SIMPLIFIED HOMINY SALAD

1 large can hominy
1/2 c. diced sweet pickle
2 hard cooked eggs

3 Tbsp. mayonnaise
1 small onion, chopped
Salt to taste

Cook hominy; drain off water and mix with next 4 ingredients. Add salt to taste. Chill to serve.

Betty J. Cowherd
Andrew Jackson Council

HONEY FRUIT SALAD

1 (15 1/4 oz.) can pine-
   apple chunks, undrained
2 medium oranges, peeled
   and sectioned
1 medium apple, peeled
   and diced

1 banana, peeled and sliced
1/2 c. chopped pecans
1/2 c. orange juice
1 Tbsp. fresh lemon juice
1/4 c. honey

Combine first 5 ingredients in a large bowl. Combine orange juice, lemon juice and honey in a small bowl; mix well. Pour over fruit, tossing gently; chill thoroughly. Yield: 4 to 6 servings.

Anita Turner
Memphis Downtown Council

HOT CHICKEN SALAD

3 chicken breasts, cut into
  small pieces, hot
4 hard boiled eggs, diced
1 1/2 c. mayonnaise
2 c. celery, diced
2 Tbsp. lemon juice
1/2 c. almonds

2 jars pimento (canned pieces)
1 tsp. salt
1/2 tsp. Accent
1 Tbsp. onion
1 c. grated sharp Cheddar
  cheese
1 1/2 c. finely crushed potato
  chips

Mix all but cheese and potato chips; let stand overnight. Next morning, mix well, adding cheese and potato chips. Bake at 400° for 25 minutes.

Ann R. Wooten
Memphis Council

HOT CHICKEN SALAD

2 c. chicken, cubed
2 c. celery
1/2 c. toasted almonds
2 tsp. grated onion

2 Tbsp. lemon juice
1 c. mayonnaise
1 can cream of chicken soup

Mix above ingredients together and put in a casserole. Sprinkle top with 1/2 cup grated Cheddar cheese and 1 cup crumbled potato chips. When ready to serve, heat in oven for 30 minutes at 400°. For the chicken, I boil a hen and bone it. This recipe serves 6.

Anne R. Rikard
Memphis Downtown Council

HOT CHICKEN SALAD

4-6 c. diced, cooked
  chicken
2 c. celery
6 hard boiled eggs
4 Tbsp. grated onion
1 c. mayonnaise
1 c. cracker crumbs

Dash of Worcestershire sauce
1/2 c. salted almonds,
  slivered
3 cans cream of chicken soup
2 Tbsp. lemon juice
Salt and pepper to taste
Small can of mushrooms

Mix all ingredients together. Put into 1 large or 2

small casserole bowls; cover with cracker crumbs. Sprinkle with paprika. Bake 45 minutes in 400° oven. This freezes well.

Dot Crouch
Clarksville Council

HOT CHICKEN SALAD

2 chicken breasts, cooked (equals about 2 c.)
1/2 c. mayonnaise
1 can cream of chicken soup
2 hard boiled eggs

1 c. chopped celery, cooked 5 minutes
1/2 c. slivered almonds
1 tsp. onion or more
1/2 c. cracker crumbs

Mix and top with potato chips, crushed. Bake at 350° for 20 minutes, no longer.

Carol McKinnon
Harpeth Council

HOT CHICKEN SALAD

2 c. diced, cooked chicken
2 c. diced celery
1/2 c. slivered almonds
1/2 tsp. salt
1/2 tsp. grated onion

2 Tbsp. freshly squeezed lemon juice
1/2 c. shredded mild cheese
1 c. mayonnaise
2/3 c. broken potato chips

Mix all ingredients, except cheese and chips. Turn into shallow buttered pan. Combine cheese and chips over top. Bake, uncovered, at 375° for 20 minutes.

Yvonne Eldridge
Knoxville Council

HOT CHICKEN SALAD

2 c. diced, cooked chicken
2 c. chopped celery
1/2 c. almonds
1 c. mayonnaise
2 hard cooked eggs, chopped

1/2 tsp. salt
2 tsp. chopped onion
2 Tbsp. lemon juice
1/2 c. grated cheese
1 c. potato chips, crumbled

Heat oven to 450°. Grease a 2 quart casserole dish. Mix together all ingredients, except potato chips, and pour into prepared dish. Add the potato chips and bake about 30 minutes. Serves 6 to 8.

Joyce Mattice
Harpeth Council

HOT TURKEY SALAD

8 c. diced turkey
2 tsp. salt
2 c. diced celery
1 1/2 c. chopped sweet
green pepper
1 1/2 c. almonds
2 c. mayonnaise

2 (10 1/2 oz.) cans creamed
chicken soup
4 hard cooked eggs
1/4 lb. sharp Cheddar cheese
1 1/2 c. crushed potato
chips

Heat oven to 350°. Butter a 2 quart casserole dish. Mix all ingredients, except the cheese and potato chips. Place in a prepared dish; top with cheese and potato chips. Bake for 25 minutes. Serves 20.

Joyce Mattice
Harpeth Council

JALUPE'S

2 lb. ground beef
2 onions
2 tomatoes
1 regular pkg. Fritos

2 pkg. Kraft cheese, grated
1 head lettuce
2 medium cans Lucks pinto
beans

Brown ground beef; drain grease. Add beans and heat together. Chop onions, lettuce and tomatoes. Serve in the following order: Fritos, meat and bean mixture, onion, tomatoes, lettuce, cheese. Serves 4 people.
Optional: Taco sauce.

Vickie Watson
Green Hills Council

KIDNEY BEAN SALAD

2 (15 oz.) cans kidney
beans
1 c. celery, cut fine
1 medium onion, chopped

4 sweet pickles, cut fine
1 green pepper, cut fine
12 stuffed olives, sliced
3 boiled eggs, diced
Mayonnaise to taste

88

Drain beans and rinse once with cold water. Add other ingredients; mix well with mayonnaise to taste. Chill in refrigerator. Serves about 6.

Mrs. Wavie Minke
Harpeth Council

BAVARIAN KRAUT SALAD

1 (No. 2 1/2) can Bavarian
   style or plain kraut
1 medium green pepper,
   chopped
1 c. sugar
1 c. chopped onion

1 c. chopped celery
1 small jar pimento, chopped
1/3 c. vinegar
1 tsp. caraway seed, if
   desired

Combine all ingredients and mix; chill.

Helen H. Stephens
Memphis Council

SAUERKRAUT SALAD

1 (No. 2 1/2) can kraut (we
   used two No. 303 cans
   or 4 c.)
1 c. celery, minced
1 medium onion, minced

1 bell pepper, minced
1 1/4 c. salad oil (Wesson,
   Crisco or corn)
1 1/3 c. vinegar
1 1/4 c. sugar

Wash and rinse kraut; wash again. Squeeze out water with hands. Add to kraut the celery, onion and green pepper. Mix oil, vinegar and sugar together; pour over vegetables. Let stand overnight before using. Salad will keep in refrigerator for days.

Linda Kitchens
Green Hills Council

SAUERKRAUT SALAD

1 can shredded kraut,
   drained
1 c. sliced raw carrots
1 c. sliced celery

1 c. sliced onion
1 c. sliced green pepper
1 c. sugar
1/3 c. vinegar

Combine kraut and sliced vegetables in a bowl or dish that has a cover. In a small saucepan, dissolve sugar in

vinegar over low heat. Pour over kraut and vegetables.
Let cool, then store in refrigerator overnight before
serving. Delicious with white beans and corn bread.

Mary R. Veal
Chattanooga Council

LAYERED JELLO SALAD

1 small pkg. lime jello
1 small pkg. orange jello

1 small pkg. lemon jello
1 small pkg. strawberry jello

Sauce:

2 c. milk
1 c. sugar
2 pkg. unflavored gelatin

2 c. sour cream
2 tsp. vanilla

Dissolve lime jello in 1 cup boiling water; add 1/2 cup
cold water. Pour into 12x9 inch pan; chill till firm. Bring
milk to boil in saucepan. Add sugar; mix till dissolved.
Add unflavored gelatin, which has been dissolved in 1/2 cup
cold water. Add sour cream and vanilla. Beat well or until
blended and cool. Divide into 3 parts. When lime jello is
set, pour 1/3 sauce over and let set till sticky to touch.
Repeat layers as same with orange jello, sauce, lemon jello,
sauce and strawberry jello. Chill between layers. Keep
sauce in a pan of warm water till all of it is used or it will
harden.

Rosa Brown
Harpeth Council

LAYERED CREAMY POTATO SALAD

8 medium potatoes
1 c. minced fresh parsley
1 large onion, minced
1 c. mayonnaise, divided

1 (8 oz.) ctn. commercial
  sour cream
1 1/2 tsp. celery seeds
1 tsp. salt
2 tsp. prepared horseradish

Cook potatoes in boiling, salted water about 30 minutes
or until tender; drain and cool slightly. Peel and thinly
slice potatoes; set aside. Combine parsley and onion; mix
well and set aside. Combine mayonnaise, sour cream, celery
seeds, salt and horseradish; stir well. Place 1/3 of the
potatoes in a 13x9x2 inch baking dish. Top with 1/3 of

90

mayonnaise mixture, then 1/3 of onion-parsley mixture. Repeat layers twice. Chill 8 hours. Yield: 8 to 10 servings.

Dorothy Bryant
Clarksville Council

LAYERED SALAD
(Food Processor Recipe)

1 medium head iceberg lettuce, washed and chilled
1 bunch green onions
1 (8 oz.) can water chestnuts
1/2 bell pepper (red or green), seeded
2 stalks celery
1 (10 oz.) pkg. frozen peas

2 c. mayonnaise*
2 tsp. sugar
1/2 c. grated Parmesan cheese
1 tsp. salt
1/4 tsp. garlic powder
3/4 lb. bacon, crisp fried and drained
3 hard cooked eggs
2 tomatoes

Insert slicing disc in processor. Core lettuce and cut in wedges that will stand in feed tube; slice. Spread lettuce over bottom of a wide 4 quart serving dish. With a knife, thinly slice green onions and part of the tops (because of their texture and shape, green onions cannot be sliced neatly in the food processor). Scatter slices over lettuce. Drain water chestnuts; drop into feed tube and slice. Sprinkle over onions. Stand pepper vertically in feed tube and slice; sprinkle over water chestnuts. Cut celery in lengths to fit feed tube and slice; sprinkle over pepper. Open package of frozen peas and break apart; sprinkle frozen peas over salad. Spread mayonnaise evenly over peas; sprinkle with sugar, Parmesan cheese, salt and garlic powder. Change to metal blade and process bacon until finely chopped; sprinkle over salad. Wash bowl and blade and reassemble. Cut eggs in quarters; drop into processor bowl and process with on-off bursts until coarsely chopped. Sprinkle over bacon. Cover and chill for 4 hours, or as long as 24 hours. Just before serving, cut tomatoes into wedges and arrange around top of salad. Makes 8 to 10 servings.

*Mayonnaise:

1 whole large egg
1 tsp. Dijon mustard
1 c. salad oil
1489-81

1 Tbsp. wine vinegar or lemon juice
Salt and pepper to taste

91

Using metal or plastic blade, process egg, mustard and vinegar for 3 seconds to blend well. With processor still running, add oil, a few drops at a time at first, then increasing to a slow steady stream about 1/16 inch wide. Taste and season with a few more drops of vinegar and salt and pepper, if desired. Makes 1 cup.

Sherree Weisenberger
Harpeth Council

LAYERED SALAD

Lettuce, cut up
Green onions, cut up
  (use the blades)
Cucumbers, cut up
4 eggs, sliced
3 stalks celery

Cheddar cheese, grated
Radishes, sliced
Green peas, drained
Mayonnaise or salad
  dressing

Place each ingredient in layers in oblong dish, starting with lettuce and ending with lettuce. Top with salad dressing and bacon bits.

Debbi Wakefield
Harpeth Council

LEMON FLUFF SALAD

1 small pkg. lemon jello
1 c. boiling water
1 (13 or 15 oz.) can crushed
  pineapple

1 large pkg. cream cheese
3/4 c. sugar
1/2 pt. whipping cream
1 c. chopped pecans

Mix sugar and pineapple; boil 15 minutes and cool. Mix jello with boiling water; add cheese and mix well, then add pineapple and nuts. Put in refrigerator and cool. Whip cream; fold in cooled mixture. Place in Pyrex dish and refrigerate. To serve, cut in squares; put on lettuce. Add 1/2 pecan on each square to add beauty.

Pattie Carpenter
Nashville Council

LIME CONGEALED SALAD

2 small boxes lime jello
1/2 pt. whipping cream
1/2 c. water

Small can crushed pineapple
Small can fruit cocktail
1 c. grated American cheese

Mix jello, water and fruit together; heat until jello is dissolved. Cool, then add cheese and fold in cream that has been whipped. Pour in mold; let congeal.

Mabel M. Wilson
Clarksville Council

LIME CONGEALED SALAD

1 large box lime jello
1 large can crushed
  pineapple

1 large container Cool Whip
1 large ctn. cream style
  cottage cheese

Combine lime jello and crushed pineapple (do not drain). Put over medium heat until it reaches a rapid boil. Take off heat; let cool. Combine Cool Whip and cottage cheese; stir until well combined. Put in refrigerator and let set for 2 or 3 hours before serving.

Gerry Panter
Columbia Council

LIME JELLO SALAD

1 (No. 2 1/2) can pears
1 (No. 2 1/2) can pineapple
1 large pkg. lime jello

2 pkg. Knox gelatine
3 drops green food coloring

Dice and drain fruit well. To juices of fruit, add 1 cup sugar and dissolve; add 3 tablespoons lemon juice. Cook and bring to rolling boil. Soften 2 envelopes of Knox gelatine, dissolved in 1/2 cup cold water; add to hot juices. Stir; add lime jello and 1 tray ice cubes. Cool; add drained chopped fruit and food coloring. Beat:

2 whole eggs
4 Tbsp. sugar
4 Tbsp. lemon juice

12 large marshmallows
2 Tbsp. butter

Cook over low heat in double boiler until thick. When

cool, add 1 pint whipped cream and 4 tablespoons powdered sugar. Spread over salad; top with grated Cheddar cheese.

Marie Gardner
Harpeth Council

MACARONI SALAD

2 c. macaroni, cooked
1 onion, chopped
1 large green pepper, chopped
1 large carrot, chopped
1 stalk celery, chopped

2 sweet pickles
1 large tomato (fresh or canned)
2 boiled eggs
Salt and pepper to taste

Combine macaroni with chopped vegetables and eggs. Mix with enough mayonnaise to moisten; add seasonings.

Joyce Mattice
Harpeth Council

MACARONI AND HAM SALAD

2 c. uncooked elbow macaroni
3 hard cooked eggs, chopped
1 c. minced, boiled ham
2 Tbsp. diced pimento

2/3 c. sour cream
1/3 c. mayonnaise
1 tsp. dry mustard
Chopped parsley (optional)
Sliced green olives (optional)
Salt to taste

Cook macaroni according to package directions; drain. Rinse with cold water; drain. Combine macaroni, eggs, ham and pimento; toss gently. Combine sour cream, mayonnaise, salt and mustard; mix well. Pour dressing over salad; toss gently. Chill; garnish with parsley or olives, if desired. Serves 8 to 10.

Shirley Buckner
Green Hills Council

MARINATED ORIENTAL SALAD

1 (17 oz.) can small peas, well drained
1 (16 oz.) can bean sprouts
1 (12 oz.) can white whole kernel corn

2 (5 1/2 oz.) cans water chestnuts, drained
1 (6 oz.) can sliced mushrooms
1 (4 oz.) jar pimiento

1 large green pepper
1 large onion, thinly sliced
1 c. diced celery
1 c. salad oil

1 c. water
1 c. sugar
1/2 c. vinegar
Seasoned salt and pepper to taste

Bring water, sugar and vinegar to boil for 1 minute; cool and add oil. Pour over other ingredients; toss. Cover and chill for 24 hours. (This salad keeps well for a long time.) Drain bean sprouts, mushrooms and pimiento.

Dorothy Bryant
Clarksville Council

MRS. COLLIER'S SUNSHINE SALAD

1 small can pineapple
1 small pkg. orange jello
1 small pkg. cream cheese

1 small can evaporated milk
1/4 c. nuts
1/4 c. celery

Bring to a boil a small can of pineapple; add 1 package orange jello and boil about 3 minutes. Grate a small package of cream cheese into above mixture; stir until almost dissolved. Put into refrigerator until it starts to congeal. Put a small can of evaporated milk in freezer to cool it off. Whip the evaporated milk and add it, 1/4 cup nuts and 1/4 cup celery to the salad.

Judy Christopher
Harpeth Council

MILLION DOLLAR SALAD

1 (10 oz.) pkg. miniature
    marshmallows
1 large (15 1/4 oz.) can
    crushed pineapple
2 Tbsp. sugar

1 (4 oz.) small ctn. Cool
    Whip
1 small (6 oz.) jar cherries
1 Tbsp. mayonnaise
1 (6 oz.) ctn. cottage cheese

Drain juice from pineapple; mix pineapple with marshmallows. Combine cherries, cottage cheese, sugar and mayonnaise. Add pineapple and marshmallows. Fold in Cool Whip and chill thoroughly before serving.

Mary G. Rogers
Memphis Council

1489-81

ORANGE SALAD

6 oz. pkg. orange jello
1 c. boiling water
1 pt. orange sherbet
Small can crushed pine-
    apple with juice

1 c. marshmallows
1 small can Mandarin oranges,
    drained
Small ctn. Cool Whip

Mix all together and let congeal.

Helen Sims
Harpeth Council

ORANGE CRANBERRY GELATIN

4 lb. 4 oz. strawberry or
    cherry jello (with sugar
    already added)
1 gal. hot water
1 gal. cold water
6 oranges

4 lb. cranberries (fresh or
    frozen)
4 c. sugar
4 c. chopped celery
4 c. apples, chopped, peeled
    and cored

Dissolve gelatin in hot water; stir in cold water. Place in refrigerator until gelatin is partially congealed. Grind oranges and cranberries together. Mix well with sugar. Mix chopped oranges, apples, cranberries and celery. Fold cranberry mixture into partially congealed gelatin. Place in refrigerator until firm. Serve on crisp lettuce and top with salad dressing. Makes 100 portions.

ORANGE CONGEALED SALAD

1 pkg. orange jello
1 c. boiling water
2 c. miniature marshmallows
1 small can frozen orange
    juice (don't add water)
8 oz. Cool Whip

1/2 c. sugar
8 oz. cottage cheese
1 small can Mandarin oranges,
    drained
1 small can crushed pine-
    apple, drained

Pour boiling water over jello and marshmallows; stir until dissolved. Combine orange juice and sugar; add to jello. Add pineapple to cottage cheese and to other. Add orange sections; stir until well mixed, then stir in Cool Whip. Pour into large container; refrigerate overnight.

Belinda Dorris
Nashboro Council

ORANGE JELLO DESSERT

2 c. water
2 small boxes orange jello
Small can frozen orange
  juice

1 can Mandarin oranges with
  juice
1 (15 1/4 oz.) can crushed
  pineapple, drained

Heat water. Add boxes of orange jello; stir till dissolved. Add orange juice. Add oranges with juice and pineapple. Pour into oblong dish, sprayed with Pam, and chill.

Topping:

1 small box instant vanilla
  pudding

1 1/2 c. milk
1 pkg. Dream Whip

Combine and mix well. Spread over jello.

Jeannine Linn
Knoxville Council

ORANGE JELLO SALAD

1 pkg. orange jello, dissolved in 1 c. hot water
2 c. miniature marshmallows
1 (3 oz.) pkg. cream cheese
1/2 c. sugar

1 small can crushed or diced
  pineapple
1 can Mandarin oranges
1/2 pt. whipping cream
1 c. nuts, if desired

Drain juice from oranges and pineapple; add water to make 1 cup. Have cream cheese at room temperature. Add to jello, which has been dissolved in 1 cup hot water. Add all ingredients, except whipping cream. Let chill until thick before adding cream. I add 1 envelope plain gelatin to make it firm.

Addie Downs
Green Hills Council

ORANGE SHERBET SALAD

1 large box orange jello
1 c. boiling water
1 c. hot water
1 pt. orange sherbet

1 (No. 2) can crushed
  pineapple, drained
1 can Mandarin oranges,
  cut in pieces
1 banana, cut fine

Dissolve jello in cup of boiling water and add remaining ingredients; mix well and congeal. Serves 10.

Mrs. Adelene Queenan
Harpeth Council

OUT OF THIS WORLD SALAD

1 (6 oz.) pkg. lemon jello
1 (3 oz.) pkg. lime jello
2 finely chopped cucumbers
1 onion
1 c. mayonnaise

2 1/2 tsp. vinegar
Scant tsp. salt
1 (24 oz.) ctn. cottage cheese
1 c. pecans (optional)

Dissolve jello in boiling water. Stir in remaining ingredients and chill.

Dot Shipe
Knoxville Council

OVERNIGHT LETTUCE SALAD

1 head lettuce, cut up
1/2 c. chopped celery
1 c. green pepper

1/2 c. onion, chopped, or green onions
1 pkg. frozen green peas, unthawed

Layer above ingredients in large bowl. Spread 1 cup mayonnaise and 2 tablespoons sugar over top of layers. Top with 4 ounces grated Cheddar cheese and 8 slices of crisp bacon, crumbled in order as listed. Refrigerate, covered with Saran Wrap or foil, overnight.

Sarah Unkenholz
Harpeth Council

OVERNIGHT VEGETABLE SALAD

1 (No. 2) can small green peas
1 (No. 2) can French style green beans
4 ribs celery, chopped fine

1 medium onion, chopped fine
1 small pimento, chopped
1 medium green pepper, chopped fine

Dressing:

1 c. white sugar

1 c. vinegar

98

1 c. apple juice   1 tsp. salt
1/4 c. Wesson oil

Bring to boil; pour over drained vegetables. Marinate overnight or longer. Drain before serving.

Jewell Mercer
Nashville Council

PHILA'S FROZEN FRUIT SALAD

1 can cherry pie filling
1 can crushed pineapple
1 can sweetened Eagle
  Brand condensed milk
1/4 c. lemon juice
1/2 c. broken pecans

1/2 c. peaches, chopped,
  drained
1/2 c. pears, chopped,
  drained
2 bananas, chopped (optional,
  good with or without)
1 c. cream, whipped (or
  whipped topping)

Mix together condensed milk and lemon juice; stir until thick. Fold in rest of ingredients and freeze. Serve in squares frozen (with a dab of mayonnaise) or may be frozen in cupcake papers and served individually. Will keep frozen for several months. Pretty as well as tasty!

Dot Crouch
Clarksville Council

PINEAPPLE-CHEDDAR SALAD

1 small pkg. lemon jello
1 c. boiling water
1 small can pineapple,
  undrained
3/4 c. sugar

1 ctn. whipping cream,
  whipped
1 c. Cheddar cheese
1/2 c. pecans

Dissolve gelatin in boiling water; stir in pineapple and sugar. Cool; fold in remaining ingredients. Put in 9 inch square pan; chill until firm. Serves 9.

Dean Tidwell
Nashboro Council

PINK CONGEALED SALAD

1 c. boiling water
1 small pkg. red jello
1 pkg. miniature
  marshmallows
1 c. pineapple juice

1 (3 oz.) pkg. cream cheese,
  room temperature
1 small can crushed pine-
  apple, drained
1 (9 oz.) container Cool Whip
Pecans (optional)

Mix boiling water and jello together; blend until jello is dissolved. Add miniature marshmallows and stir until marsh-mallows are partially dissolved. Add 1 cup pineapple juice (individual can plus juice from drained pineapple equals 1 cup). Mix thoroughly and pour all ingredients into a 13x9 inch pan and chill. Blend small cream cheese and crushed pineapple together. Add Cool Whip to this mixture; blend well. Spread over jello mixture and sprinkle chopped pecans over top, if desired. Refrigerate.

Cheryl V. Alderson
Columbia Council

PISTACHIO FRUIT SALAD

1 small box pistachio
  instant pudding mix
1 large pkg. miniature
  marshmallows

1 large can crushed pineapple
1/2 c. pecans, coarsely
  chopped
1 1/2 c. Cool Whip

Mix dry pudding mix with marshmallows; stir in Cool Whip. Add other ingredients, including juice from pine-apple. Refrigerate overnight before serving. Makes 3 quarts.

Sheila Fleming
East Memphis Council

CREAMY POTATO SALAD

1/2 c. mayonnaise
1/2 c. plain yogurt
3 Tbsp. cider vinegar
2 Tbsp. sugar
1 tsp. salt

2 lb. potatoes, cooked,
  peeled, sliced (this is
  about 4 c.)
1/2 c. sliced green onions

In a large bowl, mix together mayonnaise, yogurt,

vinegar, sugar and salt. Add potatoes and onions; toss.
Cover and chill for about 4 hours. This can be garnished
by sprinkling chopped parsley on top.

Shirley Buckner
Green Hills Council

POTATO SALAD

3 lb. potatoes, cooked, cooled, peeled, diced	2 pimentos, diced
1 c. celery, chopped	1/2 green pepper, diced
1/4 onion, cut fine	1/2 c. pickles, diced

Mix above ingredients.

Dressing:

3/4 c. mayonnaise	1/8 tsp. pepper
1 Tbsp. mustard	1 1/2 tsp. salt
3 Tbsp. vinegar	1 Tbsp. sugar

Mix well and toss with potato mixture.

Sivalene Rouse
Morristown Council

POTATO SALAD

1 can Veg-All mixed vegetables	6 salami slices
2 c. diced, cooked potatoes	3 hard boiled eggs
1/4 c. chopped green pepper	3/4 c. mayonnaise
1/4 c. diced sweet pickles	2 tsp. horseradish
1 bunch green onions	Dash of hot pepper sauce
	1 tsp. salt

Drain Veg-All well; combine with potatoes, pepper,
pickles, onions, 4 slices salami and 2 eggs. Chill thoroughly. Mix together mayonnaise, horseradish, pepper sauce
and salt. Add to chilled mixture; toss gently. Garnish with
other salami slices and egg.

Polly Kirby
Andrew Jackson Council

POTATO SALAD

4 medium Irish potatoes
2 hard boiled eggs
1 small can pimento
3 medium sweet cucumber
    pickles
Salt

2 pieces celery, chopped
1/2 c. finely chopped onion
Salad dressing
Vinegar
Sugar

Boil potatoes with jackets on until you can prick easily with a fork. Allow to cool until you can dice. Remove jackets; dice and add the chopped eggs, pimentos, pickles, celery and onion. Mix well, adding salt to taste. Add about 3 tablespoons of salad dressing, diluted with 1 tablespoon of vinegar, again mixing thoroughly. After placing in serving bowl, add paprika, if desired. Serves 6.

Joyce Mattice
Harpeth Council

YOGURT POTATO SALAD

1 c. plain yogurt
2 tsp. prepared mustard
2 tsp. horseradish
2 c. cooked, cubed potatoes

1/2 c. diced celery
1 medium cucumber, sliced
1/2 c. sliced onion
1 Tbsp. chopped chives

In a large bowl, combine yogurt, mustard and horse-radish. Add remaining ingredients; toss to mix well. Chill.

Helen H. Stephens
Memphis Council

PRETZEL SURPRISE

1 1/2 c. crushed pretzels
1/2 c. sugar

1 stick butter, melted

Mix and press above ingredients into an 8x8 inch dish, saving half of the pretzels for the top. In a large bowl, mix 3 ounces cream cheese and 1 cup powdered sugar together. Fold in 1 (20 ounce) can crushed pineapple, well drained. Add 1 (8 ounce) carton Cool Whip. Sprinkle remaining half of crumbs over top; chill.

Beverly Vaughn
Harpeth Council

RASPBERRY TANG

1 (3 oz.) pkg. raspberry
   jello
1 (4 oz.) pkg. cream
   cheese, softened
1/2 c. chopped pecans
1/2 pt. whipping cream

1 (8 oz.) can crushed
   pineapple
1/2 c. hot water
3 bananas, mashed
1/2 c. mayonnaise

Add jello to hot water. Add all other ingredients, but add whipping cream last. Pour into mold; let chill until firm. Serves 4-6.

Mike and Charlotte Tate
Harpeth Council

SALAD BOWL PUFF

2/3 c. water
1/4 c. margarine or butter
1 c. Bisquick baking mix

4 eggs
Ham Salad Filling (below) or
   your favorite luncheon
   salad

Heat oven to 400°. Generously grease pie plate, 9 x 1 1/4 inches. Heat water and margarine to boiling in 2 quart saucepan. Add baking mix, all at once. Stir vigorously over low heat until mixture forms a ball, about 1 1/2 minutes; remove from heat. Beat in eggs, 1 at a time; continue beating until smooth. Spread in pie plate (do not spread up side). Bake until puffed and dry in center, 35 to 40 minutes; cool. Just before serving, fill with Ham Salad Filling. Cut into wedges. Makes 6 to 8 servings.

Ham Salad Filling:

1 (10 oz.) pkg. frozen
   green peas
2 c. cubed, fully cooked
   smoked ham
2 Tbsp. chopped onion

1 c. (about 4 oz.) shredded
   Cheddar cheese
3/4 c. mayonnaise or salad
   dressing
1 1/2 tsp. prepared mustard

Rinse frozen peas under running cold water to separate; drain. Mix all ingredients; cover and refrigerate at least 2 hours.

   Small Salad Bowl Puff: Cut all ingredients in half.

   Do-Ahead Salad Bowl Puff: After baking Salad Bowl Puff, cool completely. Wrap and freeze no longer than 1 week. To serve, place on serving plate; let stand, uncovered, at room temperature until thawed: Large salad bowl, about 60 minutes; small salad bowl about 30 minutes.

High Altitude Directions (3500 to 6500 feet): Cut all ingredients for Salad Bowl Puff in half. (Dough will form ball in about 30 seconds.)

Frances Nevette
Harpeth Council

SALMON SALAD

1 large can red sock-eye
  salmon
4 hard boiled eggs
Mayonnaise
Olives

1 medium-large onion,
  chopped very fine
1/2 c. sweet pickles, diced in
  small pieces

Strain salmon and discard juice; also discard any darkened pieces of the salmon. Chop 3 of the eggs in small pieces. Crumble salmon in large mixing bowl. Add the 3 chopped eggs, pickles and onion. Stir well and add just enough mayonnaise to form a soft mixture of all the above ingredients. Decorate top with olives and slices of remaining egg.

(Much tastier if prepared early in the morning, refrigerated all day and served during the evening meal.)

Audrey Spiceland
Green Hills Council

SCANDINAVIAN SALAD

1 c. LeSueur peas (canned)
1 c. French style green
  beans
1 c. shoe peg corn (12 oz.
  Green Giant)
1 c. chopped onion
1 c. chopped celery

Green pepper to taste
Pimentos to taste
1/3 c. oil
1/3 c. white vinegar
1/2 c. sugar
1 tsp. salt
1/2 tsp. pepper

Drain vegetables; mix. Pour dressing mixture over vegetables. Let set at least 12 hours. Will keep a long time.

Mary Beth McLaurine
Harpeth Council

SHRIMP MOLD

1 1/2 env. unflavored
 gelatin
1/2 c. cold water
1 (3 oz.) pkg. cream cheese
 at room temperature
1 1/2 c. mayonnaise

2 tsp. lemon juice
1 c. chopped celery
2 c. cooked shrimp, chopped
1 tsp. minced onion
1 tsp. minced parsley
Salt to taste

Dissolve gelatin in cold water; place over hot water to melt. Whip cream cheese; add melted gelatin. Add mayonnaise and lemon juice. Fold in other ingredients; salt to taste. Place in oiled 1 quart mold; chill until congealed. Serve with Sociable crackers.

Rosemary Grand
Harpeth Council

SHRIMP SALAD (400)

35 lb. shrimp
2 gal. mayonnaise
1 c. salt
10 doz. eggs, hard cooked
 and diced

2 c. lemon juice
6 c. green pepper, chopped
 fine
6 c. pickle relish
Chopped onion

Mix together.

SIX CUP SALAD

1 c. white grapes (seedless)
1 c. Mandarin oranges
1 c. pecans

1 c. Angel Flake coconut
1 c. miniature marshmallows
1 c. sour cream

Drain juice off completely and mix all above ingredients together. Put into refrigerator; chill until firm.

Katie Castleman
Memphis Downtown Council

SOUR CREAM FRUIT SALAD

1 (6 oz.) can crushed
 pineapple slices
1 (11 oz.) can Mandarin
 orange slices

1 can (cup) green grapes
1 can miniature marshmallows
1 c. coconut
2 c. sour cream
1 c. pecans

Drain fruit juices; mix. Let set in sour cream overnight.

Kay Boswell
Andrew Jackson Council

SOUR CREAM STRAWBERRY SALAD

2 regular or 1 family size
  pkg. strawberry gelatin
2 c. boiling water
1 (10 oz.) pkg. frozen
  strawberries

1 (No. 2) can crushed
  pineapple
3 mashed or chopped bananas
1 1/2 - 2 c. sour cream
1 c. pecans, broken

Dissolve gelatin in boiling water. Add frozen strawberries, pineapple and bananas. Pour half of mixture into large mold or 12x8x2 inch pan. Chill until firm while other half remains at room temperature. Let sour cream come to room temperature and spread on top of congealed mixture. Top with remaining gelatin mixture. Chill again until firm. Yield: 8-10 servings.

Mickie Herrell
Harpeth Council

SNOW SALAD

8 oz. pkg. cream cheese
1 medium can crushed
  pineapple
2 large jars maraschino
  cherries, drained

1 1/2 c. chopped nuts
1 small pkg. miniature
  marshmallows
1/2 pt. Cool Whip

Soften cream cheese and drain pineapple. Combine cream cheese, pineapple, cherries, nuts and marshmallows; mix well. Add Cool Whip; mix well, then chill.

Elizabeth Kitts
Knoxville Council

SPINACH SALAD

1 1/4 lb. fresh spinach
6 green onions, sliced

5 boiled eggs, chopped
8 slices bacon, cooked and
  crumbled

Wash and break spinach, then refrigerate 2 hours.

Mix all and cover with dressing.

Dressing:

2 tsp. garlic oil   Dash of pepper
1/2 c. salad oil   3 Tbsp. lemon juice
1 tsp. salt   1/4 c. cider vinegar

Combine all, except oil. As you beat, gradually add oil. This dressing will thicken.

Mary Jane Bailey
Green Hills Council

7 LAYER SALAD

Lettuce, torn in bite   4 hard boiled eggs, sliced
   size pieces   1/2 lb. bacon, cooked and
1 medium onion, chopped   crumbled
   or sliced (purple)   1/2 - 1 c. mayonnaise
1 pkg. frozen green peas,   1/2 - 1 c. shredded Cheddar
   uncooked   cheese

Layer lettuce, onion, peas and eggs. Sprinkle with bacon bits. Ice top with mayonnaise. Sprinkle top with shredded cheese.

Edna Cate
Green Hills Council

7-UP SALAD

1 small bottle 7-Up   1 (8 oz.) pkg. cream cheese
1 small can crushed   1 pkg. orange jello
   pineapple, drained   1 tsp. vanilla
2 Tbsp. sugar   1 c. hot water

In a bowl, mix cream cheese; add slowly the bottle of 7-Up and vanilla. In another bowl, mix jello, sugar, hot water and pineapple. Mix together and chill.

Topping: (For 7-Up Salad or Jello)

1/2 c. pineapple juice   2 Tbsp. cornstarch
1/2 c. sugar

Cook till thick; set aside. When cooled, add 1 package

Cool Whip. (*At this point, you can also add 1 (8 ounce) package of softened cream cheese to make it richer.) This topping can be stored in covered container in refrigerator for 2 weeks.

Linda Earp
Clarksville Council

SHIRLEY'S SUMMER SALAD

1 (7 oz.) pkg. (2 c. uncooked) elbow macaroni
1 (16 oz.) can Veg-All, drained
1 (7 oz.) can tuna, drained and flaked
1 c. Cheddar cheese, diced

1/2 c. sweet pickles, diced
1/2 c. onion, diced
1/2 c. sour cream
1/2 c. salad dressing
1 1/2 Tbsp. lemon juice
1 tsp. seasoned salt
1/4 tsp. black pepper

Prepare macaroni according to package directions; drain. Add Veg-All, tuna, cheese, onion and pickles. Mix remaining ingredients and toss with macaroni mixture; chill.

Barbara Stanfill
Harpeth Council

STARDUST SALAD

1 box lemon jello
1 box orange jello
2 c. hot water
1 1/2 c. cold water

1 (No. 2) can crushed, drained pineapple
40 small marshmallows
2 bananas

Dissolve 1 box lemon jello, 1 box orange jello in 2 cups hot water. Add 1 1/2 cups cold water, 2 bananas, crushed pineapple and marshmallows, or cover top with marshmallows and then let this congeal.

Sauce: Second Layer -

1 c. sugar
2 Tbsp. flour

1 c. pineapple juice
1 egg, beaten until foamy

Cook until thick and let get cold.

Third Layer: Whip 1/2 pint (1 cup) heavy cream. Blend in (with cream) a small package of cream cheese, then spread on second layer. Grate sharp Cheddar or American cheese on top.

Mrs. Harvey Cummings
Harpeth Council

FROZEN STRAWBERRY SALAD

1 (3 oz.) pkg. cream cheese
2 rounded tsp. salad
  dressing
2 Tbsp. pineapple juice
2 medium bananas, sliced

1 can crushed or chunk
  pineapple, drained
1 (10 oz.) pkg. frozen
  strawberries
1/2 pt. whipping cream or
  Cool Whip

Soften cheese in salad dressing and pineapple juice. Fold in whipped cream or Cool Whip. Add strawberries, bananas and pineapple; mix well and pour in molds.

Anne R. Rikard
Memphis Downtown Council

STRAWBERRY SALAD

1 small box strawberry jello
1 (15 1/2 oz.) can crushed
  pineapple

1 c. buttermilk
1 medium container Cool Whip

Heat pineapple (juice included) and jello until boiling. Cool in freezer until partially congealed. Mix Cool Whip and buttermilk with mixer. Combine with pineapple mixture and pour into oblong Pyrex dish; refrigerate.

Connie M. Davis
Knoxville Council

TACO SALAD

1 lb. lean ground beef
1 (16 oz.) can stewed
  tomatoes
1 (4 oz.) can chopped green
  chilies, drained
2 tsp. beef flavor instant
  bouillon
1/4 tsp. hot sauce

1/8 tsp. garlic powder
1/8 tsp. pepper
1 medium head shredded
  lettuce
1 1/2 c. corn chips
1 medium tomato, chopped
1 c. shredded Cheddar
  cheese

1489-81

Brown meat; pour off fat. Add next 6 items. Simmer, uncovered, for 30 minutes. Combine meat mixture and remaining ingredients in large bowl or platter; toss. Serves 4 people.

Sandra H. Bullock
Harpeth Council

TANGY CHICKEN SALAD

1/2 c. mayonnaise or salad
   dressing
1 (11 oz.) can Mandarin
   oranges, drained, cut up
1/4 tsp. curry powder or
   poultry seasoning

2 c. cubed, cooked chicken
1/2 c. chopped celery
1/4 c. chopped green pepper
1/4 c. toasted, slivered
   almonds
1/4 tsp. seasoned salt

In large bowl, combine mayonnaise, oranges, curry powder and seasoned salt. Stir in chicken, celery, green pepper and almonds; chill. Serve on salad greens. Makes about 3 1/2 cups.

Helen DeWolfe
Nashville Council

TASMANIAN FRUIT SALAD

2-3 bananas, sliced
2-3 apples, cored and cut
   into 1/2 inch cubes
Lettuce (optional)

1 (15 1/2 oz.) can pineapple
   chunks, drained
1 (8 oz.) ctn. Mandarin
   orange flavored yogurt

Combine fruit and yogurt; mix well. Chill thoroughly. Serve on lettuce, if desired. Yield: 6 to 8 servings.
Note: May also be served for breakfast or as a dessert.

Inda Adams
Andrew Jackson Council

THREE LAYER SALAD

First Layer:

1/2 box lemon jello
1/2 box orange jello

1/2 c. miniature marshmallows
1 small can crushed pineapple
1 1/2 large bananas, diced

110

Dissolve jello in 1 cup boiling water. Add 1/2 cup cold water; mix well. Chill until thick. Add fruits and marsh-mallows. Put in 8 inch square pan; chill several hours.

Second Layer:

1 c. pineapple juice
1/2 c. sugar

2 Tbsp. flour
1 egg, beaten

Mix sugar and flour thoroughly in saucepan. Add egg and juice; cook until thick. Cool and spread on top of first layer.

Third Layer: Cream 1 (3 ounce) package cream cheese. Whip 1 package Dream Whip; fold whip into cream cheese. Spread on top of second layer. Sprinkle with 1/2 cup grated Velveeta cheese; chill.

Robi Akers
Harpeth Council

TOMATO SALAD
(Tomatensalat)

5 medium tomatoes, chopped
1 Tbsp. sugar
1 tsp. salt
1 tsp. dried basil
1/4 tsp. dried thyme

1/4 tsp. freshly ground
    pepper
1/2 c. vegetable oil
6 Tbsp. vinegar
1 Tbsp. Worcestershire sauce
1 large onion, diced

Blend all ingredients together and chill for 1 hour before serving. Serve on lettuce. Makes 4 servings.

Beverly Jones
Andrew Jackson Council

TOMATO ASPIC

16 oz. can tomato juice
2 tsp. vinegar
Juice of a whole lemon
1 pkg. Knox gelatine
2 Tbsp. water
1 button finely chopped
    garlic

2 green onions, finely
    chopped, including stems
Celery, finely chopped,
    including the leafy leaves
    (use your own judgment
    as to how much)
Pinch of salt and sugar
    added to taste

Bring tomato juice to a boil; set aside. Add vinegar, lemon juice, chipped garlic and small green onions, celery, salt and sugar. Mix water and package of gelatine together; stir into the tomato juice. Be careful in mixing so as not to cause it to ball up or lump. This can be poured into a casserole to congeal or use a regular size mold. Let stand at least 8 hours or overnight.

Nell Young
Harpeth Council

TWENTY FOUR HOUR SALAD

3 egg yolks
2 Tbsp. sugar
Dash of salt
2 Tbsp. vinegar
2 Tbsp. pineapple syrup
1 Tbsp. butter

1 c. heavy cream, whipped
2 c. pitted white cherries
2 c. quartered marshmallows
2 c. pineapple bits
2 oranges, cut in pieces

Cook egg yolks, sugar, salt, vinegar, pineapple syrup and butter in double boiler until thick; cool. Fold in whipped cream, white cherries, marshmallows, pineapple and oranges; chill 24 hours. Decorate top with orange sections and maraschino cherries, if desired.

Metty C. Fain
Andrew Jackson Council

TWENTY-FOUR HOUR SALAD

2 eggs, well beaten
5 Tbsp. lemon juice
5 Tbsp. sugar
1 Tbsp. butter
1 (No. 2) can fruit cocktail

1 (No. 1) can diced pineapple
1/2 lb. miniature
marshmallows
1/2 c. chopped pecans
2 c. heavy cream, whipped

Mix eggs, lemon juice and sugar in a double boiler. Cook, stirring, until smooth. Remove from heat; add 1 tablespoon butter and cool. Drain fruit cocktail and pineapple; mix with marshmallows, pecans and whipped cream. Add to cooked mixture. Chill at least 24 hours before serving. Yield: 8 servings.

Evalyn Morris
Harpeth Council

24 HOUR CABBAGE SALAD

2 lb. cabbage, thinly sliced
1 carrot, grated
1/2 Tbsp. unflavored
  gelatin
3/4 c. sugar
1/2 tsp. celery seed
1/8 tsp. pepper

1 green pepper, chopped thin
1 small onion, grated
1/4 c. cold water
1/2 c. vinegar
1/2 tsp. salt
1/2 c. salad oil

Combine cabbage, green pepper, carrot and onion. Dissolve gelatin in cold water. Heat sugar and vinegar; add dissolved gelatin. Cool and add celery seed, salt and pepper. Allow to cool until mixture is thickness of cream. Add salad oil; pour over sliced and grated vegetables and toss to blend. Place in refrigerator for 24 hours. Makes 8 servings.

Jennifer C. Alley
Harpeth Council

WATERGATE SALAD

1 box Jell-O pistachio
  instant pudding mix
1 can chunk pineapple

1 can fruit cocktail, drained
1/4 c. chopped pecans
1 large ctn. Cool Whip

Mix jello with juice from pineapple. Mix all other ingredients together. Keeps 1 week. Let set 1 day to set flavors.

Brenda L. DeVault
Knoxville Council

WILTED SPINACH SALAD

1 lb. fresh spinach, at
  room temperature
4 green onions, sliced,
  tops and all
1/2 tsp. coarsely ground
  black pepper

5 slices bacon, diced
2 Tbsp. wine vinegar
1 Tbsp. lemon juice
1 tsp. sugar
1/2 tsp. salt
2 hard cooked eggs, sliced

Wash spinach; discard stems. Dry and tear into bite size pieces in large bowl. Add onions and pepper. Fry diced bacon until crisp. Add vinegar, lemon juice, sugar and salt to bacon and drippings; heat to boiling. Pour over spinach. Toss until all leaves are coated and slightly wilted. Serve at once in individual salad bowls, garnished with egg slices.

Rosemary Grand
Harpeth Council

BLUE CHEESE SALAD DRESSING

2 c. mayonnaise
1 tsp. lemon juice
1 tsp. white vinegar
1/4 c. buttermilk
1/2 c. sour cream
1/2 tsp. salt
1/4 tsp. pepper
1/4 tsp. garlic powder
1 (4 oz.) pkg. Blue cheese, crumbled

Combine all ingredients but Blue cheese; blend well. Gently stir in Blue cheese. Refrigerate until needed. Yield: 3 cups.

Evelyn Carrico
Nashboro Council

CHEF SALAD DRESSING

1 c. Hunt's tomato sauce
1 c. Wesson oil
3/4 c. vinegar
1 tsp. salt
3/4 tsp. black pepper
1 1/2 tsp. oregano
1 1/2 tsp. dry mustard
3/4 tsp. soy sauce

Put in shaker or mix in blender; refrigerate.

Claudia Davenport
Clarksville Council

CUCUMBER DRESSING

1 large cucumber, grated and drained
1 c. mayonnaise
1 Tbsp. lemon juice
1/8 tsp. garlic salt
1 small onion, grated
1 tsp. sugar
1 tsp. Worcestershire sauce
1 tsp. Accent
About 3 drops green food coloring

Mix above ingredients and refrigerate.

Mrs. A.C. Mullins
Jackson Council

114

FRENCH DRESSING

1 can tomato soup
1/2 c. vinegar
1/2 c. sugar
1/2 c. vegetable oil

1/2 tsp. onion salt
1 tsp. mustard
1/2 tsp. salt

Put all ingredients in jar and shake. Keep refrigerated.

Clara Rainey
Harpeth Council

FRENCH DRESSING

1 can tomato soup
1 c. Wesson oil
1/2 c. vinegar
1/2 tsp. sugar
2 tsp. salt
1 tsp. mustard (powder)

1 tsp. paprika
1 tsp. Worcestershire sauce
Garlic button
Juice of 1 lemon or 2 Tbsp.
    lemon juice

Mix all the above ingredients in blender and blend until smooth. Makes about 1 quart.

Judy Christopher
Harpeth Council

MERICHKA'S FRENCH DRESSING

1 1/4 c. salad oil
3/4 c. vinegar
3/4 c. sugar
1 can tomato soup
1 tsp. dry mustard

2 tsp. salt
1 tsp. paprika
1 tsp. pepper
1 tsp. garlic powder

Place in quart jar and shake well. Let stand overnight in refrigerator before serving.

Sylvia Kaffer
Clarksville Council

POPPY SEED DRESSING

1 1/2 c. sugar
2 tsp. dry mustard
2 tsp. salt
2/3 c. vinegar

3 Tbsp. fresh onion juice
2 c. salad oil
3 Tbsp. poppy seed

Put first 4 ingredients in bowl; beat well. Add onion juice; mix, then very slowly add oil, beating constantly until thick. Stir in poppy seed. Refrigerate until ready to use. This keeps very well.

Dee Schell
Columbia Council

FRUIT SALAD SAUCE

2 c. pineapple juice
1/3 c. sugar
1 tsp. flour

2 eggs
1/4 c. lemon juice

Mix and cook over low heat until thick; refrigerate until cool. Pour over sliced fruit and serve.

Shirley Robertson
Harpeth Council

HAM SAUCE

Broil tenderized ham in butter.

1/2 c. currant jelly or
    apple jelly
1/2 c. brown sugar

1/2 tsp. paprika
2 Tbsp. vinegar
1 Tbsp. water, if desired

Pour over cooked ham and simmer for a few minutes.

Lillian Reynolds
Harpeth Council

HOMEMADE SALAD DRESSING

1/4 c. Bisquick baking mix
2 Tbsp. sugar
1 tsp. dry mustard
2 c. milk

2 egg yolks, slightly beaten
1/3 c. white vinegar
1 Tbsp. margarine or butter

116

Mix all ingredients in 2 quart saucepan. Heat to boiling over medium heat, stirring constantly. Boil and stir 1 minute. Cool slightly; refrigerate until chilled. Stir well before serving. Makes about 2 cups salad dressing.

Creamy Onion Dressing: Mix 1 cup Homemade Salad Dressing, 1/2 cup dairy sour cream, 1 tablespoon sugar, 2 tablespoons milk and 2 green onions, finely chopped. Makes 1 1/4 cups dressing.

Russian Dressing: Mix 1/2 cup Homemade Salad Dressing and 1/4 cup chili sauce. Makes 3/4 cup dressing.

Thousand Island Dressing: Mix 1/2 cup Homemade Salad Dressing, 2 tablespoons sweet pickle relish, 1 tablespoon catsup and 1 hard cooked egg, chopped. Makes 3/4 cup dressing.

Tomato-Cucumber Dressing: Mix 1 cup Homemade Salad Dressing, 1/2 cup drained, finely chopped tomato, 1/2 cup drained, finely chopped cucumber, 1 teaspoon finely chopped onion and 1/2 teaspoon dried dill weed, if desired. Makes 1 3/4 cups dressing.

High Altitude Directions (3500 to 6500 feet): No adjustments necessary.

Pat Ferguson
Hardeth Council

MARINADE

1/2 c. salad oil	1 tsp. oregano
1/4 c. lemon juice	1/2 tsp. pepper
1 tsp. salt	1 clove garlic, minced

Mix together and let marinate for 24 hours at least. Good on steak, chicken or pork.

Ann Hughes
Green Hills Council

MAYONNAISE

1 egg	1/4 tsp. dry mustard
2 Tbsp. lemon juice	1 scant c. salad oil

Put salt, mustard, egg and lemon juice into container of blender; cover. Mix well; remove cover and pour oil very slowly, while beating. Stop frequently and use spatula to lift mixture. Takes a little more than a minute. Makes 1 pint.

Frances McLaughlin
Harpeth Council

ROQUEFORT DRESSING

1 qt. mayonnaise	1 tsp. salt
1 large white onion, minced	1/2 tsp. black pepper
2 (3 oz.) wedges Roquefort	1/2 tsp. garlic powder
cheese, crumbled	1 tsp. parsley, chopped
1 small jar pimento	1 Tbsp. lemon juice

Mix all ingredients in order and store in a large jar in the refrigerator. Recipe makes slightly over 1 quart of dressing. Dressing will keep for weeks.

Katie Braden
Harpeth Council

SALAD DRESSING
(For Potato or Macaroni Salad)

3 Tbsp. mayonnaise	1 tsp. mustard
1 Tbsp. vinegar	1 tsp. sugar
1 tsp. salt	1/2 tsp. pepper
1 Tbsp. water	

Mix above ingredients and pour over potato or macaroni salad.

Joyce Mattice
Harpeth Council

TASTY SALAD DRESSING

2/3 c. olive or salad oil	1/3 c. vinegar
4 Tbsp. (heaping) sugar	1 tsp. lemon juice
3/4 tsp. salt	2 large cloves fresh garlic
1/2 tsp. celery seeds	1/2 tsp. rosemary leaves,
1/2 tsp. thyme	crushed
4 bay leaves, crushed	1/2 tsp. sweet basil leaves,
1/2 tsp. parsley flakes,	crushed
crushed	1/2 tsp. minced onion

Mince fresh garlic. Combine all ingredients in blender.
Blend until sugar is dissolved.

Phyllis Whaley
Andrew Jackson Council

TWENTY DOLLAR DRESSING

1 pt. salad oil	2 tsp. grated onion
2 tsp. salt	1 c. sugar
2 tsp. paprika	1/2 c. vinegar
2 tsp. dry mustard	

Heat salad oil until warm; add remaining ingredients.
Beat on medium speed until thickened. Yield: 1 pint.

Pat Prosser
Columbia Council

TWENTY DOLLAR SALAD DRESSING

1 pt. salad oil (Wesson)	2 tsp. celery salt
2 tsp. salt	2 tsp. grated onion
2 tsp. paprika	1 c. sugar
2 tsp. dry mustard	1/2 c. vinegar (not white)

Heat salad oil until just warm. Add remaining ingredients. Beat until thickened at medium speed. Makes 1 pint.

Gerry Panter
Columbia Council

BEEF BURGER SOUP

1 1/2 lb. ground beef	3 small cans celery soup
1 c. onion, chopped	1 tsp. pepper
1 1/2 qt. tomato juice	3 bay leaves
2 c. water	1 Tbsp. garlic salt
1 qt. raw carrots, blended	1 Tbsp. sugar

Brown beef; add onion. Cook until soft. Add other
ingredients and put in crock pot. Let simmer about 2
hours. Makes 1 gallon.

Johnnie Foster
Harpeth Council

CHICKEN AND OKRA GUMBO

1 (about 2 - 2 1/2 lb.)
  fryer, cut up
Salt and pepper to season
1 tomato, cubed
1 c. onion, chopped
3 Tbsp. shortening
1 1/2 lb. fresh okra, sliced
2 Tbsp. flour

3 Tbsp. shortening (from
  that used to fry chicken)
1 c. celery, diced
1 bell pepper, diced
1 1/2 qt. water (little more
  if needed)
1 can tomato sauce
Additional salt and pepper to
  taste

Season chicken and dredge in flour; fry until brown. In another saucepan, heat shortening and fry okra, onion and tomato until almost dry. In the saucepan in which chicken was cooked, brown flour; add celery and cook a few minutes before adding water, chicken and okra mixture. Cover closely; lower heat to simmer and cook about 2 hours. Adjust seasoning as needed. Serves 6 to 8.

Linda Kitchens
Green Hills Council

CHILI

1 lb. ground chuck
20 oz. canned tomatoes,
  mashed
2 cans Boone County chilli
  beans

1 large onion, chopped (can
  substitute 4 Tbsp. dried
  onion chips)
2 heaping Tbsp. chilli powder
1 tsp. salt
3 1/2 c. boiling water

Drop meat gradually into boiling water; add salt and cook 5 minutes. Add all other ingredients. Simmer several hours. Add small amount of cooked spaghetti. Serves 10.

Jane Wohlbold
Green Hills Council

CHILI

1 lb. hamburger
1 large onion
1 (1 lb. 12 oz.) can whole
  tomatoes

1/2 tsp. salt
1 (1 lb. 15 oz.) can pinto
  beans
2 Tbsp. chili powder

Brown hamburger, onion and salt in 2 tablespoons oil in

heavy skillet; drain and set aside. Mash the tomatoes in a large country kettle; add pinto beans, hamburger, onion and chili powder. Stir this really well. Bring to a full boil, then turn off. Let set about 20 minutes before eating. It's good made in advance, then just warm up.

Gene P. Currin
Columbia Council

CHILI

2 medium onions, diced   1 lb. hamburger
1 bell pepper, chopped   1 button of garlic

Cook until done. Add 1 stick of chili con carne, 1 large can kidney beans, 1 can tomato paste, 1 can tomato puree and salt and pepper to taste.

Beverly Vaughn
Harpeth Council

CHILI

1 lb. ground beef   1 Tbsp. cornstarch, mixed
1 large onion, chopped   with 1 can of water
1 pt. can tomatoes   1 1/2 Tbsp. chili powder
1 (15 oz.) can chili hot   1 1/2 tsp. salt
  beans   1 tsp. minced garlic
                                 Black pepper to taste

Saute chopped onion. Brown ground beef; drain off fat. Add all the remaining ingredients and simmer for 1 hour.

Vera S. Beard
Jackson Council

DORRIS ANN'S CHILI-O

1 lb. ground beef   1 (15 1/2 oz.) can kidney
1/3 c. chopped green   beans, undrained
  pepper (optional)   1 1/2 c. water
2 (8 oz.) cans tomato sauce   1 c. (or more) catsup
  with onions   1 env. Chili-O seasoning mix

Brown ground beef in shortening or corn oil until

lightly browned. Add all other ingredients to ground beef and simmer approximately 45 minutes. Serve hot. This recipe freezes well.

Pat Carpenter
Nashville Council

CORN CHOWDER
(New England Style)

4 large potatoes	2 cans cream style corn
Dash of salt	1 can evaporated milk
2 large onions	1 qt. milk
Butter or margarine	

Peel and cube potatoes; rinse and put in large pot. Cover with water; add dash of salt. Bring to a boil. Saute onions in butter; add onions to potatoes and cook until done. Do not drain potatoes. Add cream style corn and evaporated milk and milk. Stir together; let heat 5 to 10 minutes. Can be served with sliced, fried salt pork and crackers.

Mary Conrad
Harpeth Council

DAN'S FAVORITE VEGETABLE SOUP

1 (8 oz.) can tomato sauce	1 c. frozen crowder peas
1 c. water	1/2 c. rice, uncooked
1 c. frozen kernel corn	1/2 c. catsup
1 c. frozen lima beans	1 tsp. pepper
3-4 slices bacon, cooked	1 tsp. salt
2 Tbsp. bacon grease	

Combine tomato sauce and water in Dutch oven over medium heat. Add all vegetables, bacon, bacon grease, rice and catsup; stir well. Add pepper and salt. Cook over medium heat for 15 minutes; reduce to simmering and cook approximately 30 minutes longer. Serves 6-8.

Norma S. Watson
Downtown Memphis Council

EASY SOUP

1 (16 oz.) bag frozen
   vegetables
1/2 - 1 lb. ground beef
1 (28 oz.) can tomatoes,
   mashed
4 large potatoes, diced

1 chopped onion
3 bay leaves
1/2 tsp. oregano
1 Tbsp. sugar
2 Tbsp. salt

Put frozen vegetables in 2 quarts boiling water. Brown meat; drain. Add to vegetables with rest of ingredients. Simmer until vegetables are tender and seasonings are well blended. Remove bay leaves. Makes about 10 servings. Serve with corn bread. Freezes well or keeps several days in refrigerator.

Reba Gray
Harpeth Council

FRENCH ONION SOUP

8 beef bouillon cubes
8 c. water
1 bay leaf
8 slices French bread,
   toasted
1 lb. grated baby Swiss
   cheese

1 lb. grated Mozzarella
   cheese
1 1/2 lb. onions, sliced
1/4 c. butter
1/2 tsp. sugar (optional)
1 Tbsp. cognac or dry
   vermouth
Grated Parmesan cheese

In a large pot, cook onions slowly in melted butter until brown. Sugar may be added to help browning. Add cognac or vermouth, bouillon cubes, water and bay leaf. Boil slowly, uncovered, until volume is reduced to 2/3. Remove film from surface of soup; remove bay leaf. Ladle soup into 8 ovenproof bowls. Place toasted bread slices on top of soup. Mix baby Swiss and Mozzarella cheeses and sprinkle lots on top of bread and soup. Sprinkle with Parmesan cheese. Broil until cheese is melted. Serves 8.

Judy Desendorf
Harpeth Council

MEAT BALL SOUP

Meat Balls:

1 egg
1 lb. ground chuck
2 Tbsp. chopped parsley

1/2 c. soft bread crumbs
  (1 slice)
1/2 tsp. salt
Dash of pepper

Soup:

2 Tbsp. butter or margarine
1 c. sliced onion
1 (1 lb. 12 oz.) can
  tomatoes, undrained
2 (10 1/2 oz.) cans
  condensed consomme,
  undiluted
2 c. cubed, pared potato
4 carrots, pared and sliced
  1/4 inch thick on diagonal

1 (10 oz.) pkg. frozen mixed
  vegetables
1/4 c. chopped celery tops
1/4 c. chopped parsley
1 bay leaf
1/2 tsp. dried oregano
  leaves
1/8 tsp. pepper
Chopped parsley

1. Make meat balls: In medium bowl, using fork, beat egg slightly. Add chuck, 2 tablespoons parsley, the bread crumbs, salt and dash of pepper; mix until well blended. 2. Shape into 60 balls, about 3/4 inch in diameter. 3. In hot butter in medium skillet, saute meat balls, a third at a time, until browned. Remove as browned; set aside. 4. In remaining fat, saute onion until golden, about 5 minutes. 5. In large kettle or 6 quart Dutch oven, combine meat balls, onion, tomatoes, consomme, potato, carrots, mixed vegetables, celery tops, 1/4 cup parsley, the bay leaf, oregano, pepper and 1 cup water. Bring to boiling. Reduce heat; simmer, covered, 20 minutes or until vegetables are tender. 6. Serve sprinkled with chopped parsley. Makes 3 quarts; 8 servings. Costs less than $1.00 per serving.

Marian Molteni
Harpeth Council

SAUSAGE-BEAN CHOWDER

1 lb. pork sausage
2 (16 oz.) cans kidney
  beans
1 (13 oz.) can tomatoes
1 qt. water

1 large onion, chopped
Bay leaf
1 1/2 tsp. seasoned salt
1 1/2 tsp. garlic salt
1/2 tsp. thyme

Dash of pepper　　　　　　1/2 c. chopped green (bell)
1 c. diced potatoes　　　　　　pepper

Brown sausage; pour off fat. Combine remaining ingredients, except potatoes, in a large kettle and simmer approximately 1 hour. Add potatoes and cook until done.

Maxine Scott
East Memphis Council

SHRIMP GUMBO

2 lb. shrimp, peeled and　　　2 Tbsp. oil
  deveined　　　　　　　　　1 bay leaf
2 Tbsp. oil　　　　　　　　　1 large can tomatoes
3 Tbsp. flour　　　　　　　　3 pods garlic (optional)
3 c. okra, chopped　　　　　2 qt. water
2 onions, chopped

Make a dark roux of flour and oil, stirring constantly. Add shrimp, uncooked; stir in a few minutes. Set aside. Smother okra and onions in oil; add tomatoes when okra is nearly cooked. Add water, bay leaf, garlic, salt and pepper. Add shrimp mixture. Cover and cook slowly 30 minutes. Put a rice mound in soup bowl and ladle gumbo over it. Serves 6 to 8.

Dorothy Bryant
Clarksville Council

HOMEMADE VEGETABLE SOUP

3-4 lb. beef, including soup　　3-4 c. tomatoes (canned
  bone　　　　　　　　　　　stewed or fresh)
3 qt. cold water　　　　　　　5-6 medium carrots, sliced
3-4 onions, quartered　　　　1 turnip, diced
Salt to taste　　　　　　　　3-4 medium potatoes, diced
1/4 head cabbage, shredded　3-4 beef bouillon cubes

Cut half the meat from bone and brown in hot fat. Add remaining meat and bone to cold water. Add browned meat, onion and salt to the cold water with meat. Cook slowly for a couple of hours. Add vegetables; continue cooking until done. This soup is better if it is made one day and used the next. If part of the soup is used and you warm up the leftover, add water and additional bouillon cubes for flavor.

Margaret Slack
Green Hills Council

CARAMEL-MALLOW SAUCE

15 cellophane wrapped
  caramels
1/2 c. milk
14 large marshmallows
Dash of salt

1 Tbsp. butter
1/4 tsp. burnt sugar
  flavoring (optional)
1/4 tsp. butter flavoring
  (optional)

Combine all ingredients in a heavy saucepan over low heat. Cook, stirring constantly, until melted into a smooth sauce. Use over ice cream, white cake or spice cake. Store sauce in refrigerator.

Beverly Pettigrew
Harpeth Council

HOT FUDGE SAUCE

1 (6 oz.) pkg. chocolate
  chips
1 stick butter or margarine

1 tsp. vanilla flavoring
1 c. evaporated milk
2 c. powdered sugar

Melt chocolate chips and butter over low heat. Add evaporated milk and cook 5 minutes. Remove from heat; add powdered sugar and vanilla. Refrigerate if kept more than a day. Makes 2 cups.

Beverly Pettigrew
Harpeth Council

SWEETENED CONDENSED MILK

1 c. instant non-fat dry
  milk solids
2/3 c. sugar

1/3 c. boiling water
3 Tbsp. melted butter or
  margarine

Combine all ingredients in the container of electric blender; process until smooth. Store in refrigerator until ready to use. Yield: About 1 1/4 cups. Can be used in any recipes calling for Eagle Brand milk.

Annie H. Harper
Nashville Council

126

CONDENSED MILK

1 c. instant nonfat dry
  milk
1/3 c. boiling water

3 Tbsp. melted butter or
  margarine
2/3 c. sugar
Pinch of salt

Put all ingredients in blender; process until smooth. Will keep several weeks in refrigerator. (This is a cheaper version of condensed milk to use in favorite recipes.) Makes 1 1/4 cups.

Judy Christopher
Harpeth Council

MILK GRAVY

2 Tbsp. flour
1-2 Tbsp. bacon grease

1 c. milk
Salt and pepper to taste

In hot skillet, stir in grease, flour, salt and pepper. Cook over medium-high heat; add milk and stir until mixture boils. Serve hot with bacon, eggs and biscuits.
Note: For thinner gravy, increase milk. For thicker gravy, decrease milk.

Kay Boswell
Andrew Jackson Council

SPICY BAR-B-QUE SAUCE

3/4 c. chopped onion
1/2 c. salad oil
3/4 c. catsup
1/3 c. vinegar
2 tsp. salt
1/2 tsp. pepper

1 (8 oz.) can tomato sauce or
  tomato paste
3/4 c. water
3 Tbsp. Worcestershire sauce
3 Tbsp. sugar
2 Tbsp. prepared mustard

Cook onion in hot salad oil until tender but not brown. Add catsup, water, vinegar, Worcestershire sauce and all other ingredients. Simmer slowly for about 1 hour. Add a little horseradish, if desired.

Beverly Pettigrew
Harpeth Council

BBQ SAUCE

1 onion
2 Tbsp. fat
2 Tbsp. vinegar
2 Tbsp. brown sugar
1/4 Tbsp. lemon juice
1 c. catsup

3 Tbsp. Lea & Perrins sauce
1/2 Tbsp. mustard
1 c. water
1/2 c. chopped celery
6 Tbsp. bottled smoke
1/3 bottle hot sauce (or less)

Brown onion in fat and mix remaining ingredients. Simmer 30 minutes or longer.

Ann Hughes
Green Hills Council

BARBECUE SAUCE

2 Tbsp. butter or margarine
1/2 c. finely chopped onion
1 c. water
1 c. ketchup
2 Tbsp. vinegar
2 Tbsp. lemon juice

2 Tbsp. Worcestershire sauce
2 Tbsp. brown sugar
1 tsp. dry mustard
1 tsp. salt
1/4 tsp. pepper

Melt butter in skillet; saute onion. Add remaining ingredients; simmer 20 minutes.

Vickie Jones
Harpeth Council

BARBECUE SAUCE

4 Tbsp. tomato catsup
2 Tbsp. lemon juice
1 Tbsp. vinegar
2 Tbsp. butter

1 Tbsp. Worcestershire sauce
1 tsp. chili powder
1 tsp. paprika
Salt and pepper

Mix well. Makes enough for a 2 1/2 pound fryer or 6 pork chops. Put in iron skillet; cover with foil. Bake in 350° oven for 1 hour and 15 minutes.

Marie Barnett
Harpeth Council

CARROT PUREE

1/2 lb. carrots, scraped and cut into 1/2 inch slices

2 tsp. orange juice
1 Tbsp. butter
Dash of nutmeg

Cover carrots with water in saucepan; bring to boil. Simmer until tender. Drain well and put into blender. Add juice and puree. Return to saucepan to heat with butter and nutmeg.

Judy Q. Arnold
Harpeth Council

CREOLE SAUCE

2 Tbsp. bacon fat or salad oil
1/2 c. chopped onion
1 clove garlic, finely chopped
1/4 c. chopped green pepper
1 tsp. celery seed

1 (1 lb. 12 oz.) can tomatoes, undrained
1 bay leaf
1 tsp. salt
2 tsp. sugar
1/2 tsp. chili powder
1 Tbsp. chopped parsley

In hot bacon fat in medium saucepan, saute onion, garlic and pepper until tender, about 5 minutes. Add remaining ingredients; simmer, uncovered, 45 minutes or until mixture is thickened. Stir occasionally; strain, if desired. Makes about 3 cups. Good over veal, meat loaf, cubed beef or breaded chops.

Joyce Mattice
Harpeth Council

PIZZA SAUCE

1 (6 oz.) can tomato paste
1/4 tsp. oregano
2 tsp. finely grated onion

1/2 tsp. salt
1/8 tsp. garlic salt
3 Tbsp. water

Combine all ingredients. Place on simmer flame if gas burner. Heat thoroughly to blend flavors. Makes approximately 1 cup of sauce.

Evelyn B. Bean
Harpeth Council

SAUCE FOR CHICKEN ON EGG BREAD

2 Tbsp. onion	1 1/2 pt. stock
2 Tbsp. celery	3/4 c. heavy cream
1/2 c. butter	Salt and pepper
6 Tbsp. flour	

Make like white sauce. If thin, mix a little flour and cream and add to thicken. Serves 6.

Joyce Mattice
Harpeth Council

SAUCE FOR ROUND STEAK

1 c. Heinz ketchup	2-4 Tbsp. Heinz wine vinegar
1/3 c. cooking oil	

1. Slash meat at edges to prevent curling. 2. Moisten meat with water; sprinkle Adolph's tenderizer over meat like salt on both sides. Pierce meat with fork. 3. Blend Heinz ketchup, oil and vinegar in small bowl. 4. Baste one side of steak with sauce. Place steak, basted side down, on hot grill set 3 inches above coals. Barbeque 25 minutes, turning frequently and basting with sauce. 5. Carve in diagonal slices across grain; serve with remaining sauce.

Claudia Davenport
Clarksville Council

SPAGHETTI SAUCE

1/2 c. onion	1 can Chef-Boy-Ar-Dee's
2 Tbsp. olive oil	spaghetti sauce
1 lb. ground beef	1 1/2 tsp. oregano
2 cloves garlic	1 tsp. salt
4 c. tomatoes	1/2 tsp. monosodium glutamate
2 c. seasoned tomato sauce	1/4 tsp. thyme
1 (3 oz.) can mushrooms	1 bay leaf
1/4 c. parsley	1 c. water

Cook onion in oil, then add meat and garlic; brown lightly. Add remaining ingredients and simmer, uncovered, until thick. (I always add 2 teaspoons sugar and dash of cinnamon.)

Joyce Mattice
Harpeth Council

SPAGHETTI SAUCE (WITH MEAT)

1 lb. ground chuck
1 medium onion, chopped
  fine
2 pieces celery, chopped
  fine
1 1/4 tsp. parsley flakes
1 pod garlic, chopped fine
4 Tbsp. oil or butter

2 (6 oz.) cans tomato paste
1 (8 oz.) can tomato sauce
  with mushrooms
1/4 tsp. oregano
3/4 tsp. Italian seasoning
2 tsp. sugar
2 bay leaves (optional)

Lightly brown onion, celery, garlic and parsley in oil or butter; add ground chuck and cook until redness is out. Stir often; salt and pepper to taste. Add 2 cans of tomato paste, plus 3 cans of water to each of paste, and 1 can tomato sauce with mushrooms. To this mixture, add more salt and pepper to taste, 2 teaspoons sugar, 1/4 teaspoon oregano, 3/4 teaspoon Italian seasoning and bay leaves. Cover pot with lid and cook slowly, 1 1/2 to 2 hours, or longer depending on thickness desired. Stir often to avoid sticking. Grated cheese may be added the last 15 minutes of cooking.

Rosemary Catalani
Harpeth Council

TARTAR SAUCE

4 large dill pickles
10 sprigs parsley
1 small onion

1 Tbsp. capers
1 pt. mayonnaise

Grind pickles; drain juice. Grind other ingredients and mix together.

Ann Hughes
Green Hills Council

COOKING MEAT AND POULTRY

ROASTING
- Use tender cuts of beef, veal, pork or lamb and young birds.
- Place meat fat side up, or poultry breast side up, on rack in foil-lined shallow roasting pan. Do not add water; do not cover.
- Insert meat thermometer in center of thickest part of meat, being careful that end does not touch bone, fat or gristle.
- Roast at 300 to 350 degrees to desired degree of doneness.

BROILING
- Use tender beef steaks, lamb chops, sliced ham, ground meats and poultry quarters or halves. Fresh pork should be broiled slowly to insure complete cooking in center. Steaks and chops should be at least ½ inch thick.
- Preheat oven to "broil". Place meat on rack in foil-lined broiler pan.
- Place meat on oven rack 2 to 5 inches from the heat source, with thicker meat placed the greater distance. Brush poultry with butter.
- Broil until top side is browned; season with salt and pepper.
- Turn; brown second side. Season and serve at once.

PANBROILING
- Use the same cuts suitable for broiling.
- Place skillet or griddle over medium-high heat. Preheat until a drop of water dances on the surface.
- Place meat in skillet; reduce heat to medium. Do not add water or cover. The cold meat will stick at first, but as it cooks and browns it will loosen. If juices start to cook out of the meat, increase heat slightly.
- When meat is brown on one side, turn and brown second side.

PANFRYING
- Use comparatively thin pieces of meat, meat that has been tenderized by pounding or scoring, meat that is breaded and chicken parts.
- Place skillet over medium high heat. Add a small amount of shortening—2 tablespoons will usually be sufficient.
- When shortening is hot, add meat or poultry. Cook as in panbroiling.

BRAISING
- Use for less tender cuts of meat or older birds. You can also braise pork chops, steaks and cutlets; veal chops, steaks and cutlets; and chicken legs and thighs.
- Brown meat on all sides as in panfrying. Season with salt and pepper.
- Add a small amount of water—or none if sufficient juices have already cooked out of the meat. Cover tightly.
- Reduce heat to low. Cook until tender, turning occasionally. Meats will cook in their own juices.

COOKING IN LIQUID
- Use less tender cuts of meat and stewing chickens. Browning of large cuts or whole birds is optional, but it does develop flavor and improve the color.
- Brown meat on all sides in hot shortening in saucepan.
- Add enough water or stock to cover meat. Season if desired. Simmer, covered, until tender.
- Add vegetables to allow enough time to cook without becoming mushy.

AMERICAN CHOP SUEY

1 lb. ground beef
1 large onion, sliced
1 c. sliced carrots
1 c. sliced celery
1 c. rice, cooked
1/4 stick margarine

Brown ground beef; add remaining ingredients. Salt and pepper to taste. Cook slowly until carrots are tender, about 30 minutes.

Myrtle Baker
Nashville Council

ALL AMERICAN CHOP SUEY

6 slices bacon
1 large onion
1 piece celery
1 lb. ground beef
1 can tomatoes
2 Tbsp. Worcestershire sauce
1 dash of Tabasco sauce
Salt and pepper to taste
1 can beef consomme
1 c. uncooked rice

Cook bacon until crisp; break into pieces. In bacon grease, brown chopped onion and celery. Add ground beef; brown. Add remaining ingredients; cover and simmer for 45 minutes.

Wanda Ladd
Green Hills Council

BAKED BUFFALO FISH

1 (4-5 lb.) buffalo fish
2 sticks corn oil margarine
1 tsp. black pepper
1 lemon, thinly sliced
1/2 tsp. cayenne pepper

Build an open fire using only hickory. While the fire is burning down to gray coals, clean fish and cut almost through the backbone from end to end so that it can be laid out flat. Obtain a yellow poplar board, approximately 12x36 inches. Place the buffalo, skin side down, about 6 inches from one end of the board. Nail the fish to the board, using large headed roofing nails. In a small saucepan, melt the margarine and add the pepper and lemon. Simmer, covered, for 5 minutes. Baste the fish liberally with the lemon butter, being sure that some sauce runs between the board and the fish. When the fire has burned down to coals, lean the board over the coals, fish side down, using a small stick to prop the board up. Baste liberally every 5 minutes, being sure that some sauce runs underneath the fish. Cook 40-50 minutes until fish flakes easily. Remove nails; throw the fish back in the river and eat the board.

Charlie Ham
Memphis Council

BAKED CHICKEN

Dip chicken in melted butter; salt and pepper. Roll in crushed potato chips. Place chicken on broiler rack. Sprinkle with Kraft Romano cheese and bake in a 350° oven for 30 minutes. Turn chicken; sprinkle with cheese and continue baking until chicken is done.

Addie Downs
Green Hills Council

SISTER'S BARBECUED BEEF

3 lb. chuck roast or   3/4 c. water
   boneless stew beef

Cook until tender (can be cooked in pressure cooker for 45 minutes). Cool and shred meat.

Sauce:

2 Tbsp. oil or shortening   1/2 tsp. salt
1 c. onion   1/2 tsp. garlic salt
2 tsp. paprika   3 Tbsp. cider vinegar
1 tsp. black pepper   3 Tbsp. sugar
1 tsp. dry mustard   3 Tbsp. Worcestershire sauce
3/4 tsp. red pepper   1 (6 oz.) can tomato paste

In iron skillet, cook onion in oil or melted shortening until tender. Add other sauce ingredients; simmer slowly for 20 minutes. Add beef and liquid. Cover and cook slowly for 30 minutes. Can be frozen for several days. Fills about 20 buns. Makes a good meal with slaw, French fries, baked potato or potato chips.

Flora Moore
Knoxville Council

BARBECUED CHICKEN

1/3 c. ketchup	1 tsp. dry mustard
1/3 c. vinegar	1 1/2 Tbsp. sugar
1/3 c. Worcestershire sauce	1/4 tsp. Tabasco sauce
1 Tbsp. lemon juice	1 c. water
2 Tbsp. margarine	2 Tbsp. minced onion

Pour sauce over prepared chicken. Sprinkle paprika over. Bake at 350° for 1 1/2 hours; turn at half the time.

Mrs. Adelene Queenan
Harpeth Council

BARBECUED CHICKEN

2/3 c. Bisquick baking mix	1/4 tsp. pepper
1 1/2 tsp. paprika	2 1/2 - 3 1/2 lb. broiler-
1 1/4 tsp. salt	fryer chicken, cut up

Mix baking mix, paprika, salt and pepper; coat chicken. Place chicken pieces, skin side up, on grill 5 inches from hot coals. Grill 20 to 30 minutes. Turn chicken; grill until done, 30 to 40 minutes longer. Makes 6 servings.

High Altitude Directions (3500 to 6500 feet): Not recommended for use.

Pat Ferguson
Harpeth Council

QUICK AND EASY BAR-B-Q CHICKEN

1 c. chicken	Coca-Cola
1 c. catsup	

Place chicken in a skillet; salt and pepper. Pour catsup over chicken, then cover with Coke. Bake at 325° for approximately 1 hour or until liquid is almost gone.

Debbi Wakefield
Harpeth Council

BAR-B-QUED CHOPS

4 or 5 large chops   Seasoned salt and pepper
1/2 c. chopped onion   2 c. barbeque sauce

Season chops with salt and pepper. Dip in barbeque sauce and place on grill; turn once or twice. Drop onions on top of each chop; turn over again and let onion flavor go through.

Curtisene Johnson
Memphis Council

BARBECUED FRANKFURTERS

1/3 c. chopped onion   2 Tbsp. brown sugar
1/3 c. chopped celery   2 Tbsp. Worcestershire sauce
1/2 clove garlic, minced   2 Tbsp. lemon juice or vinegar
3 Tbsp. shortening   2 Tbsp. prepared mustard
1 can (1 1/4 c.) condensed   4 drops Tabasco sauce
   tomato soup   1 lb. frankfurters

Brown onion, celery and garlic in shortening. Stir in the remaining sauce ingredients; simmer for a few minutes. Add the frankfurters; cover and simmer for 20 minutes. Serves 4 to 5.

Joyce Mattice
Harpeth Council

BAR-B-QUE MEAT BALLS

1 1/2 lb. ground beef   2 Tbsp. Worcestershire sauce
1 env. Lipton dry onion soup   1/2 c. milk

Mix all ingredients together and form into balls; place on flat baking pan. Bake until brown, approximately 30 minutes. Drain grease from pan and put balls in fondue base or another type container that you can keep warm. Pour Kraft's barbeque sauce over balls; let simmer. Makes about 50 meat balls. This is a perfect hot and spicy hors d'oeuvres for parties.

Frankie M. Atkins
Knoxville Council

BEER BARBECUED PORK CHOPS

8 (3/4 inch thick) pork chops	2 tsp. celery salt
Garlic salt to taste	4 tsp. Worcestershire sauce
2 (12 oz.) cans beer	2 bay leaves
1 1/3 c. catsup	1 tsp. pepper
1 c. water	1/2 tsp. basil
2/3 c. lemon juice	1/8 tsp. hot sauce

Place chops in shallow pan; sprinkle with garlic salt. Pour beer over chops and marinate in refrigerator 4 hours. Combine remaining ingredients in a saucepan; bring to a boil. Simmer over low heat 10 minutes. Remove chops from marinade. Grill to desired doneness, basting frequently with sauce. Serves 8.

Mary Crabtree
Knoxville Council

BARBECUED MEAT BALLS

1 1/2 lb. ground beef	1/2 c. milk
2 tsp. salt	1/4 tsp. pepper

Mix together; shape into 16 balls and fry in small amount of fat until browned. Combine:

1 c. catsup	1 tsp. sugar
1/4 c. Worcestershire sauce	2 Tbsp. vinegar
3 Tbsp. chopped onion	1 Tbsp. water

Pour over meat in skillet. Cover and cook slowly 30 minutes, turning meat occasionally. Makes 16 meat balls.

Rachel Yarbrough
Clarksville Council

BBQ RIBS

Spareribs	Salt and pepper
1 bottle barbecue sauce	

Place ribs in crock pot and season with salt and pepper. Pour sauce over. Cook on low all day (8 hours).

Mrs. Lewis (Pam) Lawley
Green Hills Council

BARBECUED RIBS

4 lb. pork spareribs
  (country style), cut in
  serving pieces
1 c. catsup
1/2 c. Worcestershire sauce
1 tsp. chili powder

1 tsp. salt
1/2 tsp. pepper
1 lemon, thinly sliced
1 medium onion, peeled and
  thinly sliced

Heat oven to 450°. Salt and pepper ribs lightly and arrange them in a large, shallow roasting pan, meaty side up. Bake ribs, uncovered, for 30 minutes. While ribs are baking, mix together in a saucepan the catsup, Worcestershire sauce, chili powder, the 1 teaspoon salt and 1/2 teaspoon pepper. Place saucepan over moderate heat and bring mixture to a boil, stirring frequently. Remove sauce from heat. Reduce oven temperature to 350°. Remove ribs from oven and drain excess fat from pan. Brush ribs generously with sauce. Arrange lemon and onion slices on ribs. Return ribs to oven and bake, uncovered, 1 1/2 hours, brushing frequently with sauce. Serves 6.

Mary Crabtree
Knoxville Council

BARBECUE SPARERIBS

Salt and pepper each sparerib and put into baking pan, then add 1 bottle of Kraft Miracle French dressing. Put in oven and bake 1 to 1 1/2 hours.

Addie Downs
Green Hills Council

BAR-B-Q SHRIMP

1 doz. jumbo unpeeled
  shrimp
1 lb. margarine, not whipped

1/2 big bottle Wish-Bone
  Italian dressing
Black pepper

Place unpeeled shrimp in 12x9x2 inch Pyrex baking dish. Sprinkle well with pepper. Combine melted margarine and Italian dressing; pour over shrimp. Total cooking time is 15 minutes. Bake at 350° for 5 minutes; turn shrimp over. Bake 5 more minutes at 350°; turn shrimp over again. Cook last 5 minutes under broiler. Dip hot French bread in sauce along with the shrimp. (Remove shrimp shells before dipping in sauce.)

Glory Sharp
Green Hills Council

BAR-B-QUE SHRIMP

Figure 20 shrimp per pound.

Sauce:

1 lb. butter	1 tsp. rosemary
1 lb. oleo	4 lemons, sliced
6 oz. Lea & Perrins sauce	1 tsp. Tabasco sauce
8 Tbsp. black pepper	4 tsp. salt
2-4 cloves garlic	

Melt butter and oleo in large saucepan. Add Lea & Perrins sauce, pepper, rosemary, lemon slices, Tabasco sauce, salt and garlic; mix thoroughly. Divide shrimp between 2 large pans and pour heated sauce over each. Stir well. Bake at 400° for 15 to 20 minutes, turning shrimp once. Shells should be pink, meat white and not translucent. Cook with shells on. Sauce may be stored and used again.

Bessie Crosby
Harpeth Council

BEEF RAGUE

6 Tbsp. Mazola corn oil	2 (16 oz.) cans tomatoes
2 lb. stew beef, cut in 2 inch pieces	1/3 c. dry white wine
	1 tsp. dried rosemary
1 large onion, sliced	1/2 tsp. garlic salt
2 c. sliced celery	1/4 tsp. pepper
2 (4 oz.) cans mushrooms, drained (reserve liquid)	1/3 c. cornstarch
	Cooked rice or noodles

In 5 quart Dutch oven, heat 2 tablespoons of corn oil over medium heat. Add beef; brown on all sides, turning as needed. Remove meat. Heat remaining corn oil; add onion, celery and mushrooms. Saute, stirring frequently, until onion is transparent. Add meat, tomatoes, wine, salt, rosemary, garlic salt and pepper. Bring to boil; reduce heat. Simmer, covered, about 3 hours or until meat is tender. Mix cornstarch and 1/2 cup reserved mushroom liquid. Add to meat mixture. Bring to boil, stirring constantly; boil 2 minutes. Serve hot over noodles or rice.

Polly Kirby
Andrew Jackson Council

EASY BEEF STROGANOFF

1 lb. round steak, cut into
   thin strips
1/2 c. chopped onion
Garlic to taste
2 Tbsp. butter

1 can cream of mushroom soup
1/4 c. water
1/2 c. sour cream
1/2 tsp. paprika
Salt and pepper to taste
2 c. cooked rice

Brown the steak, onion and garlic in the butter. Remove the garlic. Stir in the soup, water, sour cream, paprika, salt and pepper; cover. Cook over low heat for 45 minutes or until the steak is tender, stirring frequently. Serve over rice. Yield: 4 servings.

Dorothy Bryant
Clarksville Council

EASY BEEF STROGANOFF

1 1/2 lb. round steak, cut
   in thin strips
1/4 c. flour
Dash of pepper
1/4 c. oleo

4 oz. sliced mushrooms
1/2 c. chopped onion
1 can beef broth or consomme
1 c. sour cream

Cover steak strips with the flour and pepper; brown in the margarine. Add drained mushrooms and onion; brown lightly. Stir in 1 can clear beef broth. Cover and cook until meat is tender, approximately 1 hour; stir several times. Gradually stir in 1 cup sour cream. Cook over low heat 5 minutes. Serve over cooked noodles.

Marian Molteni
Harpeth Council

BEEF STROGANOFF

1 1/2 lb. steak, 3/4 inch
   thick
2 medium onions
1/4 lb. fresh mushrooms
   or 1 (4 oz.) can
6 Tbsp. salad oil
1/2 c. flour

1 1/2 c. water
1 1/2 tsp. salt
1/4 tsp. pepper
1 Tbsp. tomato paste
1 c. thick sour cream
Dash of Tabasco sauce
1 Tbsp. Worcestershire sauce

Slice steak into thin pieces. Wash and slice fresh mushrooms or drain canned mushrooms. Heat oil in a <u>large</u> skillet. Add <u>sliced</u> onions and mushrooms; cook until tender but not browned, about 5 minutes. Remove from skillet. Roll steak in flour; brown in remaining oil on all sides. Add water, salt and pepper; cover and cook slowly about 45 minutes until tender. Meanwhile, mix together onions, mushrooms, tomato sauce or paste, sour cream, Tabasco sauce and Worcestershire sauce. Pour sauce over meat; stir gently to blend and simmer, uncovered, 5 minutes. Serve over noodles, rice or mashed potatoes. Serves 4.

Virginia Q. Kaderabek
Harpeth Council

BEEF STROGANOFF

1 lb. lean round steak
1 Tbsp. paprika
2 tsp. butter or margarine
2 garlic cloves, crushed
1 1/2 c. beef broth
1 c. sliced green onions
   with tops

2 green peppers, cut in
   strips
2 Tbsp. cornstarch
1/4 c. water
1/4 c. soy sauce
2 large fresh tomatoes
   (optional)
Sour cream (optional)

Pound steak to 1/4 inch thick; cut into chunks and sprinkle with paprika. Let stand for a few minutes. Using a large skillet, brown meat in butter; add garlic and beef broth. Cover and simmer for 30 minutes. Stir in onions and green peppers; cover and cook 5 minutes more. Blend cornstarch, water and soy sauce; stir into meat mixture. Cook, stirring until clear and thickened, about 2 minutes. Add tomatoes and stir gently. Serve over rice or noodles. Top with sour cream, if you like. Serves 6.

Donna Perry
Harpeth Council

BEEF STROGANOFF

1 round steak
1/4 c. flour
1/4 c. margarine
1 (4 oz.) can mushrooms, sliced
1/2 c. sliced onion

2 beef bouillon cubes, dissolved in 2 c. hot water
1 c. sour cream
1 Tbsp. Worcestershire sauce
3 c. cooked noodles

Cut steak into slices of 3/8 inch strips, then into 3 inch pieces. Dust with flour. Melt oleo in heavy skillet; brown steak. Add mushrooms and onion; brown. Add bouillon and Worcestershire sauce; simmer 45 to 50 minutes. Five minutes before serving, stir in sour cream. When warm, pour over cooked noodles in a large container.

Mary Jane Bailey
Green Hills Council

BOEUF BOURGUIGNONNE

2 lb. cubed beef
3-4 carrots, cut up and partially cooked
1 c. chopped celery
2 onions, sliced
16 oz. canned tomatoes
8 oz. tomato sauce

1 clove garlic, minced
3 Tbsp. Minute Tapioca
1 Tbsp. sugar
1/2 c. burgundy
8 oz. canned mushrooms
2 cans small Irish potatoes

Combine first 10 ingredients in large casserole or Dutch oven; bake at 250° for 4 hours. Add mushrooms and potatoes; bake for 1 more hour. Serves 6-8.

Note: If freezing a portion, leave out potatoes until ready to serve.

Judy Desendorf
Harpeth Council

BRAISED SIRLOIN TIPS OVER RICE

2 Tbsp. shortening
2 lb. beef sirloin tip (or round steak), cut into 1 inch cubes
2 (10 1/2 oz.) cans condensed beef consomme or bouillon

2/3 c. burgundy
2 Tbsp. soy sauce
2 cloves garlic, minced
1/2 tsp. onion salt
4 Tbsp. cornstarch
1/2 c. water
4 c. hot, cooked rice

Melt shortening in large skillet; brown meat on all sides. Stir in consomme, wine, soy sauce, garlic and onion salt; heat to boiling. Reduce heat; cover and simmer 1 hour or until meat is tender. Blend cornstarch and water; stir gradually into meat mixture. Cook, stirring constantly, until mixture thickens and boils. Boil and stir 1 minute. Serve over rice. Serves 6.

Judy Desendorf
Harpeth Council

CANELLONI FLORENTINE

Filling:

1/2 lb. ground beef	1/8 tsp. thyme
1/2 lb. ground pork	1/8 tsp. pepper
1 box frozen chopped	1/2 tsp. salt
spinach	1/8 tsp. oregano
1 chopped onion	1/2 c. grated Romano cheese

Brown meat and onion; add all seasonings. Thaw spinach and drain; add to meat. Set aside.

Pancake Batter:

1 c. milk	1 tsp. baking powder
2 Tbsp. butter	1/2 tsp. salt
2 eggs	Oil
1/2 c. flour	

Heat milk and butter in saucepan until butter is melted. Let cool. Meanwhile, beat eggs, flour, baking powder and salt. Add milk slowly; beat until mixed. Lightly oil 6 inch iron skillet and heat. Pour 1/8 cup batter in skillet and tilt to distribute batter. Bake until bubbles appear; remove to cool. Makes 12 pancakes. Put meat on pancakes and roll up.

Cheese Sauce:

3 Tbsp. butter	Dash of nutmeg
3 Tbsp. flour	1/2 c. grated Parmesan or
1 1/2 c. light cream	Romano cheese
1/2 tsp. salt	

Melt butter in top of double boiler; blend in flour.

Add cream, salt, nutmeg and cheese. Pour 1/2 (16 ounce) can of tomato sauce into a greased baking dish. Add meat rolls. Mix any leftover meat with remaining tomato sauce and pour around pancakes. Pour cheese sauce over pancakes and sprinkle with more cheese. Place in 350° oven; heat until brown and bubbly.

Vangie Whitley
Harpeth Council

CAROLINA MEAT BALLS

1 lb. ground beef
2 slices bread
1/2 c. sweet milk

1/2 tsp. salt
1/2 tsp. pepper

Soak bread in milk; mix with meat. Add salt and pepper. Form in balls, not too large; place in greased baking dish.

Sauce:

1/2 c. water
1/2 c. catsup
1/2 c. vinegar

2 Tbsp. Worcestershire sauce
1 Tbsp. white or brown sugar
1/2 c. chopped green pepper
1/2 c. onion, chopped

Mix well and pour over meat balls. Bake at 350° for 45 minutes.

Pattie Carpenter
Nashville Council

CHEDDAR BURGER SKILLET

1 lb. ground beef
1 onion, chopped
1 can Cheddar cheese soup
1/2 c. water

4 medium potatoes, sliced, boiled
1 tsp. salt
1/4 tsp. black pepper

Brown onion and beef in skillet. Add soups, water, salt and pepper. Simmer 5 minutes; add potatoes. Simmer 5 minutes. Serve.

M. Carolyn Hunter
Harpeth Council

IMPOSSIBLE CHEESEBURGER PIE

1 lb. ground beef
1 c. chopped onion
1/2 tsp. salt
1/4 tsp. pepper

1 c. shredded Cheddar
  cheese
1 1/2 c. milk
3/4 c. Bisquick baking mix
3 eggs

Heat oven to 400°. Lightly grease 10 inch pie plate. Cook and stir beef and onion until brown; drain well. Stir in salt and pepper. Spread beef in pie plate; sprinkle with cheese. Beat remaining ingredients until smooth, 15 seconds in blender on high speed, or 1 minute with hand beater. Pour into pie plate. Bake until golden brown and knife inserted in center comes out clean, about 30 minutes. Let stand 5 minutes. Serves 6 to 8.

> Pat Ferguson
> Harpeth Council
> Beverly Simpkins
> Harpeth Council

CHEESEBURGER PIE

1 stick or 1/2 packet pie
  crust mix
1 lb. ground beef
1 tsp. salt
1/2 tsp. oregano
1/4 tsp. pepper

1/2 c. dry bread crumbs
1 (8 oz.) can tomato sauce
1/4 c. chopped onion
1/4 c. chopped green pepper
Cheese Topping (below)
1/2 c. chili sauce (optional)

Heat oven to 425°. Prepare pastry for one 9 inch pie. In medium skillet, cook and stir meat until brown; drain off fat. Stir in salt, oregano, pepper, crumbs, 1/2 cup tomato sauce, onion and pepper. Turn into pastry lined pie pan. Spread cheese topping over filling. Bake about 30 minutes; cut into wedges. (Stir together remaining tomato sauce and the chili sauce; serve with pie.) Makes 6 to 8 servings.

Cheese Topping:

1 egg
1/4 c. milk
1/2 tsp. salt
1/2 tsp. dry mustard

1/2 tsp. Worcestershire sauce
2 c. (about 8 oz.) shredded
  natural Cheddar cheese

Beat egg and milk; stir in seasonings and cheese.

Billie Fleming
Nashboro Council
Pat DeMatteo
Nashboro Council

CHEESE PUFF - TUNA BAKE

3 Tbsp. butter or margarine
1/4 c. Martha White self-
  rising flour
1 (10 1/2 oz.) can con-
  densed celery soup

3/4 c. milk
6 1/2 or 7 oz. can tuna
1 c. small lima beans, drained
1 Tbsp. lemon juice

Heat oven to 425° F. Melt butter in saucepan. Blend in flour, then celery soup and milk. Cook until thickened, stirring constantly. Fold in tuna, lima beans and lemon juice. Pour into greased 8 inch square baking dish.

Vickie Jones
Harpeth Council

FRIED CHICKEN

2 lb. frying chicken,
  skinned
1 1/2 c. buttermilk
2 eggs

1/4 tsp. garlic powder
1/4 tsp. onion powder
Dash of salt
2 c. flour

Mix buttermilk, eggs, onion powder, garlic powder and salt. Dip chicken in this mixture, then roll the chicken in the flour. Fry in 2 inches of cooking oil. Turn once only. This makes a very tasty, crisp crust. Can be served hot or cold.

Brenda Craig
Chattanooga Council

MICHELE'S OVEN FRIED CHICKEN

2 1/2 - 3 lb. broiler-fryer
1/4 c. shortening
1/4 c. margarine
1/2 c. flour

1/2 tsp. salt
1 tsp. paprika
1/4 tsp. pepper

Heat oven to 425°. Wash chicken and pat dry. Melt

shortening and margarine in pan in oven. Mix remaining ingredients; coat chicken with mixture. Place chicken with skin side down in melted shortening. Bake, uncovered, for 30 minutes. Turn chicken and bake 30 minutes longer.

Barbara Stanfill
Harpeth Council

SOUTHERN   FRIED   CHICKEN

Dip pieces of chicken in boiling water; immediately coat with seasoned flour. Quickly place in hot skillet, 300°, skin side down. Cover; fry 5 minutes. Remove cover and cook 4 minutes longer. Turn chicken; cover 5 minutes longer. Remove cover and cook 4 minutes. By now the chicken should be brown, crunchy and done. Sprinkle with more salt and pepper, if desired; do not overcook.

Mary Beth McLaurine
Harpeth Council

CHICKEN

Chicken parts (about 8 pieces)
1 jar apricot preserves
1 bottle Russian dressing
1 pkg. Lipton onion soup mix

Combine preserves, dressing and soup mix. Pour mixture over chicken and bake, uncovered, at 350° for 1 1/4 to 1 1/2 hours. Serves 4.

Addie Downs
Green Hills Council

CHICKEN   AND   RICE

2 c. cooked, diced chicken
1 (8 oz.) ctn. sour cream
1 can cream of chicken soup

Mix above and pour over cooked rice.

Cooked Rice:

1 1/4 c. water
Salt to taste
1/2 c. Uncle Ben's converted rice
1 Tbsp. margarine

In a greased Pyrex dish, layer the rice with the chicken mixture on top. Pour 1/4 to 1/2 cup chicken broth over the casserole. Crush 3/4 cup Ritz crackers and dot with butter. Sprinkle 1/4 cup slivered almonds on top. Bake 30 to 35 minutes at 350°.

Nancy Cochrane
Harpeth Council

BAKED CHICKEN BREASTS WITH ALMONDS

5 chicken breasts
Cooking oil (enough to
  brown chicken pieces)
1 can cream of mushroom
  soup
1/2 c. sherry cooking wine

1/4 c. sharp Cheddar cheese
3 Tbsp. grated onion
2 Tbsp. Worcestershire sauce
1/2 c. slivered almonds
1/3 c. water
Salt and pepper to taste

Brown chicken in cooking oil; place in baking dish. Combine soup, wine, cheese, onion and Worcestershire sauce together and pour over chicken. Place almonds on top. Cover with foil; bake at 350° for 45 minutes or longer.

Mrs. Adelene Queenan
Harpeth Council

CHICKEN BREASTS IN WINE

1/2 c. flour
1 1/2 tsp. salt
1 1/2 tsp. garlic salt
1 1/2 tsp. paprika

1/4 c. cooking oil
1 can dark sweet cherries
1 c. sauterne wine
Rice

Mix together flour, salt, garlic salt and paprika. Coat chicken breasts with flour mixture; brown in oil. Drain cherries; measure 1/2 cup of the cherry juice. Add cherries, juice and wine to chicken. Cover and simmer until chicken is tender, about 1 hour at 350°. Serve over rice.

Peggy Burr
Harpeth Council

CHICKEN CORDON BLEU

Chicken breasts, boned
and beaten flat

Boiled ham slices
Swiss cheese slices

Pound chicken breasts between 2 sheets of waxed paper until very thin (twice the original size). Layer these with the ham and cheese slices and pound the edges of breasts together.

1/2 c. flour
1/2 tsp. salt
1/4 tsp. pepper
1/4 tsp. monosodium
glutamate
1/4 tsp. paprika
1 egg

2 tsp. milk
1/2 c. bread crumbs
3 tsp. margarine
1/2 c. chicken broth
2 tsp. dried parsley flakes
1 (10 oz.) can chicken soup
1/2 c. sour cream

Mix dry ingredients and coat each breast with mixture. Dip in beaten egg and milk; roll in crumbs. Brown slowly in margarine. Add chicken broth; sprinkle with parsley and simmer until chicken is tender, about 1 hour. Blend soup and pan drippings; stir in sour cream and heat gently. Serve over rice.

Addie Downs
Green Hills Council

MARGIE'S CHICKEN IN WINE

1 whole chicken, cut up,
or about 6 chicken
breasts
2 env. dry onion soup

1 can mushroom soup
1/2 c. water
Red cooking wine

Lay pieces of chicken in Corning Ware. Pour over chicken the dry onion soup, mushroom soup, water and enough red cooking wine to cover chicken. Cover and bake in 350° oven for 2 hours.

Margie Switzer
Memphis Council

CHICKEN CRUNCH

1 frying chicken, boiled
1 pt. stock
2 cans mushroom soup
1/2 c. onion, chopped

3/4 c. celery, chopped
1 can water chestnuts
1 can chow mein noodles

Boil chicken; pick meat from bones and add all the ingredients. (Noodles can be sprinkled on top.) Put in an 11x7 inch casserole. Bake 30-45 minutes at 350°.

Linda Whitaker
Harpeth Council

CHICKEN EASY

Chicken breasts
1 can cream of chicken soup
1 can cream of mushroom
  soup
1 can cream of celery soup

3/8 c. sugar (optional)
Salt and pepper to taste
Basil to taste (optional)
1 1/2 c. instant rice

Mix soups and spices (do not dilute the soups). Heat and take out 1 cup of mixture (for reserve). Add instant rice to remaining mixture; bring to a boil. Spread in a long baking dish; place pieces of chicken breast on top and spread reserved cup of soup over top. Bake at 300° for about 2 hours (or microwave chicken until almost done, then add to above for shorter cooking time).

Marian Molteni
Harpeth Council

CHICKEN IMPERIAL

3 c. cooked chicken
1 pkg. Uncle Ben's
  combination white and
  wild rice, cooked
1 can celery soup

1 medium jar sliced pimento
1 medium onion, chopped
2 c. French style green beans
1 c. Hellmann's mayonnaise
1 can water chestnuts

Mix ingredients. Pour into 2 1/2 or 3 quart casserole. Bake 25 to 30 minutes at 350°. To freeze, do not bake.

Katie Braden
Harpeth Council

150

CHICKEN AND RICE
(Diabetics)

1/2 c. cooked chicken, diced   1 tsp. onion, chopped
1/2 c. rice, cooked   1 oz. cheese, grated
1 tsp. chicken fat

    1. The rice should be cooked in advance in chicken broth, which has been made from chicken bones. 2. Using 1/2 cup of cooked rice and 1/2 cup cooked, diced chicken, mix them together well. 3. Brown the finely chopped onion in chicken fat until golden brown; add to the chicken and rice. 4. Turn out onto a hot dish and garnish with grated cheese. Exchange: 5 meat exchanges; 1 bread exchange; 478 calories.

PARMESAN CHICKEN BREASTS

1/2 lb. melted butter   8 chicken breasts, boned
1 c. Parmesan cheese   Fresh parsley (for
1 1/2 - 2 c. bread crumbs   decoration)
     Garlic salt

    Dip breasts in melted butter. Roll in mixture of cheese, bread crumbs and garlic salt. Top with parsley in uncovered glass baking dish. Pour unused butter over top of breasts. Bake 1 1/2 hours at 350°.

Ginger Lewis
Harpeth Council

PARMESAN CHICKEN BAKE

1 chicken, cut up   Garlic salt (may use other
2 c. Parmesan cheese   spices to suit your taste,
1/2 c. chopped onion   i.e., salt, pepper, etc.
   (optional)   Note: When mixing garlic
2 c. melted margarine (or   salt and table salt, be
   butter)   careful not to get too
1 egg   salty)
     2 1/2 c. bread crumbs

    Mix egg and margarine. Mix bread crumbs, spices and onion. Dip chicken thoroughly in egg and margarine, then into cheese, then into crumbs. Place in greased baking dish and cover. Bake at 350° for 45 minutes, then uncover and continue baking for 15 minutes.

Donnalee Langston
Memphis Council

CHICKEN PICCATA

4 whole chicken breasts,
  skinned, boned, halved
1/2 c. flour
1 1/2 tsp. salt
1/4 tsp. freshly ground
  pepper
Paprika
1/4 c. clarified butter

1 Tbsp. olive oil
2-4 Tbsp. wine or water
3 Tbsp. fresh lemon juice or
  lemon slices
3-4 Tbsp. capers (optional)
1/4 c. minced parsley
  (optional garnish)

Pound chicken breasts about 1/4 inch thick. Combine flour, salt, pepper and paprika. Add breasts and coat well; shake off excess. Heat butter and olive oil in large skillet until bubbling. Saute chicken pieces, a few at a time, 2 to 3 minutes on each side; do not overcook. Drain on paper towels and keep warm. Drain off all but 2 tablespoons of butter and oil. Stir wine or water into drippings, scraping bottom of skillet to loosen any browned bits. Add lemon juice and heat briefly. Return chicken to skillet, interspering with lemon slices and heat until sauce thickens. Add capers; sprinkle with minced parsley. Makes 4 to 8 servings.

Mary Lynn Johnson
Harpeth Council

CHICKEN PIE

1 whole chicken
1 1/2 c. chicken broth
1 can cream of celery soup

1 stick melted oleo
1 c. self-rising flour
1 c. milk

Cook whole chicken until tender and debone. Spray Pam in bottom of casserole and spread chicken pieces over bottom. Combine broth and soup; pour over chicken. Mix oleo, milk and flour; pour on top. Bake at 350° for 1 hour or until top is golden brown.

Carol Minshew
Memphis Council

152

CHICKEN LIVERS SUPREME
(Ulcer Diet)

2 Tbsp. butter
2 Tbsp. flour
1 c. milk
Salt
1/2 lb. chicken livers

2 whole eggs
2 egg yolks
6 Tbsp. heavy cream
1 Tbsp. cognac
1 can cream of celery soup

Set oven at 350°. Melt butter in the top of a double boiler. When melted, stir in flour and mix well. Add milk, salt to taste and stir constantly until sauce is smooth and begins to thicken. Set aside to cool slightly, but do not refrigerate. Stir sauce occasionally while it is cooling. Put chicken livers, whole eggs and egg yolks in a blender; blend for 1 minute. Add the cooled sauce, cream and cognac; blend for 15 seconds. Pour mixture into a 1 quart baking dish and set baking dish in a pan of hot water. Bake in preheated 350° oven for 30 minutes or until set. Unmold onto a warm platter. Serve with this quick celery sauce: About 10 minutes before chicken livers are done, put the contents of 1 can cream of celery soup, undiluted, in a blender. Blend until soup is smooth and has a sauce-like consistency, about 15 seconds. Pour into saucepan and heat over low flame until sauce is hot. Makes 4 servings.

CHICKEN LIVERS PAGLIACCI

1 packet chicken broth or
   golden seasoning and
   broth mix
1 lb. chicken livers, cut
   in thirds
1 c. sliced mushrooms

1 Tbsp. Worcestershire sauce
1 tsp. salt
1/2 tsp. pepper
1/2 clove garlic, minced
2 c. buttered cauliflower or
   creamed potatoes

Combine chicken broth mix and 1 cup boiling water; stir until broth is dissolved. Brown chicken livers on all sides over moderate heat in nonstick skillet. Reduce heat to low; add mushrooms, chicken broth, Worcestershire sauce, salt, pepper and garlic. Cook over low heat for 10 minutes or until livers are done. Serve over cauliflower or potatoes. Garnish with parsley. Yields 2 servings.

Peggy Burr
Harpeth Council

CHICKEN POJARSKY
(Food Processor Recipe)

Prepare mixture and refrigerate. Saute just before serving.

3 chicken breasts, split, skinned and boned	1 tsp. salt
1 c. soft bread crumbs (about 2 slices)	1/2 tsp. white pepper
	1/4 tsp. ground nutmeg
1/2 c. milk	1-2 Tbsp. brandy
1/4 c. (1/2 stick) butter, softened	1 egg yolk
	Flour
1/3 c. heavy cream	Butter for sauteing

Cut chicken into approximately 1 inch pieces; place in the bowl of a food processor, fitted with the steel blade, and "chop". Do this with short on/off motions until the chicken meat resembles coarse ground beef. Soak bread crumbs in milk 10 minutes; squeeze out excess milk. Add bread crumbs to chicken along with butter, cream, salt, pepper, nutmeg, brandy and egg yolk. Blend until well mixed. With wet hands, shape into oval patties and pat with flour. Refrigerate until ready to saute. Heat butter in large skillet. Cook chicken over low heat until browned on both sides, 10 to 15 minutes, depending on thickness. Serves 6.

Note: Shallots, lemon, tarragon or other herbs may be added to pan while cooking.

Sherree Weisenberger
Harpeth Council

CHICKEN SPAGHETTI

2 lb. chicken breast, chopped fine	1 can French fried onions
	1 can chopped pimento
1/2 c. green pepper, chopped	1/2 c. chopped celery
	1 small can sliced mushrooms
1 1/2 c. grated Cheddar cheese	7 or 8 oz. box spaghetti
	1 can cream of mushroom soup
	1 can cream of celery soup

Cook chicken breasts; save broth to cook spaghetti. Cook spaghetti until tender. Mix pepper, onion rings, pimento, celery and mushroom soups with spaghetti. Place in baking dish; cover with cheese. Bake at 250° for 1 1/2 hours.

Florence Stubblefield
Morristown Council

154

CHICKEN WITH COOKING SHERRY

1/2 c. cooking sherry
1/2 c. milk
1 chicken, cut

1 can mushroom soup
1 can water

Brown chicken in skillet. Mix sherry, milk and mushroom soup and water in pan. Add chicken and bake in oven 1 1/2 hours at 350°.

Judy Gibson
Harpeth Council

CHICKEN SUPREME

4 or 5 chicken breasts
1 can cream of mushroom
  soup

1 container sour cream
1 pkg. bacon
Sliced chipped beef

1. Season and boil chicken till done; drain and let cool. 2. Debone chicken; place some chicken on top of 1 slice of chipped beef, then roll into a little roll the width of 2 fingers. Wrap half of a slice of bacon around the roll to hold it. Make as many rolls as possible. Place in casserole dish. 3. Make soup, then add sour cream; let come to a boil. 4. Pour over rolls. Bake at 350° for 25-30 minutes or till sides bubble.

Janet Sexton
Harpeth Council

CHICKEN TETRAZZINI

1 (4 lb.) chicken, quartered
1 diced carrot
1 medium onion, chopped
2 stalks celery, coarsely
  chopped
Salt and pepper
3 Tbsp. butter or chicken
  fat
3 Tbsp. flour

1 c. half & half
1/2 lb. mushrooms, sauteed
  in butter
2 Tbsp. sherry
1/4 lb. grated Parmesan or
  Cheddar cheese
1/2 c. buttered bread crumbs
1/2 lb. spaghetti
2 c. chicken broth

Boil chicken until tender in water to cover, to which has been added diced carrot, onion, celery and salt and pepper to taste. Allow chicken to cool in broth, then remove and cut into bite sized pieces; strain broth. Make a medium sauce with the butter or chicken fat, flour, chicken broth and half & half. Add mushrooms and sherry. Boil spaghetti according to package directions in chicken broth. Combine sauce, mushrooms, chicken and spaghetti in greased baking dish. Sprinkle with grated cheese and bread crumbs. Bake in 375° oven until heated thoroughly and lightly browned. Serves 8 to 10.

Patsy Carter
Harpeth Council

CHICKEN TURNOVERS

1/2 c. shredded cheese
1/4 c. chopped celery
2 Tbsp. chopped onion

1 (5 oz.) can chicken
1 can (10) biscuits
2 jalapeno peppers, chopped

Combine cheese, celery, onion, chicken and peppers. Roll out biscuits on a lightly floured board. Place 1-2 tablespoons chicken mixture on each biscuit. Fold over and seal edges. Bake in 400° oven for 12 minutes or until brown. Yield: 10 turnovers.

Linda Cavazos
Jackson Council

COMPANY CHICKEN WITH GRAVY

6-8 chicken breasts
1/2 - 1 stick margarine
1 tsp. paprika

1/2 tsp. salt
1/2 tsp. pepper
1 can mushroom soup

Brown chicken breasts in butter, adding in seasonings. Add in can of mushroom soup; this will make your gravy. Bake the complete mixture at about 325° until your chicken is tender, about 30 to 45 minutes. You also have your gravy for rice or potatoes.

Mindy Yates
Harpeth Council

CREAMED CHICKEN AVEC MUSHROOMS

6 whole deboned chicken
   breasts
2 pkg. frozen broccoli
2-3 cans cream of mushroom
   soup

1 c. Parmesan cheese
1/3 c. mayonnaise
1 c. whipped cream (8 oz.
   Cool Whip)

156

Brown the chicken in butter first. Cook broccoli.
Spread 1 can of soup over broccoli; sprinkle generously
with Parmesan cheese. Place chicken on top and spread
another can of soup over chicken; again sprinkle generously
with Parmesan cheese. Place in 350° oven for 45 minutes,
covered. Mix 1/3 cup mayonnaise with 1 cup whipped
cream. Spread on top and sprinkle with Parmesan cheese.
Place in broiler until toasted; watch, browns quickly.
Serve over rice.

Serene Schwartz
Memphis Downtown Council

HAWAIIAN CHICKEN BY JUDIE

Mix together:

1 jar apricot preserves   1 pkg. Lipton onion soup mix
1 bottle Russian dressing

Dip chicken pieces in mixture, covering each piece
well. Put on foil covered cookie sheet and spoon leftover
mixture on each piece. Bake at 325° for 1 1/2 hours.
Freezes well, too.

Marie Barnett
Harpeth Council

HUNGARIAN CHICKEN

1 broiler-fryer, cut in parts	2 Tbsp. cooking oil
1 1/2 Tbsp. paprika	1/2 tsp. salt
1/8 tsp. pepper	1 c. sliced onion
1 c. chicken broth	1/2 c. sour cream

Place flour in shallow dish. Add chicken, one piece at
a time; dredge to coat. In fry pan, place oil and heat to
medium temperature. Add chicken and cook, turning, about
10 minutes or until brown on all sides. Sprinkle paprika,
salt and pepper on all sides of chicken until actually coated
with paprika. Remove chicken from fry pan; add onion and
cook 3 minutes, stirring occasionally. Return chicken to
fry pan; add chicken broth. Simmer 30 minutes or until
fork can be inserted in chicken with ease. Arrange chicken
on heated platter. Strain liquid into saucepan; boil over
high heat 3 minutes. Reduce heat; add sour cream. Cook,

stirring, until heated through and well mixed. Do not allow
to boil; pour sauce over chicken. Makes 4 servings.

Dot Crouch
Clarksville Council

MEXICAN CHICKEN

4 large chicken breasts
2 cans cream of chicken soup
1 can Ro-Tel tomatoes
1 c. chopped bell peppers
1 c. chopped onion

1 Tbsp. garlic powder
1 Tbsp. chili powder
1 c. grated cheese
1 large bag regular flavor
   Doritos

Boil chicken; peel off skin and take off the bone. Mix
together soup, tomatoes, bell pepper, onion, garlic powder,
chili powder and 1/2 cup of cheese. Grease large Pyrex pan;
line bottom with 1/2 cup of crushed Doritos, then place
chicken pieces on top. Pour in mixed ingredients. Bake at
350° for 30 minutes. Pour remaining Doritos and cheese
over top; put in oven until cheese melts. (When crushing
Doritos, cut a corner of bag and mash with hand.)

Sarah Craig
Chattanooga Council

OVEN-FRIED CHICKEN PARMESAN

1/2 c. (2 oz.) Kraft grated
   Parmesan cheese
1/4 c. flour
1 tsp. paprika
1/2 tsp. salt
Dash of pepper

2 1/2 - 3 lb. broiler-fryer,
   cut up, or 5-6 fryer
   breasts
1 egg, slightly beaten
1 Tbsp. milk
1/4 c. Squeeze Parkay
   margarine

Combine cheese, flour and seasonings. Dip chicken in
combined egg and milk; coat with cheese mixture. Place in
baking dish; pour margarine over chicken. Bake at 350° for
1 hour or until tender. Makes 3 to 4 servings.

Note: This recipe can easily be doubled or tripled for
a crowd.

Peggy L. Parker
Chattanooga Council

QUICK CHICK TRICK

4 chicken breasts
8 oz. sour cream
1 can cream of chicken soup

40 Ritz crackers
1 stick butter

Boil and debone chicken; tear into small pieces and line bottom of dish. Mix together soup and sour cream; heat just to boiling and pour over chicken. Crumble all crackers over mixture. Melt butter and pour over crackers. Bake about 20 minutes at 350°.

Renell Yarbrough
Memphis Downtown Council

SAUCY CHICKEN BREASTS

2 small whole chicken
   breasts, split in halves
1 chicken bouillon cube
1/4 tsp. instant minced onion
2 Tbsp. sauterne (sherry)
   or water

1/4 tsp. seasoned salt
Paprika
1/4 tsp. curry powder (good
   with more)
1 (2 oz.) can sliced
   mushrooms

Sprinkle chicken with seasoned salt and paprika. Place in small baking dish. Dissolve bouillon cube in 2/3 cup boiling water; add wine, onion, curry powder and dash of pepper. Pour over chicken. Cover; bake at 350° for 30 minutes. Uncover; bake 30 minutes or until tender. Remove chicken to platter. Blend 1 tablespoon flour and 2 tablespoons cold water to pan juices. Cook and stir until thickened; add drained mushrooms and heat. Spoon gravy over chicken.

Dot Crouch
Clarksville Council

SUNDAY SUPER CHICKEN

1 pkg. Uncle Ben's wild
   rice mix
3 c. cooked, cubed chicken
   or turkey

1 can cream of chicken soup
1 can cream of mushroom soup
1 pkg. onion soup mix
1 c. sour cream

Prepare rice mix according to package directions. Add

all other ingredients; mix well. Place in casserole and bake at 350° for 25-30 minutes. Serves 10.

Darlene S. Roach
Knoxville Council

SWEET AND SOUR CHICKEN

1/2 c. white vinegar
3 Tbsp. brown sugar
1 Tbsp. soy sauce

1 (20 oz.) can crushed pineapple with juice
1/2 tsp. pepper
4 chicken breast halves

Place chicken in baking dish. Heat the other ingredients to boiling; pour over chicken. Bake at 250° for 2 1/2 to 3 hours.

Pat Prosser
Columbia Council

SWEET-SOUR CHICKEN

2 1/2 c. cut up, cooked
   chicken
1 egg, slightly beaten
1/4 c. cornstarch
2 Tbsp. shortening
1 (13 1/2 oz.) can pineapple
   chunks, drained (reserve
   juice)
1/2 c. vinegar

1/2 c. sugar
1 medium green pepper, cut
   into 1 inch squares
1/4 c. water
2 Tbsp. cornstarch
1 tsp. soy sauce
1 (16 oz.) can small carrots,
   drained
3 c. hot, cooked rice

Toss chicken and egg until all pieces are coated. Sprinkle 1/4 cup cornstarch over chicken; toss until all pieces are coated. Melt shortening in medium skillet; add chicken pieces. Cook over medium heat until brown. Remove chicken from skillet; set aside. Add enough water to reserved pineapple syrup to measure 1 cup. Stir liquid, vinegar and sugar into skillet; heat to boiling, stirring constantly. Stir in green pepper; heat to boiling. Reduce heat; cover and simmer 2 minutes. Blend water and 2 tablespoons cornstarch; stir into skillet. Cook, stirring constantly, until mixture thickens and boils. Boil and stir 1 minute. Stir in pineapple chunks, soy sauce, carrots and chicken; heat through. Serve over rice. Makes 4 servings.

Vickie L. Sutphin
East Memphis Council

SWEET-SOUR CHICKEN KABOBS

2 whole chicken breasts, skinned, boned, cut into 1 1/4 inch pieces
2 green peppers, cut into eighths

1 (16 3/4 oz.) can pineapple chunks, drained (reserve juice)
1 small can water chestnuts (whole), drained
10 mushroom caps

Marinade:

1/2 c. soy sauce
1/2 c. reserved pineapple juice
1/4 c. cooking oil
1 tsp. dry mustard

1 Tbsp. brown sugar
2 tsp. ground ginger
1 tsp. garlic salt
1/4 tsp. ground pepper

Combine marinade ingredients in a small saucepan; simmer 5 minutes. Cool. Marinate chicken pieces for 1 hour, stirring occasionally. Drain, reserving marinade. Thread chicken pieces, pineapple chunks, green pepper pieces, water chestnuts, cherry tomatoes and mushroom caps on metal skewers. Grill for 20 minutes, basting with reserved marinade. Serves 4.

Emily Townes
Harpeth Council

CREAM OF CHICKEN

2 pkg. frozen broccoli spears
2 c. condensed cream of chicken soup
1/2 c. chopped sharp Cheddar cheese

2 Tbsp. melted butter
2 or 3 c. boiled chicken
1 c. mayonnaise
1 Tbsp. lemon juice
1/2 c. soft bread crumbs

Preheat oven to 350°. Cook broccoli until tender and drain. Arrange stalks in long, greased casserole dish. Place chicken on top. Combine soup, mayonnaise, lemon juice and pour over chicken; sprinkle with cheese. Combine bread crumbs and butter; sprinkle on top and bake 30 minutes. Serves 4-6 people.

Sarah R. Smith
Green Hills Council

1489-81

CREAMED CHICKEN ON CORN BREAD

Boil a 2 pound chicken or 2 pounds chicken breasts with 3/4 stick butter, salt and pepper.

1 small onion
1 stick butter
4 Tbsp. flour
2 c. chicken broth
1 can green peas, drained

1 can cream of chicken or
mushroom soup
3/4 c. (small can) evaporated
milk
1 can diced pimentos, drained

Saute onion in butter until tender; add flour and stir well. Add soup, milk and broth; cook until thick. Add diced chicken, green peas and pimentos. Simmer 30 to 45 minutes; stir often. Serve on corn bread.

Beverly Vaughn
Harpeth Council

CHICKEN CORN BREAD

4 c. boned chicken
1 can cream of celery soup

1 can cream of chicken soup
2 boxes "Jiffy" corn bread
mix

Combine chicken with soup and about 1 1/2 soup cans of milk. Mix well; add to greased 9x13 inch casserole. Prepare corn bread according to directions. Spread corn bread mixture on top of mixture. Bake at 425° until brown. (If you want to, divide soup mixture into 2 smaller Corning Ware dishes; freeze one until needed. Mix up only one box of corn bread mix.)

Catherine Taylor
Green Hills Council

CHICKEN ON EGG BREAD

1 hen, cooked and sliced
(save broth for sauce)
1 stick oleo
1 small onion, chopped
3/4 c. evaporated milk

1/4 c. chopped celery
4 Tbsp. flour
2 c. chicken broth
1 can cream of chicken soup

Saute onion and celery in butter until tender. Add flour; stir well. Add soup, cream and broth. Cook until thickened. Make your favorite egg bread; cut in serving portions, split. Put a layer of chicken between slices. Add a little sauce. Do the same on top slice when put together.

Mrs. Betty Officer
Green Hills Council

EASY   CHICKEN   AND   DRESSING

1 chicken or at least 2 c.
1 can cream of celery soup
1 can cream of chicken soup

1 can water
1 pkg. Pepperidge Farm
   corn bread stuffing
1/2 c. melted butter

Debone chicken; cut up into bite size pieces. Mix with soups and water. Put in a 9x11 inch or similar size pan (you do not want to use a small deep type bowl). Sprinkle bread stuffing over this mixture; pour butter over it. Bake about 30 minutes at 350°. Stir a little before finished baking. If you don't want it very dry, reduce baking time.

Glenda S. Lunn
Columbia Council

CRUNCHY   PARMESAN   CHICKEN

1 (3 oz.) can French fried
   onions, crushed
3 oz. grated Parmesan
   cheese
1/4 c. dry bread crumbs
1 tsp. paprika
1/2 tsp. salt

Dash of pepper
1 broiler-fryer (about 3 lb.)
   chicken, cut up
1 egg, beaten
1 Tbsp. milk
1/4 c. butter/margarine,
   melted

Combine onion, cheese, bread crumbs and seasonings. Dip chicken in combined egg and milk, then coat with cheese mixture. Place in baking dish; pour margarine over all. Bake at 350° for 55-60 minutes or until golden brown.

Carol Nunnery
Memphis Council

163

EASY CHICKEN POT PIE

3 chicken breasts
2 pkg. frozen mixed
  vegetables
Several potatoes
3 pkg. chicken gravy mix
Bisquick

Boil chicken breasts until done, about 20 minutes; set aside to cool. Peel and dice potatoes into bite sized pieces. Combine potatoes and mixed vegetables; bring to a boil and simmer until tender. Cut chicken into bite sized chunks. Put into large casserole dish. Drain potatoes and vegetables; add to chicken in dish. Season to taste. Make up chicken gravy mix; pour over other ingredients. Preheat oven to 450°. Mix up enough Bisquick (just as if making biscuits) to cover top of your casserole dish. Bake until crust is browned and done.

Dinah Randolph
Harpeth Council

GOLDEN CHICKEN OR TURKEY BAKE

3 c. cooked chicken or
  turkey
1 1/2 c. thin celery slices
1 c. cubed Cheddar or
  American cheese
3/4 c. mayonnaise
1/4 c. chopped onion
1 Tbsp. lemon juice
1/2 c. corn flake crumbs

Combine all ingredients, except corn flake crumbs. Spoon into a 10x6 inch baking dish; cover with corn flake crumbs. Bake at 325° for 35 minutes. Serves 6.

John H. Wilds
Knoxville Council

GRILLED POLYNESIAN GAME HENS

Have ready 2 Cornish game hens, split in halves.

Marinade:

1/2 c. soy sauce
1 (6 oz.) can pineapple juice
1 small can pineapple slices
  (use juice and save
  slices for garnish)
1 tsp. dry mustard
2 Tbsp. brown sugar
2 tsp. ground ginger
1/2 tsp. garlic powder
1/2 tsp. garlic salt
1/4 tsp. ground pepper
1/4 c. cooking oil

Combine marinade ingredients in a small saucepan; simmer 10 minutes. Cool. Marinate Cornish hen halves for 2-3 hours, turning occasionally. Cook on grill, basting with reserved marinade until done, about 20 minutes each side. Garnish with pineapple slices. Serves 4. Can be served over rice (wild or plain) or with baked potato, salad and Hawaiian bread.

Emily Townes
Harpeth Council

"CHINESE HASH"

1 lb. ground beef, browned in 2 Tbsp. salad oil
2 medium onions, chopped
1 c. celery, chopped
1/2 c. uncooked rice (not instant)
1 can cream of mushroom soup
1 can cream of chicken soup
1 1/2 c. warm water
1/4 c. soy sauce
1 large can Chinese noodles

Mix all ingredients, except noodles. Pour into 9x13 inch baking dish. Bake at 375°, covered, for 30 minutes; uncover and stir. Bake 30 minutes, uncovered. Spread can of noodles over top and bake 15 minutes longer.

Virginia Thomas
Nashville Council

CHINESE PEPPER STEAK

Boneless chuck roast (approx. 1 lb.), cut into 1 inch strips
1 tsp. salt
1/4 c. oil
2 Tbsp. soy sauce
1 clove garlic, minced, or garlic powder
1 1/2 c. water, divided
1 c. green pepper strips
1 large onion, sliced
1/2 c. sliced celery
2 tomatoes, cut into wedges
1 Tbsp. cornstarch
Hot cooked rice
Sliced mushrooms (optional)

Sprinkle meat with salt; brown meat quickly in hot oil. Add soy sauce, garlic and 1/2 cup water; bring to a boil. Cover and simmer about 45 minutes or until tender. Add green pepper, onion, celery and mushrooms. Cover and simmer until vegetables are crisp tender. Add tomato wedges; toss lightly. Dissolve cornstarch in 1 cup water; add to meat mixture. Cook over medium heat, stirring constantly, until mixture boils and thickens. Serve over hot rice. Serves 4 to 6.

Addie Downs
Green Hills Council

DEEP FRIED CHITTERLINGS

1 lb. chitterlings
1 c. meal
2 Tbsp. self-rising flour
2 eggs, beaten

1 oz. Lea & Perrins sauce
1 oz. Tabasco sauce
Pepper and salt to taste

Mix ingredients thoroughly; add 1 cup white wine. Soak chitterlings for 1 hour. Drop in Fry Daddy until they come to top. Very good with pinto or white beans.

Reba G. Powers
Columbia Council

CORN DOGS

1 c. self-rising meal
1 c. self-rising flour
1 tsp. salt
3 Tbsp. prepared mustard

2 eggs
1 1/2 c. milk
2 lb. wieners

Mix the batter with all ingredients, then put wooden skewer in each wiener. Heat oil to 370°.

Joyce Mattice
Harpeth Council

CROCK POT STEAK

Round steak
3 Tbsp. flour
1 can tomato wedges

1 can cream of mushroom soup
1 onion
1 bell pepper
Salt and pepper to taste

Cut steak into strips; put in crock pot. Cover strips with flour; make sure it is well covered. Pour cream of mushroom soup over this. Add tomatoes, diced onion and peppers. Cook on high for 1 hour, then turn down to low for 6 to 7 hours.

Mary Chaudoin
Harpeth Council

FANCY PANTS

2 lb. hamburger, seasoned
   to taste
1 small can tomato sauce

4 slices American cheese (not
   cheese food)
1 small onion, diced

Shape hamburger into 8 patties. Fold slices of cheese into 4 small squares; put each square between 2 hamburger patties. Press edges firmly together so cheese won't melt through. Makes 4 servings. Brown hamburgers on both sides in skillet; add onion while browning patties. Add tomato sauce; reduce to simmer. Cover with lid and cook about 1/2 hour or until done.

Barbara Weatherford
Nashboro Council

FILET OF SOLE EAST INDIAN

6 filets of sole or flounder
1/4 lb. fresh mushrooms,
   quartered
1 scallion, chopped
1/4 c. white wine

2 Tbsp. flour
2 Tbsp. butter
1/2 c. milk
1 tsp. curry powder
Salt and pepper to taste

Put filets and onion in buttered skillet. Season with salt, pepper and curry powder. Add wine and cook slowly on top of stove until fish is white, about 10 minutes. Remove filets to casserole. Make sauce of butter, flour and milk, using same pan in which fish was cooked. Pour over fish in casserole. Garnish with mushrooms; dot with butter. Bake, uncovered, at 350° for 20 minutes.

Peggy Burr
Harpeth Council

FLUFFY OVEN EGGS AND BACON

1/2 lb. bacon (about 12
   slices)
1/2 lb. chopped onion
1/2 c. Bisquick baking mix
3 eggs

1 1/4 c. milk
1/4 tsp. salt
1/8 tsp. pepper
1/2 c. shredded Cheddar or
   Swiss cheese

Heat oven to 375°. Grease 1 1/2 quart round casserole. Cut bacon slices into thirds. Cook and stir bacon in 10 inch skillet over medium heat until almost crisp. Add

1489-81

onion. Cook, stirring frequently, until bacon is crisp; drain. Spread bacon and onion in bottom of casserole. Beat baking mix, eggs, milk, salt and pepper with hand beater until almost smooth. Slowly pour egg mixture over bacon; sprinkle with cheese. Bake, uncovered, until knife inserted in center comes out clean, about 35 minutes. Makes 4 to 6 servings.

Fluffy Oven Eggs and Ham: Substitute one cup of 1/4 inch cubes fully cooked, smoked ham for the bacon. Spread ham and onion in bottom of casserole. Continue as directed.

High Altitude Directions (3500 to 6500 feet): Heat oven to 400°. Bake 35 to 40 minutes.

Frances Nevette
Harpeth Council

BAKED HICKORY SMOKED HAM IN A BROWN PAPER BAG

Take wrappings off of ham; place in a plain brown grocery bag, fat side up. Twist ends of bag together as tightly as possible; place in a deep broiler type pan. Bake in a slow oven at 300°, uncovered, for 30 minutes per pound, allowing an extra 30 minutes for the ham to heat through and through. Example: 8 pound ham would be in oven for 4 1/2 hours. At the end of cooking, the brown bag will be greasy and there will be liquid in the bottom of the pan. Carefully tear bag open and discard (don't get steamed fingers). Cut away the hard skin; discard this too and score the fat on both sides of the ham. Mix sauce and spoon over top side of the ham. Return it to oven at 375°-400° for 10-15 minutes of browning. Take out; turn the ham over and repeat the sauce and browning on that side. This will be golden brown and luscious tasting!

Sauce for Ham:

1 c. brown sugar	2 Tbsp. orange juice
1/2 c. honey	1 tsp. lemon juice

This will be thick; stir and mix well. Spoon over ham.

Dorothy Crouch
Clarksville Council

HAM LOAF

2 lb. smoked ham
1 lb. pork loin (lean)
1 c. milk

2 eggs
1 c. cracker crumbs

Have butcher grind ham and pork 2 times. Combine all ingredients; shape into 2 loaves. Place in skillet or casserole, lined with foil. Rub loaves with brown sugar. Bake in 350° oven for 1 hour or until done.

Deanna Baker
Harpeth Council

GLAZED HAM STEAK

1 (1 1/2 lb.) ham steak,
    1 inch thick
1 small orange, peeled
1/4 c. molasses
2 Tbsp. water

1/4 c. orange juice
2 Tbsp. sugar
1/8 tsp. dry mustard
1/8 tsp. ground cloves

Preheat oven to 375° F. Place ham steak in a shallow, 11x7 inch, baking dish. Cut orange into very thin slices. Place on top of ham. In a small bowl, combine molasses, water, orange juice, sugar, dry mustard and cloves. Pour over ham. Bake, uncovered, 30 minutes; baste occasionally. Cut into wedges. Serve with a slice or two of orange on each wedge. Makes 6 servings. Excellent for brunch.

Doris Binkley
Nashboro Council

GLORIFIED HAMBURGERS

1 1/2 lb. ground lean chuck
1 c. sour cream
1 Tbsp. instant onion

1 1/2 tsp. salt
Pepper, if preferred
1 1/4 c. crushed corn flakes

Mix all ingredients together and grill over a charcoal fire to preferred doneness.

Jewell Mercer
Nashville Council

GLORIFIED HAMBURGERS

1 lb. hamburger
1 c. tomato ketchup
3 small onions, chopped
3/4 bell pepper, chopped
Garlic powder
1 c. grated cheese
Worcestershire sauce

Mix the above ingredients and make into patties.

Joyce Mattice
Harpeth Council

HAMBURGER CORN-PONE PIE

1 lb. ground beef
1/3 c. chopped onion
1 Tbsp. shortening
2 tsp. chili powder
3/4 tsp. salt
1 tsp. Worcestershire sauce
1 c. canned tomatoes
1 c. drained kidney beans
1 c. corn bread batter (1/2
standard recipe)

Brown meat and onion in melted shortening. Add seasonings and tomatoes. Cover and simmer 15 minutes. Add kidney beans. Pour into a greased casserole dish. Top with corn bread batter and bake in 425° oven for 20 minutes.

Patty McElroy
Harpeth Council

M.E. Womble, Jr.
Memphis East Council
Emma Jo Perry
Green Hills Council

HAMBURGER FLIP

2 lb. hamburger (chuck)
1 medium onion, chopped
1 small green pepper,
chopped
4 or 5 fresh mushrooms, sliced
Cheddar cheese, grated
Mustard

Press hamburger flat on waxed paper until 1/4 inch thick. On 1/2 of the meat, spread mustard; place all other ingredients on top of mustard. Fold the plain half of the meat over the half with all ingredients; pinch edges together. Put in freezer on a plate to stiffen while the grill is heating. Cook over low heat on grill until done, about 10 minutes on each side.

Mary Lynn Johnson
Harpeth Council

HAMBURGER-NOODLE BAKE

2 lb. ground beef
1 1/2 c. chopped onion
1/2 c. green pepper
8 oz. medium noodles
2 (10 3/4 oz.) cans con-
  densed tomato soup
2 c. shredded American
  cheese

6 oz. chili sauce
1/8 c. chopped pimiento
1 tsp. salt
1 tsp. chili powder
1/4 tsp. pepper
2 1/4 c. soft bread crumbs
1/8 c. butter, melted

In a large skillet, cook beef, onion and green pepper
till meat is brown; drain off fat. Cook noodles according to
package directions; drain well. Return noodles to kettle.
Stir in meat mixture, tomato soup, cheese, chili sauce,
pimiento, salt, chili powder, pepper and 1 cup water; mix
well. Pour in a 13x9x2 inch baking dish. Toss bread
crumbs with melted butter; sprinkle atop casserole. Bake,
uncovered, at 350° till heated through, about 45 minutes.
Garnish with green pepper rings. Makes 6 servings.

Beverly Simpkins
Harpeth Council

HAMBURGER PIE

1 lb. ground beef
1 c. cheese
2 Tbsp. parsley
1/2 c. milk

1/4 c. onion
1/4 c. mayonnaise
1 1/2 c. Bisquick

Sauce:

1 can cream of mushroom
  soup

1 (8 oz.) can mixed
  vegetables
1/3 c. milk

Cook beef and onion until browned; stir in cheese,
mayonnaise and parsley. In separate bowl, combine Bisquick and milk. Roll out on floured board to make two 8
inch circles. Line one in a well greased pie plate. Spread
meat mixture over pie shell. Add the other pie shell over
the meat and bake for 20-25 minutes at 375°. Heat sauce
and serve over each slice of hamburger pie.

Barbara Drukenbrod
Harpeth Council

HAMBURGER QUICHE

2 unbaked pie crusts
1 lb. hamburger beef
4 eggs
2 Tbsp. cornstarch

1 c. mayonnaise
1 c. sweet milk
1 c. chopped onion
3 c. grated cheese (Cheddar)

Brown beef and onion; mix all other ingredients. Combine with meat mixture. Save enough cheese to put on top. Bake at 350° for 35 to 45 minutes; let cool.

Linda Earp
Clarksville Council

HOPPING JOHN
(An old dish; hearty and easy to make.)

1 lb. ground beef
1 (1 lb.) can red kidney
  beans

2 Tbsp. bacon drippings
1 (1 lb.) can tomatoes
Salt and pepper to taste

Brown ground beef in bacon drippings. Add beans and tomatoes; season to taste. Allow to simmer until desired thickness has been reached. Serves 6.

Cornelia L. Mangrum
Harpeth Council

HOT DOG KABOBS

4 hot dogs
1 (10 1/2 oz.) can pineapple
  chunks

4 tsp. vegetable oil
8 hot dog rolls, toasted
8 tsp. barbecue sauce

Cut each hot dog into 5 chunks; alternate each on a skewer with pineapple chunks. Brush with vegetable oil. Broil over heat, turning until browned. Meanwhile, spread each roll with barbecue sauce. Slide hot dogs off skewers and onto the rolls. Serves 4.

Judy Q. Arnold
Harpeth Council

ITALIAN SAUSAGE

6-12 Italian sausages
   (Maria Rosa brand)
2 bell peppers, sliced
2 onions, sliced
Italian oil (olive oil)

Salt and pepper
Onion salt
Garlic salt
Red pepper, crushed, to
   taste

Boil sausage until tender; brown in a skillet. In another skillet, cook onions and bell peppers in olive oil until tender. Combine sausage with onions and peppers; add all other ingredients. Simmer for 10 minutes. Serve on Italian or French bread or buns.

Othelia Taylor
Harpeth Council

LASAGNE

1 lb. hamburger or Italian
   sausage
1 clove garlic, minced
1 1/2 Tbsp. salt
10 oz. lasagne noodles
1/2 c. Parmesan or Romano
   cheese
2 beaten eggs
1/2 tsp. pepper

2 c. (1 can) tomatoes
2 (6 oz.) cans tomato paste
3 c. Ricotta or cottage
   cheese
2 Tbsp. parsley flakes
2 tsp. salt
1 lb. Mozzarella cheese,
   grated

Preheat oven to 375°. Brown meat slowly, spooning off excess fat. Add garlic, tomatoes, tomato paste and salt. Simmer, uncovered, for 30 minutes, stirring occasionally. Cook noodles according to package directions; drain and rinse. Combine remaining ingredients, except Mozzarella cheese. Place half the noodles in 13x9x2 inch baking dish. Spread with the cottage cheese mixture; add half the meat sauce and half the Mozzarella cheese. Repeat layers. Bake for about 30 minutes.

Bessie Crosby
Harpeth Council

LA VERNE'S PASTA WITH MEAT

Flour and brown minute steaks until done. Pour off excess grease and put the following over meat:

1 small can tomatoes
1 small can tomato sauce
Chopped onion

Chopped green pepper
Salt and pepper to taste

Sprinkle 1/4 cup Parmesan cheese over top. Cover and cook for 30 minutes. Cook macaroni, spaghetti or rice and pour meat and sauce over pasta.

Debbie Burton
Harpeth Council

LITTLE HOT DOGS IN CURRANT SAUCE

10 or 11 oz. jar currant or
    quince jelly

3 heaping tsp. prepared
    mustard
20 hot dogs

Cut hot dogs in quarters. Mix jello and mustard; heat. Add hot dogs and simmer for 1/2 hour. Serve with toothpicks as hors d'oeuvres.

Judy Desendorf
Harpeth Council

SKILLET MACARONI 'N' BEEF
(Low Calorie)

12 oz. ground beef
3/4 c. beef bouillon
1/2 c. sliced celery
2 oz. chopped onion

2 Tbsp. tomato paste
1 1/2 c. cooked elbow
    macaroni, warm (cook in
    unsalted water)

Place beef on a rack in a pan; broil 6 inches from source of heat, about 5 minutes or until rare. Crumble beef into a large nonstick skillet. Add remaining ingredients, except macaroni, and simmer about 20 minutes or until vegetables are tender and liquid is reduced by 1/2. Add macaroni; toss gently. Cook about 1 minute until macaroni is heated. Makes 2 servings; 383 calories per serving.

Johnnie Foster
Harpeth Council

MARINATED CHUCK ROAST

3-5 lb. chuck roast
1/2 c. strong coffee
1/2 c. soy sauce
1 Tbsp. Worcestershire
  sauce

Meat tenderizer
1 Tbsp. vinegar
1 Tbsp. sesame seeds
Dab of butter
1 large onion, chopped

Sprinkle meat with tenderizer. Brown sesame seeds in the butter. Add other ingredients; pour over the roast. Let stand, turning every few hours, at room temperature all day. Charcoal broil for about 45 minutes.

Marie Barnett
Harpeth Council

MARINATED FLANK STEAK

2 c. soy sauce
1 c. water
2 Tbsp. Worcestershire
  sauce
1 tsp. salt

1 tsp. sugar
2 cloves garlic, crushed
2 Tbsp. wine
1/8 tsp. pepper
1 1/4 lb. flank steak

Combine first 8 ingredients, mixing well; pour over steak. Cover and marinate in refrigerator overnight; drain meat. Broil, outdoors is best, for very few minutes on either side. Store the liquid and use to marinate steak several times. This is good to use on chuck steak, too.

Dorothy Bryant
Clarksville Council

MEAT BALLS EXTRAORDINARE

4 lb. ground beef
1 large onion, grated
1 (12 oz.) bottle chili sauce
Juice of 1 lemon

1 egg, slightly beaten
Salt to taste
1 (12 oz.) jar grape jelly

Blend together meat, egg, onion and salt; form into 100 small meat balls. Combine chili sauce, jelly and lemon juice; pour over meat balls and simmer in electric skillet for 1 hour. Serve in heated chafing dish.

Bessie Crosby
Harpeth Council

MEAT BALLS IN BUTTERMILK SAUCE

1 1/2 lb. ground beef
1 small onion, finely chopped
3 Tbsp. chopped green
    pepper
1/3 c. sliced celery
1 c. cooked rice
1 tsp. salt

1/2 tsp. pepper
1 egg
1 (10 1/2 oz.) can mushroom
    soup
1 soup can of buttermilk
1 (2 oz.) can mushroom stems
    and pieces

Put the ground beef, onion, green pepper, celery, rice, salt, pepper and egg into a large bowl. Work together with hands until well mixed. Divide into 12 portions; roll each into a ball. Place in a greased 2 quart casserole. Place the soup, buttermilk and liquid from the mushrooms in a bowl; beat until smooth. Pour over the meat balls, along with the mushrooms. Bake in a moderate 350° oven for 1 hour. The extra gravy is good to spoon over baked potatoes. Yield: 6 servings.

Debby Maddox
Harpeth Council

DOT'S MEAT LOAF

1 1/2 lb. ground beef
1 c. tomato juice
1/4 c. oats, uncooked
1 egg, beaten

1/4 c. chopped onion
1 1/2 tsp. salt
1/4 tsp. pepper

Combine all ingredients; mix well. Press firmly into ungreased 8 1/2 x 4 1/2 x 2 1/2 inch loaf pan. Bake in preheated moderate oven, 350° F., for about 1 hour. Let stand 5 minutes before slicing. Makes 8 servings.

Jane York
Harpeth Council

MEAT LOAF SUPREME

1 lb. ground beef
2 carrots, shredded
1/2 c. sour cream
1 onion, chopped

1 tsp. salt
Dash of pepper
1/4 c. oats or bread crumbs

Mix well and press into baking dish. Bake at 350° for about 45 minutes. Slice when done and pour sauce over meat loaf.

Sauce:

1 can cream of mushroom
  soup

1 bouillon cube and drippings
  from meat loaf

Combine and heat to boiling.

Jessie S. Taylor
Harpeth Council

15-MINUTE MEAT LOAVES

Preheat oven to 450°. Mix together:

2 beaten eggs
1 lb. ground beef
1 c. rolled bread crumbs

2 Tbsp. A.1. sauce or your
  favorite meat sauce
1 tsp. salt
3/4 c. milk

Pack mixture level into greased muffin pans. Bake 15 minutes. Serves 6.

Frances R. Lauderdale
Memphis Downtown Council

MOZZARELLA-LAYERED MEAT LOAF

1 lb. ground beef
1/2 lb. highly seasoned
  bulk sausage
1 c. bread crumbs
1/2 c. chopped onion
1/2 c. Parmesan cheese
1/2 c. milk

1 egg, beaten
2 Tbsp. parsley
2 tsp. salt
1/2 tsp. Accent
1/4 tsp. pepper
1 (8 oz.) pkg. sliced
  Mozzarella cheese

Combine all ingredients, except Mozzarella cheese. Spoon 1/2 of mixture into lightly greased 9x5x3 inch loaf pan. Place Mozzarella cheese on top, leaving 1 inch border on all sides. Spoon remaining mixture over cheese, pressing lightly on sides to seal. Bake at 350° for 1 hour.

Debbie Bullock
Harpeth Council

1489-81

SOUPED UP MEAT LOAF

1 env. Lipton beef flavor
  mushroom soup mix
2 lb. ground beef

1 1/2 c. soft bread crumbs
2 eggs
3/4 c. water
1/3 c. catsup

Preheat oven to 350°. In large bowl, combine all ingredients. In large shallow baking pan, shape into loaf. Bake 1 hour or until done. If desired, garnish with parsley. Makes 6 to 8 servings.

Ruby Cloud
Harpeth Council

ONION SOUP MEAT LOAF

1 env. onion soup dry mix
2 eggs
1 lb. ground beef

8 oz. can tomato sauce
1 1/2 c. soft bread crumbs
3/4 c. warm water

Break eggs in a bowl; beat slightly. Stir in tomato sauce, warm water and soup mix. Add bread crumbs and ground beef; mix well. Shape into loaf or pack in pan. May be shaped into 2 loaves. Bake at 350° for 1 hour. Serves 6 to 8.

Beverly Pettigrew
Harpeth Council

MIDGET MEAT BALLS

Meat Balls:

1 1/2 lb. ground beef
1/2 c. Quaker or Mother's
  oats (quick or old
  fashioned), uncooked

1 1/2 tsp. salt
1 1/2 tsp. dry mustard
1/4 tsp. pepper
2 Tbsp. milk

Sauce:

2 c. boiling water
2 beef bouillon cubes
2 Tbsp. all-purpose flour

1/4 c. cold water
1 tsp. paprika
1/4 c. dairy sour cream

For meat balls: Combine all ingredients thoroughly. Shape into 36 meat balls. Brown in small amount of

178

shortening in large skillet.

For sauce: Combine boiling water and bouillon cubes. Pour over browned meat balls. Cover; simmer for 15 minutes. Combine flour with cold water; add to sauce, stirring constantly. Simmer about 5 minutes or until thickened. Remove from heat; stir in paprika and sour cream. Pour into chafing dish. (Be sure heat is very low to prevent separation.) Makes 6 servings.

Betty Coleman
Green Hills Council

MINSK BEEF
(Ulcer Diet)

1 1/2 lb. sirloin steak, cut into strips 2 inches long and 1/2 inch thick	1/2 c. chicken broth
	1 c. commercial sour cream
2 Tbsp. water	Salt

In a teflon pan or a heavy iron skillet, put 2 tablespoons water and the meat. Cook over low heat for 5 to 10 minutes until the meat has lost its pinkness and is just slightly brown; do not overcook. Add chicken broth to meat. Cover; cook for about 10 minutes over low heat. Uncover; let liquid cook down for another 10 minutes. Add sour cream; mix well. Makes 4 servings.

MINUTE STEAKS

4-6 cubed steaks	Flour
Salt and pepper	Small amount of oil
Garlic salt	2 cans creole sauce
Onion salt	

Season meat with small amount of salt, pepper, garlic and onion salt. Roll in flour; brown in oil. Remove meat from skillet; drain off oil. Return meat and pour creole sauce over. Place lid on and cook on low for 45 minutes to 1 hour.

Mrs. Lewis (Pam) Lawley
Green Hills Council

1489-81

OVEN-FRIED FISH

1 lb. sole or flounder fillets   1/2 tsp. salt
1/4 c. mayonnaise   1/4 tsp. pepper
Bread crumbs   Lemon wedges
Paprika

Thinly coat fish fillets with mayonnaise; dredge in bread crumbs. Arrange in a greased 13x9x2 inch baking pan. Sprinkle fillets with paprika, salt and pepper. Bake at 450° for 25 minutes. Garnish with lemon wedges.

> Debbie Bullock
> Harpeth Council

OYSTER-ROCKEFELLER

Drain oysters dry; place in individual shell dishes (or bottom of casserole dish). Combine:

1 Tbsp. chopped onion   1 Tbsp. melted butter or
2 Tbsp. parsley   margarine

Spread over oysters. Season with salt, pepper and paprika. Top with:

1/2 c. chopped, cooked,   1/3 c. fine bread crumbs
   drained spinach

Dot with butter or margarine. Brown in very hot, 450°, oven for 10 minutes.

> Margaret Sells
> Morristown Council

PEPPER STEAK

1 1/2 lb. round steak, cut   1 3/4 c. water
   in small strips   1/2 c. chopped onion
1/4 c. flour   Dash of garlic salt
1/2 tsp. salt   2 Tbsp. brown gravy mix
1/4 tsp. pepper   1 1/2 Tbsp. Worcestershire
1/4 c. oil   sauce
8 oz. can tomatoes   1 green bell pepper

Mix flour, salt and pepper; coat meat in flour mixture. Brown steak in oil. Drain tomatoes; save juice. Add juice to meat; add water, onion, garlic salt and gravy mix. Combine; cover and simmer until tender, 1 to 1 1/2 hours. Uncover; stir in Worcestershire sauce. Add green pepper, cut in small strips. Add tomatoes and cook about 10 to 15 minutes more. Serve over rice.

Wanda Ladd
Green Hills Council

PIZZA

Crust:

1 pkg. dry yeast	4 c. plain flour
1 1/2 c. warm water	1 tsp. salt
2 Tbsp. oil	

Sauce:

1 (6 oz.) can tomato paste	1 tsp. oregano
1 (6 oz.) can hot water	1/8 tsp. pepper
1 tsp. salt	

Additional Ingredients:

1 lb. Mozzarella cheese, grated	Own taste preference such as onion, pepper, olives, pepperoni
1 lb. sausage	

Crust: Dissolve yeast in warm water; stir in oil. Sift flour and salt; add to yeast mixture. Knead about 10 minutes. Shape into ball and place in bowl, covered with damp cloth (be sure and oil bowl and also brush ball with oil). Let rise 1 hour. Spread on well greased pan.

Mix sauce ingredients and spread on dough. Brown sausage and spread on top. Cover with other ingredients if you choose to do so. Cover with grated cheese. Bake at 425° for about 15 minutes. Even though this crust is thick, it will be done.

Margaret Slack
Green Hills Council

MINI PIZZAS

1 lb. hamburger
1 lb. sausage
1 lb. box Velveeta cheese
Shredded Mozzarella cheese

1/2 tsp. oregano
1/2 tsp. Worcestershire sauce
1/2 tsp. garlic powder
Cocktail rye bread

Brown hamburger and sausage in separate pans. Drain grease from both. Combine browned hamburger and sausage; add seasonings and chopped Velveeta cheese. When cheese is melted, put a teaspoon of mixture on cocktail rye bread. Sprinkle with shredded Mozzarella cheese. Bake at 350° for 6 minutes. Makes about 45 mini-pizzas. Recipe may be doubled and put in Tupperware with waxed paper between layers and freeze, then use as needed, baking them for 10 minutes.

Judy Christopher
Harpeth Council

MINI PIZZAS

English muffins
Mozzarella cheese
Grated Cheddar cheese

Pizza sauce (canned)
Crumbled, cooked sausage

Split muffins onto baking sheet. Butter and toast under broiler. Place slice of Mozzarella cheese on each muffin; sprinkle with meat. Top each with about 2 tablespoons pizza sauce and a little grated Cheddar cheese. Bake about 10-15 minutes in 350° oven. Allow 2 mini-pizzas per person. These are terrific and easy.

Barbara Drukenbrod
Harpeth Council

MINI PIZZAS

1 can refrigerator biscuits
1 (8 oz.) can tomato sauce
1/4 c. finely chopped onion
1/2 tsp. salt
1 tsp. garlic salt

2 Tbsp. grated Parmesan
cheese
3/4 tsp. crushed oregano
leaves
1 c. shredded Mozzarella
cheese

Flatten biscuits to small circles; place on cookie sheet. Mix tomato sauce, onion, garlic salt, salt, Parmesan cheese and oregano for sauce. Spoon about 1 tablespoon sauce on each biscuit; top with Mozzarella cheese. Bake in preheated 400° oven for 10 minutes. Meat topping may also be used, if desired.

Pat Ferguson
Harpeth Council

EASY DEEP-DISH PIZZA

3 c. Bisquick baking mix
3/4 c. water
1 lb. ground beef
1/2 c. chopped onion
1/2 tsp. salt
2 cloves garlic, crushed
1 (15 oz.) can tomato sauce

1 tsp. Italian seasoning
1 (4 1/2 oz.) jar sliced
  mushrooms, drained
1/2 c. chopped green pepper
2 c. (about 8 oz.) shredded
  Mozzarella cheese

Heat oven to 425°. Lightly grease jelly roll pan, 15 1/2 x 10 1/2 x 1 inches, or cookie sheet. Mix baking mix and water until soft dough forms. Gently smooth dough into ball on floured surface; knead 20 times. Pat dough on bottom and up sides of pan with floured hands; or, roll into rectangle, 13x10 inches, and place on cookie sheet. Pinch edges of rectangle, forming 3/4 inch rim. Cook and stir ground beef, onion, salt and garlic until beef is brown; drain. Mix tomato sauce and Italian seasoning; spread evenly over dough. Spoon beef mixture over sauce; top with mushrooms, green pepper and cheese. Bake until crust is golden brown, about 20 minutes. Makes 8 servings. Additional ingredients can be added.

Grace Carnes
East Memphis Council

ENGLISH MUFFIN PIZZAS

1/4 lb. ground beef
1/4 lb. hot Italian sausage
1 can condensed tomato
  soup
2 Tbsp. water
1 tsp. crushed oregano

1 clove garlic, minced
Dash of pepper
3 English muffins, lightly
  toasted
10 slices Mozzarella cheese
Green pepper strips
Stuffed green olives

Saute ground beef and sausage until browned; drain excess fat. Add soup, water, oregano, garlic and ground

pepper. Cover and simmer for 5 minutes over low heat.
Place a slice of cheese on each toasted muffin half. Top with
meat mixture, then place an "X" of cheese strips, made from
the remaining slices of Mozzarella cheese. Decorate with
pepper strips and olive slices. Bake at 400° for 5 to 10 minutes or until the cheese melts and the pizzas are heated
through.

Cornelia L. Mangrum
Harpeth Council

POLYNESIAN HOT DOGS

8 hot dogs
8 slices bacon

1 (10 1/2 oz.) can crushed
pineapple

Slit the hot dogs lengthwise to form a pocket. Fill hot
dogs with drained pineapple. Wrap a slice of bacon around
each stuffed hot dog, securing ends with toothpicks.
Barbecue in hand grill over medium heat, turning several
times, until the bacon is crisp.

Judy Q. Arnold
Harpeth Council

DEB'S PORK CHOPS

1 small can Mandarin
    oranges (reserve juice)
3 Tbsp. butter

1 tsp. mustard
1/3 c. brown sugar
4 pork chops

Mix butter, mustard, juice and sugar; place in a
greased Corning Ware dish. Add the pork chops and brown
in a 375° oven. Turn the chops over; pour the oranges on
top. Cook until tender. Pears may be substituted for
oranges.

Jane York
Harpeth Council

PORK CHOPS AND BROWNED RICE

6 pork chops
1 c. uncooked rice
1 medium onion, chopped
Salt and pepper to taste

1/2 green bell pepper,
    chopped
2 bouillon cubes, dissolved in
    2 1/2 c. hot water

184

Brown pork chops; set aside. Pour rice into pan that chops were cooked in, stirring constantly, until golden brown, about 10 minutes. Add onion and pepper; cook until tender. Add bouillon water; simmer over low heat until liquid is gone, about 20-25 minutes. Lay pork chops on top for last 10 minutes.

Goldie B. Davis
Knoxville Council

PORK CHOP AND RICE CASSEROLE

4 pork chops
1 c. Minute Rice
Chopped green pepper

1 can cream of mushroom
  soup
Sliced American cheese

Fry pork chops in small amount of oil. Place chops in casserole dish. Mix soup, 1 can water and chopped pepper; pour over pork chops. Sprinkle rice over this and press into soup. Bake at 350° until rice is done. Cover with cheese. When cheese is melted, remove from the oven and serve.

Debbie Burton
Harpeth Council

PORK CHOPS A L'ORANGE

6 (1/2 inch) pork chops,
  with fat trimmed off
2 Tbsp. margarine
1/4 c. flour
1 tsp. dried sage

1/2 tsp. salt
1/2 tsp. pepper
1/8 tsp. garlic powder
1 can chicken broth
1/2 c. orange juice

Heat margarine in large skillet; rinse chops and set aside. Combine flour and spices in a large bowl; dip chops in mixture, coating lightly. Reserve remaining flour. In hot fat, brown chops on both sides. Remove from pan; set aside. To drippings in skillet, stir in flour mixture. Add broth and orange juice; bring to a boil and add chops. Simmer, covered, 40 to 50 minutes until chops are tender. Add more salt and pepper, if necessary.

Paula Akin
Green Hills Council

PORK CHOP SPECIAL

2 (1/2 inch thick) pork
  chops
1 Tbsp. flour
1 Tbsp. vegetable oil
2 1/2 Tbsp. grated Parmesan
  cheese
1/4 tsp. salt
1/8 tsp. pepper
2 c. thinly sliced potatoes
2 beef bouillon cubes
1/4 c. plus 2 Tbsp. hot water
1 1/2 tsp. lemon juice

Dredge pork chops in flour; brown in hot oil in a
medium skillet. Combine cheese, salt and pepper; sprinkle
1 tablespoon mixture over chops. Arrange potatoes over
meat; sprinkle 1 tablespoon cheese mixture over potatoes.
Arrange 1/3 cup chopped onion on top. Dissolve cubes in
hot water; stir in lemon juice and pour over onion. Sprinkle
remaining cheese mixture on top. Cover and simmer 40 minutes. Serves 2.

Debbie Bullock
Harpeth Council

PORK CHOPS WITH MUSHROOM SAUCE

6 pork chops
Salt and pepper
3 cans cream of mushroom
  soup

Broil pork chops for 30 minutes. Remove from oven;
salt and pepper the pork chops and layer the chops and the
soup in a casserole dish. Cover and bake at 350° for 1 hour.

Sharon Rawlings
Harpeth Council

PORK CHOP SKILLET DINNER

4-10 pork chops
2-3 potatoes
2 large onions
1 head cabbage
2 cans cream of mushroom
  soup (any kind)

Place pork chops in electric skillet; brown on both
sides (no grease). On top of chops, slice onions and potatoes. Quarter cabbage and place in each corner of skillet.
Add mushroom soup; cover with water (2-3 cans). Bake at
300°-350° for approximately 1 hour or until cabbage is done.

Debbi Wakefield
Harpeth Council

SAUCY PORK CHOPS

6 pork chops
1/2 c. all-purpose flour
1 c. salad oil, divided
Salt and pepper to taste
3/4 c. vinegar

1/4 c. water
1 tsp. salt
3 Tbsp. brown sugar
3 Tbsp. catsup

Dredge pork chops with flour; brown in 1/2 cup hot salad oil; drain. Add salt and pepper to taste. Combine 1/2 cup salad oil, vinegar, water, 1 teaspoon salt, brown sugar and catsup to make sauce; heat just to boiling temperature. Pour sauce over pork chops; let simmer for about 20 minutes in the oven or on top of the stove.

Shirley Buckner
Green Hills Council

POT ROAST NEW ORLEANS

1/2 tsp. pepper
1/2 tsp. ground cloves
1/2 tsp. ground allspice
1 Tbsp. salt
1 (4 lb.) pot roast of beef
1 large onion, chopped
1/2 c. cooking oil
2 onions, peeled and
   sliced
1 clove garlic, finely
   chopped

2 Tbsp. lemon juice
1 Tbsp. vinegar
Flour
2 c. tomato juice or canned
   tomatoes
1 1/2 c. water
2 beef bouillon cubes,
   crushed
4 carrots, peeled, quartered
4 potatoes, peeled, quartered
2 or 3 bay leaves

Mix spices and salt; rub into roast. Combine onion, garlic, 1/4 cup cooking oil, lemon juice and vinegar. Marinate roast in mixture in refrigerator for about 5 hours, turning occasionally. Remove roast from marinade; save marinade. Sprinkle roast with flour; brown in remaining cooking oil in large heavy Dutch oven with lid. Add marinade, tomato juice or tomatoes, water, bouillon cubes and bay leaves. Cover and simmer about 2 1/2 hours. Add vegetables; continue cooking over low heat about 45 minutes or until vegetables are done.

Note: If desired, marinating step may be eliminated by adding spices, etc., to liquid after meat has been browned.

Nikki Ballard
Andrew Jackson Council

1489-81

QUICHE LORRAINE

This is the classic version. If you choose to be non-traditional, use Cheddar cheese and 1/2 cup chopped ham in place of Swiss cheese and bacon.

1 (9 inch) pie shell
8 slices bacon, cooked crisp, drained and crumbled
1 1/4 c. half & half or milk
1/8 tsp. nutmeg
6 eggs, beaten
1 c. (4 oz.) shredded Swiss cheese
1/2 tsp. salt
1/8 tsp. pepper

Brush pie shell with small amount of the beaten eggs. Prick bottom and sides with fork. If using metal pie pan, bake shell in preheated 450° F. oven until golden brown, about 5 minutes. If using pie plate, bake shell at 425° F. Cool on wire rack. Reduce oven temperature to 375° F. for metal pan or 350° F. for pie plate. Sprinkle bacon and cheese in pie shell. Beat remaining ingredients together until well blended; pour into pie shell. Bake in preheated oven until knife inserted near center comes out clean, 35-40 minutes. Let stand 5 minutes before serving.

Jennifer C. Alley
Harpeth Council

QUICK AND EASY POTATO STEW

1 lb. ground beef
1 tsp. salt
3 Tbsp. chopped onion
1 can cream of mushroom soup
1 soup can water
1/4 - 1/2 tsp. garlic powder
4 or 5 potatoes, cut into bite size pieces, cooked

Brown meat, salt and onion in skillet; drain off liquid. Add soup and water; mix well. Sprinkle with garlic powder; cover and simmer gently for 20 minutes. Pour over cooked potatoes when ready to serve. Serves 4 generously.

Emma Jo Perry
Green Hills Council

REGAL RUMP ROAST

1 c. Catalina dressing
2 Tbsp. Worcestershire
   sauce
1/2 tsp. garlic salt

1/4 tsp. cracked black
   peppercorns
1 tsp. sunflower oil

Rinse 3 to 5 pound Regal rump roast. Sprinkle meat tenderizer over roast, then prick meat with fork tines. Cover meat completely with marinade. Cover and refrigerate overnight. Bake in same marinade sauce at 225° for about 4 hours.

Nancy Cochrane
Harpeth Council

ROLLED STEAK

2 1/2 - 3 lb. round steak,
   pounded or sliced very
   thin
Salt and pepper to taste
Paprika
1/2 lb. fresh sauteed
   mushrooms
2 or 3 medium onions, sliced
Flour or cornstarch

1 c. beef stock
Large jar chopped pimentos
1/2 c. Pepperidge Farm
   crumbs
1 stick melted butter
1 Tbsp. water
1 egg
18-24 stuffed olives
1 c. rich red wine

Pound steak out; overlap 2 rectangles. Make square. Season with salt, pepper and paprika. Cover square with mushrooms, onions, pimento and crumbs. Combine butter, water and egg; pour over steak. Double over steak. (Note: Before rolling, cut 12 nine inch strings and have at hand.) Line up olives at end of doubled over steak; roll up. Be patient! Slip strings under rolled steak and tie. Place in baking dish. Pour over roll 1 cup or more wine and beef stock. Bake at 350° for 1 1/2 hours; baste every 15 minutes.

Gravy: Stir in cornstarch with wine and beef stock. Add more wine and beef stock if necessary.

Betty Marek
Harpeth Council

1489-81

ROUND STEAK CASSEROLE

1 c. chopped onion
1 c. chopped bell pepper
1 c. chopped celery
1 round steak, cut into
   bite size pieces
1 can golden mushroom soup

2 c. Minute Rice
1/2 stick butter/margarine
American cheese
Almonds (optional)
Mushrooms (optional)

Brown onion, bell pepper and celery in butter. In separate skillet, brown the round steak. Combine onion, bell pepper, celery and round steak. Stir in soup and 1/2 can water. Add uncooked rice, almonds and mushrooms, if desired. Cook 10 minutes over low heat. Pour into 1 1/2 quart casserole dish and cover. Bake at 325° for about 20 minutes. Remove lid; top with cheese. Bake until cheese melts.

Carol Nunnery
Memphis Council

ROULADEN

Stuffing:

2 Tbsp. butter or margarine
1/2 c. chopped onion
1/2 c. grated carrot
1/4 c. chopped celery
1/4 c. chopped parsley
1 c. packaged stuffing mix

3/4 tsp. salt
1/4 tsp. pepper
2 Tbsp. salad oil
1 can mushroom soup,
   undiluted, or 1 env. brown
   gravy mix (I prefer gravy
   mix)

Have ready 4 slices round steak, cut 1/4 inch thick (about 2 pounds), or you may use sandwich steaks, allowing 2 per person.

1. Make stuffing: In hot butter in large skillet, saute onion, carrot and celery about 5 minutes. Remove from heat; stir in parsley, stuffing mix and 1/3 cup water until well blended. Set aside. 2. Wipe steak with damp paper towels and cut each piece in half crosswise (if round steaks are used; sandwich steaks will already be correct size). Pound with mallet to 1/8 inch thickness. 3. Sprinkle meat with salt and pepper. Spread about 3 tablespoons stuffing on each piece, almost to edge; roll up in jelly roll fashion and tie with cord or skewer with toothpicks. 4. In hot salad oil in Dutch oven or skillet, brown beef roulades, half at a time,

on all sides. Remove as they brown. 5. Stir soup and 1/2 cup water into pan drippings (or the gravy mix, made up according to package directions). Return roulades to skillet; bring to boiling. Reduce heat; simmer, covered, 2 hours or until tender. Serve with mashed potatoes and gravy. (Rice is also good.) Makes 4 to 6 servings.

Metty C. Fain
Andrew Jackson Council

SALMON CROQUETTES

Make a cream sauce by blending 1 tablespoon butter with 1 tablespoon flour and 1/8 teaspoon salt. Stir 1 cup milk into this and cook until thickened (use rounded tablespoon measures in this recipe so your sauce will be quite thick). Set aside until cold. Drain a 1 pound can of salmon; take out skin and bone. Add 1 slightly beaten egg, 2 tablespoons lemon juice and the white sauce to the salmon. Place in refrigerator to chill for at least an hour, then shape into croquettes. Roll in fine cracker crumbs and fry in hot fat. Drain on paper towels to remove excess fat before serving.

Ruth and Deborah Cole
Harpeth Council

SALMON CROQUETTES

Make a cream sauce by blending 3 tablespoons butter with 3 tablespoons flour and 1/8 teaspoon salt. Stir in 1 cup milk; cook until thickened. (Use rounded tablespoon measure in this recipe so your sauce will be quite thick.) Set aside until cold. Drain a 1 pound can of salmon; take out skin and bone. Add 1 slightly beaten egg, 2 tablespoons lemon juice and the white sauce to the salmon. Place in refrigerator to chill for at least an hour, then shape into croquettes. Roll in fine cracker crumbs and fry in hot fat. Drain on paper towels.

Joyce Mattice
Harpeth Council

SALMON LOAF

1 tall can salmon
2 eggs
1 c. cracker crumbs

1/2 c. cream of celery soup, undiluted
1 Tbsp. grated onion
1 Tbsp. butter

Mince salmon with a fork; add eggs and other ingredients. Form into a loaf; put in a greased pan. Bake for 30 minutes at 350°. The remaining soup can be diluted slightly with water to make a sauce.

Eugenia W. Smith
Chattanooga Council

SALMON LOAF - DELUXE

1/2 c. buttered bread crumbs
1/2 tsp. salt
2 Tbsp. melted butter
Dash of black pepper
1 (1 lb.) can salmon, flaked

2 eggs, slightly beaten
1/2 c. milk
1 tsp. sage
2 Tbsp. chopped onion
1 tsp. lemon juice
1 Tbsp. parsley (optional)

Mix in order given and pack in greased baking dish. Bake 30-40 minutes in 350° oven. Serve with sliced, boiled eggs or 1 can of mushroom soup, heated and poured over loaf. Serve warm. Serves 6.

Dorothy Bryant
Clarksville Council

IRRESISTIBLE SALMON MOUSSE

2 env. unflavored gelatin
1/2 c. water
1 (15 1/2 oz.) can red salmon
1 c. mayonnaise
2 Tbsp. vinegar
2 Tbsp. catsup
Dash of cayenne pepper
Dash of pepper

15 pimiento-stuffed olives, sliced
2 hard cooked eggs, chopped
2 Tbsp. sweet pickle relish
1 c. whipping cream, whipped
Lettuce
Lemon halves (optional)
Paprika (optional)
Parsley sprigs (optional)

Combine gelatin and water in a small saucepan; place over medium heat until gelatin is dissolved, stirring constantly. Remove from heat; set aside. Drain salmon; remove skin and bones. Flake salmon with a fork; add mayonnaise, vinegar, catsup, cayenne pepper and pepper. Mix well, then stir in olives, eggs, relish and dissolved gelatin. Fold in whipped cream. Spoon mixture into a well greased 5 1/2 to 6 cup mold; chill overnight. Unmold on lettuce. If desired, garnish with lemon halves dipped in paprika and topped with parsley sprigs. Yield: One 5 1/2 cup mousse.

Judy Christopher
Harpeth Council

SCALLOPED SALMON

1/2 c. chicken broth
2 eggs, slightly beaten
1 Tbsp. minced onion
1 (16 oz.) can salmon, drained
2 c. seasoned stuffing croutons

2 Tbsp. parsley flakes
1/2 tsp. dry mustard
1/4 tsp. salt
1/8 tsp. pepper
1 c. Cheddar cheese, grated
1/2 c. milk
1 recipe Vegetable Sauce

Vegetable Sauce:

2 Tbsp. all-purpose flour
1/4 tsp. salt

Dash of pepper
1 c. milk

Cook until bubbly. Cook 2 minutes more; add 1 cup green peas on top. Combine chicken broth, eggs, milk, parsley, onion, mustard, salt and pepper. Stir in salmon, croutons and cheese. Turn into 9 inch pie plate. Bake, uncovered, at 350°. Serve with Vegetable Sauce.

Lena Roberson
Andrew Jackson Council

SAUSAGE CHEESE SOUFFLE

Beat:
2 c. milk
6 eggs

1 tsp. dry mustard
1/2 - 1 tsp. salt

Fold in:
6 slices cubed bread
1 c. grated sharp Cheddar cheese
1/4 c. ripe olives, chopped

1 lb. mild sausage, fried, drained and chopped up
1/2 c. chopped mushrooms (pieces)

1489-81

Pour into baking dish; let stand 12 hours or longer in refrigerator. Bake in preheated oven at 350° for 1 hour. Serves 8.

Jane Wohlbold
Green Hills Council

SHEPHERD'S PIE
(Ulcer Diet)

2 c. cooked beef or lamb, cubed
1 c. mixed leftover vegetables, drained (string beans and carrots, for example)

2 c. cooked dehydrated mashed potatoes
1/4 c. cream
1 egg, beaten
1 Tbsp. butter

Preheat oven to 400°. Lightly butter a 1 1/2 quart casserole. Place meat in casserole; add drained vegetables. Makes 2 cups dehydrated mashed potatoes, following directions on box. Add cream. Beat egg until light; fold into the potato mixture. Spread mixture over meat and vegetables. Dot the top with butter. Bake 20 minutes or until lightly brown. Makes 3 to 4 servings.

SHRIMP-CRAB DIVINE

1 can crabmeat (or pkg. frozen crabmeat)
1 lb. cooked shrimp
1/2 green pepper, chopped
1/2 c. chopped onion
1 small jar pimento, chopped
1 Tbsp. Worcestershire sauce

1/8 tsp. pepper
1/2 c. raw rice
1 c. chopped celery
1 small can mushrooms, chopped
1 c. mayonnaise
1/2 tsp. sage
3/4 c. light cream

Cook rice according to package instructions; drain. Combine all ingredients; pour into large casserole and bake at 375° for 30 minutes. Serves 10. (If mixture does not seem moist enough, use mushroom soup to thin down.)

To vary: Two to 3 hard boiled eggs, chopped, can be added.

Hazel Moore
Green Hills Council

SHRIMP MOUSSE

1 1/2 lb. cooked, peeled, deveined shrimp (fresh or frozen)
1 (10 3/4 oz.) can condensed tomato soup
1 (8 oz.) pkg. cream cheese
2 Tbsp. unflavored gelatin
1 c. mayonnaise or salad dressing
3/4 c. finely chopped celery
1/2 c. finely chopped green pepper
1 tsp. Worcestershire sauce
1 tsp. lemon juice
Rich buttery crackers

Thaw shrimp if frozen; chop shrimp. Heat tomato soup and cream cheese in the top of double boiler until cream cheese melts; cool slightly. Stir in gelatin; mix well. Add shrimp, mayonnaise, celery, green onion, green pepper, Worcestershire sauce and lemon juice; mix well. Pour into a well greased 1 1/2 quart mold. Cover and refrigerate at least 8 hours. Serve with crackers. Makes approximately 50 appetizers.

Judy Christopher
Harpeth Council
Nell Young
Harpeth Council

AUNT JENNY'S SPAGHETTI

1 1/2 lb. ground beef
1 large onion, chopped
1 green pepper, chopped
1 can sliced mushrooms, drained
1 can tomato puree
1 jar Ragu spaghetti sauce
Salt and pepper to taste
1 box long, thin spaghetti, broken up
1/2 tsp. oregano
1 tsp. garlic powder

Saute ground beef, onion, green pepper and mushrooms; drain off all fat. Add garlic powder, oregano, salt and pepper. Add puree and spaghetti sauce and simmer for about 30-45 minutes. Prepare spaghetti according to package directions. Strain in colander; rinse with hot water. Drain well, then stir in spaghetti sauce.

Kay Boswell
Andrew Jackson Council

ITALIAN SPAGHETTI

Brown 1 small onion and 1/4 small green pepper in 2 tablespoons bacon drippings. Add 1 pound ground beef and brown; dip off excess grease. Mix in large pan:

1 (12 oz.) can tomato paste	2 pinches of leaf oregano
3 cans water	2 bay leaves
1 pkg. Italian spaghetti sauce mix (McCormick or Lawry's)	1 can sliced mushrooms
	2 Tbsp. butter
	Salt and pepper to taste
3 or 4 sifts of celery salt	

Add hamburger mixture and simmer for 2 hours. Stir every 15 minutes; remove bay leaves when done.

Dean Tidwell
Nashboro Council

SPAGHETTI - ITALIAN STYLE

1 tsp. basil	1 bay leaf
1 tsp. oregano	2 small cans tomato sauce
1 tsp. garlic salt	1 small can tomato paste
1 tsp. onion salt	2 cans water

Combine all ingredients; bring to a boil. Simmer for 3-5 hours, stirring occasionally. Add bay leaf and meat balls the last hour.

Meat Balls - Italian Style:

1 tsp. basil	1-2 eggs
1 tsp. oregano	1/2 c. bread crumbs
1 tsp. garlic salt	Pepper
1-2 lb. ground beef	

Combine all ingredients; form in walnut size balls. For best texture, use microwave oven. If using skillet, brown on all sides until well done. Add to sauce and serve.
This is enough sauce for 1 pound spaghetti; cook spaghetti as directed on box.
Note: Green peppers, chopped finely, and mushrooms can be added as extra touch.

Reba Owens
Knoxville Council

SULLIVAN'S ISLAND PEEL 'EM AND EAT 'EM

8 c. water
3 Tbsp. Old Bay seasoning
6 whole lemons

2 cans regular beer
1 lb. fresh deheaded shrimp
  (any size)

Put water in 1 gallon pot; add Old Bay seasoning and beer. Squeeze the juice from 5 of the lemons into the water; slice up the sixth, letting the slices float on top. Bring water to fast boil. Clean shrimp, leaving shells on to cook. Empty all shrimp into boiling water; let cook for 4-5 minutes until water has just begun to boil again. Remove shrimp and enjoy with any seafood cocktail sauce.

Betty Swindle
Knoxville Council

SWEET AND SOUR RIBS

1/2 c. vinegar
1 c. water
1 c. chunk pineapple
1/2 c. tomato ketchup

1/2 c. sugar
1 tsp. cornstarch or 2 tsp.
  flour
1 tsp. soy sauce

Cook ribs by placing in large pot; cover them with water. Add a little salt and black pepper; simmer for an hour or two (until meat is almost falling off the bone). Prepare the sweet and sour sauce by combining vinegar, sugar, water and cornstarch, stirring until smooth. Add the pineapple, soy sauce and tomato ketchup; stir thoroughly. Place the cooked ribs in a large pan and pour sauce over them. Bake in oven at 300° to 350° for about an hour. Baste the ribs frequently.

Richard Underwood
Harpeth Council

SWISS STEAK CHEESE SKILLET

2 lb. boneless round steak
1/4 c. all-purpose flour
1/4 c. butter or margarine,
  melted
1 (16 oz.) can tomatoes
1/2 tsp. salt

1/4 tsp. whole basil leaves
1/8 tsp. pepper
1/2 c. chopped onion
1/3 c. chopped green pepper
1 1/2 c. (6 oz.) shredded
  Mozzarella cheese

Trim excess fat from steak; cut into serving size

1489-81

pieces. Dredge steaks in flour; saute in butter until browned. Add tomatoes, salt, basil and pepper to steak; cover and simmer 1 hour. Stir in onion and green pepper. Cook an additional 30 minutes. Sprinkle cheese over meat and heat just until melted. Yield: 4 to 6 servings.

Johnnie Foster
Harpeth Council

SWISS STEAK

1 1/2 lb. round steak
1 can mushroom soup
1/4 c. chopped onion
Dash of pepper

2 Tbsp. shortening
1/2 c. chopped canned
 tomatoes
1/4 c. water
Salt to taste

Cut steak into serving size pieces. Brown steak in a skillet; pour off fat. Add remaining ingredients; cover and cook over low heat for 1 hour and 15 minutes or until tender, stirring often. Makes 4-6 servings.

Evelyn Easley
Harpeth Council

SYMPHONY BEEF
(This one is a nice brunch dish.)

2 Tbsp. butter
1/2 lb. chipped beef of
 dried beef, torn into bite
 size pieces
1 Tbsp. flour
1 pt. sour cream
1/2 c. dry white wine or
 dry vermouth

1 heaping Tbsp. grated
 Parmesan cheese
1 (10 oz.) can artichoke
 hearts, thinly sliced
Split, toasted and buttered
 English muffins, buttered
 toast or noodles
Paprika

Melt butter in a skillet over low heat (an electric skillet set at 180° is safest). In it, frizzle the beef until crimpy and crisp on the edges. Sprinkle on the flour; mix and add the sour cream and wine. Stir thoroughly until smooth. Add the cheese and finally the artichoke hearts. Stir gently; don't disintegrate the artichoke hearts. Keep warm at 180° until serving time. Spoon over muffins, toast or noodles and sprinkle paprika on top. Serves 4.

Addie Downs
Green Hills Council

TUNA CHOW MEIN

Saute 1 cup chopped celery, 1/3 cup chopped onion and 2 tablespoons chopped green pepper in 2 tablespoons butter in medium saucepan until onion is tender. Stir in 2 tablespoons flour; heat about 1 minute. Slowly add:

2/3 c. water
1 1/4 c. (9 1/4 oz. can)
   drained tuna

1 c. undiluted evaporated
   milk
1 chicken bouillon cube
1/8 tsp. pepper

Heat until thickened over medium heat; stir often. Stir in 3/4 cup salted peanuts and 2 1/2 cups chow mein noodles. Heat through over medium heat. Spoon mixture into 1 1/2 quart buttered casserole. Sprinkle 1 cup chow mein noodles over top. Bake in moderate oven, 350° F., for 15-20 minutes or until bubbling. Makes 1 1/2 quarts.

Polly Kirby
Andrew Jackson Council

TURBOT OR COD WITH MORNAY SAUCE

1/2 c. dry white wine
1 1/2 lb. frozen turbot or
   cod fillets or steaks
3 Tbsp. flour
3 Tbsp. butter or margarine,
   melted

3/4 c. hot milk
1/2 c. grated Cheddar
   cheese
Salt and pepper to taste
Buttered bread crumbs

Pour wine into a 9 inch skillet; bring to boiling point. Arrange the fish in a single layer in wine; cover and cook over moderately low heat until the fish flakes when tested, 5 to 6 minutes. Keep the fish warm while making the sauce. Blend flour with butter; stir and cook 1 to 2 minutes. Remove from heat and beat in the milk. Return to heat and cook until the sauce is very thick, stirring constantly. Thin sauce with 1/3 cup wine from cooking fish. Add cheese, salt and pepper. Place fish in a buttered 9x9x2 inch baking dish; pour sauce over it. Sprinkle with buttered bread crumbs. Brown quickly, about 10 minutes, in a preheated oven, 425° F. Makes 4 to 5 servings.

Emily Townes
Harpeth Council

1489-81

TURKEY ALFREDO

8 oz. noodles
1/2 c. butter

1 c. grated Parmesan cheese

Cook noodles; drain. Add cheese and 5 tablespoons butter; toss. Set aside and keep hot.

1 egg
1 tsp. oregano
1/2 tsp. salt
Dash of pepper
2 Tbsp. water

3/4 c. fine bread crumbs
8 slices turkey breast
3 Tbsp. olive oil or salad oil
(olive oil is best)

Beat egg with oregano, salt and pepper. Place bread crumbs in separate plate; dip turkey in egg, then in crumbs. Fry in 3 tablespoons butter and olive oil. Put noodles in casserole; arrange turkey, overlapping, on top.

Supreme Sauce:

2 Tbsp. butter
2 Tbsp. flour

1 c. broth
1/2 c. milk

Cook over low heat until thick. Whip 1/4 cup whipping cream and fold into above cooked mixture when it has cooled slightly. Spoon sauce on turkey. Broil 4 inches from heat for approximately 5 minutes. Eat immediately.

Addie Downs
Green Hills Council

TURKEY CASSEROLE

1 c. broth and milk
2 eggs
2 slices bread
1/4 green pepper

1 stalk celery
2 tsp. salt
2 c. canned turkey

Drain broth from the canned turkey; add enough milk to make 1 cup liquid. Beat eggs; add to milk mixture. Tear bread into small pieces. Chop green pepper and celery; mix all ingredients. Put into greased baking pan. Bake at 350°, moderate oven, for 30 minutes or until browned. Makes six servings, about 1/2 cup each.

Judy Gibson
Harpeth Council

TURKEY TETRAZZINI

2 Tbsp. butter
2 Tbsp. flour
1/2 tsp. salt
2 c. turkey broth
1 c. milk

1/4 c. sliced mushrooms
2 c. shredded turkey
1/2 lb. egg noodles, cooked
and drained
1/2 c. grated Cheddar cheese

Melt butter; add flour and mix until smooth. Add salt, broth and milk; cook until thickened. Add mushrooms and turkey. Alternate turkey mixture and noodles in dish; cover with cheese. Bake 15 minutes at 350°.

Patricia Hire
Harpeth Council

TURKETTE

1 1/4 c. spaghetti
2 c. chopped turkey or ham
1/4 c. chopped pimento
1 can mushroom soup,
undiluted
1/2 c. stock from turkey

1/4 c. green pepper and 1/2
c. onion, chopped fine,
sauteed in small amount of
butter
1/2 tsp. salt
1/2 tsp. pepper
1 3/4 c. grated cheese

Cook spaghetti; drain. Mix other ingredients with spaghetti. Save some cheese to cover top of casserole. Makes enough for 2 small or 1 large casserole (freeze one and eat one). Bake 45 minutes at 350°.

Linda Whitaker
Harpeth Council

"TURKETTY"

1 1/2 c. elbow spaghetti
(measure before cooking),
cooked 7 to 10 minutes
2 c. cooked turkey or
chicken, diced
1 onion, diced
1/2 c. green pepper, diced

1/2 c. pimento, diced
1/2 tsp. black pepper
1 can cream of mushroom
soup
1 c. chicken stock or 2
bouillon cubes
1 1/2 c. Cheddar cheese

Mix all ingredients, except cheese. Place in 9x12 inch

1489-81

baking dish; cover with foil. Bake 40 minutes at 300°. Remove foil; spread cheese and return to oven until cheese is melted.

Opal A. Jones
Harpeth Council

TURKEY TOMORROW

3 c. cubed, cooked turkey
2 cans cream of mushroom
   soup
4 hard cooked eggs, diced
2 c. chopped celery
2/3 c. uncooked Minute Rice

2 Tbsp. lemon juice
2 Tbsp. onion juice
1 c. mayonnaise
1/2 tsp. salt
Dash of cayenne pepper
4 c. crushed potato chips

Combine all ingredients, except potato chips. Mix lightly, then add 2 cups potato chips to mixture. Add the remaining 2 cups potato chips to top of mixture. Bake 30-35 minutes at 375°. Makes 8-10 servings.

Barbara Reynolds
Chattanooga Council

BARZIZZA'S VEAL PARMIGIANA

3/4 tsp. salt
1/8 tsp. pepper
1 c. crushed corn flakes
1/2 c. Parmesan cheese
2 eggs, lightly beaten
1/3 c. olive oil

6 veal cutlets
2 (8 oz.) cans tomato sauce
1 tsp. oregano
1/4 tsp. onion salt
6 slices Mozzarella cheese

Combine salt, pepper, corn flake crumbs and Parmesan cheese. Dip each cutlet into egg, then crumbs; repeat. In large skillet, heat olive oil; brown cutlets on each side. Add a few tablespoons of water; cover and cook over low heat for 30 minutes. In saucepan, combine tomato sauce, oregano and onion salt. Heat and, if necessary, keep hot over boiling water. Place veal in dish; cover with piece of cheese and sauce. Bake in 400° oven for about 3-5 minutes.

Marian Molteni
Harpeth Council

BREAD, ROLLS, PASTRY

BREAD BAKING GUIDE

The pleasure of baking homemade bread is matched only by eating it, except when something goes wrong. Most problems can be determined and easily avoided the next time.

WHAT WENT WRONG...	WHY...
Bread or biscuits are dry	Too much flour; too slow baking; over-handling
Bread has too open or uneven texture	Too much liquid; over-handling in kneading
Strong yeast smell from baked bread	Too much yeast; over-rising
Tiny white spots on crusts	Too rapid rising; dough not covered properly while rising
Crust has bad color	Too much flour used in shaping
Small flat loaves	Old yeast; not enough rising or rising much too long; oven temperature too hot
Heavy compact texture	Too much flour worked into bread when kneading; insufficient rising time; oven temperature too hot
Coarse texture	Too little kneading
Crumbly bread	Too much flour, undermixing; oven temperature too cool
Yeasty sour flavor	Too little yeast; rising time too long
Fallen center	Rising time too long
Irregular shape	Poor technique in shaping
Surface browns too quickly	Oven temperature too hot
Bread rises too long during baking and is porous in center and upper portion of loaf	Oven temperature too cool

ANGEL BISCUITS

5 c. self-rising flour
1 tsp. soda
4 Tbsp. sugar
1 c. shortening

1 pkg. dry yeast, dissolved
in 1/4 c. lukewarm water
2 c. buttermilk

Combine flour, soda and sugar; cut in shortening. Add yeast mixture and buttermilk; mix with hands until dough is formed. May be made into biscuits immediately or kept in refrigerator as long as 2 weeks (if air is worked every day), then make into biscuits as needed. Bake 15 minutes at 375°. Makes 3 to 4 dozen biscuits.

Mrs. A.C. Mullins
Jackson Council

ANN'S ANGEL BISCUITS

1 pkg. dry yeast
2 Tbsp. warm water
4 Tbsp. sugar

1 c. Crisco
5 c. self-rising flour
2 c. buttermilk

Add yeast to warm water; let set while mixing other ingredients. Sift flour; add sugar and shortening. Mix well. Add yeast and buttermilk; blend (do not overwork). You can roll out immediately or place in refrigerator and use as needed. Bake at 450° for 15-20 minutes or until brown.

Ann Kinser
Knoxville Council

DROP BISCUITS

3 c. Quick Mix

3/4 c. milk or water

Preheat oven to 450°. Grease a baking sheet. Combine Quick Mix and milk or water in a medium bowl; stir until just blended. Drop by tablespoonfuls onto prepared baking sheet. Bake 10 to 12 minutes, until golden brown. Makes 12 large drop biscuits. Variations:

Cheese and Herb Biscuits: Add 1/3 cup grated cheese and chopped parsley, chives or herbs to taste while stirring dough.

1489-81

Buttermilk Biscuits: Substitute 3/4 cup buttermilk for milk or water.

Country Dumplings: Drop dough by tablespoons over top of boiling beef or chicken stew. Boil gently 10 minutes, uncovered. Cover and cook over medium-high heat 10 more minutes, until cooked through. Makes 12 dumplings.

Orange Biscuits: Add 1 tablespoon grated orange peel. If desired, substitute 2 tablespoons orange juice for part of milk or water.

Fruit Cobbler: Spoon dough over top of hot, sweetened fruit or berries and bake in an 8 inch square pan about 20 to 25 minutes until golden brown.

Joyce Mattice
Harpeth Council

EASY BISCUITS

1 c. self-rising flour   3 Tbsp. shortening
2/3 c. milk

Mix all ingredients together. Pour out on floured board and knead for about 5 minutes. Bake at 400° until done.

Mary Lynn Johnson
Harpeth Council

HOT CHEESE BISCUITS

1/2 c. margarine, softened   1 (5 oz.) jar pasteurized
1 c. all-purpose flour   process sharp American
1 or 2 drops hot sauce   cheese spread

Combine margarine and cheese; blend until smooth. Add flour and hot sauce; mix well. Shape into small balls. Place on ungreased cookie sheet and press with fork. Bake at 350° for 10 minutes. Yield: About 3 1/2 dozen.

Judy Gibson
Harpeth Council

NEVER-FAIL ROLLED BISCUITS

3 c. Quick Mix   2/3 c. water or milk

Preheat oven to 450°. Combine Quick Mix and milk or water in a medium bowl; blend. Let dough stand 5 minutes. On a lightly floured board, knead dough about 15 times. Roll out to 1/2 inch thickness. Cut with a floured biscuit cutter. Place about 2 inches apart on ungreased baking sheet. Bake 10 to 12 minutes, until golden brown. Makes 12 large biscuits. Variations:

Cinnamon Rolls: Preheat oven to 400°. Roll out dough to a rectangle; brush with melted butter. Sprinkle with brown sugar and cinnamon. Roll dough like a jelly roll and cut into 1/2 inch slices. Bake 10 to 15 minutes. Glaze with mixture of powdered sugar and a few drops of water.

Pizza: Use dough as crust for 12 individual pizzas or two 12 inch pizzas. Pat dough to 1/8 inch thickness. Top with tomato sauce, spices, cheese, meat and choice of toppings.

Meat Pinwheels: Preheat oven to 450°. Roll out dough to a rectangle. Chop cooked meat; combine with gravy. Spread over dough like a jelly roll and cut into 1/2 inch slices.

Pot Pie: Use as the top crust of a chicken or meat pot pie.

Joyce Mattice
Harpeth Council

SUGAR BISCUITS

2 c. all-purpose flour, sifted   1 1/2 tsp. grated orange rind
1 Tbsp. sugar   (optional)
1 Tbsp. baking powder   1/4 c. shortening
                             3/4 c. milk

In a large bowl, sift together flour, sugar and baking powder. If you use orange rind, add it at this time. Cut in shortening; stir in milk. Knead lightly on floured board. Roll out to 1/2 inch thickness; cut with a 2 inch round biscuit cutter. Place on ungreased cookie sheet and sprinkle with additional sugar. Bake at 450° for 10 minutes or until lightly brown.

Shirley Buckner
Green Hills Council

WHIPPING CREAM BISCUITS

1 c. whipping cream,   2 c. self-rising flour
  unwhipped

Mix flour and whipping cream together, then place dough on a floured pastry board. Roll out dough; cut out biscuits and place on a greased cookie sheet. Bake at 350° for 12 minutes.

Margaretta Douglas
Knoxville Council

YEAST BISCUITS

2 pkg. yeast   1 c. warm water
4 Tbsp. sugar   2 c. buttermilk
1 tsp. soda   2/3 c. oil
6 c. flour (self-rising)

Dissolve 2 packages yeast and 4 tablespoons sugar in 1 cup warm water. Add 2 cups buttermilk, 2/3 cup oil and 1 teaspoon soda. Add 6 cups flour gradually and stir. Cool and store in refrigerator. Roll gently into a roll; cut into sections. Bake at 425° for about 12 to 15 minutes. One-half recipe is enough for small family.

Dot Sells
Morristown Council

BANANA BREAD

3/4 c. shortening   1 tsp. soda
1 3/4 c. sugar   1 tsp. baking powder
1/2 tsp. vanilla   3/4 tsp. salt
3 eggs, beaten   1 c. nuts
3 bananas, mashed 1 c. buttermilk
3 c. flour

Cream shortening and sugar; add vanilla and beaten eggs. Sift together dry ingredients. Add alternately with milk and soda mixture. Mix well, adding bananas and nuts. Bake in 2 loaf pans in 350° oven for 45 minutes to 1 hour.

Joyce Mattice
Harpeth Council

BANANA NUT BREAD

2 c. crushed, ripe bananas (4-7)	5 c. flour
4 eggs	1 tsp. salt
2 c. sugar	1 tsp. baking soda
1 c. Crisco oil	1 tsp. baking powder
	1 c. chopped pecans

Mix bananas and eggs. Add sugar and oil; mix well. Stir salt, baking soda and baking powder into one of the 5 cups of flour, then add all 5 cups flour to liquid ingredients. Stir in nuts. Pour into 3 medium foil lined loaf pans and place in cold oven. Set oven to 275°; bake 1 1/2 hours or until firm to the touch. After bread cools, glaze loaves with powdered sugar, mixed with a small amount of milk.

Shelby Billmyer
Clarksville Council

BANANA NUT BREAD

1/2 c. shortening (I use Crisco)	3 mashed ripe bananas
1 c. sugar	2 c. sifted plain flour
2 eggs	1 tsp. soda
	1/2 c. chopped nuts

Mix shortening, sugar and eggs; blend well. Add bananas; beat well. Add flour and soda; beat well after each addition. Add nuts; mix well. Pour batter into well greased and floured loaf pan. Bake in a 350° oven for 1 hour.

Mary R. Veal
Chattanooga Council

BANANA OATMEAL BREAD

1/3 c. uncooked oats (regular or quick-cooking)	3 ripe bananas, mashed
1/4 c. buttermilk	2 c. all-purpose flour
1/2 c. shortening	1 tsp. baking powder
1/2 c. sugar	1 tsp. soda
2 eggs	1/2 tsp. salt

Combine oats and buttermilk; set aside. Cream shortening and sugar until light and fluffy. Add eggs, one at a time, beating well after each addition. Stir in bananas and oat mixture. Combine flour, baking powder, soda and salt; stir into banana mixture. Spoon batter into a greased 9x5x3 inch loaf pan. Bake at 350° for 1 hour and 10 minutes or until done. Yield: 1 loaf.

Inda Adams
Andrew Jackson Council

BUTTERMILK BANANA BREAD

1/2 c. butter
1 c. brown sugar
3 ripe bananas
1/4 c. buttermilk
1 tsp. soda

2 eggs
2 c. whole wheat flour
1/2 c. chopped nuts
1/8 tsp. salt

Cream butter and sugar with mixer. Add bananas; mix well. Add eggs and continue mixing. Dissolve soda in buttermilk, then add to mixture. Add flour and salt; fold in nuts. Bake in 1 well greased and floured loaf pan for about 60 minutes in a 350° oven.

Janice Moore
Harpeth Council

"FLOWERPOT" BANANA NUT BREAD

2 c. all-purpose flour
1 tsp. baking soda
1/2 tsp. salt
1/2 c. butter
1 c. sugar

2 eggs
1 c. mashed, ripened bananas
1/3 c. milk
1 tsp. lemon juice
1/2 c. chopped walnuts

Sift flour, soda and salt. Cream butter till light and fluffy. Beat in sugar, eggs and bananas, blending thoroughly. Add dry ingredients to banana mixture alternately with milk and lemon juice, beginning and ending with dry ingredients. Stir in nuts. Pour mixture into a new 6 1/2 inch (top diameter) clay flower pot, that has been washed and dried, greased, lined with waxed paper and greased again. Set flower pot in slow cooker; cover with 2 or 3 paper towels. Cover with lid and cook on high 4 or 5 hours. Do not lift lid, even to peek. Can be baked in conventional oven at 350° for 1 hour.

Sandra H. Bullock
Harpeth Council

BEER BREAD

3 c. self-rising flour or   3 Tbsp. sugar
  4 c. biscuit mix   12 oz. beer

Put flour or biscuit mix into large mixing bowl; add sugar and beer. Mix thoroughly at low speed. Spread in a well greased 9x5x3 inch loaf pan. Bake at 375° for 45-60 minutes (test with toothpick).

Butch Cooper
Harpeth Council

BREAD

2 eggs   2 c. water (tepid)
2 sticks margarine   2 pkg. dry yeast
1 c. sugar   6 1/2 c. plain flour
1 tsp. salt

Melt margarine and cool. Dissolve yeast in the 2 cups tepid water; add eggs, salt, sugar and margarine. Stir in sifted flour. Cover and set to rise in a warm place. When dough is about twice its size, remove from bowl to floured board and knead slightly. Pinch off into rolls and/or loaves. Place into greased, floured pans. Top with pats of butter on each roll. Place in a warm place to rise again; do not cover. Let rise to twice its size. Bake in 400° oven until brown, about 30 minutes. This recipe can be used as a basic for coffee cakes, cinnamon rolls, etc. by adding more sugar, etc.

Phyllis Whaley
Andrew Jackson Council

WHITE BREAD
(Sodium Restricted Diets)

1/4 c. lukewarm water   2 Tbsp. shortening
1 cake compressed yeast   Flour, about 6 c. (do not
2 c. hot water   use self-rising flour)
2/3 Tbsp. sugar

Soften yeast with lukewarm water. Pour hot liquid over sugar and shortening; cool to lukewarm. Add yeast and flour to make a stiff batter; beat well. Add additional flour to make a soft dough; turn out on board. Knead until

light and elastic and until dough does not stick to board.
Place in warm, greased bowl; grease top lightly. Cover;
keep between 80° and 85° F. When doubled in bulk, about
2 hours, punch down and round up; let rise again to double
bulk, about 1 1/2 hours. Shape into loaves; place on
greased pan. Grease top lightly; let rise again to double
bulk. Bake in hot oven, 400° F., for 40-50 minutes.
Yield: 2 pound loaves.

BRAIDED WHITE BREAD

1 pkg. dry yeast
1/2 c. warm water, 105°
   to 115°
1/3 c. sugar
2 tsp. salt

1 egg, well beaten
3 Tbsp. salad oil
6-7 c. all-purpose flour,
   divided

Combine yeast, warm water, sugar, salt and egg in a
large bowl; set aside for 5 minutes. Gradually add 3 cups
flour; beat well. Add salad oil gradually. Add 3 to 4 cups
flour to form a stiff dough. Turn dough out on a floured
surface; knead until smooth and elastic, 5 to 8 minutes.
Place in a well greased bowl, turning to grease top. Cover;
let rise in a warm, 85°, place, free from draft, for 1 1/2 to 2
hours or until double in bulk. Punch dough down; divide
into thirds. Shape each part into a 14 to 16 inch rope.
Place ropes on a greased baking sheet. Firmly pinch ends
together at one end to seal. Place right rope over center
rope to center, as in braiding. Pinch ends to seal when
braided. Cover; let rise in a warm place, free from draft,
until double in bulk. Bake at 350° for 20 to 25 minutes or
until lightly browned. Makes 1 large loaf or 2 small loaves.

Betty Finchum
Morristown Council

SWEET BRAIDED BREAD

2 pkg. active dried yeast
1/2 c. warm water
1 tsp. sugar
3 eggs
1/2 c. sugar
1 1/2 c. warm water
1/2 c. vegetable oil

1 1/2 tsp. salt
9 c. flour (used in varying
   amounts)
2 1/2 c. raisins (optional)
2 eggs, beaten with 2 Tbsp.
   water
Sesame or poppy seeds

Combine the yeast, water and sugar; set aside. Beat the eggs with sugar; add the warm water, oil and salt. Blend in the yeast mixture; beat well. Using 5 cups flour, add 1 cup at a time, beating well after each addition; the dough will be sticky. If raisins are used, add them now. Add 2 more cups of flour, beating well, until the dough leaves sides of bowl. Place the dough on a surface onto which you have shaken an additional 2 cups of flour and knead until almost all the flour is absorbed into batter. Return to bowl; cover with a towel and let rise until double in bulk, usually 1 hour in unheated oven with door closed or 2 hours on counter top). Punch down. *Divide the dough into 3 parts and divide each part into 3 parts again for braiding. Braid on a greased and floured cookie sheet; cover with a towel and let rise until double in size, 1 1/2 to 2 hours. Preheat oven to 400°. Before baking, brush with the egg-water mixture and seeds. Bake for 15 minutes; tap the loaves, which should have a hollow sound. If not, then bake 5 more minutes. Cool on a wire rack. Makes 3 loaves. This bread freezes well.

*Or, divide into 8 equal pieces. On lightly floured board, roll each piece into a rope about 20 inches long. Braid 3 ropes in standard braid; place on buttered baking pan. Braid 3 more ropes and place alongside first braid, about 1 1/2 inches away. Braid remaining 2 ropes; place in the center on top of braided sections. Cover with towel; let rise another hour. Bake in 375° oven for 45-60 minutes.

Rick Ammons
Harpeth Council

CARROT BREAD

1 c. sugar
3/4 c. vegetable oil
2 beaten eggs
1 1/2 c. flour
1 tsp. soda

1/2 tsp. salt
1 tsp. cinnamon
1 c. grated carrots
1 c. chopped pecans

Mix sugar, oil and eggs. Sift in flour, soda, salt and cinnamon. Add grated carrots and nuts. Carrots may be grated in a blender. Pour in floured, ungreased loaf pan, 9x5x3 inches. Bake at 325° for 1 hour or until done; cool. May be frozen. Makes 1 loaf.

Patsy Carter
Harpeth Council

BIG MAMA'S CORN BREAD

2 c. self-rising corn meal
1/2 c. flour (plain or self-
   rising, doesn't matter)

2 c. buttermilk
1 tsp. baking soda
2 or 3 Tbsp. bacon grease

Turn on oven to 450°. Rub iron skillet with bacon grease; place in oven to heat while mixing corn bread. Place all ingredients in mixing bowl; stir well. Pour into heated skillet and bake about 25 minutes or until sides look brown and crispy.

Kay Boswell
Andrew Jackson Council

CORN BREAD

1 1/4 c. all-purpose flour,
   sifted
1/4 c. sugar
3 tsp. baking powder
1 tsp. salt

1 c. corn meal (plain)
2 eggs
1 c. buttermilk
2 Tbsp. vegetable oil

Heat oven to 425°. Grease iron skillet with shortening. Sift flour, sugar, baking powder and salt together. Stir corn meal into dry ingredients. Place eggs, milk and oil in bowl; blend. Add dry ingredients to egg mixture; stir until dry ingredients are just moistened. Pour batter into hot skillet. Bake 20 to 25 minutes.

Mary Crabtree
Knoxville Council

LITTLE BILL'S COWBOY CORN BREAD

1 c. corn meal
2 eggs
1 c. milk
1/2 tsp. soda
3/4 tsp. salt
2 Tbsp. bacon drippings

1 (8 3/4 oz.) can cream style
   corn
1 lb. ground meat
1 onion, chopped
4 jalapeno peppers, chopped
1/2 lb. Cheddar cheese

Mix corn meal, eggs, milk, soda, salt, corn and bacon drippings; set aside. Saute meat, onion and peppers. Pour 1/2 of corn meal batter into greased casserole (preferably square or rectangular). Add meat mixture; sprinkle with cheese. Pour remaining batter on top. Bake for 45 minutes in preheated 350° oven.

Lena P. Paschall
Jackson Council

MOM'S CORN BREAD

1 1/2 c. white corn meal	1 egg
3 Tbsp. flour	2 c. buttermilk
1 tsp. salt	2 Tbsp. melted shortening
1 tsp. soda	

Stir all dry ingredients into a large bowl. Add egg and buttermilk until combined. Melt shortening in a skillet; add to batter and stir. Pour batter into hot skillet. Bake at 450° for 20 to 25 minutes.

Tricia Owens
Harpeth Council

NO FAT ADDED CORN BREAD

1/2 c. all-purpose flour	1/2 tsp. salt
1/2 c. white or yellow corn meal	1 c. skim milk
3 tsp. baking powder	1 large egg

Stir flour, corn meal, baking powder and salt together. In another bowl, beat milk and egg together. Combine ingredients; stir just until blended. Turn into a nonstick round or square 8 inch cake pan, which has been sprayed with cooking spray. Bake in a preheated 400° oven for about 20 minutes, or until a knife inserted in the center comes out clean. Cut into wedges or squares to serve. Serve warm or lightly toasted. Makes 9 servings, 70 calories each.

Ruth L. Cole
Harpeth Council

PRISSY'S CORN BREAD

1 1/2 c. self-rising corn
  meal
2 eggs
3/4 c. oil

8 oz. sour cream
1 c. yellow creamed corn
1/2 tsp. salt
1 chopped onion

Mix ingredients in a large bowl. Pour into casserole dish or preheated oiled skillet. Bake at 350° for 35 minutes. Let cool for 10-15 minutes before serving.

Ms. Kendall Clark
Memphis Council

SOUR CREAM CORN BREAD

Mix:
8 oz. sour cream
2 eggs
1 c. corn meal

1 (16 oz.) can cream style
  corn
1 small grated onion

Mix all ingredients and pour into baking dish, 8x10 inches, with 1 stick melted margarine. Bake 25-30 minutes at 350°.

Pat Steinke
Knox Council

SOUR CREAM CORN BREAD

2 c. self-rising corn meal
2 eggs, well beaten
1 (8 oz.) ctn. sour cream

1 small (8 1/4 oz.) can kernel
  corn
1/2 c. Wesson oil or cooking
  oil

Mix well. Bake in greased pan, stick pan or muffin rings. Bake at 400° for 20 minutes or till brown.

Pattie Carpenter
Nashville Council

SOUR CREAM CORN BREAD

1 c. self-rising meal
2 eggs

8 oz. sour cream
8 oz. cream style corn

Stir and put ingredients in frying pan with a little hot grease in bottom of pan. Bake at 450° for 30 minutes.

Mrs. Adelene Queenan
Harpeth Council

CORN CAKES

2 c. cooked whole kernel
  corn (canned or fresh),
  drained
1/4 c. finely chopped onion
1 c. milk

1 egg, beaten
1 1/2 c. flour
2 tsp. baking powder
3/4 tsp. salt

Combine corn, onion and milk with beaten egg. In a separate bowl, combine flour, baking powder and salt. Add corn mixture to flour mixture; stir just enough to moisten. Drop by 1/4 cupfuls on a lightly greased griddle and fry on both sides until golden brown.

Butch Cooper
Harpeth Council

SCALDED CORN CAKES

1 pt. water
11 oz. plain corn meal

1 tsp. salt

Bring water to a boil; gradually mix meal with water. Set in refrigerator for 20 minutes. Deep fry at 350° for approximately 5 minutes, or until golden brown (skillet with 1 inch of fat). Makes 18 two ounce cakes.

Judy Gibson
Harpeth Council

SCALDED CORN CAKES

1 tsp. salt
1 pt. boiling water

1 1/4 c. plain corn meal
Shortening for frying

Add salt to boiling water; gradually sift in the meal. Cool until firm. Shape into balls or patties; fry in 1 inch fat until golden brown, about 5 minutes. Drain and serve hot. Makes 18 corn cakes.

Joyce Mattice
Harpeth Council

1489-81

CORN LIGHT BREAD

2 1/2 c. corn meal	1/2 c. sugar
1 c. flour	1/4 c. melted shortening
1/2 tsp. salt	2 c. buttermilk
1 tsp. soda	1/2 c. sweet milk

Sift together all dry ingredients. Add melted shortening. Add milk and stir just enough to mix. Pour into well greased loaf pan. Bake at 350° for 1 hour.

J.C. Mallard
Nashville Council

CORN LIGHT BREAD

2 c. meal (plain)	1/2 tsp. salt
1/2 c. flour	1/2 tsp. soda
2 c. buttermilk	1/2 c. sugar
1/2 c. bacon grease	1 small egg

Mix dry ingredients; add milk and egg. Pour fat over mixture. Bake at 350°.

Janice Moore
Harpeth Council

EASY CORN LITE BREAD

2 c. plain corn meal	1 tsp. salt
1/2 c. flour	1 tsp. baking powder
3/4 c. sugar	1/2 tsp. baking soda

Mix all dry ingredients well. Add 2 cups buttermilk; stir well. Melt about 3 tablespoons shortening in loaf pan, which has been lined with brown paper (bottom only). After the shortening has soaked through the paper, pour mixture into the pan. Bake at 350° for about 1 hour. Let cool for about 5 minutes before removing from pan.

Vera S. Beard
Jackson Council

GRANNY'S CORN LIGHT BREAD

4 c. plain corn meal
1/2 c. plain flour
3/4 c. sugar
1 tsp. soda

1 tsp. dry yeast
1 tsp. salt
2 c. buttermilk
2 or 3 Tbsp. shortening

Sift together dry ingredients; add buttermilk and mix thoroughly. Melt shortening in hot oven of 375° (in loaf pan). After melting, make sure sides of the pan are covered lightly with shortening. Pour remaining shortening into prepared ingredients and mix. Bake 55 minutes or until golden brown. Especially good with barbequed meats.

Cheryl Enoch
Harpeth Council

JALAPENO HOT CORN BREAD

3 c. self-rising meal
1 small can hot El Paso
  chili peppers
2 c. milk
3 eggs, beaten
1/2 tsp. salt
1/2 tsp. baking powder

2 Tbsp. sugar
1/2 c. Wesson oil
1 1/2 c. grated Cheddar
  cheese
1 bunch green onions,
  chopped
1 small can cream corn

In mixing bowl, whip eggs and milk together; add all liquid ingredients. Add meal, to which baking powder, salt and sugar have been added; mix well. Stir in grated cheese. Pour into oiled pan. Bake at 350° for about 45 minutes. This bread freezes well. Cut into squares; wrap in foil to freeze.

Mrs. George Price
Knoxville Council

CATHRINE'S MEXICAN CORN BREAD

1 1/2 c. self-rising meal
3 beaten eggs
1 c. cream style corn
2/3 c. oil

1 c. buttermilk
1 hot pepper, chopped
1/2 large sweet pepper,
  chopped
1 c. sharp cheese, grated

1489-81

Mix all ingredients until well mixed. Bake at 375°
until golden brown.

Zoeritz Proctor
Nashboro Council

MEXICAN CORN BREAD

Mix and set aside:

1 c. yellow corn meal
1 1/4 c. flour
2 eggs
1 c. sweet milk

1/2 tsp. soda
3/4 tsp. salt
1/2 c. bacon drippings
1 (No. 303) can cream style
  corn

Prepare:

1 lb. hamburger, sauteed
  and drained
1 large onion, chopped

1/2 lb. sharp cheese, grated
1 can jalapeno peppers

Grease two 8 inch skillets; heat. Pour 1/2 of batter in
skillets, then sprinkle 1/4 of cheese, 1/4 meat, 1/4 onion
and repeat this process until all is used. Add peppers last.
Pour remaining batter on top and bake at 350° for 45 to 50
minutes.

Betty Coleman
Green Hills Council

MEXICAN CORN BREAD

2 c. self-rising corn meal
2 eggs
1 medium onion, chopped
1/4 tsp. garlic salt
1/3 c. bacon drippings

3/4 c. milk
1 small can cream style corn
3 or 4 jalapeno peppers,
  finely chopped
1 c. grated Cheddar cheese

Mix all ingredients, except cheese. Pour 1/2 the mixture into 12 inch greased pan or skillet. Sprinkle on cheese.
Pour in remaining mixture. Bake at 350° for 45 minutes or
until brown.

Evalyn Morris
Harpeth Council

MEXICAN CORN BREAD

3 c. self-rising corn meal
2 1/2 c. sweet milk
3 eggs, well beaten
1 c. Cheddar cheese, grated
1 large onion, chopped

1/2 c. diced pimento
1/2 c. jalapeno pepper, chopped
1 regular can cream style corn
2 Tbsp. sugar

Combine all ingredients in order given; blend well. Pour in well greased 13x9x2 inch pan. Bake at 400° for 30-45 minutes.

Martha Stovall
Nashboro Council

MEXICAN CORN BREAD

8 1/2 oz. can cream corn
1 c. sour cream
2 eggs
3/4 c. salad oil

1 c. self-rising corn meal
2 tsp. baking powder
1/4 c. flour
1 c. grated Cheddar cheese

Mix eggs, sour cream, corn and oil well. Mix dry ingredients, then blend in eggs, sour cream, corn and oil mixture. Have a black skillet hot. Pour half the batter in, then the cheese, then the other half of the batter. Bake at 400° for 30 minutes.

Dianne Hunter
Harpeth Council

MEXICAN CORN BREAD

2 c. self-rising corn meal
2/3 c. oil
3 eggs
1 c. buttermilk
1/2 tsp. soda
1/4 c. sugar

1 small onion, chopped
1 small bell pepper, chopped
3/4 tsp. (hot) crushed red pepper
1 c. grated cheese
1 c. whole kernel corn

Beat eggs; add oil, meal, soda, buttermilk and all other ingredients. Mix well. Pour in a hot greased pan and bake like regular corn bread until done. Bake 40 minutes at 400°.

Maxine Scott
East Memphis Council

1489-81

CRANBERRY BANANA LOAF

1 (16 oz.) can cranberry jelly sauce
1 medium apple, pared and grated
2 medium bananas, mashed
1/3 c. sifted confectioners sugar
1 tsp. vanilla
1/4 c. chopped nuts
1 c. whipping cream, whipped

Beat cranberry sauce until smooth; stir in grated apple. Pour into 11 x 7 x 1 1/2 inch pan. Fold bananas, sugar, vanilla and half the nuts into whipped cream. Spread over cranberry sauce layer. Sprinkle with remaining nuts. Freeze until firm. Let stand at room temperature before serving. Cut into squares. Serves 8.

Charles L. Hare
Andrew Jackson Council

CRANBERRY BREAD

2 c. whole wheat flour
2 c. white flour
1 Tbsp. baking powder
1 tsp. baking soda
1 tsp. salt
1/2 tsp. cinnamon
1/4 tsp. nutmeg
1 c. brown sugar
1 c. chopped nuts
1 c. white sugar
1/2 c. butter
1 Tbsp. grated orange rind
1 1/2 c. orange juice
2 eggs
2 c. fresh cranberries, coarsely chopped
2/3 c. raisins

Sift dry ingredients together; cut in butter until mixture resembles coarse meal. Combine orange rind, orange juice and eggs; add to dry ingredients, mixing just to moisten. Fold in berries, nuts and raisins. Turn into two greased and floured 9x5 inch loaf pans. Bake at 350° for 55 to 60 minutes; cool. Makes 2 loaves. Bread slices better the next day.

Barbara Harris
Harpeth Council

DILLY BREAD

1 pkg. dry yeast
1/4 c. warm water
1 c. creamed cottage cheese, heated to lukewarm
2 Tbsp. sugar
1 Tbsp. instant minced onion
1 Tbsp. butter or margarine
2 tsp. dill seed

1 tsp. salt   1/4 tsp. soda
1 egg, unbeaten   2 1/4 - 2 1/2 c. flour (plain)

1. Soften yeast in water; let stand 5 minutes. Add sugar. 2. Combine all ingredients, except flour, in bowl. 3. Add flour to form a stiff dough, beating well after each addition; knead 5 minutes. 4. Let rise in a warm place 1 hour. 5. Stir down dough; turn into well greased casserole round, 1 1/2 - 2 quarts. Let rise in warm place, 30 minutes. 6. Bake at 325° for 40-50 minutes. Brush with butter; sprinkle with salt.

Betty Finchum
Morristown Council

CRESCENT ROLL STICKS

1 pkg. refrigerated   Poppy seed
  crescent rolls   Garlic salt
Parmesan cheese   Celery seed
Onion flakes   Sesame seed

Form a rectangle by pressing 2 triangular sections of crescent roll together. Sprinkle with your favorite combination of ingredients listed above. Pat lightly and cut each rectangle into 14 small sticks. Place on ungreased sheet and bake at 350° for 15 minutes or until evenly browned. Place in warm place until serving time. These are especially good with salads; use as you would crackers. Yield: 56 sticks.

Carolyn Mitchell
Memphis Downtown Council

MRS. DAVENPORT'S REAL FRENCH BREAD

1 pkg. yeast   1 Tbsp. sugar
2 c. water   2 tsp. salt
4 c. all-purpose flour

Dissolve yeast in 1 cup lukewarm water. While yeast softens, mix flour, sugar and salt together in a large bowl, then stir in the dissolved yeast. Add just enough of the second cup of water to hold dough together. Mix until you have a soft, sticky dough. Cover with a clean cloth; set bowl in a warm spot in your kitchen. Let rise until double, 2-4 hours. When dough is high and spongy, punch it down with your fist and give it a good sound beating with your hands. Divide bread in 2 parts; place each part in a greased 6 inch round baking dish (or use 2 loaf pans). Cover again with cloth; let rise until it reaches top of baking dish. At this point, start your oven at 400° F. Bake 1 hour. Brush top of bread with butter for a softer crust. Let cool on side.

Nancy Bess Lord
Harpeth Council

GRAPE-NUT BREAD

1/2 c. Grape-Nuts cereal
1 c. buttermilk
1/2 tsp. soda
1/2 tsp. salt

1 c. sugar
2 c. flour
3 eggs

Soak the Grape-Nuts cereal in the buttermilk for 10 minutes. Combine other ingredients; beat well. Let stand 10-15 minutes before putting in oven. Bake 40 minutes at 375° in loaf pan.

Kathleen Wagner
Green Hills Council

GREEN ONION FRENCH BREAD

2 loaves French bread
1 c. melted margarine

2 Tbsp. parsley flakes
3/4 c. chopped green onions

Slice bread lengthwise almost through loaf, leaving one side like a hinge. Combine margarine, parsley and onion. Spoon mixture inside loaves; wrap in heavy duty aluminum foil. Place on grill until well heated. Serves 8.

Mary Crabtree
Knoxville Council

LEMON BREAD

1/2 c. shortening
1 c. sugar
2 eggs, slightly beaten
1 1/4 c. flour
1 tsp. baking powder
1/4 tsp. salt

1/2 c. milk
1/2 c. finely chopped walnuts
    or pecans
Grated rind and juice of 1
    lemon
1/4 c. sugar

222

Cream together the shortening and sugar; stir in the slightly beaten eggs. Sift together the flour, baking powder and salt. Stir this mixture into the creamed mixture alternately with the milk. Add the walnuts and grated lemon rind. Bake at 350° for about 1 hour in a 9x5 inch loaf pan. Remove the bread from the oven and pierce surface with a small skewer or toothpick to make small holes. Combine the sugar and lemon juice; pour over hot bread very slowly.

Patsy Carter
Harpeth Council

MONKEY BREAD

1 c. buttermilk	1/2 tsp. soda
1 stick oleo	1/4 c. sugar
1 pkg. dry yeast	2 1/2 c. plain flour
1 tsp. salt	

Combine yeast with 1/3 of the flour and all other ingredients (dry). Heat buttermilk and oleo to 120°-130°. Pour over dry ingredients; mix on medium speed of electric mixer for approximately 2 minutes. Add 1/2 cup flour; mix on high speed for 2 minutes. Stir in remaining flour and more if needed to knead. Knead about 5 minutes. Let rise until double, about 1 hour, in a warm, dry place. Turn out on floured surface and roll about 1/4 inch thick. Cut into oval 2 inch pieces; dip in melted butter. Layer in a Bundt pan or solid bottomed angel food cake pan; let rise until doubled again. Bake at 400° for 30 minutes. Turn out onto a plate; pull apart individual pieces.

Cheryl V. Alderson
Columbia Council

MY FAVORITE BREAD

2 1/2 tsp. salt	1 Tbsp. yeast (1 pkg. or 1
Oil	cake compressed)
2 Tbsp. honey	3 Tbsp. lukewarm water
2 c. skim milk or	6 c. sifted whole wheat flour
reconstituted non-fat	or unbleached white flour
dry milk, scalded	Melted butter (optional)

Place the salt, 3 tablespoons oil and the honey in a bowl. Pour the milk over all; cool to lukewarm. Dissolve the yeast in the lukewarm; add to the cooled milk mixture. Stir in enough flour to make a stiff dough. Turn onto a floured board; knead for 10 minutes or until dough is smooth and elastic. It will lose its stickiness as it is kneaded. Place dough in a clean, oiled bowl; brush top lightly with oil. Cover; set in a warm place to rise until doubled in bulk, about 2 hours. (When dough is pressed lightly with a finger, an impression will remain.) Punch dough down; fold and turn so that smooth side is on top. Let rise again until almost doubled in bulk, about 30 minutes. Divide into 2 pieces; let rest, covered, with a cloth or bowl upside down, on the board for 10 minutes. Roll or pat each piece of dough until it is twice the size of an 8 1/2 x 4 1/2 inch loaf pan. Fold in the sides, then the edges. Roll tightly into a loaf shape and set, seam side down, in pans. Cover pans; let dough rise until doubled in bulk, about 1 hour. Preheat the oven to 400°. Bake bread 35 to 45 minutes or until it sounds hollow when tapped on the bottom. Cool on a rack. Brush with melted butter if a soft crust is desired. Yield: 2 loaves.

Nancy Bess Lord
Harpeth Council

OATMEAL NUT BREAD

2 buttered (8 1/2 x 4 1/2 x 2 1/2 inch) loaf pans
2 eggs
1 c. sugar
2 c. buttermilk
2/3 c. dark molasses
1 tsp. salt
3 c. sifted regular all-purpose flour
1 1/2 c. quick cooking oats
1 1/2 c. chopped nuts
1 1/2 c. chopped dates
1 tsp. baking powder
2 tsp. baking soda

In mixing bowl, beat eggs until light. Gradually add sugar, beating constantly. Blend in buttermilk and molasses. Sift together flour, baking soda, baking powder and salt. Gradually add to buttermilk mixture, beating only until blended. Stir in rolled oats, nuts and dates, just enough to combine evenly. Divide into pans. Bake 50 to 60 minutes. Turn out of pans onto wire rack to cool. Slices better second day.

Peggy Burr
Harpeth Council

PIZZA BREAD

2 lb. Italian sausage or
   ground beef
2 small cans tomato paste
1 large can mushrooms,
   undrained
Mozzarella cheese, grated

2 Tbsp. Parmesan cheese
1 Tbsp. Worcestershire sauce
1 small can tomato sauce
2 Tbsp. brown sugar
French bread or Sunbeam
   barbeque bread

Fry meat and drain. Mix remaining ingredients, except cheeses and bread; simmer for 1 1/2 to 2 hours until thick. Slice bread 1/2 inch thick and spoon 1 tablespoon of sauce on each slice. Sprinkle with grated Parmesan and Mozzarella cheeses. Place under preheated broiler; broil for 2 or 3 minutes. Makes enough sauce for 2 loaves of bread.

Barbara Harris
Harpeth Council

PIZZA BREAD

2 lb. ground beef
2 small cans tomato paste
1 small can tomato sauce
2 Tbsp. brown sugar

1 large can mushrooms, not
   drained
1 tsp. Worcestershire sauce
2 Tbsp. Parmesan cheese

Brown ground beef; drain. Add remaining ingredients. Place approximately 2 heaping tablespoons of meat mix on (barbeque) bread slice. Top with Mozzarella cheese. Place in 350° oven until cheese melts.

Debbie Bullock
Harpeth Council

PUMPKIN BREAD

4 eggs, beaten
3 1/2 c. flour, sifted before
   measuring (plain flour)
3 c. sugar
1 c. oil
1/2 c. water

2 tsp. soda
1 1/2 tsp. nutmeg
1 1/2 tsp. salt
2 c. pumpkin
Nuts
Raisins

Grease eight No. 2 cans. Fill a little over half full. Bake at 350° for 1 hour. Cool about 10 minutes before taking out of can. Slice and spread with cream cheese and orange marmalade.

Ruth and Deborah Cole
Harpeth Council

PUMPKIN BREAD

2 c. pumpkin
4 eggs
3 c. sugar
3 1/2 c. flour
1 c. oil
2/3 c. water

1 1/2 tsp. salt
1 1/2 tsp. cinnamon
2 tsp. soda
1 c. pecans
1/2 tsp. cloves
1/2 tsp. nutmeg

Mix pumpkin, eggs, water and oil; add dry ingredients. Bake 1 hour in four 1 pound coffee cans, well greased, at 350°. Wait 10 minutes to remove.

Mrs. Harold (Nancy) Turner
Columbia Council

QUICK CHEESE BREAD

2 eggs
3/4 c. water
2 (5 1/2 oz.) pkg. Bix Mix

2 tsp. dry mustard
1 1/2 c. grated Cheddar
  cheese
2 Tbsp. melted butter

Heat oven to 350°. Grease an 8 1/2 x 4 1/2 x 2 1/2 inch loaf pan. Beat eggs in large bowl; stir in water. Add Bix Mix and beat. Add mustard and 1 cup cheese; mix thoroughly. Turn batter into pan; sprinkle with remaining cheese and dot with melted butter. Bake for 45 minutes. Cool in pan 15 minutes. Remove and cool on rack before slicing.

Paula Akin
Green Hills Council

QUICK LIGHT BREAD

1 c. boiling water
1/2 tsp. salt
2 Tbsp. shortening
1/4 c. sugar
1/4 c. lukewarm water

1 tsp. sugar
1 pkg. dry yeast
4 c. flour
1 egg

Mix first 4 ingredients; cool to lukewarm. Dissolve yeast in 1/4 cup lukewarm water and 1 teaspoon sugar. Combine mixture. Add egg and 2 cups flour. Beat well. Add remaining flour until moistened. Don't knead. Let rise until double in bulk, about 1 hour. Make into rolls or 2 loaves. Place in a warm place for about 1 hour to rise. Bake for 15-20 minutes for rolls, or 25-30 minutes for loaves in a 425° oven.

Katrina Carter
Harpeth Council

RYE   BREAD

2 1/2 c. rye flour
2 pkg. dry yeast
1/2 c. firmly packed brown
   sugar
1 Tbsp. salt
2 c. water

1/4 c. molasses
1/4 c. margarine
3 1/2 - 4 c. unbleached or
   all-purpose flour
1/4 c. caraway seed or Bran
   Buds (optional)

Lightly spoon rye flour into measuring cup; level off. Combine flour, yeast, brown sugar and salt in large mixing bowl; blend. Heat in saucepan over low heat until very warm the water, molasses and margarine. Add to flour mixture. Blend at low speed till moist; beat at medium speed 2 minutes. Stir in all-purpose flour to form a sticky dough. Knead dough, adding caraway seeds and additional flour (1/2 - 1 1/2 cups) till dough is smooth and no longer sticky, about 5 minutes. Place dough in greased bowl; turn over, then cover. Let rise in warm place until almost double in size, about 45 minutes. Grease 2 loaf pans or large cookie sheet. Punch down dough; divide into 2 parts. Shape for loaf pans, round loaves or each half will make six 7x3 inch hoagie buns. Cover; let rise till double in size in warm place. Bake at 375° for 25-30 minutes until loaf sounds hollow when tapped. Remove from pan; rub with additional margarine.

Tip: Bread will rise in allotted time if placed in electric oven with light on or in gas oven with pilot light on.

Mrs. James D. Cowan
Knoxville Council

SOUTHERN SPOONBREAD

1 1/3 tsp. sugar	3 eggs, well beaten
1 1/2 tsp. salt	1 Tbsp. baking powder
1 c. corn meal	1 1/3 c. milk
1 1/3 c. boiling water	

Preheat oven to 350°. Grease 2 quart casserole. Mix sugar and salt with corn meal; blend well. Pour boiling water over corn meal, stirring constantly; cool. Beat eggs until foamy. Add beaten eggs and baking powder to mixture; add milk. Pour mixture into greased casserole and dot with butter. Place casserole in shallow pan of hot water. Bake about 35 minutes.

Opal Pyle
Nashboro Council

SPOON BREAD

1 egg, beaten	2 c. warm water
1 pkg. yeast	1/4 c. sugar
4 c. self-rising flour	1 1/2 sticks butter, melted

Dissolve yeast in water; stir. Add flour, eggs, sugar and butter; stir until well mixed. Spoon into greased muffin pans. Bake at 350° for 20 minutes. Put in large covered bowl in the refrigerator if you have dough left over.

Katrina Carter
Harpeth Council

STRAWBERRY BREAD

1/8 c. margarine	1/4 tsp. lemon flavoring
1/2 tsp. baking soda	1/2 c. sour cream
1 1/2 c. sugar	1/2 tsp. salt
1/2 c. chopped nuts	4 eggs
1 tsp. vanilla	3 c. plain flour
	1 c. strawberry jam

Mix margarine, sugar, vanilla, salt and lemon flavoring. Add eggs one at a time, beating well. Dissolve baking soda in sour cream; add to mixture. Fold in flour, nuts and jam. Mix well; pour into well greased pans. Use 2 large pans or 4 small ones. Bake bread for 40 minutes at 350°; freezes well.

Peggy Burr
Harpeth Council

STRAWBERRY BREAD

3 c. flour
2 c. sugar
3 tsp. cinnamon
1 tsp. soda
1 c. pecans, chopped

1 (10 oz.) pkg. frozen
   strawberries, thawed
1 tsp. salt
4 eggs, beaten
1 1/4 c. oil

Mix ingredients. Grease and flour pans. Bake at 325° for 1 hour. Makes 2 loaves.

Marian Molteni
Harpeth Council

SWEET POTATO BREAD

1 c. flour
1 tsp. baking powder
Pinch of salt
2 Tbsp. shortening
1 c. (or more) grated sweet
   potato

1 egg
1/2 c. sugar
Cinnamon, nutmeg and
   vanilla
Enough milk for thick batter

Cut shortening into flour, baking powder, salt and sugar. Add egg, flavorings and milk; this batter should be very thick. Mix in grated potato and spread evenly in well greased 9 inch square pan (or small baking dish). Bake in 350° oven until lightly brown on top and center springs back when touched. Serve warm with butter in center of each slice.

Bob and Nora Chandler
Harpeth Council

YEAST BREAD

1 pkg. dry yeast
1/4 c. lukewarm water
1/2 c. sugar
1 c. water

1 c. milk
1/2 c. lard
6 c. sifted flour
1/2 tsp. salt

Dissolve yeast in 1/4 cup lukewarm water. When yeast is thoroughly dissolved, add 1/2 cup sugar; let set a while. Mix water and milk; heat to lukewarm. Put 3 cups of flour in large bowl; mix in 1/2 teaspoon salt and lard. Mix until flour is crumbly; add liquid. Mix and work as biscuits. Add flour until the mixture forms a soft dough. Let rise until double in bulk; work down. Divide dough and put in 2 loaf pans that have been greased. Let rise to top of pan. Bake in oven at 350° until well browned. (Will rise faster if covered with foil.)

Frances McLaughlin
Harpeth Council

SPICED ZUCCHINI BREAD

3 c. all-purpose flour
2 tsp. baking soda
1 tsp. salt
1/2 tsp. baking powder
1 1/2 tsp. ground cinnamon
3/4 c. finely chopped
  walnuts (or pecans)
3 eggs

2 c. sugar
1 c. vegetable oil
2 tsp. vanilla
2 c. coarsely shredded
  zucchini
1 (8 oz.) can crushed
  pineapple, well drained

Combine flour, baking soda, salt, baking powder, cinnamon and nuts; set aside. Beat eggs lightly in a large mixing bowl. Add sugar, oil and vanilla; beat until creamy. Stir in zucchini and pineapple. Add dry ingredients, stirring only until dry ingredients are moistened. Spoon batter into two well greased and floured 9x5x3 inch loaf pans. Bake for 1 1/2 hours at 325°. Cool 10 minutes before removing from pans. Turn out on wire rack to cool completely. Yields 2 loaves.

Bertice Spencer
Memphis Council

ZUCCHINI BREAD

1 c. salad oil
3 eggs, slightly beaten
2 c. sugar

2 c. grated new zucchini
2 tsp. vanilla extract

Mix the above ingredients together; blend well. Add:

3 c. self-rising flour
3 tsp. ground cinnamon

1 c. chopped nuts

Stir well, but do not beat. Spoon batter into two well greased 8 1/2 x 4 1/2 x 2 5/8 inch loaf pans. Bake at 325°

for 1 1/2 hours. Yields 2 loaves. Two cups grated zucchini is usually 1/2 of a large zucchini.

Dot Robinson
Harpeth Council

ZUCCHINI BREAD

3 c. plain flour
1 1/2 c. sugar
1 tsp. cinnamon
1 tsp. salt
1 tsp. baking powder
3/4 tsp. soda

2 c. shredded zucchini
2 tsp. vanilla
1 c. nuts (pecans)
1 c. raisins
1 c. oil
3 eggs

Mix dry ingredients with nuts, raisins and zucchini. Beat eggs with oil; pour over flour mixture and stir until moist. Add vanilla. Pour into 2 greased loaf pans and bake at 350° for 1 hour and 15 minutes. Cool in pan 30 minutes.

Mabel M. Wilson
Clarksville Council

ZUCCHINI BREAD

3 eggs
2 c. sugar
1 c. Mazola oil
2 c. grated zucchini
1 tsp. cinnamon

1 tsp. salt
1 tsp. soda
1/4 tsp. baking powder
3 c. flour
1 c. chopped pecans

Beat eggs until foamy; add other ingredients. Mix well. (I prefer to cream sugar and oil, then add beaten eggs. Next, add all dry ingredients that have been sifted together.) Pour batter into 2 greased and floured loaf pans and bake 1 hour at 350°. Test with toothpick. Cool in pan 10 minutes. Remove and finish cooling. Freezes real well.

Tillie T. Smith
Chattanooga Council

ZUCCHINI BREAD

1 c. oil
3 eggs
2 c. sugar
2 tsp. vanilla
1 tsp. baking powder
3 c. flour

1 tsp. salt
3 tsp. cinnamon
1/2 c. nuts
1 tsp. soda
2 c. grated raw zucchini
   (do not peel)

Mix in large pan. Pour into greased loaf pans. Bake 1 hour at 325°.

Jewell Hall
Memphis Downtown Council

ZUCCHINI BREAD

2 c. finely chopped zucchini
2 c. sugar
2 c. flour
1 tsp. baking soda
1/4 tsp. baking powder

1 c. chopped nuts (optional)
1 c. oil
2 tsp. vanilla
3 eggs, beaten
1 tsp. salt
1 tsp. cinnamon

Mix sugar and oil; add eggs and beat well. Add dry ingredients, then zucchini and nuts. Bake in tube pan at 325° for 1 hour. Let stand for 10 minutes after removing from oven.

Mrs. James D. Cowan
Knoxville Council

ZUCCHINI BREAD

3 eggs, beaten
2 c. sugar
1 c. vegetable oil
2 c. raw, grated, unpeeled
   zucchini
2 c. sifted flour

1 1/4 tsp. baking soda
1 tsp. salt
2 tsp. cinnamon
1/4 tsp. baking powder
2 tsp. vanilla
1 c. chopped pecans

Add sugar and oil to beaten eggs; mix well. Add zucchini. Sift dry ingredients; add to zucchini mixture. Mix well and add remaining ingredients. Bake 1 hour at 325°.

Judy Christopher
Harpeth Council

ZUCCHINI BREAD

3 eggs, well beaten
2 Tbsp. vanilla
1 c. oil
2 c. shredded zucchini
squash
3 c. flour
1 c. nuts, chopped

2 c. sugar
1 tsp. salt
1/4 tsp. baking powder
1 tsp. soda
1 tsp. cinnamon
1 c. dates, chopped

Beat eggs till light and fluffy; add sugar, vanilla and oil. Blend well; stir in grated zucchini. Sift together flour, baking powder, salt, soda and cinnamon. Blend with creamed mixture; stir in dates and nuts. Turn into two greased 9x5 inch loaf pans. Bake 1 hour at 350°; glass pans 325°.

Leola Holbert
Knoxville Council

ZUCCHINI BREAD

Mix well:
1 c. oil
1 1/4 c. brown sugar

1 c. white sugar

Add:
2 beaten eggs

2 c. grated zucchini

Sift together and add:

3 c. flour
1 1/4 tsp. baking powder
1 tsp. soda

1 Tbsp. cinnamon
1 tsp. vanilla
1 tsp. salt

We add 1 cup diced dates and 1 cup nuts or 1 cup coconut or 1 cup raisins. Bake 1 hour at 325°.

Tamera Spivey
Green Hills Council

ZUCCHINI-CHEDDAR BREAD

1 c. chopped onion
1/4 c. margarine or butter
2 1/2 c. Bisquick baking mix
1 Tbsp. snipped parsley

1/2 tsp. dried basil leaves
1/2 tsp. dried thyme leaves
1/4 c. milk
3 eggs

1489-81

1 1/2 c. shredded fresh zucchini	1 c. (about 4 oz.) shredded Cheddar cheese
	3/4 c. toasted, chopped almonds

Heat oven to 400°. Grease and flour round pan, 9 x 1 1/2 inches. Cook and stir onion in margarine until tender; cool slightly. Mix onion mixture, baking mix, parsley, basil, thyme, milk and eggs; beat vigorously 1 minute. Stir in remaining ingredients; spread in pan. Bake until wooden pick inserted in center comes out clean, about 40 minutes. Cool slightly; remove from pan.

High Altitude Directions (3500 to 6500 feet): Heat oven to 425°. Decrease baking mix to 2 cups and add 1/2 cup Gold Medal all-purpose flour. Increase milk to 1/3 cup. Bake about 35 minutes.

Frances Nevette
Harpeth Council

FLUFFY HOT CAKES

1 egg	1/2 tsp. salt
3/4 c. plus 2 Tbsp. milk	2 Tbsp. baking powder
2 Tbsp. melted shortening	2 Tbsp. sugar
1 c. flour	

Mix all together quickly. Cook on well greased, hot griddle.

Frances W. Gilliam
Columbia Council

CORN BREAD DRESSING FOR CHICKEN OR TURKEY

Many Southerners cook corn bread dressing separately from the roasting chicken or turkey; others stuff the bird with the mixture before roasting. This delicious dressing is typically used as stuffing; part, or all of it may be baked in a separate pan or dish. It is served with the roasted meat and giblet gravy.

6 c. corn bread crumbs	2 medium onions, finely chopped
6 cold biscuits or 6 slices toasted bread	1 tsp. black pepper
1/2 c. butter	3 hard cooked eggs
1 c. finely chopped celery	1-2 c. slivered almonds or roasted pecans (optional)
3 raw eggs, slightly beaten	

234

One of the following may be added:

1 c. cooked, diced chicken giblets

1 c. sliced mushrooms

1 c. chopped, drained oysters

1 tsp. or more pulverized sage (optional)

Pinch of thyme

2 or more c. chicken broth and pan drippings

Melt butter in heavy pan; add minced onion and celery. Saute until vegetables are soft but not brown. Combine crumbled corn bread and white bread or biscuits. Add onions, celery, seasoning and other ingredients, except liquid, to the bread mixture and stir/toss until well mixed. Pour on enough broth to moisten the corn bread (do not make soggy). Mix lightly and use for stuffing hen or turkey. Handle lightly; do not compact it. Allow space when stuffing poultry so mixture can swell. Extra dressing may be cooked separately in pones, mounds or spread 2 inches deep in a greased skillet or baking pan. Bake at 400° until lightly browned on top and cooked through.

Joyce Mattice
Harpeth Council

CORN BREAD DRESSING

1 large iron skillet of corn bread

6-8 pieces dry toast

3/4 c. chopped celery

1/2 c. chopped onion

1 egg

1 can cream of chicken soup

Water (as desired for moisture; fill from soup can)

Sage, as desired for taste

Cook celery and onion together until tender. Break corn bread and toast up in large bowl. Add celery and onion mixture and next 4 ingredients. After mixing, put into baking dish or pan and bake at 350° for 30 minutes or until done to your likeness.

Marianne Wright
Nashboro Council

MAMA MARIE'S DEE-LICIOUS DUMPLIN'S

3 c. plain flour

1 Tbsp. lard (not shortening)

Chicken broth (better with hen broth)

Boil chicken or hen until tender; reserve broth. Combine flour and lard; cut lard into flour with 2 knives until coarse. Add chicken broth gradually until dough forms. Remove from bowl and knead on lightly floured counter. Knead until dough becomes <u>very</u> tough, adding flour as needed to keep from sticking to counter. Roll out about 1/8 inch thick (will be very hard to roll out). Cut in 2 inch strips about 2 or 3 inches long. Drop into remaining boiling chicken broth. Cook about 30-45 minutes until tender, adding salt and pepper as desired.

Marie Bedwell
Clarksville Council

ROLLED DUMPLINGS

2 c. flour
3 Tbsp. shortening
1/3 - 1/2 c. water, meat
   stock or chicken broth

1 egg, beaten
1/2 tsp. baking powder
1/2 tsp. salt

Combine dry ingredients. Add beaten egg, shortening and liquid. Divide into 3 parts. Roll out very thin. Cut in small strips; drop in broth. Cook dumplings until tender. Makes about 6 servings. Use in meat stock or chicken broth.

Joyce Mattice
Harpeth Council

HUSH PUPPIES

3 eggs
2 tsp. baking powder
1/2 tsp. salt
2 Tbsp. flour
1 Tbsp. melted shortening

1 tsp. onion juice or minced
   onion
1 1/2 c. milk
Corn meal to make stiff batter

Beat eggs and add the liquid. Add remaining ingredients and drop from a spoon into deep, but not too hot, fat used in frying fish.

Carolyn Mitchell
Memphis Downtown Council

HUSH PUPPIES

1 c. corn meal
1 Tbsp. flour
1 1/2 tsp. double-acting
  baking powder
1/2 tsp. salt
1/4 tsp. pepper

1 large mild onion, finely
  chopped
1 egg
1/2 - 3/4 c. milk
Salad oil for frying

In medium bowl, combine corn meal, flour, baking powder, salt and pepper. Add onion and egg; mix and beat well. Add milk, a little at a time, until batter is smooth. In saucepan, heat at least 2 inches of oil to 375° F. on deep fat thermometer. Drop batter from the side of a tablespoon into hot oil; fry until golden brown. Remove with slotted spoon; drain on paper towels. Serve immediately. Makes 10 hush puppies, about 85 calories each.

Leslie Stephens
Harpeth Council

MUFFINS

2 c. plain flour
2 tsp. baking powder
2 Tbsp. sugar
1/2 tsp. salt

1 well beaten egg
1 c. milk
4 Tbsp. melted butter or
  shortening

Sift flour once; measure and add baking powder, sugar and salt. Sift again. Combine egg, milk and butter; add to flour gradually, beating only enough to blend ingredients. Bake in greased muffin pan in hot oven, 425°, for 30 minutes. Makes 12 muffins.

Jane York
Harpeth Council

BEER MUFFINS

4 c. Bisquick mix
2 Tbsp. sugar

2 eggs
1 can beer

Heat oven to 400°. Grease bottoms of 18 medium muffin cups. Mix ingredients; beat 30 seconds. Fill muffin cups 2/3 full. Bake 15 minutes until golden brown.

Jewell Mercer
Nashville Council

BRAN MUFFINS

1 (15 oz.) box Kellogg's
  Raisin Bran
5 c. plain flour
2 tsp. salt
4 eggs, beaten

4 tsp. soda
1 c. oil
1 qt. buttermilk
3 c. sugar

Mix well. Fill muffin pans about 2/3 full. Bake at 375°-400° for 15 to 20 minutes. (Batter may be stored in refrigerator as long as 6 weeks.)

Bessie Crosby
Harpeth Council

CORN MUFFINS

2 whole eggs
1 small ctn. sour cream
1/2 c. corn oil

1 small can cream style corn
1 c. self-rising corn meal
Sugar and salt to taste

Mix above ingredients and bake in 350° oven for 15 to 20 minutes.

Judy Christopher
Harpeth Council

CORN MEAL MUFFINS

1/2 c. sifted flour
1 Tbsp. sugar
1 tsp. baking powder
3/4 tsp. salt

1 1/2 c. yellow corn meal
1 egg, beaten
1/4 c. butter, melted
1 c. milk

Combine flour, sugar, baking powder, salt and corn meal. Make well in center and add remaining ingredients; stir briskly. Pour into greased muffin tins and bake in hot oven, 450°, for 15-20 minutes.

Norma S. Watson
Memphis Council

HONEY WHEAT MUFFINS

1 c. all-purpose flour
1/2 c. whole wheat flour
2 tsp. baking powder
1/2 tsp. salt
1 beaten egg

1/2 c. milk
1/2 c. honey
1/4 c. cooking oil
1/2 tsp. finely shredded
lemon peel

In a bowl, stir together flours, baking powder and salt. Make a well in center of dry ingredients. Combine egg, milk, honey, oil and lemon peel all at once to dry ingredients; stir until just moistened. Batter should be lumpy. Fill greased or paper baking cup lined muffin tins 2/3 full. Bake at 375° for 20 minutes. Remove from pan and cool slightly. Makes 10.

Peggy Burr
Harpeth Council

MAYONNAISE MUFFINS

1 c. self-rising flour
3 Tbsp. mayonnaise
1/2 c. milk

1/2 tsp. sugar
Pinch of salt

Mix all ingredients together and drop in lightly greased muffin tin. Makes 6 muffins. Bake at 425° until golden brown, 20 to 25 minutes. Watch after 15 minutes.

Rosemary Catalani
Harpeth Council

MUSHROOM CORN MUFFINS

1 (4 oz.) can mushroom
    stems and pieces
Milk
1 egg, beaten

3 Tbsp. chopped almonds
1 (12 oz.) pkg. corn muffin
    mix

Drain mushrooms; add enough milk to mushroom liquid to measure 2/3 cup. Add egg to liquid. Chop mushrooms into small pieces. Add mushrooms, almonds and liquid to muffin mix; mix well. Spoon batter into well greased muffin pan, filling cups half full. Bake according to package directions for 20 minutes. Makes 18 muffins.

Peggy Burr
Harpeth Council

SESAME MINI MUFFINS

1/2 c. vegetable shortening
1/2 c. sugar
2 eggs
3/4 c. milk
2 1/4 tsp. baking powder

2 1/4 c. unsifted all-purpose flour
1/2 tsp. salt
1 (2 1/2 oz.) jar sesame seeds, toasted in skillet

In a bowl, cream shortening with sugar. Beat in eggs one at a time; stir in milk. Add remaining ingredients and stir until smooth. Spoon dough into greased muffin pans, filling them 3/4 full. Bake in a preheated moderate oven at 350° for 15 to 20 minutes or until puffed and lightly browned.

Judy Q. Arnold
Harpeth Council

SOUTHERN BRAN MUFFINS

1 1/4 c. all-purpose flour
3 tsp. baking powder
1/2 tsp. salt
1/2 c. sugar

1 1/2 c. All-Bran cereal
1/3 c. shortening or vegetable oil
1 1/4 c. milk
1 egg

Stir together flour, baking powder, salt and sugar; set aside. Measure All-Bran cereal and milk into mixing bowl; stir to combine. Let stand 1 to 2 minutes or until cereal is softened. Add egg and shortening; beat well. Add dry ingredients to cereal mixture, stirring only until combined. Portion batter evenly into 12 greased (2 1/2 inch) muffin pan cups. Bake in oven at 400° for about 25 minutes or until golden brown. Serve warm. Yields 12 muffins.

Alison Bennett
Andrew Jackson Council

WHOLE KERNEL CORN MUFFINS

1 large egg
1 c. skim milk
1/4 c. cold water
1 c. cut corn, thawed

1 1/2 c. all-purpose flour
1 c. white or yellow corn meal
1 1/4 tsp. salt
3 1/2 tsp. baking powder

Beat egg, milk and water together until well blended; stir in corn. Combine remaining dry ingredients in another bowl and stir together, then stir into egg-corn mixture, just until batter is blended. Spray nonstick muffin cups with cooking spray. Fill muffin cups about 1/2 to 2/3 full. Bake in a preheated 425° oven for about 15 minutes. Makes 18 small muffins, about 80 calories each.

Ruth L. Cole
Harpeth Council

CHOUX PASTRY
(For eclairs, cream puffs, etc.)

1 c. fine flour	1 c. water
1 stick butter	1/2 tsp. salt
1/2 c. sugar	1/2 tsp. vanilla
2 eggs	

Put water, butter, sugar and salt in saucepan; bring to a boil. Add flour, well sieved. Cook, while stirring, for about 6 minutes. Cool slightly, then beat in eggs one at a time. Add vanilla; shape for eclairs. Bake at 350° for 15 minutes. Fill with whipped cream and top with melted chocolate when cooled.

Norma Ann Webb
Harpeth Council

PASTRY DOUGH

2 lb. flour	1 1/2 c. cold water
1 lb. 8 oz. shortening	1 1/2 Tbsp. salt

Mix flour and shortening all together. Add water and salt; mix light. Makes eight 2 crust pies or 16 shells.

CINNAMON ROLLS

These quick (no yeast) cinnamon rolls are fun to make and delicious.

3 c. self-rising flour	1/2 c. sugar
4 1/2 Tbsp. shortening (1/4 c. plus 1/2 Tbsp.)	1/2 c. brown sugar, firmly packed
1 c. milk	1 Tbsp. cinnamon
1/2 c. butter (or margarine), softened (1 stick)	3/4 c. chopped pecans (optional)
	3/4 c. raisins (optional)

Cut shortening into flour until it resembles coarse crumbs. Add milk; blend with fork until dough leaves sides of bowl. Turn onto lightly floured surface and knead 4-6 strokes; roll into 14x20 inch rectangle. Spread butter over dough, leaving a narrow margin on all sides. Combine sugar, brown sugar and cinnamon; sprinkle over butter. Add nuts and raisins, if desired. Beginning at the <u>long</u> side of dough, roll up in jelly roll fashion. Pinch ends and edges to seal. Cut roll into 1 inch slices. Place slices cut side down in greased 9x13x2 inch pan. Bake at 375° for 20-25 minutes. Remove from oven and cool.

To glaze: Combine 1 1/4 cups confectioners sugar and 3 tablespoons milk. Drizzle over cooled rolls. Makes about 20.

Kathy Pack
Harpeth Council

CINNAMON ROLLS WITH ORANGE GLAZE

2 pkg. active dry yeast
1 tsp. sugar
1 c. lukewarm water
1 c. shortening
1/2 c. sugar
2 tsp. salt
2 eggs, beaten

1 c. boiling water
6 1/2 c. Pillsbury all-purpose flour
Melted butter
1 c. sugar
2 tsp. cinnamon
1/2 c. chopped nuts

Dissolve yeast and 1 teaspoon sugar in lukewarm water. Cream shortening, sugar and salt; pour in boiling water and stir until shortening is melted. Add beaten eggs, then yeast mixture. Be sure shortening mixture is only warm before adding yeast mixture. Beat in 4 cups sifted flour; stir with a wooden spoon until well mixed. Batter will be a little thicker than cake batter. Add 2 more cups of flour; mix well. Cover bowl with a plate. Place bowl in a warm place and allow to rise until dough touches bottom of plate, about an hour. Use remaining 1/2 cup of flour on board to roll out. It may take more than 1/2 cup, depending on type of flour used. Knead 3-5 minutes. Divide dough in half; roll to 1/4 inch thickness. Spread with melted butter. Mix 1 cup sugar with cinnamon; sprinkle each half of dough with 1/2 of the sugar mixture. Cover sugar mixture with nuts. Roll up, beginning at narrow end, until roll is about 3 inches in diameter. Slice 3/4 inch thick and place in buttered pan. Let rise 2 hours in warm place. Bake in 350° oven for 12 to 15 minutes. (Glaze follows.)

242

Orange Glaze:

1 1/2 c. powdered sugar   1-2 Tbsp. undiluted frozen
                                          orange juice

Mix together and pour over baked rolls while they are
still warm.

Beverly Pettigrew
Harpeth Council

ROLLS

2 yeast cakes   1 c. Crisco
2 c. water   1/2 c. sugar
1 tsp. salt   6 c. flour
2 eggs

Do not use electric mixer; do this by hand! Crumble
2 yeast cakes in 2 cups water. Let stand while you mix 1
cup Crisco and 1/2 cup sugar. Cream; add salt. Add your
2 eggs; beat until creamy. Add yeast and water; mix
again. Add flour; will keep for a week. Let rise 1 hour.
Bake at 400°.

Dot Crouch
Clarksville Council

ALL-BRAN REFRIGERATOR ROLLS

1 c. shortening   3/4 c. sugar
1 c. All-Bran cereal   1 1/2 tsp. salt
1 c. boiling water   2 pkg. dry yeast
1 c. lukewarm water   2 eggs, well beaten
6 1/2 c. sifted flour

Combine shortening, sugar, All-Bran cereal and salt.
Add boiling water; stir until shortening is melted. Let
stand until lukewarm. Dissolve yeast in warm water. When
mixture is lukewarm, add beaten eggs, dissolved yeast and
flour. Mix very well, but do not knead too long. Place
dough in refrigerator for about 2 hours. Take from refrigerator and shape into rolls. Let rise about 2 hours. Bake
at 400° until golden brown.

Sarah Smith
Green Hills Council

BRAN REFRIGERATOR ROLLS

1/2 c. shortening
6 Tbsp. sugar
3/4 tsp. salt
1/2 c. bran
1/2 c. boiling water

1 egg
1 yeast cake or pkg. dis-
    solved in 1/2 c. warm water
3 c. flour

Put shortening, sugar, salt, bran and boiling water in bowl; stir until shortening melts. When lukewarm, add well beaten egg and yeast mixture. Add flour; beat well. Let rise till double in bulk or place in refrigerator. When ready to use, roll out; cut and let rise. Bake at 425° for 12 to 20 minutes.

Tamera Spivey
Green Hills Council

BEER ROLLS

3 c. Bisquick
3 Tbsp. sugar

1 (12 oz.) can beer

Blend ingredients with spoon. Spoon into greased muffin pan. Bake at 350°-375°. Yield: 20-21 rolls.

Jean Huggins
Harpeth Council

BEER ROLLS

3 c. Bisquick
1 (12 oz.) can beer

2 Tbsp. sugar

Mix and bake in muffin pan (like cake batter) at 400° until brown.

Sylvia Kaffer
Clarksville Council

DELUXE ROLLS

1 1/4 c. scalded milk
1 c. shortening
1 c. sugar
1 tsp. salt
2 cakes yeast

1/4 c. lukewarm water
6 1/2 c. flour
4 beaten eggs
2/3 c. brown sugar
2 tsp. cinnamon

Combine milk, shortening, sugar and salt; cool until lukewarm. Soften yeast in water; stir and combine with cooled milk mixture. Add half the flour; add the beaten eggs. Beat well. Add remaining flour; mix thoroughly. Place in greased bowl; cover and let rise until double in size. Turn out on board and roll into rectangle 1/4 inch thick and 8 inches wide. Brush with melted butter. Combine brown sugar and cinnamon; spread over dough. Roll like jelly roll. Shape on greased baking sheet into a ring, sealing ends together. From outside, cut through the ring towards the center, almost all the way through in 1 inch slices. Turn slices on side. Cover; let rise until double. Bake at 300° for 25 to 30 minutes. While warm, brush with mixture of confectioners sugar, milk and vanilla flavoring. Sprinkle with nuts.

Joyce Chapman
Harpeth Council

DINNER ROLLS
(Sodium Restricted Diets)

1 1/2 c. warm water (105° to 115°)
1 pkg. or cake yeast
2 Tbsp. sugar
6 Tbsp. unsalted margarine
4 c. unsifted flour (approx.)
2 tsp. poppy seeds

Measure warm water into large bowl; sprinkle or crumble in yeast. Stir until dissolved. Add sugar, softened unsalted margarine and half of the flour. Beat until margarine is blended in. Stir in enough additional flour to make a soft dough. Turn out on lightly floured board; knead until smooth and elastic, about 10 minutes. Place in greased bowl, turning to grease all sides. Cover; let rise in warm place, free from draft, until doubled in bulk, about 30 minutes. Punch down and turn out on lightly floured board; divide dough in half. Form into long rolls and cut each roll into 12 equal pieces. Form each piece of dough into a smooth ball. Place in two greased 9 inch round cake pans (12 rolls per pan). Cover; let rise in warm place, free from draft, until doubled in bulk, about 45 minutes. Lightly brush rolls with melted, unsalted margarine; sprinkle with poppy seeds. Bake in moderate oven, 375° F., for 25-30 minutes or until done. Makes 24 rolls.

DINNER ROLLS

2 pkg. active dry yeast	2 1/2 c. lukewarm water
1/3 c. oleo, melted	1 Tbsp. sugar
6 1/2 - 7 1/2 c. flour	1 Tbsp. salt

Dissolve yeast in water. Add 2 tablespoons oleo, sugar, salt and 3 cups flour; beat until smooth. Stir in remaining flour to form a stiff dough. Place dough in greased bowl; brush with margarine. Cover; let rise in a warm place until double in bulk. Punch down; shape into 1 inch balls. Place 3 balls in each greased medium size muffin cup. Cover; let rise until double in bulk. Brush with margarine. Bake at 400° for 18 to 20 minutes or until lightly brown. Makes 3 dozen.

Carolyn Mitchell
Memphis Downtown Council

EGG ROLLS

1 1/2 c. milk	1 env. dry yeast, dissolved
1/2 c. water	in 1/2 c. warm water
3/4 c. sugar	2/3 c. melted shortening
2 eggs, beaten thoroughly	4-5 c. plain flour

Combine milk with 1/2 cup water and sugar in a saucepan; heat until barely warm. Remove from heat; add yeast mixture. Stir well. Add beaten eggs to milk mixture and enough flour to make a thin batter. Add melted shortening and enough flour to make a soft dough. Place in refrigerator for 2 hours before shaping into rolls. Allow rolls to rise 1 1/2 hours and bake at 400° for about 15-25 minutes. (Will keep at least a week in the refrigerator.)

Hazel Moore
Green Hills Council

GRANNY BAKER'S DINNER ROLLS

1 pkg. dry yeast	1 egg, beaten
1/4 c. sugar	4 c. self-rising flour
1 1/2 sticks margarine	2 c. warm water

Melt margarine; add sugar and beaten egg. Combine the yeast and warm water; add to margarine and sugar mixture. Add flour; mix well. Place in airtight container; no need to let rise. Bake in greased muffin tins. Unused portion may be kept in refrigerator. Bake 20 minutes at 375°.

Elizabeth Kitts
Knoxville Council

ICEBOX ROLLS

1 yeast cake or pkg.
  dry yeast
1/2 c. warm water
1/3 c. sugar
1/2 c. butter

1 egg
1 c. warm water
4 c. flour
1 tsp. salt

Dissolve yeast in 1/2 cup warm water; add 1 teaspoon sugar. Cream together 1/3 cup sugar, 1/2 cup butter and 1 egg. Add 1 cup warm water; beat. Add dissolved yeast. Beat in 4 cups unsifted flour and 1 teaspoon salt. Cover; let rise in warm area about 2 hours. Punch down; refrigerate overnight. Roll dough out 1/2 inch thick on floured board; cut with biscuit cutter. Place in greased pan. Brush with melted butter. Cover; let rise until double in size. Bake at 400° for 15-20 minutes.

Jane Allen
Jackson Council

LINDA'S ROLLS

2/3 c. sugar
2/3 c. shortening
1 tsp. salt
1 egg

1 pkg. dry yeast
2 c. lukewarm water
6-8 c. flour

Put all in a bowl; add flour last as it may not take 8 cups. Stir well; put in refrigerator until ready to use. Roll out and dip rolls in melted oleo. Let rise until ready to bake, about 1 hour. Bake about 20 minutes at 350°.

Linda Earp
Clarksville Council

MAYONNAISE ROLLS

1 c. self-rising flour	1/2 c. milk
3 Tbsp. mayonnaise	1/2 tsp. sugar

Mix all ingredients together and drop lightly in greased muffin tins. Bake at 425° until golden brown. Makes 6 rolls.

Shirley Buckner
Green Hills Council

NON'S ROLLS

1 c. butter or margarine	2 eggs, beaten
1 c. boiling water	5 c. unsifted flour
1 c. warm water	1 1/2 tsp. salt
3/4 c. sugar	2 pkg. dry yeast

Pour boiling water over butter, sugar and salt; cool. Add beaten eggs; sprinkle yeast in warm water. Stir until dissolved. Add to mixture. Add flour; blend well. This will be soft. Place in refrigerator for 4 hours. About 3 hours before using, place in greased pan. Allow to rise at room temperature for 3 to 4 hours. Bake at 425° for 12-15 minutes. Makes 80 rolls.

Jane York
Harpeth Council

QUICK ROLLS

4 c. self-rising flour	2 c. warm water
3/4 c. (1 1/2 sticks) melted	2 eggs
oleo	1/4 c. sugar
1 pkg. dry yeast	1 tsp. salt

Dissolve yeast in warm water. Beat eggs; add sugar and butter. Pour in yeast. Add flour, 1 cup at a time, and salt; mix with electric mixer. Batter will be somewhat runny. Fill muffin tins 3/4 full. Bake at 400° for 15-20 minutes.

Peggy Boatwright
Memphis Council

QUICK ROLLS

1 egg (optional)	1 1/2 sticks melted butter
1/4 c. sugar	2 c. warm water
2 pkg. dry yeast	4 c. self-rising flour

Mix yeast in warm water; add sugar, egg and melted butter. Add flour; does not need to rise. Batter will be runny. Fill greased muffin tins 3/4 full. Bake at 425° for 15 to 20 minutes. Makes 24. Make 1/2 recipe for 12.

Peggy L. Parker
Chattanooga Council

HOT CROSS BUNS

4 c. self-rising flour	1 egg
1 oz. yeast	1 c. currants
1/2 stick butter	1/2 c. candied peel
1/2 c. sugar	About 1 c. milk
2 tsp. mixed spice	

Put flour, sugar, salt and spice in large bowl; mix. Make a well; pour in the yeast, dissolved in a little warm milk. Add egg and melted butter. Knead to a nice clean and smooth dough, using as much liquid as you need (should be stiff). Add the fruit; knead into the dough. Cover with a damp cloth; leave to rise about 2 hours in a warm place. Dough should double in size. Knock the dough down and shape into about 18 medium sized buns. Place on cookie sheet; leave to rise again, for about 30 minutes. Cut cross on top with blunt knife. Bake at 350° for about 20 minutes. Brush with milk and sugar syrup to glaze them when they come out of the oven.

Norma Ann Webb
Harpeth Council

QUICK STICKY BUNS

2 Tbsp. margarine	1/4 c. chopped nuts
1/4 c. firmly packed brown sugar	1/4 c. raisins
1/4 tsp. ground cinnamon	1 (8 oz.) can refrigerated biscuits (do not use buttermilk biscuits)
1/4 c. Karo light or dark corn syrup	

In 8 or 9 inch layer pan, melt margarine in preheating oven. Remove from oven; stir in sugar, cinnamon, corn syrup, nuts and raisins. Place biscuits on top. Bake according to package directions or at 400° for 15 minutes or until biscuits are well browned. Let stand 5 minutes; invert on serving plate and remove pan. Yield: 10 buns.

Kathleen Wagner
Green Hills Council

REFRIGERATOR ROLLS

2 c. lukewarm water
1 pkg. dry yeast
3/4 stick margarine

1/3 c. sugar
1 egg, beaten
4 c. self-rising flour

Mix all ingredients together and store in refrigerator. When ready to use, spoon batter into greased muffin tins. Do not let rise before baking! Bake at 375° for 15 or 20 minutes. (Batter will keep for several days in refrigerator.) Makes about 2 dozen.

Carolyn Mitchell
Memphis Downtown Council

REFRIGERATOR ROLLS

3/4 c. shortening
1 c. scalded milk
2 beaten eggs
3/4 c. sugar
2 tsp. salt

1 c. cold water
2 cakes yeast
1/2 c. lukewarm water
7 1/2 c. flour

Combine shortening and scalded milk. Combine eggs, sugar and salt; beat in cold water. Soften yeast in lukewarm water. Mix all together and add flour. Mix well and cover; leave in refrigerator until needed. When ready to use, roll out dough and cut into rolls. Let rise at least 1 hour. Bake at 425°.

Patty McElroy
Harpeth Council

250

SPOON ROLLS

1 pkg. dry yeast	1/4 c. sugar
2 c. water (warm)	4 c. flour (plain)
1 egg	1/4 tsp. salt
3/4 c. salad oil	

Dissolve yeast in water; add oil and sugar. Add liquid ingredients and egg to dry ingredients. Let stand in refrigerator for 24 hours. Spoon into greased muffin tins. Bake 20 minutes at 475°. Keeps 1 week in refrigerator.

Brenda L. DeVault
Knoxville Council

EASY YEAST ROLLS

4 c. self-rising flour	1 egg
1 pkg. dry yeast	1/4 c. Wesson oil
1/4 c. sugar	2 c. warm water

Mix flour, yeast and sugar; beat in water, oil and egg. Cover bowl; refrigerate until ready to bake. Grease muffin tins and fill 2/3 full. Bake at 425° for about 20-25 minutes. Does not have to rise before baking. Will keep in refrigerator 3-4 days.

Cheryl Enoch
Harpeth Council

YEAST ROLLS

1 pkg. dry yeast	2 c. flour
1 c. warm water	2 Tbsp. butter
4 Tbsp. sugar	1 beaten egg
2 tsp. salt	2 c. flour

Dissolve yeast in warm water. Add sugar and salt; dissolve. Add 2 cups of flour and mix. Add butter and egg; mix. Add remaining 2 cups of flour; knead until smooth. Put in large, greased bowl and let rise until doubled, 2 hours at room temperature or overnight in refrigerator. Punch down and shape into rolls. Let rolls rise 2 hours and bake in hot oven until lightly browned.

Dinah Randolph
Harpeth Council

CRISPY WAFFLES

2 c. flour (plain)
1 tsp. soda
1 Tbsp. sugar
1 tsp. salt

2 eggs, separated
1/4 c. vinegar
1 3/4 c. sweet milk
4 Tbsp. melted shortening

Sift dry ingredients. Beat egg yolks, vinegar and milk together. Add dry ingredients, then melted shortening; blend well. Fold in egg whites, stiffly beaten. Bake on hot, well greased waffle iron.

Frances W. Gilliam
Columbia Council

** NOTES **

CANDY & COOKIES

CANDY CHART

PRODUCT	TEST IN COLD WATER*	DEGREES F. ON CANDY THERMOMETER			
		SEA LEVEL	2000 FEET	5000 FEET	7500 FEET
FUDGE, PENUCHE AND FONDANT	SOFT BALL (can be picked up but flattens)	234° to 240°	230° to 236°	224° to 230°	219° to 225°
CARAMELS	FIRM BALL (holds shape unless pressed)	242° to 248°	238° to 244°	232° to 238°	227° to 233°
DIVINITY, TAFFY AND CARAMEL CORN	HARD BALL (holds shape though pliable)	250° to 268°	246° to 264°	240° to 258°	235° to 253°
BUTTERSCOTCH AND ENGLISH TOFFEE	SOFT CRACK (separates into hard threads but not brittle)	270° to 290°	266° to 286°	260° to 280°	255° to 275°
BRITTLES	HARD CRACK (separates into hard and brittle threads)	300° to 310°	296° to 306°	290° to 300°	285° to 295°

* Drop about 1/2 teaspoon of boiling syrup into one cup water, and test firmness of mass with fingers.

CAN SIZE CHART

Can Size	Can Number	Cups
8 ounces		1
10 1/2 ounces		1 1/4
12 ounces		1 1/2
14 - 16 ounces	300	1 3/4
16 - 17 ounces	303	2
20 ounces	2	2 1/2
29 ounces	2 1/2	3 1/2
46 ounces		5 3/4
6 1/2 to 7 1/2 pounds	10	12 - 13

BOURBON BALLS

3/4 c. chopped nuts
2 boxes powdered sugar
1 stick margarine

8 Tbsp. bourbon (soak nuts in bourbon 24 hours)
Dash of salt

Mix all ingredients; roll in balls. (Let set in cold place to chill.) Dip in:

5 sq. semi-sweet chocolate   1/3 cake paraffin

Melt in top of double boiler; dip with hat pin.

Anne Gebhardt
Harpeth Council

BOURBON BALLS

2 boxes confectioners sugar
1 stick or 1/4 lb. butter
1/2 c. bourbon

Pecan halves
1 bag semi-sweet chocolate
1/2 bar paraffin (Gulf Wax)

Mix butter and sugar together by hand in a large bowl. Add bourbon; mix well. Shape into balls. Put a pecan half in the middle of each ball. Put the balls in the refrigerator for at least 1/2 hour. In double boiler, melt chocolate and paraffin. Using a toothpick, dip the balls in chocolate mixture and lay on waxed paper until dry. Store in refrigerator.

Dale Bushulen
Harpeth Council

BROWN SUGAR FUDGE SQUARES

1 lb. brown sugar
4 beaten eggs
1 1/2 c. flour

1 tsp. baking powder
1 tsp. vanilla
1 c. broken pecans

Beat eggs and sugar together. Cook over hot water for 15 minutes; cool. Sift flour and baking powder together. Add to sugar mixture. Stir in pecans and vanilla.

Pour into 9x9 inch square, greased and floured pan. Bake
30 minutes at 350°. Cool and cut into squares.

Beverly Pettigrew
Harpeth Council

BUTTERSCOTCH CONFECTIONS

2 small bags butterscotch
  morsels

1/2 c. peanut butter
5 c. corn flakes

Melt together butterscotch morsels and peanut butter.
Add corn flakes; mix well. Drop by teaspoon on waxed
paper. Let set until firm.

Frances McLaughlin
Harpeth Council

CARAMELS

2 c. white sugar
1 1/2 c. dark Karo syrup
1 pt. whipping cream

1/4 c. margarine
1/2 tsp. salt

Combine sugar, Karo syrup, salt and 1 cup cream on
medium heat. When temperature reaches 236° add 1/2 cup
cream slowly, so as not to stop boiling. Continue until 236°
has been reached again. Slowly add 1/2 cup more cream
and margarine; continue cooking until 240°. Near end of
cooking time, stir with wooden spoon. Take from heat; add
vanilla. Pour into well buttered cookie sheet with sides.
Let cool. Take from pan with silver knife. Cut into squares
and wrap in heavy waxed paper. When you take it out of
the pan, put in on a buttered bread pan.

Ginger Lewis
Harpeth Council

CARMELITAS

1 c. flour
1 c. quick cooking oats
3/4 c. brown sugar, packed
1/2 tsp. soda
1/4 tsp. salt
3/4 c. butter

1 c. or 6 oz. semi-sweet
  chocolate bits
1/2 c. chopped pecans
3/4 c. caramel ice cream
  topping
3 Tbsp. flour

Combine first 6 ingredients; press half in a 10x10 inch pan. Bake 10 minutes at 350°. Sprinkle chocolate bits and pecans on top. Blend caramel and flour; pour over nuts and chocolate bits. Sprinkle remaining crumbs over top and bake 15 or 20 minutes or until golden brown. Cool completely and cut into squares.

Emma Jo Perry
Green Hills Council

CARAMEL CORN

5 qt. popped corn	1 tsp. baking soda
2 c. brown sugar	1 tsp. vanilla
2 sticks butter	1 tsp. salt
1/2 c. white corn syrup	

Pop 5 quarts of popcorn; place one layer thick on baking sheets and set aside. In a large saucepan, combine brown sugar, butter and corn syrup. Boil 5 minutes; remove from heat. Add baking soda, vanilla and salt; stir thoroughly. Mixture will foam up. Pour over popped corn; mix well. Place baking sheets in 250° oven for 40 minutes; stir every 15 minutes.

Kathy Pack
Harpeth Council

CARAMEL CORN

1 c. light brown sugar	1/8 tsp. soda
1 c. white corn syrup	1 1/2 qt. popcorn, popped
1 Tbsp. water	1/8 lb. butter
1/2 tsp. salt	

Put sugar, syrup and water in pan; cook to 280°, then immediately add salt, soda and butter. Remove from fire. Pour over popped corn; stir vigorously until all the corn is coated. Pour on waxed paper to cool. This keeps well in Tupperware and makes a great holiday treat.

Dee Schell
Columbia Council

CHOCOLATE BALLS

2 1/2 boxes powdered sugar
2 sticks oleo, melted
1 can Eagle Brand milk
1 block paraffin wax
2 c. chopped pecans
1 tsp. vanilla extract
1 (12 oz.) pkg. chocolate chips

Mix sugar, oleo, nuts, vanilla and milk. Form into balls; chill. Melt wax and chocolate chips in double boiler. Use wooden toothpicks to dip balls in chocolate. Place on waxed paper.

Jeanette W. Palmer
Harpeth Council

CHOCOLATE BALLS

1 large pkg. flaked coconut
1 1/2 boxes powdered sugar
1/4 lb. butter
1 tsp. vanilla
1 can Eagle Brand milk
2 c. nuts, finely chopped

Mix all ingredients; shape into small balls. Refrigerate for 2 hours or overnight.

1 large pkg. chocolate chips (use real chocolate)
1 (2 inch) sq. paraffin

Melt chocolate and paraffin in a heavy saucepan over low heat. Dip coconut mixture balls in chocolate mixture. Place on foil. Store in refrigerator.

Nancy Bess Lord
Harpeth Council

EASY CHOCOLATE CANDIES

1 (12 oz.) bag semi-sweet chocolate chips
1 can Eagle Brand milk
2 c. miniature marshmallows
2 c. whole pecans

Combine chocolates and milk in saucepan over low heat. When completely melted, remove from heat and fold in nuts and marshmallows. Drop by spoonfuls onto cookie sheet. Freeze for 2 hours. Remove from freezer; let stand at room temperature for several hours. The longer they stand, the easier they will be to remove from the cookie sheet.

Leslie Stephens
Harpeth Council

CHOCOLATE CREAMS

2 boxes confectioners
   sugar, sifted
1 can Eagle Brand milk
1 stick oleo

1 c. nuts
1 Tbsp. vanilla flavoring
1 Tbsp. flour

Mix; place in refrigerator for an hour. Remove; shape in small balls. Place in refrigerator for another hour. Melt two 6 ounce packages chocolate chips and 3/4 cake paraffin in top of double boiler (direct heat melting will cause chocolate to lump). Place balls on toothpick; dip in hot mixture. Put on waxed paper; remove toothpick and coat hole with chocolate. Place in refrigerator for another hour.

Judy Gibson
Harpeth Council

CHOCOLATE COATED CREAMS

1 stick butter, melted
4 tsp. vanilla
2 boxes 10X powdered sugar

1 can sweetened condensed
   milk
2 c. cocoanut
2 c. chopped nuts

Mix and make into balls about the size of a walnut; store in refrigerator overnight. Melt 1 large cake of semi-sweet chocolate and about 1/4 cake of paraffin. Take the balls from refrigerator and stick a toothpick in each one. Dip in chocolate and paraffin mixture; place on waxed paper until cold. Makes about 4 pounds.

I leave the toothpicks in the balls. Makes it easy to handle. You can use other things besides cocoanut and nuts. Last Christmas I divided the mixture before I added those and just added candied cherries to part of it.

Addie Downs
Green Hills Council

COCONUT BONBONS

1 can Eagle Brand milk
1/2 stick oleo
2 cans pecans, chopped

2 boxes 10X sugar
2 cans Angel Flake coconut
1 tsp. vanilla

Mix together and form into balls the size of a walnut.

In double boiler, melt together 1 stick paraffin, 1 stick oleo and 2 packages chocolate chips. When melted, dip each ball into mixture, using round toothpick. Coat each ball and place on dish to dry.

Carolyn Mitchell
Memphis Downtown Council

FUDGE

4 1/2 c. sugar
1 (13 oz.) can evaporated milk
3 (6 oz.) pkg. semi-sweet chocolate chips

1 pt. or 2 (7 oz.) jars marshmallow creme
2 sticks (1/2 lb.) butter
1 c. nuts

Boil sugar and evaporated milk for exactly 12 minutes (start timing when mixture starts boiling). Stir continuously. Pour over chocolate chips, marshmallow creme and butter; add nuts. Stir until chocolate chips are melted. Pour into buttered pans. Allow to cool before cutting.

Katie Braden
Harpeth Council

CARNATION FIVE MINUTE FUDGE

2/3 c. undiluted Carnation evaporated milk
2 Tbsp. butter
1 2/3 c. sugar

2 c. miniature marshmallows
1/2 c. chopped nuts
1 1/2 c. semi-sweet chocolate bits
1 tsp. vanilla

Combine evaporated milk, butter and sugar in saucepan; heat to boiling. Cook 5 minutes, stirring constantly. Remove from heat. Add marshmallows, nuts, chocolate bits and vanilla. Stir until marshmallows are melted. Pour into 8 or 9 inch square pan. Garnish with nuts, if desired; cool. Cut in squares.

Donna Maxwell
Harpeth Council

CHOCOLATE FUDGE

1 stick butter
3 c. sugar
2/3 c. cream
1 tsp. vanilla

1 (12 oz.) pkg. chocolate chips
1 (7 oz.) jar marshmallow cream

Cook butter and cream to soft ball stage (it will form a soft ball in cold water). Add chocolate chips; blend well. Stir in marshmallow cream and vanilla. Pour into buttered dish; cut into squares when cool.
Note: Almond or caramel chips may be substituted for chocolate chips.

Pat Carpenter
Nashville Council

CHOCOLATE FUDGE

2 c. sugar
1/2 stick margarine
1/2 c. milk

1/4 c. white Karo syrup
1/4 tsp. salt
1/2 c. cocoa

Place all ingredients in pan; boil for 2 or 3 minutes. Take from heat. Cool and beat with electric mixer (takes considerable beating). Add nuts.

Wanda Thomas
Nashboro Council

CHRISTMAS FUDGE

1 c. candied pineapple
1 c. candied cherries
1 1/2 c. broken Brazil nuts
2 c. broken pecans

1 1/2 c. broken English walnuts
3 c. granulated sugar
1 c. white corn syrup
1 1/2 c. light cream
1 tsp. vanilla

Grease two 9x9x2 inch pans. Combine first 5 ingredients. Stir sugar with next 3 ingredients and dissolve over low heat. Continue gentle cooking until soft ball forms when dropped in cold water; remove from heat. With electric mixer or spoon, beat until mixture is creamy and begins to hold shape. Thoroughly mix in nuts and fruit; press into pans; chill until firm enough to cut. Makes about 4 pounds.

Anne Gebhardt
Harpeth Council

FOOLPROOF FUDGE

3 (6 oz.) pkg. semi-sweet   Dash of salt
   chocolate morsels   1 1/2 tsp. vanilla extract
1 (14 oz.) can Eagle Brand   1/2 c. chopped nuts
   sweetened condensed milk   (optional)

In top of double boiler, over boiling water, melt morsels with sweetened condensed milk. Remove from heat; stir in remaining ingredients. Spread evenly into waxed paper lined 8 inch square pan. Chill 2 hours or until set. Turn fudge onto cutting board; peel off paper and cut into squares. Cover and store at room temperature.

Kay Boswell
Andrew Jackson Council

GRAHAM CRACKER FUDGE SQUARE

2 c. graham cracker crumbs   1 (6 oz.) pkg. chocolate
1 can Eagle Brand milk   chips
                             1/2 c. chopped pecans

Stir with spoon and bake in 8 inch greased pan at 325° for 35 minutes. Cool and cut in squares.

Mrs. Adelene Queenan
Harpeth Council

NEVER FAIL FUDGE

5 1/2 c. white sugar   1 (7 oz.) jar marshmallow
1 large can Pet milk   cream
1 stick oleo   3 (6 oz.) bags pure chocolate
2 tsp. vanilla   chips

Mix sugar, milk and oleo together in saucepan; stir until creamy. Bring to a boil and cook 7 minutes. Add marshmallow cream and chocolate chips; stir until melted. Add vanilla, then pour into buttered pans.

Gerry Panter
Columbia Council

QUICK NUT FUDGE

1 (16 oz.) box powdered
  sugar
1/2 c. cocoa
1/4 tsp. salt

1 stick butter (or oleo)
1/4 c. milk
1 tsp. vanilla
1 c. chopped nuts

Combine all ingredients, except nuts, in top of double boiler. Place over simmering water and stir until smooth. Add nuts and spread quickly in a buttered 9x5 inch pan. Cool and cut in squares. A buttered glass pie plate may also be used.

Barbara S. Stanfill
Harpeth Council

REFRIGERATOR FUDGE

3/4 c. undiluted evaporated
  milk
2 1/4 c. sugar
2 (6 oz.) pkg. chocolate
  chips

1/3 c. Karo syrup (red label)
2 Tbsp. butter or margarine
1 tsp. vanilla
1 c. chopped nuts (optional)

Combine milk and sugar in heavy saucepan; cook over medium heat, stirring constantly, until mixture boils. Turn heat low and cook 10 minutes, stirring constantly. Remove from heat immediately; add chocolate chips, Karo syrup, butter and vanilla. Stir until chocolate melts and fudge is smooth. Stir in nuts, if desired. Pour into a buttered baking dish to cool.

Sheila Fleming
East Memphis Council

SOFT FUDGE

2/3 c. (small can) undiluted
  Carnation milk
1 2/3 c. sugar
1/2 tsp. salt
1 tsp. vanilla

1 1/2 c. diced or miniature
  marshmallows
1/2 c. semi-sweet chocolate
  bits
3/4 c. chopped nuts

Combine milk, sugar and salt in saucepan over low heat. Heat to boiling, then cook 5 minutes, stirring constantly. Remove from heat; add marshmallows and chocolate bits, vanilla and chopped nuts. Beat vigorously 1 or

2 minutes or until marshmallows are melted. Pour into buttered 9 inch square pan. Top with whole or chopped nuts, if desired.

Dot Gilliland
Harpeth Council

COCONUT BALLS CANDY

2 boxes powdered sugar
2 sticks butter
1 can Eagle Brand milk
7 oz. coconut

1 Tbsp. vanilla
1 lb. chopped pecans
1 1/2 large pkg. chocolate
   chips
1 block paraffin

Melt butter; add 1 box sugar. Add milk; add second box of sugar. Add nuts, coconut and vanilla. Put in refrigerator overnight; shape in small balls. Melt chocolate chips and paraffin in double boiler. Dip balls in chocolate while warm.

Betty Stewart
Harpeth Council

DATE BALLS

1 stick oleo
1 c. sugar
1 small pkg. chopped dates
1 egg, well beaten

1/2 c. chopped nuts
2 c. Rice Krispies
Angel Flake coconut

Mix oleo, sugar, dates and egg together. Bring to a boil for about 1 minute, stirring all the while. Remove from heat and when cool; add nuts and Rice Krispies. Mix well. Shape into balls and roll in Angel Flake coconut.

Jeanette W. Palmer
Harpeth Council

MOTHER'S DIVINITY

5 c. sugar
1 c. white Karo syrup
1 c. water

Whites from 3 eggs
2 tsp. vanilla
1-2 c. nuts

Cook sugar, syrup and water to soft ball. Take out 1 cup and stir into stiffly beaten egg whites. Put remaining

262

mixture back on fire and cook to hard ball. Pour slowly into egg mixture, beating continuously. Add vanilla and nuts; beat until it starts to harden. Pour into greased pan to cool. Cut into squares while still warm.

Nancy Bess Lord
Harpeth Council

CHOCOLATE COVERED CHERRIES

2 lb. confectioners sugar
1 (15 oz.) can sweetened
  condensed milk
1/2 c. butter or margarine

Maraschino cherries with
  stems or you can use
  toothpicks for stems

Let cherries drain on paper towels for 15 minutes. Place on cookie sheet and freeze in freezer. (If using toothpick, stick in cherry before freezing.) When cherries are frozen (leave in freezer and only remove a few at a time), mix sugar, milk and butter. Shape into 1 inch balls. Flatten to about the size of a half dollar. Place frozen cherry in center and wrap mixture completely around. Repeat; chill cherries overnight.

For variety, you can use your imagination and make plain cream drops or cream nuts in center.

For pina colada candy, use pineapple chunks instead of cherries and add rum flavoring and cocoanut to cream mixture. I use 1/2 of the mixture for cherry candy, then add the rum flavoring and cocoanut for about the same amount of pina colada candy. The secret to this recipe is to be sure the fruit and cream mixture is frozen when working with it.

Chocolate Coating for Candy:

12 oz. semi-sweet chocolate
  chips

1/2 bar paraffin

Melt chocolate chips and paraffin in double boiler. Dip cherries by holding stem into chocolate; let cool on waxed paper. Dip a second time if desired, to make them even more attractive.

Golda Colbert
Jackson Council

MY DAD'S CHOCOLATE COVERED CHERRIES

1 lb. box powdered sugar 2-3 Tbsp. milk or rum
1 stick margarine, softened Maraschino cherries

Mix first 3 ingredients and chill. Roll in ball around cherries. Dip in melted chocolate.

Nancy Bess Lord
Harpeth Council

ORANGE BONBONS

1 (12 oz.) box vanilla 1 c. chopped nuts
  wafers, crushed 2 Tbsp. oleo
1 small can frozen orange 1/4 c. orange juice
  juice (do not dilute) Baker's cooky coconut
1/2 box powdered sugar

Mix vanilla wafers, nuts and orange juice. Roll into small balls. Blend together remaining ingredients, except coconut. Dip balls in this mixture and roll in coconut. Let set for an hour or so and store in covered container in refrigerator. These keep for several weeks.

Jean Bethel
Memphis Council

PEANUT BRITTLE

1 c. raw peanuts 1/2 c. white syrup
1 c. granulated sugar Pinch of salt
1/4 c. water

Combine together in pan and cook until peanuts "pop", then watch carefully until mixture smokes. Remove from heat; add 2 teaspoons baking soda and 4 teaspoons butter. It will rise to top of pan. Stir, then pour onto a greased pan and let cool till it hardens. Break into bite size pieces.

Johnnie Foster
Harpeth Council

PEANUT BRITTLE

2 c. sugar
1 c. clear Karo syrup
1/2 c. water

1/4 c. butter or margarine
4 c. raw peanuts
1 tsp. baking soda

Blend sugar, corn syrup, water and butter. Cook to 230° F. Add peanuts and cook to 280° F. Stir constantly and continue to 305° F. Remove from heat; add baking soda and stir quickly until mixture foams. Quickly pour into two buttered 15x10x1 inch pans. Spread thinly over entire surface of pans. Cool until hard and break into pieces.

Nancy Bess Lord
Harpeth Council

PEANUT BUTTER BALLS

3/4 c. peanut butter
3/4 c. melted butter
1 c. uncooked oatmeal
1 lb. powdered sugar

1/2 c. raisins
1 tsp. vanilla
1 small can coconut
Nuts

Mix all the above ingredients together and form into small balls. Melt 1 package chocolate chips with 1/4 stick paraffin and dip peanut butter balls in this mixture.

Mrs. Harvey Cummings
Harpeth Council

PEANUT BUTTER BALLS

10 oz. jar peanut butter
1 box powdered sugar

1 1/3 sticks softened
margarine

Cream together peanut butter and margarine; add powdered sugar. Roll into balls and dip in chocolate mixture prepared as below:

3/4 bar paraffin
6 oz. milk chocolate chips

1 large pkg. Nestle's
chocolate bar

Melt above in double boiler. Dip balls in chocolate. Cool on waxed paper.

Judy Hagar
Harpeth Council

1489-81

PEANUT BUTTER CANDY

4 c. sugar	Pinch of salt
1 c. milk	1 pt. peanut butter
1/4 c. Karo syrup	1 tsp. vanilla

Mix sugar, Karo syrup, milk and salt together. Boil for 5 minutes after mixture starts to boil. Remove from stove; add peanut butter. Boil 3 minutes after mixture begins to boil. Add vanilla and beat until stiff, then pour into buttered pan.

Margaret McCafferty
Nashboro Council

PEANUT BUTTER CANDY

1 Tbsp. butter, melted	1 Tbsp. milk
1/2 box powdered sugar	Peanut butter

Combine sugar, butter and milk; roll into a ball on waxed paper. Put small amount of powdered sugar on paper to keep from sticking. Roll out ball and spread with peanut butter. Roll out with fingers into a long roll and wrap in waxed paper. Put in refrigerator to harden. Cut into small pieces.

Barbara Wells
Knoxville Council

PEANUT BUTTER FUDGE

3 c. sugar	3/4 c. evaporated milk
1 1/2 sticks margarine	

Cook on medium heat, stirring constantly. When this mixture comes to a boil, boil exactly 5 minutes. Remove from heat; add 1 cup crunchy peanut butter, 1 (17 ounce) jar marshmallow cream and 1 teaspoon vanilla. Beat until smooth. Pour into buttered pan; let cool and cut into squares.

Linda Rigell
Knoxville Council

PEANUT BUTTER LOGS

2 sticks melted oleo
1/2 c. crunchy peanut
  butter
1 1/2 c. oats

1 tsp. vanilla
1 lb. powdered sugar
1/2 c. raisins
1 c. coconut

Mix well and shape into logs.

Glaze:

1 (6 oz.) pkg. chocolate
  chips

2 oz. paraffin

Melt in double boiler. Dip logs in glaze and place on waxed paper to dry.

Linda Cavazos
Jackson Council

PECAN SANDIES

2 sticks margarine
1/2 c. sugar
2 tsp. water

2 tsp. vanilla
2 c. self-rising flour
1 c. chopped pecans

Cream margarine and sugar; add water and vanilla. Add flour and pecans; roll into balls. Bake at 325° for 20 minutes. Cool slightly and roll in confectioners sugar.

Dean Tidwell
Nashboro Council

PENUCHE

2 c. brown sugar
2 c. white sugar
4 Tbsp. syrup

2 Tbsp. butter
3/4 c. milk

Combine all ingredients and bring to soft ball (on candy thermometer). If mixture curdles while cooking, a pinch of salt may stop it, but don't worry, mixture will blend together as it cooks. Stir constantly. Add about 2 teaspoons vanilla and nuts. Pour into buttered pan to cool. Cut while still warm.

Nancy Bess Lord
Harpeth Council

POTATO CANDY

1 medium potato   Peanut butter
1 box powdered sugar

Boil potato in jacket until soft. Peel potato, then mash. Stir in sugar until mixture is stiff. Roll out mixture like biscuits. Spread peanut butter over all. Roll up and refrigerate until cool; cut into slices.

Judy M. Gray
Harpeth Council

PRALINES

2 c. brown sugar   1 c. white sugar
1 c. milk   2 Tbsp. butter
1 tsp. vanilla   1 1/2 c. pecans

Mix all ingredients, except vanilla and pecans. Cook until mixture forms soft ball. Beat and cool until slightly thick; add vanilla and pecans. Beat until it stands in soft peaks. Spoon onto waxed paper until cool. If too thick, add hot water.

Carolyn Mitchell
Memphis Downtown Council

NEW ORLEANS PRALINES

1 1/2 c. sugar   1 c. buttermilk
1/2 c. light brown sugar   1/2 tsp. soda

Cook to soft ball stage. Cool; add 2 tablespoons butter and 1 teaspoon vanilla. Beat until creamy. Add 1 1/2 cups whole pecans; beat until gloss is gone. Drop by teaspoon (very hurriedly) on salted aluminum foil before it begins to harden.

Jean Hunt
Nashboro Council

SEASIDE CANDY ROLL

1 c. pecans
1/3 c. margarine
1/3 c. Karo light corn syrup

1 tsp. maple flavoring
1/2 tsp. salt
1 lb. confectioners sugar, sifted

Chop 1/2 cup of the nuts finely and 1/2 cup coarsely. Mix together margarine, corn syrup, maple flavoring and salt. Add confectioners sugar all at once; mix thoroughly. Knead until smooth. Add finely chopped nuts. Shape mixture into two rolls 2 inches thick. Brush with additional syrup and roll in coarsely chopped nuts. Wrap and chill. Slice into 1/4 inch pieces.

Helen Hardison
Columbia Council

TURKISH DELIGHT

2 c. confectioners sugar
4 c. granulated sugar
1 pkg. lemon gelatin
1 Tbsp. rum

1/2 c. water
Orange flavoring
1/2 c. chopped almonds

Place sugar, water and gelatin in saucepan. Bring to a boil, stirring constantly. Cool and add rum, flavoring and nuts. Pour into wetted shallow dish. When cool, turn out and cut in squares.

Norma Ann Webb
Harpeth Council

AMBER COOKIES

1 lb. candy orange slices,
    finely cut with scissors
    or hot water knife (can
    use less)
1 (7 oz.) can flaked coconut

1 tsp. orange flavoring or
    orange juice
2 cans Eagle Brand milk
1 c. finely chopped pecans
1 tsp. vanilla extract
Powdered sugar

Combine all ingredients, except powdered sugar; mix thoroughly. Spread mix into lightly greased 10 x 15 x 1/2 inch pan and bake for 45 minutes at 275°. Remove from oven; use a teaspoon to scoop out cookies. Form them into balls with fingers; be careful, it's hot. Roll cookies in powdered sugar and place on waxed paper to cool.

Richard Underwood
Harpeth Council

APPLESAUCE COOKIES

1 (2 layer) pkg. spice
  cake mix
1 c. raisins

1/2 c. cooking oil
1/2 c. applesauce
1 egg

In large bowl, combine spice cake mix, raisins, cooking oil, applesauce and egg; beat at medium speed of electric mixer for 1 minute. Drop from teaspoon 2 inches apart on ungreased cookie sheet. Bake cookies at 350° for 12 to 15 minutes. Makes 6 dozen.

Debbie Bullock
Harpeth Council

FRESH APPLE COOKIES

1/2 c. shortening
1 1/3 c. brown sugar
1 tsp. salt
1 tsp. cinnamon
1 tsp. cloves
1/2 tsp. nutmeg
1 egg

2 c. sifted flour (plain)
1 tsp. baking soda
1 c. finely chopped apples,
  unpeeled
1 c. chopped nuts
1/4 c. apple juice or milk

Put first 7 ingredients in mixing bowl; beat until smooth. Sift flour and soda; add 1/2 flour mixture to shortening and blend. Add fruit, nuts and liquid. Add remaining flour; mix well. Drop heaping teaspoonful of dough on greased cookie sheet. Bake 8 to 10 minutes at 350° F. Glaze while warm with mixture of confectioners sugar and milk (fairly thick).

Donna Perry
Harpeth Council

BAKED FUDGE

1 stick butter
3 sq. unsweetened chocolate
  (Baker's)
1 1/8 c. sugar
2 eggs

1/2 c. plain flour
1 tsp. vanilla
1/2 c. nuts (pecans or black
  walnuts)

Melt butter and chocolate. Add sugar after removing from fire, then add unbeaten eggs, flour, vanilla and nuts. Mix well. Bake in 11x7 inch cake pan in 375° oven for 20 to 25 minutes.

Dot Gilliland
Harpeth Council

BLARNEY STONE BARS

3 egg yolks
1 c. sugar
1 tsp. vanilla
1 c. all-purpose flour

1 tsp. baking powder
4 stiffly beaten egg whites
Sweet Butter Icing
1 c. finely chopped peanuts

In large bowl, beat egg yolks; add sugar and vanilla. Beat till thick and lemon colored. Stir together flour and baking powder; stir into yolk mixture. Add 1/2 cup boiling water; mix well. Fold in egg whites. Spread in greased 15 1/2 x 10 1/2 x 1 inch baking pan. Bake at 350° till done, about 20 minutes. Cool; frost with Sweet Butter Icing. Top with nuts, lightly pressing into frosting. Cut into bars. Makes 36.

Sweet Butter Icing: In small bowl, combine 2 cups sifted powdered sugar and 6 tablespoons margarine, melted. Add 1 egg yolk; beat till smooth. Add enough milk (about 1 tablespoon) till of spreading consistency.

Debbie Bullock
Harpeth Council

BONBON COOKIES

1/2 c. soft butter
3/4 c. sifted confectioners
  sugar
1 Tbsp. vanilla

1 1/8 c. sifted flour
1/8 tsp. salt
Filling

Thoroughly cream butter and sugar; stir in vanilla.
Mix in, by hand, the flour and salt. For filling, use candied
or well drained maraschino cherries, pitted dates or gumdrops. Wrap level tablespoon of dough around filling.
Place 1 inch apart on ungreased baking sheet. Bake at 350°
for 12-15 minutes until cookies are set, but not brown.

Icing for Bonbon Cookies:

1 c. sifted confectioners   1 tsp. vanilla
  sugar   Food coloring
2 Tbsp. milk

Combine ingredients. Dip top of warm cookie in icing.
Drain on waxed paper.

Cathy Petrosky
Green Hills Council

BROWNIES

1/2 c. cocoa   2 c. sugar
1 c. pecans (optional)   2 sticks butter, melted
1 1/2 c. plain flour   4 eggs
2 tsp. vanilla

Mix all ingredients together and bake 30 minutes in a
350° oven.

Icing:

1/2 box confectioners sugar   1 tsp. vanilla
3 Tbsp. cocoa   A little milk
1/2 stick butter, melted

Mix together and spread on cake.

Pamela Brashear
Green Hills Council

BROWNIES

2 sq. unsweetened chocolate   1 tsp. baking powder
3/4 c. sifted cake flour   1/2 c. butter
2 eggs   Dash of salt
1 c. sugar   1 c. chopped walnuts
1 tsp. vanilla

Melt chocolate and butter in double boiler; mix well. Remove from heat. Gradually add sugar and eggs to chocolate, beating well. Add sifted baking powder, flour and salt. Add vanilla and nuts. Pour into greased 8 inch square pan and bake at 350° for 25-30 minutes. Cut into squares. Cool in pan. Makes 20-24.

Jeannine Linn
Knoxville Council

BROWNIES SUPREME

Combine and beat well:

1 stick margarine	1 c. sugar

Add and beat well 4 eggs. Add:

1 large (16 oz.) can Hershey's chocolate syrup	1 c. flour 1/2 c. nuts

Put on a large cookie sheet or broiler pan and bake 25 minutes at 350°.

Frosting: Combine -

6 Tbsp. margarine	1 1/3 c. sugar
6 Tbsp. milk	

Boil just 1 minute; remove from heat and add 1/2 cup chocolate chips. Beat until of spreading consistency.

Marge Yates
Harpeth Council

SYRUP BROWNIES

1 c. sugar	4 eggs
1 stick (1/2 c.) margarine	1 tsp. baking powder
1 (16 oz.) can chocolate syrup	1 c. all-purpose flour
1 tsp. vanilla	1/2 c. chopped nuts

Cream sugar and margarine. Add vanilla and eggs; beat well. Combine flour and baking powder; add alternately with syrup to egg mixture. Stir in nuts. Bake in a 9x13 inch pan at 350° for 20 to 25 minutes.

Barbara Harris
Harpeth Council

BETTER-THAN-BROWNIES

2 sq. (2 oz.) unsweetened
  chocolate
1/2 c. shortening
1 c. sugar

3 eggs
3/4 c. sifted cake flour
1 tsp. baking powder
1 c. chopped nuts

Melt chocolate and shortening; cool slightly, then stir in sugar. Add eggs one at a time, beating well after each addition. Sift together flour and baking powder. Add to chocolate mixture. Stir in chopped nuts. Pour into greased 2 quart dish. Bake in moderate oven, 325°, for about 35 minutes.

Metty C. Fain
Andrew Jackson Council

"DELICIOUS" BROWNIES

1/2 c. melted butter or
  margarine
1 c. sugar
1 tsp. vanilla

2 eggs
1/2 c. self-rising flour
1/3 c. Hershey's cocoa
1/4 tsp. salt
1/2 c. nuts

Blend butter, sugar and vanilla in a mixing bowl. Add eggs; beat well with spoon. Combine flour, cocoa and salt; gradually add to egg mixture until well blended. Stir in nuts. Spread in a 9 inch square pan. Bake at 350° for 20 to 25 minutes. Cool in pan.

Jean Hunt
Nashboro Council

CARAMEL-CHOCOLATE BARS

60 light caramels
1/2 c. evaporated milk
1 pkg. German chocolate
  cake mix
1/3 c. evaporated milk

3/4 c. butter or margarine,
  melted
1 c. chopped nuts
1 c. semi-sweet chocolate
  pieces

In a heavy saucepan, combine caramels and 1/2 cup evaporated milk. Cook over very low heat, stirring constantly, until caramels are melted; set aside. Grease and flour a 9x13 inch baking pan. In a large bowl, combine cake mix, melted butter, 1/3 cup evaporated milk and nuts.

Press 1/2 of the dough into the pan; reserve the rest for topping. Bake at 350° for 8 minutes. Sprinkle chocolate pieces over baked crust. Spread caramel mixture over chocolate pieces. Crumble the rest of the dough over the caramel layer. Return to oven and bake for another 18-20 minutes at 350°. Cool slightly, then refrigerate about 30 minutes to set the caramel layer. Cut into 36 bars or even smaller if you wish.

Patricia Hire
Harpeth Council

CARROT ORANGE COOKIES

1 c. softened oleo
3/4 c. firmly packed brown
  sugar
1 egg
1 1/2 c. grated carrots
1 1/2 tsp. vanilla

2 c. all-purpose flour
2 tsp. baking powder
1 tsp. cinnamon
1 tsp. salt
Orange Glaze

Preheat oven to 350°. In large mixer bowl, cream together oleo and sugar; beat in egg, carrots and vanilla. Combine dry ingredients; stir into creamed mixture. Mix well. Drop from tablespoon, 2 inches apart, onto greased cookie sheet. Bake 10 to 12 minutes or until lightly browned. Frost with Orange Glaze while still warm.

Orange Glaze:

2 c. confectioners sugar
3 Tbsp. orange juice

1 Tbsp. grated orange rind

In small bowl, combine ingredients; mix well and spread on cookies while still warm.

Jeanette W. Palmer
Harpeth Council

CHEESE CAKE CUPCAKES

3 (8 oz.) pkg. cream cheese
1 c. sugar

5 eggs
1 Tbsp. vanilla

Soften cheese and blend in sugar, eggs and vanilla, using mixer until smooth and creamy. Pour into 24 cupcake liners. Bake at 300° for 35 minutes. Remove from oven.

Smooth frosting on top and return to oven for 10 minutes (with oven turned off).

Topping: Mix together and spoon onto cupcakes -

1 (8 oz.) ctn. sour cream   1/2 tsp. vanilla
1/4 c. sugar

Judy Christopher
Harpeth Council

CHEESECAKE COOKIES

Crust:

1/2 c. brown sugar, packed   1/2 c. chopped nuts
3/4 c. all-purpose flour   1/3 c. melted butter

Preheat oven to 350°. Grease an 8 inch square baking pan; set aside. In small bowl, mix sugar, flour and nuts until blended, then stir in butter until well mixed. Reserve 1/3 cup of crumbs. Pat remaining crumbs into pan; bake 15 minutes.

Filling:

1 (8 oz.) pkg. softened   2 Tbsp. milk
  cream cheese   1 egg
1/2 c. sugar   1 tsp. vanilla extract

Beat cream cheese and sugar at high speed until smooth; beat in remaining ingredients. Pour over crust and sprinkle with reserved crumbs. Bake 25 minutes until set. Cool on a wire rack; when cool, cut into 2 inch squares and cut each square diagonally in half. Makes 32 triangle cookies.

Paula Akin
Green Hills Council

CHIP DREAMS

2 egg whites   3/4 c. sugar
1/8 tsp. cream of tartar   1 c. chocolate chips
1/8 tsp. salt

Beat together egg whites, cream of tartar and salt until

it forms stiff peaks. Continue beating and slowly add sugar. Fold in chocolate chips. Cover cookie sheet with heavy brown paper and drop mixture by teaspoons. Bake at 280° until lightly brown, about 20 minutes.

Cathy Petrosky
Green Hills Council

CHOCOLATE CRINKLES

1/2 c. oil	2 tsp. vanilla
4 sq. (4 oz.) unsweetened chocolate, melted	2 c. all-purpose flour
	2 tsp. baking powder
2 c. granulated sugar	1/2 tsp. salt
4 eggs	1 c. confectioners sugar

Mix oil, chocolate and granulated sugar. Blend in one egg at a time, until well mixed; add vanilla. Measure flour, baking powder and salt; stir into the oil mixture. Chill several hours or overnight. Heat oven to 350°. Drop teaspoons of dough into confectioners sugar; roll in sugar and shape into balls. Place about 2 inches apart on greased baking sheet. Bake for 10 to 12 minutes; do not overbake. They will become hard if overbaked. Makes 6 dozen.

Jeanette W. Palmer
Harpeth Council

DOUBLE CHOCOLATE COOKIES

Cake mix (chocolate)	2 eggs
1/2 c. self-rising flour	6 oz. chocolate chips
2/3 c. oil	1/2 c. nuts

Mix above ingredients. Drop on cookie sheet and bake 8-10 minutes at 350°.

Kathy Franck
Harpeth Council

CHOCOLATE OATMEAL COOKIES

2 c. sugar	1/4 c. cocoa
1/2 c. milk	1/2 c. peanut butter (do not cook)
1/2 c. margarine or butter	3 c. oats (do not cook)

Mix together sugar, milk, margarine and cocoa in saucepan over medium heat; boil 1 minute. Remove from heat and quickly add peanut butter and raw oats. Scoop by spoonfuls onto waxed paper; let cool. Makes about 3 dozen.

Gerry Panter
Columbia Council

CHOCOLATE OATMEAL COOKIES

2 c. sugar
1/4 c. cocoa
1/2 c. milk
1 stick margarine
1 tsp. vanilla
1/3 c. peanut butter
2 1/2 c. quick cooking oats

Mix sugar, cocoa, milk and margarine. Heat to boil; let boil for 2 minutes. After mixture reaches boiling, remove and cool. Beat and add flavoring, oats and peanut butter. Drop by teaspoon onto waxed paper. After cookies are firm, place them into airtight container while they are still warm. This will make them moist.

Sharon Rawlings
Harpeth Council

CHRISTMAS FRUIT COOKIES

1 c. brown sugar
1/2 c. butter
4 eggs, well beaten
1 Tbsp. milk
3 scant tsp. baking soda
3 c. all-purpose flour
1 tsp. nutmeg
1 tsp. cinnamon
1 tsp. cloves
1/2 lb. pecan pieces
1 small glass whiskey
1 lb. pecan halves
1/2 lb. candied cherries, chopped
1/2 lb. candied pineapple, chopped
3/4 lb. white raisins

Cream butter; add sugar to butter and cream well. Add well beaten eggs; mix thoroughly. Coat cherries, pineapple and raisins with 1 1/2 cups flour of the 3 cups required. Combine all ingredients. Heat oven to 250°. Drop cookies onto greased cookie sheet. Place a pecan half on each cookie. Bake slowly until cookies dry out; do not brown cookies. These cookies are best if baked 3 weeks ahead of time and stored in an airtight container.

Mary L. McCracken
Columbia Council

CHRISTMAS FRUIT COOKIES

3 c. flour
1 c. brown sugar
1/2 c. or 1 stick butter
4 eggs, well beaten
1 tsp. soda
3 Tbsp. buttermilk
1 tsp. nutmeg
1 tsp. cinnamon

1/2 c. whiskey
1 tsp. vanilla
1 lb. seedless white raisins
1 lb. candied pineapple
1 lb. candied cherries (red
  and green)
1 1/2 lb. pecans, chopped

Cut fruit in tiny pieces; add chopped pecans and raisins. Sprinkle with 3/4 cup of the flour; toss to mix well and coat all fruit. In separate bowl, cream butter and sugar. Add beaten eggs. Add remainder of flour and dry ingredients gradually. Add whiskey while beating, then vanilla. Pour batter over fruit and stir until all fruit is coated. Spoon with a teaspoon onto ungreased cookie sheet. Bake 15 minutes at 350° or until brown.

Jane Wohlbold
Green Hills Council

COCONUT LOG

1 lb. box vanilla wafers
1 can Eagle Brand milk
2 c. chopped pecans

1 c. raisins
1 can coconut

Crush vanilla wafers until fine (rolling wafers between waxed paper with rolling pin is an easy way). Pour into large bowl; add other ingredients and mix well with large spoon or faster by hands. It will be a very stiff mixture. Form into logs any size you choose by putting margarine on your hands to make them roll out smoothly. Powdered sugar can be added to the rolls to handle better (so they will not be tacky). They can then be wrapped tightly in Saran Wrap, waxed paper or foil and stored in refrigerator. They slice like a jelly roll after chilling and can be made days or weeks ahead of a special occasion.

Jean Holt
Chattanooga Council

COCO-NOT COOKIES

1 stick oleo
1 c. sugar
1 tsp. coconut extract

1 egg
1 (5 1/2 oz.) pkg. Bixmix
1 (2 oz.) pkg. spud flakes

Mix melted oleo, sugar, coconut extract, egg, Bixmix and spud flakes. Cover bowl and refrigerate for 1 hour. Heat oven at 375°. Shape dough into marble size balls; place 2 inches apart on cookie sheet, ungreased. Bake 8 minutes.

Sylvia Kaffer
Clarksville Council

CREAM CHEESE AND BUTTER COOKIES

1 c. margarine
1/2 c. sugar
2 c. sifted flour

1 (3 oz.) pkg. cream cheese
1 tsp. vanilla

Cream butter and cheese; add sugar and cream well. Add vanilla. Slowly add sifted flour; mix thoroughly. Fill cookie press 1/2 full. Form cookies on unbuttered cookie sheet, using your favorite shape. Bake 8-10 minutes at 375°. If you don't have a cookie press, chill the dough and form logs. Chill the logs and slice cookies off the logs. Bake on ungreased cookie sheet. The time may have to be adjusted.

Carolyn Mitchell
Memphis Downtown Council

CREME DE MENTHE BALLS

1 c. vanilla wafer crumbs
3/4 c. pecans, finely
   chopped
1 c. confectioners sugar

2 Tbsp. light or dark corn
   syrup
1/2 c. white or green creme
   de menthe

Combine vanilla wafer crumbs, pecans and sugar. Add corn syrup and creme de menthe, blending with a fork to make a stiff dough. Form into balls and roll in confectioners sugar. Chill overnight. Store in an airtight container.

Peggy Burr
Harpeth Council

CRISP MOLASSES COOKIES

1 c. shortening	1/2 tsp. salt
1 c. molasses	1 tsp. soda
2 eggs, beaten	1/4 tsp. cinnamon
1 c. sugar	1/2 tsp. cloves
3 1/2 c. sifted flour	1/4 tsp. ginger

Heat shortening and molasses in saucepan until shortening is melted; stir constantly. Slowly pour this mixture over the eggs. Add dry ingredients; mix thoroughly. Chill. Roll into sticks and chill until firm. Cut into 1/4 inch pieces and bake, or roll on a floured board or pastry cloth and cut with cooky cutter. Bake in a moderate oven, 350°, for 10 minutes. Makes about 10 dozen cookies.

Joyce Mattice
Harpeth Council

DATE MUFFINS

1 c. water	1 tsp. ground cinnamon
1 (8 oz.) pkg. pitted dates	1/2 tsp. salt
1/4 c. margarine	1 c. shredded coconut
1/4 c. firmly packed brown sugar	1 pkg. (6) English muffins

Combine water, dates, margarine, sugar, cinnamon and salt. Heat and stir until dates are mashed and mixture is well blended. Fold in coconut. Split muffins with a fork spread halves with margarine (squeeze type) and toast under broiler. Spread with date-coconut mixture. Broil for 1 or 2 minutes longer. Serves 6. Excellent for brunch.

M. Carolyn Hunter
Harpeth Council

DATE SWIRL COOKIES

Dough:

4 c. flour	1 tsp. soda
2 c. brown sugar	1 tsp. salt
2 eggs (whole)	1 tsp. vanilla
1 c. (1/2 lb.) butter	1 Tbsp. lemon juice

Cream the butter and sugar together; add eggs. Mix

soda and salt with flour; add to above, including vanilla and lemon juice. Let cool before rolling. (Divide dough into 4 sections before rolling.)

Filling:

1 1/4 c. chopped dates
1/2 c. water
1/2 c. white sugar

1 Tbsp. lemon juice
1/2 c. chopped nuts

Cook dates, water and sugar slowly at low temperature until dates are soft. Remove from heat; beat until smooth. Add lemon juice and nuts. Let cool before filling dough, which is rolled long but narrow. Keep in refrigerator overnight if possible; slice thin. Bake at 400° for about 10 minutes (watch).

Katie Braden
Harpeth Council

FORGOTTEN COOKIES

2 egg whites
2/3 c. sugar
Pinch of salt

1 tsp. vanilla
1 c. chocolate chips
1 c. chopped pecans

Beat egg whites to a peak. Gradually add sugar and continue beating until stiff. Add salt and vanilla; mix well. Fold in nuts and chocolate chips. Preheat oven to 350°. Drop by ice teaspoonfuls on lightly oiled cookie sheet. Place cookies in the oven and immediately turn off oven. Leave cookies in closed oven overnight. Makes about 25 cookies.

Dot Crouch
Clarksville Council

FRENCH BUTTER CREAM COOKIES

1 stick (1/2 c.) butter
1/2 c. shortening
1 1/2 c. sifted powdered
  sugar
1/4 tsp. salt

1 tsp. vanilla
1 egg
2 c. sifted flour
1 tsp. soda
1 tsp. cream of tartar

Cream butter and shortening. Add powdered sugar gradually, continuing to cream. Add salt, vanilla and egg; beat thoroughly. Add flour, soda and cream of tartar; mix

282

well. Chill at least 10 minutes. Form into 1/2 inch balls. Flatten with a fork on baking sheet. Bake in a 350° oven about 13 minutes. Cool slightly before removing from baking sheet. Makes about 80 cookies, 2 inches in diameter.

Joyce Mattice
Harpeth Council

FROSTED CASHEW COOKIES

1/2 c. butter	3/4 tsp. baking powder
1 c. brown sugar	3/4 tsp. soda
1 egg	1/4 tsp. salt
1/2 tsp. vanilla	1/3 c. sour cream
2 c. sifted flour (plain)	1 3/4 c. salted cashew nuts

Mix above ingredients and drop by teaspoon on greased cookie sheet. Bake at 400° for 10 minutes.

Frosting: Lightly brown 1/2 cup butter, 3 tablespoons coffee cream and 1 teaspoon vanilla. Stir in 2 cups sifted confectioners sugar. Spread on top of cookies.

Marie Barnett
Harpeth Council

FRUIT CAKE COOKIES
"MELT IN YOUR MOUTH COOKIES"

2 sticks margarine	3 1/2 c. flour
2 c. brown sugar	1 tsp. soda
2 eggs	1 tsp. salt
1 tsp. vanilla	2 c. candied cherries, halved
1 1/2 c. pioneer pecans	1 c. chopped dates
1 c. coconut	1/2 c. buttermilk

Mix margarine, sugar, eggs and vanilla thoroughly; stir in buttermilk. Sift dry ingredients together; add to creamed mixture. Stir in nuts, coconut, cherries and dates. Chill at least 1 hour. Drop by teaspoons 2 inches apart onto lightly greased baking sheet. Bake 8-10 minutes at 400°.

Mrs. Lamar (Jean) Edwards
Knoxville Council

FRUIT CAKE COOKIES

1/2 c. brown sugar
2 eggs
6 oz. (1/2 box) raisins
1 1/2 c. flour
1/2 c. butter
1 c. candied cherries

3 slices candied pineapple
1 c. dates
1/2 tsp. soda
1/2 tsp. cinnamon
1/4 c. wine or brandy
3 1/2 c. pecans

Cream butter, sugar and eggs. Sift flour, soda and cinnamon together; add to sugar mixture, then add wine. Mix well. Pour this over fruit and nuts, which have been cut into pieces. (Break nuts once; cut cherries in halves, pineapple about the size of cherries or smaller.) Work this mixture with hands. Drop by spoon on a greased cookie sheet. Bake at 250° until light brown, about 20 or 30 minutes.

Jane York
Harpeth Council

GERMAN CREAM CHEESE BROWNIES

1 (4 oz.) pkg. Baker's
  German's sweet chocolate
5 Tbsp. butter
1 (3 oz.) pkg. cream cheese
1 c. sugar
3 eggs

1/2 c. plus 1 Tbsp. unsifted
  flour
1 1/2 tsp. vanilla
1/2 tsp. baking powder
1/4 tsp. salt
1/2 c. coarsely chopped nuts
1/4 tsp. almond extract

Melt chocolate and 3 tablespoons butter over very low heat, stirring constantly; cool. Cream remaining butter with the cream cheese until softened. Gradually add 1/4 cup sugar, creaming until light and fluffy. Stir in 1 egg, 1 tablespoon flour and 1/2 teaspoon vanilla until blended. Beat remaining eggs until fluffy and light in color. Gradually add remaining 3/4 cup sugar, beating until thickened. Fold in baking powder, salt and remaining 1/2 cup flour. Blend in cooled chocolate mixture; stir in nuts, almond extract and remaining 1 teaspoon vanilla. Measure 1 cup chocolate batter; set aside. Spread remaining chocolate batter in a greased 9 inch square pan. Pour cheese mixture over the top. Drop measured chocolate batter from tablespoon onto the cheese mixture; swirl the mixtures together with a spatula just to marble. Bake in a moderate oven, 350° F., for 35 to 40 minutes; cool. Cut in bars or squares. Cover and store in the refrigerator. Makes about 20 brownies.

Norma Foster
Harpeth Council

GINGER COOKIES

3/4 c. shortening
1 c. sugar
1 egg, slightly beaten
1/4 c. molasses
2 c. flour

2 tsp. soda
1/4 tsp. salt
1 tsp. cinnamon
1 tsp. ginger
Sugar

Cream shortening; add 1 cup sugar and continue creaming. Add egg and molasses; beat well. Sift flour with soda, salt and spices. Add to shortening mixture; mix well. Shape into balls about 1 1/2 inches in diameter; roll in sugar. Place 3 inches apart on baking sheet. Bake in 350° oven for 15 minutes. Yields about 3 dozen.

Mrs. Harvey Cummings
Harpeth Council

GLAZED DONUTS

1 c. very warm liquid
(1/2 c. water, 1/2 c. milk)
1 pkg. dry yeast (use 2 to rise quickly)
1/4 c. shortening (use half Crisco and half oleo is best)

1/3 c. plus 1 Tbsp. sugar
1 tsp. salt
1 large whole egg
1 tsp. vanilla
3 drops lemon extract
4 - 4 1/2 c. all-purpose flour, sifted

Soften yeast in liquid; add shortening next to soften (stir and break apart with spoon). Add sugar, salt and flavorings. Stir in enough flour, about 2 1/2 cups, so that you can beat the batter until smooth. Add the egg; beat again. Gradually add more flour until stiff enough to turn out and knead. Knead until smooth and elastic; dough will be soft. Return to a lightly greased bowl; cover and let rise until double. Turn out on floured surface and roll to about 1/2 inch thick; cut with donut cutter. Place on lightly greased cookie sheet; let rise again, about 1 hour. Fry in deep fat, turning with fork to brown on both sides. After putting more donuts in to fry, dip first ones in glaze and stand on cookie sheet. Continue until all are fried and glazed.

Glaze: Add just enough milk to approximately 3/4 box confectioners sugar to mix well and smooth out lumps, then gradually add more milk until thin enough to dip donuts. (Glaze will be about the thickness of pancake syrup.) Stir in 1 tablespoon vanilla and 3 drops lemon extract. (This makes about 1 1/2 dozen donuts. I double the recipe to make 3 dozen.)

Donna Maxwell
Harpeth Council

GRAHAM CRACKERS WITH "GOO"

2 Tbsp. butter or margarine
1/2 tsp. vanilla
1/8 tsp. salt

1 c. confectioners sugar
3-4 Tbsp. half & half
Graham crackers

Melt butter. Add remaining ingredients and blend until it is spreading consistency. If necessary, thin with additional cream. Spread mixture between graham crackers.

Sue Roller
Harpeth Council

GUMDROP COOKIES

1 c. shortening
1 c. brown sugar
1 c. granulated sugar
2 eggs
1 tsp. vanilla
1 c. coconut
2 c. sifted all-purpose flour

1 tsp. baking powder
1/2 tsp. soda
1/2 tsp. salt
2 c. quick cooking rolled oats
1 c. gumdrops, cut in small
   pieces

Thoroughly cream shortening and sugar. Add eggs and vanilla; beat well. Sift dry ingredients; add to creamed mixture. Add remaining ingredients. Drop from teaspoons onto greased cookie sheet. Bake at 375° for about 10 to 12 minutes. Makes about 6 dozen.

Marie Barnett
Harpeth Council

HEATH BLONDE BROWNIES

1 1/2 c. sifted flour
2 tsp. baking powder
1/2 tsp. salt
1/2 c. butter or margarine
1 c. granulated sugar

1/2 c. brown sugar, packed
2 eggs
1 tsp. vanilla
4 Heath bars, chopped

Sift together flour, baking powder and salt. Cream butter or margarine with both sugars. Add eggs and vanilla; beat until fluffy. Blend in dry ingredients; stir in chopped Heath bars. Spread over well greased 9x13 inch baking pan. Bake at 350° for 25-30 minutes. When cool, cut into bars, 3x1 inches. Yield: 3 dozen bars.

Ophelia Baker
Harpeth Council

HELLO DOLLY COOKIES

1 stick butter (or oleo)
1 c. graham cracker crumbs
1 c. grated coconut
1 small bag butterscotch
  chips

1 large bag chocolate chips
1 can sweetened condensed
  milk
1 c. chopped pecans or
  walnuts

Place each ingredient into an 11x13 inch Pyrex pan in the order shown above. Bake at 350° for 20-25 minutes. Cool; cut and serve.

Ginger Lewis
Harpeth Council

HERSHEY KISSES COOKIES

1 c. margarine
1/2 c. powdered sugar
1 tsp. vanilla

2 c. flour
1 c. walnuts, chopped fine
1 (5 3/25 oz.) pkg.
  Hershey's kisses

In large bowl, soften margarine at medium speed. Add powdered sugar and vanilla; beat well until light and fluffy. Fold in flour and nuts; beat until well mixed. Put dough around kisses to form a ball with kisses inside. Place on ungreased cookie sheet and bake for 12 minutes at 375°. Roll warm cookies in powdered sugar.

Carol Hudgens
Harpeth Council

1489-81

ICEBOX COOKIES

2 c. all-purpose flour
1 c. brown sugar
1 egg
1 stick butter
1/2 tsp. vanilla

1/2 tsp. baking soda
1/2 c. nuts or fruit
(optional)
1/4 tsp. salt

Roll into 2 long rolls; wrap in foil. Chill before cutting into 1/4 inch slices. Bake at 350° for 8 to 10 minutes.

Ruby O. Bayless
Knoxville Council

JELLY BEAN COOKIES

1/2 c. butter or shortening
1/3 c. sugar
1/3 c. firmly packed light
  brown sugar
1 egg
1 c. jelly beans, chopped

1/2 tsp. baking soda
1/2 tsp. baking powder
1/2 tsp. salt
1/2 tsp. vanilla
1 1/4 c. flour
1/2 c. rolled oats

Cream together butter and sugars. Beat in egg, baking soda, baking powder, salt and vanilla. Stir in flour and oats. Add cut up jelly beans. Heat oven to 375°. Drop rounded spoonfuls of batter about 2 inches apart on lightly greased cookie sheet. Bake 10 to 12 minutes or until lightly brown. Makes 3 to 3 1/2 dozen cookies.

Polly Kirby
Andrew Jackson Council

LEMON BARS

2 c. flour
1/2 c. powdered sugar

1 c. (2 sticks) oleo

Melt oleo in 9x13 inch pan. Mix flour and sugar together; add melted oleo. With fingers, pat into bottom of pan. Bake 20 to 25 minutes in a 300° to 325° oven.

Filling:

2 c. sugar
4 Tbsp. flour
1 tsp. baking powder
1/4 tsp. salt
288

4 well beaten eggs
4 Tbsp. lemon juice
4 Tbsp. grated lemon rind

Mix together and pour over crust. Return to oven and bake 30 minutes at 350°.

Carolyn Mitchell
Memphis Downtown Council

MRS. BOYD'S LEMON BARS

2 c. flour
1/2 c. XX sugar

1 c. (2 sticks) butter (not oleo)

Sift flour and sugar together; cut in butter. Press into 13x9x2 inch pan (or Pyrex). Bake at 350° for 20 to 25 minutes.

4 eggs
2 c. sugar
1/2 tsp. baking powder

1/3 c. lemon juice
1/4 c. flour

Beat eggs, sugar and lemon juice. Sift flour and baking powder together; stir into egg mixture. Pour over crust and bake about 25 minutes at 350°. Sprinkle top with confectioners sugar. Cut in squares when cool.

John Owen
Harpeth Council

LEMON BARS

1 c. all-purpose flour
1/4 c. sifted powdered
   sugar
1/2 c. butter
2 eggs

3/4 c. sugar
1 tsp. shredded lemon peel
3 Tbsp. lemon juice
2 Tbsp. all-purpose flour
1/4 tsp. baking powder

Stir together 1 cup flour and 1/4 cup powdered sugar; cut in butter till mixture clings together. Pat into un- greased 8x8x2 inch baking pan. Bake at 350° for 10 to 12 minutes. In mixer bowl, beat eggs; add sugar, lemon peel and juice. Beat till slightly thick and smooth. Stir to- gether 2 tablespoons flour and baking powder; add to egg mixture. Blend just till all is moistened; pour over baked layer. Bake at 350° for 20 to 25 minutes. Sift powdered sugar over top. Cool; cut into bars. Makes 20.

Debbie Bullock
Harpeth Council

LEMON COOKIES

1/2 c. butter	1/4 c. powdered sugar
1 c. flour	

Mix together. Put in 8 or 9 inch square pan. Bake at 325° for 15-20 minutes.

2 eggs, beaten	3 Tbsp. lemon juice
1 c. sugar	Rind of 1 lemon, grated
2 Tbsp. flour	

Mix together; pour over above crust. Bake at 325° for 15-20 minutes; cool. Cut into small squares. Sprinkle with powdered sugar.

Ann Hughes
Green Hills Council

MAGIC COOKIE BARS

1/2 c. butter or margarine	1 (6 oz.) pkg. semi-sweet chocolate morsels
1 1/2 c. graham cracker crumbs	1 (3 1/2 oz.) can flaked coconut
1 (14 oz.) can Eagle Brand milk	1 c. chopped nuts

Preheat oven to 350° (325° for glass dish). In 13x9 inch baking pan, melt butter. Sprinkle crumbs over butter; pour sweetened condensed milk evenly over crumbs. Top evenly with remaining ingredients; press down gently. Bake 25 to 30 minutes or until lightly browned. Cool thoroughly before cutting. Store, loosely covered, at room temperature. Makes 24 bars.

Jean Hunt
Nashboro Council

MINCEMEAT CRESCENTS

1/2 c. margarine	3/4 c. ready-to-use mincemeat
1 (3 oz.) pkg. cream cheese	1/3 c. sugar
1 c. unsifted flour	1 tsp. ground cinnamon

Cream together margarine and cream cheese until well blended. Mix in flour and shape dough into a smooth ball. Wrap in waxed paper or foil and chill 1 hour or until ready to use. Roll dough out on a lightly floured board to 1/8 inch thickness; cut with 3 inch round cookie cutter. Place about 1 teaspoonful of mincemeat in center of each round. Fold over; press edges together. Place on ungreased cookie sheet and bake at 375° for about 15 minutes or until done. Combine sugar and cinnamon; roll cookies in mixture. Cool on wire racks. Makes 2 dozen.

Frances R. Lauderdale
Memphis Downtown Council

NO BAKE COOKIES

1 c. white Karo syrup	1 c. coconut
1 c. sugar	5 c. Special K cereal
1 (12 oz.) jar peanut butter	1 c. pecans, if desired

Combine Karo syrup and sugar; bring to rolling boil (do not cook too long). Take syrup mixture from store and stir in peanut butter till smooth. Pour over cereal and coconut (and pecans). Drop by spoon on waxed paper.

Rosemary Catalani
Harpeth Council

OATMEAL COOKIES

1/2 c. butter	1 tsp. soda
1/2 c. other shortening	1 tsp. salt
1 c. white sugar	3 c. raw oatmeal
1 c. dark brown sugar	1 c. chopped nuts
1 1/2 tsp. vanilla	1 c. chopped dates or 1 c.
2 eggs	raisins
1 1/2 c. flour	

Cream butter and shortening. Add white and brown sugars gradually; blend well. Add vanilla, then eggs; beat well. Add dry ingredients. Fold in oatmeal, nuts and raisins. Drop by teaspoon onto greased cookie sheet. Bake at 350° for about 12 minutes. Makes approximately 8 dozen.

Virginia Kaderabek
Harpeth Council

OATMEAL COOKIES

1 c. all-purpose flour	1/4 tsp. salt
1/2 c. sugar	1/2 c. shortening
1/2 c. packed brown sugar	1 egg
1/2 tsp. baking powder	1/4 tsp. vanilla
1/2 tsp. baking soda	3/4 c. oats

Stir together first 6 ingredients. Add shortening, egg and vanilla; beat well. Stir in oats. Form into small balls; dip tops in additional sugar. Place on ungreased cookie sheet. Bake at 375° for 10 to 12 minutes. Makes 3 1/2 dozen.

Debbie Bullock
Harpeth Council

AUNT KLONDA'S OATMEAL COOKIES

Beat:

1 c. oleo	2 eggs
1 c. granulated sugar	1 tsp. vanilla
1 c. brown sugar	

Sift and add to above ingredients:

1 1/2 c. all-purpose flour	1 tsp. baking soda
1 tsp. salt	

Add and mix by hand:

3 c. (3 minute) oatmeal	1 (6 oz.) pkg. chocolate
1 c. chopped pecans	chips
1 c. coconut	

Mixture will be very thick. Drop by teaspoon onto greased baking sheet. Bake at 375° for 10 minutes.

Ginger Lewis
Harpeth Council

OATMEAL BUTTERSCOTCH COOKIES

Sift together:

1 c. Amway nutrilite protein	3/4 tsp. soda
1 c. flour	1 tsp. cinnamon
1 tsp. salt	

Combine in bowl and beat until creamy:

1 c. brown sugar
2 eggs

3/4 c. softened butter or
margarine

Gradually add flour mixture alternately with 1/3 cup milk. Stir in:

1 1/2 c. rolled oats
1 (16 oz.) pkg. butterscotch
bits

1 c. raisins
1/2 c. chopped nuts

Drop by tablespoon on greased cookie sheet. Bake at 325° F. (160° C.) for 12 to 14 minutes. Cool on cookie rack. Makes 4 dozen.

Carolisa Coley
Harpeth Council

OATMEAL CHOCOLATE CHIPPERS

1 c. shortening (don't use
oil)
1 c. granulated sugar
1 c. brown sugar
2 eggs
2 c. sifted all-purpose flour

1 tsp. salt
1 tsp. soda
2 c. quick cooking oatmeal,
uncooked
1 c. chopped walnuts
1 (6 oz.) pkg. (1 c.) semi-
sweet chocolate pieces

Thoroughly cream together shortening, granulated sugar and brown sugar. Add eggs; beat well. Sift together flour, salt and soda; add to creamed mixture, mixing well. Stir in oats, walnuts and chocolate pieces. Shape dough into 1 inch balls; place on ungreased cookie sheet about 2 inches apart and flatten. Bake in moderate oven, 375°, for 8 to 10 minutes or till lightly browned. Cool on rack. Makes about 6 dozen.

Alison Bennett
Andrew Jackson Council

OATMEAL GUMDROP COOKIES

1 c. gumdrops or orange
slices, cut in small
pieces
1 1/2 c. plain flour, sifted
1/2 tsp. soda

1/2 c. shortening
1/2 c. margarine
1/2 c. brown sugar
1/2 c. white sugar
1 tsp. vanilla

1 c. coconut
1/2 tsp. baking powder
1 egg

1/2 tsp. salt
1 1/2 c. oats, uncooked

Mix all ingredients thoroughly. Shape into balls and flatten slightly on greased cookie sheet. Bake in 375° oven for about 10 minutes.

Joyce Mattice
Harpeth Council

OATMEAL REFRIGERATOR COOKIES

1 c. shortening
1 c. sugar
1 c. packed brown sugar
2 eggs
1 tsp. vanilla

1 tsp. salt
1 tsp. baking soda
1 tsp. ground cinnamon
1 1/2 c. all-purpose flour
1 1/2 c. oats

Cream together shortening, sugar and brown sugar till light and fluffy. Add eggs, one at a time, beating well after each; add vanilla. Thoroughly stir together flour, salt, soda and cinnamon; stir into creamed mixture. Stir in oats. Shape dough into two 8 inch rolls. Wrap in waxed paper or clear plastic wrap; chill. Cut into 1/4 inch slices. Place on greased cookie sheet. Bake at 350° for 8 to 10 minutes. Makes 5 dozen.

Debbie Bullock
Harpeth Council

OATMEAL SURPRISE COOKIES

1/2 c. granulated sugar
3/4 c. vegetable shortening
1 c. brown sugar
2 eggs
1/4 c. water
1/2 c. raisins

1 tsp. vanilla
3 c. oats, uncooked
1 c. self-rising flour
1/2 c. coconut
1/2 c. chocolate chips
1/2 c. pecan pieces

Preheat oven to 350° F. Beat together shortening, sugars, eggs, water and vanilla until creamy. Add combined remaining ingredients; mix well. Drop rounded teaspoonfuls onto greased cookie sheet. Bake at 350° F. for 12 to 15 minutes. Makes about 5 dozen cookies.

Barbara Wells
Knoxville Council

OLD-FASHIONED LEMON DROP COOKIES

Zest (yellow part of rind)
  from 1/2 lemon
1/3 c. sugar
1/2 c. butter
1 egg

3 Tbsp. squeezed lemon juice
1/2 tsp. baking powder
2/3 c. flour
Pinch of salt

With a vegetable peeler, lightly peel the yellow part only from 1/2 lemon; mix well with sugar. Add butter and with an electric mixer, blend thoroughly until creamy. Add remaining ingredients; continue mixing until smooth, scraping down side of bowl as needed. Drop batter by tablespoons in mounds onto lightly greased cookie sheet. Bake in a 375° oven until nicely browned around the edges, about 10-12 minutes.

Ruth and Deborah Cole
Harpeth Council

MEXICAN WEDDING CAKES

1 c. soft butter
1/2 c. powdered sugar
1 tsp. vanilla

2 1/4 c. sifted flour
1/2 tsp. salt
3/4 c. finely chopped nuts

Mix butter, sugar and vanilla. Sift together flour and salt; add to butter mixture. Add nuts; chill dough. Roll into 1 inch balls. Place on ungreased cookie sheet. Bake at 400° until set but not brown. Roll warm cookies in additional powdered sugar; cool. Roll in powdered sugar again.

Debbie Bullock
Harpeth Council

NUT BARS

1/2 c. margarine, melted
  and cooled
1/2 c. light brown sugar

1 c. sifted all-purpose flour
Topping (follows)
Confectioners sugar

Combine margarine and sugar; cream until fluffy. Stir in flour until blended. Spread on bottom of well greased 13x9x3 inch pan. Bake in preheated oven, 350°, for 10 minutes; spread on topping. Bake 20 minutes longer. Cool on rack and cut into 2x1 inch bars. Sift confectioners sugar over tops. Makes 3 1/2 dozen.

Topping:

2 eggs
1/4 tsp. salt
1 c. light brown sugar
1 tsp. vanilla

1 Tbsp. flour
1 c. chopped nuts
1 (3 1/2 oz.) can flaked
  coconut

Pat Prosser
Columbia Council

CLARA'S ORANGE NO-BAKE COOKIES

3/4 box powdered sugar
1 (1 lb.) pkg. vanilla
  wafers, crumbled very
  fine

1 stick oleo or butter, melted
1 c. chopped nuts
1 (6 oz.) can frozen orange
  juice
1 (7 oz.) bag coconut

Mix all ingredients with hand, except coconut. Shape dough into small size balls and roll in coconut. Yields about 4 dozen.

Jane York
Harpeth Council

ORANGE-CHOCOLATE CHIPPERS

1 c. shortening
2 (3 oz.) pkg. softened
  cream cheese
1/2 c. sugar
1/2 c. packed brown sugar
2 eggs
1 tsp. grated orange peel

1 tsp. vanilla
2 c. all-purpose flour
2 tsp. baking powder
1 tsp. salt
1 (6 oz.) pkg. semi-sweet
  chocolate pieces

Cream together shortening, cheese and sugars. Add eggs, peel and vanilla; beat well. Stir together flour, baking powder and salt; add to cream mixture. Mix well. Stir in chocolate. Drop from teaspoon 2 inches apart on ungreased cookie sheet; sprinkle with sugar. Bake at 350° for about 10 minutes. Makes 6 dozen.

Debbie Bullock
Harpeth Council

ORANGE MUFFINS

1/2 c. shortening
1 c. sugar
2 eggs, well beaten
2/3 c. buttermilk
2 c. flour, minus 3 Tbsp.

1/2 c. nuts and 1/2 c. dates,
  chopped fine and mixed
  with reserved 3 Tbsp.
  flour
1 tsp. soda
1/4 tsp. salt

Cream shortening and sugar; add eggs. Add sifted dry ingredients alternately with the buttermilk. Add the dates and nuts last. Fill small muffin pans 1/2 full. Bake at 375° for 12 minutes. Recipe makes 50 small muffins.

Sauce:

Juice of 2 oranges
Grated rind of 1 orange

1 c. sugar

Combine and heat until sugar is dissolved. Immediately after removing from oven, pour 1 tablespoon of sauce on each muffin; remove from pan.

E.T. Greer, Jr.
Green Hills Council

PAN FRIED COOKIES

2 eggs
1 c. sugar

2 Tbsp. butter or oleo
1/2 lb. dates, cut fine

Cook in skillet about 8 minutes over low heat, stirring constantly. Take off fire and add:

2 c. Rice Krispies
1 c. chopped nuts

1 tsp. vanilla

Let cool; form in balls and roll in coconut.

Rosemary Catalani
Harpeth Council

PEANUT BLOSSOM COOKIES

1 3/4 c. flour
1 tsp. soda
1/2 tsp. salt
1/2 c. butter (or oleo)
1/3 c. peanut butter

1/2 c. sugar
1/2 c. brown sugar
1 egg, unbeaten
1 tsp. vanilla
Hershey's chocolate kisses

Sift the dry ingredients together. Cream butter, peanut butter, sugar and brown sugar together. Add the egg and vanilla; blend in the dry ingredients. Shape dough into balls and roll each in granulated sugar. Place on greased cookie sheet. Bake at 375° for 8 minutes (I usually do only 6 minutes). Top each cookie with a solid milk chocolate candy kiss, pressing down firmly so cookie cracks around the edge. Return to oven; bake 2 to 5 minutes. (I usually do about 2 to 3 minutes at the most.)

Margaret Slack
Green Hills Council

PECAN COOKIES

1 c. sugar
2 c. flour
1 egg white

2 sticks butter, room
temperature
Pinch of salt

Mix and spread on cookie sheet with sides. Mixture will be thick. Spread with spatula to wafer thin thickness. Pour egg white, unbeaten, on mixture. Spread with fingers; pour off excess. Sprinkle 1 cup pecans over top. Bake at 300° for 40 minutes. Cut while hot.

Louise Breeden
Nashboro Council

PECAN DAINTIES

3 sticks butter
1 c. confectioners sugar
4 c. flour
1/2 tsp. salt

2 Tbsp. water
2 tsp. vanilla
1/2 c. chopped pecans
1/4 tsp. baking powder

Cream butter and sugar; add flour, salt and baking powder. Add water, vanilla and nuts. Shape into small balls or crescents. Bake on ungreased cookie sheets in oven at 300°. When baked, roll in powdered sugar.

Cathy Petrosky
Green Hills Council

PECAN PUFFS

1/2 c. butter
4 Tbsp. sugar
1 tsp. vanilla

1 c. flour (plain)
1 c. pecans, chopped

Cream butter and sugar; add rest of ingredients. Roll in small balls. Place on greased cookie sheet. Bake at 300° for 30 minutes. Roll while hot in confectioners sugar. Put in bag and shake; repeat when cool. Makes about 3 dozen.

Donna Perry
Harpeth Council

PECAN ROLL COOKIES
(Christmas Cookies)

1 lb. butter, softened
1 c. confectioners sugar, sifted
4 c. sifted cake flour (not self-rising)

2 c. chopped pecans
1 Tbsp. vanilla
Sifted confectioners sugar to roll cookies in

Cream butter and sugar; stir in flour, nuts and vanilla. Mix well; shape into 1 inch balls. Bake 15-20 minutes at 325°. Roll in confectioners sugar while still warm. Yield: About 10 dozen. This recipe freezes well. Put waxed paper between layers of cookies in airtight container to freeze.

Kathy Pack
Harpeth Council
Sheila Fleming
East Memphis Council

PECAN TASSIES

1 (3 oz.) pkg. cream cheese	1 Tbsp. butter or margarine,
1/2 c. butter or margarine	softened
1 c. sifted flour	1 tsp. vanilla
1 egg	Dash of salt
3/4 c. brown sugar	2/3 c. coarsely broken pecans

Cheese Pastry: Let cream cheese and 1/2 cup margarine soften at room temperature; blend together. Stir in flour; chill about 1 hour. Shape in two dozen 1 inch balls. Place in ungreased 1 3/4 inch (mini) muffin tins. Press dough evenly against bottom and sides of each.

Pecan Filling: Beat together egg, brown sugar, 1 tablespoon butter, vanilla and salt just until smooth. Divide half the pecans among pastry lined pans. Add egg mixture and top with remaining pecans. Bake in slow oven, 325°, for 25 minutes or until filling is set. Cool before removing from pans. Makes 2 dozen.

Jean Winters
Memphis Council

NO BAKE PEANUT BUTTER COOKIES

1 c. white corn syrup	4 1/2 c. Special K cereal
1 c. granulated sugar	1 can flaked coconut
1 c. peanut butter	

Combine sugar and corn syrup; bring to a boil. Remove from heat; stir in peanut butter. Pour this mixture over the cereal and coconut; mix well. Drop by teaspoon on waxed paper.

Judy Gibson
Harpeth Council

PEANUT BUTTER COOKIES WITH CHOCOLATE TOPPING

1/2 c. shortening	1/2 tsp. soda
1/2 c. peanut butter	1/2 tsp. salt
1 c. sugar	2 Tbsp. milk
1 egg	6 oz. pkg. semi-sweet
1 tsp. vanilla	chocolate bits
1 1/4 c. sifted flour	

Cream together shortening, peanut butter and sugar.

Add egg and vanilla; beat well. Sift together flour, soda and salt; add to peanut butter mixture alternately with milk. Turn dough onto lightly floured board or pastry cloth. Roll 1/4 inch thick. Cut and place cookies on baking sheet. Bake in 350° oven for about 10 minutes; cool. Melt chocolate bits over hot water and cook slightly. Spread chocolate on cooled, baked cookies. (I roll dough into 1 1/2 inch thick sticks. Chill and cut into 1/4 pieces.)

Joyce Mattice
Harpeth Council

PRALINE GRAHAMS

Thoroughly grease cookie sheet (or use teflon). Cover sheet with graham crackers. In small saucepan, melt 1 stick butter and 1 stick margarine (or 2 sticks butter but not 2 margarine). As it melts, pour in 1 cup sugar. When it comes to a boil, let it cook for 10 minutes, stirring as needed to keep from sticking and burning. Stir in 1 cup broken pecans. Quickly spoon onto graham crackers, smoothing out with a spatula; it will thicken fast. Place in preheated 350° oven and bake for 10 minutes. Remove from oven; let cool. Loosen with a spatula. Remove from pan and break into serving size pieces.

Tenia Stone
Harpeth Council

SANDIES

1 c. butter or margarine
1/3 c. granulated sugar
2 tsp. water

2 tsp. vanilla
2 c. sifted all-purpose flour
1 c. chopped pecans

Cream butter and sugar. Add 2 teaspoons water and vanilla; mix well. Blend in flour and nuts; chill 4 hours. Shape in balls or fingers. Bake on ungreased cookie sheet at 325° for about 20 minutes. Remove from pan; cool slightly. Roll in confectioners sugar. Makes about 3 dozen cookies.

David Lewis
Clarksville Council

SEVEN LAYER COOKIES

1 stick oleo
1 1/4 c. graham cracker
  crumbs
1 1/4 c. coconut

1 medium pkg. chocolate chips
1 medium pkg. butterscotch
  chips
1 c. chopped nuts
1 can Eagle Brand milk

In 9x13 inch pan, melt oleo in bottom of pan. Sprinkle graham cracker crumbs evenly. Sprinkle coconut, chocolate chips, butterscotch chips and nuts; press firmly. Spread milk over whole mixture. Bake at 350° for 30 to 40 minutes.

Sylvia Kaffer
Clarksville Council

SKILLET COOKIES

1 c. sugar
1 stick butter or margarine

2 egg yolks, beaten
1 (8 oz.) pkg. dates

Cook sugar and butter in skillet on low heat 5 minutes, stirring constantly. Stir in egg yolks. Add dates and cook 5 minutes longer, still stirring. Remove from heat and add 1 cup chopped pecans, 2 cups Rice Krispies and 1 teaspoon vanilla. Stir until well mixed. Divide mixture in 2 or 3 sections and put on waxed paper dusted with powdered sugar; roll as jelly roll. Place in refrigerator several hours, then slice in thin slices. This is very rich, almost like candy. Will keep wrapped or in covered container for weeks.

Ella M. Crockett
Columbia Council

SNICKERDOODLES

1 c. shortening
2 eggs
2 tsp. cream of tartar
1 tsp. soda
4 tsp. sugar

1 1/2 c. sugar
2 3/4 c. all-purpose flour
1/2 tsp. salt
1 tsp. vanilla extract
4 tsp. ground cinnamon

Cream shortening, 1 1/2 cups sugar and eggs until light and fluffy. Combine flour, cream of tartar, salt and soda; stir into creamed mixture. Stir in vanilla. Shape the dough into balls the size of walnuts. Combine remaining sugar and cinnamon, mixing well; roll each ball in mixture. Place on a greased cookie sheet; flatten cookies slightly. Bake at 400° for 8 minutes or until the first cookies begin to fall. Yield: 5 dozen.

Judy Christopher
Harpeth Council

SUGAR COOKIES

1 c. oleo, softened	4 c. plain flour
1 c. cooking oil	1 tsp. cream of tartar
1 c. granulated sugar	1 tsp. soda
1 c. powdered sugar	1/4 tsp. salt
2 eggs	4 tsp. vanilla

Cream first 4 ingredients. Add eggs, one at a time; beat after each egg. Add dry ingredients and vanilla; mix with beater. Chill at least 1 hour. Make small balls; roll in granulated sugar. Place on cookie sheet and flatten with fork. Bake at 350° for 10 minutes.

Ann R. Wooten
Memphis Downtown Council

BASIC SUGAR COOKIES

2/3 c. shortening	4 tsp. milk
3/4 c. granulated sugar	2 c. sifted all-purpose flour
1 tsp. vanilla	1 1/2 tsp. baking powder
1 egg	1/4 tsp. salt

Thoroughly cream shortening, sugar and vanilla. Add egg and milk; beat till light and fluffy. Sift together dry ingredients; blend into creamed mixture. Divide dough in half; cover and chill at least 1 hour. On lightly floured surface, roll to 1/8 inch thickness.* Cut in desired shapes with cutters. Bake on ungreased cookie sheet at 375° for about 8 to 10 minutes. Cool slightly; remove. Makes about 3 dozen.
*Chill other half till ready to use.

David Lewis
Clarksville Council

DROP SUGAR COOKIES

2 1/2 c. sifted flour
3/4 tsp. salt
1/2 c. Crisco
1 tsp. vanilla
2 Tbsp. milk

1/2 tsp. soda
1/2 c. butter
1 c. sugar
1 egg

Cream butter, Crisco and sugar thoroughly. Add egg. Cream until mixture is fluffy. Stir in dry ingredients until mixture is smooth. Blend in 2 tablespoons milk. Drop on ungreased cookie sheet; flatten with glass or hand. Sprinkle with sugar. Bake in 400° oven for 12 minutes.

Marie Barnett
Harpeth Council

MAMA'S SUGAR COOKIES

1/2 c. Crisco
1 c. sugar
2 eggs

1 tsp. vanilla
2 c. self-rising flour
Sugar

Mix; cook on greased cookie sheet at 350° for 10 minutes or until lightly browned. Sprinkle tops with sugar while hot.

Peggy Hunter
Harpeth Council

STUFFED DATE DROPS

1 lb. pitted dates
Pecan halves
1/4 c. shortening
3/4 c. light brown sugar
1 egg

1 1/4 c. sifted flour
1/2 tsp. baking powder
1/2 tsp. soda
1/4 tsp. salt
1/2 c. sour cream

Stuff dates with nut halves. Cream shortening with sugar until light; beat in egg. Sift dry ingredients and add alternately with sour cream to shortening mixture. Cover each date with mixture. (Use a teaspoon to roll dates around in batter; they do not need to be completely coated.) Bake on greased cookie sheet at 350° for about 10-15 minutes.

Frosting: Melt 1/2 cup oleo. Remove from heat and

gradually beat in 3 cups powdered sugar. Add 3/4 teaspoon vanilla. Slowly add 3 tablespoons hot water till spreading consistency. Spread on tops of cookies.

Peggy Hunter
Harpeth Council

SUN-MAID RAISIN CUPCAKES

1 c. Sun-Maid puffed
  raisins
1/4 c. butter
3/4 c. sugar
1 egg

1 3/4 c. flour
3 tsp. baking powder
1/2 c. milk
1 tsp. lemon extract

Slice or chop raisins. Cream butter with sugar; add beaten egg. Sift flour with baking powder and add alternately with milk to creamed mixture, mixing thoroughly. Add raisins and lemon extract; blend well. Fill greased muffin pans 1/2 full. Bake about 20 minutes in a moderate oven, 375° to 400°. This will make 12 to 14 medium sized cupcakes.

Joyce Mattice
Harpeth Council

TEXAS COOKIES

1 1/3 c. plain flour
3 Tbsp. sugar
1/4 lb. oleo, room
  temperature

1 can vanilla sour cream
  frosting
Almond extract

Mix flour, sugar and oleo together till it forms a soft dough; roll into 1 inch balls. Place on ungreased cookie sheet. Press down each ball with your thumb to make an indentation. Bake at 250° for 20 minutes. Mix can of vanilla sour cream frosting with 1 cap of almond extract. Tint to desired color and frost each indentation.

Cheryl V. Alderson
Columbia Council

THUMBPRINT COOKIES

3/4 c. butter or margarine
1 (3 oz.) pkg. cream cheese
2 c. flour
2 Tbsp. sugar

1/2 tsp. salt
1/4 tsp. baking powder
1/2 c. jam or jelly

Cream together butter and cream cheese until light and fluffy. Sift together flour, sugar, salt and baking powder. Stir into creamed mixture. Roll out on lightly floured surface into a square about 1/2 inch thick. Cut into 1 1/2 inch squares. Place on ungreased baking sheet. With your thumb, make an indentation in the center of each cookie. Fill with 1/2 teaspoon jam or jelly. Bake in a moderate oven, 350°, for 20 to 25 minutes. Makes 2 1/2 dozen.

Nancy Bess Lord
Harpeth Council

VALENTINE CRUNCHIES

1/2 c. butter
1/2 c. brown sugar
1/2 c. white sugar
1 egg, well beaten
1/2 tsp. vanilla
1 c. flour
1/2 tsp. soda

1/4 tsp. salt
1/4 tsp. baking powder
1 c. oatmeal
1 c. corn flakes
1/2 c. coconut
1/2 c. pecans, chopped

Cream butter and sugars, then add eggs and vanilla. Sift dry ingredients together; add to creamed mixture. Add corn flakes, oatmeal, coconut and pecans. Roll into small balls; place 2 inches apart on greased cookie sheet. Bake at 350° for 10-15 minutes. Yield: 6 dozen.

Bernie Wright
Green Hills Council

VIENNA CHOCOLATE BARS

2 sticks butter
1 1/2 c. sugar
2 egg yolks
2 1/2 c. flour
1/4 tsp. salt
4 egg whites

1 (10 oz.) jar jelly (raspberry jelly or apricot preserves; I use cherry preserves)
1 c. semi-sweet chocolate bits
2 c. finely chopped nuts

Cream the butter with the egg yolks and 1/2 cup sugar. Add the flour; knead with the fingers. Pat batter out on a greased cookie sheet to about 3/8 inch thickness. Bake for 15 to 20 minutes at 350° until lightly browned. Remove from oven; spread with jelly and top with chocolate bits. Beat egg whites with salt until stiff. Fold in remaining cup of sugar and nuts. Gently spread on top of jelly and chocolate. Bake for about 25 minutes at 350°. Cut into squares or bars. Yield: Two dozen bars, 3x1 inches.

Edyth H. Castello
Green Hills Council

** NOTES **

.

DESSERTS

CAKE BAKING GUIDE

PROBLEM...	CAUSE...	
	Butter-Type Cakes	Sponge-Type Cakes
Cake falls	Too much sugar, liquid, leavening or shortening; too little flour; temperature too low; insufficient baking	Too much sugar; overbeating egg whites; underbeaten egg yolks; use of greased pans; insufficient baking
Cake cracks or humps	Too much flour or too little liquid; overmixing; batter not spread evenly in pan; oven temperature too high	Too much flour or sugar; temperature too high
Cake has one side higher	Batter not spread evenly; uneven pan; pan too close to side of oven; oven rack or range not even; uneven oven heat	Uneven pan; oven rack or range not level
Cake has hard top crust	Temperature too high; overbaking	Temperature too high; overbaking
Cake has sticky top crust	Too much sugar or shortening; insufficient baking	Too much sugar; insufficient baking
Cake has soggy layer at bottom	Too much liquid; underbeaten eggs; undermixing; insufficient baking	Too many eggs or egg yolks; underbeaten egg yolks; undermixing
Cake crumbles or falls apart	Too much sugar, leavening or shortening; undermixing; improper pan treatment; improper cooling	
Cake has heavy, compact quality	Too much liquid or shortening; too many eggs; too little leavening or flour; overmixing; temperature too high	Overbeaten egg whites; underbeaten egg yolks; overmixing
Cake falls out of pan before completely cooled		Too much sugar; use of greased pans; insufficient baking

JUANITA"S ANGEL PIE

Crust:

4 egg whites
2/3 c. sugar

1/2 c. powdered sugar

Beat whites until stiff; add 2 tablespoons at a time of the 2/3 cup sugar, beating at high speed. When finished, add the same way 1/2 cup powdered sugar. Have metal pie pan lightly buttered and floured. Spread meringue in pan, covering pan around edge. Bake at 300° for 45 to 50 minutes; cool and fill.

Filling:

4 egg yolks
1/2 c. sugar
1 heaping Tbsp. flour
1 c. milk

Pinch of salt
1 tsp. vanilla
1/2 pt. cream
Grated chocolate

Combine in top of double boiler pan the egg yolks, sugar, flour and milk. Cook, stirring until thick. Remove from heat; add salt and vanilla. Cool and put into meringue shell. Top with cream, whipped. Top with grated chocolate; chill overnight.

Joe Holdway
Harpeth Council

RUTH'S ANGEL PIE

24 cream filled chocolate
cookies
1/4 c. melted butter or
margarine

1/4 c. creme de noyaux
1 large jar marshmallow creme
2 c. heavy cream, whipped
stiffly

Crush cookies; reserve half for topping. Mix crumbs with butter and press into bottom of a spring form pan. In a bowl, mix creme de noyaux and marshmallow creme until smooth. With wire whisk, fold in whipped cream. Pour mixture into pan; sprinkle with remaining crumbs.

Freeze immediately until ready to use. May use 1/8 cup creme de noyaux and 1/8 cup creme de cacao for a variation.

Ruth L. Cole
Harpeth Council

APPLE PIE

3 lb. York or Winesap apples
2 c. sugar

Juice of 1 lemon
1 stick butter

Combine apples in pan with sugar and juice. Simmer over medium heat until apples are transparent, stirring to bring apples from bottom of pan. Put in pie shell; lay pastry strips on top. Slice butter on top. Bake in 350° oven for 30 to 40 minutes or until brown.

Joyce Mattice
Harpeth Council

APPLE PIE

1 Tbsp. flour
4 Tbsp. melted butter
1/2 tsp. nutmeg
1/2 c. orange juice

1 c. sugar
3 medium pared, chopped apples
1 unbaked pie shell and pastry strips

Blend flour into melted butter; add juice, apples, sugar and nutmeg. Pour into pie shell. Crisscross pastry strips on top. Bake in preheated oven, 450°, for 15 minutes; reduce to 300° for 25 minutes.

Pastry:

2 c. plain flour
3/4 tsp. salt

2/3 c. Crisco
1/3 c. ice water

Blend Crisco and salt into flour; work in ice water. Reserve a portion for pastry strips. Roll out enough for 9 inch pie pan. Roll out remainder and cut into 1/2 inch wide strips.

Pattie Hoffman
Nashboro Council

310

APPLE CRUMB PIE

Place 4 apples, sliced, in unbaked pie shell. Sprinkle over apples 1/2 cup sugar and 1 teaspoon cinnamon. Mix together and crumble on top of apples:

3/4 c. flour	1/3 c. butter
1/2 c. sugar	

Bake 40-50 minutes at 400°. Top will be golden brown when done.

Bob and Nora Chandler
Harpeth Council

SOUR CREAM APPLE PIE

1 c. (8 oz.) sour cream	1 c. sugar
2 Tbsp. flour (plain)	Dash of salt
1 tsp. vanilla	1 egg

Mix well. Add 2 cups diced apples to above. Pour into 8 inch unbaked shell. Bake at 400° for 25 minutes.

1/2 c. brown sugar	1/3 c. flour
1/4 c. butter	1 tsp. cinnamon

Sprinkle on top of pie. Bake another 20 minutes. Serves 8.

Katrina Carter
Harpeth Council

APPLE PIE IN A SACK

Filling:

3 medium Winesap apples, chopped	1 tsp. nutmeg
	1/2 c. sugar
2 Tbsp. flour	

Mix apples with all other ingredients and place in one unbaked 9 inch pastry shell. Sprinkle the following topping over this.

Topping:

1 stick margarine	1/2 c. flour
1/2 c. sugar	

Mix these ingredients until crumbly. Place assembled pie in a brown paper bag and close with wrapper wire. Place on cookie sheet and bake at 400° for approximately 1 hour.

Jessie S. Taylor
Harpeth Council

LEMON GLAZED APPLE TART

2 c. unsifted flour	1/2 c. sugar
3/4 c. margarine	1 egg yolk
6 c. golden apples, diced	3 Tbsp. ice water
1 1/2 c. granola	1 c. unsifted powdered sugar
1/2 c. slivered almonds	2 Tbsp. lemon juice

Measure flour and 1/4 cup sugar into a bowl. Cut in margarine with pastry blender or 2 knives until mixture resembles coarse meal. Combine egg yolk and ice water. Stir into flour mixture; mix lightly. Form dough into ball. Press pastry evenly over bottom and sides of ungreased 15 1/2 x 10 1/2 x 1 inch jelly roll pan. Bake at 350° for 15 minutes. Arrange apple slices over partially baked pastry. Combine granola, remaining 1/4 cup sugar and slivered almonds; sprinkle over apples. Bake at 350° for 55 minutes, or until apples are tender. Cool on wire rack. Stir together confectioners sugar and lemon juice; drizzle over slices.

Carolyn Mitchell
Memphis Downtown Council

BANANA SPLIT PIE

2 eggs	3 medium bananas
2 sticks margarine	1 (No. 2) can crushed
2 c. confectioners sugar	pineapple, drained
Whipped topping	Nuts
2 (8 inch) graham cracker crusts	Maraschino cherries

Beat together eggs, margarine and confectioners sugar

15 minutes or until fluffy. Pour into graham cracker crusts. Slice bananas and layer over mixture. Pour drained pineapple over bananas; cover with whipped topping. Top with nuts and cherries; chill.

Dot Crouch
Clarksville Council

BANANA SPLIT PIE

2 1/2 c. graham cracker
   crumbs
2 1/2 sticks oleo
1 (No. 2) can crushed
   pineapple
Large tub of Cool Whip

2 eggs
1 box powdered sugar
5 or 6 bananas
Chopped nuts
Cherries

Mix graham cracker crumbs and 1 stick of oleo; spread in a 9x13x2 inch pan. Bake 8-10 minutes; cool. Whip margarine, eggs and sugar until smooth; spread onto crust. Slice bananas and top with drained pineapple. Spread Cool Whip on top. Sprinkle with chopped nuts and decorate with cherries.

Carolyn Mitchell
Memphis Downtown Council

BANANA SPLIT PIE

1 (12 oz.) box vanilla
   wafers, crushed
3/4 c. melted butter or
   margarine
2 c. powdered sugar
1 c. butter or margarine,
   softened
2 eggs

5 bananas, sliced
1 (20 oz.) can crushed
   pineapple, drained
1 (13 oz.) ctn. frozen
   whipped topping, thawed
1 c. chopped nuts
Maraschino cherry halves
   (optional)

Combine crushed vanilla wafers and melted butter; mix well and press onto bottom and sides of a 13x9x2 inch pan. Combine powdered sugar, softened butter and eggs; beat on high speed of electric mixer 15 minutes. Do not underbeat. Spread sugar mixture on top of crust and top with bananas, then cover with pineapple. Spread whipped topping over fruit and sprinkle with nuts. Garnish with cherries, if desired; chill thoroughly. Cut into squares to serve. Yield: 20 to 24 servings.

Inda Adams
Andrew Jackson Council

BLACKBERRY COBBLER

1 c. flour
1 c. sugar
1 tsp. baking powder
1/2 c. sweet milk

1 stick butter or margarine
2 c. hot sweetened
  blackberries

Melt butter in 10x6x2 inch Pyrex dish. Mix together flour, sugar, baking powder and milk; pour into Pyrex dish. Cover with hot, sweetened blackberries and stir slightly to mix in blackberries. Bake at 350° for 30 minutes. Use apples, cherries, peaches or any fruit instead of blackberries, if desired.

Pat Carpenter
Nashville Council

BLACKBERRY COBBLER

1 c. self-rising flour
1 c. sugar
1 c. milk

1 stick margarine
1 qt. blackberries

Melt margarine in a 2 quart baking dish. Mix flour, sugar and milk; beat until well mixed, then pour over melted butter. Do not stir. Pour the berries over this and again, do not stir. Bake in a preheated 350° oven until crust rises to the top and browns. You can also use strawberries.

Jane York
Harpeth Council

BLACK FOREST PIE

1 (7 oz.) jar Kraft
  marshmallow creme
2 (1 oz.) sq. unsweetened
  chocolate, melted
1 tsp. vanilla
1 c. heavy cream, whipped

2 Tbsp. maraschino cherry
  juice
1/2 c. quartered maraschino
  cherries
1 Johnston's chocolate
  flavored pie crust

314

Combine marshmallow creme, chocolate and vanilla; mix until well blended. Gradually add cherry juice, blending until smooth. Fold in whipped cream and cherries. Pour into crust; freeze. Garnish with additional cherries, if desired.

Leslie Stephens
Harpeth Council

BLACK WALNUT PIE

1 stick butter	1 c. black walnuts
4 eggs	1 tsp. vanilla
1 c. sugar	1/2 tsp. lemon juice
1 c. dark syrup	Pinch of salt

Brown butter. Beat eggs; add all other ingredients. Bake in preheated oven, 425°, for 10 minutes, then 325° for 40 minutes.

Bobbie Blackwell
Nashboro Council

BLUEBERRY PIE

8 oz. cream cheese	Blueberry pie filling
1 c. sugar	Bananas
8 oz. Cool Whip	Graham cracker crust

Beat 8 ounces cream cheese with 1 cup sugar until light and fluffy; fold in Cool Whip. Slice bananas onto graham cracker crusts; top with cream cheese mixture, then spread pie filling on top. Refrigerate. Makes 2 pies.

Note: Cherry pie filling can be substituted for blueberry.

Cheri Dickson
Harpeth Council

BLUEBERRY PEACH COBBLER

1 pkg. wild blueberries	1/2 c. chopped pecans
Muffin mix	2 cans peach pie filling
1/4 c. sugar	1/4 c. sugar
1/2 tsp. cinnamon	1 tsp. cinnamon
1/2 stick butter	1 tsp. almond extract

1489-81

315

Preheat oven to 350°. Wash blueberries; set aside to drain. In a medium size bowl, combine dry muffin mix, 1/4 cup sugar and 1 teaspoon cinnamon. Cut in butter, then stir in nuts. In a 13x9 inch pan, combine pie filling, 1/4 cup sugar, 1 teaspoon cinnamon, the almond extract and the blueberries. Spoon crumbled muffin mix on the peach mixture. Bake at 350° for 35 to 45 minutes or till topping is golden brown. Serve with ice cream.

C. Juandell Stogsdill
Knoxville Council

BUTTERMILK PIE

1 1/2 c. sugar
3 whole eggs
1/2 c. buttermilk

1/2 stick margarine
1/2 tsp. vanilla
3 Tbsp. flour

Cream sugar and margarine. Add flour, eggs, milk and vanilla. Pour into unbaked pie shell. Preheat oven to 450°, then bake at 350° for 35 minutes.

Linda Earp
Clarksville Council

BUTTERMILK PIE

1 1/2 c. sugar
Pinch of salt
1/2 c. buttermilk

3 whole eggs
1 tsp. vanilla

Mix well. Put in unbaked 9 inch pie shell. Bake 30 minutes at 325°.

Dot Gilliland
Harpeth Council

BUTTERMILK PIE

3/4 c. buttermilk
1 1/2 c. sugar
3 eggs (whole)

1 Tbsp. lemon juice
2 Tbsp. flour (plain)
1/2 stick margarine, melted

Combine all ingredients; mix well with electric mixer. Pour into an unbaked 9 inch pie shell. Bake at 325° until firm.

Mrs. Frankie R. Totty
Nashboro Council

316

OLD FASHIONED BUTTERMILK PIE

1 1/4 c. sugar
3 whole eggs
1 Tbsp. flour
3 Tbsp. butter

1/2 c. buttermilk
1 tsp. vanilla
Unbaked pie shell

Cream butter and sugar; add remaining ingredients and mix well. Pour into unbaked pie shell and bake at 300° for about 45 minutes.

David Lewis
Clarksville Council

BUTTERMILK COCONUT PIE

3/4 stick margarine
1 1/4 c. sugar
1 Tbsp. flour
3 eggs

1/2 tsp. vanilla
1/2 c. buttermilk
1 c. coconut

Melt margarine in large bowl. Mix together flour and sugar; add to margarine. Add eggs one at a time, beating well. Add vanilla, buttermilk and coconut. Pour into 9 inch unbaked pie shell. Bake at 350° for 35 minutes or until filling is set and golden brown.

Bertha C. Weigel
Knoxville Council

CANTALOUPE PIE

1 baked pie crust
1 medium size ripe
  cantaloupe
3/4 c. sugar
1/8 tsp. salt

3 egg yolks
2 Tbsp. cornstarch, dis-
  solved in 1/4 c. water
1 tsp. vanilla
Never-Fail Meringue

Put cantaloupe in top of double boiler and cook until dissolved; mash as you stir. Add sugar, salt, egg yolks and cornstarch mixture; cook until thick. Add vanilla. Pour in baked crust; cover with meringue and bake in 350° oven until browned. Serves 8.

Frances R. Lauderdale
Downtown Memphis Council

CARAMEL PIE

2 c. sugar
1 stick butter
1 Tbsp. vanilla

3 egg yolks
3 c. milk
2 Tbsp. cornstarch

Brown sugar and butter in a heavy skillet. Beat together remaining ingredients; gradually add to browned sugar and butter mixture. Heat and stir until mixture thickens. Pour into unbaked pie shell. Bake at 350° for 30 minutes. Add meringue, if desired.

M.G. Meeks
Clarksville Council

CARAMEL PIE

First, you must caramelize 1/2 cup white sugar. This is done by placing an iron skillet on low heat and placing the 1/2 cup sugar in the skillet and melting it. You must stir constantly so it does not stick. A wooden spoon is best for this. Set this aside and combine the following ingredients.

5 Tbsp. flour (and about 2
    Tbsp. flour may be used
    with this to thicken the
    liquid)

3/4 c. sugar
1 3/4 c. sweet milk
2 egg yolks (no whites)

Mix all dry and liquid ingredients; place over a double boiler to cook. Let come to a light simmer and add the caramelized sugar. You may want to add a little of the warm liquid first so as not to lump. After this is combined, you stir constantly until it begins to thicken to pie consistency. Pour into a baked pie shell and use a meringue top or a whipped cream topping.

Nell Young
Harpeth Council

CARAMEL PIE

2 1/2 c. granulated sugar
3 Tbsp. butter
3 c. sweet milk
Few grains of salt

3 Tbsp. flour
2 Tbsp. cornstarch
5 egg yolks, beaten
2 (9 inch) baked pastry shells

318

Combine 2 cups sugar with flour and cornstarch. Blend in egg yolks, milk, butter and salt. Place in large saucepan over low heat. Place remaining 1/2 cup sugar in heavy skillet and place over medium heat and keep an eye on this, but do not stir until melted. Stir the custard mixture, and by the time it begins to thicken, the sugar in skillet should be melted. Stir well as it should be caramelized and bubbly all over. As soon as this stage is reached, combine the two mixtures, stirring constantly. Continue cooking until the custard is smooth, creamy and thickened. Fill pastry shells and top with meringue and brown. These pies can be frozen for later.

Mary Louise Guinn
Nashville Council

CARAMEL PIE

1 baked pie shell	2 heaping Tbsp. flour
1 1/2 c. sugar	1/4 c. water
1 Tbsp. butter	6 Tbsp. sugar
3 egg yolks, beaten	3 egg whites, stiffly beaten
1 c. milk	

Brown 1/2 cup sugar and 1 tablespoon butter in a skillet, stirring constantly to prevent burning. Mix egg yolks, 1 cup sugar, milk and flour together. Add water; combine well. Pour into browned sugar and cook until mixture is thick. Pour into baked pie shell. Beat egg whites until stiff; gradually add sugar and beat until it makes stiff peaks. Heap over caramel filling, sealing edges. Bake at 350° for about 12 minutes or until golden brown.

David Lewis
Clarksville Council

NO CRUST CHEESE PIE

2 (8 oz.) pkg. cream cheese	2/3 c. granulated sugar
3 large eggs	1/2 tsp. vanilla extract

Blend mixture until smooth; pour into 9 inch pie plate. Bake in 350° oven for 25 to 35 minutes, or until puffed up and light brown on the edges. Remove from oven and allow to cool for 20 minutes. When cool, cover with the following mixture.

1/2 pt. sour cream   3 Tbsp. granulated sugar
1 tsp. vanilla extract

Place pie in 350° oven again and bake 15 to 20 minutes.
Ann Harmon
Harpeth Council

CHERRY-O-CREAM CHEESE PIE

Crust:

2 sticks butter   1 c. pecans, chopped
2 c. flour (plain)

Mix well. Bake in 2 quart Pyrex dish at 350° until golden brown.

Filling:

8 oz. Philadelphia cream   1 pkg. Dream Whip, prepared
  cheese   as directed on pkg.
1 box confectioners sugar

Chill. Top with Comstock cherry pie filling.
Metty C. Fain
Andrew Jackson Council

CHEERY CHERRY CHEESE PIE

1 (8 oz.) pkg. cream   1 tsp. vanilla extract
  cheese, softened   1 graham cracker Ready-
1 (14 oz.) can Eagle Brand   Crust pie crust
  sweetened condensed milk Cherry pie filling, chilled
1/3 c. ReaLemon juice

In medium bowl, beat cheese until light and fluffy. Add sweetened condensed milk; blend thoroughly. Stir in lemon juice and vanilla; pour into crust. Chill 3 hours or until firm. Top with desired amount of pie filling before serving. Refrigerate leftovers.
Inda Adams
Andrew Jackson Council

CHERRY PIE

1 (1 lb.) can tart pitted
   cherries
3/4 c. sugar

2 rounded Tbsp. flour
4 Tbsp. butter

Pour cherries and juice into bottom of 9 inch <u>deep</u> pie shell. Combine flour and sugar; pour over cherries. Dot with butter; top with lattice pastry. Bake at 400° for 50 minutes.

> Deenie Thornton
> Green Hills Council

NO-ROLL CHERRY PIE

1/2 c. butter
1 Tbsp. sugar
1 c. flour

1 (1 lb. 5 oz.) can prepared
   cherry or blueberry pie
   filling

In saucepan, melt butter with sugar over low heat. Add flour and stir until mixture forms a ball. Press onto bottom and sides of 9 inch pie pan; form an edge. Pour in pie filling. Spoon topping over filling. Bake at 350° for 50 to 60 minutes, until crust is golden brown; cool.

Topping:

1 egg
1/2 c. sugar

1/4 c. flour
1/4 c. milk

In small bowl, beat egg with sugar. Blend in flour and milk until smooth.

> Lauraette Cheatham
> Harpeth Council

QUICK CHERRY PIE (OR OTHER FRUIT)

1 3/4 c. sugar*
3 Tbsp. soft margarine
1 c. flour
1/2 c. milk

1 tsp. baking powder
1/4 tsp. salt
1 can sour cherries (or
   other fruit)

Mix batter of 3/4 cup sugar, flour, baking powder, salt, margarine (cut in) and milk. Pour in lightly greased baking dish. Mix cherries (or fruit) with remaining sugar.

Pour over batter. Bake at 350° for 1 hour or less. Crust comes to top.

*I never use this much sugar. Suit your taste.

Mrs. George Price
Knoxville Council

SNOW THE RELATIVES CHERRY COBBLER

1 c. self-rising flour, sifted
1 c. sugar
3/4 c. milk
1 can cherry pie mix
1 stick butter

Melt butter in baking pan in oven. Coat over all sides of pan. Mix flour and sugar; stir in milk; batter will be consistency of pancake batter. Pour batter into pan on melted butter; do not stir. Spoon cherry pie mix over batter. Bake in preheated 350° oven for 50 minutes to 1 hour or until golden brown. Apple, peach or cherry mix can be used.

Harriet Darnell
Clarksville Council

CHESS PIE

2 lb. 8 oz. oleo, melted
7 lb. 8 oz. sugar
4 oz. cornstarch
6 oz. flour
1/4 c. vanilla

Blend all together and mix well.

36 eggs
3 lemon rinds, grated
1 qt. buttermilk

Add to above mixture and mix 10 minutes. Pour into unbaked pie shells and bake at 350° for 45 minutes. Yields eight 9 inch pies.

CHESS PIE

1 stick butter or oleo
1 1/2 c. sugar
3 eggs, lightly beaten
1 1/2 tsp. white vinegar
1 1/2 tsp. meal
1 tsp. vanilla
2 Tbsp. thick buttermilk

Melt butter in saucepan; stir in sugar and remove from heat. Add eggs, buttermilk, vinegar, meal and vanilla. Pour into unbaked pastry shell. Bake at 425° for 10 minutes; reduce heat to 350° and bake until filling shakes slightly and is brown, about 20 minutes.

Mary P. Russell
Jackson Council

CHESS PIE

1 stick butter	1/4 c. milk
3 eggs	1 1/2 c. sugar
1 tsp. vanilla	

Melt butter. Add sugar, vanilla and milk; beat well. Add eggs, one at a time; beat well. Pour into unbaked pie crust. Bake at 350° for 35 minutes.

Ernie Simpson
Memphis Council

CHESS PIE

1/2 c. butter	1 tsp. vanilla
1 1/2 c. sugar	Pinch of salt
1 Tbsp. vinegar	1 (8 inch) pie shell, unbaked
3 eggs	

Combine butter, sugar and vinegar in a saucepan. Stir constantly over low heat until sugar is dissolved. Pour hot mixture over beaten eggs, beating constantly and thoroughly. Fold in vanilla and salt; pour into pastry pie shell. Bake at 350° for 30 minutes.

Dot Gilliland
Harpeth Council

SOUTHERN CHESS PIE

3 eggs	1 1/2 c. sugar
1 stick butter	1/2 tsp. vanilla
1/2 Tbsp. vinegar	1 Tbsp. meal

Cream butter and sugar; add eggs one at a time. Add

vinegar and meal; pour in unbaked pie shell. Bake at 325°
for about 45 minutes.

Evalyn Morris
Harpeth Council

SOUTHERN CHESS PIE

3 whole eggs	1 1/2 c. sugar
1 stick butter, melted	1/2 tsp. vanilla
1 Tbsp. vinegar	1 Tbsp. meal

Combine all ingredients in order and stir only enough
to mix. <u>Don't beat</u>. Pour in unbaked pie shell. Bake at
350° for 1 hour.

Denise Gill
Harpeth Council

MY GRANDMOTHER'S CHESS PIE

1/2 c. butter	3 whole eggs
1 1/2 c. sugar (blend 1	1 Tbsp. vinegar
Tbsp. corn meal)	1 Tbsp. vanilla

Melt butter in saucepan; add sugar mix. While warm,
add beaten eggs. Add vinegar and vanilla. Pour in unbaked crust. Bake very slow, about 30 minutes or until
firm, at 350°.
For variations: Omit vinegar; add cocoa, lemon juice,
cocoanut or pecans. These are <u>very very</u> rich.

Evelyn Causey
Nashville Council

MY BEST MERINGUE CHESS PIE

1 stick butter	3 egg yolks
2 Tbsp. corn meal	1 whole egg
1 tsp. vanilla	2 c. sugar
1 c. milk	2 Tbsp. flour
	1 Tbsp. vinegar

Melt butter and add sugar to it slowly. Mix corn meal
and flour; add to mixture. Add vinegar. Beat eggs and
add. Add milk and vanilla; mix well. Pour into unbaked
pastry shell. Bake 15 minutes at 400°, then at 350° for 35

minutes. Beat egg whites until fluffy, then add 4 table-spoons sugar gradually. Beat until sugar is dissolved. Spread on top of pie and bake at 325° until brown.

Dorothy Bryant
Clarksville Council

CHOCOLATE PIE

2 pie shells, cooled
1 (8 oz.) pkg. cream cheese
1 large container Cool Whip

1 c. confectioners sugar
3 c. milk
2 small boxes instant
    chocolate pudding

Let cream cheese get soft; add sugar, milk and confectioners sugar. Add 1 cup Cool Whip and chocolate pudding. Put in pie shell. Add additional Cool Whip for topping.

Lena Roberson
Andrew Jackson Council

CHOCOLATE PIE

1 can Eagle Brand milk
1 stick oleo or butter
4 egg yolks

1 bar Baker's German's
    chocolate
1 tsp. vanilla or 1/4 tsp.
    almond extract

Over low heat, melt chocolate and butter, stirring with wooden spoon, about 5 minutes. Add Eagle Brand milk and continue stirring until hot and bubbling. Beat eggs; add vanilla or almond extract. Cover and when cool, pour into graham cracker crust. Serve with whipped cream. (For a really delicious pie shell, use the egg whites to make the pie shell. Use chocolate shavings to garnish whipped cream.)

Chuck and Gail Dickson
Harpeth Council

CHOCOLATE PIE

1 1/2 c. sugar
4 Tbsp. Hershey's cocoa
1/4 tsp. salt
2 Tbsp. cornstarch
1 Tbsp. flour
1489-81

2 c. milk
3 egg yolks, slightly beaten
2 Tbsp. butter or margarine
1 tsp. vanilla

Heat milk in saucepan. Mix sugar, salt, cornstarch, flour and cocoa. Add milk to dry mixture, mixing well. Boil 1 minute over medium heat, stirring constantly. Remove from heat. Stir half of mixture into beaten egg yolks, then blend into hot mixture in saucepan. Boil 1 more minute, stirring constantly. Remove from heat; blend in butter and vanilla. Cool. Pour into baked pie shell; top with meringue. Bake in 400° oven for 8 to 10 minutes until a delicate brown.

Margaret H. Brooks
Harpeth Council

CHOCOLATE PIE

You will need a double boiler for this. Combine the following dry ingredients:

3/4 c. sugar	Pinch of salt
1/3 c. flour or 3 large level Tbsp.	1/3 or 1/2 c. cocoa (or however dark you want it)

You will also need 3 or 4 eggs. Stir into this 2 cups of sweet milk; mix well. Place in double boiler and stir constantly until it comes to a light simmer. At this point, drop a lump of butter or margarine the size of a small egg into this and stir well. Now, in a separate bowl or a cup, beat only the 3 or 4 egg yolks. This depends on the size of the eggs. If large, use 3 yolks; if small, use 4 yolks. Do not use whites. Now, add some of the hot mixture to this and blend well. Gradually add this mixture back to the liquid in the double boiler and continue to stir. Let this thicken to a pie filling consistency and remove from heat. Stir in 1/2 teaspoon of vanilla flavoring. Pour into a baked pie shell or use as a pudding. May be topped with a meringue or with whipped cream.

Nell Young
Harpeth Council

CHOCOLATE PIE

1 c. sugar	3 eggs, separated
1/2 c. plain flour	1 Tbsp. butter (or oleo)
2 Tbsp. cocoa	1 tsp. vanilla flavoring
1 1/2 c. sweet milk	

Mix flour, sugar and cocoa together. Add milk; blend all together and put mixture in top of double boiler and let get hot before you add the egg yolks and butter. Stir occasionally as it thickens, 20-25 minutes. When done, take off stove and add flavoring. Set aside as you beat the egg whites for the meringue. This will thicken more as it cools. Beat egg whites for 10-15 minutes, slowly adding 1 tablespoon sugar per egg white used. Beat till can be cut with a knife. Pour chocolate mixture in baked pie shell. Smooth meringue on top; brown in 400° oven for 5-10 minutes. Best in town-up and down-and all around.

Dot Crouch
Clarksville Council

CHOCOLATE PIE

3 c. sugar
1 stick oleo, melted
4 eggs
7 Tbsp. cocoa

1 tsp. vanilla
1 large can Pet milk
2 c. coconut
1 c. chopped pecans
1/4 tsp. salt

Mix all ingredients well and pour into unbaked pie shells. Bake in 350° oven for 40 minutes. Yield: 3 pies.

Linda Cavazos
Jackson Council

CHOCOLATE PIE

1 c. sugar
3 or 4 Tbsp. cocoa
4 Tbsp. flour

1 small can Carnation milk
1 small can water
3 eggs, separated

Blend all together, except egg whites; cook until thick. Add 2 tablespoons butter and 1 teaspoon vanilla. Pour into a baked 9 inch pie shell. Beat egg whites until almost dry; add 6 tablespoons sugar and beat until stiff. Swirl on top of cooled pie filling and brown in 400° oven, approximately 5-10 minutes.

Pattie Hoffman
Nashboro Council

CHOCOLATE PIE

2 sq. chocolate	1 c. sugar
2 Tbsp. butter	1/4 tsp. salt
1/3 c. flour	2 1/2 c. milk
3 eggs	3/4 tsp. vanilla

Melt chocolate and butter in top of double boiler. Scald milk. Add dry ingredients to chocolate; mix well. Add 1 cup milk and mix well. Add remaining milk and cook approximately 15 minutes. Beat egg yolks; add to mixture and cook all together 5 minutes more. Add vanilla and pour into baked pie shell.

Bonnie Sneed
Harpeth Council

CHOCOLATE PIE

Filling:

1 c. sugar	3 egg yolks, beaten
2 heaping Tbsp. flour	1 1/3 c. sweet milk
2 heaping Tbsp. cocoa	1 tsp. vanilla extract

Meringue:

3 egg whites	1/2 tsp. cream of tartar
3 Tbsp. ice water	6 tsp. sugar

Mix all dry ingredients for filling, making sure there are no lumps. Add beaten egg yolks, then milk gradually. Place over medium heat; stir constantly until mixture thickens. Remove from burner; add vanilla. Stir well. Place in baked pie shell.

For meringue: Place egg whites, ice water and cream of tartar in mixing bowl; beat until it stands in peaks. Fold in sugar gradually. Cover pie filling and peak with back of spoon. Bake in preheated 350° oven until brown.

Jane Wohlbold
Green Hills Council

IRON SKILLET CHOCOLATE PIE

1 c. sugar
2 Tbsp. cocoa
2 eggs, separated
1 tsp. vanilla

2 rounded Tbsp. flour
2 rounded Tbsp. butter
1 c. milk

Melt butter in skillet over low heat. Add sugar, flour and cocoa; mix lightly. Combine egg yolks and milk; add to above mixture. Stir constantly until thick; add vanilla. Pour into baked pie shell and cover with meringue made of 2 egg whites and 1/4 cup sugar. Brown in 325° oven.

Ann Harmon
Harpeth Council

KATHERINE LEEGON'S CHOCOLATE PIE FILLING

Combine and mix in iron skillet:
1 c. sugar
1 Tbsp. chocolate

7 Tbsp. flour
1/2 tsp. salt

Blend in 3 egg yolks. Next, add 2 cups milk. Cook until thick; remove from heat. Add 1/4 stick butter and 1 tablespoon vanilla; stir until cool.

Zoerita Proctor
Nashboro Council

MOM'S OLD FASHIONED CHOCOLATE PIE

1 c. sugar
2 Tbsp. cornstarch or flour
2 Tbsp. cocoa
2 c. sweet milk
3 egg yolks, beaten

1 Tbsp. butter
Dash of salt
1 Tbsp. vanilla
1 baked pastry shell
2 egg whites, beaten stiff

Cook first 5 ingredients, stirring constantly until thick. Add butter, salt and vanilla. Stir well; pour into pastry shell. Top with meringue and bake until golden brown.

Mary C. Jackson
Memphis Council

CREAMY CHOCOLATE PIE

Whip 1 (4 1/2 ounce) package instant chocolate pudding, using 1 cup milk, for 1 minute in mixer. Blend in 1 1/2 cups Cool Whip and 1/4 cup chopped pecans. Spoon into a baked pie crust. Garnish with 1/2 cup Cool Whip. Sprinkle chopped pecans on top.

Imogene H. Suttles
Knoxville Council

CHOCOLATE PIE DELIGHT

1 (3 1/2 oz.) pkg. chocolate
   pudding and pie filling
3 Tbsp. sugar
2 c. milk
1 (9 inch) pie shell, baked

Prepare pudding mix according to directions. Stir in sugar and cool thoroughly. Fill pie shell with cool pudding; set in refrigerator.

Joyce Hill
Harpeth Council

CHOCOLATE CHESS PIE

1 1/2 c. sugar
2 eggs
1 small can Pet milk
1 c. nuts
1 tsp. vanilla
1/2 stick butter
3 Tbsp. cocoa

Mix cocoa, sugar, eggs, milk, nuts and butter. Heat in double boiler until butter melts; add vanilla. Pour in large unbaked pie shell and bake 30 minutes at 350°.

Shirley Duncan
East Memphis Council

CHOCOLATE CHESS PIE

1 small can evaporated milk
1 1/2 c. sugar
3 1/2 Tbsp. cocoa
1/2 stick butter, melted
2 eggs
1 tsp. vanilla

Mix and put in an unbaked pie shell; test for doneness

by shaking gently until it looks firm. Bake at 350° for 30 to 45 minutes.

Frances McLaughlin
Harpeth Council
Tricia Owens
Harpeth Council

CHOCOLATE CHIFFON ICEBOX PIE

Cream:
1 stick butter (margarine)   2 Tbsp. cocoa
3/4 c. sugar

Add:
1/4 tsp. vanilla   1 egg, unbeaten

Beat with mixer at high speed for at least 5 minutes. Add another egg and beat 5 more minutes. Pour into baked pie shell; refrigerate. Top with whipped cream and shaved chocolate.

Mrs. Harold (Nancy) Turner
Columbia Council

CHOCOLATE CHIP PIE

1 stick butter, melted   1 c. light corn syrup
4 eggs, beaten   1 c. broken pecans
1 c. sugar   1 small pkg. chocolate chips

Divide nuts and chips in bottoms of 2 unbaked pie shells. Mix butter, eggs, sugar and syrup; pour in pie shells. Bake 30-40 minutes at 350°.

Barbara S. Stanfill
Harpeth Council

CHOCOLATE CHIP PIE

1 stick margarine   1 (6 oz.) pkg. semi-sweet
1 c. sugar   chocolate chips
1/2 c. flour   1/2 c. chopped nuts
2 eggs, well beaten   1 unbaked pie crust (don't
1 tsp. vanilla   cook in advance)

Combine sugar and flour. Melt margarine and cool.

Add to flour and sugar with eggs and vanilla. Add chocolate chips and nuts to mixture; pour in pie shell. Bake in conventional oven at 375°; reduce heat to 350° after 10 minutes and finish baking.

C. Juandell Stogsdill
Knoxville Council

CHOCOLATE ICE CREAM PIE

1 pkg. chocolate instant
  pudding mix
1 pkg. vanilla instant
  pudding mix
2 (8 inch) graham cracker
  crusts (or 1 larger one)

1 1/3 c. milk
3 c. vanilla ice cream,
  softened
Non-dairy whipped topping
Chocolate bar or toffee bar,
  crumbled finely

Beat milk and softened ice cream together with electric mixer. Add chocolate pudding mix and beat 2 minutes. Add in vanilla pudding mix; beat 2 minutes. Pour into pie shell(s); freeze. For 2 hours before serving, place in refrigerator. Top with non-dairy whipped topping and garnish with grated chocolate or toffee bar.

Ruth L. Cole
Harpeth Council

CHOCOLATE PECAN PIE

1/2 c. sugar
1 c. dark corn syrup
1/4 tsp. salt
1 Tbsp. flour
1 c. pecan halves

2 eggs
1 Tbsp. butter or oleo
2 sq. unsweetened chocolate
1 tsp. vanilla

Beat together sugar, syrup, salt, flour and eggs. Melt butter and chocolate together; add with vanilla and pecans to first mixture. Pour into shell. Bake in slow oven, 300°, for 50 to 60 minutes, until filling is set. Cool and serve with ice cream or whipped cream. Makes a 9 inch pie.

Ann Harmon
Harpeth Council

COBBLER PIE

1 stick butter
1 c. sugar
1 c. flour

1 c. milk
1 (21 oz.) can pie filling
(berries or fruit)

Melt stick of butter in pan. Mix sugar, flour and milk; pour in berries or fruit. Pour mixture in a baking dish and bake at 400° until tested done with a fork.

Barbara Wells
Knoxville Council

AMAZING COCONUT PIE

4 eggs, unbeaten
3/4 c. sugar
1/2 c. self-rising flour
2 c. milk

1/4 c. melted butter
1 1/2 tsp. vanilla
1 c. coconut

Mix all ingredients, except coconut; beat on low speed 3 minutes. Pour into 9 inch greased pie pan. Let set in pan 5 minutes, then add coconut. This pie makes its own crust. Bake at 350° for 40 minutes.

Nellie V. Brewer
Jackson Council

IMPOSSIBLE COCONUT PIE

2 eggs, well beaten
1 c. sugar
1/4 c. self-rising flour
1 c. milk

1/2 tsp. vanilla
1/4 stick margarine, melted
1 (3 1/2 oz.) can or pkg.
coconut

Beat eggs and blend in other ingredients; mix well. Turn into a buttered 9 inch pan. Bake 30 minutes at 350°.

Inda Adams
Andrew Jackson Council

COCONUT PIE
(Creates-its-own-crust)

1/4 c. margarine
1 c. sugar
2 eggs

1 c. milk
1/4 c. self-rising flour
1/2 (3 1/2 oz.) can flaked
coconut

1489-81

Cream margarine and sugar. Add eggs, one at a time, mixing well after each addition. Add milk and flour, blending well; add coconut. Pour into a lightly greased 9 inch pie pan. Bake at 350° for 45 minutes or until set. Yield: 6 to 8 servings.

Judy Gibson
Harpeth Council

COCONUT CREAM PIE

3 egg yolks
Pinch of salt
2 1/2 c. milk
1/2 c. sugar

1/4 c. flour
1 tsp. vanilla
1 c. flaked coconut
9 inch baked pie crust

Combine egg yolks, salt and milk. Stir over medium heat till warm. Combine sugar and flour, mixing well. Gradually add to milk mixture, stirring constantly; cook until thickened. Stir in vanilla and coconut. Remove from heat and pour into pie shell; chill. Top with sweetened whipped cream before serving.

Norma S. Watson
Downtown Memphis Council

COCONUT CREAM PIE

3 eggs
6 Tbsp. flour
2 c. sweet milk
1 can coconut

1 c. sugar
1 tsp. vanilla
Pinch of salt

Separate eggs. Mix egg yolks, sugar, vanilla and salt in top of double boiler. Add flour and milk alternately to egg mixture; stir over boiling water until it thickens. Remove from heat. Add 1/2 can coconut. Pour into baked pie shell. Beat egg whites until they stand in peaks. Spread over cooled pie mixture. Put remaining coconut on meringue. Bake in 350° oven until golden brown.

Alberta McCroskey
Knoxville Council

334

FRENCH COCONUT PIE

3 eggs
1 1/2 c. sugar
1 tsp. vanilla

1 stick margarine, melted
6 Tbsp. buttermilk
1 c. coconut

Mix all ingredients together. Pour in unbaked pie shell. Bake at 350° for 30-40 minutes until done.

Eunice Buffaloe
Knoxville Council

FRENCH COCONUT PIE

3 eggs
2 c. sugar
1/2 stick melted margarine
1 tsp. vanilla

3 Tbsp. flour
1 c. milk
2 c. coconut

Combine all ingredients; pour in 2 unbaked pie shells. Bake about 40 minutes at 350° in preheated oven.

Billie C. Moore
Knoxville Council

KAT'S COCONUT PIE

2 c. milk
4 eggs
3/4 c. sugar

1/2 stick butter or margarine
1 1/2 tsp. vanilla

Blend 3 minutes with 1/2 cup Bisquick. Pour in pie pan; sprinkle 1 cup of Angel Flake coconut on top. Bake 40 minutes in 350° oven.

Jane York
Harpeth Council

COFFEE TOFFEE PIE

1 c. flour
1/2 tsp. salt
1/2 c. shortening
1/4 c. brown sugar, packed
3/4 c. ground walnuts
1 Tbsp. ice water
1/2 c. butter
1/2 c. sugar
1489-81

1 sq. melted unsweetened
  chocolate
2 Tbsp. instant coffee
2 eggs
2 c. heavy cream
2 Tbsp. instant coffee
1/2 c. confectioners sugar
1 Tbsp. dark rum

Combine flour and salt in bowl; cut in shortening. Lightly stir in brown sugar and walnuts. Sprinkle in the ice water; mix quickly. Pack mixture in 10 inch pie pan. Bake at 375° for 15 minutes or until firm. Beat butter until creamy; add sugar and beat until fluffy. Blend in chocolate and coffee. Add 1 egg; beat 5 minutes. Add second egg and beat 5 minutes. Pour into pie shell. Refrigerate, covered, overnight. Combine the last 4 ingredients; refrigerate 15 minutes, covered. Beat until stiff; swirl on pie. Freeze 2 hours. Serves 8.

Addie Downs
Green Hills Council

CREAM PIE FILLING

Separate 4 eggs; place whites in refrigerator. Mix in top of double boiler or a very heavy pan 1/4 teaspoon salt, 1 1/4 cups sugar and 1/2 cup plain flour. Add to blended mixture 2 1/2 cups milk, adding 1/2 cup first to make a paste. Place filling mixture over boiling water and cook, stirring constantly, until it begins to thicken. Pour hot mixture slowly over beaten egg yolks; return to double boiler and continue cooking until mixture is quite thick. Remove from heat; add 3/4 stick butter or margarine. To complete pie filling, use one of the following flavors. Will fill two 9 inch pie crusts.

Coconut: Add 3 1/2 ounce can moist flaked coconut and 2 teaspoons vanilla.

Pineapple: Add 1 (8 ounce) can crushed pineapple, drained, and 2 teaspoons vanilla.

Chocolate: Add 6 tablespoons cocoa or 2 squares chocolate and 2 teaspoons vanilla.

Raisin: Put 1 1/2 cups raisins in enough water to barely cover; bring to boil. Boil 5 minutes; drain and add to filling with 2 teaspoons vanilla.

Banana: Slice 2 very ripe bananas very thin. Add 2 teaspoons vanilla to filling. Pour part of filling in pie shell; add sliced bananas and fill with rest of filling.

Meringue:

4 egg whites   8 Tbsp. sugar
1/2 tsp. cream of tartar

Beat egg whites and cream of tartar until frothy. Add

sugar 1 tablespoon at a time; beat until egg whites stand in a stiff peak. Bake 8 to 10 minutes at 350° or until brown.

Joyce Mattice
Harpeth Council

DAIQUIRI PIE

1 (8 oz.) pkg. cream cheese	1/3 c. light rum
1 (14 oz.) can sweetened condensed milk	1 (9 inch) graham cracker crust
1 Tbsp. grated lemon rind	1 Tbsp. light rum
1/2 c. fresh lime juice	1 c. whipping cream
	1 tsp. grated lime rind

Beat cheese; gradually add condensed milk till well blended. Add 1 tablespoon lime rind, juice and 1/3 cup rum; pour into crust. Refrigerate 3 to 4 hours or overnight. Gradually add 1 tablespoon rum to cream; beat till stiff. Spread over pie and sprinkle with 1 teaspoon lime rind. Serves 8.

Debbie Bullock
Harpeth Council

DATE NUT PIE

1 c. butter	2 c. sugar
1 c. pecans	4 eggs, separated
1 c. dates	1 tsp. vanilla

Preheat oven to 250°. Cut up nuts and dates; roll in flour. Mix butter and sugar; add egg yolks that have barely been beaten. Add dates, nuts and vanilla. Fold in stiffly beaten egg whites. Put in an unbaked pie shell and bake in 250° oven for about an hour. Makes 2 pies.

Metty C. Fain
Andrew Jackson Council

RUTH'S EGG CUSTARD PIE

3 eggs, separated	3/4 c. milk
1 c. sugar	1 stick butter (not margarine)
1 1/2 Tbsp. flour	

Mix flour in sugar; add to egg yolks alternately with

the milk. Stir until smooth. Mrs. Brock's mother used no
flavoring. Pour mixture into unbaked pie shell; cut butter
into slices and let float in pie filling. Bake in a 300° oven
until custard is set, then brown the top, being very careful
not to burn. Add 1 tablespoon water to egg whites and beat
until peaks form. Add 3 tablespoons sugar; beat in quickly.
Heap meringue on pie; return to oven and let brown.
Delicious when served hot.

Ruth and Deborah Cole
Harpeth Council

8-MINUTE LIGHT AND FRUITY PIE

1 (3 oz.) pkg. jello	1 (8 oz.) ctn. Cool Whip,
2/3 c. boiling water	thawed
2 c. ice cubes	9 inch graham cracker crust
	Fruit

Dissolve gelatin completely in boiling water, stirring
about 3 minutes. Add ice cubes; stir until gelatin is thickened. Remove any unmelted ice cubes. Using wire whip,
blend in Cool Whip and whip until smooth. Stir in fruit.
Spoon into pie crust and chill 2 hours before serving.

Suggested Fruits: Fresh strawberries, raspberries,
blueberries, canned and drained apricots or peaches,
canned crushed pineapple in syrup.

Sheila Fleming
East Memphis Council

FOUR LAYER PIE

3/4 c. nuts, chopped	1 1/2 sticks oleo, melted
1 1/2 c. flour	

Bake at 400° until light brown; allow to cool. Mix in
mixer:

1 c. sugar	1 (8 oz.) pkg. Philadelphia
1/2 large ctn. Cool Whip	cream cheese

Spread over crust. Mix:

2 small pkg. instant	3 c. milk
chocolate pudding	2 tsp. vanilla

Spread over Cool Whip-cream cheese layer. Spread rest of Cool Whip on this. Sprinkle with shredded chocolate or nuts. Refrigerate several hours.

Shirley Turner
Memphis Council

FRIED FRUIT PIES

1 (8 oz.) pkg. dried
  peaches, cut in halves
  or 1 (6 oz.) pkg. dried
  apricots
2 c. water

1 Tbsp. honey
1/2 c. sugar
1 can (10) biscuits
Shortening for frying

In medium size saucepan, combine fruit, honey, sugar and water. Cook on medium-low for about 45 minutes, stirring occasionally, until tender and thickened. More water may be needed. On floured surface, roll each biscuit round and as flat as possible. Place about 2 tablespoons of fruit mixture on each pastry; fold and seal edges with fork. Fry in shortening until brown on each side. Drain on paper toweling. Makes 10 pies.

Emily Townes
Harpeth Council

FRUIT COBBLER

1/2 c. butter or margarine
1 c. flour (plain)
1 1/2 tsp. baking powder

1 c. sugar
1 c. milk
1 qt. fruit pie filling

Melt 1/2 cup butter in 2 quart baking dish. In bowl, sift flour, baking powder and sugar together. Add milk; mix well, then pour mixture over melted butter in baking dish. Add 1 quart pie filling. Bake in 400° oven until crust rises to top and browns, about 50-60 minutes.

Kay Boswell
Andrew Jackson Council

QUICK FRUIT COBBLER

1/2 c. flour   1/2 tsp. baking powder
1/2 - 2/3 c. sugar   1 1/2 - 2 c. fruit
1/2 c. milk   1 stick margarine

Melt margarine and put in small baking dish. Mix flour, baking powder, sugar and milk; pour over butter. Do not stir. Put in fruit; do not stir. Bake 30 to 40 minutes at 350°; crust will rise to top.
Suggested Fruits: Peaches or blackberries frozen in syrup or canned, undrained.

Mrs. Harold (Nancy) Turner
Columbia Council

QUICK COBBLER

1 stick butter or margarine   1 c. milk
3/4 c. flour   1 Tbsp. nutmeg or cinnamon
1 c. sugar   1 large can peaches

Melt butter in baking dish. Mix flour, sugar, nutmeg and milk; add to melted butter. Add a large can of peaches; stir. Bake at 350° until crust rises to the top and browns. Serve with whipped cream or ice cream.

Sheila Fleming
East Memphis Council

QUICKIE COBBLER

1 stick butter or margarine   1/2 c. flour (self-rising)
1/2 c. milk   1 can pie filling or fruit
1/2 c. sugar

Melt butter in baking dish. Mix together milk, flour, sugar and pour into butter; pour in filling. Bake at 350° for 30-40 minutes.

Debbi Wakefield
Harpeth Council

FRENCH CREAM PIES

1/2 lb. graham cracker
   crumbs
1/2 pt. whipping cream
2 (10 oz.) pkg. straw-
   berries, drained

1/2 c. pecans, chopped
2 sticks oleo
1 box powdered sugar
4 eggs
3 bananas, sliced

Grease 9x13 inch Pyrex dish; line with crumbs. Cream oleo, eggs and sugar; place on crumbs for second layer. Beat the cream; fold in strawberries, bananas and pecans for the third layer. Top with crumbs; refrigerate overnight. Serves 12.

Carolyn Mitchell
Memphis Downtown Council

CHOCOLATE FUDGE PIE

4 1/2 c. sugar

8 Tbsp. cocoa

Mix together and add:

1 can evaporated milk
6 eggs

1 tsp. vanilla
1 1/2 sticks melted butter

Mix thoroughly; pour in pie shells. Bake for 50 minutes at 325°. You must keep a close watch on this pie while baking. Makes 3 pies.

Alene White
Green Hills Council

FUDGE PIE

2 sq. unsweetened chocolate
1/2 c. butter
2 eggs
1 c. sugar

2 Tbsp. flour
1 tsp. vanilla
1/2 c. chopped nuts

Melt chocolate and butter. Add eggs, sugar, flour, vanilla and nuts. Bake in greased pie pan for 30 minutes at 325°, starting in cold oven. There's no need for crust. Delicious served with peppermint ice cream!

Brenda D. Brown
Harpeth Council

FUDGE PIE

1 stick margarine or butter
3/4 c. sugar
3 Tbsp. cocoa
1 tsp. vanilla

2 eggs
1/4 c. flour
1/2 c. nuts

Melt butter in 8 or 9 inch pie plate. Mix dry ingredients. Beat eggs slightly with fork and add to dry ingredients. Add vanilla, nuts and butter. Mix just enough to get all ingredients blended. Pour into pie plate and bake 30 minutes at 300°.

Kathy Irvin
Harpeth Council

FUDGE PIE

1/2 stick margarine
1 1/2 c. sugar
3 Tbsp. cocoa

1 tsp. vanilla
2 whole eggs
1/2 c. evaporated milk

Melt margarine in heavy saucepan; add sugar and cocoa. Stir well; add eggs. Stir mixture; do not beat. Add milk and vanilla. Pour into a 9 inch unbaked pie shell and bake at 400° for 10 minutes. Reduce to 350° for 20 to 25 minutes, or till crust is brown.

Joyce Mattice
Harpeth Council

FUDGE PIE

1 c. sugar
1/4 c. plain flour
1/4 c. cocoa

2 eggs
1 stick butter
1 tsp. vanilla

Beat eggs slightly; add melted butter. Mix all ingredients together and pour into unbaked pie shell. Bake at 325° for about 25 minutes or until firm. Serves 6.

Wanda Ladd
Green Hills Council
Cindy Martin
Harpeth Council

FUDGE PIE

1 c. sugar
1/4 c. cocoa
1/4 c. flour

2 whole eggs
1 tsp. vanilla
1 stick butter, melted

Combine cocoa and flour. Mix ingredients together in the order listed. Pour into unbaked pie shell. Bake at 300° for 45 minutes.

Tammy Raines
Eastgate I Council

FUDGE PIE

2 eggs
1 c. sugar
1 stick oleo

1/4 c. flour
1/4 c. cocoa
1 tsp. vanilla

Melt oleo and beat eggs slightly. Mix all ingredients thoroughly; pour into unbaked 8 inch pie shell. Bake at 325° until filling is firm.

Meringue:

3 egg whites
1/2 tsp. cream of tartar

6 Tbsp. sugar
1/2 tsp. vanilla

Beat egg whites, cream of tartar and vanilla until stiff. Add sugar; beat until stiff again. Bake at 400° until brown.

Ginger Lewis
Harpeth Council

FUDGE PIE

Melt:
1 1/2 sticks butter

1 1/2 sq. unsweetened chocolate

Add:
1 c. sugar
2 Tbsp. flour

2 eggs, well beaten
1 tsp. vanilla

Beat well. Pour in 9 inch unbaked pie shell. Bake 30 minutes at 350°.

Nancy D. Loftin
Columbia Council

FUDGE PIE

1 graham cracker pie shell	2 whole eggs
1/2 stick melted butter	1 Tbsp. vanilla
1 1/2 c. sugar	Small can evaporated milk
3 Tbsp. cocoa	

Combine the sugar and cocoa, then add the other ingredients. Pour into the graham cracker pie shell. Bake for 1 hour at 325°. You may need to adjust time to your oven.

Sharon Rawlings
Harpeth Council

EASY FUDGE PIE

1 c. sugar	2 eggs
2 Tbsp. flour	3 Tbsp. butter, melted
4 Tbsp. cocoa	1 tsp. vanilla
1/2 c. milk	

Mix all ingredients with electric mixer. Pour into prepared pie shell. Bake for 45 minutes at 325°. Serve warm with whipped cream or ice cream.

Beverly Vaughn
Harpeth Council

FRUIT PIE

Mix together in a large bowl:

1 large ctn. Cool Whip	1 medium can fruit cocktail, drained
1 can Eagle Brand milk	
1 small can crushed pineapple, drained	1 small can Mandarin oranges, drained
1 c. chopped pecans	1/3 c. lemon juice (add last)
3 bananas, sliced	4 graham cracker pie shells

Mix all ingredients together and pour into pie shells. Chill for 2 hours or overnight.

Othelia Taylor
Harpeth Council

GERMAN CHOCOLATE PIE

1 stick butter ·	1 Tbsp. vanilla
3 eggs	Pinch of salt
2 c. sugar	1 full bar German's
1 large can Pet milk	chocolate

Melt butter with chocolate; stir in sugar. Cook for a minute or two. Beat eggs with electric mixer, then add to chocolate mixture. Add Pet milk, salt and vanilla. Pour into an unbaked pie shell in a 9 or 10 inch metal pie pan. Chopped nuts may be added if you like just before pouring into pie shell.

Barbara S. Stanfill
Harpeth Council

GERMAN SWEET CHOCOLATE PIE

1 (4 oz.) pkg. German's sweet chocolate	1/8 tsp. salt
	2 eggs
1/2 c. butter	1 tsp. vanilla
1 2/3 c. (14 1/2 oz. can) evaporated milk	1 unbaked (10 inch) pie shell
	1 1/3 c. Angel Flake coconut
1 1/2 c. sugar	1/2 c. chopped pecans
3 Tbsp. cornstarch	

Melt chocolate with butter over low heat; stir until blended. Remove from heat; gradually blend in milk. Mix sugar, cornstarch and salt. Beat in eggs and vanilla. Gradually blend in chocolate mixture; pour in pie shell. Mix coconut and pecans; sprinkle over chocolate filling. Bake at 375° for 45 minutes. Cool at least 4 hours before serving.

Joyce Taylor
Green Hills Council

GLAZED PEACH PIE

1 c. sugar
3 Tbsp. cornstarch
Dash of salt
1/2 c. water

3 peaches, peeled and mashed
4 peaches, peeled and sliced
1 baked (9 inch) pastry shell
Whipped cream

Combine sugar, cornstarch and salt in a medium saucepan; stir in water and mashed peaches. Cook over medium heat, stirring constantly, about 5 minutes or until mixture is smooth and thickened; cool. Place sliced peaches in pastry shell. Pour cooled peach mixture over top and chill at least 2 hours. Serve with whipped cream. Yield: One 9 inch pie.

Beverly Pettigrew
Harpeth Council

GOLDEN BREEZE PIE

1 can condensed milk
1 small can frozen orange
  juice concentrate, thawed
1 (9 oz.) ctn. frozen dessert
  topping (Cool Whip),
  thawed

1 can Mandarin oranges, cut
  into bite size pieces,
  saving a few whole sections
  for garnish
1 baked pie crust (either
  graham cracker or regular)

Mix condensed milk and thawed orange juice concentrate. Fold in whipped topping and Mandarin oranges. Spread into prepared pie crust. Garnish with reserved Mandarin orange sections; chill thoroughly. Makes 2 thin or 1 piled high pie.

Joyce M. Crump
Knoxville Council

GOOBER PIE

Make graham cracker crust for 3 pies (I put mine in a 9x13 inch and one 2x8 inch pan.)

6 sticks whipped Kraft
  margarine

2 c. peanut butter
2 lb. confectioners sugar

In mixer, blend margarine, peanut butter and confectioners sugar. Put into pan. Melt in double boiler 1 (12 ounce) package chocolate chips and 1/3 bar paraffin. Pour over above mixture. Serves 36.

Charlotte and Mike Tate
Harpeth Council

HAWAIIAN PIE

1 deep dish pie crust
1/2 c. chopped pecans
1 small can crushed
  pineapple
3 bananas, chopped

1 pkg. frozen coconut or
  fresh, grated
1 medium bowl Cool Whip
1 c. sugar
2-3 Tbsp. cornstarch

Bake crust according to directions; cool. Spread pecans over bottom of crust. Mix sugar and pineapple in saucepan; bring to boil. Mix cornstarch in small amount of water in shaker or jar with lid and add to thickened mixture, stirring constantly. Spread over pecans. Spread bananas over pineapple; spread coconut over bananas, then cover with Cool Whip. Let set in refrigerator for about 1 hour before serving to let all ingredients chill through. Just double or triple for more pies.

Dot Murphy
Memphis Council

HEAVENLY PIE

Crust:

2 c. plain flour
1 c. chopped nuts

2 sticks oleo

Combine flour, nuts and melted oleo. Pat into 13x9x2 inch pan and bake for 30 minutes at 350°; cool.

Filling:

1 (8 oz.) pkg. cream cheese
1 box powdered sugar

1 (8 oz.) ctn. Cool Whip

Mix cream cheese and sugar well, then fold in Cool Whip. Spread over cooled crust.

Topping: Spread 1 can cherry pie filling (or your

favorite fruit filling) over. Chill several hours before serving.

Sue W. Grizzard
Clarksville Council

HERSHEY BAR PIE

6 Hershey's bars (plain or almond)	1/2 c. milk
	1/2 pt. whipping cream
16 marshmallows	Graham cracker pie crust

Melt Hershey's bars and marshmallows in milk over low heat in double boiler. Remove from heat and cool. Fold in whipped whipping cream; pour in crust. Refrigerate overnight.

Deenie Thornton
Green Hills Council

IMITATION PECAN PIE

1 1/2 c. sugar	3/4 c. mashed pinto beans
3 eggs	2 tsp. vanilla flavoring
1/3 c. butter or margarine	

Cook beans well; mash. Reheat and measure. Beat eggs; blend with beans. Add remaining ingredients. Pour into 9 inch unbaked pie shell. Bake 40 minutes at 350°.

Judy Gibson
Harpeth Council

IMPOSSIBLE PIE

1/2 c. flour	2 c. milk
1 c. sugar	4 eggs
1 c. coconut	1 1/2 tsp. vanilla
1 stick oleo	

Mix all ingredients in blender or mixer at once. Put in a large buttered pie pan. Bake at 400° for 15 minutes, then at 350° for 30 minutes.

Sarah Unkenholz
Harpeth Council

JAPANESE PIE

2 eggs, well beaten
1 c. sugar
1/2 c. chopped nuts
1/2 c. raisins

1 can Angel Flake coconut
1/2 stick butter or margarine
1 Tbsp. vinegar

Mix and bake in unbaked pie shell. Bake at 350° for 20 to 25 minutes.

Pattie Carpenter
Nashville Council

JAPANESE FRUIT PIE

1 stick oleo
1 c. sugar
2 eggs
1/2 c. pecans, cut in halves

1/2 c. raisins
1/2 c. coconut
1 Tbsp. vinegar

Melt oleo and cool. Add the remaining ingredients; mix well. Pour into pie crust and bake 40 minutes at 325°.

Metty C. Fain
Andrew Jackson Council

JAPANESE FRUIT PIE

1 c. sugar
2 eggs
1/2 c. raisins
1/2 c. coconut

1/2 c. chopped nuts
1 Tbsp. vinegar
1 tsp. vanilla
3/4 stick melted butter

Mix all ingredients together and pour into an unbaked pie shell. Bake at 300° for 45 minutes to 1 hour.

Jasymine E. Bass
Columbia Council

JAPANESE FRUIT PIE

3/4 stick margarine, melted
1 c. sugar
1/8 tsp. salt
2 eggs, beaten
1/2 c. coconut

1/2 c. raisins
1/2 c. pecans, broken
1 tsp. vinegar
1 (9 inch) pastry shell,
   unbaked

Blend margarine, sugar, salt, eggs, coconut, raisins, pecans and vinegar. Pour into pastry shell. Bake at 350° for 40 minutes or until golden brown and set. Serve warm.

Ruby Smith
Knoxville Council

KENTUCKY PIE

3/4 c. semi-sweet chocolate
  chips
1 c. English walnuts,
  chopped
2 eggs, beaten

1 c. sugar
1 stick oleo, melted, cooled
1/2 c. flour
1 tsp. vanilla

Mix all together and pour into an unbaked pastry shell. Bake at 350° for 30 minutes.

Ruth L. Cole
Harpeth Council

KEY LIME PIE

Crust: Chill -

1 2/3 c. crushed graham
  crackers
1/4 c. sugar

1/4 c. soft butter or
  margarine
8 inch pie pan

Filling:

2 eggs, separated
1 can Eagle Brand milk

1/2 c. fresh lime juice
1 grated lime rind

Beat yolks until light; add milk and beat well. Fold in lime juice and rind. Beat egg whites until stiff; fold into lime filling. Pour into crust; freeze.

Virginia Q. Kaderabek
Harpeth Council

BETTY'S SPECIAL LIME PIE

1 can sweetened condensed
  milk
10 oz. can crushed pineapple
2 drops green food coloring

1/2 c. fresh lime juice
(bottled juice doesn't
give the same results)

350

Mix together milk and lime juice; add pineapple and food coloring. Put the mixture into baked pie shell. Refrigerate at least 3 hours.

Betty J. Cowherd
Andrew Jackson Council

KOOL-AID PIE

1 pkg. Kool-Aid
1 large can evaporated milk, stiffly whipped

1 c. sugar
Graham cracker crust pie shell

Cool milk until it is cool enough to be whipped. Add sugar; whip until blended. Add Kool-Aid and pour into shell. Keep in freezing storage until ready to serve.

David Lewis
Clarksville Council

LEMONADE PIE

1 small can frozen lemonade
1 small container non-dairy whipped topping

1 can Eagle Brand milk
1 graham cracker pie crust

Combine thawed lemonade, whipped topping and Eagle Brand milk; blend thoroughly. Pour into pie crust and chill.

David Lewis
Clarksville Council

Cheryl V. Alderson
Columbia Council
Patricia McRough
East Memphis Council

LEMON CHESS PIE

Put in large bowl:
2 c. sugar
1 Tbsp. flour

1 Tbsp. meal

Toss lightly with fork and add:

4 eggs, unbeaten
1/4 c. butter, melted (or
   1/2 c. cream)

1/4 c. milk
1/4 tsp. salt
Grated rind, juice of 1 lemon

Beat until smooth (thoroughly). Pour in uncooked pie shell. Bake at 370° for 10 minutes, then reduce heat to 300° for 35 to 40 minutes. Serve with whipped cream or top with ice cream. This will make 2 small pies or 1 large pie shell; depends on how thick you like your pie. Real rich.

Ruth L. Cole
Harpeth Council

LEMON PIE

1 prepared graham cracker
  pie shell
3 eggs, separated

1 can Eagle Brand milk
1/2 c. lemon juice
  (concentrate)
6 Tbsp. sugar

Separate the eggs. Mix together the egg yolks and Eagle Brand milk, then add the lemon juice; mix well. Pour mixture into prepared graham cracker pie shell. Beat egg whites until stiff. Add 3 tablespoons sugar and continue to beat. Add 3 more tablespoons sugar; beat until creamy. Top pie with meringue mixture and bake at 350° for 15 minutes.

Elaine Beard
Clarksville Council

LEMON ICEBOX PIE

1 (8 oz.) can Borden's
  Eagle Brand milk
1 (9 inch) prepared graham
  cracker pie crust

1/3 c. lemon juice
1 1/2 c. Cool Whip
Few drops yellow food
  coloring, added to filling
  (optional)

Mix milk, lemon juice and Cool Whip in large bowl until smooth. Pour into pie crust. Chill in refrigerator for 1 hour before serving.

Margaretta Douglas
Knoxville Council

LEMON ICEBOX PIE

1 box vanilla wafers
2/3 c. lemon juice
1 grated lemon rind

1 can Borden's sweetened
   condensed milk
1 small ctn. whipping cream

In bottom of 9 inch pie pan, crumble enough vanilla wafers to cover bottom of pan completely. Stand whole vanilla wafers around edge of pan to make crust. Add grated rind to lemon juice. Mix thoroughly with the sweetened condensed milk and pour into pie shell. Whip cream; sweeten to taste. Cover pie with cream and chill for several hours.

Vesta Frazier
Knoxville Council

MILE HIGH LEMON PIE

8 egg yolks, beaten
1 c. sugar
1 env. unflavored gelatin
1/2 c. water
1 Tbsp. grated lemon peel

1/2 c. lemon juice
1/4 tsp. salt
8 egg whites
1/4 tsp. cream of tartar
1 c. sugar

Mix egg yolks, 1 cup sugar, gelatin, water, lemon peel, lemon juice and salt. Cook over medium heat, stirring constantly, just until mixture boils. Chill in refrigerator, stirring once, until mixture mounds slightly when dropped from a spoon. Beat egg whites and cream of tartar until stiff and glossy. Add 1 cup sugar; beat again. Fold meringue into lemon mixture; pile into baked pie shell. Chill until set.

Mary McCracken
Columbia Council

RUTH'S LEMON MERINGUE PIE

2 Tbsp. cornstarch
1 c. sugar
1 c. boiling water
2 Tbsp. butter or margarine

1/2 c. lemon juice
Grated rind of 1 lemon
1/4 tsp. salt
3 egg yolks

Meringue:

3 egg whites
6 Tbsp. sugar

1/8 tsp. cream of tartar

1489-81

Mix cornstarch, sugar and salt; stir in boiling water gradually. Add butter; cook in top of double boiler until thick and clear, about 30 minutes. Remove from heat; beat in lemon juice and rind. Beat in egg yolks, one at a time. Cook over hot water 2 or 3 minutes longer, stirring constantly; cool. Fill baked pie shell. Cover with meringue, made by beating egg whites with cream of tartar until stiff, adding sugar gradually while beating. Place in slow oven, 300° F., until meringue is golden brown, about 1/2 hour. Cool away from drafts.

Ruth L. Cole
Harpeth Council

MA MA'S COBBLER

1 stick butter or margarine
1 c. self-rising flour
1 c. sugar
1 c. milk
1 can fruit (sweet or add sugar to make sweet)

Put stick of butter in 2 quart dish. Melt in oven at 425°. While butter is melting, mix flour, sugar and milk. After butter melts, pour flour mixture on top of butter, then pour fruit on top of flour mixture. Bake 30 minutes or until top is golden brown.

Neva Ferguson
Harpeth Council

MILLION DOLLAR PIE

1 can Eagle Brand milk
1/4 c. lemon juice
1 large can crushed
  pineapple
1 c. coconut
1 c. chopped nuts
1 large container Cool Whip
Yellow food coloring, if
  desired
Graham cracker crust

Drain pineapple. Mix all ingredients well and fold into graham cracker crust; chill well. (Can use different colors of food coloring for variation.)

Gerry Panter
Shelbyville Council

MILLION DOLLAR PIE

1 large ctn. Cool Whip
1 can Eagle Brand milk
1 small can crushed
   pineapple, drained

1 c. chopped pecans
1/4 c. lemon juice
1 small can Angel Flake
   coconut

Mix lemon juice and milk with mixer; add other ingredients. Pour into 2 graham cracker pie shells. Refrigerate.

Evelyn Carrico
Nashboro Council

MILLIONAIRE PIE

1 can condensed milk
1 (9 oz.) ctn. Cool Whip
1 large can crushed pine-
   apple, drained well

4 Tbsp. lemon juice
1/4 - 1/2 c. chopped pecans
2 graham or butter crusts

Combine condensed milk and lemon juice; mix well. Fold in Cool Whip; stir in well drained pineapple and pecans. Spread in prepared crust and chill. Makes 2 pies.

Joyce M. Crump
Knoxville Council

OATMEAL PIE

2/3 c. sugar
2/3 c. melted butter
2 eggs

2/3 c. white Karo syrup
2/3 c. oats

Bake in unbaked pie shell at 325° for 40 minutes.

Judy Christopher
Harpeth Council

OREO PIE

1. Crush 1 large package Oreo cookies while still in package (coarse crumbs). Pour into bowl and add 1 stick melted margarine; toss until all crushed cookies are covered with melted margarine. Lightly press cookies evenly into 9x13 inch Pyrex pan. Place in freezer. 2. About an hour later, set 1/2 gallon vanilla ice cream out of freezer

and let it get soft enough to spread evenly over first layer
of cookies, then refreeze. 3. Make sauce of:

3 Tbsp. cocoa	1 large can evaporated milk
1 1/2 c. sugar	3 Tbsp. margarine

Combine in saucepan; let boil 8 to 10 minutes, stirring
continuously. Allow to <u>completely</u> cool. Pour over second
layer of ice cream. Top with maraschino cherries and
chopped pecans. Allow to freeze overnight before serving.
Freeze any leftovers.

Jerry Doub
Chattanooga Council

PECAN PIE

4 whole eggs	1/3 c. butter
1 c. white Karo syrup	1 c. pecans
1 c. white sugar	1 tsp. vanilla

Brown pie crust. Mix together all of the above ingredients, adding pecans last. Pour pie mixture into crust
and bake at 350° for 40 to 45 minutes.

Dinah Randolph
Harpeth Council

PECAN PIE

Small	Large
3 eggs	4 eggs
1/4 c. (4 Tbsp.) soft butter	1/4 c. soft butter
1/2 c. sugar	2/3 c. sugar
2 Tbsp. flour	2 1/2 Tbsp. flour
1 c. light corn syrup	1 1/3 c. light corn syrup
1/2 c. chopped pecans	2/3 c. chopped pecans

Mix flour thoroughly with sugar. Beat eggs lightly;
add butter, sugar, pinch of salt, syrup and nuts. Mix
well and pour into unbaked pie shell. Bake at 375° for 10
minutes, then reduce heat to 350° and bake 50 minutes.
Place pie pan on cookie sheet to bake.

Ruth Wood
Harpeth Council

PECAN PIE

3 eggs
1 c. light Karo syrup
1 tsp. vanilla
1 c. chopped pecans
1/2 stick margarine, melted

1/2 c. sugar
1/2 tsp. salt
1/2 tsp. cinnamon
1 Tbsp. plain flour

Beat eggs well with fork; add syrup and vanilla. Mix well; add sugar, salt, cinnamon and flour. Mix well; add pecans and melted margarine. Mix well and pour into unbaked pie shell. Bake at 375° for 10 minutes. Reduce heat to 350° and bake for 30-35 minutes; if center is not firm, bake about 7 more minutes.

Wilma Hunt
Knoxville Council

PECAN PIE

3/4 c. pecans
1/2 c. sugar
1 Tbsp. flour

1 Tbsp. butter, melted
3/4 c. dark Karo syrup
2 whole eggs

Mix ingredients, adding melted butter and pecans last. Pour into unbaked pastry shell and bake at 350° for 50 minutes.

Edna S. Farrell
Nashville Council

PECAN PIE

1/3 lb. butter, at room
    temperature
1/2 c. sugar
1/4 tsp. salt

1 c. dark corn syrup
1/4 tsp. vanilla
3 eggs
1 c. pecan halves

Preheat oven to 350°. Stir butter until well softened and smooth. Add sugar slowly, blending until smooth. Add salt, dark corn syrup and vanilla; mix well. Add eggs, one at a time, beating thoroughly after each egg. Stir in pecan halves and pour into unbaked pie crust. Place filled pie on a cookie sheet in center of oven. Bake at 350° for about 50 minutes or until deep, golden brown. Cool for 3 hours before serving.

Debbie Lowe
Knoxville Council

AUNT SALLYE'S KARO PECAN PIE

2/3 c. sugar
1/2 tsp. salt
1 Tbsp. cornstarch
1 c. Karo syrup

2 eggs
1 tsp. vanilla
2 Tbsp. melted butter
1 c. pecans

Mix sugar, salt and cornstarch; add Karo syrup. Beat and add eggs and vanilla. Add butter and pecans; pour into pie shell. Bake 1 hour at 325°.

Ginger Lewis
Harpeth Council

BEST PECAN PIE

1 c. sugar
1 c. dark corn syrup
1/2 stick butter
4 eggs

1 tsp. vanilla
1 pinch of salt
1 heaping c. broken pecan
　meats
1 unbaked pie shell

Melt the sugar and syrup over low heat. Cut the butter in slices; add to the hot syrup until it melts. In separate bowl, beat eggs; add salt and vanilla. Slowly add the hot syrup, beating all the time. Add pecans; pour into pie shell. Bake at 350° for about 45 minutes or until pie is almost firm. I make 1 1/2 recipes and it makes two 9 inch pies.

Peggy L. Parker
Chattanooga Council

DELUXE PECAN PIE

1 unbaked (9 inch) pastry
　shell
3 eggs
1 c. Karo dark corn syrup
1 c. sugar

2 Tbsp. margarine, melted
1 tsp. vanilla
1/8 tsp. salt
1 c. pecans

Beat eggs slightly. Mix in next 5 ingredients, then nuts. Pour into unbaked shell. Bake in 400° F. oven for 15 minutes. Set oven temperature control at 350° F.; continue baking 30 to 35 minutes. (Filling should be slightly less set in the center than around the edge.)

Beatrice Lunday
Green Hills Council

FRANCES'S PECAN PIE

1 deep Pet-Ritz pie shell
1 c. sugar
2 Tbsp. flour
1/2 tsp. salt
2 Tbsp. milk
2 eggs

1 tsp. vanilla
1/2 c. dark syrup
3/4 stick butter (real
   butter), melted
1 c. pecans

Mix sugar, flour and salt, then add butter, milk, syrup, vanilla, eggs and pecans. Mix well; pour into a deep Pet-Ritz pie shell. Bake at 300° for about an hour or until golden brown.

Linda Earp
Clarksville Council

GOLDEN PECAN PIE

3 eggs
1 c. Karo light corn syrup
1 c. sugar
2 Tbsp. margarine, melted

1 tsp. vanilla
1/8 tsp. salt
1 c. pecan halves
1 unbaked (9 inch) pastry
   shell

In medium bowl, beat eggs slightly. Beat in next 5 ingredients; stir in pecans. Pour into pastry shell. Bake in 350° oven for 55 minutes or until knife inserted halfway between center and edge comes out clean; cool. Serves 8.

Jewel Calvin
Nashboro Council

KARO PECAN PIE

1/2 c. light Karo syrup
1/2 c. dark maple syrup
   or preference
1/2 c. sugar
2 eggs, unbeaten (if you
   beat, it will boil over
   or bubble)

2 Tbsp. flour (plain)
1/2 tsp. or dash of salt
1 tsp. vanilla flavoring
1 c. finely chopped pecans
1 uncooked pie shell

Add all ingredients together; blend well without beating. Small slices of butter may be added to the top before baking. Bake at 350° for 35 to 45 minutes, depending on whether you have an electric stove or gas.

Nell Young
Harpeth Council

KARO PECAN PIE

1 stick oleo, melted
3 eggs
1 tsp. flour
1 c. pecans

1/2 c. sugar
2 Tbsp. vanilla flavor
1 c. light Karo syrup
Dash of salt

Mix oleo and sugar together well. Add other ingredients, pouring pecans in last. Bake in 450° oven for 10 minutes; reduce heat to 300° and bake for 50 minutes or until it gets firm. Use deep dish pie crust.

Carolyn Mitchell
Memphis Downtown Council

KARO PECAN PIE

1 c. white Karo syrup
3 eggs
3/4 c. sugar
2 Tbsp. flour

2 Tbsp. butter
1 tsp. vanilla
1 c. pecans

Beat eggs. Mix flour and sugar, then add to eggs. Add syrup, vanilla, butter and pecans. Pour into unbaked deep dish pie shell. Bake at 350° for 50-60 minutes until center of pie is well done.

Sheila Fleming
East Memphis Council

SOUTHERN PECAN PIE

1 c. dark Karo syrup
2 eggs
1/3 c. sugar
1/4 c. flour

2 Tbsp. melted butter
1 tsp. vanilla
1 c. pecans, broken

Line a 9 inch crust, unbaked, with pecans. Mix flour and sugar; add syrup and beaten eggs, then melted butter and vanilla. Mix well; pour over pecans. Bake at 400° for 10 minutes; reduce heat to 325° and bake for 25 minutes.

Pattie Hoffman
Nashboro Council

SOUTHERN PECAN PIE

1 c. white corn syrup
1 c. light brown sugar
1/3 tsp. salt
1 tsp. vanilla

1/3 c. melted butter or
  margarine
3 whole eggs, slightly beaten
1 heaping c. chopped pecans

Combine syrup, sugar, salt, butter and vanilla; mix well. Add slightly beaten eggs; add pecans. Pour into a 9 inch unbaked pie shell. Bake in a preheated 350° oven for approximately 45 minutes. When cool, you may top with whipped cream or ice cream.

Vera S. Beard
Jackson Council

SUMMER PECAN PIE

10 saltines
1 c. pecan pieces
1 c. sugar

1 tsp. vanilla
3 egg whites

Crumble saltines. Beat egg whites until stiff; mix all ingredients. Put into greased pie pan. Bake at 350° for about 30 minutes.

Jo Ann Hindsley
Harpeth Council

PINA COLADA CREAM PIE

1 env. unflavored gelatin
1/4 c. cold water
1 c. pineapple juice
12 oz. cream of coconut
  (Coco Lopez)

1/4 c. light rum
1/2 c. cream, whipped
8 or 9 inch graham cracker
  pie crust

Soften gelatin in water. Heat pineapple juice to boiling, stirring in gelatin until dissolved. Add cream of coconut and rum; chill until set. Beat until smooth on low speed of mixer. Fold in 1/2 of whipped cream; pour into pie crust. Chill until firm. Garnish with drained, crushed pineapple and whipped cream.

Peggy Burr
Harpeth Council

PINEAPPLE PIE

2 sticks oleo
2 c. sugar
4 eggs, beaten
1 tsp. vanilla

1 small can crushed pine-
  apple, undrained
2 Tbsp. corn meal
2 Tbsp. flour

Melt oleo; add remaining ingredients. Pour into 2 unbaked pie shells and bake at 350° for 45 minutes.

Margaret Powers
Harpeth Council

PINEAPPLE-COCONUT PIE

1 stick melted butter
4 well beaten eggs
2 c. sugar

1 small can crushed
  pineapple, drained
1 can flaked coconut

Mix and pour into an unbaked pie shell. Bake at 350° for 30 to 40 minutes.

Barbara S. Stanfill
Harpeth Council

PINEAPPLE RHUBARB PIE

3 Tbsp. flour
1 1/2 c. sugar
1 egg
3 c. diced rhubarb

3/4 c. pineapple
2 Tbsp. lemon juice
4 Tbsp. melted butter

Mix together flour and sugar. Separate egg. Mix egg yolk, lemon juice, butter and pineapple. Combine these two mixtures thoroughly; fold in beaten egg white. Add rhubarb. Place in an unbaked pie shell and bake in 425° oven until rhubarb is well done and brown.

Joyce Mattice
Harpeth Council

SOUR CREAM PINEAPPLE PIE

1 1/3 c. sugar
1/3 c. all-purpose flour
1 (13 1/2 oz.) can crushed
pineapple in syrup
2 Tbsp. lemon juice

1 c. (1/2 pt.) dairy sour
cream
1/4 tsp. salt
3 egg yolks, slightly beaten
1 (9 inch) baked pie shell

Combine sugar, flour, pineapple with syrup, sour cream, lemon juice and salt; mix well. Cook over low heat, stirring constantly, until mixture thickens. Stir small amount of the hot pineapple mixture into egg yolks; mix and return to hot mixture. Cook, stirring constantly, about 2 minutes. Cool, stirring frequently. Pour filling into the baked crust. Make your favorite meringue recipe. Spread over filling and seal to edge of crust. Bake at 325° until meringue is browned.

Barbara S. Stanfill
Harpeth Council

PRALINE PIE

9 inch pie shell, unbaked
1/3 c. butter
1/2 c. brown sugar, packed
1/3 c. chopped pecans

1 (5 oz.) pkg. vanilla
pudding and pie mix
1 ctn. Cool Whip

Bake pie shell for 5 minutes. Remove from oven and pour mixture of melted butter, brown sugar and pecans into pie shell. Return to oven for 5 minutes; cool. Make vanilla pudding according to directions on package for pie filling. Pour pie filling over top of pecan mixture, reserving 1 cup of pie filling. Cool reserved pie filling, then add half the carton of Cool Whip and stir. Pour this over the pie filling already in pie shell; cool in refrigerator. Use remaining Cool Whip on top of pie and garnish with whole pecan halves. Chill thoroughly before serving.

Sue Roller
Harpeth Council

PUMPKIN PIE

1 1/2 c. pumpkin, cooked
3/4 c. sugar
1/2 tsp. salt
1/2 tsp. ginger
1 tsp. cinnamon
1/4 tsp. nutmeg

1/4 tsp. cloves
3 eggs, slightly beaten
3/4 c. evaporated milk
1 1/4 c. milk (I use much less because we like a drier pie)

Thoroughly combine pumpkin, sugar, salt and spices. Add eggs and both milks; blend. Pour into pastry lined pie pan. Bake at 450° for 10 minutes, then at 325° for about 45 minutes or until mixture does not adhere to a knife.

Bob and Nora Chandler
Harpeth Council

PUMPKIN PIE

2 eggs, beaten
1 (16 oz.) can Del Monte pumpkin
1 c. firmly packed brown sugar

1 Tbsp. pumpkin pie spice
1 Tbsp. flour
1/2 tsp. salt
1 1/3 c. (13 oz.) evaporated milk

Combine eggs and pumpkin. Blend in sugar, spice, flour and salt; mix well. Add milk; mix well. Pour into pastry shell. Bake at 425° for 15 minutes. Reduce heat to 350° and continue baking 35-40 minutes or until knife inserted near center comes out clean; cool. Store in refrigerator. One pie is 8 servings. (You may substitute 1 teaspoon cinnamon, 1/2 teaspoon nutmeg, 1/2 teaspoon ginger and 1/4 teaspoon cloves for 1 tablespoon pumpkin pie spice.)

Joyce Mattice
Harpeth Council

RAISIN PIE

1 c. raisins
1 c. sugar

1 pt. whipping cream, not whipped
1 tsp. vanilla

Mix well the above ingredients and bake in unbaked pie shell. Put pastry strips on top. Bake in 300° or 350° oven till done. This is over 80 years old.

Pattie Carpenter
Nashville Council

364

RAISIN NUT TARTS

3 eggs
1/2 c. (1 stick) butter
  (or margarine), melted
1 1/2 c. sugar
1/2 tsp. cinnamon
1 tsp. vinegar

1 tsp. vanilla
Pinch of salt
1 tsp. plain meal
1/2 tsp. allspice
1/2 c. raisins
1/2 c. chopped pecans

Beat eggs, sugar and butter. Add all other ingredients; beat. Fill <u>unbaked</u> tart shells (Bama ready made are good). Bake at 350° for 15-20 minutes until golden brown. These freeze well. Serve with whipped cream or ice cream on top. Makes 10-12 servings.

Marietta (Marie) Gray
Jackson Council

RHUBARB-STRAWBERRY PIE

1 1/3 c. sugar
2 c. fresh rhubarb (about
  1 lb.), cut into 1 inch
  pieces

1/3 c. unsifted flour
1 pt. strawberries, washed,
  hulled and cut into pieces

In a large mixing bowl, combine sugar and flour. Add rhubarb and strawberries, tossing lightly; let stand 30 minutes. Place mixture into pie crust, mounding in center. Dot with butter. Bake in 400° oven for 50 minutes or until filling bubbles.

Margaret McCafferty
Nashboro Council

RITZ PIE

3 egg whites
22 Ritz crackers, crushed

1 tsp. vanilla
1 c. sugar
1 c. chopped pecans

Beat egg whites until stiff; slowly add sugar. Fold in crushed crackers, pecans and vanilla. Pour into buttered pie plate. Bake at 350° for 30 minutes. Cool and top with whipped cream.

Mrs. Harold Turner
Columbia Council

ROCKY ROAD PIE

1 qt. chocolate ice cream,
  softened
1/2 c. chopped peanuts
1/4 c. chopped semi-sweet
  chocolate pieces

1/2 c. marshmallow creme
1/4 c. chocolate syrup
1 (9 inch) baked graham
  cracker crust

In large bowl, combine ice cream with peanuts and chocolate pieces. Gently swirl marshmallow cream and 2 tablespoons chocolate syrup into ice cream to create a marbled effect. Spoon into prepared crust. Drizzle on remaining 2 tablespoons syrup; freeze until firm or up to 2 days. Makes 10 servings, about 315 calories each.

Leslie Stephens
Harpeth Council

STRAWBERRY PIE

1 pie shell
Strawberries
1 1/2 c. water
3/4 c. sugar

2 Tbsp. cornstarch
1 small pkg. strawberry jello
Cool Whip

Brown pie shell; set aside to cool. Stir water and cornstarch over medium heat until thick and clear red in color. Let boil 2 minutes; add jello and stir until dissolved. Arrange strawberries in pie shell; pour mixture over top. Let cool. Store in refrigerator. Top with Cool Whip when served.

Dinah Randolph
Harpeth Council

STRAWBERRY PIE

1 can Eagle Brand milk
3 Tbsp. lemon juice

1 pt. strawberries, thawed
9 oz. Cool Whip
Graham cracker crust

Mix together Eagle Brand milk and lemon juice. Add strawberries and Cool Whip to the Eagle Brand mixture; mix well. Pour into graham cracker crust; refrigerate.

Cheryl V. Alderson
Columbia Council

STRAWBERRY PIE

1 c. sugar	4 Tbsp. strawberry jello
6 tsp. cornstarch	1/2 pt. whipping cream
1 pt. strawberries	1 baked pie shell
1 c. boiling water	

Mix cornstarch and sugar with water; bring to a boil. Add jello; remove from heat and cool. Add strawberries. Pour into pie shell; top with whipped cream.

Betty Stewart
Harpeth Council

STRAWBERRY PIE

3/4 c. sugar	2 1/2 Tbsp. cornstarch
2 1/2 Tbsp. strawberry jello	1 c. water

Boil until thick. Let cool; pour over berries, which have been hulled, washed and placed in baked pie shell. Cover with whipping cream.

Ruth L. Cole
Harpeth Council

FRESH STRAWBERRY PIE

1 c. water	Red cake coloring (enough
1 c. sugar	to make red)
3 Tbsp. cornstarch	4 Tbsp. strawberry jello
	1 baked pie shell, cooled

Cook sugar, cornstarch and water until thick and clear; remove from heat. Add red cake coloring and 4 tablespoons dry strawberry jello. Spoon a few spoonfuls of cooked mixture in bottom of cool pie shell. Line pie shell with whole strawberries. Pour rest of cooked mixture over the berries; refrigerate. Serve with whipped cream or Cool Whip. (You may use fresh peaches and peach jello.)

Imogene H. Suttles
Knoxville Council

FRESH STRAWBERRY PIE

1 1/2 c. sugar
1 1/2 c. water
1/4 c. cornstarch
Dash of salt
1 Tbsp. red food coloring

1 small pkg. strawberry
gelatin
Fresh unsweetened
strawberries
1 baked pie shell
Whipped cream

Combine sugar, water, cornstarch and salt; cook until clear. Remove from heat; add food coloring. Add gelatin; stir well. Let cool. Put strawberries into baked pie shell. Pour sauce over them; chill. Top with whipped cream before serving.

Carolyn Utley
Memphis Downtown Council

FRESH STRAWBERRY PIE

1 (9 inch) baked pie shell
1 c. sugar
3 Tbsp. cornstarch
4 Tbsp. strawberry jello

1 c. boiling water
1 pt. fresh strawberries or
1 pkg. frozen strawberries

Mix sugar, cornstarch, jello and water; cook until clear. Let cool. Place strawberries in baked pie shell. Pour cooled mixture over strawberries; chill 3 to 4 hours. Top with whipped topping, if desired.

David Lewis
Clarksville Council

GLAZED STRAWBERRY PIE

1 baked (9 inch) pastry
  shell
3/4 c. water
3 Tbsp. cornstarch
1/2 c. whipping cream

4 c. (1 qt.) strawberries
3/4 c. sugar
1/4 tsp. salt
1 Tbsp. sugar (to sweeten
  whipped cream)

Crush 1 cup of the berries; add water and simmer 3 minutes. Strain juice from cooked berries; add water if needed to make 1 cup. Reserve. Combine sugar, corn-starch and salt. Add strawberry juice and cook until clear; cool slightly. Arrange remaining strawberries in baked pastry shell. Spoon glaze over berries and chill. Serve with sweetened whipped cream.

Ruth L. Cole
Harpeth Council

QUICK STRAWBERRY PIE

1 single frozen pie crust,   1 c. sugar
  cooked   3 Tbsp. dry strawberry jello
1 1/2 pt. fresh strawberries   3 Tbsp. cornstarch
1 c. water   Whipped topping

Bake pie crust as directed on package. Fill with fresh strawberries, slicing if necessary. In a saucepan, combine sugar, cornstarch and water. Cook over medium heat, stirring constantly, until thick. Add dry jello; stir until dissolved. Pour over strawberries in pie shell; chill. Cover with whipped topping; garnish with strawberries and serve.

Linda A. Gifford
Chattanooga Council

SHONEY'S STRAWBERRY PIE

1 qt. strawberries, drained   6 Tbsp. cornstarch
1 c. sugar   3 Tbsp. strawberry jello
1 c. water   1 (9 inch) pie crust, baked
Few drops of red food   until lightly browned
  coloring

Cook sugar, water and cornstarch until thick and clear. Add cake coloring and jello; let cool. Put strawberries in cooled pie crust; spoon filling over berries. Chill before serving and add whipped cream.

Laura M. Cheslock
Memphis Council

SHONEY'S ORIGINAL STRAWBERRY PIE

1 c. sugar   1 c. 7-Up
1 small pkg. strawberry   4 Tbsp. cornstarch
  jello

Heat 7-Up with cornstarch; add jello and sugar.

Simmer and stir until slightly thick; let cool. Bake pie shell and cool. Pour in cooled pie shell 1 1/2 cups strawberries; pour mixture over strawberries. Refrigerate until cool and thick. Top with Cool Whip.

Maxine Scott
East Memphis Council

STRAWBERRY YOGURT PIE

1 pt. fresh strawberries
1 env. Knox unflavored
  gelatine
1/2 c. sugar
2 eggs, separated
1/2 c. milk

1 c. (8 oz.) Dannon
  strawberry yogurt
1 tsp. lemon juice
4 drops red food coloring
  (optional)
1 butter flavored ready-crust
  pie crust

In blender, puree enough strawberries to equal 3/4 cup; reserve remaining berries for garnish. In medium saucepan, mix unflavored gelatine with 1/4 cup sugar. Blend in egg yolks, beaten with milk; let stand 1 minute. Stir over low heat until gelatine is completely dissolved, about 5 minutes. With wire whip or rotary beater, blend in pureed strawberries, yogurt, lemon juice and food coloring. Chill, stirring occasionally, until mixture mounds slightly when dropped from spoon. In medium bowl, beat egg whites until soft peaks form. Gradually add remaining sugar and beat until stiff. Fold into gelatine mixture. Turn into prepared crust and chill until firm. Garnish with reserved strawberries.

Polly Kirby
Andrew Jackson Council

24 HOUR FRUIT PIE

1 can Eagle Brand milk

1/3 c. lemon juice

Beat together until thick.

1 1/2 c. drained peaches
1 1/2 c. crushed pineapple

1 jar cherries, cut in halves
1 large pkg. Cool Whip

Mix together and let stand 24 hours.

Judy Christopher
Harpeth Council

VANILLA ICE CREAM PIE

1/2 gal. vanilla ice cream,
   softened

1 large ctn. Cool Whip
Small pkg. (2 rows) Oreo
   cookies

Mix ice cream and Cool Whip. Crush 2 rows of Oreo cookies and mix with ice cream and Cool Whip. Put in freezer.

Linda Whitaker
Harpeth Council

VANILLA PIE

3 eggs, separated
1 c. sugar

3 Tbsp. flour or cornstarch
1 1/2 c. sweet milk
1 1/2 tsp. vanilla

Combine sugar and flour; mix well. Stir in egg yolks. Add milk and cook on top of stove until thick. Add vanilla; pour into baked pie shell. Cover pie with 3 beaten egg whites and brown under broiler.

Helen Jones
Nashville Council

RUTH'S VINEGAR PIE

For an 8 inch pie:

1/2 c. sugar
2 Tbsp. butter
3 Tbsp. flour
2 tsp. cinnamon
1/2 tsp. powdered cloves

1/2 tsp. allspice
2 Tbsp. vinegar
1 egg
1 c. water

1. Prepare pastry for a one crust pie; line a pie tin.
2. In a mixing bowl, cream the sugar and butter together.
3. Blend in the flour, cinnamon, cloves and allspice. 4. Beat the egg with the vinegar and water. 5. Stir into the dry ingredients; mix well. 6. Transfer to the top part of a double boiler; cook over hot water until the mixture is thickened. Stir frequently. 7. Place the empty pie shell in a 350° oven for about 3 minutes. 8. Remove from the

oven and pour in the pie mixture. 9. Return to 350° oven and bake for about 45 minutes or until pie is puffy and set.

Ruth L. Cole
Harpeth Council

VINEGAR NUT PIE

1 c. firmly packed light
  brown sugar
1/4 c. flour
1/4 tsp. ground nutmeg
Dash of salt
3 eggs, lightly beaten

3 Tbsp. butter or margarine,
  melted
1 1/2 c. hot water
2 Tbsp. cider vinegar
3/4 c. chopped pecans or
  walnuts
9 inch baked pie shell

In the top of a double boiler, combine brown sugar, flour, nutmeg and salt. Add eggs and butter; mix well. Add hot water and vinegar; beat with a wire whisk. Cook and stir over simmering water until thickened, about 10 minutes. Stir in 1/2 cup of the pecans; pour into prepared pie shell and sprinkle with remaining 1/4 cup pecans. Set aside until cooled. Not necessary to bake after filling is added to crust. Serve with whipped cream, if desired.

Dot Gilliland
Harpeth Council

PIE CRUST
(Never Fail)

3 c. flour
1 tsp. salt
2 tsp. sugar

1 c. shortening
1 egg, beaten, plus enough
  milk added to make 3/4 c.

Mix all ingredients. Makes 2 or more large crusts.

Jewell Mercer
Nashville Council

NEVER FAIL PIE CRUST

2 c. plain sifted flour
1/2 tsp. salt
1 c. Crisco shortening

1/3 c. sweet milk
1 tsp. white vinegar

Cut shortening into flour and salt; be sure it is well

blended. Measure 1/3 cup sweet milk and add the teaspoon of vinegar to this. Cut into flour mixture and, if need be, you may add a few drops of milk or cold water to get it to blend and make a ball. Roll into 1 large ball and cut in half. Place on well floured surface; roll out. Makes 2 pie crusts.

Nell Young
Harpeth Council

ANGEL FOOD SURPRISE

1 large prepared angel food cake	1 large container Cool Whip
	1 pkg. frozen strawberries

Take fresh angel food cake and cut a 1 inch layer off the top. Spoon out a "tunnel" in the center of the cake, leaving a thick wall on each side. Mix together the strawberries, slightly thawed, and 1/2 the container of Cool Whip. (Cake pieces spooned from middle may be added to this mixture if desired.) Spoon strawberry mixture into tunnel. Place 1 inch layer back on top of cake; secure with toothpicks. Place in freezer for 30 minutes. Remove and frost with remaining Cool Whip. Garnish with fresh strawberries, if desired. Replace in freezer and freeze at least 1 1/2 hours. Remove 30 minutes ahead of serving time. Cut directly out of freezer, then place in refrigerator.

Leslie Stephens
Harpeth Council

APPLE CRISP

1 can apple pie filling	1 box "Jiffy" cake mix
1 tsp. cinnamon	(yellow)
1/2 c. chopped nuts	1 stick margarine
	1/8 c. milk

Spread apples in 13x9 inch pan. Sprinkle cinnamon and nuts over apples; sprinkle cake mix over all. Melt margarine and mix with milk; pour evenly over cake mix. Bake at 350° until golden brown, approximately 30 minutes. Serves 8. Good with vanilla ice cream. Can also be made with cherry pie filling.

Amy Wade
Green Hills Council

APPLE KUCHEN

1/2 c. butter or margarine,
  softened
1 pkg. Duncan Hines yellow
  cake mix
1/2 c. flaked coconut
1/2 c. sugar
1 tsp. cinnamon

1 (20 oz.) can pie sliced
  apples, well drained, or
  2 1/2 c. sliced, pared
  baking apples
1 c. dairy sour cream
2 egg yolks or 1 whole egg

Heat oven to 350°. Cut butter into cake mix (dry) until crumbly; stir in coconut. Pat mixture lightly in ungreased oblong pan, 13x9x2 inches, building up slight edges. Bake 10 minutes. Arrange apple slices on warm crust. Mix sugar and cinnamon; sprinkle on apples. Blend sour cream and egg yolks; drizzle on apples (topping will not completely cover apples). Bake 25 minutes or until edges are light brown; do not overbake. Serve warm. Makes 12 servings.

Bernie Wright
Green Hills Council

AILEEN'S FAST APPLE DUMPLINGS

Pastry (or biscuits)
Apples
Cinnamon

Butter
Sugar

Sauce (for 6 dumplings):

1 c. sugar
Juice of 1 lemon

1 c. water

Peel and core apples; slice or leave whole. Make pastry (or use canned refrigerator biscuit dough; just roll each one out for the perfect individual size). Roll pastry and cut into squares or circles. Place apple slices in center and add sugar, cinnamon and a pat of butter to each. Fold points together on top; press together. Lay them in a baking dish. Boil the sauce; pour over dumplings. Bake at 400° for 10 minutes, then turn down to 350° and bake another 20 or 25 minutes until apples are tender. (Pierce with toothpick to check.) Serve with ice cream or Cool Whip.

Marian Molteni
Harpeth Council

BAKED APPLE DUMPLINGS

2/3 c. shortening
1 tsp. salt

2 c. sifted flour
5-6 Tbsp. cold water

Cut shortening into flour, then add salt. Add cold water; mix. Add more water, if needed. Divide pastry into 2 balls. Roll pastry about 1/8 inch thick (thinner, if possible); cut into squares. Place a cored, pared apple in center of each square. Fill each apple with 1 teaspoon sugar and 1 teaspoon lemon juice. Top the apple with a piece of butter; sprinkle with cinnamon. Pinch edges of dough together on top. Place in a well greased pan, a few inches apart. Bake in a 450° oven for 10 minutes. Combine in another pan:

2 c. sugar
1/4 c. flour
1/4 tsp. salt

2 Tbsp. butter
3/4 c. water
1 tsp. vanilla

Bring to a boil; let boil 5 minutes. Pour over baked apples and reduce heat to 350° and bake about 25 minutes longer, basting occasionally. Serve with cream.

Joyce Mattice
Harpeth Council

APRICOT CREAM CHEESE DELIGHT

1 (6 oz.) pkg. apricot or pineapple-orange jello
1 (No. 2) can crushed pineapple
2 small or 1 large jar junior apricot baby food

1 (8 oz.) pkg. cream cheese
1 pkg. Dream Whip, whipped
2/3 c. nuts, finely chopped
3/4 c. sugar

Combine gelatin and pineapple; heat until mixture simmers. Add sugar, baby food and softened cream cheese. Continue heating, stirring occasionally, until cheese melts. Remove from heat; chill until mixture mounds when dropped from a spoon. Whip Dream Whip until stiff peaks form. Fold in apricot mixture. Pour in 9x13x2 inch pan; chill until firm. Top with chopped nuts.

Mrs. Harvey Cummings
Harpeth Council

BAKLAVA
(Greek Traditional Dessert)

4 c. (one 16 oz. pkg.)
  California walnuts,
   finely chopped
1/2 c. sugar
1 tsp. ground cinnamon

1 lb. phyllo (strudel leaves)*
1 c. butter or margarine,
  melted
1 (12 oz.) jar honey

About 2 1/2 hours before serving or up to 2 days
ahead: 1. Grease 13x9 inch baking dish. In large bowl
with spoon, combine chopped walnuts, sugar and ground
cinnamon until blended; set mixture aside. 2. In baking
dish, place 1 sheet of phyllo, allowing it to extend up sides
of dish; brush with some butter or margarine. Repeat to
make 5 more layers of phyllo; sprinkle with 1 cup walnut
mixture. Cut remaining phyllo into approximately 13x9 inch
rectangles. 3. Place one sheet of phyllo in baking dish
over walnut mixture; brush with butter or margarine. Repeat to make at least 6 layers, overlapping small strips of
phyllo to make rectangles, if necessary. Sprinkle 1 cup
walnut mixture evenly over phyllo. 4. Repeat step 3 two
more times. Place remaining phyllo on top of last walnut
layer. Trim any phyllo that extends over top of dish.
With sharp knife, cut just halfway through all layers in a
diamond pattern to make 28 servings. Bake in 300° oven for
1 hour and 25 minutes or until top is golden brown. 5.
Meanwhile, in 1 quart saucepan over medium-low heat, heat
honey until hot but not boiling. Spoon hot honey evenly
over Baklava. Cool in pan on wire rack at least 1 hour,
then cover and leave at room temperature until serving time.

To serve: With sharp knife, finish cutting through
layers. Makes 28 servings.

Note: While working with the phyllo dough, a moistened tea towel placed over the dough will keep it from
drying out.

*Phyllo is available in Greek pastry shops or in the
frozen food section of most supermarkets.

Sherree Weisenberger
Harpeth Council

BANANAS FOSTER

3 bananas, sliced in chunks
  2 1/2 inches long
3 Tbsp. butter
6 Tbsp. cream de banana

6 Tbsp. (heaping) brown
  sugar
6 Tbsp. rum
1 tsp. cinnamon

Melt butter in a heavy skillet; roll bananas in melted butter to coat on all sides. Sprinkle with brown sugar and cinnamon; cook for 2 minutes, stirring constantly. Warm liqueurs (lukewarm). Remove bananas from heat; pour in warm liqueurs. Ignite and spoon over vanilla ice cream.

Sheila Hardin
Nashboro Council

COLD BANANA PUDDING

1 box vanilla wafers
6 medium bananas, sliced

1 can Borden's Eagle Brand
  sweetened condensed milk

Use 2 quart covered dish. Crumble vanilla wafers and layer with bananas. Pour Eagle Brand milk over each layer. Refrigerate 2 hours.

Emily Townes
Harpeth Council

BANANA PUDDING

3 c. milk
1 large pkg. instant vanilla
  pudding
1 can Eagle Brand milk

1 large ctn. Cool Whip,
  divided
1 box vanilla wafers
4 large bananas

Mix milk and instant pudding until thick. Add Cool Whip (1/2 carton) and Eagle Brand milk; mix well. Layer vanilla wafers, bananas and pudding mixture. Top with Cool Whip.

Ann R. Wooten
Memphis Downtown Council

BANANA PUDDING

2 egg yolks
2 Tbsp. flour
1 c. milk
1/2 tsp. salt

1 c. sugar
2 Tbsp. butter
1 tsp. vanilla

Mix flour and sugar. Beat egg yolks; mix with milk. Add dry ingredients; cook in double boiler until it forms a smooth sauce. Add vanilla. Cut bananas in slices and alternate layers with vanilla wafers; cover each with sauce. Beat egg whites and add 4 tablespoons sugar. Cover pudding with meringue. Bake in 350° oven until brown.

Dorothy Bryant
Clarksville Council

BANANA PUDDING

3/4 c. sugar (save 1/4 c. for meringue)
1/3 c. flour
1/4 tsp. salt
2 c. milk

2 eggs (save whites for meringue)
1 Tbsp. vanilla
Bananas
Vanilla wafers

Blend 1/2 cup sugar, flour and salt in top of double boiler. Add milk; cook until thick, stirring constantly. Beat egg yolks slightly; add custard gradually to eggs. Return to double boiler and let cook 2 minutes more, stirring constantly. Add vanilla. Alternate bananas, wafers and custard in baking dish, ending up with custard on top. Beat egg whites until stiff. Gradually add 1/4 cup sugar and spread over custard. Bake in 325° oven until brown.

Imogene H. Suttles
Knoxville Council

BANANA PUDDING

1/2 c. sugar
2 Tbsp. plain flour

1/4 tsp. salt
2 c. milk

Combine above ingredients; cook in double boiler until thickened, approximately 15 minutes. Beat 3 egg yolks; stir into hot mixture and cook for 5 minutes. Layer a casserole dish with vanilla wafers and bananas, alternating. Pour mixture over bananas and wafers; cool. Beat 3 egg

whites until stiff. Add 1/4 cup sugar. Pile on top of banana pudding and bake in preheated oven, 425°, for 5 minutes or until brown.

Othelia Taylor
Harpeth Council

BANANA PUDDING

3/4 c. sugar	3 eggs, separated
2 Tbsp. plain flour	1 tsp. vanilla extract
1/4 tsp. salt	1 box vanilla wafers
2 c. milk	6 medium bananas, sliced

In thick saucepan, combine sugar, flour and salt; stir
in milk. Cook over medium heat, stirring constantly, until
thickened. Simmer, uncovered, for 15 minutes, stirring
occasionally. Beat egg yolks; add 2 tablespoons hot mixture and blend, then pour yolks into hot mixture. Cook 5
minutes, stirring constantly. Remove from heat and add
vanilla. Line bottom of 1 1/2 quart casserole dish with
wafers, then top with layer of sliced bananas. Pour a thin
portion of custard over bananas. Continue to layer wafers,
bananas and custard, ending with custard on top. Bake 5
minutes or until delicately browned in 425° oven, or make
meringue by beating 3 egg whites with 1 teaspoon vanilla
until soft peaks form, then slowly add 6 tablespoons sugar
and beat until glossy. Spread over pudding and place in
350° oven for 12-15 minutes or until delicately browned.

Kay Boswell
Andrew Jackson Council

BANANA PUDDING

5 c. milk	1 small ctn. sour cream
3 small boxes vanilla instant	1 small ctn. Cool Whip
pudding	

Mix milk and pudding together. Add sour cream and
1/2 carton Cool Whip. Layer 1 large box vanilla wafers,
bananas and pudding mix. Top with rest of Cool Whip.

Jewell Mercer
Nashville Council

EASY-CREAMY BANANA PUDDING

2 large pkg. Jell-O instant
   vanilla pudding mix
1 (8 oz.) pkg. Cool Whip

1 (8 oz.) pkg. sour cream
1 pkg. vanilla wafers
4-6 bananas

Mix pudding as box directs. Add to pudding the Cool Whip and sour cream; stir. When pudding is mixed, layer pudding, vanilla wafers, bananas, pudding, vanilla wafers, bananas, etc.

Debbi Wakefield
Harpeth Council

BAVARIAN DELIGHT

Line pan with 1/2 pound crushed vanilla wafers. Mix well:

3/4 c. butter
1 lb. powdered sugar

2 eggs, separated and beaten
4-6 Tbsp. whiskey

Spoon mixture on crumbs. Add layer of whipped cream (1/2 pint). Add layer of crushed pineapple (No. 2 can), drained, then layer of nuts (1/2 cup). Sprinkle vanilla wafer crumbs. Let set for 24 hours.

Addie Downs
Green Hills Council

BERRY-MERRY SWEETS

2 c. (1 lb. 2 oz. can)
   sweet potatoes
1 c. miniature marshmallows

1 (10 oz.) pkg. frozen
   cranberry orange relish,
   thawed, or 1 small jar

Place sliced potatoes in baking dish. Top with cranberry-orange relish. Bake 30 minutes in 350° oven. Sprinkle with marshmallows and broil until lightly browned. Serves 6.

Jean Bethel
Memphis Council

BLUEBERRY DELIGHT

Crust:

1 c. flour
1 c. chopped nuts

1/4 c. brown sugar
1 stick melted margarine

Mix well and pour in a greased Pyrex dish. Bake 10 minutes at 325°, then cool.

Filling:

1 pkg. Dream Whip, mixed
   by box directions
1 (8 oz.) pkg. cream cheese

3/4 c. sugar
1/2 tsp. vanilla flavoring

Mix and pour over crust; refrigerate before adding topping.

Topping: Add 1 chilled can of blueberry pie filling (favorite). Keep in refrigerator.

Mildred I. Brady
Harpeth Council

AUNT JULIET'S BREAD PUDDING

2 c. milk
1/2 c. sugar
1/4 tsp. salt
1 Tbsp. butter

Grated rind of lemon
2 egg yolks
1 tsp. vanilla
1 c. bread crumbs

Scald milk; add sugar, salt, butter and lemon rind. Pour this mixture over well beaten egg yolks. Add vanilla and bread crumbs. Pour into a buttered baking dish; set in a pan of hot water. Bake in 350° F. oven until firm. Top with meringue and return to oven to brown meringue.

Meringue: Beat egg whites in a small bowl until they hold stiff peaks. Add 1/4 teaspoon cream of tartar and 3 tablespoons sugar. Spread on top of pudding when you take it from oven. Return to oven for about 5 minutes or until meringue is golden brown.

Mary R. Veal
Chattanooga Council

BREAD PUDDING

1/2 c. sugar
1/2 tsp. cinnamon
1/4 tsp. salt
2 eggs
1 qt. (4 c.) fluid milk

1 tsp. vanilla extract
8 slices bread, cut in cubes
1/2 c. seedless raisins
2 Tbsp. butter, melted

Mix sugar, cinnamon and salt in a large bowl. Beat in eggs and slowly stir in milk and vanilla. Stir in bread cubes, raisins and butter. Pour into 9 inch square pan. Bake at 350° F. (moderate oven) for about 1 hour until knife stuck near center comes out clean. Makes 6 servings, about 1 cup each.

Violet R. Purcell
Knoxville Council

BUTTER BRICKLE DESSERT

1 stick butter
1 c. plain flour

1 c. butter brickle

Mix together and pat in 9x13 inch pan. Bake 20 minutes at 350°.

8 oz. cream cheese
1 c. powdered sugar

1 c. Cool Whip

Beat together and pour over crust.

2 small pkg. instant butter
  pecan pudding

3 c. milk

Beat until thick; spread over second layer. Cover with Cool Whip and butter brickle. Keep in refrigerator.
Katrina Carter
Harpeth Council

Marie Barnett
Harpeth Council

CHERRY DELIGHT

Use about 8 inch square pan. Line the bottom with whole graham crackers. Make filling of:

1 large pkg. vanilla instant pudding, mixed with 2 c. milk

1 (9 oz.) ctn. Cool Whip

Spread 1/2 of this on first layer of crackers. Add another layer of crackers, layer of pudding, another layer of crackers, then pour 1 can of cherry pie filling on top of last layer of crackers. Chill for 3 hours.

Doris Crowell
Knoxville Council

CHERRY CREAM FREEZE

1 1/3 c. (15 oz. can) Eagle Brand sweetened condensed milk
1/4 c. lemon juice
2 1/2 c. cherry pie filling

3/4 c. (9 oz. can) crushed pineapple, well drained
1/4 tsp. almond extract
2 c. (1 pt.) heavy cream, whipped

Combine first 5 ingredients in large bowl; mix well. Gently fold in whipped cream until evenly blended. Turn mixture into 9x5x3 inch loaf pan. Cover tightly with aluminum foil. Freeze 24 hours or until thoroughly firm. Makes about 2 quarts.

Judy Christopher
Harpeth Council

CHERRY DESSERT

1 can cherry pie filling
1 can Eagle Brand milk

1 (8 oz.) ctn. Cool Whip
1 (15 oz.) can crushed pineapple

Drain pineapple. Mix together all 4 ingredients; spread evenly in oblong refrigerator dish, 9x11 inches. Cool for several hours before serving.

Optional: Cool Whip can be spread over cherry mixture.

Rosemary Catalani
Harpeth Council

CHERRIES JUBILEE

2 sticks oleo
2 c. flour
1 c. nuts (pecans), ground

Mix above ingredients; pat into 9x13 inch pan. Bake at 400° for 20 minutes.

8 oz. cream cheese
1 lb. confectioners sugar

Mix cheese and sugar. Prepare 2 packages Dream Whip and fold into cheese mixture. Spread cheese mixture over cooled crust; cool in refrigerator. Add 1 can cherry pie filling on top. It's delicious!

Sarah Unkenholz
Harpeth Council

CHERRY PIZZA

2 cans cherry pie filling
1 stick margarine
1 box white cake mix
1/2 - 1 c. chopped nuts

Pour pie filling into greased 13x9 inch cake pan. Put dry cake mix on top of this. Cut up stick of butter, dotting top of cake mix. Top with nuts. Bake at 350° for about 35 minutes or until brown. Very good!

Mindy Yates
Harpeth Council

CHERRY YUM-YUM

2 c. graham cracker crumbs
1 stick melted butter
1 (8 oz.) pkg. cream cheese
3/4 c. sugar
1 c. milk
2 env. Dream Whip
1 large can cherry pie filling

Mix graham cracker crumbs and butter. Spread half of mixture on bottom of pan; press. Mix together cream cheese, sugar, milk and Dream Whip; beat until stiff. Pour half of this Dream Whip mixture on top of graham cracker mixture, then add all of cherry pie filling. Top with another layer of Dream Whip mixture and sprinkle remaining graham cracker crumbs over all. Chill 2 to 4 hours.

Myrna Phillips
Clarksville Council

Wilma O. Kelly
Knoxville Council

CHOCOLATE DESSERT

1 c. plain flour, mixed
  with 1 tsp. salt
1 stick butter
1 c. chopped pecans,
  toasted
1 c. powdered sugar

1 large (8 oz.) pkg. cream
  cheese, softened
1 giant ctn. Cool Whip
2 small pkg. chocolate fudge
  instant pudding
3 c. milk

Mix first 3 ingredients; press in 9x13 inch Pyrex dish.
Bake for 20 minutes at 350°. Mix cream cheese, sugar and
1/2 carton Cool Whip; spread over cooled crust layer. Top
with remaining Cool Whip; refrigerate overnight. Sprinkle
grated chocolate on top. (Freezes well.)

Cheri Dickson
Harpeth Council

CHOCOLATE MOUSSE

1 qt. whipping cream
1 c. sugar

1 (8 oz.) semi-sweet
  chocolate bar
7 egg yolks

Whip cream until stiff; chill. Melt chocolate in double
boiler. Beat egg yolks and sugar. Fold chocolate in egg
mixture; add whipped cream. Reserve some whipped cream
to top each serving.

Tricia Owens
Harpeth Council

CHRISTMAS PUDDING
(Plum Pudding)

1 pkg. dry yeast
1 c. flour
1 c. raisins
1/2 c. mixed peel
1 tsp. nutmeg
1 tsp. cinnamon
1 c. milk
1 tsp. mixed spice

1/2 c. rum or brandy
1 c. bread crumbs
1 c. currants
1 lemon
1 c. shredded coconut or
  shredded almonds
1/2 tsp. salt
4 eggs

Put all dry ingredients in large bowl and mix. Add
eggs one at a time; add liquor and juice of the lemon. Mix
thoroughly. Add the yeast, dissolved in warmed milk.

1489-81

Mix thoroughly. Put in greased bowl; cover with cheese-cloth. Seal sides. Steam in double boiler for at least 5 hours.

Norma Ann Webb
Harpeth Council

BREAD CUSTARD
(Diabetics)

1 slice bread
1 c. milk
1 egg

1/4 tsp. cinnamon or nutmeg,
    sprinkled
1/2 tsp. vanilla

1. Assemble all ingredients. 2. Cut the slice of bread into small cubes and toast until light brown and crisp. 3. Place toasted bread cubes in an 8 ounce Pyrex baking dish. 4. Beat the egg; add to the milk. Pour this mixture over the bread. 5. Add vanilla to the milk and egg mixture when beating. 6. Sprinkle the nutmeg or cinnamon over the top. Place the dish in a pan of warm water. 7. Bake in a moderate oven until the custard is set. This may be tested by inserting a silver knife. If it comes out clean, remove the bread custard from the oven at once.
Exchange: 1 bread exchange, 1 meat exchange, 1 milk exchange. Calories: 311.

CUSTARD SAUCE
(Low Fat - Low Cholesterol Diet)

Shake together in a covered jar:

2 c. skim milk or 1/2 c.
    skim milk powder and
    2 c. water
2 Tbsp. skim milk powder

1 Tbsp. corn oil
2 Tbsp. cornstarch
1/4 c. sugar
1/8 tsp. salt

Pour into a pan; cook over low heat until thickened, stirring constantly. When slightly cooled, add 1 teaspoon vanilla (or sherry or rum) and 1 drop yellow food coloring. Makes 2 1/2 cups. Total recipe:

Oil - 3 teaspoons
Cholesterol - 17 milligrams
Saturated fat - 2 grams
Linoleic acid - 8 grams

Protein - 19 grams
Carbohydrate - 91 grams
Calories - 565

386

DAIRY DELIGHT

1 (4 1/2 oz.) ctn. Cool Whip
1 small can crushed pine-
   apple, drained
1 can Eagle Brand milk
1 can cherry pie filling

    Combine all ingredients and store in refrigerator until ready to serve. It can also be frozen.

                Ura Blanks
                Harpeth Council

DANISH PUDDING

1 c. butter
1 3/4 c. sugar
3 eggs, beaten
1 1/2 tsp. baking soda
1 tsp. salt
1 c. buttermilk
3 Tbsp. orange juice
3 orange rinds
1 c. chopped dates
1 c. chopped nuts
3 c. cake flour

    Mix thoroughly and bake in a tube cake pan in a pre-heated 350° oven for 1 hour. Pour sauce over cake while still hot.

    Sauce for Danish Pudding:

5 Tbsp. grated orange rind
1 c. sugar
Fresh orange juice

    Rub grated orange rind into sugar. Add juice of orange to make 1 1/4 cups; heat to boiling. Stir until sugar is dissolved. Pour over pudding while pudding is still hot.

                Katie Braden
                Harpeth Council

CHOC-O-DATE DESSERT
(Date Delight)

12 packaged cream filled
   chocolate cookies, crushed
1 (8 oz.) pkg. (1 c.)
   pitted dates, cut up
3/4 c. water
1/4 tsp. salt
2 c. tiny marshmallows or
   16 marshmallows
1/2 c. chopped California
   walnuts
1 c. heavy cream
1/2 tsp. vanilla
Walnut halves

1489-81

Reserve 1/4 cup cooky crumbs; spread remainder in 10 x 6 x 1 1/2 inch baking dish. In saucepan, combine dates, water and salt; bring to boiling. Reduce heat and simmer 3 minutes. Remove from heat; add marshmallows and stir till melted. Cool to room temperature; stir in chopped nuts. Spread date mixture over crumbs in dish. Combine cream and vanilla; whip. Swirl over dates. Sprinkle with reserved crumbs; top with walnuts. Chill overnight. Cut in squares. Makes 8 servings.

Evelyn Causey
Nashville Council

DATE DELIGHT

12 packaged cream filled chocolate cookies (Oreo)
3/4 c. water
1 (8 oz.) pkg. or 1 c. pitted dates

1 pt. whipping cream
3/4 c. tiny marshmallows
1/4 tsp. salt
1/2 c. chopped pecans

Reserve 1/4 cup crumbled cookies. Spread remainder in 10 x 6 x 1 1/2 inch baking dish. In saucepan, combine chopped dates with water and salt; bring to boil. Reduce heat; simmer 3 minutes. Remove from heat; add the marshmallows and stir until melted. Cool to room temperature; stir in chopped pecans. Spread over crumbs in dish. Whip cream and spread over date mixture. Sprinkle with remainder of cookie crumbs. Top with pecan halves; chill overnight. Cut in squares. Makes 8 generous servings.

Jane Wohlbold
Green Hills Council

DUMP PUDDING

1 can cherry pie filling
1 can crushed pineapple
1/2 c. sugar

1 yellow cake mix
2 sticks oleo
1/2 c. chopped pecans

Preheat oven to 325°. Butter dish. Mix pie filling, pineapple and sugar together; spread in pan. Sprinkle cake mix over all; slice oleo over top. Sprinkle pecans on top. Bake 1 hour.

Linda Kitchens
Green Hills Council

FOUR LAYER DELIGHT

Make crust of 1 cup flour, 1 stick margarine and 1/2 cup chopped nuts. Pat in bottom of Pyrex dish, 12x8 inches. Bake at 350° for 15 minutes; set aside and cool. Mix:

1 c. powdered sugar
1 small container Cool Whip

1 (8 oz.) pkg. cream cheese

Mix well and spread over crust.

2 small pkg. instant
    chocolate pudding

3 c. milk

Beat until real stiff; spread over cheese mixture. (You can make your own chocolate pudding and it is better than the instant pudding.) Top with Cool Whip. Grate sweet chocolate over top; refrigerate.

Sandra Duke
Jackson Council

FROZEN DESSERT

3 c. graham crackers

1 stick butter, melted

Combine above and press into a long dish.

1 can Borden's condensed
    milk

3 Tbsp. lemon juice

Mix together until milk thickens; pour over graham crackers.

2 pkg. Dream Whip, prepare
    as instructed on pkg.
8 oz. cream cheese
1 can crushed pineapple
1 can fruit cocktail

1 c. miniature marshmallows
1/2 c. pecans
1/2 c. coconut
1/2 c. cherries

Mix; pour on top of graham cracker crumbs and freeze.

Ruby Smith
Knoxville Council

FRUIT SQUARES

1 c. sugar
4 Tbsp. cornstarch
1 c. Crisco
2 eggs
2 cans fruit pie filling

4 c. flour
1 1/2 tsp. baking soda
1 tsp. baking powder
1/2 c. milk
1 Tbsp. vinegar

Stir vinegar into milk to sour milk; set aside. Combine flour, baking soda and baking powder together. Cream Crisco and sugar until well blended, then add eggs. Mix flour and milk alternately into egg mixture. (Start and end with flour.) Divide dough in half; press half of dough onto an 11x14x1 inch cookie sheet. Mix cornstarch into pie filling; spread filling over dough on cookie sheet. Roll remaining dough between 2 pieces of waxed paper. Remove waxed paper and place dough on top of filling. Bake at 400° for 20 minutes. Sprinkle with powdered sugar after baking.

Pat Becker
Harpeth Council

FRUIT SQUARES

1 c. shortening
2 c. sugar
4 eggs
3 c. sifted flour
1 tsp. baking powder

1 1/2 tsp. vanilla
1 can fruit filling (blueberry, cherry, apple, lemon or strawberry)

Cream shortening and sugar. Add eggs, one at a time, beating after each addition. Add flour, baking powder and vanilla; mix well. Spread 1/2 of batter in the bottom of a greased 13x9x2 inch pan. Spread can of fruit filling over batter. Spread remaining batter over fruit, covering as best as you can. Bake at 350° for 45 minutes. Cut in squares and serve.

Sheila Fleming
East Memphis Council

GLAZED FRUIT COMPOTE

1 small pkg. regular
vanilla pudding
1 1/2 c. pineapple juice
3 tsp. lemon juice
4 bananas

2 1/2 cans pineapple chunks
(save juice for pudding)
1 (14 oz.) can Mandarin
oranges
1 c. red grapes or cherries

Cook pudding with juice until thick. Drain fruit very well; add dressing to fruit after cooling slightly. Add bananas just prior to serving.

Marcia Jackson
Harpeth Council

HEAVENLY CREAM SQUARES

1 3/4 c. vanilla wafer
crumbs
1/2 c. pecans, chopped
1/2 c. margarine, melted

1 pkg. vanilla pudding
1/4 tsp. imitation rum
flavoring
1 (8 oz.) pkg. cream cheese

Combine crumbs, pecans and margarine, reserving 1/2 cup of mixture for topping. Press onto the bottom of a 9 inch square pan. Prepare pudding according to directions on package; remove from heat. Add cream cheese, stirring until blended. Add rum flavoring; mix thoroughly. Pour into crumb lined pan. Sprinkle with the remaining crumb mixture; chill.

Sudie Sredonja
East Memphis Council

HEAVENLY DELIGHT

1 large can crushed pine-
apple, well drained
1 large ctn. Cool Whip
1 can Baker's Angel Flake
coconut

3 c. miniature marshmallows
1/4 c. chopped maraschino
cherries (red)
1/2 c. chopped pecans
(optional)
3 Tbsp. sweet milk

Mix all together well and chill.

Pattie Carpenter
Nashville Council

HEAVENLY HASH

1 1/2 lb. miniature
  marshmallows
1 large pkg. cream cheese

1 large can pineapple chunks
1 pt. whipping cream
1 c. nuts

Cream cheese, room temperature. Mix with 1/4 cup pineapple juice. Add nuts, marshmallows, pineapple chunks, whipping cream and stir. Chill.

Ruby Smith
Knoxville Council

HOT FRUIT

2 c. Ritz crackers, crushed   1 stick butter, melted

Mix and press lightly in a 9x13 inch dish. Drain and arrange:

1 large can pear halves
1 large can chunk pineapple

1 large can apricot halves
Cherries

Sprinkle over fruit 3/4 box dark brown sugar. Pour over sugar not more than 1/2 cup of the fruit juices. Bake 45 minutes at 350°.

Patricia Hire
Harpeth Council

HUNTER'S PUDDING

3/4 lb. butter or oleo
1 1/4 lb. (2 1/2 c.) sugar
1 Tbsp. cinnamon
1 Tbsp. cloves
1 Tbsp. nutmeg
3 eggs

3 c. milk
1 1/3 lb. bread (whole
  wheat), cubed
1 c. chopped nuts
1 lb. raisins
2 tsp. baking powder
3/4 tsp. soda

1. Cream margarine and sugar. 2. Add remaining ingredients; blend well. 3. Bake in a moderate oven at 350° for 1 1/2 hours. 4. Serve with hard sauce or whipped cream. Makes 25 portions.

Note: If shortening other than butter or margarine is used, add 1/2 teaspoon salt.

JELLIED CITRUS LOAF

1 env. unflavored gelatin
1/4 c. cold water
1 c. boiling water
1 (3 oz.) pkg. orange jello
1/2 c. sugar
1/4 c. orange juice

1 pt. orange sherbet
12 ladyfingers or sponge
  cake, cut in 24 strips
1/2 c. heavy cream, whipped
  and sweetened

Sprinkle unflavored gelatin over cold water in large mixing bowl; let stand until softened. Add boiling water, orange jello and sugar; stir until dissolved. Stir in orange juice and sherbet; beat with whisk until sherbet melts and mixture is smooth. Let stand until mixture mounds when dropped from spoon. Line bottom of 9x5x3 inch loaf pan with 8 ladyfingers. Spread with 1/3 of orange mixture. Repeat layers twice, ending with orange mixture; chill until firm. Unmold on serving plate. Garnish with whipped cream and mint sprigs. Makes 6 servings.

Billie Fleming
Nashboro Council

JELLO PUDDING DELIGHT

1 (20 oz.) can crushed
  pineapple
1 (17 oz.) can fruit cocktail
1 large or 2 small boxes
  instant vanilla Jell-O
  pudding and pie filling
4 or 5 bananas

1/2 c. lemon juice
2 (1/2 pt.) ctn. whipping
  cream or Cool Whip or
  Dream Whip
Coconut, sprinkled on top
  (optional)
Cherries (optional)
Powdered sugar
Vanilla flavoring

Combine first 3 ingredients; do not drain. Put in oblong container. Slice bananas. Pour lemon juice over bananas but do not put lemon juice in mixture. Place bananas on top of mixture. Prepare topping, using 2 tablespoons powdered sugar, 1/4 teaspoon vanilla flavoring and whipping cream. Spread over mixture; sprinkle with coconut, if desired. Chill overnight.

Dot Jenkins
Knoxville Council

MANDARIN ORANGE DELIGHT

1 (16 oz.) can Mandarin
   oranges
1 (8 oz.) can crushed
   pineapple

12 large marshmallows
1 (6 oz.) pkg. orange jello
6 oz. cream cheese
1/2 pt. whipping cream

Drain oranges and pineapple; set fruit aside. Add enough water to this liquid to make 2 cups. Heat liquid and dissolve marshmallows and cream cheese. Pour over jello; dissolve. Add 2 cups cold water. Pour into 9x13 inch pan. Refrigerate until salad has congealed slightly. Whip whipping cream until stiff. Fold whipping cream, oranges and pineapple into salad. Return to refrigerator and allow to congeal before serving.

Dorothy Bryant
Clarksville Council

NORTH CAROLINA GRATED SWEET POTATO PUDDING

5 c. coarsely grated, raw
   sweet potatoes
3/4 c. brown sugar, packed
1 1/2 c. milk
1/2 c. melted butter
3 eggs, well beaten
1/4 tsp. powdered nutmeg
1/2 tsp. powdered cinnamon

1/4 tsp. powdered allspice
1/4 tsp. ground cloves
1/2 c. seedless raisins
1/2 c. shredded coconut
1/2 c. chopped pecans
1/2 tsp. grated orange
   or lemon rind

Mix all ingredients and pour into a buttered medium size casserole dish or skillet. Bake in a preheated 400° oven for 50-60 minutes. As crust forms around edges, remove from oven and stir pudding well to mix crust throughout. Do this several times until baking is finished. Serve warm or cold; plain or topped with whipped cream or ice cream. Yield: 8 servings.

Agatha J. Wilson
Clarksville Council

OREO DELIGHT

1/2 gal. vanilla ice cream
1 (8 oz.) ctn. Cool Whip

1 small pkg. Oreo cookies

Let ice cream set out until it becomes soft and easy to

work with. Blend in Cool Whip and mix these 2 ingredients well. In another bowl, crush the Oreo cookies into small tidbits. Add these to the previous mixture of ice cream and Cool Whip; mix well. Place the mixture into an oblong Tupperware container and place in the freezer. Let freeze, then cut into squares and serve.

Kathy O. Brock
Green Hills Council

FREAK OUT

1/2 gal. vanilla ice cream
1 large container Cool Whip

1 large pkg. Oreo chocolate
    cookies

Let ice cream soften. Crumble cookies; mix all ingredients. Freeze and eat. Freak out!

Jo Ann Hindsley
Harpeth Council

PEACHES AND CREAM CREPES

4 large fresh peaches,
    peeled and sliced
2 Tbsp. sugar
1 (14 oz.) can sweetened
    condensed milk

1/4 c. lemon juice
1/2 c. heavy cream, whipped
8-10 cooked crepes
Whipped cream (optional)

Sprinkle peaches with sugar; set aside. In medium bowl, beat sweetened condensed milk with lemon juice until thick. Fold in whipped cream and sweetened peaches. Fill cooked crepes; fold over. Serve with additional whipped cream, if desired. Makes 8 to 10 crepes.

Basic Dessert Crepe Batter:

4 eggs
1 c. flour
2 Tbsp. sugar

1 c. milk
1/4 c. water
1 Tbsp. melted butter

In medium mixing bowl, beat eggs. Gradually add flour and sugar alternately with milk and water, beating with electric mixer until smooth. Beat in melted butter. Refrigerate batter at least 1 hour. Cook on upside-down crepe griddle or in traditional pan. Makes about 20-25 crepes.

Doris Binkley
Nashboro Council

1489-81

PRETZEL SURPRISE

1 (8 1/2 oz.) pkg. Keebler
  butternut pretzels,
  crushed (about 2 c.)
3 Tbsp. sugar
3/4 c. margarine, softened
1 c. sugar
8 oz. cream cheese

8 oz. Cool Whip
2 c. boiling water
1 (6 oz.) pkg. strawberry
  jello
1 (20 oz.) pkg. frozen
  strawberries (if whole,
  slice in halves)

Mix crushed pretzels, 3 tablespoons sugar and margarine. Press mixture in Pyrex dish, 13x9x2 or 12x8x2 inches. Bake at 400° for 10 minutes; cool. Beat 1 cup sugar, cream cheese and Cool Whip; add to cooled pretzel layer. Mix boiling water with jello; add strawberries. Let stand 10 minutes; add to casserole. Chill 1 hour. Store in refrigerator. Serves 12 or more.

Emily Townes
Harpeth Council

PUDDING AND SAUCE

1/2 c. lard
1 c. sugar
1/2 tsp. salt
1/2 tsp. vanilla

2 eggs
2 c. flour
2 1/2 tsp. baking powder
3/4 c. milk

Blend lard, sugar, salt, flavoring and eggs. Add alternately the sifted ingredients and milk. Bake at 325° for about 25 minutes. Makes 2 layers.

Sauce:

2 Tbsp. cocoa
2 c. milk
1 c. sugar
2 1/2 tsp. flour

1/8 tsp. salt
2 Tbsp. butter
1 tsp. vanilla

Add cocoa and flour to sugar; mix well. Add milk. Boil until thick; add butter and vanilla. Serve over the above pudding.

Marie Barnett
Harpeth Council

PUDDING DESSERT BUTTERSCOTCH

1 c. flour (plain)
1 (8 oz.) pkg. cream cheese
1 (13 oz.) ctn. Cool Whip
3 c. milk

1 stick butter or margarine
1 c. powdered sugar
2 boxes instant butterscotch
   pudding
1 c. nuts, chopped

Melt 1 stick butter or margarine; add 1/2 cup chopped nuts and 1 cup flour. Mix together and press into 9x13 inch pan. Bake 15 minutes at 350°; cool. Cream cheese; add 1 cup powdered sugar and 1 cup Cool Whip. Mix well; spread over cooled crust. Mix 2 boxes instant butterscotch pudding with 3 cups milk; cook until thick. Cool; spread on cheese layer. Add remaining Cool Whip and sprinkle with nuts.

Margaret Sells
Morristown Council

PUMPKIN PUDDING

2 c. cooked pumpkin
2 c. sugar
1 c. self-rising flour
3 eggs

2 1/2 c. evaporated milk
1/2 tsp. cinnamon
1/2 tsp. nutmeg
1 tsp. vanilla
1 stick margarine, melted

Combine pumpkin, sugar and flour; beat until well blended. Add eggs; beat well. Blend in evaporated milk, cinnamon and nutmeg. Stir in vanilla and margarine. Pour mixture into a buttered 9x13 inch pan. Bake at 450° for about 25 minutes or until brown.

Elizabeth Kitts
Knoxville Council

QUICK AND EASY CHOCOLATE DESSERT

1 stick margarine
2 Tbsp. cocoa
1 c. sugar
2 eggs

1/4 c. flour
1/2 tsp. vanilla
Pinch of salt

Melt margarine; pour into a large bowl. Add cocoa; stir well. Add remaining ingredients; pour into buttered Pyrex dish. Bake at 350° for 35 to 40 minutes.

Patricia Hire
Harpeth Council

1489-81

RASPBERRY DESSERT

1 small angel food cake	1 c. sugar
1 pkg. red raspberries	1/2 c. marshmallows
1 pkg. raspberry jello	1/2 pt. whipping cream

Drain berries. Mix juice with jello and sugar; bring to a boil. Let cool and congeal slightly. Break cake into bite size pieces; fold into jello mixture and fold in whipped cream. Pour into casserole dish and refrigerate a few hours. Slice and serve.

Judy Gibson
Harpeth Council

RASPBERRY ICE
(Food Processor Recipe)

Using metal blade, process 4 cups raspberries until pureed. Pour through a sieve and discard seeds. Return puree to processor along with 1/2 cup water, 3/4 cup sugar and 1 tablespoon lemon juice. Process for 2 seconds to mix. Freeze puree in divided ice cube trays. To serve, use metal blade to process 4 to 6 cubes of puree at a time. Use on/off bursts to break up cubes, then run processor continually until you have a velvety slush. Spoon into serving containers and serve at once. Makes about 2 3/4 cups.

Sherree Weisenberger
Harpeth Council

OLD-FASHIONED RICE PUDDING
(Diabetics)

2 Tbsp. rice, uncooked	1 tsp. vanilla
1 c. whole milk	1/4 tsp. cinnamon

1. Wash the rice and place in a large individual casserole. 2. Pour 1/2 cup milk over the rice; set the dish in a pan. Place in a moderate oven. 3. Allow to bake until a brown crust forms. With a spoon, turn the crust under and mix with the rice. Do this 2 or 3 times during the baking. 4. As the milk is absorbed by the cooking rice, pour the remaining milk into the dish. 5. During the last part of the cooking, add the vanilla and the cinnamon. 6. As soon as the rice is soft, remove from the oven and chill.

Note: A serving of fruit such as a peach or pear may

be combined with the pudding. For example, 1 serving may equal 1 medium sized peach or pear (100 grams).

Exchange: 1 milk exchange, 1 bread exchange, 1 fruit exchange. Calories: 238.

FRENCH STRAWBERRY PUDDING

1 (12 oz.) box vanilla
  wafers
1 stick butter
1 1/2 c. powdered sugar
1 tsp. vanilla

1 c. Dream Whip
1 (10 oz.) pkg. frozen
  strawberries
1 c. chopped pecans
2 eggs

Crumble wafers into fine crumbs. Put half of crumbs in bottom of 13x9x2 inch pan. Whip butter, sugar, vanilla and eggs together until light and creamy. Spread evenly over crumbs. Whip cream or topping mix; spread over butter mixture. Spread strawberries over whipped cream. Mix chopped pecans and remaining wafer crumbs; sprinkle over strawberries. Chill overnight in refrigerator or put into freezer for later. Thaw about 30 minutes before eating.

Katrina Carter
Harpeth Council

FROZEN STRAWBERRY DELIGHT

1 c. flour
1/4 c. brown sugar
1/2 c. chopped pecans
1/2 c. melted butter
2 egg whites, stiffly beaten
1 c. sugar

2 c. sliced strawberries or
  1 (10 oz.) pkg. frozen
  strawberries, thawed
2 Tbsp. lemon juice
1 c. heavy cream, whipped,
  or 1 (10 oz.) pkg. Cool
  Whip

Mix flour, sugar, nuts and butter together. Crumble onto a shallow pan or cookie sheet. Bake at 350° for 20 minutes; stir occasionally. Combine egg whites, sugar, berries and lemon juice. Whip Cool Whip; fold in. Sprinkle 2/3 of crumbs in 9x13 inch pan. Spoon cream mixture over crumbs. Top with remaining crumbs. Freeze 6 hours before serving.

Bettye Inman
Green Hills Council

FROZEN STRAWBERRY SQUARES

Crumb Crust and Topping: Melt 1 stick butter (margarine) in 9x12 inch pan. Add 1 cup flour, 1/4 cup brown sugar and 1/2 cup chopped nuts. Bake at 350° for approximately 20 minutes. Stir at least once while baking and remove from oven and stir again. Let cool. Reserve 1/3 of crumbs to sprinkle on top.

2 egg whites	2 c. strawberries, drained
1 c. sugar	

Combine in large mixing bowl. Beat at high speed until stiff peaks form, 10 to 15 minutes. Your bowl will be almost full. Fold in 1 carton Cool Whip. Pour on the crumb crust; sprinkle reserved crumbs on top, then freeze.

Kathy Franck
Harpeth Council

STRAWBERRY CHIFFON SQUARES

1/3 c. butter or margarine	1 (14 oz.) can Eagle Brand
1 1/2 c. finely crushed	sweetened condensed milk
vanilla wafers (about 45)	(not evaporated)
1 (3 oz.) pkg. strawberry	1 (10 oz.) pkg. frozen sliced
flavored gelatin	strawberries in syrup,
3/4 c. boiling water	thawed
4 c. miniature marshmallows	1 c. (1/2 pt.) whipping
	cream, whipped

In a small saucepan, melt butter; stir in crumbs. Pat firmly on bottom of 11x7 inch baking dish; chill. In large bowl, dissolve gelatin in boiling water; stir in sweetened condensed milk and undrained strawberries. Fold in whipped cream and marshmallows. Pour into prepared pan. Chill 2 hours or until set. If desired, garnish with whipped topping and strawberries. Refrigerate leftovers.

Jewell S. Brabston
Morristown #12 Council

STRAWBERRY TRIFLE

1 large box vanilla pudding and pie filling (not instant)
2 pt. strawberries
1 large container Cool Whip
Milk as directed on pie filling box
Angel food cake (about 1/4 cake)
Few Tbsp. orange juice

Cook pie filling as directed on box with amount of milk as per box instructions; cool. Add 1 cup Cool Whip to cooled pie filling. Cut angel food cake into 1 inch squares and put in bottom of dish or souffle bowl. Cover with cut up strawberries, non-sweetened. Sprinkle strawberries with small amount of orange juice. Pour pudding mix over strawberries. Cover and chill for 3-4 hours or overnight. Before serving, add additional Cool Whip as topping and garnish with whole strawberries. Any other fruit may be used.

Cassandra Jones
Nashville Council

TEXAS HEAVENLY HASH

3 c. sugar
1/2 c. light corn syrup
1 tsp. vanilla
1 c. milk
1 c. pecans
3/4 c. cocoa
1/2 c. glazed cherries, chopped
4 Tbsp. oleo
1/2 lb. marshmallows, diced

Combine cocoa, sugar, corn syrup and milk. Cook over low heat until sugar is dissolved. Continue to cook over medium heat, stirring frequently, to soft ball stage. Remove from heat; cool to lukewarm. Add vanilla; beat until creamy. Stir in pecans, marshmallows and cherries. Continue to beat until thick. Cut into squares when cold.

Carolyn Mitchell
Memphis Downtown Council

ANGEL STREET CAKE

1 baked angel food cake
1 qt. cherry vanilla ice cream
1 qt. mint chip ice cream
Whipped cream for garnish (optional)

Place a 9 inch tube pan in freezer. Tear cake into bite

1489-81

sized pieces. Remove pan from freezer; arrange layer of cake pieces in bottom of pan. Working quickly, alternate scoops of mint chip and cherry vanilla to make next layer; press firmly into cake. Add a layer of cake pieces, then a second layer of ice cream scoops. Finish with layer of cake pieces. Press cake down firmly. Cover and freeze 6 hours or overnight. To serve: Invert cake onto serving plate. Return to freezer until ready to serve. If desired, pipe whipped cream around top and bottom edges.

Leslie Stephens
Harpeth Council

APPLE DAPPLE CAKE

1 1/2 c. cooking oil
2 c. sugar
3 eggs
2 tsp. vanilla
3 c. plain flour
1 tsp. salt

1 tsp. soda
1 tsp. cinnamon
1 c. chopped pecans (or raisins)
3 c. chopped apples

Mix first 4 ingredients. Sift the next 4 and add to the above. Fold in pecans and apples last. Mix by hand as batter is very stiff. Bake in greased and floured tube pan at 350° for 1 hour or 13x9 inch pan for 40-45 minutes.

Topping:

1 c. packed brown sugar
1/4 c. fresh milk

1 stick margarine

Mix and bring to boil for 3 minutes. Pour over hot cake. Punch holes in cake to allow sauce to soak in better. Let remain in pan for 2 hours.

Jessie S. Taylor
Harpeth Council

APPLESAUCE CAKE

3 1/2 c. flour, sifted (plain flour, sift before measuring)
1 1/4 c. shortening or 1 c. oil (I use oil)
3 tsp. cocoa

1 1/2 c. sugar or 2 c. with oil
2 c. (1 can) applesauce
2 tsp. cinnamon
3 tsp. soda
1/2 tsp. salt

2 tsp. allspice
1/2 - 3/4 c. raisins, floured
  before adding to batter

Pecan or black walnuts (I
  use approx. 1 c. black
  walnuts)

Mix shortening (or oil), sugar and applesauce together; mix well. Sift all dry ingredients together. Gradually add dry ingredients to oil mixture. Bake at 350° for
30 to 40 minutes; I use 13x9 inch pan.

Dorothy Stanton
Knoxville Council

FRESH APPLE CAKE

3 c. raw apples
1 1/2 c. all vegetable
  cooking oil
2 c. sugar
3 eggs
2 1/2 c. sifted flour

1 tsp. salt
1 tsp. soda
2 tsp. baking powder
1 tsp. vanilla
1 c. nuts

Peel apples and chop. I pour the juice of a small lemon
over the apples. Beat eggs; add oil and sugar. Beat well.
Sift flour with salt, baking powder and soda. Gradually
add flour to creamed mixture; add vanilla. If mixture is
too thick, I add 1/4 cup buttermilk. Fold in chopped apples and nuts. Bake at 350° for 1 hour or until done.
When cake is cool, remove from pan and drizzle with Sugar
Glaze.

Sugar Glaze:

1 1/2 c. powdered sugar
3 Tbsp. water

2 tsp. vanilla

Sue Malone
Harpeth Council

FRESH APPLE CAKE
(Easy and Quick)

1 1/2 c. vegetable oil
2 c. granulated sugar
3 whole eggs
2 1/2 c. sifted self-rising
  flour
1 tsp. vanilla

2 tsp. cinnamon
3 good sized apples, peeled
  or unpeeled, cubed in
  1/2 inch pieces (I use
  red Delicious)
1 c. pecan pieces

Mix first 3 ingredients in large bowl. Add flour (some at a time) and add remaining ingredients; stir until well mixed. Pour into greased tube pan or Bundt pan. Bake at 325° for 1 hour; cool in pan until firm, about 30 minutes. Turn out, leaving pan over released cake an additional 30 minutes. This keeps cake from getting crusty. Use plain or with a sugar glaze on top. It's already excellent, but the glaze really makes it yummy.

Pat DeMatteo
Nashboro Council

FRESH APPLE CAKE

2 c. sugar
1 1/2 c. vegetable oil
3 eggs
3 c. all-purpose flour
1 tsp. soda
1 tsp. baking powder
1 tsp. salt

1 tsp. ground cinnamon
1 tsp. ground nutmeg
2 tsp. vanilla extract
3 c. chopped firm apples
1 c. chopped, pitted dates
1 c. chopped pecans

Combine sugar and vegetable oil in large bowl; stir to mix well. Add eggs, one at a time, beating well after each addition. Combine dry ingredients; stir into the oil mixture. Add vanilla, chopped apples, dates and pecans; mix well. Spoon batter into greased 10 inch tube pan and bake at 325° for 1 1/2 hours or until cake tests done.

Ruth L. Cole
Harpeth Council

FRESH APPLE CAKE

1 c. salad oil
2 eggs
1 tsp. baking soda
1 tsp. vanilla
1 c. pecans

2 c. sugar
1 tsp. salt
1 tsp. baking powder
2 1/2 c. all-purpose flour
3 c. fresh apples

Mix together sugar and oil. Add eggs; beat until creamy. Add vanilla. Combine salt, baking soda, baking powder and flour. Add a small amount at a time to sugar and oil mixture. Add sliced, peeled apples and pecans. Mix by hand. Bake in greased Bundt pan in 350° oven for about 1 hour and 10 minutes. No icing is necessary.

Ginger Lewis
Harpeth Council

FRESH APPLE CAKE

2 c. sugar	2 1/2 c. flour
2 eggs	2 tsp. baking powder
1/2 c. water	1 tsp. soda
1 c. salad oil (corn oil)	1 tsp. salt
3 diced apples (2 1/2 c.)	1 tsp. cinnamon
1 c. chopped nuts (optional)	1 pkg. Nestle's butterscotch chips

Combine sugar, eggs, water and oil. Add dry ingredients, mixing well while adding apples and nuts. Pour into greased and floured pan, 13x9x2 inches. Sprinkle butterscotch morsels over top of batter. Bake at 350° for 1 hour. Better when served after first day. Use spatula to remove in small squares so the moist part won't be left in the pan.

Elizabeth E. Bennett
Knoxville Council

FRESH APPLE CAKE

Bake in a large loaf pan or a regular Bundt pan. Requires a large bowl or container to mix all ingredients. Bake in oven at 325° for 50 to 60 minutes, depending on whether you have a gas or an electric oven. Mix the following ingredients as listed:

2 c. sugar	1/2 tsp. salt
1 c. oil	1 tsp. soda
3 eggs, should be well beaten, then add at this point	2 tsp. cinnamon (if person does not like cinnamon, may be omitted)
3 c. well diced, fresh apples	2 Tbsp. vanilla
3 c. plain, sifted flour	1 c. finely chopped pecans

Walnuts and a walnut flavoring may be used instead of the pecans and vanilla flavoring. Also can be baked several days ahead of time and allows the cake to become moist. A thin glaze could be used on this cake.

Nell Young
Harpeth Council

1489-81

FRESH APPLE CAKE

2 c. sugar
1 1/4 c. oil
3 eggs
3 c. self-rising flour
1 tsp. cinnamon

1 tsp. nutmeg
1 tsp. vanilla
1 c. nuts
3 c. chopped apples

Mix together and bake in tube pan approximately 1 hour.

Topping:

1/4 c. brown sugar
1/4 c. white sugar

1/4 c. milk
1/2 stick margarine

Bake for 2 1/2 minutes; pour over hot cake.

Betty Hale
Harpeth Council

FRESH APPLE CAKE

1 1/2 c. Crisco oil
2 c. sugar
3 eggs
1/2 tsp. soda
1 tsp. baking powder
1/2 tsp. salt

1 tsp. vanilla
2 1/2 c. cake flour
1 c. pecan pieces
3 c. raw, chopped apples, peeled
2 tsp. cinnamon

Mix oil, eggs and sugar; beat at low speed. Sift flour and dry ingredients; add to first mixture. Add vanilla, apples, pecans and cinnamon; mix well. Bake in greased tube pan at 325° for 1 hour or until done.

Sauce (optional):

1/2 c. sugar
1/4 c. buttermilk
1/4 tsp. baking soda

1/2 stick margarine
1/2 tsp. vanilla

Mix all ingredients together; boil 1 minute. Pour over cake.

Martha Stovall
Nashboro Council

FRESH APPLE CAKE

1 1/2 c. Wesson oil	1 tsp. salt
2 c. sugar	1 tsp. cinnamon
3 eggs	1 tsp. vanilla
3 c. flour (plain)	3 c. chopped apples
1 tsp. soda	1 c. black walnuts or pecans

Mix in order given. Bake 1 hour and 15 minutes in tube pan at 350° to 375°.

Caramel Frosting:

1/2 c. evaporated milk	1/2 stick margarine
1 1/2 c. brown sugar	1 Tbsp. vanilla

Cook until it forms soft ball. Cool; beat until of spreading consistency.

Dorothy Stanton
Knoxville Council

FRESH APPLE CAKE

1 c. oil	3 c. chopped apples
2 c. sugar	3 eggs
2 1/2 c. self-rising flour	1 c. chopped nuts
1 tsp. vanilla	

Mix sugar, eggs, oil and vanilla. Add flour; mix well. Fold in apples and nuts. Bake 45 minutes to 1 hour at 350° in greased 9x13x2 inch pan.

Icing:

1 c. brown sugar, packed	1/2 c. Pet evaporated milk
1 stick margarine	

Cook until thick. Pour over cake while cake and icing are still warm.

Emma Jo Perry
Green Hills Council

FRESH APPLE CAKE

1 1/2 c. Crisco oil	3 c. sugar
3 c. cake flour	3 c. sliced apples
1 tsp. soda	3 eggs
1 tsp. salt	3/4 c. chopped pecans
1 Tbsp. cinnamon	3/4 c. chopped walnuts
1 Tbsp. allspice	3/4 c. dark raisins

Do not use mixer. Combine oil, sugar and eggs; mix well. Add apples; mix. Add dry ingredients; mix well. Add nuts and raisins; mix well. Pour into well greased and floured 13x9 inch pan. Bake at 350° for 1 hour and 15 minutes (if glass pan is used, bake at 325° for 1 hour). Have the following glaze ready when cake is removed from oven:

Glaze:

2/3 c. sugar	1/4 c. buttermilk
1/4 c. butter or margarine	1/4 tsp. soda
1 tsp. vanilla	

Melt butter; add other ingredients. Bring to boil; boil 1 minute, then pour over hot cake.

Wilma Hunt
Knoxville Council

FRESH APPLE NUT CAKE

An easy to mix, moist cake that is full of rich, spicy flavor.

2 eggs	1 c. chopped pecans
1 c. cooking oil	3 c. pared, chopped apples
1 3/4 c. sugar	1 tsp. cinnamon
2 1/2 c. sifted self-rising flour	1 tsp. vanilla

Heat oven to 300°. Grease 13x9x2 inch baking pan. Beat together eggs, oil and sugar. Add remaining ingredients; mix well. Turn batter into prepared pans and bake 1 hour and 10 minutes. Let cake cool in pan. Frost with Cream Cheese Icing and cut in squares.

Note: This batter will be very stiff. If using plain flour, use 1 teaspoon each of salt, soda and baking powder.

Mabel M. Wilson
Clarksville Council

LITTLE GRANNY'S FRESH APPLE CAKE

1 c. Wesson oil
2 c. sugar
4 eggs
3 c. sifted plain flour
1 tsp. salt
1 tsp. soda

3 c. peeled, sliced raw
  apples
1 tsp. vanilla
1/2 c. chopped walnuts or
  pecans

In a large mixing bowl, combine oil, sugar and eggs; beat well. Add vanilla and nuts. Add combined dry ingredients, beating well after each addition. Add sliced apples; mix well. Pour batter into well greased 9x13 inch pan and bake in a 325° oven for 1 hour.

Glaze: Combine in a small saucepan -

1 c. light brown sugar,
  packed
1 stick oleo

1/2 c. cream (canned, or I
  substitute milk)
1 tsp. vanilla

Cook for 2 1/2 minutes over medium heat after mixture comes to a boil. Pour over warm cake. This cake stays moist for several days.

Mary R. Veal
Chattanooga Council

OLD FASHION APPLE STACK CAKE

3 c. self-rising flour
1 1/2 c. sugar
1 c. Crisco
3 eggs
1 tsp. vanilla flavoring

1 tsp. lemon flavoring
2 pkg. dried apples, cooked
  and mashed
2 Tbsp. allspice
1 1/2 c. sugar

Sift flour and sugar together; make a well. Add Crisco, eggs and flavoring. Mix into stiff dough; let set in refrigerator a couple of hours or overnight in covered bowl. Divide into 4 or 5 portions. Grease and flour 9 inch pans and roll or pat dough out to fit pans. Bake at 350° until golden brown. Brown usually about 12 minutes. Do not overbake; invert layers to cool. They will be hard layers when cool. Cook dried apples until tender; mash. Add 1 1/2 cups sugar and spice; spread between cooled layers. Put in airtight container; let set overnight or longer before serving. Cake should be moist before serving. Slice thin. Makes about 20 servings.

Virginia Jaynes
Morristown Council #12

BABY FOOD CAKE

2 c. self-rising flour
2 c. sugar
1 c. Crisco oil
3 eggs

2 small jars baby food (plums)
1 tsp. cinnamon
1/2 tsp. cloves
1 c. chopped nuts

Blend together. Bake 1 hour in tube pan at 350° (electric oven) or 325° (gas oven).

Inda Adams
Andrew Jackson Council

BABY FOOD CAKE

2 c. sugar
1 c. Wesson oil
3 eggs
2 c. self-rising flour
1/2 c. nuts
1 tsp. cinnamon

1/2 tsp. nutmeg
1/2 tsp. allspice
1 small jar baby food apricots
1 small jar baby food plums
1 small jar baby food prunes

Mix all together well. Pour into Bundt or tube pan. Bake at 300° for 1 1/4 hours.

Judy Gibson
Harpeth Council

BANANA NUT CAKE

3/4 c. butter or margarine
2 1/4 c. sugar
4 eggs
1 1/2 c. mashed bananas
1 c. chopped pecans

1 1/2 tsp. vanilla
8 Tbsp. buttermilk
1 1/2 tsp. soda
2 1/4 c. self-rising flour

Cream butter, sugar and eggs one at a time; mix well. Add bananas, pecans and vanilla; mix well after each addition. Mix soda and buttermilk in separate container; let stand a few minutes. Add flour and liquid. This fills three 9 inch pans. Grease pans with Crisco and flour lightly.

410

Bake at 350° for 25 minutes or till cake springs back when touched.

Creamy Nut Icing: Melt in stewer 1 stick margarine. Blend level 2 1/2 tablespoons flour and 1/4 teaspoon salt; stir in slowly 1/2 cup sweet milk. Bring to boil, stirring all the time; boil 1 minute. Remove from stove; stir in 1 box powdered sugar. Add 1/2 teaspoon vanilla and 1/2 cup of finely chopped pecans.

Marlyn Russell
Harpeth Council

BANANA SPICE CAKE

1/4 c. butter	2 tsp. soda
2 c. sugar	1 tsp. vanilla
3 c. flour	4 eggs
3 tsp. cinnamon	1 c. Wesson oil
1/2 tsp. salt	1 1/2 c. raisins
1/2 tsp. nutmeg	6 bananas
1 1/2 tsp. cloves	1 c. nuts

Mix all ingredients well. Mash bananas and add to batter. Bake at 350° for 30 minutes. Bake in 3 layers. Frost with your favorite caramel icing.

Carolyn Mitchell
Memphis Downtown Council

BANANA SPLIT CAKE

First Layer:

2/3 c. melted butter	2 c. crushed graham crackers

Mix in bottom of 9x13 inch pan; press around edge.

Second Layer: Beat until firm; spread on first layer -

2 sticks soft butter	2 c. powdered sugar
2 eggs	1 tsp. vanilla

Third Layer: Add 3 large sliced bananas.
Fourth Layer: Add 1 (16 ounce) can crushed pineapple, drained.

Fifth Layer: Add 1 large carton Cool Whip.
Sixth Layer: Sprinkle with chopped nuts and cherries.
Refrigerate 8 hours or overnight.

Sylvia Kaffer
Clarksville Council

BANANA SPLIT CAKE

2 c. graham cracker crumbs
3 sticks margarine
2 eggs
2 c. powdered sugar
1 tsp. vanilla
3-4 bananas, sliced

2 lb. can crushed pineapple,
drained well
9 oz. Cool Whip
3/4 c. pecans, chopped
1 small jar cherries, chipped

Mix 2 cups graham cracker crumbs and 1 stick melted margarine. Press into bottom of 13x9 inch pan. In mixing bowl, cream 2 eggs, 2 sticks melted margarine, 2 cups powdered sugar and 1 teaspoon vanilla. Beat with mixer for 15 minutes, no less. Spread over crumbs. Slice 3 to 4 bananas, thin, and layer with 2 pound can crushed pineapple, well drained. Top with 9 ounces Cool Whip; spread over top of all. Sprinkle 3/4 cup chopped pecans and chips of cherries over Cool Whip. Cover and refrigerate overnight.

Cynthia D. Holton
Harpeth Council

BEER CAKE

1 c. shortening
2 c. light brown sugar,
packed
2 eggs
1 c. chopped nuts (pecans)
2 c. chopped dates
1 Tbsp. cinnamon

1/2 tsp. allspice
3 c. sifted all-purpose flour
2 tsp. baking soda
1/2 tsp. salt
2 c. beer
1/2 tsp. ground cloves

Cream together sugar and shortening; stir in eggs, nuts, dates, cinnamon, allspice and cloves. In a separate bowl, sift together flour, soda and salt; stir in beer. Combine flour mixture with creamed mixture; mix until well blended. Bake in a greased large tube pan in a moderate oven, 350°, for 1 1/4 hours. Ice cooled cake with Caramel Icing, if desired.

412

Caramel Icing:

1/2 c. butter
1 c. brown sugar, firmly
  packed
1/4 c. milk

1/4 tsp. salt
1 tsp. vanilla
2 c. confectioners sugar

Melt butter and brown sugar in saucepan, stirring constantly over low heat until sugar is dissolved. Add milk and continue cooking until mixture boils. Remove from heat; cool slightly, then add salt, vanilla and confectioners sugar. Stir until the consistency to spread.

Inda Adams
Andrew Jackson Council

BETTER THAN SEX CAKE

1 box cake mix with pudding
  (yellow or white)
1 large can crushed
  pineapple

1 c. sugar
1 small pkg. vanilla pudding
  and pie mix
1 large ctn. Cool Whip

Bake cake in 9x13 inch pan according to directions on box. When done, poke holes in cake. While cake is baking, combine pineapple and sugar; boil for 5 minutes. Pour over cake while hot. Let cake cool, then prepare instant pie and pudding mix according to directions on box. Spread over cake. Spread Cool Whip over this.

Bobby Moore
Harpeth Council

BLACKBERRY CAKE

2 c. sugar
2 c. blackberries with
  juice, mashed up
2 tsp. soda
1/2 tsp. cinnamon

1/2 tsp. allspice
1/2 tsp. nutmeg
1 c. butter
3 c. flour
3 eggs

Cream butter and sugar with mixer. All other ingredients, add and mix by hand. Add berries and juice alternately with flour, sifted with soda and spices. Add eggs one at a time, slightly beaten. Bake at 350° for 1 hour in tube pan. Use Cream Cheese or Sour Cream Icing.

Helen Clowers
Knoxville Council

FRESH BLACKBERRY CAKE

1 c. cooking oil
2 c. sugar
2 c. fresh blackberries
3 whole eggs
3 c. plain flour

1 tsp. soda
1 tsp. allspice
1 tsp. cinnamon
1 tsp. cloves

Combine cooking oil, sugar and blackberries; beat until sugar dissolves. Beat in eggs, then blend in the dry ingredients. Pour into 3 greased and floured cake pans or a 9x13 inch pan. Bake at 350° for about 40 minutes. Top with Caramel Icing.

Never Fail Caramel Icing:

2 1/2 c. sugar
1 slightly beaten egg
1 stick margarine

3/4 c. sweet milk
1 tsp. vanilla

Melt 1/2 cup sugar in iron skillet slowly until browned and runny. Mix egg, butter and remaining sugar and milk in saucepan; cook over heat until butter is melted. Turn heat to medium; add browned sugar. Cook until it forms a soft ball when dropped in water. Remove from heat; cool slightly. Add vanilla; beat until right consistency to spread. If too thick, add a little cream.

Note: Instead of using the egg in the icing, you can mix 1 tablespoon of flour with the sugar (which I do).

Marie Barnett
Harpeth Council

BLUEBERRY COFFEE CAKE

Mix 3/4 cup sugar, 1/4 cup soft shortening and 1 egg. Stir in 1/2 cup milk. Sift 2 cups sifted flour, 2 teaspoons baking powder and 1/2 teaspoon salt; stir into first mixture. Carefully blend in 2 cups blueberries. Spread batter into greased and floured 9 inch square pan. Sprinkle top with mixture of 1/2 cup sugar, 1/3 cup flour, 1/2 teaspoon cinnamon and 1/4 cup soft butter. Bake at 375° for 25-35 minutes.

Mickie Herrell
Harpeth Council

BROWN SUGAR CAKE

2 c. brown sugar	1-2 c. pecans
2 c. white sugar	1 tsp. vanilla
3 c. cake flour	1/2 tsp. salt
1 lb. butter	6 eggs

Mix only until blended. Bake at 300° for approximately 1 hour and 30-45 minutes. Bake in oblong pan; cut in squares.

Joyce Mattice
Harpeth Council

E-Z BROWNIES

Mix:

2 c. sugar	4 eggs
1 c. Crisco	1/2 c. cocoa

Add:

1/4 tsp. salt	1/2 tsp. vanilla
1 c. self-rising flour	1 c. chopped nuts
1/2 c. Carnation milk	

Bake 20-30 minutes at 350°. Ice while hot with a mixture of:

3/4 stick melted margarine	3 Tbsp. cocoa
1/2 tsp. vanilla	Dash of salt
2 c. powdered sugar	

Cream for spreading texture.

Stephen (Yogi) Steinke
Knox Council

ICED BROWNIES

2 c. sugar	1/2 c. evaporated milk
1/2 c. cocoa	1 c. flour
1 c. Crisco	1/2 tsp. vanilla
Pinch of salt	1 c. nuts
4 eggs	

Cream first 4 ingredients. Add remaining ingredients, adding nuts last; mix well. Bake in a greased and floured

1489-81

pan at 350° for 20 or 30 minutes.

Icing:

1 box powdered sugar	3 Tbsp. cocoa
Pinch of salt	3/4 stick margarine, melted

Add enough evaporated milk (1/4 to 1/2 cup) to mixture to bring to spreading consistency.

Peggy L. Parker
Chattanooga Council

JEWELL'S BUNKO CAKE

1 large angel food cake	2 tsp. sugar
2 pkg. semi-sweet chocolate	1 tsp. vanilla
chips	1 pt. whipping cream
4 eggs	1 c. nuts
Pinch of salt	

Melt chocolate in double boiler. Add salt and beaten egg yolks. Whip egg whites. Add sugar and vanilla; add to chocolate mixture. Fold in whipped cream and nuts. Break cake in small pieces and form layers. Pour filling over layers. Refrigerate overnight. Serve with whipped cream.

Jewell Calvin
Nashboro Council

GOOEY BUTTER CAKE

1 egg	1 stick butter
1 box yellow cake mix	1 c. chopped nuts

With hands, mix together the above ingredients until crumbly; put in bottom of 13x9 inch pan.

1 box powdered sugar	2 eggs
1 (8 oz.) pkg. cream cheese	

Pour this mixture over crumb mix and bake at 350° for 35 to 40 minutes.

Judy M. Gray
Harpeth Council

BUTTER PECAN CAKE

2 c. sugar
1 stick butter
1/2 c. Crisco
1 c. buttermilk
1 tsp. vanilla
5 eggs, separated

2 c. cake flour
1 tsp. salt
1 tsp. soda
1 c. flaked coconut
1/2 c. chopped pecans (I
   usually add a few more)

Beat egg whites; set aside. Cream butter, Crisco, sugar and egg yolks together. Gradually add flour, salt, soda and buttermilk; add vanilla. Fold in beaten egg whites. Add coconut and pecans. Bake in three 8 or 9 inch cake pans at 350° for 30 minutes or until done.

Icing:

1 stick butter
1 box powdered sugar

1 large (8 oz.) pkg. cream
   cheese

Mix small amount of each ingredient until well blended. Add vanilla to taste; mix thoroughly. Add 1/2 cup coconut and 1/2 cup chopped pecans. Mix well and spread on cake.

Linda Reus
Chattanooga Council

BUTTERNUT CAKE

1 c. Crisco
2 c. sugar
4 eggs

2 c. self-rising flour
1 Tbsp. butternut flavoring
1 c. milk

Bake at 350° in tube pan for 50 to 60 minutes or two 2 quart Pyrex dishes for 30 or 35 minutes. Superior butternut flavoring is best if you can find it.

Icing:

1 (8 oz.) pkg. Philadelphia
   cream cheese
1 stick butter

1 box confectioners sugar,
   sifted
1 Tbsp. butternut flavoring
1 c. chopped pecans

If baked in tube pan, cut cake and put icing in center. Put back together and put remaining icing on top.

Metty C. Fain
Andrew Jackson Council

CARAMEL KICK BARS

1 pkg. yellow cake mix
1 c. chopped pecans
1/2 c. Mazola oil
2 eggs
1 c. caramel ice cream topping
2 Tbsp. hot water
1 c. coconut

Mix together above ingredients for 3 minutes. Spread in greased pan, 9x12 inches. Bake at 325° until done, approximately 55 minutes; let cool.

Icing:

2 c. powdered sugar
3 Tbsp. caramel syrup
2 Tbsp. milk
1/2 c. melted oleo

Beat until smooth and spread over cake. Sprinkle with chopped nuts.

Mable R. Daniel
Clarksville Council

CARROT CAKE

2 c. plain flour
2 tsp. soda
1 tsp. salt
2 c. sugar
1 tsp. cinnamon
4 eggs, slightly beaten
1 1/2 c. Wesson oil
3 small jars carrot baby food
1 small can crushed
    pineapple, drained
3/4 c. raisins
1 c. nuts

Mix dry ingredients together, then add other ingredients. Grease and flour 9x13 inch pan. Bake at 350° for 45-55 minutes.

Icing:

1 box confectioners sugar
1 stick butter
1 tsp. vanilla
1 (8 oz.) pkg. cream cheese, softened
Small amount of milk to make smooth consistency

Emily Pruitt
Harpeth Council

CARROT CAKE

Prepare three round 8 inch pans; use waxed paper lining. Grease pan before lining and grease lining (normally with Crisco shortening); no flour. Set up all your ingredients before starting. Preheat oven to 325°.

2 c. flour (preferably
   Pillsbury plain)
2 c. sugar
2 tsp. baking soda
2 tsp. baking powder
2 tsp. cinnamon

1 1/2 c. Wesson oil
3 c. carrots
4 eggs
1 c. pecans
Dash of salt

In large bowl, combine flour, baking soda, baking powder, cinnamon and dash of salt. In small bowl, beat eggs gently, not much, with fork. In medium bowl, combine oil, sugar, eggs from small bowl, carrots and pecans. Stir together by hand, not mixer. Combine medium bowl with ingredients in larger bowl. Stir all ingredients well; do not use mixer. Pour in 3 round pans and bake for 30 minutes or until done. Test with toothpick. Set to cool before frosting.

Cream Cheese Frosting for Carrot Cake:

1 box confectioners sugar
1 (8 oz.) pkg. Philadelphia
   cream cheese

1 stick butter
2 tsp. vanilla

Let cream cheese and butter soften. Use mixer to blend all ingredients.

Winola Wills
Green Hills Council

MACPINE CARROT CAKE

3 eggs
2 c. sugar
1 1/2 c. cooking oil
2 tsp. vanilla extract
1 small can crushed pine-
   apple, juice included
2 c. raw carrots, grated
3 c. cake flour

1 tsp. baking soda
1 tsp. salt
1 tsp. cinnamon
1 tsp. nutmeg
2 Tbsp. confectioners sugar
1 c. Hawaiian Holiday
   chopped macadamia nuts

Peel carrots; remove tips. Grate coarsely. In a large mixing bowl, cream together eggs, sugar and oil. Continue beating as you add vanilla extract, crushed pineapple and juice and carrots. Combine cake flour, baking soda, salt, cinnamon and nutmeg, sifting 3 times. Slowly beat dry ingredients into batter. Add chopped macadamias; blend thoroughly. Bake in a greased and floured circular tube pan for 1 hour and 15 minutes in a 350° oven. Dust while still warm with confectioners sugar, or allow cake to cool and frost with butter based icing.

Bernie Wright
Green Hills Council

CHEESE CAKE

Mix well:

1 c. granulated sugar	1 tsp. vanilla
3 (8 oz.) pkg. cream cheese	4 whole eggs

Pour into unbaked graham cracker crust*. Bake 50 minutes in 350° preheated oven. Do not turn oven off. Remove cake; top with 1 pint sour cream and return to oven for 5 minutes. Remove cake (now turn off oven!) and let it cool. Top with favorite pie filling or leave plain. Chill overnight before eating.

*Crust:

1/3 c. powdered sugar	1 1/2 c. graham cracker
1/4 c. margarine	crumbs

Melt margarine; add to sugar and crumb mixture. Line bottom of spring form pan, packing firmly.

Mary Grey Jenkins
Green Hills Council

CHEESE CAKE

Blend until smooth:

12 oz. cream cheese	1/2 c. sugar
2 eggs	1 Tbsp. vanilla

Pour into graham cracker crust (use a 10 inch pie pan) made by combining the following ingredients.

420

9 double graham crackers   1/4 lb. melted butter or
1/4 c. sugar   margarine

Bake 25 minutes at 350°. Top with blended:

1 c. sour cream   1/2 tsp. vanilla
2 Tbsp. sugar

Return to oven; bake an additional 10 minutes.
Virginia Kaderabek
Harpeth Council

MOM'S EASY CHEESECAKE

2 (8 oz.) pkg. cream   1 c. sugar
   cheese, softened   A few drops of yellow food
1 large container Cool Whip   coloring (optional)
1 graham cracker pie crust

Mix cream cheese, Cool Whip and sugar in large bowl.
Add food coloring; pour into crust and chill.
Judy Perkins
Harpeth Council

BAKED CHEESECAKE

1 pkg. Duncan Hines yellow   1/2 c. sugar
   deluxe cake mix   4 eggs
2 Tbsp. salad oil   1 1/2 c. sweet milk
2 (8 oz.) pkg. cream cheese, 3 Tbsp. lemon juice
   room temperature   3 tsp. vanilla

Preheat oven to 300°. Reserve 1 cup dry cake mix.
In a large bowl, combine the remaining cake mix with 1 egg
and oil (mixture will be crumbly). Press crust mixture
evenly over the bottom and 3/4 way up the sides of a
13x9x2 inch pan, that has been greased. In same bowl,
blend cream cheese and sugar. Add 3 eggs and reserved
cake mix; beat 1 minute at medium speed. At low speed,
slowly add the milk and flavorings; mix until smooth. Pour
into crust. Bake at 300° for 45 to 55 minutes, or until center is firm. Let cool and spread over top 1 can pie filling
(pineapple, cherry or blueberry). Cover with aluminum foil

and store in refrigerator to chill before serving. Cut into squares.

Myrtle Porter
Knoxville Council

UNBAKED CHEESE CAKE

Dissolve 1 small package lemon jello in 1 cup boiling water. Add 3 tablespoons lemon juice to jello; let jello cool. Whip 1 tall can Pet milk (chill ahead before whipping). Cream together:

1 (8 oz.) pkg. cream cheese   1 c. sugar

Mix cheese mixture and jello together, then fold in whipped cream. Pour into graham cracker crust in 9x13 inch dish. Sprinkle with graham cracker crumbs; chill overnight.

Louise Breeden
Nashboro Council

ORIGINAL NEW YORK CHEESE CAKE

2 c. sugar	1 Tbsp. vanilla
4 (8 oz.) pkg. cream cheese	2 eggs
	1/2 c. heavy cream

Mix all ingredients thoroughly with a mixer.

Crust:

1 1/3 c. graham cracker   3/4 stick butter
   crumbs

Melt butter over low heat. Pour butter over crumbs; mix well. Pack crust into 9 x 1 1/2 inch spring form pan. Pour cheese mixture over crust. Bake at 300° for 2 1/2 hours; let cool. Remove sides of pan.

Betty Baird
Nashboro Council

CHESS CAKE

1 box Duncan Hines butter   1 stick margarine, softened
  cake mix   1 egg

Combine these 3 ingredients; mixture will be like dough. Pat into ungreased 11x13 inch pan.

8 oz. cream cheese,   3 eggs
  softened   1 box powdered sugar

Beat cream cheese. Add eggs one at a time, beating well after each. Add sugar; beat well. Pour over mixture in pan and bake at 350° for 45 minutes. Let cool before cutting.

Deanna Baker
Harpeth Council

CHESS CAKES

4 eggs   1 c. pecans, chopped
1 c. sugar   1/4 tsp. vanilla
1 box light brown sugar   2 c. flour
2 1/2 sticks margarine,   2 tsp. baking powder
  melted   1/4 tsp. salt

Combine and sift flour, baking powder and salt. Add all other ingredients, except egg whites. Beat egg whites until stiff and fold into mixture. Spread in a large broiler pan that has been greased and floured. Bake at 325° for 30 minutes. Cut into squares.

Linda Fields
Clarksville Council

CHESS CAKE

Mix:
1 box yellow butter cake mix   1 stick butter
2 eggs

Mix:
1 box powdered sugar   1 (8 oz.) pkg. Philadelphia
2 eggs   cream cheese
1 tsp. vanilla   1 stick butter

Pour cake mixture into greased and floured 9x13 inch pan. It will be stiff (I take a wooden spoon dipped in water to spread). Pour sugar-cheese mixture over cake and bake 45 minutes at 350°. Do not bake any longer.

Annabelle Fry
Memphis Council

CHESS CAKE

1 c. butter	1 tsp. baking powder
1 box light brown sugar	1 tsp. vanilla
1/2 c. white sugar	Pinch of salt
4 eggs	1 c. broken pecans
2 c. all-purpose flour	

Heat butter and brown sugar on low heat. Remove from heat; add other ingredients. Mix well and put in a 9x13 inch pan that has been greased and floured. Bake 30 to 40 minutes or until done at 300°. Cut and roll in powdered sugar while still hot or cut into squares and dust tops with powdered sugar.

Barbara S. Stanfill
Harpeth Council

CHESS PIE CAKE

1 pkg. yellow Duncan Hines	1 egg
(butter) cake mix	1 stick butter, melted

Mix together and pat into dish. Combine:

1 (8 oz.) pkg. cream cheese	1/2 - 3/4 pkg. powdered
3 eggs	sugar

Mix it well with a mixer; pour over batter. Bake at 325° for 1 hour. Let cool before cutting; cut into small squares.

Linda Earp
Clarksville Council

CHESS PIE CAKE

1 box Duncan Hines yellow
  butter cake mix

1 egg

Mix together to make a batter. Press into a greased 9x13 inch pan. With electric mixer, beat the following:

1 box confectioners sugar
3 eggs

1 (8 oz.) pkg. cream cheese

Beat until smooth. Pour over batter and bake about 1 hour at 300°-325°.

Denise Gill
Harpeth Council

CHESS PIE CAKE

1 box Duncan Hines yellow
  butter cake mix

1 egg
1 stick melted butter

Mix and press into greased pan.

1 box powdered sugar
1 (8 oz.) pkg. cream cheese

3 eggs

Cream together and pour on top. Bake at 350° for 1 hour.

Cindy Martin
Harpeth Council

CHOCO-CARAMEL FUDGE CAKE

1/3 c. evaporated milk
1 pkg. German chocolate
  cake mix
3/4 c. melted oleo

1 c. chopped nuts (optional)
1 small pkg. chocolate chips
60 Kraft caramels
1/2 c. evaporated milk

Mix 1/3 cup milk with cake mix; add oleo and nuts. Spread half of batter in 13x9 inch greased pan. Bake 8 minutes in 350° oven. While hot, sprinkle with chocolate chips and caramels, prepared by melting caramels and 1/2 cup milk. Top with other half of cake mix. Bake 18 to 20 minutes longer. Rich and delicious.

Beverly Vaughn
Harpeth Council

CHOCOLATE CAKE

Cream:
1 stick margarine   1 c. sugar

Beat in 4 eggs, one at a time.

1 (1 lb.) can Hershey's   1 tsp. baking powder
  syrup   1 tsp. vanilla
1 c. flour, sifted

Bake in two 8 inch pans at 350° for 30 to 35 minutes.
Claudia Davenport
Clarksville Council

CHOCOLATE CAKE

2 c. flour (plain)   2 c. sugar

In saucepan, mix:
2 sticks butter   1 c. water
3 Tbsp. cocoa

Cook over low heat until smooth; add to above. Add:

2 eggs, beaten   1/2 c. buttermilk
1 tsp. soda   1 tsp. vanilla

Combine all the above; beat until smooth. Pour into
greased long cake pan. Bake at 350° for 45 minutes.

Icing: In saucepan, mix -

1 stick butter   6 Tbsp. milk
3 Tbsp. cocoa   1 tsp. vanilla

Add to 1 box confectioners sugar; mix until smooth.
Pour icing on cake while hot.
Jane B. Chaffin
Harpeth Council

TEXAS CHOCOLATE CAKE

2 c. flour
2 c. sugar
1 stick butter
4 Tbsp. cocoa
1/2 c. buttermilk
2 eggs

1 tsp. vanilla
1 tsp. soda
1 tsp. cinnamon
1/2 c. shortening
1 c. water

Put in saucepan; bring to boil 1 stick butter, 4 tablespoons cocoa, 1/2 cup shortening and 1 cup water. Pour mixture over dry ingredients above, then add 1/2 cup buttermilk, 2 eggs, slightly beaten, and 1 teaspoon vanilla. Pour into greased and floured long pan. Bake at 375° or 400° for about 35 minutes.

Icing: Start about 5 minutes before cake is finished baking -

1 stick butter
4 Tbsp. cocoa
1 box confectioners sugar

1 c. nuts
8 Tbsp. milk
1 tsp. vanilla

Melt butter; add cocoa and milk. Bring to boil; remove from heat. Add 1 box confectioners sugar and 1 teaspoon vanilla. Beat well; add 1 cup nuts.

Ruby Smith
Knoxville Council

CHOCOLATE CAKE PUDDING
(Cake on top, Pudding on bottom)

3/4 c. sugar
1 c. sifted flour
1/4 tsp. salt
2 tsp. baking powder

2 Tbsp. cocoa
1/2 c. milk
3 Tbsp. melted butter
1 tsp. vanilla

Topping:

1/2 c. granulated sugar
1/2 c. brown sugar

1/4 c. cocoa
1 1/2 c. water

Sift sugar, flour, salt, baking powder and cocoa together into a 9 inch square pan. Stir in milk, butter and vanilla. Spread batter evenly in pan. Mix topping sugars and cocoa; sprinkle over batter. Pour water over all and bake in 350° oven for 45 minutes or until top springs back when lightly touched. Best when served warm with Cool Whip topping.

Bob and Nora Chandler
Harpeth Council

CHOCOLATE CHEESECAKE

2 (8 1/2 oz.) pkg.
  chocolate cookies
1/2 tsp. cinnamon
1/2 c. butter, melted
1 c. sugar
4 eggs

1 1/2 lb. cream cheese,
  softened
16 oz. semi-sweet chocolate
1 tsp. vanilla extract
2 Tbsp. cocoa
3 c. sour cream
1/4 c. sweet butter, melted

In blender, or with a rolling pin, crush the chocolate cookies. You should have about 2 cups. Mix with cinnamon and the 1/2 cup of melted butter. Press the crumbs firmly into bottom and sides of a 9 inch spring form pan; chill. Beat sugar with eggs until light and fluffy. Add the cream cheese gradually, beating well after each addition. Melt the chocolate; add to the egg mixture along with the vanilla, cocoa and sour cream, beating constantly. Add the melted sweet butter; mix well. Pour the mixture into the chilled pie shell and bake in a 350° oven for 45 minutes. Chill overnight in the refrigerator.

Chuck and Gail Dickson
Harpeth Council

CHOCOLATE CHERRY UPSIDE-DOWN CAKE

1 (21 oz.) can cherry pie
  filling
2 1/4 c. all-purpose flour
1 1/2 c. sugar
3/4 c. unsweetened cocoa
  powder

1 1/2 tsp. baking soda
3/4 tsp. salt
1 1/2 c. water
1/2 c. cooking oil
1/4 c. vinegar
1 1/2 tsp. vanilla

Spread the cherry pie filling evenly over the bottom of a greased 13x9x2 inch baking pan. In a large bowl, stir together flour, sugar, cocoa, soda and salt. In another bowl, combine water, oil, vinegar and vanilla. Add liquid ingredients to flour mixture all at once; stir just to moisten. Pour batter evenly over cherry pie filling. Bake in 350° oven for

30 to 35 minutes or till cake tests done. Cool 10 minutes in pan; invert and cool.

Leslie Stephens
Harpeth Council

CHOCOLATE CHIP DATE CAKE

Cover 1 cup dates, cut up, with 1 cup hot water in a separate bowl. Cream 1 cup butter or margarine with 1 cup sugar. Beat in 2 eggs and 1 teaspoon vanilla. Sift together:

1 3/4 c. all-purpose flour   1 Tbsp. cocoa
1 tsp. baking soda

Add to creamed ingredients; add date mixture. Stir in 1/2 cup chocolate chips. Place in a 9x13 inch greased and floured pan. Sprinkle another 1/2 cup chocolate chips and 1/3 cup chopped nuts over the top. Bake at 350° for 30 to 40 minutes until toothpick comes out clean. Serve with whipped cream or ice cream.

Virginia Kaderabek
Harpeth Council

CHOCOLATE COOKIE SHEET CAKE

2 c. flour (plain)   3 Tbsp. cocoa
2 c. sugar   2 eggs, well beaten
1/2 tsp. salt   1 tsp. soda
1 stick oleo and 1/2 c.   1/2 c. buttermilk
  shortening   1 tsp. vanilla
1 c. water   1 tsp. cinnamon

Sift flour; measure. Resift with sugar and salt. In a saucepan, put oleo, shortening, water and cocoa. Bring to a boil; pour over flour and sugar mixture. In another bowl, put eggs, soda, buttermilk and vanilla. Add to above mixture and mix well. Bake in a greased and floured shallow cake pan, 15 1/2 x 10 1/2 x 1 inches. Bake for 20 minutes at 350°. Start making icing the last 5 minutes cake is baking.

Metty C. Fain
Andrew Jackson Council

CHOCOLATE ECLAIR CAKE

1 box graham crackers
2 boxes instant vanilla
  pudding
1 c. powdered sugar

3 c. milk
9 oz. ctn. Cool Whip
1 can light chocolate icing

Mix pudding, powdered sugar and milk together with electric mixer, about 2 minutes on low speed. Fold Cool Whip into pudding mixture; set aside. Lightly grease bottom of 13x9 inch baking pan with oil. Line bottom of pan with whole graham crackers (sometimes have to break apart to make fit). Pour 1/2 of pudding mixture over crackers. Put another layer of crackers, then another layer (remaining) pudding. Finish with another layer of crackers. Ice with chocolate icing and refrigerate.

Ann R. Wooten
Memphis Downtown Council

CHOCOLATE PEANUT BUTTER TEA CAKE

1/4 c. butter or margarine,
  softened
2/3 c. sugar
1 egg
1 tsp. vanilla extract
1 1/2 c. all-purpose flour
1/2 c. cocoa

1 tsp. baking soda
1/2 tsp. salt
1 c. buttermilk
1 (12 oz.) pkg. Reese's
  peanut butter chips
1/4 c. milk

Cream butter in medium bowl till fluffy. Beat in sugar, egg and vanilla. Combine flour, cocoa, soda and salt. Mix in cocoa mixture alternately with buttermilk, beginning and ending with dry ingredients, mixing only until ingredients are blended. Stir in 1 1/2 cups of the peanut butter chips. Pour mixture into a greased and floured 9x5x3 inch loaf pan. Bake at 350° for 60 to 65 minutes or until toothpick inserted in center comes out clean. Cool cake 10 minutes; remove and place on wire rack. Heat 1/2 cup peanut butter chips and milk in small saucepan over low heat until melted, stirring often. Drizzle over warm cake.

Sandra H. Bullock
Harpeth Council

CHOCOLATE SHEET CAKE

Sift together:

2 c. flour

2 c. sugar

1/2 tsp. salt

Bring to boil:

1 stick margarine

1/2 c. shortening

1 c. water

2 1/2 Tbsp. cocoa

Pour over flour mixture.

2 eggs, well beaten

1 tsp. soda

1/2 c. buttermilk

1 tsp. vanilla

Add together, then add to above. Bake 30 minutes at 350° in cookie sheet that has been lined with aluminum foil.

Icing: Begin frosting about 5 minutes before cake is done -

1 stick margarine

2 1/2 Tbsp. cocoa

5 Tbsp. milk

Nuts

Heat over low heat; do not boil. Remove from heat; add 1 box confectioners sugar, pinch of salt and 1/2 teaspoon vanilla. Frost immediately. Put nuts on top.

Judy Christopher
Harpeth Council

CHOCOLATE SYRUP CAKE

1 c. flour

1 c. sugar

1 stick margarine

4 eggs, creamed

1 large can Hershey's
chocolate syrup

Mix all together. Bake in two 8 inch buttered and floured square pans at 350° for 30 minutes.

Chocolate Icing:

6 Tbsp. margarine

3 sq. unsweetened chocolate

6 Tbsp. milk

1 box powdered sugar

1 tsp. vanilla

1 pinch of salt

Melt margarine and chocolate. Mix with milk, sugar, vanilla and salt. Let cake cool before icing.

Mrs. Adelene Queenan
Harpeth Council

CHOCOLATE TORTE CAKE

1 c. chopped pecans
1 stick margarine
1 c. self-rising flour
2 (8 oz.) pkg. cream cheese
1 small pkg. chocolate
instant pudding

1 small pkg. vanilla instant
pudding
2 c. cold milk
1 large ctn. Cool Whip
1 c. confectioners sugar

1. Mix pecans, margarine, flour and 1 package cream cheese. Press thin into rectangular Pyrex dish. Bake until light golden brown at 325°; cool. 2. Mix 1 package cream cheese, confectioners sugar and 1 cup of Cool Whip. Spread over cooled crust. 3. Mix both boxes of pudding together with 2 cups cold milk; pour over last layer. Top with remaining Cool Whip and refrigerate.

Pam Eleazer
Green Hills Council

LAZY DAY CHOCOLATE CAKE

2 c. sugar
2 c. all-purpose flour
1 c. water
4 Tbsp. cocoa
2 sticks oleo

2 eggs
1/2 c. buttermilk
1 tsp. vanilla
1 tsp. soda

Bring to a boiling point the water, cocoa and oleo. Add sugar and flour; mix well. Add eggs, buttermilk, vanilla and soda; stir mixture. Do not use electric mixer. Mix well and bake at 350° for 40 minutes. Bake in greased oblong pan. Frost with the following frosting.

Lazy Day Frosting:

6 Tbsp. milk
4 Tbsp. cocoa

1 stick oleo

Bring to a boiling point and add the following.

432

1 box powdered sugar   1 c. chopped nuts
1 tsp. vanilla

Mix well and pour on cake.

Carolyn Utley
Memphis Downtown Council
Jeanette Palmer
Harpeth Council

VELVET CHOCOLATE CAKE

1 1/4 c. milk   1/2 tsp. salt
2 Tbsp. white vinegar   3/4 c. butter, softened
2 c. cake flour   1 tsp. vanilla
1/2 c. cocoa   1 1/2 c. sugar
1 1/4 tsp. soda   2 eggs
1 tsp. baking powder

Grease and lightly flour two 9 inch round cake pans; set aside. Combine milk and vinegar; let stand 10 minutes. Combine flour, cocoa, soda, baking powder and salt in small bowl, mixing thoroughly. In a large bowl, cream butter and vanilla. Gradually add sugar; cream. Add eggs; beat until smooth. Add flour mixture alternately with milk mixture; beat until smooth. Pour into prepared pans. Bake at 350° until cake tester inserted in center of cake comes out clean, about 30 minutes. Cool in pans for 10 minutes. Remove from pans and place on wire racks to cool completely. Frost with icing.

Martha R. Dowlen
Green Hills Council

AUNT JIMMY'S CHRISTMAS CAKE

1 (8 oz.) pkg. cream cheese   1 1/2 tsp. baking powder
1/2 lb. margarine   1 c. candied fruit
1 1/2 c. sugar   1/2 c. chopped pecans
1 1/2 tsp. vanilla   1/2 c. finely chopped pecans
4 eggs   Candied pineapple slices
2 1/4 c. sifted cake flour   Candied cherries

Thoroughly blend softened cream cheese, margarine, sugar and vanilla. Add eggs, one at a time, mixing well after each addition. Gradually add 2 cups flour, sifted with baking powder. Combine 1/4 cup flour with candied fruit and 1/2 cup chopped pecans; fold into batter. Grease a 10 inch Bundt pan (or tube pan); sprinkle with finely chopped pecans. Pour batter into pan. Bake at 325° for 1 hour and 20 minutes. Cool 5 minutes; remove from pan. Garnish with candied pineapple and cherries.

Nancy Bess Lord
Harpeth Council

CHURCH WINDOW CAKE

1 stick margarine or butter
1 (12 oz.) pkg. chocolate
   chips

1 pkg. (colored) miniature
   marshmallows
3/4 c. chopped pecans

Melt butter and chocolate chips. When cool, add marshmallows and nuts. Butter a loaf pan and sprinkle bottom and sides with coconut. Pour mixture into pan; set in refrigerator 4-6 hours until you can slice. (Pretty to serve at Christmas time.)

Judy Christopher
Harpeth Council

COCA-COLA CAKE

2 c. unsifted flour
2 c. granulated sugar
2 sticks oleo
3 Tbsp. cocoa
1 c. Coca-Cola
1/2 c. buttermilk

1 tsp. baking soda
2 eggs, beaten
1 Tbsp. vanilla
1 1/2 c. miniature
   marshmallows

Sift flour and sugar in bowl. Heat oleo, cocoa and Coke to boiling point; pour over flour mixture. Add buttermilk, soda, eggs, vanilla and marshmallows. Batter will be thin and marshmallows will float to top. Pour batter into oiled and floured oblong pan. Bake at 350° for 30 to 35 minutes. Ice cake while still hot.

Icing for Coca-Cola Cake:

1/2 c. butter
3 Tbsp. cocoa
6 Tbsp. Coca-Cola

1 box confectioners sugar
1 c. chopped nuts

434

Combine first 3 ingredients; heat to boiling. Pour over sugar; beat well. Add remaining ingredients.

Pat DeMatteo
Nashboro Council

COCONUT CAKE

1 box Duncan Hines butter
  cake mix
2 c. sour cream

1 1/2 c. Cool Whip, thawed
2 c. sugar
2 (9 oz.) pkg. frozen
  coconut

Bake cake according to directions in 2 layers. Split layers in halves when cooled. Combine sugar, sour cream and coconut (reserve a small amount of plain coconut to put on finished cake). Chill mixture; reserve 1 cup for frosting. Spread remainder between layers and on top of cake. Combine sour cream mixture (1 cup) with Cool Whip; blend until smooth. Spread on top and sides. Sprinkle reserved coconut on cake. Store in airtight container in refrigerator for 3 days before slicing.

Denise Gill
Harpeth Council

COCONUT CAKE

1 Duncan Hines white cake
  mix
1 (8 oz.) ctn. sour cream

3 (8 oz.) pkg. frozen
  coconut
2 c. sugar

Bake cake according to box directions in oblong pan. Turn out and cut layer horizontally with a string. Lift off top layer; spread on coconut filling. Replace top and ice with coconut mixture. It will be even better if it has set overnight for filling to soak through cake.

Gerry Panter
Columbia Council

COCONUT CAKE

Overnight, soak:
2 c. sour cream
2 c. white sugar

3 (6 oz.) pkg. frozen
  coconut

Next A.M.: Bake yellow cake mix; cool. Pour sour cream mixture over cake. Leave in refrigerator 3 days, covered. Easy and delicious!

Evelyn Carrico
Nashboro Council

COCONUT SHEET CAKE

Bake 1 super moist white cake mix (any brand) in 9x13 inch pan, greased and floured. After baking and cooling, punch holes in cake and pour over top 1 cup Carnation evaporated milk. Cover with 9 ounce carton Cool Whip. Frost with 7 ounce package Angel Flake coconut. Cover tightly and refrigerate 2 days.

Deenie Thorton
Green Hills Council

COCONUT SOUR CREAM CAKE

1 (18 1/2 oz.) pkg. butter
  flavor cake mix
2 c. sugar
1 (8 oz.) ctn. commercial
  sour cream
1 (12 oz.) pkg. frozen
  coconut, thawed
1 1/2 c. whipped cream (or
  frozen whipped topping,
  thawed)

Prepare the cake according to directions, making two 8 inch layers. Split both layers horizontally after they have cooled. Blend together the sugar, sour cream and coconut; chill. Spread all but 1 cup of the sour cream mixture between the 4 layers. Blend the remaining cup of the mixture with the whipped cream and spread on the top and sides of the cake. Seal in an airtight container and refrigerate for 3 days before serving. Keep refrigerated after cutting.

Jane York
Harpeth Council

FROZEN COCONUT CAKE

Bake 1 package yellow cake mix (with pudding mix) as directed in sheet cake pan. While still hot, punch holes all over cake all the way through. Pour 1 can Eagle Brand sweetened condensed milk over hot cake; let thoroughly cool.

436

Icing:

1 medium (8 or 9 oz.) ctn.
   Cool Whip (1/2 ctn.)
1 small can or 1/2 can
   cream of coconut

1 or 2 c. (as much as you
   like) frozen coconut

Make 2 days ahead and refrigerate. This gets more delicious as it sets.

Shirley Edwards
Knoxville Council

JIFFY COCONUT CAKE

Mix 1 white cake mix and bake in sheet pan. Punch holes all over cake, then pour 1 can Eagle Brand milk all over. Spread 1 regular size carton of Cool Whip over cake. Sprinkle generous amount of coconut over the Cool Whip. This is much better made a day or so in advance. Keep refrigerated!

Betty Campbell
Knoxville Council

HEAVENLY COCONUT CAKE

2 c. sour cream
2 c. powdered sugar

2 (12 oz.) pkg. frozen coconut or 3 c. fresh, grated

Blend above together; let stand in refrigerator overnight. Bake a Duncan Hines butter or yellow cake mix in 2 layers; split to make 4 layers. Spread coconut mixture between layers, covering sides with any remaining. Cover tightly. Can be stored in refrigerator for several days.

Dot Murphy
Memphis Council

COCONUT CAKE
("Martha Makes the Difference")

4 whole eggs, beaten well
2 c. sugar
1 c. Wesson oil
1 c. buttermilk

2 c. self-rising flour
   (Martha White)
1 small can or 1 c. coconut
1 Tbsp. coconut flavoring

Bake at 350° in tube pan for about 55 minutes or two 8-9 inch layers.

Seven Minute Icing:

2 whole egg whites
1/2 c. sugar
1/4 tsp. cream of tartar or
   2 tsp. light corn syrup

1/3 c. water
Dash of salt
1 tsp. vanilla

Place all ingredients, except vanilla, in top of double boiler. Beat 1/2 minute at low speed. Place over boiling water. Cook, beating constantly, till frosting forms stiff peaks, about 7 minutes. Add vanilla.

Mrs. Lamar (Jean) Edwards
Knoxville Council

COCONUT BLACK WALNUT CAKE

2 c. sugar
4 eggs
1 c. oil
1 c. buttermilk
1 c. coconut
1 c. black walnuts

1/2 tsp. salt
1/2 tsp. soda
1/2 tsp. baking powder
1 tsp. coconut flavoring
3 c. all-purpose flour

Blend together sugar, oil and eggs. Sift flour, salt, soda and baking powder. Add to first mixture with buttermilk. Add nuts, coconut and flavoring. Bake at 325° for 75 minutes in well greased, floured pan (tube pan). When cake is about finished baking, mix together:

2 c. sugar
1 c. water

4 Tbsp. margarine
3 tsp. coconut flavoring

Mix sugar, water and butter. Boil 5 minutes; remove from heat. Add flavoring. While cake is still hot, pour over cake and let stand 4 hours. Insert knife in cake as syrup is poured over cake.

Freddie Pesterfield
Knoxville Council

COCONUT PINEAPPLE CAKE

1 box yellow cake mix with
   pudding
1 (15 1/2 oz.) can cream
   of coconut
1 can Eagle Brand milk

1 small can crushed
   pineapple, drained
1 large ctn. Cool Whip
1 pkg. coconut

Bake cake according to directions in an oblong pan. Cool and punch holes in cake with toothpick. Whip together cream of coconut and Eagle Brand milk; pour over cake. Spread drained pineapple. Spread Cool Whip or sour cream and sprinkle coconut over cake. Let set overnight. Best when chilled before serving.

Willie Jean Spurlock
Nashboro Council

EASY COCONUT PINEAPPLE CAKE

Bake 1 yellow cake mix in oblong pan. When cool, punch holes in cake. Whip together:

1 (15 1/2 oz.) can cream
   of coconut

1 can Eagle Brand milk

(This will be thin.) Pour over cake; spread 1 can crushed pineapple (large can), drained. Spread large carton of Cool Whip and sprinkle coconut over cake. Let set overnight.

Billie Fleming
Nashboro Council

COFFEE CAKE

1 box white cake mix
3/4 c. Wesson oil
1/2 c. sugar

1 small ctn. sour cream
4 eggs, added one at a time

Combine above ingredients, one at a time; beat well after each. Pour 1/2 of mixture into floured, greased tube pan. Sprinkle 1/2 of crumb mixture on top. Add rest of batter, then remaining crumb mixture. Bake about 1 hour in 350° oven. Remove from pan; glaze.

Crumb Mixture:

3 Tbsp. brown sugar
2 tsp. cinnamon

1 c. chopped pecans

Pour this glaze over cake while warm.

1 c. powdered sugar

2 or 3 Tbsp. milk

Cover cake immediately.

Jean Bethel
Memphis Council

YUM-YUM COFFEE CAKE

Topping Mixture:

1/3 c. brown sugar
1/2 c. granulated sugar

1 scant tsp. cinnamon
1 c. finely chopped nuts

First Batter Mixture:

1 stick margarine
1 c. granulated sugar

2 eggs
1 tsp. vanilla

Second Batter Mixture:

2 c. plain flour
1 tsp. baking soda

1 tsp. baking powder
1/2 tsp. salt

Add one batter mixture to another alternately with 1 cup sour cream. Start with layer of mixture, then topping. Spoon on second layer of mixture. This will make 2 small loaf pans or one 9x13 inch pan. Grease pans. Bake at 350° for 45 minutes.

Katrina Carter
Harpeth Council

CREAM CHEESE SHORTCAKE SQUARES

2 c. Bisquick baking mix
2 Tbsp. sugar
2 Tbsp. firm margarine or butter
1 (3 oz.) pkg. cream cheese, softened

1/2 c. sugar
2 egg yolks
1 c. dairy sour cream
1 tsp. grated lemon peel
2 c. cut up mixed fruit

440

Heat oven to 375°. Mix baking mix and 2 tablespoons sugar. Cut in margarine. Press in ungreased square pan, 8x8x2 inches. Bake until edges are light brown, about 10 minutes. Mix remaining ingredients, except fruit; pour over baked layer. Bake until edges are golden brown, about 35 minutes. Serve with fruit. Makes 9 servings.

High Altitude Directions (3500 to 6500 feet): Heat oven to 400°. Bake base about 10 minutes. Reduce oven to 375°; continue as directed.

Pat Ferguson
Harpeth Council

CREME DE MENTHE CAKE

1 box sour creme cake mix
3 Tbsp. creme de menthe
1 (16 oz.) can Hershey's
    chocolate syrup

1 medium size ctn. Cool Whip
3 Tbsp. creme de menthe
Sugar to taste

Follow cake directions on box, except substitute 3 tablespoons creme de menthe for 3 tablespoons water. Bake in 13x9 inch pan. When cake is done, remove from oven and poke holes in cake with fork. Pour chocolate syrup over cake while still warm; refrigerate overnight. Before serving, add 3 tablespoons creme de menthe to Cool Whip and sugar to taste. Spread over cake.

Jan Morrow
Columbia Council

CRUMB CAKE

1 c. margarine
2 c. sugar
4 tsp. baking powder

4 eggs, separated
1 c. milk
4 c. flour

Combine dry ingredients; sift. Add margarine and crumb well with fingers. Take out 1 cup crumbs; set aside. Add beaten egg yolks and milk. Beat whites until stiff; fold into batter. Pour into 2 greased loaf pans; top with crumbs. Bake at 400° for 45 minutes to 1 hour; watch for burning. Test with toothpick. Makes a great breakfast or brunch cake.

Peggy Boatwright
Memphis Council

DATE NUT CHOCOLATE CAKE

Prepare 1 box chocolate fudge cake mix according to directions on box. While cake bakes, prepare filling.

Filling:

1 1/2 c. hot water	2 Tbsp. flour
1/2 c. English walnuts	1 1/2 c. sugar
1 c. chopped dates	

Mix and cook together until thick. Cool and spread between layers of cake, saving a little out for topping.

Icing:

1 box powdered sugar	1 (6 oz.) pkg. cream cheese
1 stick butter	3 sq. chocolate, melted

Beat together until fluffy. Add a small amount of sweet milk if too thick. Spread on top and sides, using leftover filling over icing on top of cake.

Joyce Mattice
Harpeth Council

MOIST DEVIL'S FOOD CAKE

2 c. sugar	1/2 c. buttermilk
2 eggs	2 c. flour
3 Tbsp. cocoa	1 tsp. soda
1 tsp. vanilla	1 tsp. salt
1/2 c. shortening	1 c. boiling water

Mix cake by normal method, except for boiling water. Add boiling water last. Bake in two 8 inch pans at 350° for 30 minutes.

Chocolate Frosting:

2 c. sugar	1/4 lb. butter or 1 stick
3 Tbsp. cocoa	1 tsp. vanilla
1/2 c. milk	

Mix; bring to full boil for 1 minute (or more). Remove from heat; add vanilla. Beat until spreading consistency.

Dorothy Balcom
Clarksville Council

442

DUMP CAKE

1 can cherry pie filling
1 can crushed pineapple
1 medium pkg. coconut
2 sticks butter

1 medium pkg. (or 1 c.)
  pecans
1 box Duncan Hines butter
  recipe golden cake mix

Pour cherries in bottom of pan, then drain pineapple. Pour on top of cherries. Sprinkle cake mix on top of the cherries and pineapple. Melt 2 sticks butter; pour on, then add coconut and pecans. Bake 1 hour at 350°.

Imogene Chesher
Knoxville Council

DUMP CAKE

1 (No. 2) can crushed
  pineapple, drained
1 (1 lb.) can cherry pie
  filling

1/2 or 1 c. chopped pecans
  or walnuts
1 box yellow or white cake
  mix
2 sticks margarine

Grease Bundt pan. Put in pineapple, cherry pie filling and cake mix, just as it comes from the box. Top with nuts; dot with margarine. Bake for 1 hour at 350°. Serve hot or cold by scooping out on plate.
Note: Do not stir or mix ingredients in any way; it's a "dump technique".

Mrs. Adelene Queenan
Harpeth Council

DUMP CAKE

1 (1 lb. 4 oz.) can crushed
  pineapple
1 can cherry pie filling

1 box yellow cake mix
1 c. chopped pecans
2 sticks butter

Spread each in order in pan; do not mix. Slice butter and place on top. Bake at 350° for 1 hour.

Virginia J. Reid
Clarksville Council

FIG CAKE

2 c. all-purpose flour
1 Tbsp. cinnamon
1 Tbsp. cloves
1 Tbsp. nutmeg
1 Tbsp. salt
1 Tbsp. soda
1 Tbsp. vanilla

1 1/2 c. sugar
1 c. cooking oil
1 c. buttermilk
3 eggs
1 c. fig preserves
1 c. chopped nuts

Mix all dry ingredients; add oil and beat well. Add eggs one at a time, alternately with the milk. Add nuts, figs and vanilla. Bake in tube pan at 350° for 1 hour or until done.

Sauce for Fig Cake:

1 c. sugar
1/2 c. buttermilk
1 Tbsp. vanilla

1 Tbsp. corn syrup
1/2 stick butter

Boil all ingredients 3 minutes, stirring constantly. Pour over hot cake; let cake cool in pan.

Maxine Scott
East Memphis Council

FINGER LICKIN' CAKE

1 box Duncan Hines butter
   cake mix
3/4 c. cooking oil

4 eggs
1 (11 oz.) can Mandarin
   oranges, including juice

Mix and beat 3 minutes. Bake at 350° for 25 minutes.

Frosting:

1 box vanilla instant
   pudding
1 (9 oz.) ctn. Cool Whip

1 (15 oz.) can crushed
   pineapple, including juice

Mix and spread; keep refrigerated.

Sylvia Kaffer
Clarksville Council

FLOWER GARDEN CAKE
(Diabetics)

1 inch sector of an 8 inch
   diameter angel cake
1/8 tsp. grated lemon rind
1 egg

1 env. saccharin sweetened
   lemon gelatin
2 Tbsp. lemon juice
1/2 c. water
2 Tbsp. whipped cream

1. Beat egg yolk; mix well with the lemon juice and water. 2. Cook a few minutes in a double boiler until the mixture coats a spoon. 3. Dissolve the gelatin dessert powder in the mixture; add the lemon rind. 4. Fold the lemon and egg mixture into the stiffly beaten egg white. 5. Cut the cake into small bite size cubes; fold into the mixture. 6. Pile into a glass sherbet dish and place in the refrigerator 24 hours in advance of serving. 7. Lightly color the whipped cream with green vegetable coloring and use to top the dessert when serving.

Exchange: 1 bread exchange, 1 meat exchange, 1 fat exchange. Calories: 186.

MOTHER'S WHITE FRUIT CAKE

5 large eggs
1/2 lb. butter
1 c. granulated sugar
1 3/4 c. regular all-purpose
   flour
1/2 tsp. baking powder

3/4 lb. candied cherries
1 lb. candied pineapple
4 c. shelled pecans
1/2 oz. bottle vanilla extract
1/2 oz. bottle lemon extract

Chop nuts and fruits into medium size pieces; dredge with 1/4 cup of the flour. Cream butter and sugar together until light and fluffy. Add well beaten eggs; blend well. Sift remaining flour and baking powder together; fold into eggs and butter mixture. Add vanilla and lemon extracts; mix well, then add fruits and nuts, blending in well. Grease 10 inch tube pan; line with paper and grease again. Pour batter into prepared pan. Place in cold oven and bake at 250° F. for 3 hours. Cool in pan on cake rack. Makes one 5 pound cake.

Barbara J. Ball
Harpeth Council

REFRIGERATOR FRUIT CAKE

2 c. crushed graham
  crackers or box of
  graham cracker crumbs
2 c. chopped pecans

1 (8 oz.) pkg. chopped
  dates
1 1/2 c. diced marshmallows
1 c. milk or less

Mix all ingredients together, except milk. Add 1 cup (or less) milk until mixture is the right consistency to mold into a log. Roll in oiled waxed paper. Refrigerate at least 24 hours before cutting and serving.

Sheila Fleming
East Memphis Council

UNCOOKED FRUIT CAKE

1 can coconut
1 box Nabisco sugar honey
  graham crackers, rolled
  real fine

1 large can Pet milk
1 large bag marshmallows
1 jar cherries, halved
1 box raisins

Add as many nuts as you like. Melt the marshmallows and milk over low heat. Mix together and pat into covered dish. Spread coconut over top of cake. Let set for 2 days in refrigerator. Also good when 1 cup wine is poured on top.

Linda Earp
Clarksville Council

FRUIT COCKTAIL CAKE

2 c. sifted flour
1/2 tsp. salt
1 egg
1 1/2 c. sugar

2 tsp. soda
1 tsp. vanilla
1 (No. 303) can fruit cocktail

Sift dry ingredients in large bowl. Lightly beat egg; add flour mixture. Stir in 1 can fruit cocktail; mix and add vanilla. Pour in well greased 13x9x2 inch pan. Bake 40 minutes at 325° until done. Fifteen minutes before cake is done, start preparing icing.

Icing:

1 small can evaporated milk   1 stick butter or margarine

1/2 c. Angel Flake coconut   1 tsp. vanilla
1 c. sugar   1/2 c. pecans, chopped

Combine milk, sugar and butter in saucepan over low heat; stir and boil 10 minutes. Take off stove and add coconut and pecans. Pour over cake while hot.

Mary Louise Guinn
Nashville Council

FRUIT PIE CAKE

2 c. self-rising flour   1 tsp. vanilla flavoring
1 3/4 c. sugar   3/4 c. oil
1 tsp. cloves   3 whole eggs
1 tsp. nutmeg   1 can apple pie filling
1 heaping tsp. cinnamon   1 c. pecans, chopped

Mix the dry ingredients together; add all other ingredients. Mix very well. Pour into greased and floured tube pan. Bake for 1 to 1 1/4 hours at 350°. Cool in pan for 10 minutes before taking out.

Glaze for Cake:

1/2 - 3/4 box powdered   1/2 tsp. cinnamon
  sugar   1/4 tsp. vanilla
1/2 stick margarine   1 Tbsp. milk

Mix this to soft spreading consistency and smooth over top of the cake. Serves 12.

Kathy Franck
Harpeth Council

FUDGE BROWNIES

1 1/2 c. sugar   1 1/2 sticks margarine
3 eggs   4 Tbsp. cocoa
1 1/2 c. flour (self-rising)   1 tsp. vanilla
1 tsp. salt   1 c. nuts, if desired

Combine sugar and eggs. Melt butter; add cocoa. Mix together sugar mixture and butter mixture. Add salt to flour; add to rest of ingredients. Add vanilla and nuts, if desired. Bake at 350° for 25-30 minutes. If desired, ice with a chocolate confectioners icing.

Vicky Salmon
Jackson Council

FUDGE CAKE

4 whole eggs	4 sq. semi-sweet chocolate or
2 c. sugar	1/2 c. cocoa
1 c. plain flour	1 c. butter
1 tsp. vanilla	Dash of salt
3/4 c. nuts	

Melt chocolate and butter together. Add sugar, then eggs one at a time. Add remaining ingredients. Bake at 350° for 25 minutes in 9x13 inch pan. Makes 40 squares.

Icing for Fudge Cake:

1 1/2 sq. semi-sweet chocolate	1 c. sugar
1/2 c. butter	1/2 c. milk or cream

Melt chocolate and butter; add sugar, then milk. Boil about 2 minutes; pour over cake. (Will make delicious chocolate sauce if boiled 1 minute.)

Judy M. Gray
Harpeth Council

FALLEN FUDGE CAKE

2 c. sugar	4 whole eggs
1/2 lb. butter	2 c. less 2 Tbsp. flour
4 sq. chocolate	1 c. pecan meats
1/2 c. water	2 tsp. vanilla

Cream sugar and butter. Melt chocolate in water in small pan. Pour chocolate over creamed mixture; blend. Add eggs one at a time, then add flour, nuts and vanilla. Pour batter into two 8 inch square pans, that have not been greased. Bake in a 300° oven for 25 minutes. Longer baking makes this cake hard and dry; don't overbake it. Frost with Minute Fudge Frosting (follows), while still warm.

Minute Fudge Frosting:

2 c. sugar
2 sq. baking chocolate
2/3 c. milk

1/2 c. shortening
1/2 tsp. salt
2 tsp. vanilla

Combine all ingredients, except vanilla, in a saucepan. Bring mixture slowly to a boil, stirring constantly, until sugar is dissolved. Boil hard for 1 minute with no stirring. Remove from heat; cook until bubbling stops, then add vanilla. Beat until thick enough to spread. If it gets too hard, add a little cream a few drops at a time until of desired consistency. Spread on Fallen Fudge Cake while it is still warm from the oven.

Mrs. Harvey Cummings
Harpeth Council

RING OF FUDGE CAKE

2 c. sugar
1 c. Crisco oil
2 eggs
3 c. self-rising flour
3/4 c. unsweetened cocoa

1 tsp. soda
1 c. hot coffee
1 c. buttermilk
1 tsp. vanilla
1/2 c. chopped nuts

Filling:

1/4 c. sugar
1 tsp. vanilla
1 (8 oz.) pkg. cream cheese

1 egg
1 (6 oz.) pkg. semi-sweet
    chocolate pieces

Combine sugar, oil and eggs. Beat 1 minute at high speed. Add remaining ingredients, except filling and nuts; beat 3 minutes at medium speed. Stir in nuts. Pour 1/2 of batter into greased Bundt pan. Spoon filling over batter. Cover with remaining batter. Bake at 350° for 1 hour.

Helen Hardison
Columbia Council

GRAHAM CRACKER CAKE

1 pkg. white cake mix
1 1/4 c. graham cracker
    crumbs
2 Tbsp. sugar

1 1/2 c. water
2 egg whites
3/4 c. chopped walnuts

1489-81

1. Add graham cracker crumbs, sugar, water and egg whites to cake mix in large mixing bowl. Blend ingredients on No. 7 (medium speed) for 4 minutes or until smooth. 2. Scrape sides and bottom of bowl. Mix in chopped walnuts on No. 7 (medium speed) for 1/2 minute. 3. Pour batter into two greased and lightly floured 9 inch round cake pans. 4. Bake at 350° F. (moderate oven) for 45 minutes or until cake tester inserted in center comes out clean.

Betty J. Cowherd
Andrew Jackson Council

HERSHEY SYRUP CAKE

2 sticks margarine
2 c. sugar
4 eggs
1 c. flour
1 tsp. baking powder
Pinch of salt
1/3 c. evaporated milk

1 (16 oz.) can Hershey's syrup
1/2 c. Hershey's chocolate chips
1 tsp. vanilla
1 c. chopped nuts

Cake: Cream 1 stick margarine and 1 cup sugar. Add 4 eggs one at a time, beating well. Sift 1 cup flour, 1 teaspoon baking powder and salt together. Add to creamed mixture alternately with 1 can syrup. Bake 30 minutes at 325° in greased and floured 8x12x2 inch pan. Leave cake in pan.

Icing: Bring to a boil 1 stick margarine, 1/3 cup evaporated milk and 1 cup sugar. Cook 2 to 3 minutes, stirring constantly. Cut off heat; add 1/2 cup chocolate chips. Stir until chips melt. Add 1 teaspoon vanilla and 1 cup nuts. Pour over warm cake. Cut into squares when cool.

Linda Rigell
Knoxville Council

HOT COCOA CAKE

1 stick butter
1/2 c. oil

3 Tbsp. cocoa
1 c. water

Add, sifted together:
2 c. sugar

2 c. self-rising flour

Add:

1/2 c. buttermilk	1 tsp. vanilla
1 tsp. soda	2 eggs

Bake in a greased sheet pan for 25 or 30 minutes at 350°.

Icing:

1 box powdered sugar	2 Tbsp. cocoa
1 stick melted butter	1 Tbsp. vanilla
6 Tbsp. milk	1 c. chopped nuts

Heat butter, milk and cocoa in a saucepan; do not boil. Stir in sugar, vanilla and nuts. Start making icing about 5 minutes before cake is done. Pour over cake as soon as it comes from oven.

Dean Tidwell
Nashboro Council

HULA CAKE

1 box Betty Crocker butter recipe cake mix	4 eggs
1/2 c. oil	1 1/3 c. crushed pineapple (juice too)*

Mix according to package directions, adding pineapple last. Bake in three 8 inch pans, which have been greased, for 30 minutes at 325°. Let cake cool before frosting.

Frosting:

1 (12 oz.) ctn. Cool Whip	1 (15 1/4 oz.) can crushed
1 box non-instant vanilla pudding mix	pineapple, including juice

Mix all ingredients. Frost cake and refrigerate. This cake will freeze.

*I use a 15 1/4 ounce can of pineapple and what is left after 1 1/3 cups are removed, I use in the frosting.

Reba Gray
Harpeth Council

HUMMINGBIRD CAKE

3 c. flour
2 c. sugar
1 tsp. soda
1 tsp. salt
1 tsp. cinnamon
2 c. bananas, mashed

1 c. black walnuts, chopped
1 small can crushed pineapple
1 1/2 c. Crisco oil
4 eggs, beaten
1 1/2 tsp. vanilla

Mix dry ingredients together. Add remaining ingredients; mix together with a fork. Bake in a tube pan for 1 hour and 15 minutes at 325°.

Icing: Whip -

1 (4 oz.) pkg. cream cheese
1/2 box powdered sugar

1 tsp. black walnut flavoring
1 Tbsp. milk
Kathryn H. Baxley
Morristown Council

HUMMINGBIRD CAKE

3 c. all-purpose flour
2 c. sugar
1 tsp. salt
1 tsp. soda
1 tsp. ground cinnamon
3 eggs, beaten
1 1/2 c. salad oil
1 1/2 tsp. vanilla extract

1 (8 oz.) can crushed
    pineapple, undrained
2 c. chopped pecans or
    walnuts, divided
2 c. chopped bananas
Cream Cheese Frosting
    (recipe follows)

Combine dry ingredients in a large mixing bowl. Add eggs and salad oil, stirring until dry ingredients are moistened. Do not beat. Stir in vanilla, pineapple, 1 cup chopped pecans and bananas. Spoon batter into three well greased and floured 9 inch cake pans. Bake at 350° for 25 to 30 minutes or until cake tests done. Cool in pans 10 minutes; remove from pans and cool completely. Spread frosting between layers and on top and sides of cake. Sprinkle with 1 cup chopped pecans. Yield: One 9 inch layer cake.

Cream Cheese Frosting:

2 (8 oz.) pkg. cream
    cheese, softened
1 c. butter or margarine,
    softened

2 (16 oz.) pkg. powdered
    sugar
2 tsp. vanilla extract

Combine cream cheese and butter; cream until smooth. Add powdered sugar, beating until light and fluffy. Stir in vanilla. Yield: Enough for a 3 layer cake.

Judy Christopher
Harpeth Council
Inda Adams
Andrew Jackson Council

HUNDRED DOLLAR CAKE

1/2 c. oleo or shortening	2 c. sugar
2 c. cake flour	4 sq. unsweetened chocolate,
2 tsp. baking powder	melted
1/2 tsp. salt	1 1/2 c. milk
2 eggs	1 c. nuts

Combine all of the ingredients above, except nuts; mix at medium speed until smooth. Stir in nuts last. Pour into 3 greased cake pans. Bake at 350° until inserted toothpick can be removed clean.

Icing:

1/2 lb. oleo	1 tsp. lemon juice
1 lb. powdered sugar	2 tsp. vanilla
1 egg, beaten	1 c. nuts
2 chocolate sq., melted	

Beat all of the above, except nuts, until smooth at medium speed. Stir in nuts; spread over cake.

Carolyn Utley
Memphis Downtown Council

ITALIAN CREAM CAKE

Cream well:
2 c. sugar	1/2 c. Crisco
1 stick margarine	

Add:
5 egg yolks	1 tsp. soda
2 c. flour	1 c. Angel Flake coconut
1 c. buttermilk	

Fold in 5 beaten egg whites. Bake as one sheet cake

at 350° for 25 minutes. When cake is cool, ice with 1 (8 ounce) package cream cheese, 1 stick margarine or butter, 1 box powdered sugar, 1 teaspoon vanilla and 1 cup chopped pecans. Your friends will rave about this one!

Bea Hall, Sue Malone
Harpeth Council

ITALIAN CREAM CAKE

1 stick margarine	1/2 c. vegetable shortening
2 c. flour	2 c. sugar
1 small can Angel Flake coconut	5 egg whites, stiffly beaten
	5 egg yolks
1 tsp. soda	1 c. buttermilk
1 tsp. vanilla	1 c. nuts, chopped

Cream shortening and margarine. Add sugar; beat until smooth. Add egg yolks; beat well. Combine flour and soda; add to cream mixture, alternately with buttermilk. Stir in vanilla; add coconut and nuts. Fold in egg whites. Pour batter into three greased 8 inch pans. Bake at 350° for 25 minutes.

Frosting: Beat 1 (8 ounce) package cream cheese and 1/2 stick margarine until smooth. Add 1 box powdered sugar and 1 teaspoon vanilla; beat smooth. Sprinkle with 1/2 cup nuts, chopped.

Bertie Wallace   Elizabeth Kitts
Jackson Council   Knoxville Council
Marian Molteni   Pauline Barnett
Harpeth Council   Jackson Council

JAM CAKE

2 c. sugar	1 c. nuts
1 c. butter	1 c. cherries
3 c. flour (self-rising)	1 c. raisins
1 c. buttermilk	1 c. coconut
2 eggs	1 c. blackberry jam

454

Cream butter and sugar; add eggs and milk. Add flour and fruit. Bake in oven at 350° until done.

Inda Adams
Andrew Jackson Council

JAM CAKE

Batter:

1 c. buttermilk	1 tsp. cloves
3 c. flour	1 c. sugar
1 tsp. soda	2 c. jam
1 c. butter	1 c. mincemeat (canned)
5 eggs	1 c. raisins
1 tsp. nutmeg	1 c. nuts
1 tsp. cinnamon	1 c. candied cherries

To mix cake: Cream butter and sugar. Beat eggs; add to butter and sugar. Mix well. Sift dry ingredients together. Add flour mixture and buttermilk alternately. Add mincemeat, raisins, nuts, jam and cherries. Bake in 3 layers.

Filling (optional):

4 Tbsp. cake batter	1 c. jam
1 c. nuts	1 c. sugar
1 c. raisins	1 c. water

Mix and cook on low heat until mixture thickens. May use as filling or icing. (You may use caramel icing, which is delicious.)

Billie Fleming
Nashboro Council

JAM CAKE

1 c. butter	1 c. buttermilk
3 c. sugar	1 c. blackberry jam
6 whole eggs	1 c. any jam you prefer
4 c. flour	(strawberry, peach, pear)
1 tsp. soda	1 c. raisins
1 tsp. nutmeg	1 c. chopped nuts
1 tsp. cinnamon	1 tsp. pure vanilla or pure
1 tsp. allspice	lemon flavoring
1/2 tsp. salt	

1489-81

Cream butter and sugar. Add eggs one at a time, beating well after each addition. Stir soda into buttermilk. Add alternately to creamed mixture with sifted dry ingredients. Add flavoring, raisins, jam and nuts. Pour into three 9 inch round greased and floured cake pans. Bake at 350° for 25 to 30 minutes. Ice with caramel icing.

J.C. Mallard
Nashville Council

JAM CAKE

Cream:

1 c. butter　　　　　　　　1/2 c. brown sugar
1 1/2 c. white sugar

Separate 4 eggs. Beat yolks and add. Beat whites and add. Add 1 teaspoon vanilla. Sift:

2 1/2 c. flour (cake flour)　　1/2 tsp. cinnamon
1 tsp. soda　　　　　　　　1/2 tsp. spice cloves
1/2 tsp. salt　　　　　　　　1/2 tsp. nutmeg
1 heaping tsp. baking　　　　1/3 c. cocoa
　　powder

Sift all ingredients at one time. Add alternately with 1 cup buttermilk. Add 1 apple, 1 cup jam, 1 cup pecans and 1/2 box raisins (a little less raisins). Bake at 350° until done, about 30 minutes.

Joyce Mattice
Harpeth Council

CARPIE'S PLAIN JAM CAKE

1 1/2 c. Crisco　　　　　　1/2 c. buttermilk
2 c. sugar　　　　　　　　1 tsp. baking soda
6 egg yolks　　　　　　　　1 c. blackberry jam
3 c. all-purpose flour　　　　1 c. strawberry jam
1 tsp. salt　　　　　　　　6 egg whites, beaten stiff
1 tsp. cinnamon　　　　　　1 c. nuts
1 tsp. cloves　　　　　　　1 c. raisins (optional)
1 tsp. allspice　　　　　　　2 Tbsp. vanilla

Mix first 12 ingredients on medium speed. Fold in beaten egg whites, nuts, raisins and vanilla. Bake at 350°

for approximately 2 hours in any shape pan. Use favorite icing; caramel icing is good.

Pat Carpenter
Nashville Council

OLD FASHION JAM CAKE

4 c. sifted self-rising flour	1 c. chopped, cooked prunes
4 eggs	(substitute for raisins)
1 1/3 c. sugar	1 tsp. soda
1 c. Crisco oil	1 tsp. baking powder
1 c. buttermilk	1 tsp. cinnamon
2 c. blackberry jam	1 tsp. nutmeg
1 c. chopped pecans	1 tsp. allspice
1 c. pear or pineapple	1 "pinch" of salt
preserves	

Cream sugar and oil; add dry ingredients. Add eggs, one at a time; beat well. Add milk; beat well. Add jam, preserves, nuts and prunes. Pour into four greased and floured 9 inch pans. Bake 45 minutes at 350°. Cool and frost with Caramel Icing.

Note: This makes two "normal" 2 layer cakes or 1 "extra large" if all 4 layers are used together. (I generally make 2 cakes!)

Mary Grey Jenkins
Green Hills Council

OLD FASHIONED JAM CAKE

2 c. flour (plain)	1 1/2 tsp. cinnamon
1 1/4 c. sugar	1/2 tsp. nutmeg
1/2 c. shortening	1/4 tsp. salt
2 eggs	1/2 - 3/4 c. jam (blackberry,
1/2 c. raisins	dewberry or strawberry;
1 tsp. soda	your choice)
	1 c. buttermilk

Cream sugar and shortening until fluffy. Add eggs; beat well. Sift dry ingredients with flour; add alternately with milk. Fold in the jam and raisins. Bake in 3 layers in 350° oven for 20 to 25 minutes. Frost with Butterscotch Icing (follows).

Butterscotch Icing:

1 1/2 c. brown sugar
3 Tbsp. butter
1/3 c. milk
2 Tbsp. corn syrup

1/3 c. shortening
1/4 tsp. salt
1 box confectioners sugar
5 Tbsp. hot milk

Sift confectioners sugar; set aside. Cook the brown sugar, butter, 1/3 cup milk and corn syrup until a hard ball forms when dropped into cold water. When this mixture begins to boil, stir constantly. Remove from heat. Combine shortening and salt; add sugar gradually. Add hot milk, then the butterscotch mixture. Beat until smooth. Spread between layers, then on top and sides of Jam Cake. Also delicious on spice or apple cake.

Mary R. Veal
Chattanooga Council

JUANITA'S HOT MILK CAKE

2 eggs
1 c. sugar
1 c. flour
1 tsp. baking powder,
  rounded

1 tsp. vanilla
Dash of salt
1/2 c. milk
1 Tbsp. butter

Beat eggs; add sugar gradually and beat for 5 minutes. Add flour (measure after sifting), baking powder, vanilla and salt. Heat milk and butter until butter melts and milk comes almost to boil. Add to first mixture. Bake in 9 inch square pan for approximately 30 minutes at 375°. After done, top with the following mixture:

3 Tbsp. butter
2 Tbsp. cream or evaporated
  milk

5 Tbsp. brown sugar
1/2 c. chopped nuts

Melt butter; add cream, brown sugar and chopped nuts. Mix; spread over cake. Put under broiler until brown. Can be reheated in warm oven if covered.

Joe Holdway
Harpeth Council

LEMON SQUARES

1 c. sifted all-purpose flour   1/4 c. sugar
1/2 c. (1 stick) butter

Blend above ingredients in a small bowl until smooth. Press mixture into an 11 x 7 x 1 1/2 inch baking pan. Bake this shortbread crust at 325° for 20 minutes or until lightly browned. While shortbread bakes, combine the following:

1 c. sugar   1/4 tsp. salt
2 eggs, lightly beaten   2 Tbsp. flour
1 tsp. grated lemon rind   1/2 tsp. baking soda
3 Tbsp. lemon juice

Beat until well blended. Spread mixture over the hot baked shortbread crust; return to oven. Bake an additional 25 minutes; remove from oven. Cool in pan; cut in squares.

Rosemary Grand
Harpeth Council

CRUNCHY LEMON SQUARES

1 c. quick oats, uncooked   1 c. flour
1/2 c. flaked coconut   1/2 c. coarsely chopped
1/2 c. firmly packed light   pecans
  brown sugar   1 tsp. baking powder
1 can Eagle Brand   1/2 c. butter, melted
  condensed milk   1/2 c. ReaLemon reconsti-
1 Tbsp. grated lemon rind   tuted lemon juice

Preheat oven to 350° (use 325° if using glass). In medium bowl, combine oats, flour, coconut, nuts, sugar, baking powder and butter. Stir to form crumbly mixture; set aside. In medium bowl, combine sweetened condensed milk, lemon juice and rind. Pat 1/2 the crumb mixture evenly on bottom of 9x9 inch baking pan. Spread sweetened condensed milk mixture on top; sprinkle with remaining crumbs. Bake 25 to 30 minutes or until lightly browned. Cool thoroughly before cutting. Top with Cool Whip when ready to serve. Makes 9 servings.

Willine Gillespie
Nashboro Council

LEMON SUPREME SPECIAL

1 Duncan Hines lemon
  supreme cake mix
1 c. apricot nectar

1/2 c. Crisco oil
4 eggs
1/2 c. sugar

Mix cake mix, sugar, oil and nectar together. Add 1 egg at a time. Bake in tube pan at 325° for 1 hour in oven. Mix 1 cup powdered sugar and juice of 1 lemon. Pour over cake while still warm to make a glaze.

Evelyn Carrico
Nashboro Council

MAGIC LEMON ICEBOX CAKE

1 c. fine graham cracker
  crumbs
3 Tbsp. butter, melted
1 (15 oz.) can Eagle Brand
  sweetened condensed milk
1/2 c. lemon juice

1 Tbsp. grated rind
2 eggs, separated
1/4 tsp. vanilla
1/4 c. sugar
3 or 4 drops green food
  coloring, if desired

Combine crumbs and butter; reserve 1/4 cup mixture. Press remaining mixture on bottom and sides of buttered refrigerator tray; chill. Beat egg yolks until thick and light in color; mix with sweetened condensed milk. Add lemon juice, rind and vanilla; stir until mixture thickens. If desired, tint pale green. Beat egg whites into soft peaks; gradually add sugar, beating until stiff. Fold into Eagle Brand mixture. Pour into tray. Border with reserved crumbs. Decorate with peel; freeze until firm. I use lime instead of lemon sometimes. Serves 6 to 8.

Allie Lee Long
Nashville Council

LOAF CAKE

1 c. self-rising flour
1/4 c. butter, softened
1/2 c. sugar

1 tsp. vanilla
1/3 c. sweet milk
1 egg

Cream sugar and butter together. Add egg and mix well. Add vanilla to milk; mix alternately the milk, then

flour until cake is mixed. Pour in loaf pan. Bake at 350°
for 30 to 35 minutes.

JoLoy Renshaw
Jackson Council

DOROTHY PAYNE'S LOAF CAKE

2 sticks butter
4 eggs
2 c. sugar

1 small can Carnation or Pet
   milk
2 c. flour (plain)
1 tsp. rum flavoring

Blend all ingredients thoroughly. Bake in greased and
floured loaf pan at 350° for 1 hour.

Marie Barnett
Harpeth Council

MANDARIN ORANGE CAKE

1 box Duncan Hines yellow
   cake mix
1/2 c. oil

4 eggs
1 can Mandarin oranges
   (use juice also)

Place all ingredients in bowl. Beat together 3-4 minutes; do not add any other moisture. Place in 3 layers.
Bake until done at 350° for 25-30 minutes.

Icing for Mandarin Orange Cake:

1 (No. 2) can crushed
   pineapple, in own juice

1 pkg. vanilla instant
   pudding
1 (13 oz.) ctn. Cool Whip

Mix together pudding and pineapple; fold in Cool Whip.
Frost cooled layers and serve. Keep in refrigerator.

Peggy Wilkes
Chattanooga Council

MANDARIN ORANGE CAKE

2 c. sugar
2 c. flour
2 tsp. baking soda
1/2 tsp. salt

2 eggs
2 (11 1/2 oz.) cans Mandarin
   oranges

Beat all ingredients for at least 4 minutes by hand. Pour into greased and floured 9x13 inch pan. Bake at 350° for 30-35 minutes. Does well in Pyrex dish.

3/4 c. brown sugar   3 Tbsp. milk
2 Tbsp. butter

In the meantime, bring brown sugar, milk and butter to boil. Pour over hot cake as soon as it comes from oven. When cool, serve with whipped topping, if desired. Very simple and very good!

Mrs. George Price
Knoxville Council

MELBA CAKE

Mix in bowl:
1 Tbsp. cinnamon   2 c. sugar
2 c. self-rising flour

Set aside. In a saucepan, bring to a boil:

1 c. water   1/2 c. oil
1 stick margarine   4 tsp. cocoa

Pour over first mixture; add:

2 eggs   1 tsp. vanilla
1/2 c. milk

Mix well. Pour into Bundt pan or 13x9x2 inch pan, greased and floured. Bake at 350° for 35-40 minutes.

Icing:

1 stick margarine   1/3 c. evaporated milk
1 c. sugar

Mix in a saucepan. Bring to a boil; let boil for 2 or 3 minutes, stirring constantly. Add:

1/2 c. chocolate chips   1 tsp. vanilla

Cool slightly; pour over cool cake.

Barbara Rush
Knoxville Council

MILK CHOCOLATE CAKE

1/2 c. butter (cream)
1 1/2 c. sugar
2 c. flour (cake)
6 Tbsp. cocoa or 2 sq.
   chocolate
1/4 tsp. salt

1 c. buttermilk
2 eggs
1 tsp. vanilla
1 tsp. soda, dissolved in 1
   Tbsp. vinegar

Cream sugar and butter. Sift cocoa with flour. Add flour and buttermilk alternately. Add one egg at a time: end with flour. Beat 300 strokes; add vinegar and soda last. Bake at 350° in two 9 inch cake pans or 1 loaf pan.

Mrs. Harvey Cummings
Harpeth Council

MILKY WAY CAKE

8 Milky Way candy bars
3 sticks butter
4 1/2 c. sugar
4 eggs
2 1/3 c. flour
1 1/4 c. buttermilk

1 tsp. vanilla
1 c. nuts
1 (6 oz.) pkg. chocolate
   chips
1 pt. jar marshmallow cream
1 c. milk

Melt 8 Milky Way bars and 1 stick of butter; set aside. Cream 2 cups sugar, 1 stick butter and 4 eggs; beat well. Add 2 1/3 cups sifted flour, 1 1/4 cups buttermilk and 1 teaspoon vanilla; beat for 2 minutes. Add 1 cup of nuts and melted Milky Way bars and butter mixture. Stir until you put in three 9 inch baking pans. Bake 30 to 35 minutes in 350° oven.

Icing: Cook 1 cup milk and 2 1/2 cups sugar until it forms a soft ball in water. Remove from heat; add 1 (6 ounce) package chocolate chips, 1 stick butter and 1 pint jar marshmallow cream. Beat until fluffy and ready to spread.

Zoerita Proctor
Nashboro Council

MILKY WAY CAKE

2 c. sugar
2 1/2 c. flour
1 1/4 c. buttermilk
1 tsp. vanilla
8 Milky Way candy bars

1 tsp. soda
2 sticks margarine
4 eggs
1 c. broken pecans

Melt candy and 1 stick butter in double boiler; set aside. Mix the remaining ingredients as in any other cake. Stir in candy and margarine. Mix well and pour in sheet cake pan. Bake at 350° for 1 hour.

Icing:

2 1/2 c. sugar   1 c. milk

Boil to soft ball stage; remove from heat and add 1 cup of marshmallow cream, 1 (6 ounce) package semi-sweet chocolate chips and 1 stick butter. Beat until smooth and cool. Spread on cake.

Evelyn Easley
Harpeth Council

MISSISSIPPI MUD CAKE

2 sticks margarine, room
  temperature
2 c. sugar
4 eggs
2 Tbsp. coconut

1 1/2 c. chopped pecans
1 tsp. vanilla
1 1/2 c. self-rising flour
1 (7 oz.) jar Kraft marshmallow creme

Grease and flour a 13x9 inch cake pan. Preheat oven to 350°. Mix all above ingredients, except marshmallow creme. Bake at 350° for 35 to 40 minutes (cake will not spring back to test for doneness). Spread marshmallow creme on cake while still hot.

Icing:

1 box confectioners sugar
1/2 c. melted margarine
1/3 c. cocoa

1/2 c. evaporated milk
1 tsp. vanilla

Mix all ingredients; spread on top of marshmallow creme.
Debra Baker
Green Hills Council

MISSISSIPPI MUD CAKE

2 sticks butter or margarine
1/2 c. cocoa
2 c. sugar
4 eggs, slightly beaten
1 1/2 c. all-purpose flour
Pinch of salt
1 1/2 c. chopped nuts
1 tsp. vanilla extract
Miniature marshmallows

Melt butter and cocoa together. Remove from heat; stir in sugar and beaten eggs. Mix well. Add flour, salt, chopped nuts and vanilla; mix well. Spoon batter into a greased 13x9x2 inch pan. Bake at 350° for 35 to 45 minutes. Sprinkle marshmallows on top of warm cake; cover with Chocolate Frosting. Yield: 1 cake.

Chocolate Frosting:

1 (1 lb.) box powdered
  sugar
1/2 c. whole milk
1/3 c. cocoa
1/2 stick softened butter or
  margarine

Combine sugar, milk, cocoa and softened butter. Mix until smooth and spread on hot cake.

Ann Love
Morristown Council

MOUNTAIN DEW CAKE

1 small box orange jello
1 box coconut cream pie
  filling
1 c. Crisco oil
1 box orange cake mix
4 eggs
10 oz. Mountain Dew

Mix all ingredients, following directions on cake mix box. Bake in 3 layers.

.. Icing for Mountain Dew Cake:

1 (20 oz.) can crushed
  pineapple
1 (8 oz.) can crushed
  pineapple
5 Tbsp. flour
1/2 stick margarine
2 c. sugar
2 c. flaked coconut

Mix pineapple, sugar and flour in a saucepan; simmer

over medium heat until thick. Stir in butter and coconut. Spread on cooled cake. Recipe will cover 3 layers.

Bertice Spencer
Memphis Council

MUD CAKE

1 c. Wesson oil	4 beaten eggs
1 3/4 c. sugar	3 tsp. vanilla
1/3 c. cocoa	1 c. nuts
1 1/2 c. flour	

Mix well; pour into greased pan. Bake at 350° for 30 minutes. Remove from oven and pour 1 bag miniature marshmallows on top. Return to oven and melt slightly; let cake cool.

Icing:

1 1/2 sticks melted margarine	1 box powdered sugar
1/2 c. cocoa	1/2 c. Carnation milk
1 tsp. vanilla	1 c. chopped nuts

Mix well and spread on cake.

Mary Lou Foutch
Jackson Council

NEVER FAIL SPONGE CAKE

1 heaping c. flour (plain)	5 eggs
1 heaping c. sugar (granulated)	1 Tbsp. lemon flavoring

Separate eggs; beat egg whites until foamy. Add 1/2 the sugar and beat until stiff (or until stands in peaks). Beat egg yolks with remaining sugar for 5 minutes; they should be light and fluffy. Fold this mixture into egg whites and stir until smooth. Add flour a bit at a time, stirring until smooth after each addition. Add lemon extract; mix thoroughly. Bake in Pyrex dish or pan, 8x12x2 inches, at 325° for 50 minutes or until brown. (Some ovens vary; it may take more or less heat.) This is good with strawberries or peaches and whipped cream or with ice cream.

Mrs. Edna Bell
Knoxville Council

466

ORANGE CAKE

1 pkg. yellow cake mix   2/3 c. oil
1 small pkg. lemon jello   4 eggs
2/3 c. water

Mix above ingredients. Pour into greased Bundt pan. Bake at 350° for 45 minutes. Mix together 1 cup orange juice and 1/2 cup sugar; pour over cake while it's still hot.

Katrina Carter
Harpeth Council

ORANGE JELLO CAKE

1 box orange cake mix   3/4 c. Wesson oil (do not
1 small box orange jello   substitute)
3/4 c. water   4 eggs

Combine all ingredients; mix well. Bake in tube pan at 350° until golden brown and springy.

Glaze Icing: To the juice of 1 lemon, add powdered sugar until desired consistency is reached. Pour over cake while it's still hot.

Pat Carpenter
Nashville Council

ORANGE-PINEAPPLE CAKE

1 box white cake mix   1 can Mandarin oranges,
4 eggs   undrained
1/2 c. oil

Blend together slowly the first 3 ingredients. Blend in oranges and juice. Bake in two 8 inch pans for 30 minutes at 350°. When cool, slice into 4 layers.

Icing:

1 large can crushed pine-   1 pkg. instant vanilla
   apple (do not drain)   pudding

Blend together and let set for a few minutes. Fold in 1 large container of Cool Whip.

Inda Adams
Andrew Jackson Council

ORANGE SLICE CAKE

1 c. margarine	1 pinch of salt
2 c. sugar	1 lb. dates
4 eggs	1 lb. orange slices
1 1/2 c. buttermilk	2 tsp. soda
4 c. flour	2 c. nuts

Melt butter. Cream in sugar; add eggs. Add 1 cup buttermilk. Add soda to remaining 1/2 cup buttermilk and add to mixture. Using hands, add flour and salt to dates and orange slices; mix together. Add to sugar-egg mixture and mix well. Bake 3-4 hours in 275° oven in tube pan.

Topping: Mix 1 cup orange juice with 1 cup brown sugar. Heat and pour over hot cake. Wrap in foil when cool and freeze.

Patricia Hire
Harpeth Council

PEA PICKING CAKE

1 box yellow Duncan Hines cake mix (butter recipe)	4 eggs
1 stick margarine	1 (9 oz.) can Mandarin oranges (do not drain)

Mix all together at medium speed on mixer for 3 minutes. Pour into two 9 inch pans. Bake at 350° until done. Cool; split layers and frost (optional).

Frosting:

1 (9 oz.) box Cool Whip	1 small box instant vanilla pie filling
1 (No. 2) can crushed pineapple (do not drain)	

Mix together and spread between layers and on top. Keep refrigerated.

Metty C. Fain
Andrew Jackson Council

468

POCKET PEACH CAKE

2 c. all-purpose flour
1 1/4 c. packed brown sugar
2 tsp. cinnamon
1 tsp. salt
1 tsp. baking soda

1 c. sour cream
2 tsp. vanilla
2 eggs
1 1/2 c. sliced peaches, well
   drained

Topping:

1 c. chopped nuts
2/3 c. packed brown sugar

2 Tbsp. butter, softened
1 c. coconut (optional)

In small bowl, combine all cake ingredients, except peaches. Blend at low speed until moistened. Beat 2 minutes at medium speed. Pour batter into greased 9x13 inch pan. Arrange peaches over batter. In another small bowl, combine topping ingredients until crumbly; sprinkle over peaches. Bake at 375° for 45 to 55 minutes until golden brown and toothpick inserted comes out clean.

Helen Hardison
Columbia Council

PEACH GOUCHIE CAKE

1 box butter cake mix or
   yellow cake mix
2 cans sliced peaches in
   heavy syrup or 1 large
   can

1 stick margarine
Sprinkle of cinnamon
Sprinkle of nutmeg

Pour peaches in greased baking dish. Sprinkle dry cake mix on top; sprinkle with cinnamon and nutmeg. Pour melted margarine on top. Bake at 400° for 45 minutes or until golden.

David Lewis
Clarksville Council

PEANUT BROWNIES

2/3 c. peanut butter
1/4 c. butter or margarine
1 c. packed brown sugar
2/3 c. sugar
1 tsp. vanilla
3 eggs

1 c. flour
2 c. or less chocolate chips
1/2 c. salted peanuts (may
   use crunchy peanut butter
   and eliminate peanuts)

1489-81

Cream peanut butter, butter, brown sugar, sugar and vanilla in large bowl. Beat eggs. Combine dry ingredients; add to creamed mixture. Stir in baking chips and peanuts. Bake in greased 13x9x2 inch pan at 350° for 30 to 35 minutes (mixture will be stiff; spread in pan with spoon).

Peggy L. Parker
Chattanooga Council

FRESH PEAR CAKE

2 c. sugar	1 tsp. soda
3 eggs, well beaten	1 tsp. salt
1 1/2 c. salad oil	1 tsp. vanilla
3 c. all-purpose flour (do	2 tsp. ground cinnamon
not sift)	3 c. thinly sliced pears

Combine sugar, eggs and oil; beat well. Combine flour, soda and salt; add to sugar mixture one cup at a time, mixing well after each addition. Stir in vanilla, cinnamon and pears. Spoon batter into a well greased 10 inch Bundt pan or tube pan. Bake at 350° for 1 hour and 15 minutes (check to make sure it's done). Choice of icings below.

Brown Sugar Icing:

1 c. brown sugar	1/4 c. milk
1 stick butter	

Bring to a rolling boil for 3 minutes; pour over cake while hot (while in cake pan).

Powdered Sugar Glaze:

1 1/4 c. sifted powdered	2-4 Tbsp. milk
sugar	

Combine ingredients, blending until smooth. Yield: 1/2 cup.

Golda Rogers
Knoxville Council
Ruth Hunley
Harpeth Council

PECAN CAKE

4 c. plain flour
1 lb. pecans
1 lb. (2 c.) sugar
1 lb. glazed cherries
1 lb. butter or margarine, softened

6 eggs, beaten
1 1/2 c. white raisins
3/4 lb. pineapple, glazed
2 tsp. baking powder
2 tsp. vanilla

Mix all fruit in 4 cups of flour. In a large mixing bowl, cream butter and eggs together. To this mixture, add vanilla and baking powder. Bake in a tube pan, lined with waxed paper, 2 1/2 to 3 hours in a 275° oven. Place a pan of water under cake.

Inda Adams
Andrew Jackson Council

PECAN CAKE

1 box white raisins, chopped
1/2 lb. candied pineapple, chopped
1/2 lb. candied cherries, chopped
1 lb. pecans, chopped
2 1/4 c. flour
1/4 tsp. baking soda

2 sticks margarine
2 c. sugar
6 whole eggs
1 c. California white Port wine
1 tsp. allspice
1 tsp. cinnamon
1 tsp. cloves

Coat raisins, pineapple and cherries in one of the above cups of flour, then combine all ingredients. Bake in a tube pan for 2 hours at 250°; let cool in pan. To retain flavor during refrigerator storage, soak a white towel in Port wine and cover cake with towel, then seal in an airtight container.

Mary McCracken
Columbia Council

PINEAPPLE CAKE

1 (No. 2) can pineapple, crushed
1 1/2 c. sugar
2 tsp. soda

2 1/2 c. sifted all-purpose flour
1/2 tsp. salt
2 large unbeaten eggs

Mix above ingredients until blended well. Bake in

9x13 inch pan; line pan with 2 sheets of waxed paper, well greased. Bake at 350° for 30 minutes.

Icing:

1 1/2 c. sugar
1 stick butter or margarine

1 c. Carnation milk
1 c. Angel Flake coconut

Heat sugar, margarine and milk until boiling. Stir 1 time and boil for 4 minutes without stirring. Remove from heat; stir in coconut. Stir until cool and thick enough to spread.

R.G. Brasfield
Jackson Council

PINEAPPLE CAKE

2 c. flour (do not sift)
2 c. sugar
2 tsp. soda
2 eggs

1 (No. 2) can crushed
pineapple, undrained
1/4 tsp. salt
1 tsp. vanilla

Add all ingredients; mix with spoon until well blended. Bake in greased and floured baking dish, 13x9x2 inches, at 350° for 35 minutes. Let cool about 30 minutes.

Frosting:

1 1/2 c. sugar
3/4 stick margarine
1 c. evaporated milk

1 c. pecans, chopped
1 c. coconut

Mix first 3 ingredients; bring to boil, then add nuts and coconut. Boil 3 minutes at medium heat. Spoon on warm cake.

Mrs. R.C. Burton
Knoxville Council

PINEAPPLE CAKE

2 eggs
2 c. sugar
2 Tbsp. cooking oil
2 c. plain flour
2 Tbsp. soda

1 Tbsp. salt
2 1/4 c. crushed pineapple
(do not drain)
1 Tbsp. vanilla
1/2 c. chopped pecans

Sift flour, soda and salt together; set aside. Beat eggs; add sugar, cooking oil and beat well. Add pineapple, flour and vanilla; beat well. Fold in pecans. Bake in 13x9x2 inch loaf pan at 350° for 35 minutes.

Frosting:

1 (8 oz.) pkg. cream cheese
1 stick margarine

1 Tbsp. vanilla
1 box powdered sugar

Blend softened cheese and margarine. Add vanilla and sugar. Beat until smooth and put on hot cake.

Maxine Scott
East Memphis Council

LAYERED PINEAPPLE CAKE

1 (8 oz.) can crushed
  pineapple
2 c. sugar, divided
1 stick butter
1 tsp. vanilla

3 eggs
2 c. flour
1 tsp. double acting baking
  powder
1 Tbsp. sugar

In a saucepan, combine the pineapple, including juice, and 1 cup sugar. Cook the mixture over moderately low heat, stirring, for 20 minutes or until thickened; let cool. In a bowl, cream together the butter, 1 cup sugar and vanilla until mixture is smooth. Add the 3 eggs, one at a time, beating well after each addition. Stir in flour, sifted with baking powder. Spread half the batter in a well buttered 9 inch round cake pan; top it with the pineapple mixture and spread the remaining batter over the pineapple mixture. Sprinkle the top with 1 tablespoon sugar and bake the cake in a preheated moderate oven, 350° F., for 30 minutes or until cake tester inserted in the center comes out clean. Transfer to rack and let cool.

Sudie Sredonja
East Memphis Council

HAWAIIAN PINEAPPLE CAKE

1 (1 lb. 4 oz.) can crushed
  pineapple
2 c. buttermilk baking mix
1 c. sifted all-purpose flour

1 tsp. baking soda
1 c. sugar
3/4 c. dairy sour cream
1/2 c. margarine

2 tsp. vanilla   2 Tbsp. rum
2 large eggs   Glaze

Drain pineapple well, saving syrup for glaze. Stir baking mix, flour and soda together. Beat sugar, sour cream, margarine and vanilla together for 2 minutes. Add eggs; beat 1 minute. Add flour mixture; beat 1 minute longer. Mix in drained pineapple and rum. Turn into well greased 9 inch Bundt pan. Bake in moderate oven, 350° F., for about 45 minutes, until cake tests done. Remove from oven and spoon about half the glaze over cake. Let stand 10 minutes, then turn out onto serving plate and spoon on remaining glaze. Cool before cutting. Makes one 9 inch cake.

Glaze: Combine 3/4 cup sugar, 1/4 cup margarine and 1/4 cup syrup from pineapple. Stir over low heat until sugar is dissolved and margarine melted. Remove from heat and stir in 2 tablespoons rum. Rum may be omitted, if desired.

Ruth L. Cole
Harpeth Council

PISTACHIO TORTE

1 c. flour   1 stick butter, melted
2 Tbsp. sugar   1/4 c. pecans, chopped

Blend until crumbly; press in 9x13 inch pan. Bake at 350° for 15 minutes; cool.

8 oz. pkg. cream cheese 2 1/2 c. milk
2/3 c. sugar   2 pkg. instant pistachio
1/2 ctn. Cool Whip   pudding

Blend cheese and sugar well. Add 1/2 (9 ounce) carton of Cool Whip; spread over crust. Mix 2 packages of instant pistachio pudding mix with 2 1/2 cups milk. Beat 2 minutes or until thick and spread over cream cheese mixture. Spread other half of Cool Whip over top and sprinkle with pecans; chill.

L. Holbert
Knoxville Council

PLUCKETT CAKE

1 c. sugar	1 1/2 sticks oleo
4 tsp. cinnamon	1 c. chopped nuts
1/4 c. brown sugar	3 cans Hungry Jack biscuits

Make mixture of first 3 ingredients. Cut each biscuit into quarters; roll in sugar mixture and drop into Bundt pan. Pour remaining sugar mixture over top; sprinkle with nuts. Melt 1 1/2 sticks oleo; pour over top. Bake at 350° for about 30 to 35 minutes or until golden brown. Pour glaze over top of cake after you remove from pan while cake is still hot.

Glaze: Mix well and pour over cake -

2 c. powdered sugar	5 or 6 Tbsp. water

Anne Watson
Jackson Council

POUND CAKE

Cream until fluffy and light:

2 3/4 c. sugar	1/2 lb. margarine

Add 4 eggs, one at a time; beat thoroughly after each. Mix together 3 cups flour and 1/4 teaspoon soda; add alternately with buttermilk.

1 c. buttermilk	1 tsp. lemon
1 tsp. vanilla flavoring	

Bake in well greased, floured tube pan 1 hour at 350°. Sometimes the cake takes a little longer than 1 hour. Top has a slight "spring back" when done and is also golden brown.

Bob and Nora Chandler
Harpeth Council

POUND CAKE

2 c. sugar	1 lb. Nucoa margarine
3 c. plain flour	6 eggs
1 tsp. vanilla	

Cream room temperature margarine until fluffy. Add sugar and continue to beat until thoroughly blended (very important). Add eggs one at a time, beating after each addition. Gradually add flour (batter will be very thick). Add vanilla, blending thoroughly. Pour into greased tube pan. Bake at 350° for 1 1/2 hours or until cake is brown on top and slightly loosened from edges of pan. This cake freezes well; can be carried well to special occasions and is an excellent cake to serve with any fresh or frozen fruit such as strawberries or peaches.

Jean Holt
Chattanooga Council

POUND CAKE

6 eggs	1 c. Crisco
3 c. plain flour	1/2 c. oil
1 c. milk	1 tsp. vanilla
1/2 tsp. baking powder	1 tsp. lemon extract
3 c. sugar	

Mix together; beat 10 minutes. Bake 1 hour and 15 minutes at 300° (don't open oven door). Makes 2 loaf pans or one 9x11 inch oblong pan.

M.J. Roderick
Knoxville Council

POUND CAKE

1/2 c. shortening	3 c. plain flour
1 stick margarine	1/2 tsp. baking powder
3 c. sugar	1 c. milk
5 eggs	1 Tbsp. vanilla

Cream margarine and shortening with sugar. Add one egg at a time, beating well after each addition. Sift flour; add baking powder and sift again. Add milk and flour alternately to mixture. Add vanilla. Pour into greased and floured 10 inch tube pan. Put in cold oven. Bake at 350° for 1 hour and 15 minutes.

Bertha C. Weigel
Knoxville Council

POUND CAKE

1 c. butter or margarine	2 c. all-purpose flour
2 c. sugar	1 tsp. vanilla flavoring
5 eggs	1 tsp. almond flavoring

Cream butter and sugar. Add one egg at a time, while beating. Add flour gradually. Add flavorings. Beat thoroughly. Bake in stem pan at 325° for 1 hour.

Brown Sugar Frosting:

2 c. (16 oz.) light brown sugar	2/3 c. evaporated milk
1/2 c. butter or margarine	1 tsp. vanilla

Mix ingredients and boil 10 minutes after it starts boiling. Cook on low heat the entire time. (Takes a long time for it to begin boiling; stir often.) Beat until creamy and of the consistency to spread.

Allie Ruby Wells
Green Hills Council

APPLE POUND CAKE

3 c. unsifted flour	1 tsp. soda
1/2 tsp. cinnamon	1 tsp. salt
1/2 tsp. nutmeg	2 c. granulated sugar
1 1/2 c. corn oil	3 eggs
2 tsp. vanilla	1 c. chopped pecans
2 c. finely chopped, pared apples	1/2 c. raisins

Sift flour, soda, salt and spices together; set aside. Beat oil with sugar, eggs and vanilla until thoroughly blended. Gradually beat in flour mixture until smooth. Fold in apples, pecans and raisins. Turn into tube pan, well greased and floured. Bake in low oven, 325°, for 1 hour and 15 minutes or until cake tester inserted in center comes out clean. Place on wire rack to cool for 10 minutes. Turn onto rack to cool completely before storing in airtight container.

Sauce for Apple Pound Cake for Soaking: Combine 1/2 cup applejack brandy, 1/2 cup apple juice, 1/4 cup brown sugar and 2 tablespoons butter in saucepan. Bring to boil,

stirring until sugar dissolves. Prick top of cake with fork.
Carefully spoon applejack syrup over the cake on plate.
When it's cooled completely, store in airtight container.

Margie Essary
Memphis Council

AUTUMN POUND CAKE

Mix together and set aside:

2 1/2 c. sifted flour	1 tsp. baking powder
1/2 tsp. salt	2 tsp. cinnamon
1/2 tsp. soda	

Beat until fluffy on medium speed, 1 stick (1/2 cup)
butter. Add 1 1/2 cups sugar; mix well. Beat in 3 eggs,
one at a time. Beat in 1/2 flour mixture, 1 cup plain yogurt
and 1/2 cup pumpkin. Mix well, then add rest of flour.
Stir in 1 cup chopped walnuts or pecans. Bake on 300°-350°
for 45 to 55 minutes. Cool on rack for 10 minutes. Take
from pan and cool completely before icing.

Cream Cheese Icing: Beat on low until fluffy -

1 (3 oz.) pkg. cream cheese   1/2 tsp. vanilla

Beat in slowly until spreadable 2 cups of sifted powdered sugar.
Note: A few drops of warm water helps if icing starts
getting too stiff.

Doris Crowell
Knoxville Council

BROWN SUGAR POUND CAKE

1 box golden brown sugar	1/2 tsp. salt
1 c. sugar	1 tsp. baking powder
3 sticks butter, softened	1 tsp. vanilla
5 eggs	1 tsp. maple flavoring
3 c. all-purpose flour	1 c. milk

Cream butter and sugar. Add eggs, one at a time,
beating well. Mix flour, salt and baking powder together.
Add flavorings to milk. Add flour and milk mixture alternately to batter, starting and ending with flour. Put in

478

greased and floured tube pan. Bake at 350° for 1 to 1 1/4 hours until toothpick comes out clean.

Mary Jane Bailey
Green Hills Council

BUTTERMILK POUND CAKE

1 c. buttermilk
2 1/2 c. sugar
1/2 c. shortening
3 c. all-purpose flour
1/2 tsp. baking soda

1 tsp. vanilla
1/2 tsp. lemon extract
1/2 c. butter or oleo
4 eggs

In mixing bowl, cream together sugar, shortening and butter until light and fluffy. Add eggs one at a time, beating after each. Stir in vanilla and lemon extracts. Thoroughly stir together the flour and soda. Add to cream mixture alternately with buttermilk, beating well after each addition. Pour in greased and floured 10 inch tube or Bundt pan. Bake at 325° for about 1 1/4 hours. Cool in pan 10 minutes. Remove and cool on rack.

Carolyn Mitchell
Memphis Downtown Council

BUTTERMILK POUND CAKE

3 c. sugar
1/2 c. vegetable shortening
1 stick (1/2 c.) butter
5 whole eggs
1/2 tsp. soda, dissolved in
  1 Tbsp. boiling water
1 c. buttermilk

3 c. all-purpose flour
1/2 tsp. salt
2 tsp. vanilla extract
1 tsp. lemon extract
1 tsp. orange extract
1/2 tsp. almond extract

Cream together the butter, shortening and sugar. Add eggs one at a time; beat well. Combine salt and flour; add alternately to creamed mixture with buttermilk and soda mixture. Beat well; blend in extracts. Pour into greased and floured 10 inch stem pan (square or round). Bake in preheated 300° oven for about 1 hour and 15 minutes or until cake tests done. Remove from pan to cool.

Hazel Moore
Green Hills Council

1489-81

CARAMEL POUND CAKE

1 box dark brown sugar	1 c. white sugar
3 c. plain flour	1/2 tsp. baking powder
1 c. butter or oleo	1/2 c. shortening
5 large eggs	1 c. milk
1 tsp. vanilla	1 tsp. butter flavoring
1 c. nuts (optional)	

Cream together butter, shortening and sugar. Add eggs, one at a time. Sift the flour and baking powder together; add alternately with milk. Add flavoring and nuts. Put in greased and floured tube pan and bake at 350° for about 1 1/2 hours.

Bessie Crosby
Harpeth Council

CARAMEL NUT POUND CAKE

1 c. butter	3 c. sifted flour
1/2 c. shortening	1 Tbsp. vanilla
1 box light brown sugar	5 eggs
1 c. sugar	1/2 tsp. salt
1 c. finely chopped nuts	1 c. milk
1/2 tsp. baking powder	

Cream butter and shortening. Add brown sugar; blend thoroughly. Gradually add white sugar. Add eggs, one at a time, beating well after each addition. Sift baking powder, salt and flour together. Add to creamed mixture alternately with milk, beginning with milk and ending with flour. Add vanilla and nuts; blend well. Pour batter into a well greased and floured 10 inch tube pan. Bake at 325° for 90 minutes. Cool 15 minutes before inverting.

Peggy Burr
Harpeth Council

CHOCOLATE POUND CAKE

3 sticks butter	3 c. flour
3 c. sugar	1/2 tsp. salt
5 eggs	1/2 tsp. baking powder
1 c. milk	1/2 c. cocoa
1 tsp. vanilla	1 c. nuts

Cream butter and sugar; add eggs one at a time. Add milk and vanilla; add dry ingredients. When well blended, fold in nuts. Bake in a greased and floured large steeple pan at 325° for 1 hour and 25 minutes.

Dot Crouch
Clarksville Council

COCONUT FLAVORED POUND CAKE

2 sticks margarine
1/2 c. Crisco
3 c. sugar
5 eggs
1 c. milk

3 c. plain flour
1/2 tsp. baking powder
1 tsp. coconut flavoring
1 tsp. rum flavoring

Cream margarine, Crisco and sugar. Add one egg at a time, beating well after each addition. Add flour and baking powder alternately with milk. Begin with and end with flour. Add flavoring. Bake in tube pan at 300° for 1 1/2 hours or until done. Glaze while cake is hot.
Note: Do not use self-rising flour.

Glaze:

1 c. sugar
1/4 c. plus 1 Tbsp. water

1 tsp. almond flavoring

Boil until rolling. Pour over hot cake; let cool in pan.

Dorothy Stanton
Knoxville Council

DEE'S COCONUT POUND CAKE

2 c. sugar
4 eggs
3 c. all-purpose flour
1 c. margarine
1 c. buttermilk
1 c. Angel Flake coconut

3 tsp. coconut extract
1/2 tsp. salt
1/2 tsp. soda
1/2 tsp. baking powder
1 c. chopped pecans

Cream sugar and margarine; add eggs one at a time. Mix well after each. Add flavoring. Add dry ingredients alternately with milk; fold in nuts and coconut. Bake in well greased and floured tube pan for 1 hour and 20 minutes in 325° oven (heat may vary). Pour syrup over cake in

1489-81

pan when removed from oven.

Syrup:

1 c. sugar
1/2 c. water
2 Tbsp. margarine

2 Tbsp. white syrup
1 tsp. coconut extract

Mix and boil 5 minutes. Pour over cake; let cool completely before removing from pan. (Freezes well.)
Jean Bethel
Memphis Council

CREAM CHEESE POUND CAKE

3 sticks margarine
1 (8 oz.) pkg. cream cheese
3 c. sugar
Dash of salt

1 1/2 tsp. vanilla extract
6 large eggs
3 c. sifted cake flour

Cream margarine, cream cheese and sugar until light and fluffy. Add salt and vanilla; beat well. Add eggs, one at a time, beating well after each addition. Stir in flour. Spoon mixture into greased 10 inch tube pan and bake at 325° for about 1 1/2 hours. Yield: One 10 inch cake.
Margaret Kolbe
Andrew Jackson Council

CREAM CHEESE POUND CAKE

3 sticks margarine
1 (8 oz.) pkg. cream cheese
3 c. sugar
Dash of salt

1 1/2 tsp. vanilla extract
1/2 tsp. butter flavoring
6 large eggs, unbeaten
3 c. sifted plain or cake flour

Cream margarine, cream cheese and sugar until light and fluffy. Add salt, vanilla and butter flavoring; beat well. Add eggs, one at a time, beating well after each addition. Stir in flour. Spoon mixture into well greased and floured 10 inch tube or Bundt pan. Bake 1 1/2 hours at 325°. This makes a large, very moist cake.
Florence Stubblefield
Morristown Council #12

482

GRANDPA'S PERFECT POUND CAKES

Bake at 300° for 1 hour and 15 minutes. Makes one 9 inch and one 10 inch cake. You'll have 2 cakes; an extra one for second helpings, neighbors or unexpected visitors.

Beat 1 pound (4 sticks) very soft butter or margarine with 3 cups sugar for 5 minutes at low speed. Add 10 egg yolks and beat 2 minutes at low speed. Beat 10 egg whites 2 minutes at high speed with same beater. Beat creamed mixture 5 minutes longer at low speed. Sift 5 1/2 cups sifted all-purpose flour and 6 teaspoons baking powder together. Beat 1/3 of flour into bowl at low speed. Beat in 3/4 cup milk until smooth. Beat in 1/3 of the flour until blended. Add egg whites and beat until smooth. Reserve 1/4 cup flour. Add remaining flour to bowl. Increase speed to medium and beat for 5 minutes. Grease one 9 inch and one 10 inch tube pan generously. Coat evenly with reserved flour, tapping excess into bowl. Add 2 teaspoons vanilla and 1 teaspoon grated lemon rind. Beat at medium speed 2 minutes. Pour batter into prepared pans. Bake in slow oven, 300°, for 1 hour and 15 minutes or until centers spring back when lightly pressed with fingertip. Cool in pans on wire rack 10 minutes. Loosen around side and tube of pan with a knife and invert cake onto wire rack to cool completely.

Basic Points to Remember: The sugar and butter should be well creamed before adding egg yolks. The egg whites are beaten separately and set aside while you measure the flour. (Sift your flour before measuring, even if it's "presifted" flour.) Add part of the flour and baking powder gradually to the butter-egg mixture. Add egg whites, lemon rind and vanilla. You should have a creamy, smooth batter.

Mary Brown
Harpeth Council

MILLION DOLLAR POUND CAKE

1 lb. butter (not margarine)	3/4 c. milk
3 c. sugar	1 tsp. vanilla extract
6 eggs, room temperature	1 tsp. almond extract
4 c. plain flour	

Beat sugar and butter until light and fluffy. Add eggs one at a time; mix well between each addition. Alternate adding flour and milk, beating well after each addition.

Stir in vanilla and almond extract. Bake at 300° for 1 hour and 40 minutes or until light brown. Cool for 25 minutes before releasing from pan. (I use a 6 cup tube pan.)

Mary Crabtree
Knoxville Council

NANNIE'S BUTTERMILK POUND CAKE

5 large eggs, separated   1 c. buttermilk
3 c. sugar   1/2 tsp. soda
3 c. flour (plain), unsifted 1 Tbsp. vanilla
1 c. Crisco   Dash of salt (1/2 tsp.)

Dissolve soda in 1 teaspoon warm water; set aside. Cream Crisco and sugar until light. Add egg yolks to Crisco and sugar. Combine soda and buttermilk. Add flour, mixed with salt, and milk alternately to creamed mixture, beating well after each addition. Add vanilla. Beat egg whites until stiff peaks form; fold into batter. Bake in a greased and floured tube pan for approximately 1 hour at 325°. The baking times will vary slightly so you need to check your cake after 1 hour. Serve plain, with lemon or chocolate sauce, or your favorite fruit and Cool Whip.

Marian Molteni
Harpeth Council

SOUR CREAM POUND CAKE

1/2 lb. butter   3 c. sugar
3 c. sifted flour   6 eggs, separated
Dash of salt   1/4 tsp. soda
1/2 pt. sour cream   1 tsp. lemon extract
                        1 tsp. vanilla extract

Cream the butter until it is very fluffy. Add the sugar by tablespoons. Add egg yolks; beat well. Beat the egg whites till stiff; set aside. Add the sour cream and the flour to the butter, sugar and egg yolks. Add flavorings and salt; mix thoroughly. Fold in egg whites. Pour or spoon into a greased and floured tube pan. Bake for 1 1/2 hours in preheated 325° oven.

Carolyn Mitchell
Memphis Downtown Council

484

SUNDROP SUPREME POUND CAKE

1 pkg. Duncan Hines Deluxe
   II lemon supreme cake mix
1 (4 serving) pkg. pineapple
   creme instant pudding mix

3/4 c. Wesson oil
4 eggs
1 (10 oz.) bottle Sundrop

Preheat oven to 350°. Blend all ingredients in a large bowl; beat at medium speed for 2 minutes. Bake in a greased and floured tube pan (10 inch) or Bundt pan at 350° for 45-55 minutes, until center springs back when touched lightly. Cool in pan, then invert onto serving plate.

Icing:

2 eggs
1 1/2 c. sugar
1 stick margarine

2 Tbsp. flour
1 small can crushed
   pineapple

Let margarine melt. Combine eggs, sugar, flour and crushed pineapple. Cook until it thickens; cool. Spread over cake.

Dorothy Bryant
Clarksville Council

PUMPKIN POUND CAKE

1 regular size can pumpkin
2 c. sugar
2 c. flour
4 eggs
1 c. salad oil
2 tsp. baking soda

1 tsp. baking powder
1/2 tsp. salt
1 tsp. nutmeg
2 tsp. cinnamon
1 tsp. vanilla

Combine sugar, oil and eggs; beat well. Sift all dry ingredients; add to oil mixture. Mix well. Stir in pumpkin and vanilla. Bake in tube pan at 350° for 1 1/2 hours.

Cream Cheese Icing for Pumpkin Pound Cake:

1 stick softened margarine
1 box powdered sugar

1 (3 oz.) pkg. softened
   cream cheese

Blend well; spread on cake. Yield: 16 slices.

Sheila Fleming
East Memphis Council

PREACHER CAKE

2 c. sugar
2 c. flour
2 eggs
2 tsp. baking soda
1/2 tsp. salt

2 tsp. vanilla
1/2 c. nuts
1 (20 oz.) can crushed
    pineapple

Combine dry ingredients; add remaining ingredients and mix by hand. Bake in a 9x13 inch pan at 350° for 45 minutes.

Frosting for Preacher Cake:

1 (8 oz.) pkg. cream cheese
1 3/4 c. powdered sugar
1/4 c. butter or margarine

1/4 tsp. salt
1/2 c. nuts
2 tsp. vanilla

Betty Gore
Memphis Council

PRUNE CAKE

2 c. flour
1 1/2 c. sugar
1 c. buttermilk
1 c. Wesson oil
1 tsp. soda
1 tsp. cinnamon

1 tsp. nutmeg
1 tsp. allspice
1/2 tsp. salt
3 eggs
1 c. cooked prunes, mashed
1 tsp. vanilla

Combine and sift flour, soda, cinnamon, nutmeg, allspice and salt. Put in large mixing bowl; add sugar, oil, buttermilk, eggs, prunes and vanilla. Mix well; pour into greased 13x9x2 inch pan. Bake at 350° for 40 to 45 minutes

Icing:

1 c. sugar
1/2 c. buttermilk

1/2 tsp. soda
1/4 stick margarine

Combine ingredients in saucepan. Cook over medium heat; boil 3 minutes. Pour over hot cake.

Mrs. Charlie Hood
Columbia Council

486

AUNT SARA'S PRUNE CAKE

3 eggs
1 1/2 c. sugar
1 c. Wesson oil
2 c. self-rising flour
1 c. buttermilk
1 c. (12 oz. pkg.) prunes,
  cooked and mashed up

1 c. nuts, if desired
1 tsp. cinnamon
1 tsp. nutmeg
1 tsp. allspice
1 tsp. vanilla
1 tsp. soda
Pinch of salt

Bake at 350° until done. Usually baked in a sheet cake pan.

Frosting/Sauce:

1 c. sugar
1/2 c. buttermilk
1 Tbsp. white syrup
1 tsp. soda

1/2 tsp. vanilla
1/4 lb. butter (usually 1
  stick)

Let come to a boil; pour over cake while hot. Punch holes in cake to let sauce go down.

Peggy Hunter
Harpeth Council

EASY PRUNE CAKE

2 c. self-rising flour
1 tsp. cinnamon
1 tsp. cloves

1 tsp. allspice
1 tsp. nutmeg
1/4 tsp. salt

Sift self-rising flour and measure. Resift twice with the four spices and salt. Add the following ingredients:

2 jars baby food prunes
  with tapioca
2 c. sugar
1 c. oil

3 eggs, slightly beaten
1 c. chopped pecans
(optional)

Mix together thoroughly in electric mixer. Fold in 1 cup chopped pecans by hand, using light up and over strokes. Turn batter into 10 inch tube pan or Bundt pan, well greased with pastry brush and floured well. Place in oven on rack about 5 inches from bottom of oven floor. Start in cold oven. Bake about 1 1/2 hours at 300° (low heat). Check for doneness with metal skewer after 1 hour and 20 minutes baking time. Allow cake to cool 10 minutes in pan. Turn onto cake rack to cool.

Edith W. Osborne
Jackson Council

PUDDIN' CAKE AND SAUCE

1 c. sugar
1 stick butter or oleo,
  softened
1/2 c. buttermilk
1 1/2 c. flour

1 tsp. vanilla
1/2 tsp. salt
1/2 tsp. soda
1 1/2 tsp. baking powder
2 eggs

Cream butter and sugar until smooth. Mix flour, salt, soda and baking powder. Add alternately with buttermilk and vanilla to the butter sugar mix. Add eggs, one at a time, beating well after each addition. Bake about 30 minutes in a 350° oven until done and slightly brown. Test for doneness with a toothpick. Makes 1 large layer.

Chocolate Sauce:

2 c. sugar
1/2 tsp. salt
2 heaping Tbsp. flour
3 heaping Tbsp. cocoa

3 c. sweet milk
1/3 stick butter or oleo
1 tsp. vanilla

Mix all dry ingredients together in a saucepan. Add milk, butter and vanilla. Cook, stirring constantly, over medium heat until thick and smooth. Serve hot water over warm cake.

Syble L. Hilliard
Jackson Council

PUMPKIN CAKE

Combine and beat thoroughly:
4 eggs   1 c. oil
2 c. sugar

Sift together and add:
2 c. self-rising flour   2 tsp. cinnamon
2 tsp. soda   1/2 tsp. salt
1 tsp. baking powder

488

Beat well and add 1 (No. 303) can pumpkin. Bake in tube pan about 50 minutes at 325°; cool thoroughly.

Frosting: Beat until light -

1 stick butter   1 (3 oz.) pkg. cream cheese

Gradually add 1 box confectioners sugar; beat until fluffy; or, use whipped cream as a topping.

Mary Ann Pierce
Knoxville Council

PUMPKIN RING

1/3 c. oleo	1 1/3 c. sugar
1 egg	1 2/3 c. flour
1/4 tsp. salt	1/4 tsp. baking powder
1/4 tsp. allspice	1 tsp. soda
1 tsp. cinnamon	1/3 c. water
1/3 c. nuts	2/3 c. cooked raisins
1 c. pumpkin	

Mix all ingredients together. Bake in tube pan for 1 hour at 350°. Leave plain or ice with Cream Cheese Frosting.

Jeanette W. Palmer
Harpeth Council

RASPBERRY BARS

3/4 c. butter or margarine	1/2 tsp. soda
1 c. packed brown sugar	1 1/2 c. uncooked oats
1 1/2 c. flour	1 (10 oz.) jar raspberry
1 tsp. salt	preserves

Cream butter and sugar until light and fluffy. Add combined dry ingredients; mix well. Press half of crumb mixture into greased 13x9 inch baking pan; spread with preserves. Sprinkle with remaining crumb mixture. Bake at 400° for 20-25 minutes. Cool; cut into bars. Flavor improves if allowed to "set" 24 hours.

Rosemary Grand
Harpeth Council

RED VELVET CAKE

2 oz. red food coloring	1 tsp. salt
1 Tbsp. cocoa	1 tsp. baking soda
1/2 c. shortening	1 tsp. vinegar
2 eggs	1 1/2 c. sugar
1 tsp. vanilla	1 c. buttermilk
2 1/2 c. all-purpose flour	

Mix above ingredients and bake in 3 cake pans at 350° for 30 minutes. Let cool before icing.

Icing for Red Velvet Cake: Stir together 1 cup milk, 1/4 cup flour and 1/8 teaspoon salt; cook until thick. When mixture cools, beat in 2 teaspoons vanilla, 1 cup sugar, 1 stick oleo and 1/2 cup Crisco.

Tammy Raines
Chattanooga Council

RUM CAKE

1 box Duncan Hines butter cake mix	1/2 c. rum
	1/2 c. water
1 large pkg. instant vanilla pudding mix	1/2 c. oil
	1/2 c. nuts, in batter
4 eggs	

Grease tube pan and sprinkle 1/2 cup nuts, chopped.

Glaze:

1 c. sugar	1/2 c. rum
1 stick butter	

Boil 3 minutes; let set. Bake cake until it springs back when touched. Remove from oven; let it cool until just warmer than room temperature. Punch holes in cake and pour 1/2 of glaze over. Let this soak in and pour the rest over cake.

Dot Gilliland
Harpeth Council

BACARDI RUM CAKE

1 c. chopped pecans or walnuts
1 (2 layer) pkg. yellow cake mix
4 eggs
1/2 c. cold water
1 (4 serving) pkg. Jell-O vanilla flavor instant pudding and pie filling
1/2 c. vegetable oil
1/2 c. Bacardi dark rum (80 proof)

Sprinkle nuts evenly in bottom of greased and floured 10 inch tube or Bundt pan. Combine cake mix, pudding mix, eggs, 1/2 cup water, the oil and 1/2 cup rum in large mixer bowl. Blend, then beat at medium speed for 2 minutes; pour into pan. Bake at 325° for 60 minutes.

Glaze: Combine 1 cup sugar, 1/2 cup butter or margarine and 1/4 cup water in a saucepan. Bring to a boil; boil 5 minutes, stirring constantly. Remove from heat. Stir in 1/2 cup Bacardi dark rum and bring just to a boil. Remove cake from pan onto plate; prick with cake tester. Spoon warm glaze over warm cake. Garnish with pecans, if desired.

Mary Burchfield
Downtown Memphis Council
Shirley Chester
Clarksville Council

BACARDI RUM PINA COLADA CAKE

Cake:

1 (2 layer) pkg. white cake mix
1 (4 serving) pkg. Jell-O coconut cream or vanilla instant pudding and pie filling
4 eggs
1 c. flaked coconut
1/2 c. water*
1/3 c. Bacardi dark rum (80 proof)
1/4 c. Wesson oil

Frosting:

1 (8 oz.) can crushed pineapple, in juice
1 (4 serving) pkg. Jell-O coconut cream or vanilla instant pudding and pie filling
1/3 c. Bacardi dark rum (80 proof)
1 (9 oz.) container frozen whipped topping, thawed

Blend all ingredients, except coconut, in large mixer bowl. Beat 4 minutes at medium speed of electric mixer. Pour into two greased and floured 9 inch layer pans. Bake at 350° for 25 to 30 minutes or until cake springs back when lightly pressed. Do not underbake. Cool in pan 15 minutes; remove and cool on racks. Fill and frost; sprinkle with coconut. Chill; refrigerate leftover cake.

For frosting: Combine all ingredients, except whipped topping, in a bowl; beat until well blended. Fold in thawed whipped topping.

*With vanilla flavor filling, increase water to 3/4 cup; add 1 cup flaked coconut to batter.

Ruth L. Cole
Harpeth Council

SAD CAKE

2 c. Bisquick	1 can coconut
1 box light brown sugar	1 c. pecans
1/3 c. oil	1 Tbsp. vanilla
3 eggs	

Bake in 9x13 inch pan at 325° for about 30 minutes. (This cake will fall.)

Elsie D. Cole
Columbia Council

SAUERKRAUT CAKE

2/3 c. butter or margarine	2 1/4 c. sifted all-purpose flour
1 1/2 c. sugar	1 tsp. baking powder
3 eggs	1/4 tsp. salt
1 tsp. vanilla	1 c. water
1/2 c. unsweetened cocoa	2/3 c. sauerkraut, well drained
1 tsp. soda	

Cream butter and sugar well; add eggs one at a time, beating after each addition. Add vanilla. Sift dry ingredients together; add alternately with water to first mixture. Rinse drained kraut well in cold water; drain again. Chop or snip into very small pieces. Divide batter into two greased and floured 8 inch cake pans. Bake at 350° for 30 minutes. Frost with chocolate or caramel or Cream Cheese Frosting.

Ruth L. Cole
Harpeth Council

SHEATH CAKE

2 c. sugar	1/2 c. buttermilk
2 c. flour	2 eggs, slightly beaten
1/4 tsp. salt	1 tsp. soda
2 sticks butter	4 tsp. cocoa
1 c. water	1 tsp. vanilla

Sift together sugar, flour and salt in large mixing bowl. Put butter, water and cocoa in saucepan; bring to rapid boil. Pour over the sugar-flour mixture; stir well. Add buttermilk, eggs, soda and vanilla. Mix well and pour in greased 9x14 inch pan. Bake 20 minutes at 400°.

Icing:

1 stick butter	1 box powdered sugar
4 Tbsp. cocoa	1 tsp. vanilla
6 Tbsp. milk	1 c. chopped pecans

Start making icing about 5 minutes before cake is done. Melt together butter, cocoa and milk; bring to a boil. Remove from heat and beat in sugar, vanilla and pecans. Spread on cake while still hot. Leave in pan and cut in squares to serve.

Jewell Bingham
Columbia Council

SNOW-BALL CAKE

2 pkg. Knox gelatine	Juice of 1 lemon
2 c. crushed pineapple, not drained	1/2 tsp. salt
	1 large angel food cake
1 c. sugar	1 pkg. Angel Flake coconut
4 small pkg. Dream Whip	

Dissolve gelatine in 4 tablespoons ice water. Add 1 cup boiling water; let cool. Combine pineapple, sugar, salt and lemon juice. Pour gelatine mixture over this; let partially congeal. Prepare 2 packages Dream Whip by

1489-81

directions and fold into mixture. Break cake into bite size pieces; line large oblong Pyrex pan. Spoon half of mixture over cake. Add layer of cake and top with rest of mixture. Prepare 2 packages Dream Whip; spread on top. Sprinkle with coconut. Chill overnight and serve.

Dale Bushulen
Harpeth Council

SNOWBALL CAKE

1 c. sugar
1 can coconut
4 pkg. Dream Whip
2 pkg. plain gelatin

1 large can pineapple, crushed (reserve juice)
1 large angel food cake
Juice from 1 lemon

Dissolve gelatin in 4 tablespoons water. Add sugar, lemon juice and pineapple juice. Set in refrigerator until congealed, then add well drained pineapple. Add 2 packages whipped Dream Whip. Break 1/2 of cake into small chunks; place in large pan. Pour gelatin mix over cake pieces. Break remaining cake over mixture and cover with 2 packages whipped Dream Whip; cover with coconut. Serves 15 or more.

Dorotha Sells
Morristown Council #12

SOUR CREAM CAKE

2 sticks butter
3 c. sugar
6 eggs, separated
3 c. flour, sifted (plain)
1/4 tsp. soda

1 (8 oz.) ctn. sour cream
1 tsp. vanilla extract
1 tsp. almond extract
1 tsp. orange extract

Cream butter and sugar; beat in egg yolks. Alternate flour with soda added and sour cream. Beat egg whites. Fold in and add flavorings. Bake in stem pan at 300° for 1 1/2 hours.

Pattie Hoffman
Nashboro Council

SOUR CREAM COFFEE CAKE

2 sticks margarine	1 tsp. vanilla
2 c. sugar	2 c. flour
2 eggs	1 tsp. baking powder
1 c. sour cream	1/4 tsp. salt

Topping: Mix together -

1/2 c. chopped pecans	1 Tbsp. cinnamon
2 Tbsp. brown sugar	

Blend margarine; add sugar and blend. Add eggs; add flour, beating gradually. Add sour cream, vanilla, baking powder and salt; blend until smooth. Sprinkle half of topping mixture in greased and floured tube pan. Pour 1/2 cake mixture on topping. Sprinkle topping on batter; add remaining cake mixture. Smooth mixture with spoon; sprinkle remaining topping on top of batter. Bake at 350° for 50-60 minutes; test with toothpick.

Trena Seaford
Nashboro Council

JO'S SOUR CREAM TWISTS

1 c. melted margarine	1 whole egg
1 c. dairy sour cream	2 egg yolks
1 tsp. salt	3 1/2 c. flour
1 tsp. vanilla	1 c. sugar, mixed with 1 tsp.
1 pkg. dry yeast	cinnamon

Combine margarine, sour cream, salt and vanilla (mixture should be lukewarm). Sprinkle in the yeast. Combine whole egg and egg yolks; beat until creamy. Blend into yeast mixture. Sift flour; measure and blend into yeast mixture. Place in a greased bowl. Cover with a damp cloth and refrigerate 2 hours. Mix sugar and cinnamon; spread on a flat surface. Roll dough into a rectangle, 15x18 inches, turning so both sides are coated with sugar. Fold over 2 times as you would a letter. Repeat rolling and folding 3 times or until sugar is used up. Roll into a rectangle about 1/4 inch thick; cut into 1 x 1/4 inch strips. Twist strips; lay on greased baking sheet. Bake at 375° for 15 minutes. Frost while warm with Powdered Sugar Frosting.

David Darrohn
Knoxville Council

CIDER SPICE CAKE

2 1/2 c. sifted flour
2 tsp. cinnamon
1 tsp. baking soda
2 tsp. cloves
1 tsp. nutmeg
1/2 c. butter or margarine

1 1/2 c. sugar
1 egg
1 c. cider or apple juice
1 c. seedless raisins
1 tsp. salt

Combine and sift flour, baking soda, spices and salt. Cream butter or margarine. Add sugar gradually; beat until smooth. Add egg; beat well. Add dry ingredients alternately with cider or apple juice; stir in raisins. Pour into greased 10 inch tube pan. Bake at 350° for 50 minutes.

M.E. Womble, Jr.
Memphis East Council

VELVET SPICE CAKE

3/4 c. Crisco or 1 1/2
  stick margarine
1 1/2 c. granulated sugar
3 eggs, separated
2 c. cake flour, sifted
1 tsp. baking powder

1 tsp. baking soda
1/2 tsp. salt
1 tsp. nutmeg
1 tsp. cinnamon
1/2 tsp. ground cloves
7/8 c. buttermilk

Set oven at 350°. Cream the butter with the sugar; beat in the egg yolks. Sift together twice the flour, baking powder, soda, salt and spices. Add the sifted ingredients to the creamed mixture alternately with the milk. Beat the egg whites until stiff; fold into batter. Bake in a floured and greased 9 inch tube pan for approximately 1 hour. Frost with chocolate, brown sugar or white icing.

Marian Molteni
Harpeth Council

OLD FASHIONED SPICE STACK CAKE

1/2 c. shortening
1 c. brown sugar, packed
1 egg
1/2 c. molasses
1/2 c. buttermilk
6 c. flour (plain)

1/4 tsp. salt
1/2 tsp. soda
1 tsp. baking powder
1 tsp. vanilla
1/4 tsp. nutmeg
1 Tbsp. pumpkin pie spice

496

Cream shortening and sugar thoroughly. Beat in egg and vanilla; add molasses. Mix well. Sift flour; measure and sift with all dry ingredients. Add alternately with buttermilk. Divide dough into 9 balls; refrigerate overnight. Roll on waxed paper and cut through dough and paper to fit 9 inch cake pan. Roll very thin; bake on paper in pan in 450° oven for 8-10 minutes. Put together with the following:

1 lb. dried apples	2 tsp. cinnamon
1 c. brown sugar	1/2 tsp. cloves
1/2 c. white sugar	1/2 tsp. allspice

Cook apples till tender. Mash thoroughly; add sugar and spice. Cool and put between cake layers.

Myrtle Porter
Knoxville Council

STRAWBERRY CAKE

1/2 c. water	1/2 c. Wesson oil
3 eggs	1 box butter cake mix
1 small box strawberry jello	1 pkg. frozen strawberries, drained (reserve juice)

Combine jello, eggs, water and Wesson oil with dry cake mix. Beat on high speed for 2 minutes. Add strawberries; mix well. Pour into a greased and floured sheet cake pan. Bake at 350° for 30 to 35 minutes.

Icing:

1 box confectioners sugar	Reserved berry juice
1 stick butter, creamed	

Cream butter well with a mixer; do not melt butter. Add butter to confectioners sugar. Add berry juice as needed for consistency. Beat on low speed until well blended.

Sandra Jones
Green Hills Council

STRAWBERRY CAKE

1 (18 1/2 oz.) pkg. yellow
  or white cake mix
1 (3 oz.) pkg. strawberry
  gelatin
3/4 c. vegetable oil
1 c. chopped nuts
4 eggs

2 Tbsp. flour
1 (10 oz.) pkg. frozen, sliced
  sweetened strawberries,
  thawed, or 1 pt. fresh,
  sliced strawberries with
  1/2 c. sugar
1/2 pt. heavy cream,
  whipped (optional)
1 Tbsp. sugar (optional)

Preheat oven to 350° and grease a 10 inch angel food cake pan or 10 inch Bundt pan. Combine cake mix, strawberry gelatin, vegetable oil, nuts, eggs, flour and strawberries in large bowl. Beat with electric mixer at medium-high speed for 3 minutes or until well blended. Pour batter into pan and bake for 55 to 65 minutes, or until a cake tester inserted in center comes out clean. Cool 10 minutes on rack. Turn out of pan to cool completely. Serve plain or with sweetened whipped cream.

Sue Watts
Clarksville Council

STRAWBERRY CAKE

1 pkg. white cake mix
1 pkg. strawberry jello
4 eggs
1/2 c. water

1 c. Crisco oil
1 c. frozen strawberries
1/2 c. nuts

Blend mix, jello, oil, water and eggs; beat at medium speed for 2 minutes. Add strawberries and nuts. Bake at 350° for 1 hour.

Ted Wiley
Columbia Council

STRAWBERRY CAKE

1 white cake mix
1 (3 oz.) box strawberry
  jello
1 c. Crisco oil
1/2 c. milk

1 c. strawberries
1 c. nuts
1 c. coconut
4 eggs

Mix per cake mix instructions. Bake at 350° for 40 minutes or until done. Best to bake in large 13x9x2 inch pan.

Frosting:

1 stick margarine	1 box powdered sugar
1/2 c. strawberries	1/2 c. nuts
1 c. coconut	

Mix and spread on warm cake.

Brenda Brinkley
Harpeth Council

STRAWBERRY CAKE

1 box white cake mix	1/2 c. water
1 small box strawberry jello	4 eggs
4 Tbsp. flour (self-rising)	1 c. fresh strawberries,
3/4 c. Wesson oil	sliced

Add the dry jello to the cake mix. Add the remaining ingredients in the order given. Beat after the addition of each egg. Mix strawberries in last. Bake in layers or 13x9x2 inch dish at 350° for approximately 30 to 35 minutes.

Frosting:

1 box confectioners sugar	1/2 c. sliced strawberries
1 stick margarine	

Mix until light and fluffy.

Mrs. R.C. Burton
Knoxville Council

STRAWBERRY CAKE

1 box white cake mix	1 c. oil
1 (3 oz.) pkg. strawberry jello	4 eggs

Mix above well and add 1 cup juice, drained from 8 ounce package of frozen strawberries (add water if needed to make 1 cup), plus 1/4 cup drained strawberries. Bake 30 minutes at 350°.

Icing:

1 box sifted confectioners
  sugar
1 stick butter or margarine

1 (8 oz.) pkg. frozen
  strawberries (remainder
  of what was used in cake)
1 or 2 drops of red food color

Mix together and spread on cake.

Belinda Dorris
Nashboro Council

STRAWBERRY CAKE

Mix in a bowl:
1 box white cake mix
1 small box strawberry jello
  (dry)

3 tsp. self-rising flour

Add and mix:
1 c. Wesson oil
1/2 c. water

4 eggs, added separately

Mix well and add 1/2 of a 10 ounce package frozen strawberries. Distribute strawberries evenly. Bake at 350° for 30 minutes in two 9 inch pans.

Icing:

1 box confectioners sugar
1 stick margarine

Remaining 5 oz. strawberries

Cream butter and sugar. Add strawberries a little at a time until the right consistency for icing. (This makes a large cake.)

Bettye Lou Nicely
Knoxville Council

STRAWBERRY REFRIGERATOR CAKE

1 angel food cake, broken
  into pieces
1 qt. strawberries, sliced
  (save a few for garnish)
1 1/2 c. granulated sugar

2 c. water
1 pkg. strawberry gelatin
1/2 env. gelatin, softened in
  small amount of cold water
1 Tbsp. lemon juice

500

Dash of salt
1 pt. whipping cream or 2 pkg. Dream Whip

1 pkg. Dream Whip to ice cake

Boil sugar and water for 1 minute. Add strawberry gelatin and stir along with softened plain gelatin. Stir until dissolved. Add lemon juice and salt; let cool and partially set. Fold in 1/2 of whipping cream, whipped, or 2 packages of Dream Whip, made up, along with strawberries. Fold in angel food cake pieces. Pour into a greased mold (angel food cake pan). Allow to set for at least 24 hours in refrigerator. Unmold and ice with package of Dream Whip. Garnish with strawberries. When ready to serve, ice cake with Dream Whip.

Billie Fleming
Nashboro Council
Pat DeMatteo
Nashboro Council

STRAWBERRY CHEESECAKE

1/3 c. margarine
1/3 c. sugar
1 egg
1 1/4 c. flour (plain)
3 (8 oz.) pkg. cream cheese
3/4 c. sugar
2 Tbsp. flour

1 tsp. vanilla
3 eggs
2 Tbsp. milk
1 (10 oz.) jar strawberry jelly
2 c. whole strawberries

Cream 1/3 cup margarine and 1/3 cup sugar until light and fluffy; blend in 1 egg. Add 1 1/4 cups flour; mix well. Spread dough with spatula on bottom and 1 1/2 inches high around sides of a 9 inch spring form pan. Bake at 450° for 5 minutes. Combine softened cheese, sugar, flour and vanilla, mixing at medium speed on electric mixer until well blended. Add eggs, one at a time, mixing well after each addition. Stir in milk. Pour into pastry lined pan. Bake at 450° for 10 minutes. Reduce heat to 250°; continue baking for 30 minutes. Loosen cake from rim of pan; cool before removing rim. Chill. Several hours before serving, melt jelly over low heat; cool slightly. Arrange strawberries on top of cake; spoon jelly over strawberries and chill.

Evalyn Morris
Harpeth Council

STRAWBERRY PECAN CAKE

1 pkg. white cake mix
1 small box strawberry
   gelatin
1 c. salad oil
1/2 c. milk

4 eggs
1 c. frozen strawberries
1 c. coconut
1 c. chopped pecans

Combine cake mix and dry gelatin. Add other ingredients, adding eggs one at a time. Pour into 3 greased and floured cake pans and bake for 20-25 minutes in a 350° oven.

Strawberry Frosting:

1 stick margarine
1 box confectioners sugar
1/2 c. strawberries, drained

1/2 c. coconut
1/2 c. chopped pecans

Cream sugar and margarine. Add other ingredients and spread on cooled cake.

Sara F. Williams
Columbia Council
Dean Tidwell
Nashboro Council

MERINGUE-TOPPED STRAWBERRY SHORTCAKE

1 qt. fresh strawberries
1/2 c. granulated sugar
2 1/3 c. Bisquick baking mix
3 Tbsp. granulated sugar
3 Tbsp. margarine or
   butter, melted

1/2 c. milk
2 egg whites
1/4 c. powdered sugar
1/4 c. granulated sugar
1 Tbsp. granulated sugar

Slice strawberries; sprinkle with 1/2 cup granulated sugar and let stand 1 hour. Heat oven to 375°. Mix baking mix, 3 tablespoons granulated sugar, the margarine and milk until soft dough forms. Gently smooth into ball on cloth covered board, dusted with baking mix. Knead 8 to 10 times. Pat in ungreased round pan, 9 x 1 1/2 inches. Beat egg whites until foamy. Beat in powdered sugar and 1/4 cup granulated sugar, 1 tablespoon at a time. Continue beating until stiff and glossy. Spread meringue on dough; sprinkle with 1 tablespoon granulated sugar. Bake until delicate brown, 25 to 30 minutes; cool 10 minutes. Run knife around edge to loosen; turn onto cloth covered board. Invert on wire rack; cool completely. Serve with strawberries. Makes 8 servings.

High Altitude Directions (3500 to 6500 feet): Not recommended for use.

Pat Ferguson
Harpeth Council

STRIPE-IT-RICH CAKE

1 (2 layer) pkg. cake mix or pudding-included cake mix (any flavor)	4 c. cold milk 2 (4 serving) pkg. Jell-O brand instant pudding
1 c. confectioners sugar	(any complimentary flavor)

Prepare cake mix as directed on package, baking in a 9x13 inch pan. Remove from oven. Poke holes at once down through the cake to the pan with the round handle of a wooden spoon (or poke holes with a plastic drinking straw, using a turning motion to make large holes). Holes should be 1 inch apart. Only after poking holes, combine pudding mix with sugar in a large bowl; gradually stir in milk. Beat at low speed of electric mixer for not more than 1 minute (do not overbeat). Quickly, before pudding thickens, pour about 1/2 of the thin pudding evenly over warm cake and into holes to make stripes. Allow remaining pudding to thicken slightly, then spoon over the top, swirling it to "frost" the cake. Chill at least 1 hour. Store cake in refrigerator.

Linda Whitaker
Harpeth Council
Marilyn Putnam
Harpeth Council

SWEET POTATO CAKE

1 1/2 c. cooking oil	2 c. sugar
4 eggs, separated	4 Tbsp. hot water
2 1/2 c. sifted cake flour	3 tsp. baking powder
1/2 tsp. ground cinnamon	1 tsp. ground nutmeg
1 1/2 c. grated, raw sweet potato	1 c. chopped nuts
	1/2 tsp. salt
1 tsp. vanilla	

Combine oil and sugar; beat until smooth. Add egg

yolks; beat well. Add hot water; beat well. Add dry ingredients, which have been sifted together. Stir in potato, nuts and vanilla; beat well. Beat egg whites until stiff; fold into mixture. Bake in greased cake pans at 350° for about 25 to 30 minutes until done.

Frosting:

1 large can evaporated milk	1 c. sugar
1 stick margarine	3 egg yolks
1 tsp. vanilla	1 1/3 c. coconut

Combine all ingredients, except coconut. Cook in double boiler about 12 minutes. Remove from heat; add coconut and spread on cake.

Phyllis Whaley
Andrew Jackson Council

TROPICAL CAKE

1 Duncan Hines butter cake mix	11 oz. can Mandarin oranges, with juice
4 eggs	1/2 c. oil

Mix ingredients together; beat with an electric mixer until well blended, approximately 2 minutes. Pour into well greased, floured pans. Will make 2-4 layers or sheet cake. Bake in preheated 350° F. oven for 25 to 30 minutes for layers (8 or 9 inch round) and 35 to 40 minutes for sheet (9x12 inch oblong pan).

Icing:

3 oz. box instant vanilla pudding	Large can crushed pineapple with juice
	9 oz. Cool Whip

Mix instant pudding with pineapple until well blended; fold in Cool Whip. Frost cake.
Note: Use only 1/2 of icing ingredients for sheet cake.

Anne Bagwell
Green Hills Council

VANILLA WAFER CAKE

1 c. margarine
2 c. sugar
6 whole eggs
1 (12 oz.) box vanilla
  wafers

1 (7 oz.) can Angel Flake
  coconut
1/2 c. milk
1 c. chopped pecans
1/4 tsp. almond extract

Cream butter and sugar; add well beaten eggs. Add crushed vanilla wafers, then add coconut and nuts. Grease and flour 10 inch tube pan. Pour ingredients in pan. Bake for 1 1/2 to 2 hours at 275°. Frost with the following icing:

1 (8 oz.) pkg. cream cheese
1 stick margarine
1 box powdered sugar

1 tsp. vanilla
1/2 c. chopped pecans

Mix well and spread over cool cake.

Mrs. Adelene Queenan
Harpeth Council

VANILLA WAFER CAKE

1 c. butter
2 c. sugar
6 whole eggs
1 (12 oz.) box vanilla
  wafers, crushed

1 (7 oz.) can Angel Flake
  coconut
1 c. chopped pecans
1/4 tsp. almond extract

Cream butter and sugar; add well beaten eggs. Add crushed vanilla wafers. Add coconut, pecans and almond extract. Bake 1 1/2 hours at 275° in stem pan.

Cream Cheese Icing:

1 (8 oz.) pkg. cream cheese
1 stick butter

1 box powdered sugar, sifted
1 tsp. vanilla
1/2 c. chopped pecans

Melt butter; add cream cheese, powdered sugar, vanilla and nuts.

Metty C. Fain
Andrew Jackson Council

WALNUT CAKE RING

3 3/4 c. sifted cake flour
2 c. sugar
4 tsp. baking powder
1 1/2 tsp. salt
1/2 c. soft butter
1/2 c. Crisco

2 tsp. vanilla
1 1/4 c. milk, room
  temperature
6 egg whites
1 1/2 c. black walnuts,
  chopped

Sift together flour, sugar, baking powder and salt. Blend together butter, Crisco and vanilla. Add dry ingredients and 1 cup milk. Blend thoroughly, then beat 300 strokes by hand. Blend in remaining milk and egg whites. Beat 300 strokes; fold in nuts. Pour into greased and floured 3 quart ring mold. Bake at 350° for 35 to 40 minutes. Cool 5 minutes; turn out on rack. Frost bottom side up.

Frosting:

3 1/2 c. confectioners sugar
1/2 c. soft butter
4-6 Tbsp. milk

1/8 tsp. salt
1 tsp. vanilla

Combine sugar, butter, 4 tablespoons milk, salt and vanilla in mixing bowl. Blend, then beat until smooth. Add milk as needed for good spreading consistency. Spread over top and sides of cake.

Lady Ruth Horsley by
Marie Barnett
Harpeth Council

BLACK WALNUT CAKE

2 1/2 c. sugar
1/2 c. oil
1 stick margarine
4 eggs

1 tsp. vanilla
3 c. sifted self-rising flour
1 c. buttermilk
1/2 c. chopped black walnuts

Cream oil, margarine and sugar. Add eggs one at a time; add vanilla. Add flour, alternating with milk. Mix well; add nuts and mix well again. Grease and flour three 9 inch cake pans. Place batter in pans and bake at 350° for 45 minutes. For frosting, use prepared Sour Cream Frosting, adding 1/2 cup chopped black walnuts.

Carolyn Cothon
Memphis Downtown Council

WHITE FUDGE CAKE

1 c. light brown sugar
1 c. white sugar
4 eggs, added one at a
    time, beaten well

1 c. flour
1/4 lb. (1 stick) butter or
    oleo
1 c. chopped pecans

Bake in a greased 9x13 inch pan. Cut into 48 pieces.
Mary Jane Bailey
Green Hills Council

YELLOW CAKE

Remove 1 stick (1/2 cup) butter or margarine; allow to soften about 15 minutes at room temperature. Preheat oven to 350°. Generously grease one 13x9x2 inch oblong pan, then flour pan. In a large bowl, combine 1 box Duncan Hines butter recipe golden cake mix, 1 stick (1/2 cup) soft butter or margarine, 2/3 cup water and 3 eggs. Blend until moistened. Scrape bowl and beaters; beat 4 minutes at medium speed. Bake about 30-35 minutes.
Bernie Wright
Green Hills Council

ZUCCHINI CAKE

3 eggs, beaten
1 c. vegetable oil
2 c. sugar
2 tsp. vanilla
2 c. all-purpose flour
3 tsp. cinnamon

2 tsp. soda
1 tsp. salt
1/2 tsp. baking powder
2 c. peeled, coarsely grated
    zucchini

Combine eggs, oil, sugar and vanilla; mix well. Combine dry ingredients and add to the egg mixture; mix well. Stir in grated zucchini. Pour batter into a greased and floured 10 inch Bundt pan. Bake at 350° for 55 minutes. Cool 20 minutes. Spoon glaze on cake.

Powdered Sugar Glaze:

1/2 c. powdered sugar

2 Tbsp. milk
Imogene H. Suttles
Knoxville Council

CARAMEL FROSTING

1 c. granulated sugar
1 stick butter, softened to
  room temperature

1/2 c. evaporated milk
1 c. brown sugar
1 tsp. vanilla

Heat first 4 ingredients until dissolved. Bring to a rolling boil; cook for 1 minute. Set off heat; add vanilla and beat until right consistency to spread. If it becomes too thick for spreading, add small amount of milk, being careful not to add too much at a time.

Bessie Crosby
Harpeth Council

CARAMEL ICING

3 c. sugar
1 c. evaporated milk
3 Tbsp. flour

1 c. butter
2 Tbsp. white syrup

Melt 1/2 cup sugar in heavy pan until light brown. Mix rest of sugar and flour; add milk, butter and syrup. As mixture boils, add melted sugar; boil until thick, 230° on candy thermometer or soft ball stage. Cool before icing cake. If mixture is too thin, add 2 or 3 tablespoons confectioners sugar.

J.C. Mallard
Nashville Council

CARAMEL ICING

3 c. sugar
2 c. whipping cream

1/2 stick butter (not oleo)
1 Tbsp. vanilla

Boil together sugar, cream and butter until it will make a soft ball in cold water. Use a heavy saucepan. Let cool; add 1 tablespoon vanilla. Beat until creamy. Yield: Icing for a 2 layer cake.

Eugenia W. Smith
Chattanooga Council

CARAMEL ICING

1 box brown sugar	Pinch of salt
1 c. sugar	1 stick margarine
1 c. Pet milk	2 tsp. vanilla

Mix brown sugar, white sugar and salt together in pan. Add Pet milk; stir well. Bring to boil on medium heat, stirring constantly; boil for 5 minutes. Remove from heat; add 1 stick butter and 2 teaspoons vanilla. Beat by hand until of spreading consistency. This icing is very good on Duncan Hines yellow cake mix.

Caution: Do not overbeat; icing will harden as you ice cake.

Dorothy Stanton
Knoxville Council

CARAMEL ICING

3 c. granulated sugar	1 c. milk
1 tsp. flour	

Cook until it comes to hard boil. Brown 1/2 cup granulated sugar in an iron skillet. When brown, add to first mixture. Cook until a soft ball is formed in cold water. Add 2 1/2 sticks of butter; beat until creamy.

Bernie Wright
Green Hills Council

CHOCOLATE FROSTING

1 stick oleo	1 box confectioners sugar
3 Tbsp. cocoa	1/2 c. pecans, chopped
6 Tbsp. milk	1 tsp. vanilla

Mix oleo, cocoa and milk in a saucepan; heat over low flame, but do not boil. Remove from heat; add confectioners sugar, chopped pecans and vanilla. Mix well. Frost Cookie Sheet Cake as soon as removed from oven.

Metty C. Fain
Andrew Jackson Council

DELUXE CHOCOLATE FROSTING

2 sq. (2 oz.) unsweetened chocolate
1 (1 oz.) sq. sweet chocolate
3 Tbsp. butter

1 3/4 c. sifted confectioners sugar
5 Tbsp. hot milk
1/2 tsp. vanilla extract

Melt chocolate and butter; cool. Dissolve sugar in hot milk; pour into chocolate mixture. Add vanilla and beat until thick enough to spread.

Metty C. Fain
Andrew Jackson Council

CHOCOLATE FUDGE ICING

2 c. sugar
1 sq. chocolate
1 stick margarine

2/3 c. milk
2 tsp. vanilla

Mix all together, except vanilla. Let come to a boil; boil for 4 minutes. Remove from stove. Add vanilla and beat until it will spread on cake. If it gets too thick, thin with a little milk.

Martha R. Dowlen
Green Hills Council

CHOCOLATE ICING
(Cooked 1 Minute)

2 c. sugar
2 Tbsp. cocoa
1/2 c. sweet milk

1 stick margarine
1/2 tsp. vanilla flavoring

Mix well and boil in heavy pan for 1 minute (rolling boil). Remove from heat; add flavoring. Let cool and beat till spreading consistency. Tastes great; just chocolate enough.

Dot Crouch
Clarksville Council

CHOCOLATE ICING

2 c. sugar
1/2 c. cocoa

1/2 c. sweet milk
1 stick margarine

Stir on medium heat until it boils. Cook 1 minute until it boils. Put in cold water; let cool 5 minutes. Beat and pour on cake.

Claudia Davenport
Clarksville Council

CHOCOLATE ICING

2 sq. unsweetened chocolate
2 c. granulated sugar
2/3 c. milk

1/2 c. shortening (Crisco)
1/4 tsp. salt
1 tsp. vanilla

Mix above ingredients, except vanilla, in a medium size pot. Stir over low heat until mixture comes to a boil. Let boil for 1 minute without stirring. Remove from heat; add vanilla. Mix with beaters until mixture becomes thick to spread.

Beverly S. Sheehan
Green Hills Council

COCONUT PECAN FROSTING
(For German Chocolate Cake)

1 c. evaporated milk
1 c. sugar
3 egg yolks, slightly beaten
1/2 c. butter or margarine

1 tsp. vanilla
1 1/3 c. coconut
1 c. chopped pecans

Combine above ingredients, except coconut and pecans. Cook and stir over medium heat until thickened, about 12 minutes. Stir in coconut and pecans. Cook until thick enough to spread; beat occasionally. This recipe will frost a 2 layer cake or a rectangular cake.

Sheila Fleming
East Memphis Council

CREAM CHEESE ICING

2 (3 oz.) pkg. cream cheese
1/2 stick margarine
1 (1 lb.) box confectioners
   sugar, sifted
2 tsp. vanilla

Combine all ingredients and beat to blend. Spread on cake.

Mabel M. Wilson
Clarksville Council

DECORATING FROSTING

1 1/4 c. Crisco
1/2 c. water
1/4 tsp. vanilla
1/4 tsp. orange flavoring
1/4 tsp. lemon flavoring
Dash of salt
2 boxes powdered sugar
Food coloring as needed

Beat Crisco with mixer until fluffy; add flavoring and salt. Alternate adding sugar and water just a little at a time until all ingredients are well mixed. Add color desired in small portions as needed and decorate.

Shirley Robertson
Harpeth Council

LEMON GLAZE

Mix 1 cup of powdered sugar and juice of 1 lemon. Pour over cake when cool.

Inda Adams
Andrew Jackson Council

LEMON CAKE FILLING OR TOPPING
("Very Tart Taste")

1 c. sugar
1 stick butter/margarine
1/2 c. lemon juice (takes
   about 6 good size lemons)
6 egg yolks (do not use
   whites)

Mix all ingredients together. Cook mixture in a double boiler until it will coat a spoon with good consistency. A wooden spoon best serves this purpose than metal. Should be like a pudding mix when cooked. You may add some grated lemon peel for garnishment. This topping may be poured over a pound cake or over hot gingerbread. Best poured over a sweetbread baked in a loaf pan or a casserole dish.

Nell Young
Harpeth Council

NEVER FAIL FUDGE ICING

Melt in saucepan 1 stick margarine; add:

2 c. sugar   1/2 c. milk
1/3 c. cocoa (extra dark)

Let come to a good rolling boil and boil for 1 minute. Remove from heat; add 1 teaspoon almond flavoring (I prefer vanilla). Cool a few minutes in cold water, then beat well and spread on cake. Will ice two 9 inch layers.

Jean Huggins
Harpeth Council

NEVER FAIL FUDGE ICING

Melt in a saucepan 1/4 pound butter; add:

2 c. white sugar   1/2 c. sweet milk
1/2 c. cocoa

Let come to a good boil; boil for 1 minute. Remove from heat; add 1 teaspoon almond or vanilla flavoring. Cool a few minutes, then beat well and spread on cake.

Lillian Reynolds
Harpeth Council

NEVER-FAIL MERINGUE

1/2 c. water, boiling   3 egg whites
1 Tbsp. cornstarch, mixed   6 Tbsp. sugar
   with 1 Tbsp. water

Add dissolved cornstarch to boiling water, making a paste; let paste cool. Beat egg whites stiff; add sugar,

1 tablespoon at a time. Add cornstarch paste, 1 tablespoon at a time. Beat until peaks form.

Frances R. Lauderdale
Memphis Downtown Council

WHITE ICING

1 heaping c. Crisco
1 box powdered sugar

2 Tbsp. hot water
1 tsp. vanilla flavoring

Mix with mixer until smooth. Good on any cakes. This icing is used by bakeries.

Sylvia Kaffer
Clarksville Council

HOMEMADE ICE CREAM

7 egg yolks, well beaten
2 c. sugar
3 Tbsp. vanilla extract

1 can Eagle Brand sweetened
   condensed milk
1/2 tsp. salt

Mix the above ingredients well, then add enough homogenized milk to fill a 1 gallon freezer. Mix well and freeze to desired consistency.

Elvie Coffman
Harpeth Council

HOMEMADE ICE CREAM

2 cans Eagle Brand milk
4 eggs
1 c. sugar
2 tsp. vanilla

Chocolate syrup (optional)
Bananas (optional)
Strawberries (optional)
Peaches (optional)

Blend above ingredients together in a blender; blend until smooth. Pour mixture into ice cream freezer and add enough regular milk to make a gallon. Freeze by freezer directions.

Cheryl V. Alderson
Columbia Council

514

OLD FASHIONED HOMEMADE ICE CREAM

6 eggs
3 c. sugar
1 tsp. vanilla

2-3 c. fruit
Approx. 3/4 gal. milk

Beat eggs until creamy; add sugar to milk and stir well. Add eggs, fruit and vanilla; mix well. Pour into freezer container within 2 inches of top; freeze.

Inda Adams
Andrew Jackson Council

REFRIGERATOR ICE CREAM

2 eggs
1/2 c. sugar
1/2 c. white syrup
1 c. Pet milk (or cream)

1 1/2 c. milk
1 c. fruit (optional)
1 tsp. vanilla

Let freeze until nearly solid. Remove from freezer; beat with mixer. Return to freezer for about 1 hour longer, or until frozen to firmness you desire.

Joyce Mattice
Harpeth Council

BANANA ICE CREAM

4 eggs
2 1/2 c. sugar
4 c. milk

4 c. heavy whipping cream
1/2 tsp. salt
3 tsp. vanilla
8-10 bananas, mashed

Beat eggs until frothy. Add sugar, then the heavy cream, milk, salt and vanilla. Fold in the bananas. Put in freezer and freeze.

Inda Adams
Andrew Jackson Council

BITS O' BRICKLE ICE CREAM AND SAUCE

2 c. graham cracker crumbs
1 stick melted butter or oleo
1/2 (7.8 oz.) bag bits o'
  brickle

1/2 gal. vanilla ice cream,
  softened to spoon easily,
  but not melted

1489-81

Mix graham cracker crumbs and oleo. Pat in bottom of 9x13 inch pan. Spoon 1/2 of softened ice cream over graham cracker crumbs. Spoon 1/2 bag of bits o' brickle on top. Heap on remaining ice cream; freeze.

Sauce:

1 1/2 c. sugar
1 c. evaporated milk
Remaining 1/2 bag bits o' brickle

1/4 c. butter or oleo
1/4 c. light corn syrup
Dash of salt

Combine sugar, milk, butter, syrup and dash of salt. Bring to boil over low heat; boil 1 minute. Remove from heat and add remaining bits o' brickle. Cool, stirring occasionally; chill. To serve: Stir sauce well and spoon over cut-out squares.

Jan Morrow
Columbia Council

BROWNIE-PEANUT BUTTER ICE CREAM

2 c. milk
1 c. sugar
1 c. peanut butter
1/4 tsp. salt

4 c. light cream
1 c. chopped, salted peanuts
1 Tbsp. vanilla

Have 2 cups crumbled brownies (purchased from grocer's bakery or freezer section or make them from a mix).
In a blender container, combine milk, sugar, peanut butter and salt. Cover; blend till smooth. Transfer to a large bowl. Stir in cream, peanuts and vanilla. Freeze in ice cream freezer according to manufacturer's directions. Stir in brownies. If desired, cover and freeze several hours to ripen. Makes 2 quarts.

Leslie Stephens
Harpeth Council

BUTTER PECAN ICE CREAM

3 Tbsp. margarine
1 c. chopped pecans
4 eggs
2 c. sugar

3 tsp. vanilla
1 (13 oz.) can evaporated milk
1 can Eagle Brand milk
1/2 gal. sweet milk

Melt margarine. Add pecans; set aside. Beat eggs with sugar; add vanilla. Mix all ingredients and pour into freezer can. Add sweet milk. Makes 1 gallon.

Reba Gray
Harpeth Council

CHOCOLATE ICE CREAM

1 qt. milk	2 c. sugar
1 c. cocoa	1 qt. whipping cream
1 c. light corn syrup	1 Tbsp. vanilla extract
5 eggs	

In 2 quart saucepan, combine 2 cups milk, cocoa and corn syrup. Bring to a boil over medium heat, stirring constantly; cool. In a large mixing bowl, beat eggs until foamy; gradually beat in sugar. Add cocoa mixture. Stir in 2 cups milk, cream and vanilla; chill. Churn-freeze. Makes 1 gallon.

Carolyn Mitchell
Memphis Downtown Council

EASY HOMEMADE CHOCOLATE ICE CREAM

1 (14 oz.) can Eagle Brand sweetened condensed milk (not evaporated milk)	2/3 c. Hershey's syrup
	2 c. (1 pt.) whipping cream, whipped

In large bowl, stir together condensed milk and syrup. Fold in whipped cream. Pour into aluminum foil lined 9x5 inch loaf pan; cover. Freeze 6 hours or until firm. Scoop ice cream from pan or remove from pan; peel off foil and slice. Return leftovers to freezer. (The above recipe can be used to make pies instead of ice cream.) Makes about 1 1/2 quarts.

Judy Christopher
Harpeth Council

CHOCOLATE ICE CREAM

2 tsp. vanilla	2 1/2 c. sugar
2 qt. half & half	1 (16 oz.) jar Hershey's milk fudge topping
1 pt. whipping cream, whipped	1/2 bag miniature marshmallows

1489-81

In a saucepan, put marshmallows, sugar and enough of the half & half milk to mix together and moisten the ingredients. Add all the chocolate. Simmer until sugar and marshmallows have dissolved completely. Whip the whipping cream in a large bowl. Pour the chocolate and marshmallow mixture and the remaining half & half and vanilla together; mix well. Fold in the whipping cream and put in hand crank or electric freezer and freeze.

Inda Adams
Andrew Jackson Council

MILKY WAY ICE CREAM

8 regular Milky Way bars
2 c. milk
5 eggs
1 1/2 c. sugar

2 tsp. vanilla
1 large can evaporated milk
1 small can evaporated milk
1 1/2 c. half & half

In a heavy saucepan, melt candy bars in the 2 cups milk; cool. Beat eggs; add sugar and beat well again. Add vanilla, remaining milk and half & half. Combine mixtures; mix well. Pour into gallon freezer can. Add extra milk, if needed, to come up to the full line. Freeze according to freezer directions.

Barbara S. Stanfill
Harpeth Council

PEACH ICE CREAM

2 eggs
1/2 c. sugar
1 Tbsp. vanilla
1/4 tsp. salt

1 small (5.33 oz.) can
Carnation milk
1 can Eagle Brand milk
3 c. Purity milk

Mix above ingredients with mixer. Pour in freezer container. Add 2 cups sweetened crushed peaches and 1 Orange Crush. Stir well; ready to freeze. Makes 1/2 gallon plus 2 cups.

Jean Hunt
Nashboro Council

PEACH ICE CREAM

.1 large can evaporated milk
1 tsp. lemon juice
5 eggs, beaten
2 c. sugar

3 1/2 c. peaches, sliced and
    sweetened
Milk (enough to fill freezer)
2 tsp. vanilla

Chill and whip evaporated milk. Beat eggs and sugar until fluffy. Add the whipped milk, peaches and regular milk to fill to the freezer line.

Inda Adams
Andrew Jackson Council

DELUXE PEACH ICE CREAM

6 c. mashed peaches
1 c. sugar
3 eggs
1 1/2 c. sugar
2 Tbsp. plain flour

1/2 tsp. salt
1 qt. milk
1 c. whipping cream
1 Tbsp. vanilla extract

Combine peaches and 1 cup sugar; stir well and set aside. Beat eggs until frothy. Combine 1 1/2 cups sugar, flour and salt; stir well. Gradually add sugar mixture to eggs, beating until thick. Add milk; mix well. Pour egg mixture into large saucepan. Cook over low heat, stirring constantly, until mixture coats spoon, about 15 minutes. Remove from heat and cool. Stir in cream and vanilla. Add peaches, stirring well. Pour mixture into chilled freezer can of 1 gallon freezer. Freeze according to manufacturer's instructions. Let ripen at least 1 hour.

Beverly Pettigrew
Harpeth Council

PEANUT FUDGE RIPPLE ICE CREAM

3 eggs
1 3/4 c. sugar
3 c. milk
3 c. whipping cream

2 Tbsp. vanilla extract
3/4 c. chopped, salted
    peanuts
1 c. fudge sauce

In a large mixing bowl, beat eggs until foamy. Gradually add sugar; beat until thickened. Add milk, cream and vanilla; mix thoroughly. Stir in peanuts; chill. Churn-freeze. After freezing, transfer ice cream to plastic freezer container, alternating layers of ice cream with cooled fudge sauce. Swirl each layer with spatula for marbled effect. Makes 3 quarts.

Carolyn Mitchell
Memphis Downtown Council

PEPPERMINT STICK ICE CREAM

3 eggs
3/4 c. sugar
3 c. milk
3 c. whipping cream
1 Tbsp. vanilla extract

1/4 tsp. salt
1 1/2 c. (about 12 oz.)
crushed peppermint stick
candy
Red food color

In a large mixing bowl, beat eggs until foamy. Gradually add sugar; beat until thickened. Add milk, cream, vanilla and salt; mix thoroughly. Stir in 1 cup candy; add food color. Chill; churn-freeze. After freezing and before ripening, stir in remaining 1/2 cup candy. Makes 3 quarts.

Carolyn Mitchell
Memphis Downtown Council

PRALINE ICE CREAM

3 eggs
1 3/4 c. firmly packed
  light brown sugar
3 c. milk
3 c. whipping cream

1 Tbsp. vanilla extract
1/4 tsp. maple flavor
  (optional)
1 c. chopped, salted pecans

In a large mixing bowl, beat eggs until foamy. Gradually add sugar; beat until thickened. Add milk, cream, vanilla and maple flavor; mix thoroughly. Stir in pecans; chill. Churn-freeze. Makes 3 quarts.

Carolyn Mitchell
Memphis Downtown Council

TOFFEE CRUNCH ICE CREAM

3 eggs
1 1/4 c. sugar
3 c. milk
3 c. whipping cream

1 Tbsp. vanilla extract
1/4 tsp. salt
2 c. (about 3/4 lb.) crushed
  toffee candy

In a large mixing bowl, beat eggs until foamy. Gradually add sugar; beat until thickened. Add milk, cream, vanilla and salt; mix thoroughly. Stir in 1 cup crushed toffee; chill. Churn-freeze. After freezing, before ripening, stir in remaining cup of toffee. Makes 1 gallon.

Carolyn Mitchell
Memphis Downtown Council

BASIC VANILLA ICE CREAM

2 large eggs
2 cans sweetened condensed
  milk
1 qt. half & half

1 pt. whipping cream
2 tsp. vanilla
Milk

In a large bowl, beat eggs well. Add the condensed milk, half & half, whipping cream and vanilla. Pour into ice cream freezer and fill with regular milk to freezer line. If fruit is added, add the fruit first and fill with milk. You may use any type of fruit or chocolate.

Inda Adams
Andrew Jackson Council

COUNTRY VANILLA ICE CREAM

5 eggs
2 1/4 c. sugar
2 c. cream

1 large can condensed milk
5 tsp. vanilla
1/2 tsp. salt
Milk (about 6 c.)

Add sugar gradually to beaten eggs. Continue to beat until mixture is very stiff. Add remaining ingredients; mix thoroughly. Pour into gallon freezer and freeze by your freezer instructions. (Fruit may be added if you desire, about 3 or 4 cups.)

Joyce Mattice
Harpeth Council

HOMEMADE VANILLA ICE CREAM

4 eggs
3 c. sugar

3 small cans evaporated milk
1/2 gal. milk
2 Tbsp. vanilla

Beat eggs and sugar. Combine remaining ingredients; pour into freezer.

Connie M. Davis
Knoxville Council

LILA CLACK'S VANILLA ICE CREAM

6 eggs	1/2 tsp. salt
4 c. whole milk	4 c. heavy cream
2 c. sugar	5 tsp. vanilla

Combine eggs and milk in a large saucepan; beat with a wire whisk until blended. Add sugar and salt. Cook over a low heat, stirring constantly, until thick, about 10 minutes. Let cool; add cream and vanilla. Pour into 1 gallon crank freezer; freeze till firm.

Mary Jane Bailey
Green Hills Council

NANNIE'S GRAPE SHERBET

1 pt. Welch's grape juice	1 qt. milk
1 c. sugar	

Heat grape juice to lukewarm. Add sugar; stir until sugar dissolves and add milk. Freeze in ice cream freezer. Makes 1/2 gallon.

Marian Molteni
Harpeth Council

ORANGE SHERBET

1 small can crushed pineapple	1 can Eagle Brand milk
	6 bottles Orange Crush

Mix all ingredients together in ice cream freezer. Freeze until hard.

Vivian Renfro
Nashville Council

BIG ORANGE FREEZE
(" Ice Cream Sherbet")

1 can condensed Eagle
  Brand milk
1 large can crushed
  pineapple

6 orange Nehi bottled drink
  (or orange flavored)

Stir and freeze in ice cream freezer.

Mrs. Lamar (Jean) Edwards
Knoxville Council

ORANGE SHERBET

2 qt. carbonated orange
  drink
1 can Eagle Brand milk

1 can water
1 small can frozen lemonade

Pour ingredients directly into freezer container.
Makes 1 gallon.

Reba Gray
Harpeth Council

CASSEROLES

& VEGETABLES

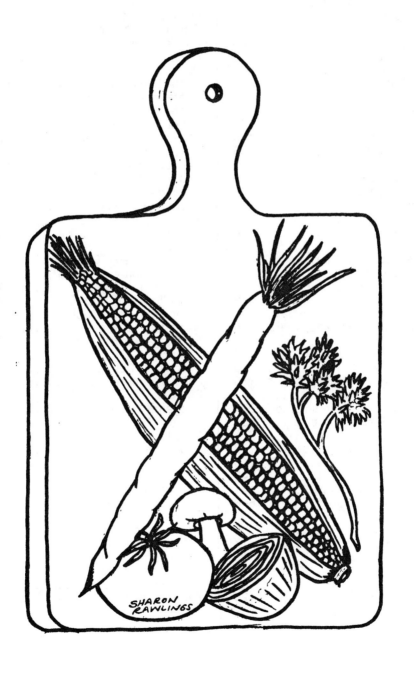

CALORIE CHART OF VEGETABLES

Artichoke:
  1 lg 88
  hearts, frozen, 3½ oz 26
Asparagus, 1 cup 35
Beans:
  green, fresh, 1 cup 35
  kidney, dried, 1 cup 635
  limas, dried, 1 cup 656
  navy, dried, 1 cup 697
  soy, dried ½ cup 95
  wax, fresh, 1 cup 30
Beets, 1 cup 58
Broccoli, 2 lg stalks 145
Brussels sprouts, 1 cup 55
Cabbage:
  green, 1 cup 36
  red, 1 cup 28
Carrots:
  raw, 1 whole 30
  cooked, 1 cup 50
Cauliflower:
  fresh, cooked, 1 cup 30
  raw, chopped, 1 cup 31
Celery, 1 lg stalk 7
Chard, 1 lb 113
Chestnuts, 1 cup 310
Collards, fresh, cooked, 1 cup .. 65
Corn:
  cream-style, ½ cup 100
  fresh, 1 ear 70
  whole kernel, ½ cup 85
Cucumber, 1 lg 45
Dandelion greens, fresh, 1 lb . 204
Eggplant, boiled, 1 cup 38
Endive:
  Belgian, 1 head 8
  curly, 1 cup 10
Kale, fresh, cooked, 1 cup 45
Kohlrabi, fresh, 1 cup 41
Lentils, dried, 1 cup 646
Lettuce:
  Bibb, 1 cup 8
  iceberg, 1 cup 7
  romaine, 1 cup 10
Mushrooms:
  canned, 1 cup 40
  fresh, 1 lb 125

Mustard greens:
  cooked, 1 cup 30
  fresh, 1 lb 141
Okra, fresh, 1 cup 36
Onions, fresh, 1 cup 65
Parsley, fresh, 1 cup 26
Parsnips, cooked, 1 cup 82
Peas:
  black-eyed, fresh, 1 cup 184
  green, fresh, 1 cup 122
Peppers:
  hot chili, ½ cup 18
  sweet green, 1 med 14
  sweet red, 1 med 19
Potatoes, sweet:
  baked, 1 med 155
  candied, 1 med 295
  canned, ½ cup 110
Potatoes, white:
  baked, 1 sm 93
  boiled, 1 sm 70
  French-fried, 10 pieces 175
  hashed brown, ½ cup 177
  mashed, ½ cup 90
  scalloped, ½ cup 120
Pumpkin, canned, 1 cup 81
Radishes, 10 whole 14
Rutabagas, fresh, 1 cup 87
Spinach:
  cooked, 1 cup 40
  fresh, 1 cup 15
Sprouts:
  alfalfa, 1 cup 10
  Mung bean, fresh, 1 cup 37
Squash:
  summer, fresh, 1 cup 25
  winter, mashed, 1 cup 129
Tomatoes:
  canned, 1 cup 50
  green, fresh, 1 lb 99
  ripe, fresh, 1 lb 88
Turnip Greens:
  fresh, cooked, 1 cup 30
Turnips, fresh, 1 cup 39
Watercress, 1 bunch 20
Water chestnuts, canned, 1 cup .70
Zucchini, fresh, 1 cup 22

CRUMB TOPPING FOR VEGETABLES

1 c. Bisquick baking mix
1/2 c. grated Parmesan
   cheese

2 Tbsp. margarine or butter,
   melted
Hot cooked vegetables or
   creamed vegetables

Heat oven to 400°. Mix baking mix and cheese in ungreased rectangular pan, 13x9x2 inches. Drizzle margarine over top. Bake until light golden brown, 8 to 10 minutes. Gently stir until well blended. Cool completely; break up, if necessary. Sprinkle over vegetables. Makes about 1 1/2 cups topping.

High Altitude Directions (3500 to 6500 feet): No adjustments necessary.

Pat Ferguson
Harpeth Council

CINNAMON APPLES

10 firm meated apples
3 c. sugar
1/2 tsp. cinnamon or cloves
   or mixture of both
2 Tbsp. red food coloring

1/4 c. or less water
8 oz. creamed cheese, room
   temperature
2 Tbsp. milk
Nuts

Wash, core, peel and cut apples in halves crosswise. Combine sugar, cinnamon, food coloring and water in large skillet. Bring mixture to a boil. Place apples in hot syrup and reduce heat to a gentle boil. Cook apples until transparent; turn apples over and cook until completely tender and transparent. Place cooked apples in serving dish; cool. Cream cheese and milk together; beat until fluffy. Mix in nuts. Add to center of apples. Pour cooled syrup around apples and garnish with celery leaves. (If you have too much syrup, it is good on toast or pancakes.) Makes 20 servings.

Peggy Hunter
Harpeth Council

FRIED APPLES

3 Tbsp. butter or margarine
1/3 c. sugar
2-4 Tbsp. sugar

3 medium size unpeeled, tart
apples, cored, quartered
and sliced

Melt butter in medium size skillet over moderate heat. Add apples to skillet; cover and cook 5 minutes or until they are juicy. Turn apples; sprinkle with the 1/3 cup sugar. Reduce heat to moderately low. Cover apples; cook 4 or 5 minutes. Uncover and cook until sugar is absorbed and apples are lightly brown on bottom, 3 or 4 minutes. Remove from heat; sprinkle apples with 2 to 4 tablespoons sugar. Serve hot.

Mary Crabtree
Knoxville Council

ASPARAGUS CASSEROLE

1/2 c. chopped onion,
   sauteed in oil
1/2 c. chopped celery,
   sauteed in oil

1 c. raw rice, cooked in 2 c. water
1 pkg. cooked asparagus

Add:
1 can cream of chicken soup
1 can cream of mushroom
   soup

18 oz. Cheez Whiz
Cracker crumbs

Bake at 400° for 12 minutes. Leave a little Cheez Whiz to put on top and cracker crumbs on top of Cheez Whiz.

Dorothy Bryant
Clarksville Council

ASPARAGUS CASSEROLE

2 cans asparagus
3 boiled eggs
1 small can chopped
   mushrooms

1 1/2 c. bread crumbs
White Sauce with 1 c. grated
   cheese added

White Sauce: Cook until thickened and add cheese -

2 Tbsp. margarine
2 Tbsp. flour

1/4 tsp. salt
1 c. milk

Mix all ingredients together, except crumbs. Put in casserole with crumbs on top. Bake at 350° until heated through and crumbs are slightly browned.

Mrs. Adelene Queenan
Harpeth Council

ASPARAGUS CASSEROLE

1 large can asparagus, well drained
1/2 c. butter, melted
2 c. cracker crumbs
1/2 lb. Cheddar cheese, grated
1 can cream of mushroom soup
1/2 c. chopped pecans

Mix cracker crumbs and melted butter well. In casserole or baking dish, place a layer of 1/2 the buttered crumbs, 1/2 the grated cheese and a layer of asparagus spears. Sprinkle with chopped pecans. Top with the remainder of grated cheese. Cover with remainder of buttered cracker crumbs. Bake 20 minutes in preheated oven at 350°. Serves 6-8 people.

Jane Wohlbold
Green Hills Council

ASPARAGUS AND PEA CASSEROLE

1 can peas, drained
12-16 soda crackers, crushed
1 can cream of mushroom soup
1/4 c. slivered almonds
1 can asparagus (save juice)
Butter
Cheddar cheese, shredded

Grease or butter pan. Put most of crackers in bottom of pan. Add peas and asparagus. Spread cream of mushroom soup over vegetables; sprinkle with almonds. Add 2 tablespoons asparagus juice; dot with butter. Spread shredded cheese on top. Add remaining cracker crumbs on top. Bake at 350° for 30 minutes. Serves 6 or more.

Margaret Minke
Harpeth Council

ASPARAGUS-PEA CASSEROLE

3 Tbsp. butter
3 Tbsp. flour
1 2/3 c. milk
2 (12 1/2 oz.) cans
  asparagus, drained

1 (17 oz.) can English peas,
  drained
3 hard cooked eggs, sliced
1 c. cheese, grated

Make white sauce of butter, flour and milk. Add 1/3 cup cheese; stir until cheese is melted. In a deep, greased casserole, arrange layers of peas, asparagus, eggs and white sauce; repeat layers. Garnish with remaining cheese. Put corn flakes or cracker crumbs on top. Bake at 325° for 30 minutes. Serves 6-8.

Mrs. Bob Unkenholz
Harpeth Council

ASPARAGUS QUICHE

4 eggs
1 1/2 c. milk
1/4 tsp. nutmeg
1/4 tsp. hot pepper sauce
1/2 tsp. salt
1/4 tsp. pepper

1 c. shredded Swiss cheese
1 (9 inch) unbaked pie shell
1 (10 oz.) pkg. frozen
  asparagus spears, cooked
  and drained

Preheat oven to 400°. In a large bowl, beat 4 eggs. Slightly beat in milk, salt, pepper, nutmeg and hot pepper sauce until well blended. Sprinkle cheese over bottom of pie shell. Arrange asparagus spears, cooled and drained, over cheese; pour in egg mixture. Place in oven and reduce heat to 375°. Bake 35 to 40 minutes or until knife comes out clean. Let cool for 15 minutes; cut into wedges.

Tricia Owens
Harpeth Council

ASPARAGUS-TUNA CASSEROLE

1 (5 oz.) pkg. fine egg
  noodles
1 (6 1/2 oz.) can white
  chunk style tuna
1 (14 1/2 oz.) can green
  asparagus (pieces)

1 can condensed cream of
  mushroom soup
3/4 c. grated American
  cheese
1/2 c. dry bread crumbs
Chopped parsley

Prepare noodles according to package directions. Line an 8x10 inch casserole dish with the drained noodles. Top noodles with remaining ingredients in order given. Sprinkle with paprika; cover and freeze. Place in cold oven. Turn oven on to 325°. Bake until hot and bubbly, about 1 1/2 hours.

Debbie Bullock
Harpeth Council

BAKED BEANS

1 medium onion, chopped
1 large can pork and beans
1 small can dried lima beans
Generous dash of soy sauce

Worcestershire sauce
1 (8 oz.) can barbecue sauce
  with onions
1 c. brown syrup or brown
  sugar

Combine all ingredients. Lay bacon strips on top and bake at 375° for 1 hour or until done.

Pat Carpenter
Nashville Council

CHUCK WAGON BEANS

1/2 lb. bacon
3 lb. ground beef
3 c. chopped onion
1 c. chopped celery
2 beef bouillon cubes
2/3 c. boiling water
1 1/2 Tbsp. garlic, minced

1 1/2 c. catsup
3 Tbsp. prepared mustard
1/2 tsp. salt
1/2 tsp. pepper
2 (29 oz.) cans molasses
  style baked beans

In Dutch oven, fry bacon till crisp; set aside. Drain fat. In same pan, cook ground beef, onion and celery till meat is brown, onion and celery are tender. Dissolve bouillon cubes in boiling water; add to meat mixture with remaining ingredients. Cover and bake 1 hour and 15 minutes in 375° oven till hot and bubbly. Crumble bacon over beans. Makes a lot of beans; you may want to halve the recipe.

Mae Hallum
Memphis Council

HAWAIIAN STYLE BEANS

1/4 lb. cooked ham, cut into pieces
1 (21 oz.) can pork and beans
1/2 tsp. dry mustard

1/4 c. firmly packed brown sugar
1 Tbsp. chopped onion
1 c. drained pineapple chunks

Combine all ingredients and put into a greased 1 1/2 quart casserole dish. Cover and bake at 350° for 1 hour. Serves 4-6.

Frances R. Lauderdale
Memphis Downtown Council

PINTO BEANS

1 smoked ham hock
1 tsp. salt
Water
2 c. dried pinto beans

1 c. coarsely chopped, peeled onion
1/4 tsp. pepper

Place ham hock and salt in large Dutch oven or saucepot. Add enough water to cover. Cook ham, covered, over moderately high heat until water comes to a boil. Reduce heat to moderately low and cook 30 minutes. Add beans, onion and pepper to ham and cook, covered, for approximately 3 1/2 hours or until beans are tender. Remove meat from the ham bone and serve a little of the meat with each serving. Serves 6.

Mary Crabtree
Knoxville Council

DISTRESS-LESS WHITE BEANS

1 lb. dried white beans
1 1/2 Tbsp. salt
1 Tbsp. sugar
1 tsp. ginger

Hunk of hog jowl or ham hocks
Red pepper to taste
10 c. water

Combine all ingredients in large covered pot. Bring to boil; reduce heat to a gentle boil. Cook until beans are tender. Be sure to stir occasionally; add more water, if needed. Use ginger in all dried beans to sweeten the stomach. It cannot be tasted in the beans. Also, use ginger in your baked beans.

Peggy Hunter
Harpeth Council

RANCH STYLE BEANS

2 lb. ground beef,
   browned and drained
1 env. onion soup mix
2 (1 lb.) cans pork-n-
   beans
1 (1 lb.) can red kidney
   beans, drained

2 tsp. vinegar
1/2 c. water
1 c. ketchup
2 Tbsp. mustard
2 Tbsp. honey

Heat to boiling in crock-pot and simmer for 30 minutes.

Kathryn Baxley
Morristown Council #12

RANCH-STYLE BEANS

1 (16 oz.) pkg. dry pinto
   beans
Water
2 Tbsp. salad oil
2 medium onions, sliced
2 garlic cloves, minced
1 (10 oz.) can whole green
   chilies, drained and cut
   into bite size pieces

1 or 2 canned jalapeno
   chilies, diced
1 Tbsp. salt
1 tsp. sugar
1 tsp. ground cumin
1 (28 oz.) can tomatoes
1/2 tsp. oregano leaves
2 c. (8 oz.) shredded
   Monterey Jack cheese

About 3 hours before serving: Rinse beans in running cold water; discard any stones or shriveled beans. In 5 quart Dutch oven over high heat, heat beans and 8 cups water to boiling; cook 3 minutes. Remove Dutch oven from heat; cover and let stand 1 hour. Drain and rinse beans; set aside. In same Dutch oven over medium heat, in hot salad oil, cook onions and garlic until tender, stirring occasionally. Add beans, chilies, salt, sugar, cumin and 3 cups water. Over high heat, heat to boiling. Reduce heat to low; cover and simmer 1 hour, stirring occasionally. Add tomatoes with their liquid and oregano, stirring to mix well and break up tomatoes. Over high heat, heat to boiling. Reduce heat to low; cover and simmer about 30 minutes longer or until beans are tender. Stir in half of the cheese and cook until cheese is melted, stirring occasionally. Spoon bean mixture into large bowl; sprinkle with remaining cheese. Makes 6 servings.

Joyce Mattice
Harpeth Council

RED BEANS AND RICE
(New Orleans Style)

2 c. chopped onions	1/8 tsp. cayenne pepper
1/2 c. chopped green pepper	2 whole bay leaves
1 1/3 Tbsp. finely minced garlic	1/2 tsp. dried thyme
	1/8 tsp. dried basil
2 Tbsp. finely minced parsley	2 qt. cold water (approx.)
	Boiled rice
1 Tbsp. salt	1/2 tsp. ground pepper

Soak 2 pounds dried red (kidney) beans overnight in cold water. Drain soaked beans and put them along with other ingredients into a large heavy pot, adding just enough cold water to cover. Bring to a boil; add 2 tablespoons bacon fat or ham bone. Lower heat to simmer for 2 1/2 to 3 hours or until beans are tender and a thick natural gravy has formed. Add water during cooking time to keep beans covered. Stir often; don't let stick. Last hour, cut up a package of smoked sausage or kielbasa and add to bean mixture. Salt and pepper to taste. Serve over boiled rice with a loaf of French bread. Bon appetite. Serves 8 or more and freezes well.

Gretchen and Louis Copp
Harpeth Council

BEEF CASSEROLE

1 lb. ground beef	1/4 c. chopped green pepper
2 Tbsp. shortening	1 (5 oz.) pkg. elbow macaroni
1 medium onion, chopped	Salt and pepper to taste
2 c. canned tomatoes	1 can cream of mushroom soup
1 Tbsp. catsup	1 c. grated Cheddar cheese
1 Tbsp. steak sauce	

Brown beef in shortening in heavy skillet until all red color disappears. Add onion, tomatoes, catsup, steak sauce and green pepper; simmer 30 minutes. Cook macaroni according to directions on box. Combine macaroni and ground beef mixture in a 2 quart baking dish. Season to taste. Gently spoon mushroom soup into mixture, lifting from bottom. Bake at 350° for 30 minutes. Sprinkle cheese over top for the last 10 minutes.

Mary McCracken
Columbia Council

BEEF CASSEROLE

1 lb. ground beef
1 can tomato soup
1 (5 1/2 oz.) pkg. noodles

1 can cream of mushroom
  soup
1/2 stick grated Cheddar
  cheese

Brown meat and cook noodles until desired tendency. Mix soup and 1/2 cheese with meat. Add noodles. Pour in baking dish and cover with remaining cheese. Bake at 300° for 30 minutes or until bubbly.

Joyce Hill
Harpeth Council

BEEF AND CHICKEN CASSEROLE

Arrange 8 chicken breasts, boned, in a large buttered dish. Break 1 package chipped beef into bits and scatter over chicken. Mix 1 can mushroom soup and 1 cup sour cream; pour over chicken and beef. Sprinkle with Bac-O's or bits of bacon. Bake for 3 hours at 275°. Serve over wild rice. Serves 8.

M. Carolyn Hunter
Harpeth Council

BEEF GARDEN CASSEROLE

1 medium onion, chopped
1 lb. ground beef
3/4 tsp. salt
1/4 tsp. pepper
1 (10 1/2 oz.) can tomato
  soup

1 (1 lb.) can (2 c.) cut
  green beans, drained
1 c. whole kernel corn,
  undrained
1 recipe Cheese Spins

Cook onion in small amount of fat until tender but not brown. Add ground beef, salt and pepper; brown lightly. Add green beans, corn and tomato soup. Pour into 1 1/2 quart casserole. Top with Cheese Spins.

Cheese Spins for Beef Garden Casserole:

1 c. sifted self-rising flour	1/3 c. milk
2 Tbsp. shortening	1/2 c. grated sharp Cheddar cheese

Cut shortening into flour; stir in milk. Turn out on floured board. Knead lightly and roll out into a rectangle. Spread cheese over biscuit dough. Roll jelly roll fashion and cut into 3/4 inch slices; place on top of mixture in casserole. Bake 15 to 20 minutes in preheated 425° oven.

A. Butler
Nashboro Council

BEEF STUFFED TOMATOES

6 large tomatoes	2 tsp. chili powder
1 Tbsp. salad oil	1 1/4 tsp. salt
1/3 c. chopped onion	2 (1 oz.) slices process
1/4 c. chopped green pepper	American cheese, cut into
1 lb. ground lean beef	12 small strips

Hold tomatoes at room temperature until fully ripe. Cut a thin slice from stem end of each tomato; scoop out pulp (use in soups, sauces, etc.). Invert shells to drain. In a medium skillet, heat oil; add onion and green pepper. Cook until onion is golden, 2 minutes. Add ground beef; brown about 5 minutes. Spoon off any fat. Stir in chili powder and salt. Place tomatoes in a shallow baking pan. Fill with beef mixture; top with cheese strips in crisscross fashion. Bake in a preheated 350° oven until hot and cheese is melted, 12 to 15 minutes. Yield: 6 portions.

Ruth L. Cole
Harpeth Council

DAIRY BEEF BAKE

1 (5 oz.) pkg. medium noodles	1/4 tsp. garlic salt
1 lb. ground beef	1/8 tsp. black pepper
1 (8 oz.) can tomato sauce	1/2 c. chopped onion
1 tsp. salt	3/4 c. shredded Cheddar cheese
1 c. cottage cheese	1 c. sour cream

534

Cook noodles according to package directions; drain and rinse. Saute ground beef until lightly browned; drain. Add tomato sauce, salt, garlic salt and pepper; simmer 5 minutes. Combine cottage cheese, sour cream, onion and noodles. Spread half of noodle mixture in a lightly greased 2 quart casserole; top with half of meat sauce. Repeat layers; top with cheese. Bake at 350° for 25 to 30 minutes or until bubbly and cheese is melted. Yield: 6 to 8 servings.

Evelyn B. Bean
Harpeth Council

FRENCH OVEN BEEF STEW

2 lb. stew beef, cut in
1 1/2 inch cubes
2 medium onions, cut in
eighths
2 stalks celery, cut into
diagonal slices
4 medium carrots, cut into
thick slices

1 medium can tomato puree or
sauce
1/3 c. quick-cooking tapioca
1 Tbsp. sugar
1 Tbsp. salt
1/2 tsp. basil
1/4 tsp. pepper
3 or 4 medium potatoes, cut
into large chunks

Combine stew beef, onions, celery and carrots in a 2 1/2 quart casserole. Mix tapioca, sugar, salt, basil and pepper into tomato puree or sauce and pour over meat and vegetables. Cover and bake for 5 hours at 250°. Add potatoes and 1 cup water, if necessary. Stir; cover and continue cooking for 1 hour or until potatoes are done.

Sheila Fleming
East Memphis Council

SUE BOOHER'S BEEF GARDEN CASSEROLE

1 lb. ground beef
1 medium onion, chopped
1 tsp. salt
1 (16 oz.) can green beans

1 small can whole kernel corn
1 can tomato soup
1 pkg. Doritos
1 small pkg. Cheddar cheese

Brown ground beef and onion; mix all ingredients. Pour in casserole dish; top with crushed Doritos. Sprinkle with shredded cheese. Bake at 400° for 20 minutes.

Zoerita Proctor
Nashboro Council

BREAKFAST CASSEROLE

1 lb. sausage, browned
  and drained
6 eggs, beaten with 1 tsp.
  salt

2 c. milk
1/2 tsp. dry mustard
1 stick oleo, melted

Layer sausage in bottom of 9x13 inch Pyrex dish. Add 1 cup grated cheese and the other ingredients. Let stand all night in refrigerator. Bake 35 minutes at 350°.

Imogene Chesher
Knoxville Council

BROCCOLI CASSEROLE

2 pkg. frozen chopped
  broccoli, cooked
1 small grated onion,
  cooked soft in butter

1 lb. grated Velveeta cheese
1 can cream of mushroom
  soup, undiluted
Several dashes of garlic
  powder

Stir soup and cheese together. Add onion, broccoli and garlic. Place in ovenproof dish; top with more grated cheese. Bake in oven at 350° till bubbly.

Memphis Downtown Council

BROCCOLI CASSEROLE

1 lb. sausage
1 c. cubed Cheddar cheese
1 can cream of cheese soup

1 can cream of mushroom soup
1/2 c. chopped onion
2 pkg. frozen broccoli
1 can onion rings

Cook sausage in frying pan with chopped onion. Add both cans of soup; let simmer for 20 minutes. Place broccoli in large casserole dish. Add sausage mixture and top with canned onion rings and cubed cheese. Place in 350° oven for 1/2 hour until bubbly and onion rings are golden brown.

Marie B. Watkins
Memphis Council

BROCCOLI CASSEROLE

1 pkg. frozen chopped
  broccoli
1/2 c. mushroom soup
1/2 c. grated Cheddar
  cheese
1 tsp. grated onion

1 egg, well beaten
1/2 c. mayonnaise (do not
  use salad dressing)
Cheese crackers for crumbs
Salt and pepper to taste

Cook broccoli in salt water for 5 minutes; strain. Combine with all other ingredients, except crackers; place in casserole. Cover with crumbs made from cheese crackers. Bake in oven at 400° for 30 minutes. Serves 6.

Jane Wohlbold
Green Hills Council

BROCCOLI CASSEROLE

1 (10 oz.) pkg. frozen
  chopped broccoli
1/2 c. sharp cheese, grated
1/2 c. mayonnaise
1 Tbsp. grated onion

1/2 can cream of chicken
  soup
1 egg, beaten
Salt and pepper to taste
Cheese crackers

Cook broccoli in small amount of boiling water until almost done; drain well. Blend all other ingredients, except cheese crackers; fold in broccoli. Spoon into buttered casserole and sprinkle top with crumbled cheese crackers. Bake at 400° for 20 minutes. Yield: 4 servings.

Jeanette W. Palmer
Harpeth Council

BROCCOLI CASSEROLE

2 boxes frozen chopped
  broccoli, cooked and
  drained
1 c. mayonnaise
2 eggs, beaten

1 medium onion, finely
  chopped
1 can cream of mushroom
  soup
1 c. Cheddar cheese, grated

Cook broccoli 5 minutes; add all other ingredients. Mix well. Pour in a greased casserole. Bake 30 minutes at 350°.

Linda Whitaker
Harpeth Council

BROCCOLI CASSEROLE

1/4 c. chopped onion
6 Tbsp. butter
2 Tbsp. flour
1/2 c. water
8 oz. jar Cheez Whiz

3 eggs, well beaten
2 pkg. frozen broccoli cuts,
  cooked and drained
1 Tbsp. butter
1/2 c. bread crumbs

Simmer onion in 6 tablespoons melted butter in large skillet. Add flour, then water. Cook until it thickens. Add Cheez Whiz, drained broccoli and beaten eggs. Put in greased 1 1/2 quart casserole. Mix bread crumbs with 1 tablespoon melted butter; sprinkle on top of broccoli mixture. Bake, uncovered, at 325° for 30 minutes. Serves 8.
    Note: If refrigerated before baked, bake at 325° for 50-60 minutes.

Judy Desendorf
Harpeth Council

BROCCOLI-CHEESE CASSEROLE

2 medium onions, chopped
1 c. melted butter or
  margarine, divided
2 (10 oz.) cans cream of
  mushroom soup, undiluted
2 (4 oz.) cans chopped
  mushrooms, drained
2 (6 oz.) rolls pasteurized
  process cheese with
  garlic, chopped

2 tsp. chopped parsley
Salt and pepper to taste
1/2 c. slivered almonds
4 (10 oz.) pkg. frozen
  chopped broccoli, partially
  cooked and drained
4 c. herb seasoned stuffing
  mix

Saute onions in 1/2 cup butter until tender. Combine onion, soup, mushrooms, cheese, parsley, salt, pepper, almonds and broccoli; mix well. Spoon into two lightly greased 2 quart casseroles. Combine stuffing mix and 1/2 cup butter; spoon over broccoli mixture. Bake at 350° for 20-30 minutes. Yields 12 to 14 servings.

Sudie Sredonja
East Memphis Council

BROCCOLI ONION DELUXE

2 (10 oz.) pkg. chopped
  broccoli
1 medium onion, chopped
4 Tbsp. margarine
2 Tbsp. flour
1/4 tsp. salt
1/2 tsp. pepper

1 c. milk
1 small pkg. cream cheese,
  cubed
Bread crumbs or Pepperidge
  Farm dressing mix
1 c. Parmesan cheese

Cook broccoli according to directions; drain. In saucepan, melt 2 tablespoons butter; blend in flour, milk, salt and pepper. Cook until thick; blend in cream cheese until smooth. Stir in vegetables. Pour into 1 1/2 quart casserole. Top with Parmesan cheese. Mix the other 2 tablespoons butter with bread crumbs; top casserole. Bake 20 minutes, covered, in 350° oven. Take top off and bake 10 minutes or until crumbs are browned.

Katie Braden
Harpeth Council

BROCCOLI-PEAS CASSEROLE

2 (10 oz.) pkg. frozen
  chopped broccoli
1 (No. 303) can green peas
1 can cream of mushroom
  soup
1 c. mayonnaise
1 tsp. salt

1/2 tsp. pepper
1 c. sharp cheese, grated
1 medium onion, chopped
2 eggs, beaten
1/2 c. crushed, round
  crackers

Cook broccoli according to package directions; drain. Arrange half of cooked broccoli in a 2 quart casserole. Cover with peas. Mix soup, mayonnaise, salt, pepper, cheese, onion and eggs to make sauce. Pour half of sauce over broccoli and peas. Add rest of broccoli; top with remaining sauce. Sprinkle crushed crackers on top. Bake at 350° for 30 minutes. Serves 8.

Margaret Powers
Harpeth Council

BROCCOLI AND RICE CASSEROLE

1 stick oleo
1/2 c. onion, chopped
2 pkg. frozen chopped
   broccoli

1 c. raw rice (not instant)
1 can cream of chicken soup
1 small jar Cheez Whiz

Saute onion in oleo. Cook broccoli for 7-8 minutes. Cook rice as directed on package. Combine all and place in dish sprayed with Pam. Bake 15 minutes at 350°. Can be made the day before and baked when ready to serve. Serves 12.

Linda Kitchens
Green Hills Council

BROCCOLI AND RICE CASSEROLE

2 Tbsp. oil
1 c. chopped onion
1 c. chopped celery
1 pkg. frozen chopped
   broccoli
1 soup can full of milk

1 can cream of chicken soup
   or cream of mushroom soup
   or cream of celery soup
1 small jar Cheez Whiz
Butter to taste
Salt and pepper to taste
2 c. rice, cooked

Thaw broccoli in 1 cup boiling water; drain. In a large skillet, saute onion and celery in 2 tablespoons oil. Add broccoli, soup, milk, Cheez Whiz, rice, butter and seasonings; mix. Turn into baking dish and bake at 350° for 30-40 minutes.

Katie Braden
Harpeth Council

BROCCOLI RICE CASSEROLE

2 boxes frozen chopped
   broccoli
3/4 c. chopped onion
1 c. uncooked instant rice

1 can cream of mushroom soup
1 can cream of chicken soup
3/4 c. chopped celery
1 stick butter, melted
1 small jar cheese spread

Cook broccoli and rice; combine with all other ingredients, except cheese. Place in buttered 13x9 inch baking dish. Dot with cheese spread; bake at 350° for 45 minutes.

Judy Gibson
Harpeth Council

BROCCOLI PUFF

2 (10 oz.) pkg. chopped
   broccoli
3 eggs, separated
1 Tbsp. all-purpose flour
Pinch of ground nutmeg
1 c. mayonnaise

1 Tbsp. butter or margarine,
   softened
1/4 tsp. salt
1/4 tsp. pepper
1/4 c. plus 1 Tbsp. grated
   Parmesan cheese

Cook broccoli according to package directions; drain well. Beat egg yolks; add flour, mixing well. Stir in nutmeg, mayonnaise, butter, salt, pepper and Parmesan cheese. Add broccoli, mixing lightly. Beat egg whites (at room temperature) until stiff but not dry. Gently fold in broccoli mixture. Pour into a lightly buttered 9 inch square baking dish. Bake at 350° for 30 minutes. Cut into squares to serve. Yield: 9 servings.

Helen C. Harris
Chattanooga Council

ZESTY CHEESE SAUCE WITH BROCCOLI SPEARS

1/4 c. butter
1/4 c. flour
2 c. milk
1 c. (about 1/4 lb.) shredded Monterey Jack cheese
1 c. (about 1/4 lb.) shredded sharp Cheddar cheese

1/2 tsp. salt
1 1/2 tsp. prepared mustard
1 1/2 tsp. horseradish
5-6 drops hot sauce, or as desired
6 servings hot, cooked, well drained seasoned broccoli spears

Melt butter in saucepan over low heat; blend in flour. Add milk gradually, stirring constantly. Cook, stirring, until thickened. Add cheeses and seasonings. Stir until cheese melts. Serve with hot, cooked, well drained broccoli spears. Yield: About 2 1/2 cups sauce; enough sauce for 6 servings of broccoli spears.

Ruth L. Cole
Harpeth Council

CABBAGE BALLS

1 lb. pork sausage
1 lb. hamburger
1 c. uncooked rice
1 small finely diced onion

2 eggs
Salt and pepper
2 loose heads of cabbage

Cut cabbage apart and dip leaves in boiling, salted water for a minute or so. Mix ingredients into balls. Put in cabbage leaves and fasten with toothpicks. Cover with 2 cups water and cook for 1 1/2 hours. Add tomato juice, chili sauce or whole tomatoes and let simmer until you're ready to eat! Makes 20 balls.

Marie Barnett
Harpeth Council

CABBAGE CASSEROLE

2 Tbsp. oleo
1 onion
1 bell pepper
1 lb. ground chuck

1 average head cabbage
1 (10 1/2 oz.) can tomato
soup
Salt and pepper

Melt oleo; saute onion and pepper in oleo. Take out and set aside. Brown meat in skillet; add onion and pepper. Salt and pepper to taste; cook slowly. Pour over shredded cabbage in casserole. Spoon tomato soup over top; do not dilute soup. Cover and cook 1 hour.

Elizabeth Morris
Jackson Council

CABBAGE CASSEROLE

1 small head cabbage,
   cut up
1 can Campbell's celery soup
1/3 c. American cheese,
   grated

1/2 can O & C French fried
   onion rings, crumbled
8 white crackers, crumbled

Steam cabbage 20 minutes; drain. Place 1/2 in casserole dish. Add 1/2 can of celery soup and 1/2 of the cheese. Add second layer of the same. Place crumbled crackers and onion rings on top. Bake 30 minutes at 300° until brown.

Sue W. Grizzard
Clarksville Council

CABBAGE ROLL
(Diabetics)

1 large cabbage leaf
4 oz. raw ground beef
  (3 oz. cooked)
1 slice onion

1 tsp. green pepper, diced
Salt and pepper to taste
1 tsp. catsup

    1. Place ground beef in a frying pan, which has been slightly greased. 2. Allow the meat to brown and add the slice of onion, which has been chopped fine, as well as the green pepper. 3. Season with salt and pepper and stir in the catsup, mixing well. 4. Choose a large cabbage leaf and place the beef mixture on the leaf. 5. Roll until all the meat is completely covered. Place in the oven, using a small frying pan or baking dish. 6. Bake until the cabbage leaf is well cooked and beginning to brown. Use a moderate oven of approximately 375°.
    Exchange: 3 meat exchanges. Calories: 219.

CREAMED CABBAGE AU GRATIN

2 slices Roman Meal or
  whole wheat bread,
  toasted
1 Tbsp. melted margarine
6 c. cabbage, finely sliced
4 c. water
1 tsp. salt

3-4 Tbsp. margarine
3 Tbsp. flour
1 1/2 c. milk
1/4 tsp. white pepper
4 slices American cheese
4 Tbsp. Oscar Mayer real
  bacon bits

    Preheat oven to 325°. Toast 2 slices of bread and make into crumbs by putting into blender at high speed. Mix 1 tablespoon margarine and 1/2 teaspoon salt in boiling water. Add cabbage; cook over high heat for 8 minutes. Drain; place in lightly buttered 1 1/2 quart casserole. Prepare a white sauce by melting the 3 to 4 tablespoons margarine over medium heat. Add flour and allow to bubble for 1 minute. Slowly add milk, 1/2 teaspoon salt and pepper. Stir until thickened and smooth; pour over cabbage. Top with cheese, crumbs and bacon. Bake, uncovered, 15 to 20 minutes or until heated thoroughly and browned. Serves 6. This can be prepared early in the day and refrigerated until baking time. Allow casserole to reach room temperature before baking.

Bertice Spencer
Memphis Council

DAGO CABBAGE

1 lb. country sausage (hot)
1 bell pepper, chopped
1 onion, chopped
1 medium head cabbage, chopped
1 qt. tomatoes
Salt and pepper

Brown sausage, bell pepper and onion in skillet. Partially cook cabbage in a quart of water. Add tomatoes and sausage mixture; add salt and pepper. Cook for 30 minutes to an hour.

Marie Barnett
Harpeth Council

OVEN CABBAGE

1 medium head cabbage
4 tsp. bacon drippings, divided
Salt and pepper
1/2 c. water, divided
3 Tbsp. picante sauce, divided

Remove and discard large outer leaves of cabbage. Cut head into 4 wedges. Place each wedge on a piece of aluminum foil. Spread each wedge with 1 teaspoon bacon drippings; sprinkle with salt and pepper. Wrap foil tightly around cabbage, leaving one end open. Spoon 2 tablespoons water and 2 1/4 teaspoons picante sauce into each packet. Seal tightly. Bake at 350° for 1 hour or until cabbage is tender.

Shirley Buckner
Green Hills Council

RED CABBAGE

In a saucepan, heat the following:
3 Tbsp. margarine
1 1/2 tsp. salt
4-6 cloves (whole)
1/3 c. sugar
1/2 c. water
1/4 c. vinegar

Add 6 cups shredded red cabbage. Cook slowly over low heat in covered saucepan; stir often. Cook about 25 minutes.

Audrey T. Lancaster
Knoxville Council

STEAMED CABBAGE WEDGES

1 firm head cabbage
Water for steaming

Seasoning to taste

A really quick meal; steamed cabbage wedges with thin slices of lean corned beef from the delicatessan. Serve with hot corn sticks and broiled peach, or other fruit halves, sprinkled with brown sugar and sherry.

Trim and wedge cabbage; leave portion of stalk attached. Place in pressure saucepan and steam according to directions, about 2 minutes; or, steam wedges in covered saucepan until just fork tender, about 15 minutes. Wedges should be crisply tender, light green color and hold shape when removed from pan. Drain; season with butter, salt and pepper as desired. Lay strips of precooked corned beef over hot cabbage wedges. Serves 2 to 4.

Joyce Mattice
Harpeth Council

CALCANNON IN PEPPER CUPS

4 large or 8 small green
  peppers
1 (10 oz.) pkg. frozen
  chopped kale, turnips
  greens or broccoli,
  defrosted

Boiling water
1 env. onion-mushroom mix
2 Tbsp. butter
3-4 c. hot, seasoned mashed
  potatoes

Cut large peppers in halves or cut slice from top of small peppers; remove membrane and seeds. Place green peppers in large saucepan. Add boiling water to cover and boil 3 to 5 minutes. Invert peppers on absorbent paper to drain. Pour off all but 1 1/2 cups boiling water; add kale, turnip greens or broccoli and cook rapidly 5 to 10 minutes, until tender. Drain thoroughly. Stir onion-mushroom mix and butter into hot vegetable; fold into hot, seasoned mashed potatoes. Spoon approximately 1/2 cup vegetable mixture into each pepper cup, mounding top. Bake in 350° oven for 15 to 20 minutes. Serves 8.

Judy Christopher
Harpeth Council

1489-81

CALIFORNIA CHICKEN AND WILD RICE

1/2 green pepper, chopped
1 1/2 c. chopped celery
4 oz. canned mushrooms
1 tsp. pepper
1/4 tsp. curry powder
1 pimiento, chopped
1 (12 oz.) pkg. wild rice
1 c. slivered almonds

1 1/2 c. chopped onion
Fat for frying
2 cans mushroom soup
1 tsp. salt
1/4 tsp. sage
4 c. cooked, diced chicken
2 beaten eggs

Saute green pepper, onion and celery in fat in large skillet until tender. Add mushrooms with liquid, 1 can soup, seasonings and pimiento. Stir in chicken gently. Cook rice according to package directions; combine rice and eggs. Blend into chicken mixture. Stir in almonds. Spoon chicken mixture into greased 3 quart casserole. Bake at 350° for 1 hour. Heat remaining soup and 1/2 cup water in saucepan until smooth. Serve mushroom sauce with chicken dish. Yield: 12 servings.

Dorothy Bryant
Clarksville Council

CARROT CASSEROLE

3 c. frozen carrots (crinkle
  cut)
1/4 c. sugar
1/2 c. orange juice

2 Tbsp. flour
1/2 tsp. salt
2 Tbsp. oleo
1/2 c. crushed pineapple

Cook carrots in water until tender; drain well. Combine all ingredients together; mix well. Place in buttered casserole. Bake at 350° for 20 minutes.

Jeanette W. Palmer
Harpeth Council

CARROT-CHEESE CASSEROLE

1/4 c. butter, melted
1 c. chopped onion
1/4 c. all-purpose flour
1 tsp. salt
1/4 tsp. pepper (black)
2 c. milk (I use 2%)

4 c. diagonally sliced carrots,
  cooked and drained
6 slices American cheese
2 c. buttered fresh bread
  crumbs (for added
  nutrition, use whole grain
  bread crumbs)

Saute onion in melted butter; stir in flour, salt and pepper. Gradually add milk, stirring constantly. Cook until it begins to thicken. Arrange a layer of carrots in a 2 quart casserole. Place 3 slices of cheese over carrots; repeat layers. Pour sauce over carrots and cheese. Top with bread crumbs. Bake at 350°, uncovered, for about 25 minutes or until nicely brown. Serves 6-8.

Note: This dish may be made ahead and refrigerated until time to bake.

Mrs. Bob Unkenholz
Harpeth Council

GINGER CARROTS

Cook carrots until done. Put in shallow pan or casserole. Dribble maple syrup over all slices. Sprinkle a little powdered ginger over top. Bake in oven 15 or 20 minutes.

Helen H. Stephens
Memphis Council

CARROTS SUNSHINE

3 c. cooked carrots	2 Tbsp. flour
1/4 c. sugar	1/2 tsp. salt
1/2 c. orange juice	2 Tbsp. butter or oleo

Combine all ingredients and place in buttered casserole. Bake at 350° for 20 minutes.

Helen H. Stephens
Memphis Council

MARINATED CARROTS

2 lb. carrots	1 small onion
1 small bell pepper	1 small bottle Italian dressing

Peel and slice carrots. Cook in water only until just tender. Dice pepper and onion; add to drained carrots. Stir in salad dressing (Kraft, preshook is best). Close tightly and allow to refrigerate overnight. Will keep about 2 weeks.

Betty Birdwell
Harpeth Council

MARINATED CARROTS

2 lb. carrots, sliced
1 (10 oz.) can tomato soup
1/2 c. salad oil
3/4 c. sugar

3/4 c. white vinegar
1/8 tsp. salt
1 green pepper, sliced
1 medium onion

Cook carrots until just barely tender; drain. Combine ingredients for marinade. Add carrots, pepper and onion slices, separated. Marinate; refrigerate overnight. Drain for serving. Serves 12-16.

Joyce Mattice
Harpeth Council

MARINATED CARROTS

5 c. sliced carrots
1 small onion, diced
1/2 small green pepper,
   diced
1/2 c. tomato soup
1/2 c. salad oil

3/4 c. sugar
1/2 c. vinegar
1 tsp. mustard
1 tsp. Worcestershire sauce
1 tsp. pepper
1 tsp. salt

Cook carrots until almost tender; drain. Mix remaining ingredients; let set 12 hours. Will keep 3 to 4 weeks. Keep refrigerated.

Sylvia Kaffer
Clarksville Council

EXOTIC CELERY

8 c. sliced celery, in 1
   inch slantwise slices
   (takes 2 extra large
   bunches of celery)
1 pkg. sliced almonds

1 (8 oz.) can water chestnuts, sliced (or slice them)
1 can cream of chicken soup
1/4 c. milk
2 Tbsp. cornstarch

Place celery in large stew cup; cover with salted (lightly) water. Bring to rolling boil; reduce heat. Cook for 3 minutes; drain thoroughly, using strainer. Mix soup, cornstarch and milk until smooth. Mix celery and water chestnuts**. Add soup mixture and mix well. Pour mixture into 7 1/2 x 12 inch flat Pyrex dish. Sprinkle liberally with sliced almonds. Bake at 350° for 30 minutes. Serves 8.
   **Return to the large cup, of course. (Note follows.)

548

Note: This dish can be prepared ahead of time, with the exception of the 30 minutes of baking. Store in refrigerator until ready to bake.

Lois P. Wells
Knoxville Council

CHEESE VEGETABLE CASSEROLE

2 c. diced potatoes
1/2 c. sliced carrots
1/2 c. sliced celery
1/4 c. chopped onion
1 c. canned green peas, drained
1/4 c. butter
3 Tbsp. flour

1 c. milk
1 c. grated Cheddar cheese
1 c. cottage cheese
Salt and pepper as desired
1 c. bread crumbs
2 Tbsp. melted butter, for crumbs

Cook first 4 vegetables in just enough water to cover until tender; add peas. Make white sauce with butter, flour and milk; add Cheddar cheese. Stir until melted; add cottage cheese. Combine with vegetables. Pour into 2 quart buttered baking dish. Cover with buttered bread crumbs. Bake in 350° oven for 15-20 minutes or until brown and bubbly. Serves 6-8.

Mrs. Bob Unkenholz
Harpeth Council

CHEESEBURGER CASSEROLE

1 lb. ground beef
1/4 c. chopped onion
1/4 c. chopped green pepper
1 (8 oz.) can tomato sauce

1/4 c. ketchup
1/8 tsp. pepper
1 c. grated cheese
1 can refrigerated biscuits

Brown beef with onion and pepper; drain off fat. Add next 3 ingredients; heat. Alternate meat mixture with cheese in 1 1/2 quart casserole dish. Arrange biscuits on top of casserole. Bake at 400° for 20 to 25 minutes. Makes 4-6 servings.

Debbie Bullock
Harpeth Council

CHEESEBURGER LOAVES

2 c. Kellogg's corn flakes cereal
1 egg
1 (8 oz.) can (1 c.) stewed tomatoes

1 tsp. salt
1/8 tsp. pepper
1 lb. ground beef
3 slices American cheese, cut in halves diagonally

1. Measure corn flakes cereal; crush to 1 cup. Place in large mixing bowl. Add egg, tomatoes, salt and pepper; beat well. 2. Add ground beef; mix only until combined. Shape into 6 loaves, about 4 inches long. Place in single layer in shallow baking pan. 3. Bake in oven at 350° F. for about 30 minutes. Remove from oven; top each loaf with 1/2 slice cheese. Return to oven; bake 10 minutes longer or until cheese melts.

Sue G. Yeager
Jackson Council

CHEESE GRITS

6-8 servings grits, cooked
1 stick (1/2 c.) butter or margarine

1 (6 oz.) roll Kraft garlic cheese spread
2 eggs
Milk (approx. 1 c.)

Cook grits per directions on package. Add butter or margarine and garlic cheese; let melt. Blend thoroughly. Break eggs into measuring cup; beat slightly. Add milk to make 1 cup. Add milk-egg mixture to grits mixture. Stir until smooth and well mixed. Pour into 9x13 inch casserole dish. Bake at 350° for 35-40 minutes or until golden brown crust forms.

Mrs. Kendall Clark
Memphis Council

CHEESY SOUR CREAM ENCHILADAS

2 (10 3/4 oz.) cans cream of mushroom soup, undiluted
1 (8 oz.) ctn. commercial sour cream
1 (4 oz.) can chopped green chiles
Hot salad oil

1/4 tsp. salt
1/4 tsp. pepper
1/2 tsp. garlic powder
2 c. shredded Cheddar cheese
1 c. chopped green onions
1 (8 oz.) pkg. or 1 doz. corn tortillas

550

Combine soup, sour cream, green chiles, salt, pepper and garlic powder in a medium saucepan; mix well. Cook over medium heat, stirring often, just until hot. Combine cheese and onion, mixing well. Cook each tortilla in hot oil for a few seconds or just until softened; drain on paper towels. Immediately spoon about 1 1/2 tablespoons cheese mixture and 2 tablespoons soup mixture onto center of each. Roll up tightly and place in a greased 13x9x2 inch baking dish. Spoon remaining soup mixture over top of enchiladas; sprinkle with remaining cheese mixture. Bake at 350° for 20 to 30 minutes. Yield: 6 servings.

Maxine Scott
East Memphis Council

CHEESE TACOS

1 medium onion, chopped	8 oz. Monterey Jack or
2 Tbsp. cooking oil	Longhorn cheese
1 (10 oz.) can Old El Paso	12 Old El Paso taco shells
tomatoes and green	1 avocado, peeled and cut
chilies	in 12 wedges
1 tsp. dried oregano,	1 c. dairy sour cream
crushed	

Cook onion in hot oil till tender but not brown. Stir in tomatoes and green chilies and oregano. Simmer 20 minutes or till very thick; keep warm. Cut cheese into 12 strips. Place 1 strip cheese in each taco shell. Arrange tacos on baking sheet. Bake, uncovered, in 350° oven for 7 to 8 minutes, or until cheese starts to melt. Top cheese with a spoonful of tomato and chilies mixture, avocado slice and a dollop of sour cream. Makes 12 tacos.

Maxine Scott
East Memphis Council

EASY CHEESE SOUFFLE

6 slices white bread with	1 tsp. dry mustard
crust removed	Dash of Worcestershire sauce
1/2 lb. sharp Cheddar	Dash of garlic powder
cheese, grated	4 eggs
1 tsp. salt	2 1/2 c. milk

Butter 9x13 inch casserole and butter one side of bread. Line casserole with bread; sprinkle grated cheese over it. Beat together eggs, milk and seasoning; pour over bread and cheese. Let stand 8 hours in refrigerator. Take out 1 hour before baking. Bake in a pan of water in a moderate oven for 1 hour and 15 minutes.

Sharon Rawlings
Harpeth Council

CHICKEN CASSEROLE

1 whole chicken	1 small can evaporated milk
1 can cream of mushroom soup	1 chopped onion
	2 eggs
1 pkg. Pepperidge Farm corn bread stuffing	1/2 tsp. sage
	3-4 c. chicken broth

Boil chicken; debone and cover bottom of casserole with bite size pieces. Cover with soup. In a separate bowl, mix stuffing, milk, chopped onion, eggs, sage and broth. Pour over chicken. Bake at 350° for 1 hour.

Susan Mayo
Chattanooga Council

CHICKEN CASSEROLE

1 pkg. wild and long grain rice	1 1/2 c. evaporated milk
	3 c. diced, cooked chicken
1/2 c. chopped onion	1/2 c. pimento
1/2 c. oleo	2 Tbsp. parsley
1/4 c. flour	1/2 tsp. salt
1 (6 oz.) can mushrooms	Dash of black pepper
Chicken broth	1/2 c. almonds (optional)

Prepare rice as directed on package. Cook onion in butter; remove from heat. Stir in flour. Drain mushrooms, saving the liquid. Add it to chicken broth to make 1 1/2 cups; add all liquids to mixture. Cook until thick, stirring constantly. Add to chicken, mushrooms, parsley, pimento and almonds; save enough almonds for top. Bake in casserole 30 minutes at 350°.

Sarah Unkenholz
Harpeth Council

CHICKEN CASSEROLE

4 c. diced chicken
3 c. cooked rice, cooled
2 c. chopped celery
1 c. mayonnaise

1 can cream of chicken soup
2 Tbsp. lemon juice
2 Tbsp. chopped onion

Combine these 7 ingredients; refrigerate overnight. Bring to room temperature and top with:

1/2 stick oleo
2 c. crushed corn flakes

1 pkg. almonds

Melt oleo; add corn flakes and almonds. Spread on casserole. Bake 50 to 60 minutes at 350°. You may have to cover with foil to keep the almonds from browning too much. Cook chicken (one whole chicken or 4 breasts) in water with celery, 1 carrot, small onion, peppercorns; add salt to taste.

Cecil Ganong
Memphis Council

CHICKEN CASSEROLE

1 can cream of chicken soup
2 c. boned, cooked chicken
1 c. chopped celery
1 c. almonds
1/2 c. chopped onion
1/2 c. mayonnaise

1/2 c. cracker crumbs
3 hard boiled eggs
1/2 tsp. salt
1/4 tsp. pepper
1 Tbsp. lemon juice

Mix all ingredients; crumble potato chips on top. Bake at 350°, covered, for 20 minutes, then uncover and bake for 15 minutes.

Frances McLaughlin
Harpeth Council

CHICKEN CASSEROLE

4 chicken breasts or 1 whole chicken, cooked, diced
1 can mushroom soup
2 Tbsp. minced onion

1/2 c. chopped almonds
3/4 c. mayonnaise
1 c. diced celery
1 (6 1/2 oz.) pkg. potato chips

1489-81

Crush potato chips; save enough to cover the top. Mix all the ingredients; top with crushed potato chips. Bake 15 minutes at 450°.

Sue Close
Harpeth Council

CHICKEN CASSEROLE

1 (3 lb.) chicken, stewed and boned
2 boxes Stove Top stuffing (corn bread)

1 c. chicken broth
1 ctn. sour cream
1 can cream of chicken soup

Mix stuffing according to package directions. Spread 1/2 of stuffing in 13x9 inch baking dish. Layer all the chicken on top of stuffing. Mix broth, sour cream and soup together; pour over chicken. Layer on remaining stuffing. Top with 1/2 cup chicken broth; sprinkle over top. Bake at 400° for 45 minutes. Can be assembled ahead and baked the next day.

Brenda L. DeVault
Knoxville Council

CHICKEN CASSEROLE

1 (10 3/4 oz.) can cream of mushroom soup
1 (10 3/4 oz.) can cream of celery soup

1 c. water
1 c. raw rice
6-8 pieces of chicken
1 (1 1/8 oz.) pkg. dried onion soup

Mix the soups and water together. Put rice in a 2 quart casserole; pour soup mixture over rice. Arrange chicken on top of rice; sprinkle onion soup over chicken. Cover; bake at 325° for 1 1/2 hours. Serves 6.

Patsy Carter
Harpeth Council

CHICKEN CASSEROLE

4 c. cooked chicken, diced
1 can cream of chicken soup
1 large onion, chopped
1 c. celery, chopped

1 stick oleo
1 pkg. stuffing mix (chicken flavor)
2 c. chicken broth

554

Melt oleo in casserole dish; spread chicken over melted oleo. Mix chicken soup and broth together; pour over chicken and oleo. Sprinkle stuffing mix over top. Bake at 350° for 1 hour.

Margie Essary
Memphis Council

CHICKEN CASSEROLE

3 whole chicken breasts
8 oz. pkg. Pepperidge Farm
   herb stuffing (blue bag)
1 bay leaf
2 stalks celery
2 or 3 chicken bouillon cubes

1 can cream of chicken soup
1 can cream of celery soup
1/2 c. chicken broth
2 Tbsp. vinegar
4 slices American cheese
1 stick margarine

Split chicken breasts; put in water. Add bay leaf, celery and bouillon cubes. Cover and cook 1 hour. Pull chicken off bones and put in large oblong Pyrex pan. Combine cream of chicken soup, cream of celery soup, chicken broth and vinegar; mix well and pour over chicken. Place slices of cheese on top, then add Pepperidge Farm stuffing. Melt margarine; pour over stuffing. Bake at 350° for 30 minutes.

Lena R. Mullins
Morristown Council

CHICKEN CASSEROLE

4 c. cooked chicken, diced
4 c. chopped celery
1 c. almonds
1 tsp. salt
4 Tbsp. chopped onion

1 c. salad dressing
6 Tbsp. pimento
4 Tbsp. lemon juice
1 can cream of chicken soup

Mix all the above ingredients; put into casserole. Top with 6 cups crushed potato chips and 1 cup grated Cheddar cheese. Bake at 350° until brown.

Marie Gardner
Harpeth Council

CHICKEN CASSEROLE

1 1/2 c. rice, cooked
2 c. chicken, cooked and
   cut in small pieces
1 c. celery, chopped
2 Tbsp. onion, chopped

3/4 c. Miracle Whip
1 can cream of chicken soup
1 c. corn flakes
2 Tbsp. butter

Mix all ingredients, except corn flakes and butter. Add about 1/4 cup of the chicken broth; pour into baking dish. Sprinkle with crushed corn flakes and pour melted butter over all. Bake at 325° for 40 minutes.

Donna Maxwell
Harpeth Council

CHICKEN CASSEROLE

2 1/2 - 3 lb. stewed chicken
   (I used 5 chicken breasts)
1 stick margarine
1 pkg. Pepperidge Farm
   stuffing mix (herb)

1 can mushrooms, sliced
1 c. sour cream
1 can cream of chicken soup
1 1/2 c. chicken broth

Melt margarine; mix the melted margarine and the stuffing mix together. Place 3/4 of the mixture in the bottom of oblong baking dish (somewhat as a crust). Place chicken pieces, broken into small bits, on top of the stuffing mix. Add drained mushroom slices. Mix together the sour cream, soup and 1 cup of the chicken broth; pour over the chicken and mushrooms. Sprinkle the other 1/4 stuffing mix over the top, then pour the remaining 1/2 cup of chicken broth over the top. Bake at 350° for 35 minutes.

Kelly Heptinstall
Knoxville Council

CHICKEN CASSEROLE

2 c. cooked chicken (white
   breast, about 6)
1 c. chopped celery
1/2 c. slivered almonds
3 sliced, hard boiled eggs
1/2 c. cracker crumbs

2 Tbsp. minced onion
1/2 c. mayonnaise
1/2 tsp. pepper
1 tsp. lemon juice
1 c. cream of chicken soup

Mix all ingredients and pour into 1 1/2 quart casserole.

Top with additional almonds and 1 cup potato chips, slightly crushed. Bake at 350° for 40 minutes.

Opal Pyle
Nashboro Council

CHICKEN-ASPARAGUS CASSEROLE

3 chicken breasts
1 can asparagus, drained

1 can cream of chicken soup
1/4 c. mayonnaise

Boil chicken breasts in salt water for 30-40 minutes. Drain asparagus and arrange in bottom of casserole dish. Bone chicken and place on asparagus layer. Mix cream of chicken soup with mayonnaise; pour over chicken. Dot with butter. Cover with bread crumbs and bake for 1 hour at 375°.

Sheila Fleming
East Memphis Council

CHICKEN-BROCCOLI CASSEROLE

2 pkg. frozen broccoli
2 c. cream of chicken soup
1 c. mayonnaise
Buttered bread crumbs

2 c. chicken, cooked, diced
1 tsp. lemon juice
1/2 c. shredded American
   cheese

Cook and drain broccoli; place in buttered casserole. Layer chicken pieces on next. Combine soup, mayonnaise and juice; pour over chicken layer. Sprinkle cheese on next. Spread crumbs on top. Bake in a 350° oven for about 30 minutes.

Carolyn Clark
Harpeth Council

CHICKEN BROCCOLI CASSEROLE

2 pkg. broccoli, cooked
   and drained
2 whole chicken breasts,
   cooked and boned
1 c. milk
1 (8 oz.) pkg. cream cheese
Salt and pepper

2 cans cream of mushroom
   soup
1 can water chestnuts or
   toasted almonds
Oregano
1 tsp. instant onion
1/4 tsp. celery salt

Pimento strips and cheese   Pepperidge Farm dressing
   for top   crumbs
                            Onion rings

Layer in large casserole: 1. Chopped chicken; 2. Dressing crumbs, sprinkle lightly; 3. Broccoli to cover; 4. Cream mixture; 5. Cheese and pimentos; 6. French fried onion rings, crushed and sprinkled with lemon juice. Bake 35 minutes at 325°. Serves 4 to 6.

                    John Owen
                    Harpeth Council

CHICKEN AND DRESSING CASSEROLE

6 chicken breasts   1 pkg. Pepperidge Farm
1 can cream of chicken soup   stuffing mix
1 can cream of celery soup   1 stick margarine
1 small can of cream   2 1/2 c. broth from chicken

Cook and debone chicken; place in bottom of dish. Mix soup and cream together; pour over chicken. Mix chicken broth and stick of margarine together (let margarine melt); mix with stuffing mix. (This will be thin when first mixed together.) Spoon on top of chicken and soup mixture; bake about 45 minutes to 1 hour at 350° or until brown. You may add a little sage to dressing, if desired.

                    Patricia G. Trotter
                    Knoxville Council

CHICKEN AND DRESSING CASSEROLE

3 lb. fryer parts   1 small can evaporated milk
2 c. chicken broth   1 pkg. Pepperidge Farm
1 can cream of chicken soup   corn bread mix

Boil the fryer parts until tender; reserve 2 cups of broth. Tear the chicken off the bone into little pieces and place in the bottom of a large casserole dish. Pour the cream of chicken soup over the meat. Next, pour on the can of evaporated milk; cover with the corn bread mix. Pour the chicken broth evenly over the entire casserole. Bake at 350° for 30 minutes.

                    Dianne Hunter
                    Harpeth Council

CHICKEN POTATO CASSEROLE

1 Tbsp. Fruit-Fresh
3 c. water
4 medium potatoes, peeled
1 (2 1/2 - 3 lb.) broiler-
    fryer chicken, cut up
1 (10 3/4 oz.) can
    condensed cream of
    mushroom soup

1 tsp. salt
1 (14 1/2 oz.) can chop suey
    vegetables, drained
1/3 c. chopped onion
1 1/2 c. grated Cheddar
    cheese
1 (3 1/2 oz.) can French
    fried onions

Mix Fruit-Fresh and water. Shred potatoes; add to Fruit-Fresh solution. Drain; pat potatoes in bottom of 13x9 inch Pyrex ware baking dish. Place chicken pieces on top of potatoes with larger pieces to the outer edge of the dish. Combine soup, salt, vegetables and onion; pour over chicken. Sprinkle cheese on top. Serves 4 to 6.

Conventional: Bake at 350° for 45 minutes. Top with fried onions and bake 10 minutes more.

Microwave: Top chicken with onions; cover with waxed paper. Microwave with high power 30 minutes or till done, giving dish a half turn during cooking.

Barbara Harris
Harpeth Council

CHICKEN RICE CASSEROLE

1 (6 oz.) pkg. long grain
    and wild rice mix
1 can cream of chicken soup
3 c. cubed chicken
1 c. sliced mushrooms
1 c. chopped celery
1/4 c. chopped onion

1 (5 oz.) can water chest-
    nuts, sliced
3 Tbsp. soy sauce
1 c. water
1 1/2 c. buttered corn flake
    crumbs on top

Cook rice as directed on the package. Add next 7 ingredients; mix well. Turn into a 3 quart casserole. Bake at 350° for 1 hour. Last 1/2 hour, add buttered crumbs on top.

Mary Jane Bailey
Green Hills Council

CHICKEN AND RICE

1 c. uncooked rice
1 can cream of mushroom
  soup

1 can onion soup
Chicken pieces
Basil to taste (optional)

Mix rice and soups in casserole dish; lay chicken pieces on top. Bake, covered, at 350° for 1 hour, then uncovered for 15 minutes. This can also be cooked in the crock pot on low for 7-8 hours or high for 5-6 hours. Serves 4.

Marian Molteni
Harpeth Council

CHICKEN AND RICE CASSEROLE

1 fryer, cut in pieces and
  seasoned with salt and
  pepper
3 c. water

1 1/2 c. uncooked rice (not
  Minute Rice)
1 env. Lipton's dry onion
  soup mix

Combine all ingredients in a casserole dish, about 2 quart size. Brush chicken pieces with melted butter. Cover with aluminum foil and bake for 2 hours at 350°.

Susan B. Joyner
Harpeth Council

CHICKEN AND RICE CASSEROLE

1 c. plain rice
1 c. cold milk
1 can cream of chicken soup
1 can cream of mushroom
  soup

1 can cream of celery soup
1 stick butter
1/2 tsp. salt
6 or 8 chicken breasts,
  skinned

Spread uncooked rice in 9x13 inch Pyrex dish. Mix salt in milk; pour over rice (add garlic salt, if desired). Mix together in saucepan all 3 cans of soup (do not dilute) and butter. (Pour soup in the melted butter and mix well; heat, but do not boil.) Pour over rice. Place chicken breasts on top of this and push down in soup. Sprinkle paprika and cover with foil. Bake at 300° for 2 hours.

Opal A. Jones
Harpeth Council

CHICKEN AND RICE CASSEROLE

2 c. Minute Rice
1 pkg. Lipton onion soup
  mix
1 can cream of mushroom
  soup

1 can cream of celery soup
1 can cream of chicken soup
1 1/2 cans water
4-6 chicken breasts

Combine the rice, soups and water; pour into a 9x13 inch baking dish. Top this mixture with the chicken breasts. Salt, pepper and butter the chicken breasts. Bake in 350° oven for 1 hour.

Sharon Rawlings
Harpeth Council

CHICKEN AND RICE CASSEROLE

1 can celery soup
1 c. uncooked rice
1 c. water
1/2 stick butter or margarine

1 can cream of chicken soup
1/4 c. diced onion
1 chicken, cut into serving
  pieces, or 4 chicken
  breasts

Combine rice, soups, water and onion; place in bottom of baking casserole. Melt butter; thoroughly spread over chicken, using it all. Salt and pepper the chicken and lay on top of rice. Bake at 350° for 45 minutes or until chicken is tender and rice is done to taste.

Judy Christopher
Harpeth Council

CHICKEN AND RICE CASSEROLE

1 can cream of chicken soup
1 c. uncooked Minute Rice
1/4 c. diced onion
4 chicken breasts or 2 lb.
  box

1 can cream of celery soup
1 c. water
1/2 stick oleo
Salt and pepper

Combine rice, soups, water and onion; place in bottom of long baking dish. Melt butter; thoroughly spread over chicken, using it all. Salt and pepper the chicken; lay on top of the rice. Bake, covered, for 30 minutes. Uncover and bake about 30 more minutes at 350° or until chicken is brown and tender to taste.

Laurie Chadwell
Green Hills Council

CHICKEN SALAD CASSEROLE

5 chicken breasts, boiled and torn into bite size pieces
2-3 stalks celery (approx. 2 c.), diced
2 tsp. grated onion
1/2 tsp. Accent

1 can undiluted mushroom soup (or cream of celery)
1/2 c. mayonnaise
1/2 tsp. salt
1 can chow mein noodles
1/2 c. Cheddar cheese, grated
1 pkg. slivered almonds

Mix first 7 ingredients together; place in casserole dish. Top with Cheddar cheese, almonds and noodles. Bake at 350° for 25 minutes.

M.J. Roderick
Knoxville Council

CHICKEN SOUR CREAM CASSEROLE

1/4 c. melted butter
1 c. crushed cracker crumbs
3 whole chicken breasts, cooked and cut into bite size pieces (2 1/2 c.)

1 (8 oz.) ctn. sour cream
1 (10 oz.) can cream of chicken soup, undiluted
1/4 c. chicken broth

Combine butter and cracker crumbs; spoon 1/2 the crumbs into a 2 quart casserole. Cover with chicken. Combine sour cream, soup and broth; pour over chicken. Top with remaining cracker crumbs. Bake at 350° for 20 to 25 minutes.

Beverly Lamb
Harpeth Council

CHICKEN-TUNA CASSEROLE

1/2 (6 oz.) pkg. (1 c.) 7-minute macaroni
1/2 c. chopped onion
1/4 c. chopped green pepper

3 Tbsp. fat
2 Tbsp. enriched flour
1 1/4 c. milk
1/4 c. chopped pimento

1 (10 1/2 oz.) can cream   1 (6 1/2 or 7 oz.) can
  of chicken soup   flaked tuna

Cook and drain macaroni, 7 minutes. Cook onion and green pepper in hot fat until tender. Add flour; blend. Add milk and cook over low heat until thick, stirring constantly. Stir in chicken soup; add remaining ingredients. Pour into a greased 1 1/2 quart casserole. Garnish with almonds. Bake in a moderate oven, 350°, for 30 minutes.

Virginia Q. Kaderabek
Harpeth Council

CHICKEN ZUCCHINI PARMESAN

2 whole chicken breasts, halved, boned, skinned
6 Tbsp. olive oil, divided
1 medium onion, diced
2 cloves garlic, minced
2 (10 3/4 oz.) cans tomato puree
1 1/4 tsp. salt
1/4 tsp. pepper

1/8 tsp. ground oregano
1 egg, beaten
1/4 c. dry bread crumbs
1/4 c. plus 3 Tbsp. grated Parmesan cheese
8 oz. Mozzarella cheese, sliced thin, divided
1 lb. zucchini, sliced

In medium saucepan, make sauce by placing 3 tablespoons of olive oil and heat to medium temperature. Add onion and garlic; cook 5 minutes or until onion is translucent. Add puree, salt, pepper and oregano; stir. Cover and simmer over low heat, stirring occasionally, for 1/2 hour. In shallow dish, place egg. In another shallow dish, mix bread crumbs and 1/4 cup of Parmesan cheese. Dip chicken in egg, then in bread crumb mixture, one piece at a time, turning to coat. In a large fry pan, place remaining 3 tablespoons oil; heat to medium temperature. Add chicken and cook, turning, about 8 minutes or until brown on both sides. Place chicken in large shallow baking pan. Spread with 1/2 of tomato sauce mixture, then with 1/2 of Mozzarella cheese. Arrange zucchini over all. Spread remaining 1/2 tomato sauce, then remaining 1/2 Mozzarella cheese. Sprinkle with 3 tablespoons Parmesan cheese. Bake, uncovered, in 375° oven for 30 minutes.

Margaret H. Brooks
Harpeth Council

HOT CHICKEN CASSEROLE

2 (5 oz.) cans boned chicken
(can use 2 c. leftover
chicken)
1 c. cream of chicken soup
1 c. diced celery
2 tsp. onion

1/4 c. mayonnaise
3 hard boiled eggs, sliced
1/2 tsp. salt
1/2 tsp. pepper
Dash of cooking sherry
Potato chips

Mix soup, celery, onion, salt, pepper and mayonnaise. Place chicken, soup mixture, potato chips, eggs and sherry in layers in casserole dish. Bake in 350° oven for about 45 minutes. Serve over crisp Chinese noodles, in prebaked pastry shells or squares of corn bread.

Jane Wohlbold
Green Hills Council

EXOTIC COLLARDS

2 pkg. frozen collards
1 c. sour cream
1 pkg. dry onion soup mix

2 Tbsp. sherry
Bread crumbs
Parmesan cheese, if desired

Cook collards in unsalted water according to directions. Drain and chop finely. Add sour cream, onion soup and sherry. Place in greased casserole. Bake at 325° for 15 to 20 minutes. Put bread crumbs and Parmesan cheese on top as desired. Yields 8 to 10 servings.

Mrs. Bob Unkenholz
Harpeth Council

BAKED CORN

1 can cream style corn
1/2 c. milk
1/2 stick margarine
2 Tbsp. flour

1/4 c. grated cheese or 1/4
tsp. grated onion and 1
Tbsp. grated pimento
3 eggs, slightly beaten

Melt margarine; add flour. Pour corn in bowl; add eggs, milk and cheese. Stir; add margarine and flour mixture. Pour into greased 1 quart casserole and bake for 60 minutes at 350°.

Frances G. Sanford
Clarksville Council

COPPER PENNIES

5 c. sliced carrots	1 c. sugar
1 medium onion	3/4 c. vinegar
1 small green pepper	1 tsp. prepared mustard
1 can tomato soup	1 tsp. Worcestershire sauce
1/2 c. salad oil	1 tsp. salt

Cook carrots; cool. Slice onion and pepper and mix with carrots. Mix other ingredients; pour over carrots. Marinate overnight or longer; drain and serve. Keep in refrigerator.

Katie Braden
Harpeth Council

COPPER CARROTS

Cut 3 bunches of carrots in slices; boil until tender and drain. Marinate for 3 hours the following:

1 large bell pepper	1 c. sugar
3 or 4 onions (red and white), ringed or chopped	1/2 c. Wesson oil
	1 Tbsp. Worcestershire sauce
1 c. vinegar	1 tsp. prepared mustard
1 can tomato soup	

After 3 hours, add carrots to this mixture and refrigerate. Serve with beans, meat, or any vegetable. Keeps indefinitely.

Sarah Nowlin
Harpeth Council

COPPER PENNIES

5 c. sliced, cooked carrots, drained	1 c. tomato soup
1 medium green bell pepper, sliced	3/4 c. vinegar
	1 c. sugar
2 medium onions, sliced in rings	1/4 c. salad oil
	1 tsp. prepared mustard
	1 tsp. Worcestershire sauce

Pour tomato soup, vinegar, sugar, salad oil, mustard

and Worcestershire sauce, combined, over carrots, pepper and onions. Let stand overnight in refrigerator.

Mrs. Adelene Queenan
Harpeth Council

CHEDDAR CHEESE AND EGG PIE

1 Pet Ritz unbaked pie shell
2 Tbsp. chopped bell pepper
1/2 c. sliced mushrooms
  (fresh or canned)
4 slices cooked bacon,
  drained and crumbled
1 tsp. salt
1/4 c. milk
1/2 tsp. margarine
1/4 c. chopped green onions
  (tops and all)
1 pkg. Buddig's smoked ham,
  torn into pieces
1 c. Cheddar cheese, grated
1/2 tsp. pepper
5 eggs

Bake pie shell in 350° oven until lightly browned. Coat inside surfaces of pie shell with margarine. Mix salt, pepper, milk and eggs together; lightly beat. Set mixture aside. Sprinkle evenly in bottom of pie shell the green pepper, onions, mushrooms, ham, bacon and Cheddar cheese. Pour egg mixture over top of pie. Bake in 350° oven for 30-35 minutes or until knife inserted in center of pie comes out clean. Serve hot, cut into wedges.

Peggy Hunter
Harpeth Council

CORN BREAD TAMALE PIE

1 lb. ground beef
1 large onion, chopped
1 can tomato soup
2 c. water
1 tsp. salt
1/4 tsp. pepper
1 Tbsp. chili powder
1 c. whole kernel corn,
  drained
1/2 c. chopped green pepper
3/4 c. corn meal
1 Tbsp. flour
1 Tbsp. sugar
1/2 tsp. salt
1 1/2 tsp. baking powder
1 beaten egg
1/3 c. milk
1 Tbsp. Mazola

Brown ground beef and onion in skillet. Add tomato soup, water, seasonings, corn and green pepper; simmer for 15 minutes. For topping, sift together dry ingredients. Add beaten egg and milk, stirring lightly until combined. Fold in melted fat. Place meat mixture in greased baking dish; cover with corn bread topping. Bake in hot, 425°, oven for 20 to 25 minutes until corn bread is brown. Yield: 6 servings.

Debby Maddox
Harpeth Council

CORN OYSTERS

2 c. cut, fresh corn	1/2 c. sifted all-purpose
2 beaten eggs	flour
1/2 c. cracker crumbs	1 tsp. salt
1/2 tsp. baking powder	1/4 tsp. pepper

Combine corn, eggs and cracker crumbs. Sift together the flour, baking powder and seasonings. Add the two mixtures together. Drop from tablespoon into small amount of hot fat in skillet. Flatten slightly and pan fry until browned, about 3 minutes, turning once.

Judy Gibson
Harpeth Council

CORN PUDDING

4 eggs	4 Tbsp. sugar
2 c. (1 can) corn	4 Tbsp. butter, melted
2 c. milk, scalded	1 tsp. salt
1/2 tsp. pepper	

Stir into corn the salt, sugar and pepper. Add well beaten eggs. Scald milk and add. Put melted butter in last. Pour into a 2 quart casserole, well greased. Place casserole in pan of water. Bake in 350° oven for 1 - 1 1/2 hours. Stir from bottom 2 or 3 times during baking.

Dot Crouch
Clarksville Council

CORN PUDDING

2 c. fresh corn (or 1 pkg.	1 Tbsp. sugar
frozen cream style corn)	2 Tbsp. butter
1 c. sweet milk	Salt and pepper to taste
2 eggs, separated	

Separate the eggs and beat the whites. In another bowl, beat the yolks and add the flour, milk, corn, sugar, salt, pepper and butter. Put into a buttered 1 quart baking dish and bake at 325° for 30 minutes or until solid.

Eugenia W. Smith
Chattanooga Council

CORN PUDDING

1 large can cream style
  corn
1 egg

1/2 stick butter or margarine
1 c. sweet milk
1 Tbsp. sugar
1 c. flour

Melt butter in Pyrex dish. Mix remaining ingredients together; pour into melted butter. Bake 15 minutes or more at 400°; add pepper to taste. This pudding thickens as it cools. It may be reheated for leftovers, if desired.

Pat Carpenter
Nashville Council

CORN PUDDING

1/2 c. sugar
3 Tbsp. all-purpose flour
3 eggs
2 c. milk

1 (17 oz.) can whole kernel
  corn, drained
1/2 tsp. salt
1/4 c. butter or margarine

Combine sugar and flour in a medium mixing bowl. Add eggs, beating well; stir in corn, milk and salt. Melt butter in a lightly greased 1 3/4 quart casserole. Pour in corn mixture. Bake at 400° for 1 hour or until firm. Serve hot. Yield: 6 servings.

Audrey T. Lancaster
Knoxville Council

CORN PUDDING

1 (1 lb.) can whole kernel
  corn, drained
2 eggs, beaten
1/4 c. chopped onion
1 tsp. sugar
Dash of pepper

1 c. milk
1 c. medium size cracker
  crumbs
1/4 c. chopped green pepper
3/4 tsp. salt
2 Tbsp. butter

In 1 quart casserole, combine all ingredients, except

butter. Bake in moderate oven, 350°, for about 30 minutes or until set.

Note: Cream style corn can be used; use 1 can cream style corn and reduce milk to 1/2 cup.

Dee Schell
Columbia Council

EASY CHINESE CASSEROLE

1 pkg. Uncle Ben's wild and long grain rice with herb seasoning packet
1 can cream of mushroom soup
1 can La Choy fancy mixed Chinese vegetables, drained
1 c. water
4 butterfly pork chops

Mix rice, seasoning, soup, water and vegetables together. Pour in large casserole. Lightly salt and pepper 4 butterfly pork chops and arrange on top of rice. Bake at 350° for 45 to 50 minutes. Delicious with Mandarin orange and pineapple salad.

Jewell Hall
Memphis Downtown Council

BAKED STUFFED EGGS

6 hard cooked eggs
5 Tbsp. margarine
1 Tbsp. Worcestershire sauce
Salt to taste
Dash of cayenne pepper to taste
1 1/2 c. ground country ham
1 1/2 c. milk
3 Tbsp. flour
1 1/2 c. grated Swiss cheese

Slice eggs; spoon out yolks. Mash yolks with margarine, pepper, salt, Worcestershire sauce and ham. Stuff whites with ham mixture. Place in large oblong Pyrex dish. Prepare the sauce with milk, flour and the remaining margarine. Add grated Swiss cheese. Pour over eggs and bake until hot and bubbly.

Peggy Burr
Harpeth Council

EGG CASSEROLE

6 eggs
Salt and pepper to taste

4 oz. grated Cheddar cheese
1 small can evaporated milk

Break eggs into buttered baking dish; do not stir. Sprinkle with salt and pepper to taste. Pour evaporated milk over eggs; cover with grated cheese. Bake in preheated oven at 350° for about 20 minutes. Serve immediately. (Excellent dish in any quantity to serve at breakfast buffet. Allows time to be with guests.)

Jane Wohlbold
Green Hills Council

EGGPLANT CASSEROLE

1 large eggplant, cooked
  and diced
1 (10 1/2 oz.) can cream
  of mushroom soup
1/3 c. milk

1 small onion, chopped fine
1 egg
1/4 tsp. salt
Dash of pepper
2 c. herb stuffing

Cook eggplant; mash. Mix soup, milk, onion, egg, salt and pepper; add to eggplant. Add 1 cup of stuffing; toss. Pour into casserole dish; sprinkle remaining stuffing on top and dot with butter. Bake 30 minutes in 350° oven.

Ann R. Wooten
Memphis Council

EGGPLANT CASSEROLE

1 eggplant, peeled and
  chopped into medium
  size cubes

1 large onion, chopped

Boil together about 10 minutes. Have ready:

2 eggs, beaten
1 small can Carnation milk
Salt and pepper to taste

1 tsp. sugar
1 Tbsp. butter, rounded
Cracker crumbs

Put eggplant and onion, egg mixture, part of cracker crumbs in baking dish in layers, topping with crumbs and remaining egg mixture; dot with butter. Bake until done and golden brown, approximately 30 to 40 minutes.

Joyce Mattice
Harpeth Council

EGGPLANT ELEGANT

1 large eggplant
1/4 c. butter
1/4 c. grated onion
1/2 tsp. salt

1/2 c. grated Cheddar cheese
2 tsp. Worcestershire sauce
1/2 c. crumbled soda
   crackers

Peel and cube a large eggplant into 1 inch pieces; cook until tender in as little water as possible for 5 minutes, stirring frequently to cook all cubes. Remove from heat; add butter, grated onion, salt and Worcestershire sauce. Blend all ingredients; add crumbled soda crackers until all moisture is absorbed. Place mixture into a greased 1 quart baking dish; cover with grated cheese. Bake at 375° for 20 minutes, until thoroughly heated and cheese is slightly browned. Serves 6.

Dorothy Jackson
Memphis Council

EGGPLANT ITALIANO

2 lb. ground beef
1 large can tomatoes, put
   in blender
1 small can tomato paste
Garlic powder
Italian seasonings
Fresh mushrooms

1 eggplant, cut in 1/4 inch
   slices
1 large ctn. cottage cheese,
   mixed with 2 eggs and
   oregano (put in blender
   until smooth)
1 pkg. Mozzarella cheese
Grated Parmesan cheese

Make sauce like you would for spaghetti or lasagna. Grease a casserole dish and alternate layers of sauce, eggplant and cheese, beginning and ending with sauce. Sprinkle grated Parmesan cheese on top and bake at 350° for about 30 minutes.

Pinky Bryant
Nashboro Council

EGGPLANT PARMESAN CASSEROLE

1 large eggplant
3 eggs, slightly beaten
2 c. Italian seasoned bread
  crumbs

1/2 c. vegetable or olive oil
8 oz. Parmesan or sharp
  Cheddar cheese, grated
1 (8 oz.) can tomato sauce

Peel eggplant and slice thinly; dip in egg, then in bread crumbs. In a large skillet, fry eggplant until tender and brown; drain on paper towels. Place alternate layers of eggplant, grated cheese and tomato sauce in 2 quart casserole. Bake at 350° until bubbling hot, about 30 minutes. Serves 10.

Patsy Carter
Harpeth Council

STUFFED EGGPLANT

1 large eggplant
3/4 c. mushrooms
2 Tbsp. onion, chopped
1 clove garlic
2 Tbsp. flour
1 tsp. salt

2 Tbsp. green pepper,
  chopped
2 Tbsp. pimiento, chopped
1/8 tsp. pepper
1/2 c. cream

Cut long lengthwise slice off top of eggplant. Remove inside and cut in cubes. Cook in small amount of salted water 10 minutes. Brown mushrooms (may use canned buttons and pieces). Stir in flour, salt and pepper; add drained eggplant, cream and pimiento. Fill shell; top with buttered bread crumbs, 2 tablespoons grated sharp cheese and 2 slices chopped bacon. Bake at 325° for 30 minutes or until done. Bacon may be omitted.

Dorothy Bryant
Clarksville Council

FIESTA CASSEROLE

1 large onion
1 clove garlic, minced
2 Tbsp. salad oil
1 lb. ground beef
1 (1 lb.) can tomatoes
1 (1 lb.) can red kidney
  beans

1 (15 oz.) can chili con carne
  (no beans)
2 tsp. salt
1/4 tsp. pepper
1 can or pkg. tortillas
1 c. grated cheese

Saute onion and garlic in salad oil until soft (in large frying pan); remove and set aside for next step. Shape beef into large patties in same pan; brown 5 minutes on one side, then break into chunks. Stir in onion mixture, tomatoes, beans, chili, salt and pepper; heat to boiling. Place 3 tortillas in 12 cup baking dish; top with 1 cup sauce. Repeat layers, ending with sauce. Sprinkle with cheese. Bake in hot oven at 400° for 30 minutes. Makes 6 servings.

C.D. Read
Green Hills Council

FIRE AND ICE TOMATOES

This is very appropriate for this time of year. Delicious served with peas and corn.

6 large ripe tomatoes, peeled and quartered	1 1/2 tsp. celery salt
1 large green pepper, cut into strips	1 1/2 tsp. mustard seed (or 3/4 tsp. dry mustard)
1 large onion, cut into slices and pulled into rings	1/2 tsp. salt
	4 1/2 tsp. sugar
	1/8 tsp. red pepper
	1/8 tsp. black pepper
3/4 c. vinegar	1/4 c. cold water

Place tomato wedges, green pepper and onion rings into shallow dish. Combine remaining ingredients and bring to a boil. Boil 1 minute; pour immediately over vegetables. Cover tightly and chill. This will keep in refrigerator several days.

Joyce Mattice
Harpeth Council

GARLIC GRITS

4 1/2 c. boiling water	1 1/2 rolls garlic cheese
1 tsp. salt	2 eggs
1 c. grits	2 c. crushed corn flakes
2/3 c. milk	Dash of Tabasco sauce
1 stick margarine	Paprika

Add salt to water and bring to boil; add grits slowly. Cook 3-5 minutes, stirring occasionally to prevent lumping. Turn off heat; add butter and cheese. Stir until melted. Beat eggs in cup; measure and finish filling cup with milk.

Add to grits mixture. Pour into well greased casserole. Sprinkle with corn flakes; dot with butter and dash of paprika. Bake at 350° for 1 hour.

Norma Foster
Harpeth Council

SOUTHERN GRITS

1 c. grits, cooked by
  directions
2 eggs

1 roll Kraft garlic cheese
Milk
1 stick margarine

Melt cheese and margarine in saucepan on low heat. Mix with cooked grits; add 2 eggs, beaten. Add enough milk to egg mixture to make 1 cup; add to other mixture. Butter dish and bake at 350° for 40 minutes or until set (test with knife). Yield: 1 1/2 quart bowl.

Mary Cate
Knoxville Council

GRITS CASSEROLE

1 c. quick cooking grits
1 roll Kraft's garlic cheese

1 stick margarine
2 eggs

Prepare grits as directed on box. After grits are cooked, turn heat off and stir in 1 roll Kraft's garlic cheese and 1 stick margarine. After this has melted, add 2 beaten eggs; mix well. Bake at 350° for 30 or 40 minutes.

Mrs. Adelene Queenan
Harpeth Council

GOURMET CASSEROLE

1 lb. fresh bulk sausage
1 medium onion, chopped
1 medium green pepper,
  chopped
1/2 c. celery, chopped
1 c. uncooked wild rice

1 c. grated American cheese
1 can cream of chicken soup
1 can cream of mushroom soup
1 (2 oz.) can mushrooms
1 small can pimientos, drained
  and chopped

Brown sausage in large skillet at 275° or use medium burner. Add onion, green pepper and celery; continue cooking until vegetables are limp. Drain off excess fat.

574

Add uncooked rice, cheese, both soups, mushrooms and pimientos; mix well. Pour into 3 quart casserole. Cover; bake in preheated oven at 350° for 1 3/4 hours. Serves 6.

Peggy Burr
Harpeth Council

GROUND BEEF AND POTATO CASSEROLE

1 lb. ground beef or chuck	1/2 tsp. pepper
1 Tbsp. oil	1 can mixed vegetables
1 large white onion, chopped	1 can cream of celery soup
1 tsp. salt	Mashed potatoes

Brown beef or chuck in oil; mix in onion. Drain this well. Add salt and pepper. Add mixed vegetables, cream of celery soup and 1/3 cup water; cover and cook 5 minutes. Pour in casserole dish; spoon potatoes into 4 heaping mounds. (Fresh mashed potatoes to make 4 good mounds.) Cover; bake in 300° oven for 30 minutes.

Teresa Beasley
Harpeth Council

HAMBURGER CASSEROLE

To 2 pounds ground beef, browned and drained, add:

2 Tbsp. onion, chopped	1 Tbsp. oregano
2 Tbsp. green pepper, chopped	1 tsp. pepper
1/2 tsp. garlic powder	4 medium potatoes, peeled and diced
2 tsp. salt	1 (16 oz.) can tomato sauce

Note: One can of celery soup and 1 can of Cheddar cheese soup are also needed for recipe. (See below.)
Cook this 20-30 minutes until potatoes are tender. Place 1/2 of recipe in casserole dish and add 1 can of celery soup, not diluted, on top of above and spread. Add remaining 1/2 of recipe on top of celery soup. Top with 1 can of Cheddar cheese soup, not diluted. Bake, covered, in oven 20 minutes at 350°.

Penny Nash
Harpeth Council

1489-81

HAMBURGER-CORN CASSEROLE

1 1/2 lb. ground beef
1 c. chopped onion
1 (12 oz.) can whole kernel corn, drained
1 can condensed cream of chicken soup
1 can condensed cream of mushroom soup
1 c. dairy sour cream
1/4 c. chopped pimento
3/4 tsp. salt
1/2 tsp. MSG
1/4 tsp. pepper
3 c. medium noodles, cooked
1 c. bread crumbs
3 tsp. melted butter

Brown meat; add onion and cook till tender. Add the next 8 ingredients; mix well. Stir in noodles and pour into a 2 quart casserole. Mix crumbs with butter; sprinkle over top. Bake quickly; cover and freeze (or if to be eaten right away, bake at 350° for 30 minutes).

Debbie Bullock
Harpeth Council

GREEN BEAN CASSEROLE

3 (No. 2) cans green beans (or equal amount cooked beans)
1/2 c. chopped celery
1/2 c. chopped green pepper
1 small can beets, sliced
1 Tbsp. minced onion
1 Tbsp. Worcestershire sauce
1 c. mayonnaise
1 c. pecans, broken (or almonds)

Cook green beans to taste. Place hot beans in casserole dish. Mix all other ingredients, except nuts. Shortly before serving, spread mixture over beans and top with pecans, toasted. Heat about 15 minutes until hot through at 350°.

Dorothy Bryant
Clarksville Council

GREEN BEAN CASSEROLE

3 pkg. French cut frozen green beans
1/2 c. butter
1 medium onion, thinly sliced
1 (3 oz.) can sliced mushrooms, drained
1/4 c. flour
1 c. milk
1 c. half & half cream
3/4 lb. sharp Cheddar cheese, grated
1/2 tsp. black pepper
1/2 tsp. salt
1/8 tsp. Tabasco sauce

2 tsp. soy sauce
1/2 c. slivered almonds

1 (5 oz.) can water chestnuts, drained and sliced

Cook green beans in salted water until tender; drain. While green beans are cooking, put butter in heavy saucepan; melt and add mushrooms and onion. Saute until onion is clear. Add flour; stir until smooth. Add milk and half & half to make a white sauce. Add the grated cheese to white sauce; stir until cheese is melted. Remove from heat; add Tabasco sauce, soy sauce, salt and black pepper. Drain and slice thin water chestnuts; add to sauce and then add to the sauce the cooked green beans, drained thoroughly. Pour this into a buttered 2 quart casserole; sprinkle with slivered almonds. Bake for 20 minutes at 375° or until bubbly. Can be made ahead and placed in refrigerator until ready to cook. Allow 40 to 45 minutes to heat through. Serves 8.

Mrs. Bob Unkenholz
Harpeth Council

IMPOSSIBLE GREEN BEAN PIE

8 oz. fresh green beans,
cut lengthwise into strips
1 (4 oz.) can mushroom
stems and pieces,
drained
1/2 c. chopped onion
2 cloves garlic, crushed

1 c. (about 4 oz.) shredded
Cheddar cheese
1 1/2 c. milk
3/4 c. Bisquick baking mix
3 eggs
1 tsp. salt
1/4 tsp. pepper

Heat oven to 400°. Lightly grease pie plate, 10 x 1 1/2 inches. Heat beans and 1 inch salted water (1/2 teaspoon salt to 1 cup water) to boiling; cook, uncovered, 5 minutes. Cover and cook until tender, 5 to 10 minutes; drain. Mix beans, mushrooms, onion, garlic and cheese in pie plate. Beat remaining ingredients until smooth, 15 seconds in blender on high speed or 1 minute with hand beater. Pour into pie plate. Bake until golden brown and knife inserted halfway between center and edge comes out clean, 30 to 35 minutes. Let stand 5 minutes before cutting. Refrigerate any remaining pie. Makes 6-8 servings.

High Altitude Directions (3500 to 6500 feet): Heat 1 cup water to boiling (omit salt). Add beans; cover and cook about 30 minutes.

Frances Nevette
Harpeth Council

GREEN BEAN STEW

1 1/2 lb. ground beef
1 (No. 2) can tomatoes
1 large onion, chopped
1 clove garlic

2 tomato cans of water
1 1/4 lb. green beans
2 medium potatoes, cubed
Salt and pepper to taste

Combine beef, tomatoes, onion and garlic in a saucepan; add water and cook over medium heat for about 40 minutes. Add green beans and cook 30 minutes. Add potatoes, salt and pepper; cook for 30 minutes or until done. Yield: 8 servings.

Alison Bennett
Andrew Jackson Council

GREEN BEAN CASSEROLE

2 (1 lb.) cans French style
  green beans
1 can cream of mushroom
  soup, undiluted

1 (4 oz.) can sliced
  mushrooms
1 can French fried onions or
  onion rings
1/2 can Cheddar cheese soup

Cook beans in salted water about 15 minutes; strain. Combine beans with mushroom soup, cheese soup and sliced mushrooms. Put into casserole dish and place in slow oven, 300°, for 15 minutes. Sprinkle top with onions or onion rings, if preferred. Return to oven long enough to heat onions thoroughly.
    Note: Sliced almonds may be used in place of onions or mushrooms.

Jane Wohlbold
Green Hills Council

SWEET AND SOUR BEANS

2 cans French style green
  beans
2 white onions
1/4 c. water

4 Tbsp. oil
1 c. sugar
3/4 c. vinegar
1 clove garlic

Arrange layer of beans and onion rings in shallow dish. Pour sugar over layers. Combine remaining ingredients;

pour over beans. Put in refrigerator overnight. Drain and serve dry.

Ura Blanks
Harpeth Council

HAM BROCCOLI CASSEROLE

3/4 lb. ham, diced	1 small jar sliced mushrooms
10 oz. pkg. frozen chopped broccoli	1 can cream of mushroom soup
6 oz. pkg. instant rice	1 c. mayonnaise
1 c. sharp Cheddar cheese	1 1/2 tsp. dry mustard
1 tsp. curry powder	1 tsp. paprika

Cook rice until tender (I use Uncle Ben's long grain rice). Thaw broccoli. Mix soup, mayonnaise, mushrooms and spices. Put ingredients in alternate layers in casserole dish. Sprinkle with cheese and paprika. Bake 45 minutes in 350° oven.

Mrs. Wavie Minke
Harpeth Council

HAM AND SCALLOPED POTATOES
(Diabetics)

1 medium raw potato	2 (1 oz.) slices ham, sliced thinly
1 tsp. grated onion	
1/2 c. milk, hot (whole)	Salt and pepper as desired

1. Using a small piece of fat from the ham, grease an individual baking dish. 2. Slice the potato and place 1/2 of it in the bottom of the dish. 3. Sprinkle with half the onion and seasoning, which should be used sparingly. 4. Add the ham; cover with the remaining half of potato and onion. 5. Add the milk and, if it is too much for the dish, hold and add gradually during the cooking process. 6. Cover the dish and bake in a moderate oven, 350°, until the potatoes are cooked through and become brown on top, approximately 20 minutes.

Exchange: 1 bread exchange, 2 meat exchanges, 1/2 whole milk exchange. Calories: 299.

RUBY'S HAMBURGER-SQUASH CASSEROLE

1 (15 oz.) can Hunt's tomato sauce
1 pkg. Success precooked rice (2 c. rice)
1 lb. hamburger
1 large onion, chopped
1 1/2 lb. yellow squash, cleaned and cooked
Dash of garlic powder (optional)
2 Tbsp. margarine
Salt and pepper to taste

Boil chopped squash in water until tender; drain. Add butter. Brown hamburger and onion; drain. Prepare rice according to directions on package. Combine squash and hamburger mixture together in a skillet with tomato sauce. Add garlic, salt and pepper; simmer 15 minutes. Mix in rice and serve.

Kay Boswell
Andrew Jackson Council

HILLBILLY CASSEROLE

1 lb. ground beef
1 c. elbow macaroni
1 onion, chopped
1 can tomato soup
1 can tomato sauce
1/4 lb. grated Cheddar cheese
Salt
Worcestershire sauce

Brown ground beef and chopped onion; season with salt and Worcestershire sauce. Add tomato soup and tomato sauce to meat mixture; cook for 15 minutes. In the meantime, cook elbow macaroni separately. When meat and macaroni are cooked, mix them all together in a baking dish and stir in Cheddar cheese. Bake 40 minutes at 325°.

Marian Molteni
Harpeth Council

HOBO DINNER FOR TWO

1 lb. hamburger (2 big patties)
3 squash
1 onion
2 carrots
1 large potato
Parsley flakes

Slice equal amounts of each on pattie; salt and pepper

to taste. Add parsley flakes. Wrap in heavy aluminum foil and bake at 375° for 1 hour and 15 minutes.

Vernon Gilliam
Columbia Council

HOMINY CASSEROLE

2 (29 oz.) cans hominy
2 (4 oz.) cans green
   chilies, minced
Butter

8 oz. sour cream
1/2 c. cream
1 1/2 c. grated Monterey
   Jack or Gruyere cheese

Drain and rinse hominy. Butter a 2 1/2 - 3 quart casserole dish. Alternate layers of hominy and chilies. Dot layers with butter and sour cream; end with hominy, salt and pepper to taste. Pour on cream and sprinkle with cheese. Bake at 350° for 25-30 minutes.

E.B. McClanahan
Memphis West Council

CHRISTMAS KRAUT

1 (No. 2) can shredded
   kraut, drained well
1 c. chopped onion
1 c. green pepper, chopped

1 c. chopped celery
1 small jar pimento, chopped
   and drained
1 c. sugar
1/3 c. white vinegar

Mix all ingredients together and cover. Put in refrigerator and let set overnight.

Dorothy Stanton
Knoxville Council

BEAUTIFUL LASAGNA

1/2 lb. ground beef
1/2 lb. ground pork
1 clove garlic, minced
2 Tbsp. chopped parsley
1 Tbsp. basil
1 1/2 tsp. salt
2 c. tomatoes
2 (6 oz.) cans tomato paste
1 Tbsp. chili powder

2 c. cottage cheese
1/2 c. Parmesan cheese
2 eggs, beaten
1 tsp. salt
1/2 tsp. pepper
1 lb. Mozzarella cheese
1 (1 lb.) pkg. lasagna,
   cooked, drained and
   washed in cold water

Cook meat until brown; drain. Add garlic, chili powder, basil, salt, tomatoes and tomato paste. Simmer for 1/2 hour; stir occasionally. Combine cottage and Parmesan cheeses; add eggs, salt and pepper. In 13x9 inch baking dish, pour a thin layer of sauce, a layer of lasagna, a layer of cheese mixture and 1/2 of Mozzarella cheese. Spread a layer of tomato sauce. Repeat layers; cover with foil and bake in a 350° oven for 20 minutes. Uncover and bake 20 minutes longer. Let stand 15 minutes before serving.

Peggy Hunter
Harpeth Council

LIMA BEAN BAKE

6 slices bacon, cooked, crumbled	3 (17 oz.) cans lima beans
3 medium onions, chopped	3 c. canned tomatoes
1 large bell pepper, chopped	2 Tbsp. sugar
	1 1/2 tsp. salt
	1/2 tsp. pepper

Saute bacon, onion and pepper until lightly browned. Pour beans and tomatoes into large greased casserole. Add seasonings and bacon mixture; mix well. Bake, uncovered, at 300° for 40-50 minutes.

Joyce Mattice
Harpeth Council

MACARONI AND CHEESE

1 1/2 c. macaroni	1 tsp. pepper
1 c. grated cheese	1/4 c. brown bread crumbs
1 Tbsp. butter	1 chopped onion
1 Tbsp. flour	1/2 tsp. dry mustard, mixed
1 c. milk	with a little water
1 tsp. salt	

Cook macaroni in boiling salt water until tender; drain. Melt butter in saucepan; stir in flour. Add milk; bring to boil, stirring constantly. Add macaroni, salt, pepper, onion and mustard. Pour in greased dish. Sprinkle cheese on top; dot with butter and cover with bread crumbs. Bake at 350° for 20 minutes until brown on top.

Norma Ann Webb
Harpeth Council

582

MACARONI AND CHEESE

Cook 12 ounces of macaroni as usual, but do not drain completely. Grate 12 ounces of mild Cheddar cheese. Mix:

1 can cream of mushroom
   soup
1 ctn. sour cream

1 c. mayonnaise
1 small jar pimento
1 small to medium chopped
   onion

Butter a large oblong oven dish. Layer half of the macaroni, half of the cheese and half of the soup mixture (and other items mixed in); repeat. Crush 1 box of Cheese-It crackers; sprinkle on top. Dot with butter. Bake at 325° for 30-35 minutes or until the crackers are brown.

Addie Downs
Green Hills Council

MACARONI AND HOT DOG CASSEROLE

2 Tbsp. shortening or 2
   Tbsp. bacon grease
1 large onion, diced

1 1/2 qt. tomato juice
1 lb. hot dogs, cut up
1 beef bouillon cube
1 lb. pkg. macaroni

Saute onion and shortening together until onion is clear; add diced hot dogs. Add tomato juice and bouillon cube; simmer while macaroni cooks. Cook macaroni until done; drain. Add to tomato juice and hot dogs. Makes large iron skillet full.

Colleen Patterson
Knoxville Council

MACARONI CASSEROLE

1 box macaroni, cooked
   and drained
1/2 c. diced onion
1/4 c. chopped sweet pepper
1/4 c. chopped pimento
1 can mushrooms

1 can cream of mushroom
   soup
Salt and pepper to taste
1 c. mayonnaise
1 pkg. shredded Cheddar
   cheese

Mix all ingredients, except macaroni. Put layer of

macaroni in baking dish, then mixture, until finished.
Sprinkle top with potato chip crumbs. Bake 30 minutes at
350°.

Imogene Chesher
Knoxville Council

DELUXE BAKED MACARONI AND CHEESE

1 1/2 c. elbow macaroni,
   cooked
1/4 c. margarine or butter
1/4 c. all-purpose flour
1 tsp. salt
1 tsp. pepper
1 tsp. dry mustard

2 1/2 c. milk
2 c. grated sharp Cheddar
   cheese
2 Tbsp. bread crumbs, tossed
   with 1 Tbsp. melted butter
   and 1/2 c. grated cheese

Preheat oven to 375°. Melt 1/4 cup margarine; stir in
flour, salt, pepper and mustard until smooth. Gradually stir
in milk; bring to a boil. Reduce heat and simmer 1 minute.
Stir in grated cheese and cooked macaroni. Pour into a 2
quart shallow baking dish. Sprinkle bread crumb mixture
over top. Bake 15 to 20 minutes, or until cheese is melted
and crumbs are golden brown. Makes 6 servings.

Paula Akin
Green Hills Council

QUICK MANICOTTI

8 manicotti shells
1 lb. ground beef
1 clove garlic, crushed
1 c. cottage cheese
1 c. (1/4 lb.) shredded
   Mozzarella cheese

1/2 tsp. salt
1/4 c. mayonnaise
1 (15 1/2 oz.) jar spaghetti
   sauce
1/2 tsp. whole oregano
About 1/3 c. grated Parmesan
   cheese

Cook manicotti shells according to package directions;
drain. Rinse in cold water; drain and set aside. Saute
ground beef and garlic, stirring to crumble beef, until beef
is no longer pink; drain off pan drippings. Add cottage
cheese, Mozzarella cheese, salt and mayonnaise to skillet;
stir well. Stuff manicotti shells with meat mixture; arrange
shells in a lightly greased 13x9x2 inch baking dish. Combine spaghetti sauce and oregano; pour over manicotti.
Sprinkle with Parmesan cheese. Cover and bake at 350° for

15 minutes. Uncover and bake 10 additional minutes.
Yield: 8 servings.

Betty J. Cowherd
Andrew Jackson Council

MARINATED VEGETABLES

1 bunch broccoli	1 head cauliflower
2-3 carrots	1 green pepper
1-2 small zucchini	1 large can black pitted
1/4 lb. fresh mushrooms	olives

Marinade:

1 c. vinegar	1 Tbsp. sugar
1 tsp. dill weed	1 Tbsp. Accent
1 Tbsp. garlic salt	1 Tbsp. pepper
1 1/2 c. vegetable oil	

Refrigerate 24 hours.

Linda Whitaker
Harpeth Council

MEXICALI CASSEROLE

1 (14 1/2 oz.) can tamales (Old El Paso)	1 (10 1/2 oz.) can condensed cream of chicken soup
1 (20 oz.) can yellow hominy, drained	1 (14 1/2 oz.) can tamales
1 (4 or 5 oz.) can Vienna sausages, cut in thirds	1/4 c. (1 oz.) shredded sharp Cheddar cheese

Remove wrappers from the first can of tamales; cut tamales in thirds. Combine the cut tamales, the hominy, sausages and soup; turn into 1 1/2 quart casserole. Bake, uncovered, in 350° oven for 35 to 40 minutes. Remove wrappers from second can of tamales; cut tamales diagonally in halves. Garnish top of casserole with cut tamales. Sprinkle cheese atop. Return to oven to melt cheese and heat top of tamales. Makes 6 servings.

Maxine Scott
East Memphis Council

MIXED VEGETABLE SUPREME

4 c. cabbage, coarsely chopped
2 c. sliced carrots
1 c. sliced celery
1 c. sliced onion
1 apple, thinly sliced
1 tsp. sugar
1/2 tsp. salt

Steam first 5 ingredients 10 to 12 minutes until tender; drain. Sprinkle with salt and sugar.

Cheese Sauce:

4 Tbsp. butter
2 Tbsp. flour
1 1/2 c. milk
1 c. sharp cheese, grated
1/2 c. sour cream

Melt butter; stir in flour. Add milk all at once. Cook and stir until thick. Remove from heat; add cheese and sour cream.

Topping:

2 Tbsp. butter
1/4 c. bread crumbs
2 Tbsp. Parmesan cheese
1 Tbsp. slivered almonds

Use oblong casserole. Layer vegetables with cheese sauce on each layer. Top with buttered crumbs and cheese; add almonds. Bake at 350° for 30 minutes.

Mrs. Bob Unkenholz
Harpeth Council

MEXICAN CASSEROLE

1 lb. ground beef
1 medium onion, chopped
2 small cans chili con carne
1/2 small ctn. sour cream
6 slices American cheese
1 medium bag Dorito chips

Brown meat and onion; mix with canned chili. Spread on bottom of oblong casserole dish. Spread sour cream carefully on top. Lay cheese slices on top of sour cream. Crush Doritos and sprinkle on top of cheese, enough to cover entire dish. Bake at 400° for 15 minutes. Make a hot sauce, using chili sauce or catsup and a dash of Tabasco sauce to be used on individual servings (optional).

Dean Tidwell
Nashboro Council

STUFFED MUSHROOM CROWNS
(This goes great with beef roast.)

12 large fresh whole
   mushrooms
1/4 c. sliced green onion
3 Tbsp. butter
1/2 tsp. dried dill weed

1/3 c. fine, dry bread
   crumbs
1/4 tsp. salt
Dash of Worcestershire sauce
1 Tbsp. red wine

Remove stems from mushrooms; chop stems. Cook stems and onion in butter until tender but not brown. Add bread crumbs, dill, salt and Worcestershire sauce. Fill mushroom crowns with onion mixture; place in buttered baking dish. Sprinkle with wine. Bake at 325° for 15 minutes. Serves 3-4.

Rosemary Grand
Harpeth Council

MUSTARD AND COLLARD GREENS

2 smoked ham hocks
Water
3 - 3 1/2 lb. mustard
   greens

3-4 lb. collard greens
2 tsp. sugar
3 tsp. salt
1/4 tsp. pepper

Place ham hocks in large saucepot or Dutch oven; cover with water and cook, covered, over moderately low heat for 2 hours. While ham is cooking, remove stems from greens and tear leaves into fairly large pieces. Rinse greens several times in warm, salted water; drain well. Stir sugar, salt and pepper into water with ham hocks. Add enough greens to fill pot; cover and when greens shrink, add more, stirring occasionally, until all the greens are added. Cook greens for 1 1/2 to 2 1/2 hours, depending on the tenderness of the greens. Remove the meat from ham hocks and serve with greens. Serves 8. (Greens may be prepared a day ahead and reheated just before dinner.)

Mary Crabtree
Knoxville Council

NOODLES-TUNA CASSEROLE

1 (6 oz.) pkg. noodles
1 green pepper (optional)
2 hard boiled eggs
3 small cans or 1 large can
   tuna

1 can condensed mushroom
   soup
1 c. milk
1/4 c. chopped pimento
1 pkg. shredded Cheddar
   cheese

Cook noodles in salt water until tender; drain. Cook pepper in salt water 10 minutes; chop pepper. Add milk to mushroom soup and heat. Add tuna, chopped pepper, chopped eggs and cheese. Pour into buttered casserole. Top with crushed potato chips and bake in moderate oven for 30 minutes.

Imogene Chesher
Knoxville Council

SPANISH NOODLE CASSEROLE

1 large green pepper,
   chopped
2 large onions, chopped
1 clove garlic, minced
   (optional)
2 lb. ground beef
3 c. tomato sauce
1 can cream style corn
1 can chopped ripe olives
1 (4 oz.) can mushrooms

1 medium pkg. flat noodles,
   cooked and drained
1/2 lb. American cheese,
   cubed
1 tsp. salt
1/4 tsp. pepper
1 or 2 dashes Tabasco sauce
1/8 tsp. paprika
1 or 2 Tbsp. Worcestershire
   sauce
1 or 2 tsp. leaf oregano

Cook pepper, onions and garlic in vegetable oil until tender; add ground beef and cook until red is out. Drain off excess fat. Add all other ingredients; mix well. Bake in large greased casserole for 30 minutes at 350°. Makes 12 servings.

Sue Gilley
Jackson Council

OKINAWAN PORK AND CABBAGE

1/2 c. sugar
1/2 c. soy sauce

1 1/2 lb. pork, cut in thin
  strips
1 medium head cabbage,
  chopped

Combine sugar, 1/2 cup water and soy sauce in large saucepan. Add pork; cook until tender. Add cabbage and cover; cook until cabbage is tender.

Peggy Burr
Harpeth Council

OKRA CREOLE STYLE

4 Tbsp. Wesson oil or
  bacon drippings
1 large onion, chopped
1 small green pepper,
  chopped
3 medium tomatoes, chopped
  (green or ripe)

1 doz. (3 inch) okra pods,
  chopped
1 c. fresh cut corn (optional)
Salt and pepper to taste
1/2 - 3/4 c. water

Heat Wesson oil or drippings in heavy skillet. Cook onion and green pepper over low heat about 10 minutes, stirring often to keep from burning. Add tomatoes, okra, corn, seasonings and water. Add more water as needed during cooking. Cook over medium heat, covered, about 30-45 minutes, or until done, stirring often and adding additional water to keep from sticking.

Joyce Mattice
Harpeth Council

CRISPY FRIED ONION RINGS

1 extra large onion
1 1/4 c. all-purpose flour
1 tsp. baking powder
1/4 tsp. salt

1 c. beer
1 egg, beaten
1 Tbsp. vegetable oil
Vegetable oil for deep frying

Peel onion; cut into 1/4 inch slices. Separate into rings. Place onion rings in a large bowl; cover with ice water. Let stand 30 minutes; drain on paper towels. Combine dry ingredients, beer, egg and 1 tablespoon vegetable oil in electric blender; process until smooth. Place batter in a shallow pan. Using a fork, dip onion rings into batter, coating both sides well. Fry in deep, hot oil, 375°, until golden brown on both sides, 3-5 minutes. Drain well on paper towels. Yield: 4-6 servings. This batter is good for zucchini also.

Note: These onion rings may be frozen in a single layer on baking sheets for later use. When frozen, package rings in foil. To reheat, place onion rings on baking sheets; bake at 400° for 7 minutes.

Nancy Ligon
Green Hills Council

FRENCH FRIED ONION RINGS

2 large (1 lb.) peeled onions	1 Tbsp. Wesson oil
1 c. sifted all-purpose flour	1 egg white
1/2 tsp. salt	Extra flour to dip in
1/4 tsp. pepper	Fat to fry 1/2 inch deep
1 c. milk	Salt

Slice onions into 1/4 inch thick slices; separate. Combine flour, salt and pepper in small, deep bowl; add milk, 1 tablespoon fat and egg white. Beat until smooth. Coat onion rings with extra flour; dip into batter. Dip back into flour. Cook 3 minutes in electric skillet. Drain on brown paper bag and salt.

Judy Christopher
Harpeth Council

CREAMED ONIONS AND CARROTS

1/4 c. sliced celery	2 Tbsp. butter or margarine
1 can Campbell's cream of chicken soup	1/2 c. sour cream
1/4 c. dry white wine	2 Tbsp. chopped parsley
1 lb. cooked medium carrots, cut in halves lengthwise	1 lb. (about 16) cooked small whole white onions

In saucepan, cook celery in butter until tender. Blend in soup and sour cream; add wine and parsley. Cut carrot halves in 2 inch pieces; add carrots and onions to soup mixture. Heat; stir occasionally. Makes about 4 cups.

Casandra Key
Harpeth Council

CREAMED ENGLISH PEAS

Make White Sauce:

3 tsp. flour   3 tsp. butter
1 c. milk

Grate 1/3 pound cheese into this. Add 1 small can pimento, chopped. Add 1 (No. 2) can English peas, drained. Salt and pepper to taste.

Joyce Mattice
Harpeth Council

EASY CHEESY PEAS

1 (10 oz.) can condensed   1 (17 oz.) can English peas,
  cream of mushroom soup   drained
1/3 c. milk   6 Ritz crackers, crushed
1 c. shredded Velveeta   1 tsp. paprika
  cheese   1 medium size baking dish

Stir soup in a small saucepan over medium heat until smooth; gradually add milk and 1/2 cup Velveeta cheese. Stir until cheese melts; pour over drained peas. Sprinkle remaining 1/2 cup cheese over pea mixture; add crushed crackers over top of other ingredients. Sprinkle 1 teaspoon of paprika over top. Bake 8-10 minutes in a 450° oven or until mixture is slightly bubbly. Serves approximately 8.

Mrs. Bob Unkenholz
Harpeth Council

ENGLISH PEA CASSEROLE

1/2 c. chopped onion   1/3 c. chopped pimento
1/4 c. chopped bell pepper   1 can cream of mushroom
3/4 c. chopped celery   soup
1 stick butter   1 (8 oz.) can mushrooms
2 (16-17 oz.) cans green   Bread crumbs
  peas, drained

Saute onion, bell pepper and celery in butter. Add to peas; stir in pimento, mushroom soup and mushrooms. Place in greased 2 quart casserole; top with bread crumbs. Bake at 350° for 30 minutes. Serves 8.

Rosemary Grand
Harpeth Council

1489-81

PARTY PEAS

1 (8 oz.) can green peas
1 can cream of mushroom
   soup

1 c. grated cheese (Cheddar,
   American, etc.)
2 hard boiled eggs
1 small jar chopped pimento

Combine all ingredients. Place in Pyrex dish and cover with cracker crumbs. Bake at 350°.

Pat Carpenter
Nashville Council

STUFFED PEPPERS

6 medium bell peppers
1 lb. hamburger meat
1/3 c. chopped onion
1/2 tsp. salt
1/2 tsp. black pepper
1 lb. can tomatoes

1/2 c. water
1/2 c. uncooked long grain
   rice
1 tsp. Worcestershire sauce
4 oz. (1 c.) sharp process
   American cheese, shredded

Cut off top of peppers; remove seeds. Put peppers in boiling, salted water about 5 minutes; drain (for crisp peppers, omit precooking). Sprinkle inside of peppers generously with salt. Cook hamburger meat and onion until brown, seasoned with salt and pepper. Add tomatoes, water, rice and Worcestershire sauce. Cover and simmer till rice is tender. Stir in cheese; stuff peppers. Bake, uncovered, at 350° for about 20-25 minutes.

Belinda Dorris
Nashboro Council

STUFFED PEPPERS

6 green peppers
1 1/4 c. ground beef
1 1/4 c. moistened bread
   crumbs

Salt and pepper
1 Tbsp. fat
1/2 onion, grated
1 c. water or stock

Cut a slice from stem end of each pepper. Remove seeds and parboil pepper 10 minutes. Mix minced, cooked meat with bread crumbs; add salt, pepper, melted fat and onion. Stuff peppers with mixture and place in baking pan.

Add water or stock. Bake in 375° oven for 30 minutes, basting frequently. Serves 6.

Joyce Mattice
Harpeth Council

STUFFED GREEN PEPPERS

1/2 c. Nutrilite protein (Amway)	1 c. tomato juice
3/4 lb. ground beef	1/4 c. chopped celery
6 medium green peppers	1/4 c. chopped parsley
2 c. cooked rice	2 Tbsp. chopped onion
	1 1/2 Tbsp. salt

Mix protein with tomato juice. Scoop out seeds and stringy sections of peppers; boil them 5 minutes in lightly salted water. Drain pepper shells. Toss all ingredients together and stuff shells. Use shallow pan with a little hot water and bake shells at 350° F. (175° C.) for 30 minutes until lightly browned.

Carolisa Coley
Harpeth Council

STUFFED GREEN PEPPERS

25 lb. (1 bushel; 100) peppers, green, large	5 lb. (2 3/4 gal.) dry bread, broken
2 lb. 8 oz. (1 3/4 qt.) onions, chopped	21 lb. (2 1/2 gal.) beef, cooked, ground
8 oz. (1 c.) fat	1 Tbsp. pepper
4 oz. (1/2 c.) salt	3/4 qt. milk (variable)

1. Wash and cut stem end from peppers; remove seeds and white membrane. 2. Cook chopped onions in fat until tender. 3. Soften bread with water; press out excess water. Mix thoroughly. 4. Combine onions, softened bread, ground meat, seasoning and milk (the milk will vary with the consistency of meat mixture). 5. Fill each pepper with 1/2 cup (6 ounces) of meat mixture. Place filled peppers on end in greased baking pan. Pour about 1 1/2 inches water around peppers. 6. Bake at 350° for 1 1/2 hours or until peppers are tender (cooking time may be reduced by steaming peppers 5 minutes before stuffing). Yields 100 large peppers, 100 portions; 1 stuffed pepper a portion.

HELMA'S STUFFED PEPPERS

1 lb. ground beef
3/4 c. chopped onion
Dash of pepper
1/2 small bay leaf
1 (1 lb.) can tomatoes
1 c. regular rice

1 tsp. cooking oil
1 1/2 tsp. salt
1/8 tsp. garlic
1/8 tsp. thyme
1/8 tsp. oregano
1 can cream of mushroom soup

Brown meat in oil; add onion. Cook until tender. Stir in other ingredients in order given; bring to boil. Reduce heat; simmer 5 minutes, stirring occasionally. Spoon in green peppers, that have been parboiled for 2 minutes. Bake 45 minutes at 350°; freezes well.

Optional: Top with grated cheese the last few minutes. If freezing, do not top with cheese until reheating.

Florence Stubblefield
Morristown Council

SCALLOPED PINEAPPLE

3 eggs
2 c. sugar
1/2 lb. butter

1 (No. 2) can crushed pineapple
4 c. bread cubes or bread pieces

Mix together the eggs, sugar and butter. Blend in pineapple and bread cubes. Bake 1 hour at 350°. Superb with ham.

Doris Binkley
Nashboro Council

DILLY BAKED POTATOES

Scrub or pare 6 potatoes; slice each into 3 or 4 slices. Between each potato slice, place a 1/4 inch slice of onion. Place each potato with onions on a double thickness of heavy duty aluminum foil. Sprinkle with salt, pepper and dill weed; dot with butter. Wrap tightly. Place on coals for 45 minutes to 1 hour, or on grill for 1 1/2 hours. Turn once or twice during cooking. Yield: 6 servings.

Jane York
Harpeth Council

DONNA KAY'S HASHED BROWN POTATOES

2 small baking potatoes   1/4 tsp. salt
1 Tbsp. finely chopped onion   2 Tbsp. butter or margarine

Boil potatoes in jackets; chill. Peel and coarsely shred (1 1/2 cups). Add onion, salt and dash of pepper. Melt butter in skillet. Pat potatoes into pan, leaving about 1/2 inch space around edge of pan. Brown about 9 minutes. Reduce heat, if necessary. Turn; brown about 5 minutes longer or until golden. Serves 2.

Kay Boswell
Andrew Jackson Council

SCALLOPED POTATOES

3 Tbsp. butter   3 c. milk
2 Tbsp. flour   1/2 c. American cheese
1 1/2 tsp. salt   6 medium potatoes, thinly
1/8 tsp. pepper   sliced
                        2 Tbsp. chopped onion

Make white sauce of first 5 ingredients; add cheese. Place 1/2 of the potatoes in a greased casserole (2 quart). Cover with 1/2 the onion and 1/2 the sauce; repeat layers. Bake 1 hour at 350°; uncover and bake 1/2 hour.

Linda Whitaker
Harpeth Council

POTATO CHEESE CASSEROLE

6-8 potatoes (2 c.)*   Dash of garlic
2 c. cottage cheese   1 tsp. salt
1/2 pt. sour cream   3/4 c. Cheddar cheese,
1/4 c. onion, finely chopped   grated

Boil potatoes in jackets; cool and dice. Combine next 5 ingredients; mix with potatoes. Pour into casserole. Sprinkle with grated Cheddar cheese. Bake at 350° until cheese melts and casserole is hot.
*Can use 18 ounces frozen hash brown potatoes.

Kathy Franck
Harpeth Council

POTATO CASSEROLE

2 lb. pkg. hash brown
  potatoes
1/4 tsp. black pepper
1 tsp. salt

1 can cream of chicken soup
1 stick butter, melted
8 oz. sour cream
8 oz. American cheese, grated

Stir together and put in baking dish.

Topping:

2 c. crushed corn flakes   1 stick butter

Mix together. Bake at 350° for 45 minutes.
Patricia Hire
Harpeth Council

POTATO CASSEROLE

1 (2 lb.) bag frozen hash
  brown potatoes
1/2 c. chopped onion
1/2 c. melted oleo (save
  half for top)

10 oz. grated Cheddar cheese
1 can cream of chicken soup
1 tsp. salt
1/2 tsp. black pepper
1 c. sour cream
Bread crumbs

Mix all ingredients together, except reserved oleo and bread crumbs. Put in well greased casserole; sprinkle top with crumbs and oleo. Bake 1 hour and 10 minutes in 350° oven.
Della D. Sullivan
Green Hills Council

EASY POTATO CASSEROLE

1 (32 oz.) pkg. frozen
  shredded hash brown
  potatoes, thawed
1 medium onion, chopped
1/2 c. chopped green pepper
1 (10 3/4 oz.) can cream of
  potato soup, undiluted

1 (10 3/4 oz.) can cream of
  celery soup, undiluted
1 (8 oz.) ctn. commercial
  sour cream
1/2 tsp. salt
1/8 tsp. pepper
1 c. (4 oz.) shredded
  Monterey Jack cheese

Combine all ingredients, except cheese; stir well.

Spoon potato mixture into a greased shallow 2 quart casserole. Bake at 325° for 1 hour and 15 minutes. Sprinkle with cheese and bake an additional 15 minutes. Makes 8 servings.

Billie Fleming
Nashboro Council

Peggy Burr
Harpeth Council
Norma Foster
Harpeth Council

NEW POTATOES

Scrape thin skin from small new potatoes. Potatoes smaller than a golf ball should remain whole; larger ones cut in halves or quarter accordingly. Boil in salt water until they can be penetrated with fork; do not overcook. Drain off water. Use salt and black pepper to taste on potatoes, then brown in skillet of hot bacon drippings, about 1/3 inch deep. Turn or roll potatoes over while browning. These small whole potatoes or quarters have a delicious and destinctive new potato taste.

Henry Marshall
Clarksville Council

FAT RASCALS

5 medium baking potatoes,
   grated
5 Tbsp. shredded cheese
   (Cheddar)
1/2 tsp. salt

Vegetable oil
2 Tbsp. all-purpose flour
2 eggs, beaten
Dash of cayenne pepper

Combine all ingredients, except oil, in large mixing bowl; mix well. Drain liquid that may accumulate. Pour oil into large skillet to the depth of 1/2 inch. Heat oil to 350°. Drop potato mixture into hot oil 1/4 cup at a time; flatten slightly with a spatula, forming circle. Cook 3 minutes on each side or until potatoes are brown. Add oil as necessary. Yield: 8 to 10 servings.

Wendell Harmon
Nashville Council

GRATED POTATO CASSEROLE

1/2 c. milk
1/2 tsp. salt
1 c. cubed process American
   cheese
1/2 small onion, cut up

3 eggs
1/8 tsp. pepper
2 Tbsp. butter
3 medium potatoes, peeled
   and cubed

Heat oven to 375°. Grease 10 x 6 x 1 1/2 inch baking dish. Place milk, eggs, salt, pepper, cheese, butter, onion and cubed potatoes in blender container in the order listed. Cover and blend on high speed just until all potatoes are grated; do not overblend. Pour into prepared dish. Bake for 35 to 40 minutes. Garnish with green pepper rings. (If you have no blender, grate cheese, potatoes and onion and combine well with other ingredients.) Serves 6.

Joyce Mattice
Harpeth Council

SUPREME POTATO CASSEROLE

6 medium potatoes, boiled
1 c. sour cream
1 tsp. salt
1/8 tsp. garlic powder
   (optional)

2 c. cottage cheese
2 Tbsp. green onion, chopped
2 tsp. sugar
1 c. grated Cheddar cheese

Peel and dice potatoes, which have been boiled in jackets until tender. Combine with cottage cheese, sour cream, onion and seasonings. Pour into a lightly greased 1 1/2 quart baking dish; top with grated cheese. Bake at 350° for about 45 minutes. Serves 10-12.

Joyce Mattice
Harpeth Council

PARMESAN POTATOES

6 large potatoes
1/4 c. sifted flour
1/4 c. Parmesan cheese
3/4 tsp. salt

1/8 tsp. pepper
1/3 c. butter or oleo
Chopped parsley

Pare potatoes; cut into quarters. Combine flour, cheese, salt and pepper in a bag. Moisten potatoes with water and shake a few at a time in a bag, coating potatoes well with cheese mixture. Melt butter in a 13x9 inch baking pan or dish. Place potatoes in a layer in pan. Bake at 375° for about 1 hour, turning once during baking. When golden brown, sprinkle with parsley. (You can also shake your cut up chicken pieces in this same coating mixture and bake in the same dish.)

Jan Morrow
Columbia Council

POTATOES WITH CARROTS

1 1/2 lb. potatoes   1 lb. young carrots

Cook separately in usual way. Drain each well and puree or blend together; add a good "hunk" of butter and 1 teaspoon hot mustard. Cream to desired consistency. Goes well with roast beef.

Betty Marek
Harpeth Council

RIVERTOWN POTATO CASSEROLE

2 c. cream style cottage cheese	2 tsp. salt
	5 c. cooked, diced potatoes
1 c. sour cream	1/2 c. shredded cheese
1/3 c. sliced onion	Paprika

Combine cottage cheese, sour cream, onion and salt. Fold in potatoes and pour into greased 1 1/2 quart shallow casserole. Sprinkle with cheese and paprika. Bake in 350° oven for 40 minutes. Serves 6.

Helen H. Stephens
Memphis Council

TOP-OF-THE-STOVE SCALLOPED POTATOES

Potatoes (to fill saucepan)	Salt and pepper to taste
Sliced onion (optional)	Cheese (optional)
2 Tbsp. butter	

Cut potatoes into crosswise slices, approximately 1/4 inch thick. Drop potatoes immediately into water while slicing to keep them from turning brown. Layer potatoes in a saucepan (onion may be sliced and sandwiched between potato layers) until saucepan is full. Add butter, salt and pepper and 1/4 cup water. Jiggle pan so water will find its way to the bottom. Place on top of stove on high heat until you hear pressure, then decrease heat to low and cook 20 minutes.

Optional: My family likes me to put them in a casserole and put shredded or sliced cheese on top and put under broiler to brown. If potatoes are drier than you like (this depends on the moisture in the potatoes), add a little milk or water in casserole.

Sheila Fleming
East Memphis Council

TWICE BAKED POTATOES

2 large baking potatoes	1/2 c. sour cream
4 strips bacon	1/2 tsp. salt
1/4 c. chopped onion	1/2 tsp. white pepper
2 Tbsp. grated Parmesan cheese	2 Tbsp. melted butter or margarine
	Paprika

Scrub potatoes; dry and prick with fork. Bake at 400° for 1 hour. While potato is cooling slightly, fry bacon in small skillet until crisp. Drain off excess drippings, leaving about 3 tablespoons in skillet. Add onion; saute until tender but not brown. Remove skillet from heat. Cut potatoes in halves lengthwise; scoop out potato insides carefully and add to skillet. Add cheese, cream and seasonings, mixing and mashing to blend thoroughly. Return skillet to low heat until mixture is heated through. Spoon mixture into potato shells; drizzle with melted butter and sprinkle with paprika. Bake at 350° for 15 to 20 minutes or until lightly browned. Can be made ahead and heated just before serving time. Serves 4. Topping -

Sour Cream and Chives: Combine 1 cup sour cream with 2 tablespoons minced chives and 1/2 teaspoon grated onion; add salt and pepper to taste.

Cheese-Sour Cream Topping: Combine 2 cups grated Cheddar cheese, 1/2 cup softened butter, 1 cup sour cream and 1/4 cup minced green onions; add salt and pepper to taste.

Bacon Topping: Add 1/4 cup crumbled, crisp cooked bacon to one of the above toppings.

Linda Smith
Harpeth Council

POTATO CAKES

3 c. mashed potatoes,
  cooled
1/2 c. chopped onion
1 tsp. salt

1 pkg. dry yeast, dissolved
  in 1/2 c. warm water
1/2 c. plain flour
1 tsp. pepper

Mix all dry ingredients thoroughly. Make a well in center of mixture; add yeast and mix well. Fry on griddle at 350° until well browned. Serve with butter or your favorite sauce or ketchup.

Norma Ann Webb
Harpeth Council

POTATO CAKES

1 lb. hot, boiled potatoes,
  peeled (2 c.)
1/3 c. melted butter

Salt and pepper
1 c. flour
1 tsp. baking powder

Mash potatoes with butter, salt and pepper to taste. Beat in flour and baking powder; knead well. Shape into rectangle 1/2 inch thick. Cut into squares or triangles. Brown well on both sides on greased medium-hot griddle.

Shirley Buckner
Green Hills Council

POTLUCK POTATOES

1 (No. 2) pkg. frozen hash
  brown potatoes
1 can cream of chicken soup
2 c. (10 oz.) shredded
  cheese
1/2 c. melted butter

1/4 tsp. pepper
1/2 c. chopped onion
1 pt. sour cream
2 c. crushed corn flakes
1/4 c. melted butter

Combine first 7 ingredients. Pour into buttered 13x9 inch baking dish. Combine corn flakes with melted 1/4 cup butter; top casserole. Bake at 350° for 45 minutes. Serves 20.

Naomi J. Martin
Clarksville Council

1489-81

PARK AVENUE HAMBURGER CASSEROLE

4-6 slices bacon, diced
1 lb. lean ground beef
2 medium onions, cut up
1 can cream of chicken soup
Salt and pepper

Garlic salt
1 c. sour cream
1 can mushroom stems and
  pieces
Noodles

Fry the bacon; add the ground beef and onions and cook until browned. Add the soup, mushrooms, seasonings and simmer. Add the sour cream last and reheat, but do not allow to boil. Cook the noodles; drain. Add butter and some poppy seeds. Arrange the noodles in a shallow casserole and top with the meat mixture. Bake 30 to 35 minutes at low temperature, about 225°. The low temperature is necessary because of the sour cream in the meat mixture. Garnish with parsley. Serves 4-6.

Peggy Burr
Harpeth Council

PARTY HAM CASSEROLE

4 oz. egg noodles
1 can cream of mushroom
  soup, undiluted
1 tsp. instant minced onion
1 1/2 Tbsp. melted butter
1/2 c. milk

2 c. leftover cooked ham, cut
  in 1 inch slivers or cubed
2 Tbsp. mustard
1 c. dairy sour cream
1/4 c. bread crumbs
1 Tbsp. Parmesan cheese

Preheat oven to 325° F. Grease 1 1/2 quart casserole. Cook noodles as directed on package. In a small saucepan, combine soup and milk, stirring until smooth. Add onion, mustard and sour cream, stirring to combine well. In the prepared casserole, make layer with half the noodles, ham and sauce; repeat layers. Toss bread crumbs with melted butter; sprinkle over casserole. Top with cheese. Bake, uncovered, for 25 minutes or until golden brown. Serves 6.

Mary R. Veal
Chattanooga Council

PORK AND ENGLISH PEA CASSEROLE

2 lb. lean pork, cut in
   1 inch cubes
2 Tbsp. salt
1 Tbsp. pepper
2 Tbsp. sugar
2 cans peas, drained

4 Tbsp. flour
2 Tbsp. bread crumbs
1 can mushroom soup
3 Tbsp. butter
1 medium bag potato chips

Put pork in covered pan with just enough water to cover. Add salt, pepper and sugar; cook until tender. Mix together peas, flour, bread crumbs, soup and butter. Drain pork; add to soup mixture. Pour into large, oiled casserole dish. Bake at 350° until thick and bubbly. Just before serving, crush chips and spread over top. Put back in oven and reheat. Serves 8-10.

Peggy Burr
Harpeth Council

QUICHE

4 c. thinly sliced zucchini   1 c. chopped onion

Saute about 10 minutes in 1/4 to 1/2 cup margarine. Add:

2 Tbsp. parsley flakes
1/2 tsp. salt
1/2 tsp. black pepper

1/4 tsp. garlic powder
1/4 tsp. basil leaves
1/4 tsp. oregano leaves

In a large bowl, beat 2 eggs. Add 2 cups shredded Mozzarella cheese; stir in vegetables. Line bottom of baking dish with 1 package of Pillsbury crescent rolls. Spread with 2 teaspoons mustard; pour mixture in dish. Bake at 375° for 18 to 20 minutes or until knife inserted comes out clean. Cool 10 minutes and serve with fresh fruit.

Note: If you think it is browning too fast, place foil over it for the last 5 minutes of baking time.

Mabel M. Wilson
Clarksville Council

QUICHE

2 Pet Ritz pie shells, baked
   light brown, then brushed
   with 1 tsp. margarine
2 c. grated Cheddar cheese

6 eggs, plus 1/2 c. milk,
   1 1/2 tsp. salt and 1 tsp.
   black pepper

Use any combination of the following:

1/2 c. chopped green pepper
1/2 c. chopped green onions
   (tops included)
1/2 c. chopped green olives
1 c. chopped mushrooms
1 pkg. Buddig smoked ham,
   chopped

1 c. smoked sausage,
   chopped, fried, drained
6 slices bacon, chopped,
   fried, drained
1/2 c. fresh tomatoes,
   chopped, drained, plus
   1/2 tsp. oregano, 1 tsp.
   sugar, mixed

Bake pie shells; brush with margarine. Sprinkle 1/2 of grated cheese in shells. Add any combination of ingredients. Add remaining cheese. Pour egg mixture over ingredients. Bake at 350° for 30 minutes or until knife inserted into center comes out clean.

Peggy Hunter
Harpeth Council

QUICK CASSEROLE DINNER

1 1/2 lb. ground beef
1/2 c. chopped onion
1/2 c. chopped celery
2 Tbsp. flour
2 (8 oz.) cans tomato sauce
   with mushrooms

1 tsp. salt
1/4 tsp. oregano
1/8 tsp. pepper
1 (10 oz.) pkg. frozen peas
1 can biscuits
1 c. grated Cheddar cheese

Brown beef, onion and celery; drain. Stir in flour, tomato sauce, peas and seasoning; simmer 5 minutes. Pour into casserole dish; top with cheese and biscuits. Bake at 350° for 20 minutes.

M.J. Roderick
Knoxville Council

RAILROAD PIE

1 lb. ground beef	1 large onion, chopped

Brown beef and onion in skillet. Pour off excess fat; add the following ingredients:

1 (12 oz.) can whole kernel corn, drained	1 tsp. salt
	1 Tbsp. chili powder
1 can tomato soup	1/2 c. bell pepper, chopped
1 soup can water	Dash of black pepper

Bring to boil and simmer 15 minutes; turn into large, greased casserole (1 1/2 quart).

Corn Bread Topping:

3/4 c. plain corn meal	1/4 tsp. soda
3/4 tsp. sugar	1 egg, beaten
1 tsp. salt	1/2 c. buttermilk
1 Tbsp. plain flour	1 Tbsp. bacon drippings
1 tsp. baking powder	

Mix dry ingredients; add buttermilk, egg and bacon drippings. Blend well; pour over meat mixture. Bake, uncovered, in 350° oven for 30-40 minutes or till topping is done and brown crusted. Scrumptious.

Dot Crouch
Clarksville Council

BAKED RICE

1/2 stick butter	1 onion, chopped fine

Glaze onion in butter and add:

1 can consomme	1 can onion soup
1 small can chopped mushrooms	1 c. uncooked long grain rice

Bake at 350°, uncovered, for 1 1/2 hours.

Robert and Terry Johnson
Harpeth Council

BROWN PARTY RICE

2 c. chopped onion
2 c. uncooked brown rice
1 stick margarine

4 cans Campbell's beef
  consomme
8 oz. can sliced mushrooms

Saute onion in margarine. Combine this with other ingredients. Bake at 350° for 2 hours. Add small amount of water if it becomes dry. Yields 8 to 10 servings.
Frankie Johnston
Chattanooga Council

BROWNED RICE

1 medium onion, chopped
1 stick oleo or butter
1 c. rice, uncooked

1 can consomme
1 can mushrooms
1 c. water

Saute onion in butter in heavy skillet; remove onion. Add rice to remaining butter. Very slowly let uncooked rice brown, moving the rice constantly. Mix with onion and other ingredients. Bake in 9x13 inch uncovered casserole in 350° oven, stirring occasionally while it cooks. Serves 4. Bake 30 to 45 minutes.
Harmon Foster
Nashville Council

RICE CASSEROLE

3/4 stick butter
1 can onion soup
1/2 can water

6 oz. can mushrooms
1/2 c. uncooked rice
1 can sliced water chestnuts

Melt butter in casserole dish; add mushrooms and chestnuts. Remove from heat. Add remaining ingredients; stir slightly. Cover and bake 1 1/2 hours at 325°.
Betty Marek
Harpeth Council

RICE CONSOMME

1 stick oleo
1 medium onion
1 can mushroom stems and
  pieces

1 c. Uncle Ben's converted
  rice, uncooked
2 cans beef consomme

Melt oleo in skillet; add chopped onion. Saute until tender, not browned. Pour into a 2 quart flat casserole. Add rice and mix. Add mushrooms and the 2 cans beef consomme. Stir until well mixed. Cover with foil, airtight. Bake at 350° for 1 hour. Makes delicious brown rice. Serves 6-8. Only 1 skillet to wash.

Ethel Louise Sparkman
Jackson Council

QUICK AND EASY FRIED RICE

1 lb. bacon, crumbled
1 large onion, diced

2 c. prepared Minute Rice

Prepare rice; set aside. Fry bacon very crisp, reserving last skillet of drippings. Saute large diced onion in last skillet of drippings till lightly browned. Add crumbled bacon to sauteed onion and mix. Just add rice and mix well, using medium heat. Remove when well blended and serve as main dish. Serves 6-8 hungry people.

Sandra Bullock
Harpeth Council

RICE AND CHICKEN CASSEROLE

1 stick butter or oleo
1 1/2 c. rice, slightly
  cooked
1 fryer, cut up

1 can cream of mushroom
  soup
1 can cream of celery soup
1 1/2 soup cans of water

Melt butter in casserole; layer rice in bottom of casserole. Arrange chicken parts on bed of rice. Pour soups over chicken and rice; add water. Bake at 300° for 2 hours or until chicken and rice are done. Yield: 8-10 servings.

Ura Blanks
Harpeth Council

SUPER CONTINENTAL RICE

1 pkg. Lipton's onion soup
   mix
1 stick butter

1 c. long grain rice
1 (4 oz.) can sliced
   mushrooms, drained

Prepare soup mix according to directions on package, then add 1 stick butter; bring to a boil. Add 1 cup long grain rice plus 1 (4 ounce) can sliced mushrooms, drained. Bring to a boil and cover rice mixture. Simmer until all liquid is absorbed, 15 minutes or longer.

Ethel V. Palmer
Memphis Council

SALMAGUNDE BAKE

3/4 c. uncooked rice
2 1/2 tsp. salt
Dash of pepper
2 (8 oz.) cans tomato sauce
1 c. hot water
1 large onion, chopped
1 c. chopped green pepper

1 lb. ground beef
1/2 tsp. monosodium
   glutamate
1 (12 oz.) can whole kernel
   corn, drained
2-3 tsp. chili powder
2-4 slices bacon

In ungreased 2 quart casserole, place rice and sprinkle with the pepper and 1 1/2 teaspoons salt. Over the rice, pour 1 can of the tomato sauce and the hot water. Add the onion, green pepper and beef in layers in that order. Sprinkle with the monosodium glutamate and remaining teaspoon salt. Add the corn in a layer; top with the remaining can of tomato sauce and chili powder. Lay the bacon slices on top. Cover and bake in 375° oven for 1 hour; uncover and bake 15 minutes longer or until rice is done. Garnish with green pepper rings, tomato wedges and crisp bacon, if desired.

Barbara Stanfill
Harpeth Council

SAUSAGE CASSEROLE

1 lb. sausage, browned
   and drained
6 beaten eggs
1 c. cheese

5 slices day old bread, cubed
2 c. milk
1 tsp. dry mustard
1 tsp. salt

Mix all in casserole (rather shallow); soak overnight. Bake, covered, for 45 minutes at 350°. Serves 6 to 8.

Bessie Crosby
Harpeth Council

SAUSAGE FRUIT BAKE

1 lb. pork sausage
1 medium can sweet potat-
   toes, drained and sliced
1 medium can sliced peaches

3 tart cooking apples, cut
   into eighths
2 Tbsp. margarine or butter,
   melted
1/3 c. brown sugar

Pan fry crumbled sausage 15 to 20 minutes; drain off excess fat. In a buttered 2 quart casserole, alternate layers of sausage, sweet potatoes and fruit. Pour melted butter over top; sprinkle with brown sugar. Bake, covered, for 20 minutes at 375°. Remove cover and bake 15 minutes until apples are tender. Yield: 6 servings.

Mrs. Wavie Minke
Harpeth Council

EASY SAUSAGE CASSEROLE

1 lb. sausage
1 c. rice, uncooked
2 pkg. chicken noodle soup
1/4 c. chopped onion

1/4 c. chopped green pepper
1 c. chopped celery
2 1/2 c. water
1 tsp. soy sauce
1/4 tsp. salt

Brown sausage; combine with other ingredients. Bake at 350° for about 30 minutes. Sprinkle with 1/2 cup toasted almonds when almost done.

Ann Oakley
Harpeth Council

SAUSAGE AND RICE CASSEROLE

2 pkg. saffron rice (comes
   in small pkg.)
1 lb. sausage
1 hen, cooked and diced

2 cans cream of mushroom
   soup
1/4 c. water, milk or
   chicken broth
1 can mushrooms

Cook rice as directed; cook sausage and drain. Mix together with diced hen. Place in casserole and top with cracker crumbs and butter. Heat in 350° oven.

Teresa Beasley
Harpeth Council

SAUSAGE-RICE DISH

2 lb. bulk sausage
1 large onion
1 green pepper
12 c. boiling water
2 c. raw rice

3 pkg. Lipton chicken noodle soup
Celery
Blanched, slivered almonds

Brown sausage; add chopped onion and green pepper and cook until tender, but not brown. Bring 12 cups water to a boil; add 3 packages soup and 2 cups rice. Cook slowly 7 minutes. Combine with chopped celery and 1/2 the sausage mixture in a large baking dish. Put the remaining sausage on the top and sprinkle with almonds. Bake 1 1/2 to 2 hours in slow oven. Makes 15 generous portions.

Virginia Q. Kaderabek
Harpeth Council

SAUSAGE-RICE CASSEROLE

Brown:
1 lb. mild sausage   1 onion
1 green pepper

Mix 2 packages Wyler's or Lipton dry chicken noodle soup mix well with 2 - 2 1/2 cups water. Cook 2 cups Minute Rice according to directions on package. Mix together with browned ingredients and bake at 325° for 30 minutes.

Betty Stewart
Harpeth Council

SAUSAGE AND WILD RICE

1 lb. sausage
1 small onion, chopped
1/2 c. celery, chopped

1 box Uncle Ben's wild rice with seasonings
1 can chopped mushrooms
1 can water chestnuts, sliced

Brown sausage; crumble and drain. Reserve drippings. Saute onion and celery in sausage drippings. Cook rice according to package directions; add sausage, onion and celery, then add mushrooms and water chestnuts. Turn into a casserole; bake at 350° for 15 minutes. This recipe may be prepared ahead and heated about 30 minutes at 300°.

Doris Binkley
Nashboro Council

SCALLOPED TOMATOES - CHEESE

1 c. herb bread stuffing
1/2 tsp. garlic salt
1/4 tsp. oregano
2 tsp. sugar

1 (13 oz.) can tomatoes
1 c. grated Cheddar cheese
1 large onion, thinly sliced
2 Tbsp. butter

Combine stuffing, garlic salt, oregano and sugar. Arrange half of tomatoes in 10 x 16 x 1 1/2 inch pan. Top with layer of bread stuffing; sprinkle with 1/2 cup of the cheese and onion. Spread with remaining tomatoes; sprinkle with remaining cheese. Dot with butter. Bake in 350° preheated oven for 30 minutes. Makes 6 to 8 servings.

Ella M. Crockett
Columbia Council

7-LAYER CASSEROLE

2 medium potatoes, thinly
  sliced
2 or 3 carrots, thinly sliced
1 (No. 2) can English peas
1 medium onion

2 or 3 stalks celery
1 lb. ground beef
1 can condensed tomato
  soup

Grease 2 1/2 quart casserole dish. Bottom Layer: Potatoes, seasoned with salt (salt this layer only). Second Layer: Carrots; Third Layer: English peas, drained (save juice); Fourth Layer: Onion; Fifth Layer: Celery; Sixth Layer: Browned ground beef; Seventh Layer: Undiluted tomato soup, to which pea juice has been added. Pour over vegetables. Bake in 325° oven for 1 hour, covered. Remove cover and bake 45 minutes more. Serves 6-8.

Betty Pruitt
Green Hills Council

SHRIMP AND CRAB CASSEROLE

1 medium green pepper,
  chopped
1 medium onion, chopped
1 c. celery, chopped
1/2 lb. shrimp, peeled and
  deveined
1/2 lb. crabmeat
1/2 tsp. salt
1/8 tsp. pepper
1 Tbsp. Worcestershire sauce
1 c. mayonnaise
1 c. buttered crumbs

Combine all ingredients, except crumbs. Place in buttered casserole dish. Sprinkle top with crumbs. Bake at 350° for 30 minutes. Serves 8.

Margaret Powers
Harpeth Council

SKILLET DINNER

1/4 c. cooking oil
1 c. chopped onion
1 green pepper, diced
1 piece of celery, sliced
1 1/2 lb. ground beef
1 can stewed tomatoes
2 c. elbow macaroni
3 c. water
1 Tbsp. pepper
1/2 tsp. salt
Corn or green beans*

Cook in oil the onion, pepper and celery until golden. Add meat and stir to break up as it cooks. Drain; add tomatoes, macaroni, water, salt and pepper. Stir; cook and cover 15 to 20 minutes.
    *Can also be added, 1 can each or both.

Linda Earp
Clarksville Council

SOUTH-OF-THE-BORDER CASSEROLE

3 Tbsp. salad oil
8 (6 inch) packaged corn
  tortillas
1/2 lb. ground beef
1 medium onion, diced
1 small garlic clove, minced
2 (15 1/2 oz.) cans pinto
  beans
1 (28 oz.) can tomatoes
1 (6 oz.) can tomato paste
1 (4 oz.) can chopped green
  chilies, drained
2 tsp. sugar
1 tsp. salt
1/2 tsp. oregano leaves
1/4 tsp. pepper
1 c. coarsely shredded sharp
  Cheddar cheese

About 1 1/4 hours before serving: In 12 inch skillet

over medium heat, in hot salad oil, fry 1 tortilla at a time, a few seconds on each side until soft and blistered Remove tortilla to paper towels to drain. Cut tortillas into 1/2 inch strips. In same skillet over medium-high heat, cook beef, onion and garlic until pan juices evaporate and beef is browned, stirring occasionally. Remove from heat; stir in pinto beans with their liquid, tomatoes with their liquid and remaining ingredients, except cheese. Preheat oven to 350° F. In 13x9 inch baking dish, arrange 1/3 of ground beef mixture; top with 1/3 of tortilla strips. Repeat layering, ending with tortilla strips. Sprinkle cheese on top. Bake 30 minutes or until hot. Makes 6 servings.

Joyce Mattice
Harpeth Council

SURFER'S SEAFOOD CASSEROLE

1/2 lb. fresh crabmeat	1/2 c. chopped green pepper
1/2 lb. cooked shrimp	1/2 tsp. salt
1 c. mayonnaise	1 tsp. Worcestershire sauce
1 1/3 c. chopped celery	1 c. crushed potato chips*
1/2 c. chopped onion	

Mix all ingredients together, except potato chips. Place in greased casserole and cover with crushed potato chips; sprinkle with paprika. Bake 30 to 40 minutes at 350°. Serves 6.
*Crushed potato chips are optional. Also canned meat can be used in place of fresh.

Peggy Wilkins
East Memphis Council

SPAGHETTI AND BEEF CASSEROLE

3 Tbsp. vegetable oil	2 (7 oz.) pkg. spaghetti
2 lb. ground beef	1 (8 oz.) pkg. cream cheese, softened
2 medium onions, chopped	
2 (4 oz.) cans mushroom stems and pieces, undrained	2 c. cottage cheese
	1 tsp. garlic powder
	1/2 c. chopped fresh or frozen chives
2 (8 oz.) cans tomato sauce	
1 (6 oz.) can tomato paste	1/2 c. sour cream
1 tsp. ground oregano	1/2 c. buttered bread crumbs

Heat oil in heavy skillet; add ground beef and onion. Saute until meat is browned, stirring to crumble; drain. Combine mushrooms, tomato sauce, tomato paste, oregano and garlic powder; add to meat mixture. Mix well; simmer, uncovered, 15 minutes. Cook the spaghetti according to package directions; drain. Place half of the spaghetti in a buttered 13x9x2 inch baking dish. Combine cream cheese, cottage cheese, chives and sour cream; mix well. Spoon cheese mixture over spaghetti layer, spreading evenly. Place remaining spaghetti over cheese mixture. Pour meat sauce over spaghetti; sprinkle with bread crumbs. Bake at 350° for 30 minutes or until bubbly. Serves 12.

Mary Crabtree
Knoxville Council

SPAGHETTI CASSEROLE

1 box Kraft dinner with
   meat sauce
1 lb. hamburger, salted
1 large onion

1 large ctn. cottage cheese
1 small ctn. sour cream
1 large pkg. cream cheese

Cook spaghetti according to directions and put in bottom of casserole. Brown meat and onion; add meat sauce. Mix cheeses; cut cream cheese in chunks. Place over spaghetti. Put meat mixture and top with Parmesan cheese. Bake in 350° oven until it bubbles and is hot through.

Pat DeMatteo
Nashboro Council

SPAGHETTI CASSEROLE

1 lb. ground chuck
1 small green pepper,
   chopped
1 small onion

1 can tomato soup
1 can golden mushroom soup
1/2 lb. grated sharp cheese
8 oz. vermicelli spaghetti

Brown ground chuck with the pepper and onion. Add tomato soup and the golden mushroom soup. Cook spaghetti until tender; drain. Alternate layers of spaghetti, ground chuck mixture and sharp cheese in a covered casserole. Bake, covered, at 350° for 1 hour. Recipe can be doubled for a crowd.

Mrs. M.E. Womble, Jr.
Memphis East Council

614

SPAGHETTI PIE

6 oz. spaghetti
2 Tbsp. butter or margarine
1/3 c. grated Parmesan
cheese
2 well beaten eggs
1 c. (8 oz.) cottage cheese
1 lb. ground beef or bulk
pork sausage
1/2 c. chopped onion
1/4 c. chopped green pepper

1 (8 oz.) can (1 c.)
tomatoes, cut up
1 (6 oz.) can tomato paste
1 tsp. sugar
1 tsp. dried oregano,
crushed
1/2 tsp. garlic salt
1/2 c. shredded Mozzarella
cheese (2 oz.)

Cook the spaghetti according to package directions; drain (should have about 3 cups spaghetti). Stir butter or margarine into hot spaghetti; stir in Parmesan cheese and eggs. Form spaghetti mixture into a "crust" in buttered 10 inch pie plate. Spread cottage cheese over bottom of spaghetti crust. In skillet, cook ground beef or pork sausage, onion and green pepper till vegetables are tender and meat is browned. Drain off excess fat; stir in undrained tomatoes, tomato paste, sugar, oregano and garlic salt. Heat through. Turn meat mixture into spaghetti crust. Bake, uncovered, in 350° oven for 20 minutes. Sprinkle the Mozzarella cheese atop. Bake 5 minutes longer or till cheese melts. Makes 6 servings.

Kathy Pack
Harpeth Council

SPINACH BALLS

2 (10 oz.) boxes chopped
spinach, cooked, drained
2 small chopped onions
3 c. packaged herb poultry
dressing
6 eggs, beaten
3/4 c. melted margarine

1/2 c. grated Parmesan
cheese
1 1/2 tsp. garlic salt
1/2 tsp. crumbled thyme
1/2 tsp. black pepper
1 Tbsp. monosodium
glutamate (optional)

Drain spinach well; mix with all other ingredients and shape into small balls. Bake at 325° for about 20 minutes on lightly greased pans or cookie sheets. Serve warm or freeze for future use. To use after freezing, thaw slightly and bake 20-25 minutes at 325°. Makes about 100 balls.

Kathy Womble
Memphis East Council

SPINACH BALLS

2 pkg. frozen chopped
  spinach
6 eggs, well beaten
1/2 c. Parmesan cheese,
  grated
1/2 tsp. thyme

3 c. stuffing mix (blend)
1 large onion, finely chopped
3/4 c. melted margarine
1 Tbsp. ground black pepper
1 1/2 tsp. garlic salt

Cook spinach according to package directions and mash dry; mix all ingredients. Roll into bite size balls. Bake at 325° for 15 to 20 minutes.

Bernice Curtis
Knoxville Council

SPINACH CASSEROLE

3 boxes frozen chopped
  spinach
2 c. sour cream

1 pkg. dry onion soup mix
4 or 5 Tbsp. melted oleo
3/4 c. herb bread stuffing

Cook spinach as directed; drain. Mix all ingredients, except bread stuffing. Pour into greased casserole. Top with herb stuffing. Bake 20 minutes at 400°.

Dorothy Bryant
Clarksville Council

SPINACH CASSEROLE

2 pkg. frozen chopped
  spinach
1 c. grated sharp Cheddar
  cheese

1/2 c. mayonnaise
1 can mushroom soup
1/2 c. chopped onion

Drain spinach; mix with remaining ingredients. Top with buttered croutons and bake for 45 minutes at 325°.

Rick and Sue Harder
Harpeth Council

SPINACH WITH SOUR CREAM

1 pkg. frozen chopped
  spinach
1 Tbsp. grated onion
2 eggs
1/2 c. sour cream

1 c. grated Parmesan cheese
1 Tbsp. flour
2 Tbsp. butter
Salt and pepper to taste

Cook frozen spinach in small amount of water with onion until thawed. Beat eggs and mix remainder of ingredients with spinach and onion. Bake in greased casserole for 25 or 30 minutes in 350° oven or until center is set. Do not overcook as it will separate. Serves 6.

Harriette Green
Memphis Council

ITALIAN SPINACH

2 (12 oz.) pkg. chopped
  frozen spinach
2 Tbsp. garlic juice
6 beaten eggs

1/2 c. grated Parmesan
  cheese
2 Tbsp. olive oil
Salt and pepper to taste

Cook and strain spinach. Pour into skillet; slowly cook in olive oil. Add garlic juice and raw eggs. When eggs turn white, remove spinach mixture from heat. Adjust seasonings and add Parmesan cheese.

Ginger Lewis
Harpeth Council

SPINACH RING

1 1/2 c. chopped spinach
  (2 pkg. frozen, thawed)
1 small onion, grated
3 well beaten eggs

1 pt. warmed milk
20 crushed soda crackers
3 Tbsp. melted butter

Mix all ingredients together and put in a greased casserole or ring mold. Bake 35 to 40 minutes at 350°.

Beverly Pettigrew
Harpeth Council

ACORN SQUASH SOUFFLE

3 c. cooked, mashed squash   1/2 c. milk
1 c. sugar   1/2 stick margarine, melted
3 eggs, slightly beaten   1 Tbsp. vanilla

Combine all ingredients; pour into buttered baking dish and top with:

1 c. brown sugar   1/2 stick margarine
1 c. chopped nuts   1/2 c. flour (self-rising)

Mix and blend by hand the ingredients. Spread on squash mixture in baking dish. Bake in 350° oven until topping is brown. Sweet potatoes may be used also.

Dorotha Sells
Morristown Council #12

BAKED SQUASH

2 1/4 lb. yellow squash   1/2 stick butter
1/2 c. sour cream   Salt and pepper to taste
1 green onion, minced   Buttered bread crumbs

Cook squash until tender; drain and mash. Combine with butter, sour cream, onion, salt and pepper. Place in buttered casserole; top with bread crumbs. Reheat when ready to serve in oven at 350° for 15 to 20 minutes. Serves 6.

Marie Barnett
Harpeth Council

SQUASH CASSEROLE

6-8 yellow squash   1 tsp. salt
1 large onion   3/4 c. Cheddar cheese,
1/4 c. sugar   grated
1/4 c. oleo   1 can French fried onions
1/4 c. water

Cook squash and onion with sugar, oleo, water and salt until squash is tender. Alternate with cheese in casserole. Bake at 350° for 20 minutes. Just before serving,

add the French fried onions on top. Place back in oven
for about 15 minutes. Serve while hot.

Jeanette W. Palmer
Harpeth Council

SQUASH CASSEROLE

2 lb. squash, sliced
1 small onion, chopped
Salt and pepper to taste
1 Tbsp. melted margarine
1 (10 3/4 oz.) can cream
   of chicken soup, undiluted

1 (8 oz.) ctn. commercial
   sour cream
2 Tbsp. chopped pimento
1/2 c. melted margarine
1 (8 oz.) pkg. herb
   seasoned stuffing mix

Cook squash and onion until tender in a small amount
of salted water; drain. Season with salt, pepper and 1
tablespoon margarine. Stir in chicken soup, sour cream
and pimento. Combine 1/2 cup margarine and stuffing mix,
stirring until well blended. Combine half of stuffing mix
and squash mixture. Spoon into a 2 quart casserole dish.
Top with remaining stuffing mix. Bake at 375° for 30
minutes. Yield: 8 to 10 servings.

Leslie Stovall
Jackson Council

SQUASH CASSEROLE

Mix the following and add to 2 cups cooked, mashed
squash:

1 can mushroom soup
1 ctn. (1 c.) sour cream
2 carrots, grated

1 medium onion, chopped
1 small jar pimentos, chopped
Salt and pepper to taste

Melt 1 stick oleo; pour over 1 package corn bread
stuffing. Put 1/2 of this in bottom of baking dish. Pour
squash mixture into dish. Put rest of the dressing on top.
Bake 30 minutes at 350°.

Imogene H. Suttles
Knoxville Council

SQUASH CASSEROLE

6 small yellow squash or
   enough to make 1 qt.,
   sliced
1 tsp. salt
3 Tbsp. margarine

1 egg, beaten
1 c. grated cheese
1/4 c. chopped onion
1/2 c. milk
1 c. cracker crumbs

Cook squash in small amount of salted water until tender; drain and mash. Add margarine, cheese, beaten egg, onion, milk and 3/4 cup cracker crumbs. Put into buttered baking dish and sprinkle top with remaining cracker crumbs. Bake in 425° oven for 20 to 25 minutes. Serves 6.

Beverly Pettigrew
Harpeth Council

SQUASH CASSEROLE

3 medium yellow squash
1 Tbsp. oleo
1/2 tsp. salt
1 beaten egg yolk
About 1/4 lb. fried, drained,
   crumbled sausage

Bread crumbs and oleo for top
1/4 c. sour cream
1/2 c. grated Cheddar cheese
1/8 tsp. pepper
1 Tbsp. chopped onion

Cook squash until tender; drain. Combine sour cream, oleo, cheese, salt and pepper; stir over low heat until melted. Take off; add egg, onion and sausage. Add the squash. Place in casserole. Top with bread crumbs and oleo. Bake at 350° for 20-25 minutes.

Marie Barnett
Harpeth Council

SQUASH CASSEROLE

2 lb. squash
1/4 c. butter
1/2 c. onion
1/4 c. sugar

2 eggs plus 1/2 c. milk,
   beaten together
1 c. cheese
Salt and pepper

Cook squash with butter, onion and sugar until tender; let cool. Add egg and milk mixture with salt and pepper to taste. Cover with cheese and bake at 375° for 45 minutes to 1 hour.

Kathy Franck
Harpeth Council

SQUASH CASSEROLE

1 can squash or cook down about 2 c. fresh squash	1 can cream of chicken soup
1 can mushroom soup	2 c. "Pepperidge Farm" herb stuffing mix

Mix all wet ingredients together. Add in all of stuffing mix, except enough to sprinkle on top. Bake till bubbly brown at 325°. Good main dish.

Mindy Yates
Harpeth Council

SQUASH CASSEROLE

2 (10 oz.) pkg. squash	2 boiled eggs, grated
1 can golden cream of mushroom soup	8 oz. Cheddar cheese, grated
	Ritz cracker crumbs

Cook squash until tender. In a large buttered casserole dish, layer squash, eggs, cheese, soup and crumbs, making 2 layers. Bake in 350° oven for about 45 minutes or until brown.

Deanna Baker
Harpeth Council

SQUASH CASSEROLE

3 cans squash	2 1/2 oz. sliced mushrooms (canned)
1 large onion, chopped	2 eggs, beaten
2 Tbsp. bacon drippings	4 c. grated mild Cheddar cheese
4 Tbsp. chopped pimientos	

Combine drained squash, chopped onion, bacon drippings and salt and pepper to taste in saucepan. Cook over medium heat until done and all liquid is absorbed; remove from heat. Stir in pimientos, mushrooms, beaten eggs and 1 cup grated cheese; mix well. Pour into casserole dish and top with remaining cheese. Sprinkle with black pepper. Bake in 375° oven for 15 or 20 minutes or until cheese is thoroughly melted.

Joyce M. Crump
Knoxville Council

SQUASH CASSEROLE

1 stick butter
1 pkg. Pepperidge Farm
  dressing mix
2-3 c. cooked, drained
  squash

1 medium onion
1 can cream of chicken soup
8 oz. sour cream

Cook squash and onion until tender; mash and drain. Melt butter in 13x9 inch baking dish. Mix in 2/3 of the package of dressing mix. Mix squash, soup and sour cream; pour over crumb mixture. Sprinkle rest of dressing mix over top and bake at 350° for 20 minutes.

Beverly Lamb
Harpeth Council

SUMMER SQUASH CASSEROLE

2 lb. squash, sliced (6 c.)
1/4 c. onion, chopped
1 tsp. salt
1 can condensed cream of
  chicken soup

1 c. dairy sour cream
1 c. carrots, shredded
1 (8 oz.) pkg. stuffing mix
1/2 c. butter, melted

Boil squash and onion 5 minutes in salted water; drain. Combine soup and sour cream; stir in carrots. Fold this into squash and onion. Combine stuffing mix and butter. Spread half of the stuffing mixture in bottom of 12 x 7 1/2 x 2 inch baking dish. Spoon vegetable mixture on top and sprinkle remaining stuffing over vegetables. Bake for 25 to 30 minutes or until thoroughly heated. Makes 6 servings.

Sally Jones
Nashboro Council

TENNESSEE SQUASH CASSEROLE

2 lb. yellow squash, sliced
1 medium onion, chopped
1 can cream of mushroom
  soup

Salt and red pepper to taste
1 c. Parmesan cheese, grated
1 c. cracker crumbs
Garlic powder to taste

Cook squash and onion together until tender; drain. Add soup; season to taste. Put into a buttered casserole.

Top with cheese and bread crumbs. Bake at 350° for 15-20 minutes. Yield: 8 servings.

Judy Christopher
Harpeth Council

THERESA WILSON'S SOUTHERN SQUASH CASSEROLE

6 or 8 small squash
2 medium onions, chopped
1 stick butter
3 large eggs

1 can cream of chicken soup
1/2 tsp. salt
1 c. buttered bread crumbs

Boil squash and onions until tender; drain and mash. Stir in remaining ingredients, except bread crumbs. Pour into 1 1/2 quart baking dish; top with bread crumbs. Bake at 350° for 25 minutes. Serves 8.

Zoerita Proctor
Nashville Council

SQUASH-CARROT CASSEROLE

6 c. yellow squash, sliced
1/2 tsp. salt
1 (8 oz.) pkg. stuffing mix
1/2 c. sour cream
1 c. grated carrots

1/2 c. onion, chopped
1/2 c. margarine, melted
1 (10 3/4 oz.) can cream of
  chicken soup

Heat oven to 350°. Grease 2 quart casserole. Cook squash and onion in small amount of salted water about 5 minutes. Combine margarine and stuffing mix. Drain squash and onion; add soup and sour cream. Fold in carrots. In prepared casserole dish, place alternate layers of stuffing mix and squash mixture, beginning and ending with stuffing mix. Bake 25 minutes. Serves 6-8.

Joyce Mattice
Harpeth Council

BUTTERNUT SQUASH SOUFFLE

3 Tbsp. margarine
2 c. cooked, mashed
  butternut squash
1 c. sugar (or less)
1/3 c. milk
1/2 tsp. salt

1/4 tsp. cinnamon
1/4 tsp. nutmeg
3 eggs
1 tsp. vanilla
Marshmallows, if desired

1489-81

623

Add margarine to hot squash; stir until melted. Add sugar, milk, salt and spices; beat until well blended. Stir in flavoring and turn into lightly buttered casserole. Top with marshmallows, if desired. If using marshmallows, bake at 300° until souffle is set and marshmallows are brown. If marshmallows are not used, bake at 325°. Yield: 6 servings.

Mrs. Wilma M. Christopher
Memphis Council

SQUASH SOUFFLE

1 pkg. frozen squash,
  sliced, or 6-8 fresh,
  small yellow squash
2 eggs, slightly beaten
1/2 c. milk, scalded
1 tsp. salt

1/2 c. shredded cheese
4 Tbsp. melted fat
2 Tbsp. finely chopped onion
1 c. sugar
1 c. bread crumbs or cracker
  crumbs

Thaw squash till separated; toss with bread crumbs. Mix eggs, sugar, salt, onion and melted fat. Combine with milk and pour over squash. Top with shredded cheese and bake at 400° for about 30 minutes, until done.

Phyllis Whaley
Andrew Jackson Council

CALMA'S SQUASH WITH CHEESE
(Sage is the surprise ingredient.)

2 lb. summer squash
1 medium onion, chopped
1 1/4 c. grated sharp cheese
1 Tbsp. sugar
1 egg, beaten
1 tsp. sage, ground

1/2 c. toasted bread crumbs
  (2 slices)
3 Tbsp. butter or margarine,
  melted
Salt and pepper to taste
Paprika

Cook squash in small amount of boiling, salted water until just tender. Combine all ingredients, except 1/2 cup cheese and paprika; pour into buttered casserole dish. Bake for 20 minutes at 350°, stirring occasionally. Place remaining cheese on top; sprinkle with paprika. Bake again for 20-25 minutes at 350° until mixture bubbles and cheese on top is melted.

Judy Gibson
Harpeth Council

GARDEN STUFFED YELLOW SQUASH

8-10 medium yellow squash
1/2 c. green pepper,
   chopped
1 medium tomato, chopped
1 medium onion, chopped
1/2 tsp. salt

2 slices bacon, fried crisp
   and crumbled
1/2 c. shredded Cheddar
   cheese
Dash of pepper
Butter

Wash squash and simmer in water 8 minutes or until just tender; drain and cool slightly. Cut a thin slice from top of each squash; remove seeds. Combine remaining ingredients, except butter. Mix well and spoon into squash shells. Dot each with a pat of butter. Bake at 400° for 20 minutes. Serves 8-10.

Peggy Burr
Harpeth Council

STUFFED YELLOW SQUASH

6 yellow crookneck squash
1 c. fine bread crumbs
1 Tbsp. minced parsley
1 tsp. salt

2 Tbsp. butter, melted
1 1/2 Tbsp. finely minced
   onion
1 egg

Cook squash in boiling, salted water until barely tender, but not soft; cool. Cut a slice lengthwise from squash, leaving the stem whole. Carefully scoop out the pulp. Stir crumbs into melted butter, saving half of crumbs for topping. Combine other half with remaining ingredients and squash pulp; fill squash shells. Sprinkle with crumbs. Bake at 400° until crumbs are evenly browned and squash is thoroughly heated, about 20 minutes. Serves 6. (This may be prepared and refrigerated until time to bake.)

Joyce Mattice
Harpeth Council

STUFFED SQUASH

12 yellow squash (gourd
   type)
6 Tbsp. melted butter
12 soda crackers, rolled to
   meal

2 small onions, minced (4
   Tbsp. if using dried)
6 Tbsp. bacon drippings
1/2 tsp. sugar
1/8 tsp. pepper
1/2 tsp. salt

1489-81

Wash squash; place in container covered with water. Boil 20 minutes (be careful not to break ends off). Let cool; slice off tops, about 2 inches long. Take teaspoon and carefully scoop pulp out; mash pulp. Add all ingredients; mix with cracker meal until it is stiff enough to place in opening of squash. Place stuffed squash on well greased* pan so stems will not break. Bake slowly, 300°, until light brown. Serve hot. Bacon crumbles or grated cheese added to top 5 minutes before removing from oven adds flavor as well as decoration.

*I prefer to use Pyrex baking dish that can be used for serving, which requires less handling of the stuffed squash.

Jane Wohlbold
Green Hills Council

SEDBERRY STUFFED SQUASH

6 large yellow squash, boiled 20 minutes, drained, cooled
3 Tbsp. melted butter
1 onion, minced
3 Tbsp. bacon drippings

1/4 tsp. sugar
Salt
Black pepper
Soda crackers, rolled to a meal (about 1/2 c.)

Slice the top off squash and hollow out inside pulp. Mix with other ingredients. Bake slowly till light brown at 275°. Pretty and good.

Mary Jane Bailey
Green Hills Council

CREAMY SUCCOTASH

1 (10 oz.) pkg. frozen corn
1 (10 oz.) pkg. frozen cut green beans
1 (10 oz.) pkg. frozen lima beans
1 large onion, chopped
1-2 stalks celery, chopped

1 (10 3/4 oz.) can condensed cream of celery soup
1 tsp. salt
Dash of pepper
1/4 tsp. dried basil leaves
3/4 c. cubed American cheese

Put all ingredients in greased crock-pot; stir to mix well. Cover and cook on low 6 to 8 hours (high 2 1/2 to 3 1/2 hours).

Sherree Weisenberger
Harpeth Council

626

SWEET POTATOES

Boil and drain 4 medium sweet potatoes. Mash potatoes and add:

1/4 c. sugar
1 stick oleo

1 tsp. vanilla
2 eggs

Place in baking dish.

Topping: Mix -

3/4 c. brown sugar
1/3 c. flour

3/4 stick oleo
1 c. chopped pecans

Crumble over potato mixture. Bake at 350° for 20 minutes.

Louise Norris
Chattanooga Council

AMARETTO SWEET POTATOES

3 large cans sweet potatoes
1/2 c. brown sugar
2 Tbsp. orange juice
1/2 c. Amaretto liqueur

1/2 c. sugar
1/2 c. melted butter
2 tsp. grated orange rind
1 c. miniature marshmallows

Heat potatoes through; drain and whip with electric beater. Add remaining ingredients, except for marshmallows; whip well. Pour into a well greased 2 1/2 - 3 quart casserole; top with marshmallows. Cover and bake at 350° for 30 minutes.

Rick and Sue Harder
Harpeth Council

CANDIED SWEET POTATOES

5 medium sweet potatoes
1 c. sugar

2 Tbsp. flour (self-rising)
1 stick butter

Peel potatoes; cut into strips about 1 inch thick. Place in 3 quart baking dish. Mix sugar and flour together well; sprinkle over potatoes. Top with stick of butter. Cover casserole and bake 1 hour at 350°.

Pat Riggs
Memphis Council

1489-81

SPICED LOUISIANA SWEET POTATO PIE

Pastry for a 9 inch pie shell
1 c. firmly packed light
  brown sugar
1 tsp. ground cinnamon
1/2 tsp. ground ginger
1/2 tsp. ground nutmeg
1/2 tsp. salt
1/8 tsp. ground cloves
1 (1 lb. 2 oz.) can sweet
  potatoes in syrup, drained
  and mashed (2 c.)
3 eggs, well beaten
1 1/2 c. hot milk
1/2 c. pecan halves

Preheat oven to 375°. In a medium bowl, combine brown sugar, cinnamon, ginger, nutmeg, salt and cloves. Blend in sweet potatoes; beat in eggs. Stir in milk; pour into pie shell. Bake 25 minutes; remove from oven. Arrange pecans on top of pie; return to oven and bake until filling is firm in center, about 30 minutes. Cool on a wire rack. Serve at room temperature, topped with whipped cream and ground nutmeg, if desired. Approximately preparation and cooking time is 1 1/2 hours.

Dot Gilliland
Harpeth Council

SWEET POTATOES DELUXE

2 c. mashed sweet potatoes
2 eggs
3/4 stick butter
1/2 tsp. cinnamon
1 1/4 c. sugar
1/2 c. milk
3/4 stick butter
1/2 tsp. nutmeg

Topping:

3/4 c. crushed corn flakes
1/2 c. brown sugar
4 Tbsp. melted butter
1/2 c. finely chopped nuts

Mix sweet potatoes with sugar, eggs, milk, butter and spices. Bake in a greased casserole for 20 minutes at 350°. Add topping and bake 10 minutes more.

Debbie Mays
Harpeth Council

SWEET POTATO CASSEROLE

3 c. cooked white sweet potatoes, mashed	1/2 c. cream
	1 stick butter, melted
1 c. sugar	1 Tbsp. vanilla
3 eggs, well beaten	1/2 tsp. nutmeg

Mix well; beat with mixer until smooth.

Topping:

1/2 c. light brown sugar	1/2 stick butter
1/2 c. self-rising flour	1 c. pecans

Mix well or until mixture is grainy. Bake at 350° for approximately 30 minutes.

Myrtle Porter
Knoxville Council

SWEET POTATOES HAWAIIAN

6 sweet potatoes	1 tsp. cinnamon
1 (8 1/2 oz.) can crushed pineapple	1/2 c. chopped pecans
	1/3 c. light brown sugar, firmly packed
1/2 c. butter, softened	
1/3 c. granulated sugar	1/4 c. butter, melted

Cook potatoes in water in skins until tender; remove skins and cream. Preheat oven to 375° F. Drain pineapple. In large bowl, combine sweet potatoes, pineapple, 1/2 cup butter, granulated sugar and cinnamon; beat until well blended and creamy. Fold in pecans. Put into casserole dish; sprinkle with brown sugar and drizzle with melted butter. Bake 20 minutes at 375° F. Serve immediately.
Optional: For company, decorate top with pineapple chunks and whole pecans before baking.

Anne Bagwell
Green Hills Council

SWEET POTATO CASSEROLE

3 c. mashed sweet potatoes	1/4 c. milk
1 c. sugar	2 eggs
1 stick margarine	1 tsp. vanilla
1 c. coconut	

Mix together until creamy; pour into casserole dish.

Topping:

1 c. brown sugar	1 stick margarine
1/2 c. plain flour	1 c. chopped pecans

Mix margarine, sugar and flour. Add pecans to mixture; spread over top. Bake at 325° for about 30 minutes.

Linda Rigell
Knoxville Council

SWEET POTATO SOUFFLE

3 c. sweet potatoes, mashed well	1/3 c. butter
1 c. sugar	2 eggs
1/2 c. milk	1 tsp. vanilla

Combine all ingredients and pour in baking dish.

Topping:

1 c. coconut	1/3 c. flour
1 c. chopped pecans	1/3 c. melted butter
1 c. brown sugar	

Blend ingredients well; spread over potatoes. Bake at 375° for 25 minutes.

Betty Houser
Knoxville Council

WALNUT SWEET POTATO PUFFS

2 c. mashed, cooked sweet potatoes	1 tsp. salt
1/2 c. chopped English walnuts	1/4 tsp. nutmeg
	3 Tbsp. melted butter
6 marshmallows	6 slices pineapple, drained
	6 walnut halves

Mix potatoes, salt and nutmeg; form into 6 balls and roll in chopped walnuts. Place balls on pineapple; brush with butter. Bake 20 minutes at 350°. Press marshmallow into center of each ball; top with walnut half. Return to oven until marshmallow is golden, about 5 minutes.

Rachel Yarbrough
Clarksville Council

TACO PIE

1 pkg. crescent rolls	1 c. crushed Fritos
1 1/2 lb. hamburger	1 small onion, chopped
1/2 bell pepper, chopped	1 pkg. taco seasoning
1/4 - 1/2 c. water	8 oz. ctn. sour cream
1 1/2 c. Cheddar cheese	

Preheat oven to 350°. Pat rolls on bottom and sides of 8 inch casserole; sprinkle with half of Fritos. Cook together hamburger, onion and green pepper; drain. Add taco seasoning mix and water; simmer until dry. Pour mixture over Fritos. Spread sour cream on top of meat mixture; sprinkle grated cheese, then add remaining Fritos. Bake for 20 minutes or until rolls are brown.

Bessie Crosby
Harpeth Council

TAMALE BAKE
(Canned tamales are the base for this prize casserole.)

1 (14 1/2 oz.) can tamales	1 (16 oz.) can cream style corn
2 Tbsp. all-purpose flour	1/2 c. pitted ripe olives, halved
1 tsp. chili powder	1/2 c. (2 oz.) shredded sharp Cheddar cheese
1/4 tsp. garlic salt	
3 beaten eggs	

Drain tamales, reserving sauce. Slice tamales crosswise; set aside. In mixing bowl, combine reserved tamale sauce, flour, chili powder, salt and the garlic salt. Add eggs, corn, olives and sliced tamales. Turn into a 10x6x2 inch baking dish. Bake, uncovered, in a 350° oven for 40 minutes or until set; sprinkle with cheese. Bake 3 minutes longer, until cheese melts. Cut into squares. Makes 4 servings.

Maxine Scott
East Memphis Council

TIAJUANA TAMALE
(Tamale Pie)

1/2 c. oil
1 large chopped onion
1 garlic clove, minced
1 lb. ground beef
2 tsp. chili powder
2 1/2 tsp. salt

Dash of Tabasco sauce
No. 2 1/2 can tomatoes
1 c. corn meal
1 c. milk
No. 2 can cream style corn
1 c. pitted ripe olives

Saute the onion and garlic in oil for 5 minutes; add beef and brown it. Next, add the salt, chili powder, tomatoes and Tabasco sauce; cover and cook 15 minutes. Stir in the corn meal and milk; cook another 15 minutes, stirring frequently. Add the corn and olives. Pack all this into 2 greased loaf pans; brush the tops with oil and bake at 325° for 1 hour. Serves 5 or 6.

W.E. Silvertooth
Columbia Council

TEXAS HASH

1 lb. ground beef
1 onion, chopped
1 green pepper

2 c. canned tomatoes
1 c. spaghetti or rice
Grated Cheddar cheese

Brown beef; add onion, pepper and tomatoes. Let cook about 3 minutes. Add spaghetti pieces or rice. Pour into 1 1/2 quart covered casserole and bake at 350° for 45 minutes. Top with Cheddar cheese and return to oven; let cheese melt.

Mary Lynn Johnson
Harpeth Council

CURT'S FRIED GREEN TOMATOES

2 large green tomatoes,
  sliced

Flour (enough to cover)
Salt and pepper to taste

Mix flour, salt and pepper in shallow bowl. Cover both sides of sliced tomatoes with flour mixture. Fry in deep grease until golden brown; drain on paper towels.

Curtisene Johnson
Memphis Council

FRESH TOMATO PIE

2 medium tomatoes	4 eggs
Pastry for 9 inch pie	1 c. milk
3 Tbsp. butter or margarine	1 1/2 c. shredded Cheddar
1 c. chopped onion	cheese
1 c. diced green pepper	1 1/2 tsp. salt
1 clove garlic, minced	1/4 tsp. ground black pepper

Hold tomatoes at room temperature until fully ripe. Slice tomatoes; set aside. Roll pastry to fit a 9 inch pie pan. Fit pastry into pan; flute edges. Prick bottom and sides of pastry with fork tines; refrigerate for 10 minutes. Bake in a preheated 450° oven until golden, about 8 minutes. Remove pie shell; reduce oven temperature to 325°. In a medium skillet, melt butter. Add onion, green pepper and garlic; saute for 5 minutes. In a medium bowl, lightly beat eggs. Stir in milk, cheese, salt, black pepper and sauteed vegetables. Arrange tomato slices in the bottom of the pie shell. Pour egg mixture over all. Bake in slow oven until a knife inserted in center comes out clean, about 50 minutes. Let pie stand at room temperature for 5 minutes before cutting. Garnish with parsley, if desired. Yield: 6 portions.

Ruth L. Cole
Harpeth Council

JIFFY TOMATO STACK-UPS

3 large tomatoes	1 (10 oz.) pkg. frozen
4 oz. cheese, grated (1 c.)	chopped broccoli, cooked
1/4 c. chopped onion	and drained

Cut tomatoes in halves or in 3/4 inch slices; sprinkle lightly with salt. Set aside 2 tablespoons grated cheese. Combine remaining cheese, broccoli and onion. Place tomato slices on baking sheet; spoon mixture onto tomatoes. Sprinkle with reserved grated cheese. Broil 7 to 8 inches from heat for 10 to 12 minutes or until cheese bubbles and tomato slices are hot. Yield: 6 servings.

Nancy Liles
Harpeth Council

MARINATED SLICED TOMATOES

4 large ripe tomatoes
1 Tbsp. lemon juice
1/2 tsp. salt

1/4 c. salad oil
1/2 tsp. minced garlic
1/2 tsp. oregano

Peel and slice tomatoes (each tomato should yield 4 or 5 slices). Combine remaining ingredients and mix. Pour over tomatoes; cover and chill thoroughly. Serves 8-10. (Good as a side dish, salad or on a sandwich. Thin cucumber slices may be added.)

Joyce Mattice
Harpeth Council

STUFFED TOMATOES

Make dressing as for baked chicken, seasoned with chicken stock, ham or bacon drippings. Hollow out tomatoes that have been capped. Mix pulp with stuffing and stuff tomatoes. Put in greased baking dish and bake in 350° oven until dressing is light brown.

Peggy Burr
Harpeth Council

TUNA CASSEROLE

1 pkg. noodles
1 medium onion, diced
1 can cream of mushroom
  soup

1/2 can milk to rinse out soup
  can
1 (6 1/2 oz.) can chunk tuna
1 can mixed vegetables
Salt and pepper

Cook noodles in salted water and drain. Put diced onion in buttered baking dish; put noodles on top. Add other ingredients; sprinkle with paprika and bake about 45 minutes. One can vegetable soup or 1 can peas or leftover green beans can be used instead of mixed vegetables.

Helen DeWolfe
Nashville Council

UPSIDE DOWN PIE
(Main Course)

1 lb. ground beef
1/2 c. chopped celery
1/2 c. chopped onion
1/4 c. chopped green pepper
1 Tbsp. shortening

1/2 tsp. salt
1 can tomato soup
1 1/2 c. biscuit mix
1/2 c. milk
3 slices cheese, cut
　diagonally

In ovenproof skillet (10-11 inches), brown beef and cook celery, onion and green pepper in shortening until tender; stir in salt and soup. Combine biscuit mix and milk; roll or pat dough into a circle slightly smaller than skillet. Spread meat mixture evenly in skillet; top with biscuit dough. Bake at 450° for 15 minutes. Turn upside down on platter; top with cheese. Cut into wedges and serve. Makes 6 servings.

Bob and Nora Chandler
Harpeth Council

WILMA'S VEGETABLE CASSEROLE

1 pkg. mixed frozen
　vegetables
1 c. grated American cheese
1 medium onion, chopped
3-4 Tbsp. mayonnaise

1/2 tsp. sugar
4 Tbsp. butter, melted
Salt and pepper to taste
1 c. cracker crumbs

Mix vegetables, cheese, onion, mayonnaise, salt, pepper and sugar; put in casserole. Mix butter and cracker crumbs; sprinkle on top. Bake in 375° oven for 30 to 35 minutes or until topping is brown.

Barbara Stanfill
Harpeth Council

BRANDY YAMS

6 medium yams, cooked
1/2 c. orange juice
1/2 c. brandy
2 tsp. grated orange rind
1 Tbsp. cornstarch
1/2 tsp. salt

3 Tbsp. melted butter or
　margarine
1/3 c. firmly packed brown
　sugar
1/3 c. sugar

Place yams in a greased 2 quart baking dish. Combine remaining ingredients and cook, stirring constantly, until thickened. Pour sauce over the yams and bake at 350° for 30 minutes. Yield: 6 servings.

Maxine Scott
East Memphis Council

GRAHAM CANDIED YAMS

6 yams (about 3 lb.)
2/3 c. graham cracker
  crumbs
1/4 tsp. allspice
1/4 c. brown sugar

1 tsp. grated orange rind
  (optional)
3 Tbsp. shortening or
  margarine, melted
1 c. light or dark corn syrup
1 c. orange juice

Boil yams until tender. Skin and cut each into 3 or 4 slices lengthwise, keeping slices to a uniform thickness. Place a layer in shallow casserole with 1/3 of sliced yams. Mix crumbs with allspice, sugar and orange rind; sprinkle 1/3 of crumbs over yams and drizzle with 1 tablespoon shortening. Repeat layers twice. Mix syrup and orange juice well; pour over and around yams. Bake, uncovered, in slow oven, 325°, for 45 minutes. Yield: 6 to 8 servings.

Imogene H. Suttles
Knoxville Council

NEW ENGLAND YAM BAKE

1 medium can pineapple
  slices
2 (17 oz.) cans yams
1/4 c. flour
3 Tbsp. brown sugar

1/2 tsp. cinnamon
1/8 tsp. salt
3 Tbsp. margarine
1/4 c. nuts
1 c. miniature marshmallows

Drain pineapple, reserving 1/4 cup syrup. Line sides of 10x6 inch baking dish with pineapple, slightly overlapping in center. Pour pineapple syrup over yams. Combine flour, brown sugar, cinnamon and salt. Mix with margarine until it resembles coarse crumbs; stir in nuts. Sprinkle over yams and bake at 350° for 25 minutes. Top with marshmallows and let brown.

Dean Tidwell
Nashboro Council

636

YAP YAP CASSEROLE

1 (8 oz.) pkg. noodles
3 celery stalks, chopped
1 onion, chopped
Butter (small amount)
1 lb. ground beef

1 can vegetable soup
1 can tomato soup
1 can mushroom soup
Sharp cheese, grated

Cook noodles according to directions on package; drain. Saute celery and onion in small amount of butter. Add ground beef; brown. Stir in soups and mix with noodles. Pour into 2 greased medium casseroles; top with cheese. Bake at 350° for 1 hour. Casserole may be frozen before baking. Yield: 10-12 servings.

Margaret H. Montgomery
Nashville Council

ZUCCHINI CASSEROLE

6 c. cubed zucchini
1 medium onion, chopped
1 stick margarine or butter
1 c. sour cream

8 oz. pkg. Pepperidge Farm
  stuffing
1 can cream of chicken soup
Grated cheese

Steam onion and zucchini for 5 minutes. Melt butter; mix with stuffing. Add sour cream and undiluted soup to zucchini and onion. Put half of the stuffing in a baking dish; add the zucchini and layer the remaining, dressing on top. Sprinkle with grated cheese. Bake for 30 minutes at 350°.

Mrs. Wavie Minke
Harpeth Council

ZUCCHINI CASSEROLE

5 c. sliced zucchini
1 tsp. salt
1 tsp. sugar

1 medium onion, chopped
1 1/2 c. water

Cook above together until zucchini is tender; drain and add:

1 large can chopped
  tomatoes

1/2 tsp. oregano

1489-81

Cook until thick. Pour 1/2 of mixture in buttered casserole dish; dot with margarine. Sprinkle with bread
crumbs. Spoon 1/2 carton of sour cream on top of crumbs.
Repeat layers. Top with more bread crumbs and Mozzarella
cheese. Bake at 350° for 20 minutes until cheese is bubbly.

Peggy Hunter
Harpeth Council

ZUCCHINI SQUASH CASSEROLE

2 lb. zucchini squash,
   grated
2 medium chopped onions
2 eggs, beaten

2 c. Pepperidge Farm herb
   dressing
1 stick butter or melted
   margarine

Mix together; add salt and pepper. Bake at 350° till
bubbly. Add grated sharp Cheddar cheese. Put back in
oven till cheese melts.

Marie Barnett
Harpeth Council

ZUCCHINI PIE

1 uncooked pie crust
2 medium zucchini squash

1 small onion
1 Tbsp. chopped green
   pepper

Put 2 tablespoons cooking oil in skillet and fry the
squash, onion and green pepper; salt to taste. Line bottom
of pie crust with sliced tomatoes, then spread mixture of
squash, onion and pepper. Mix 1/2 cup mayonnaise and 1
cup grated cheese; spread over top and bake at 350° or
until crust is done and top is brown, about 20 minutes.

Gilbert Steele
Columbia Council

ZUCCHINI PIE

3 c. unpeeled zucchini
1 small chopped onion
1 c. packaged biscuit mix
4 eggs
1/4 c. olive oil
1/4 tsp. salt

1/4 tsp. pepper
2 Tbsp. parsley flakes
1/2 c. grated Parmesan,
   Romano or other Italian
   cheese

Trim ends off zucchini; do not peel. Cut into 1/4 inch slices. Mix all ingredients and stir until well blended. Bake in a 10 inch pie plate 45 minutes at 350°.

Helen H. Stephens
Memphis Council

ITALIAN ZUCCHINI PIE

4 c. thinly sliced, unpeeled
  zucchini
1 c. coarsely chopped onion
1/2 c. margarine
2 Tbsp. parsley flakes
1/2 tsp. salt
1/2 tsp. pepper

1/4 tsp. garlic powder
1/4 tsp. basil leaves
1/4 tsp. oregano
2 eggs, well beaten
8 oz. shredded Muenster or
  Mozzarella cheese

Dough Mixture: Spread with 2 teaspoons mustard -

1 3/4 c. biscuit mix
2 Tbsp. shortening

1/2 c. milk

Heat oven to 375°. In large skillet, cook zucchini and onion in margarine until tender, about 10 minutes; add seasonings. In large bowl, beat eggs and blend in cheese. Stir in vegetable mixture. Make a soft dough and line 11 inch quiche pan or 10 inch pie plate with dough. Spread dough with mustard. Pour vegetable mixture evenly into crust. Bake 18-20 minutes until knife inserted comes out clean. Let set 10 minutes before serving. Serves 6.

Mrs. Jas. D. Cowan
Knoxville Council

ZUCCHINI-AND-CORN MEDLEY

1 Tbsp. bacon drippings
1/3 c. chopped onion
1/2 c. chopped green pepper
1 clove garlic, minced

1 (16 oz.) pkg. frozen whole
  kernel corn, thawed
4 c. thinly sliced zucchini
1 tsp. salt
1/4 tsp. pepper

Heat bacon drippings in a large skillet; add remaining ingredients. Cover; cook over medium heat 5 to 10 minutes or until zucchini is crisp-tender. Stir occasionally. Yield: 8 to 10 servings.

Dorothy Bryant
Clarksville Council

ZUCCHINI STICKS

3 medium sliced zucchini
Salt and pepper
Flour
Lemon wedges

1 egg, beaten
1 Tbsp. milk
3 Tbsp. fine cracker crumbs

Wash, but do not peel, zucchini; slice off ends. Cut into lengthwise sticks about 1/2 inch thick. Sprinkle with salt and pepper; roll in flour. Dip into mixture of egg and milk; roll in crumbs. Fry in hot oil until lightly browned and crisp on all sides, about 5 to 6 minutes. Sprinkle with lemon juice; garnish with wedges. Serves 6.

Joyce Mattice
Harpeth Council

** NOTES **

LOW CALORIE

&

MICROWAVE

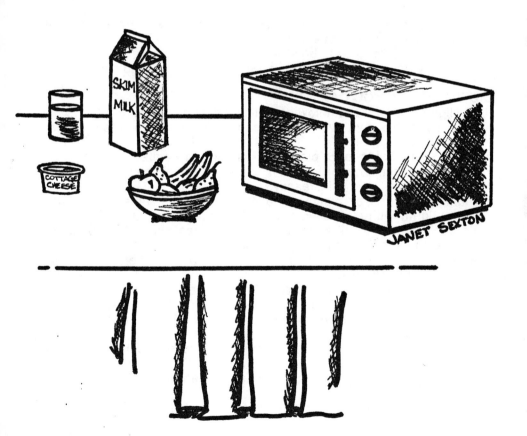

MICROWAVE TIPS

- Always choose the minimum cooking time. Remember, food continues to cook after it is removed from the microwave.
- Keep your microwave clean. Built-up grease or spatters can slow cooking times.
- When poaching or frying an egg in a browning dish, always prick the center of the yolk with a fork to keep the egg from exploding.
- Do not try to hard-cook eggs in a shell in a microwave. They will build up pressure and burst.
- To prevent soggy rolls, elevate rolls on roasting rack or place on paper towels while heating.
- Do not use metal dishes or aluminum foil except as specifically recommended by the manufacturer of your microwave.
- Never use a foil tray over 3/4 inch deep in your microwave.
- When heating TV-style dinners, remove the foil cover, then place tray back in carton. Food will heat only from the top.
- Be sure to prick potatoes before baking to allow steam to escape.
- Cut a small slit in pouch-packed frozen foods before heating in microwave to allow steam to escape.
- When placing more than one food item in microwave, arrange foods in a circle near edges of oven.
- Cover foods that need to be steamed or tenderized.
- Do not try to pop popcorn without a microwave-approved corn popper.

DID YOU KNOW YOU CAN ...?
(Use High setting for the following unless otherwise indicated.)
- Use your microwave oven to melt chocolate, to soften cream cheese and butter.
- Roast shelled nuts for 6 to 10 minutes, stirring frequently.
- Peel fruit or tomatoes. Place in 1 cup hot water. Microwave for 30 to 45 seconds; remove skins easily.
- Plump dried fruit by placing in a dish with 1 to 2 teaspoons water. Cover tightly with plastic wrap. Heat for 1/2 to 1 1/2 minutes.
- Precook barbecued ribs or chicken until almost done, then place on the grill to sear and add a charcoal flavor.
- Soften brown sugar by placing in a dish with a slice of bread or apple. Heat for 30 to 45 seconds, stirring once.
- Dry bread for crumbs or croutons. Place cubed or crumbled bread on paper towels. Heat for 6 to 7 minutes, stirring occasionally.
- Warm baby food or bottles by removing metal lid and heating for 10 to 20 seconds.
- Freshen chips and crackers by heating for 15 to 30 seconds. Let stand for 2 to 3 minutes.
- Dry herbs by placing on paper towels and heating for 2 to 3 minutes or until dry.
- Ripen an avocado by heating on Low for 2 to 4 minutes.

LOW-CALORIE BLEU CHEESE DRESSING

1 pt. cottage cheese
1/2 c. skim milk
1/4 c. Bleu cheese

1/4 tsp. garlic salt
1/4 tsp. sweet basil, crushed
1 tsp. Worcestershire sauce

Place all ingredients in blender container; blend at high speed until smooth. Store in covered container in refrigerator for several hours before serving. Yield: 8 servings.

Barbara Stanfill
Harpeth Council

DANISH DRESSING
(24 calories per tablespoon)

1 c. cream style cottage
cheese

2 Tbsp. crumbled Bleu
cheese
2 Tbsp. skim milk

Combine cottage cheese, Bleu cheese and skim milk in blender container; cover. Beat until smooth; chill. Yield: 8-10 servings.

Barbara Stanfill
Harpeth Council

FRENCH DRESSING
(5 calories per tablespoon)

1 cut garlic bud
1 c. tomato juice
2 Tbsp. grated onion

3 or 4 Tbsp. catsup
Juice of 1 1/2 lemons
2 tsp. sugar

Rub salad bowl with garlic bud; discard bud. Combine all ingredients; shake well. Place in a covered jar in refrigerator. Yield: 25-30 servings.

Barbara Stanfill
Harpeth Council

LOW-CALORIE FRENCH DRESSING

1 (10 oz.) can tomato soup
3 Tbsp. French dressing
1/4 tsp. onion salt
Dash of garlic salt
Dash of black pepper
1 tsp. artificial sweetener

Blend all ingredients well; store in the refrigerator. Yield: 2 cups dressing.

Sharon Rawlings
Harpeth Council

HONEY 'N' FRUIT SALAD DRESSING
(20 calories per tablespoon)

1/4 c. pineapple juice
2 Tbsp. frozen orange
 juice concentrate
2 Tbsp. lemon juice
2 Tbsp. strained honey
1/8 tsp. salt
1 egg, well beaten
1/3 c. instant nonfat dry
 milk solids
1/4 c. water
1/4 c. sieved cottage cheese

Blend fruit juices, honey, salt and egg in saucepan; cook over low heat until mixture coats spoon. Cool. Place water and dry milk solids in electric mixer; whip until very stiff. Fold in cottage cheese and fruit juice mixture; chill. Serve on fresh or canned fruit salads.

Sharon Rawlings
Harpeth Council

LOW-CALORIE SALAD DRESSING
(45 calories per serving)

1 garlic clove, minced
1/4 c. vinegar
1/2 c. orange juice
1/4 tsp. paprika
5 drops Sweeta
1/2 tsp. salt
1/8 tsp. pepper

Add garlic to vinegar; let stand 1 hour. Strain; add remaining ingredients to garlic-vinegar mixture. Shake well; chill. Shake again before using. Yield: 3/4 cup.

Kathy Pack
Harpeth Council

LOW-CALORIE SALAD DRESSING

1/2 c. sugar
1/2 c. vinegar
1/2 c. vegetable oil

1/2 tsp. salt
1/4 tsp. pepper

Mix ingredients in a jar; shake well. Store in refrigerator until ready to use. Pour over finely ground cabbage and marinate for at least 1 hour before serving. Yield: 10-12 servings.

Sharon Rawlings
Harpeth Council

LOW CALORIE DRESSING

1 c. buttermilk
3 Tbsp. catsup
3 Tbsp. wine vinegar
1/2 tsp. garlic salt

1/4 c. mayonnaise
1/2 tsp. onion salt
1/2 tsp. seasoned salt
Dash of pepper

Combine ingredients; mix well.

C.D. Read
Green Hills Council

LOW-CALORIE DRESSING
(3 calories per tablespoon)

1 c. buttermilk
1/2 tsp. onion juice
3/4 tsp. salt

Dash of pepper
1 1/2 Tbsp. lemon juice

Place all ingredients in a jar or bottle; cover tightly and shake thoroughly. Store in refrigerator. Shake well before using. Yield: 1 cup dressing.

Kathy Pack
Harpeth Council

LOW CALORIE MILKSHAKE
(35 calories per cup)

1 c. water
1/3 c. instant dry milk

3/4 tsp. vanilla extract
10 ice cubes

Place all ingredients in blender; process on high speed

for 45 seconds, stopping to scrape down blender container, if necessary. Pour in glasses; serve with straws. Yield: 3 cups.

Note: Lemon, orange, rum or any other extract can be used in place of vanilla.

Judy Gibson
Harpeth Council

LO-CAL PIZZA

3 oz. pepperoni (approx.
  10 slices)
2 oz. Mozzarella cheese

2 medium fresh tomatoes
2 Tbsp. Weight-Watcher's
  mayonnaise
1/2 small can mushrooms

Slice tomatoes in cake or pie dish. Put mayonnaise over the tomatoes. Place pepperoni and mushrooms on top of tomatoes and mayonnaise. Sprinkle grated cheese on top. Bake at 400° until cheese is melted and dish is hot. Serves 1 person.

Molly Heber
Andrew Jackson Council

LOW SODIUM MAYONNAISE

1 egg yolk
1/2 tsp. dry mustard
2 Tbsp. lemon juice

1 tsp. sugar or equivalent
  sweetener
1 c. salad oil

Beat together egg yolks, mustard, sugar and 1 tablespoon lemon juice. Slowly add oil, beating constantly. Beat in remaining lemon juice; chill. Yield: 1 cup.

Sharon Rawlings
Harpeth Council

MARINATED FRESH VEGETABLE SALAD
(Low in Calories)

6 medium tomatoes, cut in
  wedges
2 c. unpared cucumbers,
  sliced
2 medium onions, thinly
  sliced
1 c. carrots, thinly sliced

1 c. celery, thinly sliced
1 1/2 c. tarragon vinegar
1 c. water
1/2 c. sugar
2 tsp. basil
1 tsp. salt
1/2 tsp. black pepper

644

Place vegetables in large airtight container. Combine other ingredients; pour over vegetables. Seal and chill at least 4 hours or overnight. Makes 10 to 12 servings.

David Lewis
Clarksville Council

MOCK SOUR CREAM DRESSING

1 c. buttermilk	1/8 tsp. Accent
1/4 tsp. salt	1 Tbsp. mayonnaise
1/8 tsp. garlic salt	Finely chopped chives or
1/8 tsp. black pepper	onion to taste (optional)

Mix all ingredients well in shaker or covered jar. Serve on green salad or baked potato. May be stored in refrigerator. Yield: 6-8 servings.

Barbara Stanfill
Harpeth Council

OVEN FRENCH FRIES
(Low Fat - Low Cholesterol Diet)

Peel and cut into French fry size 4 medium size potatoes. Remove all excess moisture and place the potatoes in a medium size bowl. Sprinkle with 2 tablespoons vegetable oil. Toss the potatoes as if making a tossed green salad. When the oil and potatoes are thoroughly mixed, spread the potatoes out on a cookie sheet and place in a hot oven, 475°-500° F., for 35 minutes. Turn the potatoes so they will brown evenly on both sides. For added browning, place under the broiler 1 to 2 minutes. Sprinkle with salt before serving. Makes 6 servings. One serving equals:

Oil - 1 teaspoon	Cholesterol - 0 milligrams
Saturated fat - 1 gram	Protein - 2 grams
Linoleic acid - 3 grams	Carbohydrate - 14 grams
	Calories - 110

LOW CALORIE SOUP

1 head cabbage	1 green pepper
6 onions	1 can whole tomatoes
1 bunch celery	1 pkg. onion soup mix

Shred cabbage; chop onions, celery and pepper. Combine all ingredients along with enough water to cover well. Cook until vegetables are done; you may need to add more water.

Optional: Add a beef bouillon cube or a sprinkling of Parmesan cheese.

Barbara S. Stanfill
Harpeth Council

NO CALORIE TOMATO-CELERY SOUP

2 bouillon cubes
1 c. celery, finely diced
1 c. tomato juice
Pepper to taste

2 c. boiling water
1 c. onion, finely chopped
Salt to taste

Dissolve bouillon in water in saucepan. Add remaining ingredients and simmer until vegetables are tender.

Judy Gibson
Harpeth Council

RUBY JAMES'S LAYER SALAD

1 can tomato soup
1 c. sugar
1/2 c. vinegar

1 tsp. prepared mustard
1 tsp. Worcestershire sauce
3/4 c. oil

Put into pan and bring to a boil for 1 minute. Pour over vegetables while hot.

2 lb. carrots, sliced and
   cooked 10 minutes in
   salt water, drained
1 green pepper

1 onion
4 stalks celery
1 head cauliflower

Zoerita Proctor
Nashboro Council

STRING BEANS AND TOMATOES
(Low Fat - Low Cholesterol Diet)

Combine and simmer 10 minutes:
1 small onion, chopped
2 c. canned tomatoes
1 bay leaf

1 tsp. sugar
1 tsp. salt
Dash of pepper

Add 2 cups cut, uncooked string beans. Cover tightly and cook until almost tender. Mix together 2 tablespoons flour and 2 tablespoons water. Add slowly, stirring constantly, and cook until the mixture thickens and beans are tender. Makes 6 servings. One serving equals:

Oil - 0 teaspoons
Cholesterol - 0 milligrams
Saturated fat - 0 grams
Linoleic acid - 0 grams

Protein - 2 grams
Carbohydrate - 11 grams
Calories - 50

SKINNY APPLE FRITTER

1 large slice bread
1 small coreless apple
1 tsp. cinnamon

1/2 env. Sweet 'N Low
1 large egg

Use blender or tear bread in small pieces. In separate bowl, beat egg; add cinnamon and Sweet 'N Low. Finely chop apple; leave peel on. Mix apple with egg mixture. Add the bread crumbs; mix well. Pan fry in Pam or 1 tablespoon of butter. Other fruit (approximately 1/4 cup), well drained, may be substituted. Serves 1 person.

Molly Heber
Andrew Jackson Council

SUGARLESS CAKE

1/2 c. butter
2 eggs
1 Tbsp. liquid sweetening
1 1/2 c. unsweetened
  applesauce
3 medium bananas, mashed
1/2 c. dates or raisins

1/2 tsp. cinnamon
1/4 tsp. allspice
1 tsp. vanilla
2 c. flour
2 tsp. soda
1 c. pecans (or less)

Mix all ingredients together. Bake in greased and floured tube pan for 40 minutes at 300°.

Mrs. R.C. Burton
Knoxville Council

WEIGHT WATCHERS CORN BREAD

1 oz. corn meal (self-rising)
1 slice bread (put in
   blender)
1 egg

1/4 tsp. baking soda
1 Tbsp. diet soda
Sprinkle of salt
1/4 c. buttermilk

Blend all together and bake in a nonstick pan at 400° for 15-20 minutes or until golden brown. Serves 1.

Judy Gibson
Harpeth Council

MICROWAVE

BACON-WRAPPED WATER CHESTNUTS

1 (8 1/2 oz.) can water
   chestnuts
8 slices bacon, cut in halves

1/4 c. soy sauce
1/2 tsp. ginger
1/2 tsp. garlic salt

Wrap chestnuts in bacon; secure with toothpicks. Combine remaining ingredients; heat 45 seconds to blend. Pour over water chestnuts; refrigerate overnight. Place on bacon grill; cover with paper towels. Cook 6 minutes and remove the crisp ones. Continue cooking at 1 minute intervals, removing those that are crisp.

Barbara Harris
Harpeth Council

CHEDDAR CHEESE DIP

1 can Cheddar cheese soup
2 Tbsp. catsup

1/8 tsp. oregano
1/16 tsp. garlic powder

In small bowl, blend all ingredients. Cook 2 minutes, or until hot. Makes 1 1/2 cups of dip. This is delicious served with fresh vegetables.

Mrs. Bob Unkenholz
Harpeth Council

HOT DOG APPETIZERS

4 hot dogs   1 Tbsp. prepared mustard
1/4 c. apricot preserves

Cut each hot dog into 8 pieces. Mix preserves with mustard; pour over hot dogs. Stick a colored toothpick into each piece. Place on a paper plate. Cook for 2 minutes. Serve hot.

Mrs. Bob Unkenholz
Harpeth Council

OLD-FASHIONED BAKED BEANS

Power Level: High (10) and Automatic Simmer.
Microwave Time: 9 to 11 hours, total.
To prepare beans: In 4 quart casserole, place 1 1/2 pounds (3 1/2 cups) navy (pea) beans with enough water to cover, about 2 quarts. Let stand at room temperature to soak several hours or overnight. After soaking, drain water from beans; add 1 teaspoon soda, 1 teaspoon salt and 6 cups hot water. Cover casserole with lid or plastic wrap. Microwave at high for 1 hour, stirring after 30 minutes, until beans are almost tender; drain.

1 c. brown sugar, packed	1/4 c. molasses
1 c. ketchup	1/4 c. vinegar
2 c. hot water	1 Tbsp. salt
1/2 c. chopped onion	6 slices bacon
1/4 c. prepared mustard	Additional 1/2 c. water

In small mixing bowl, stir together well the brown sugar, ketchup, water, onion, mustard, molasses, vinegar and salt. Add and blend well into drained beans. Layer bacon on top of beans. Over back of spoon, gently pour additional water onto top surface; do not stir. Cover tightly with plastic wrap, arranging loosely around probe to vent. Attach cable end at receptacle. Microwave at Automatic Simmer 8 to 10 hours. Stir before serving. Makes 8 to 10 servings.

Mrs. Harvey Cummings
Harpeth Council

FRESH BROCCOLI

Wash 1 bunch broccoli and trim away tough stalks. Arrange in dish with the stalks toward the outside of the dish. Add 2 tablespoons water; cover dish and cook 8-10 minutes. Halfway through cooking time, rearrange the stalks in the middle. Let stand 5-10 minutes.

Cheese Sauce:

2 Tbsp. margarine   1 c. milk
2 Tbsp. flour   1 c. cheese
1/2 tsp. salt

Melt butter 30 seconds. Stir in flour to make a smooth paste. Stir in milk and cheese; cook for 3 minutes. Stir well at 30 second intervals.

Barbara Harris
Harpeth Council

SPICY CARROTS

4 or 5 large carrots, cut in   1 tsp. salt
  julienne strips   1/4 tsp. cinnamon
1/2 c. sugar   2 Tbsp. butter, cut in pieces

Place carrots, sugar, salt and cinnamon in 1 quart casserole; toss to combine. Dot with butter; cover. Microwave 7-8 minutes on High until carrots are tender-crisp. Serves 4.

Mrs. Bob Unkenholz
Harpeth Council

CORN-ON-THE-COB

Corn may be cooked right in the husk in your microwave oven. Place on a paper towel and turn ears over and rearrange after 1/2 of the cooking time.

1 ear - 1 1/2 minutes   4 ears - 8 minutes
2 ears - 4 minutes   6 ears - 9 minutes
3 ears - 6 minutes

Wrap corn in a tea towel as soon as it comes out of the oven for 5 minutes. Because all the heat is contained in the food, it continues to cook when covered even after it comes out of the oven.

Mrs. Bob Unkenholz
Harpeth Council

CORN PUDDING

2 Tbsp. butter or margarine	1 (12 oz.) can cream style
2 eggs, slightly beaten	corn
1 c. milk	1 tsp. salt
2 Tbsp. all-purpose flour	1/2 tsp. pepper

1. Place butter in 1 quart glass casserole. 2. Microwave on Roast for 1 minute or until butter melts. Add remaining ingredients; cover with glass lid or plastic wrap. 3. Microwave on Roast for 9 minutes. Stir and continue cooking on Roast for 7 to 8 minutes or until pudding is slightly soft in center. Let stand, covered, 5 minutes or until pudding is set in center. Makes 4 to 6 servings.

Mrs. Bob Unkenholz
Harpeth Council

OVEN MACARONI AND CHEESE

1/4 c. chopped onion or 1	1/2 c. milk
Tbsp. instant minced onion	1 1/4 c. water
1 can condensed Cheddar	2 c. uncooked macaroni
cheese soup	

In 2 quart casserole, combine all ingredients; cook, covered, for 10 minutes, or until macaroni is just about tender, stirring occasionally. Let stand, covered, 3 to 5 minutes to finish cooking. Yield: 3-4 servings.

Mrs. Bob Unkenholz
Harpeth Council

BAKED ONIONS

4 medium white onions or	Butter
8-10 small, peeled	Salt and pepper

Place peeled onions in a glass baking dish. Top each onion with a pat of butter and desired amount of salt and pepper. Cover with plastic wrap. Microwave on High 7 to

8 minutes, rotating dish once or twice, until onions are fork tender. Let stand, covered, 3 minutes. Makes 4 servings.

Mrs. Bob Unkenholz
Harpeth Council

FRENCH ONION CASSEROLE

4 medium onions, sliced
3 Tbsp. butter
2 Tbsp. all-purpose flour
Dash of pepper
3/4 c. beef bouillon
Paprika

1/4 c. dry sherry
1 1/2 c. plain croutons
2 Tbsp. melted butter
1/2 c. process Swiss cheese, shredded
3 Tbsp. grated Parmesan cheese

Saute onions in butter, using 1 1/2 quart casserole, for 7 minutes. Turn dish halfway through cooking. Blend in flour and pepper; pour in bouillon and sherry. Cook until thickened. Stir every 30 seconds. Toss croutons with melted butter. Spoon onto onion mixture; top with paprika and cheese. Cook 3 minutes.

Barbara Harris
Harpeth Council

STUFFED GREEN PEPPERS

3 medium green peppers
3/4 lb. ground beef
1/3 c. quick cooking rice, uncooked
1 tsp. salt

1/4 tsp. pepper
1 egg
1/3 c. water
1 (8 oz.) can tomato sauce

Cut peppers in halves, removing core and seeds. Place peppers in 2 quart, 12x7 inch, baking dish. In medium mixing bowl, combine remaining ingredients, using only half of tomato sauce. Spoon mixture into pepper halves. Spoon remaining tomato sauce over the meat. Cook, covered with waxed paper, 10 minutes or until meat is done. (Cooking the peppers for 10 minutes leaves them somewhat crunchy. For softer texture, cook 12-13 minutes.) To reheat frozen peppers, cook 3 peppers for 7 minutes and 6 peppers for 10 1/2 minutes.

Mrs. Bob Unkenholz
Harpeth Council

BAKED POTATOES

Select potatoes of equal size and weight. Scrub skins and pierce with a fork in several places. Place potatoes near the corners and microwave on High according to the time chart. Turn and reposition potatoes halfway through cooking time. When potato feels slightly soft to the touch, remove and wrap in foil or a terry towel. If there are a few hard spots, roll wrapped potato lightly on the counter top.

	Time on High
1 medium	4-6 minutes
2 medium	8-11 minutes
4 medium	13-15 minutes

Mrs. Bob Unkenholz
Harpeth Council

GOURMET STUFFED POTATOES

4 medium baking potatoes
1 c. (8 oz.) sour cream
1/2 tsp. salt
1/8 tsp. pepper
1/2 tsp. Beau Monde sea-
   soning or your favorite

1/4 c. milk
1 (8 oz.) can sliced
   mushrooms, drained
1/4 c. green onion, chopped
1/4 c. butter
1/4 c. buttered bread
   crumbs

1. Bake potatoes in the microwave until slightly soft to the touch so the skin will stay firm when stuffed. See chart above for cooking time. Cut hot potatoes in halves lengthwise and carefully scoop out pulp. Beat with electric mixer until smooth. 2. Add sour cream, salt, pepper and Beau Monde seasoning; beat until fluffy. 3. Heat milk in microwave 1 minute on High; add gradually. 4. In a 4 cup measure, saute mushrooms and onion in butter on High 3 minutes. Fold into potato mixture; fill potato shells. 5. Sprinkle with bread crumbs. Place on glass serving platter and microwave on High 2-3 minutes or until heated through. Freezes satisfactorily. Makes 8 servings. Cooking time: 22 minutes. Utensils: 4 cup glass measuring cup; glass serving plate.

Mrs. Bob Unkenholz
Harpeth Council

1489-81

SWEET POTATOES

Cook 4 or 5 medium sweet potatoes in Radarange (allow approximately 4 minutes for each potato) until tender. Allow at least 5 minutes standing time. Peel and slice potatoes. Place potatoes in baking dish.

Sauce:

1 c. brown sugar
1 1/2 Tbsp. cornstarch
1/4 tsp. salt
1/8 tsp. cinnamon
1 c. apricot nectar or
　orange juice

1/2 c. hot water
2 tsp. grated orange peel
　(optional)
2 Tbsp. butter
1/2 c. chopped pecans
1/2 c. raisins (optional)

Combine sugar, cornstarch, salt and cinnamon in a glass bowl. Stir in nectar, hot water and orange peel. Cook on Full Power 2 minutes; stir. Cook until thick, stirring after each minute. Stir in butter, pecans and raisins. Pour sauce over potatoes, making sure all potatoes are glazed. Cover; cook in Radarange approximately 6 minutes or until heated through. Leave covered and allow at least 10 minutes standing time.

Barbara Harris
Harpeth Council

YELLOW SQUASH

4 c. yellow squash, sliced
　or diced
1/2 c. onion, chopped

4 Tbsp. margarine
1 tsp. salt
1/4 tsp. white pepper

(It is not necessary to add water.) Place squash, onion and margarine in a 2 quart dish. Cover with waxed paper; microwave on High 18-20 minutes or until squash is tender. Stir once or twice. Season with salt and pepper. Makes 4 servings, two cups.

Mrs. Bob Unkenholz
Harpeth Council

BAKED FISH IN LEMON BUTTER

1 lb. firm fish fillets (such
   as sole or haddock)
1/2 - 1 tsp. salt
1/8 tsp. pepper
1/2 c. (1/4 lb.) butter

1/2 c. chopped fresh parsley
1 Tbsp. lemon juice
1/2 c. buttery cracker
   crumbs
1/2 tsp. paprika

In a 12x8x2 inch dish, arrange fillets with thickest, meaty areas to outside edges of dish. Sprinkle with salt and pepper. In 1 quart casserole, place butter. Microwave on High for 1-2 minutes, until melted. Blend in parsley and lemon juice; pour over fish. Top with crumbs, then sprinkle on paprika. Microwave on High for 9-11 minutes, rotating dish 1/2 turn after 5 minutes. Serves 4.

Packaged fish fillets may be thawed in about 3 minutes for a 1 pound package. The fish will not be completely thawed, but it will be thawed just enough to separate the pieces.

Mrs. Bob Unkenholz
Harpeth Council

BARBECUED CHICKEN DELUXE

1/2 c. onion, chopped
1/2 c. green pepper,
   chopped
1 1/2 Tbsp. butter or
   margarine
1 (8 oz.) can tomato sauce
   with onions
2 Tbsp. soy sauce

1 Tbsp. lemon juice
1 Tbsp. vinegar
1 tsp. prepared mustard
1 Tbsp. brown sugar
1 tsp. Worcestershire sauce
1/8 tsp. salt
1/8 tsp. pepper
3 lb. broiler-fryer, cut up

Place onion, green pepper and butter in 1 quart casserole. Cook in Radarange oven on Full Power for 2 1/2 to 3 1/2 minutes, or until onion and green pepper are tender. Add remaining ingredients, except chicken. Cook in Radarange oven on Full Power for 1 1/2 minutes. Arrange chicken pieces in 10 inch ceramic skillet or 2 quart utility dish with larger pieces, such as thighs and breasts, at corners, skin side down. Place small pieces such as legs and wings toward center. Pour sauce over chicken. Cook in Radarange oven, covered, on Full Power for 18 to 20 minutes, or until chicken is tender. Turn chicken pieces over halfway through cooking time. Baste with sauce.

Barbara Harris
Harpeth Council

BASIC MEAT LOAF

1 1/2 lb. ground chuck beef	1 c. milk
3/4 c. chopped onion	1 tsp. salt
1/2 c. fine dry bread	1/4 tsp. pepper
crumbs	1/8 tsp. paprika
1 egg	2 Tbsp. ketchup
2 Tbsp. ketchup	

Mix together beef, onion, crumbs, egg, ketchup, milk and seasonings. Mold into a rounded, flat loaf in a 9 inch pie plate. Meat loaf may be topped with additional 2 tablespoons of ketchup before baking. Insert temperature probe and cover; attach cable end at receptacle. Microwave on High. Set temperature at 170°. This will take approximately 15-20 minutes. Let stand about 10 minutes to firm before serving. Serve in wedges. Serves 6.

Mrs. Bob Unkenholz
Harpeth Council

BASIC MEAT BALLS

1 lb. ground chuck beef	1 tsp. salt
1 egg	1/4 tsp. paprika
1/2 c. fine bread crumbs	1/8 tsp. pepper

Mix together beef, egg, crumbs, salt, paprika and pepper. Shape into 12 balls and arrange in a circle in 9 or 10 inch pie plate. Cover with waxed paper. Microwave at High 6 to 8 minutes, rotating dish 1/4 turn after 3 minutes, until done. If desired, serve with Italian Sauce. Makes 12 meat balls.

Variations: Add one of the following flavor combinations: 1 tablespoon Worcestershire sauce and 1/4 cup chopped onion; 1 tablespoon steak sauce and 1 clove crushed garlic (or 1/2 teaspoon garlic powder); 1 tablespoon chili sauce and 1/4 cup finely chopped green pepper; 1 tablespoon ketchup and 1 teaspoon prepared mustard; 2 tablespoons red wine and 1 teaspoon oregano.

Mrs. Harvey Cummings
Harpeth Council

BEEF BARBECUE

1 (3 1/2 lb.) boneless beef   Tangy Barbecue Sauce
  chuck cross rib pot
  roast, trimmed of all
  separable fat

Cut meat into strips about 3 inches long and 1/2 inch thick. Mix strips with cold barbecue sauce in a 2 1/2 quart casserole. Cover with plastic wrap and refrigerate several hours or overnight. Turn back one corner of plastic wrap to vent and place casserole in a microwave oven. Cook 10 to 15 minutes on high, stirring after 5 minutes. Stir; cook 30 to 35 minutes on low, stirring every 10 minutes. Makes 4 1/2 cups; 6 to 8 servings.

Marian Molteni
Harpeth Council

CHICKEN FRICASSEE

2 medium onions, sliced   1 bay leaf
1 (4-6 lb.) stewing   3 stalks celery, sliced
  chicken, cut up   2 carrots, pared and sliced
2 tsp. salt   1 c. chicken broth
1 tsp. paprika   Water

In 5 quart casserole, spread out onions in even layer. Cover with chicken pieces, bony side up with meatiest pieces to edges of dish. Sprinkle with salt and paprika; top with bay leaf. Add celery and carrots. Pour chicken broth over top. Add additional water to cover (up to 5 cups). Insert temperature probe so tip rests in broth on bottom of dish, halfway between center and side. Cover tightly with plastic wrap, arranging loosely around probe to vent. Attach cable end at receptacle. Microwave at Automatic Simmer 11 to 12 hours; cool. Strip off skin and remove bones from chicken. Skim fat from broth and thicken (see below) just before serving.

To Thicken Broth: Stir together 1 cup flour, 1 teaspoon salt and 1 cup water well. Add chicken pieces to broth; stir in flour-water mixture. Microwave at High 10 to 13 minutes, until hot and bubbly. Serve over mashed potatoes or noodles.

Mrs. Harvey Cummings
Harpeth Council

1489-81

CHICKEN KABOBS

2 lb. boned chicken breasts
1/3 c. soy sauce
1 Tbsp. sugar
1 tsp. salt
1/8 tsp. pepper
1/4 tsp. garlic powder

1/4 tsp. ground ginger
2 green peppers, cut in 1/2
  inch cubes
1 (8 oz.) can mushrooms,
  drained
3 Tbsp. honey

Remove skin from chicken breasts; cut chicken into 1 inch cubes. Combine soy sauce, sugar, salt, pepper, garlic powder and ground ginger. Add chicken cubes and toss lightly to coat each piece. Alternate chicken pieces, green pepper and mushrooms on wooden skewers. Combine honey with remaining soy sauce mixture; brush each kabob liberally. Place kabobs in single layer on bacon grill for 5-9 minutes. Turn kabobs occasionally and remove as the chicken is done and green pepper is tender.

Barbara Harris
Harpeth Council

CHICKEN LIVERS CHABLIS

2 Tbsp. butter or margarine
Salt and pepper
3/4 c. chablis (or other
  dry wine)

2 Tbsp. catsup
16 to 20 chicken livers
2 1/2 Tbsp. all-purpose flour
1/4 c. minced onion

Melt butter in 10 inch ceramic skillet in radar oven for 1 minute. Season livers with salt and pepper. Dredge livers in flour; arrange in butter. Cook in radar oven, uncovered, for 7 minutes. Turn livers over halfway through cooking time. Remove and stir in wine, onion and catsup. Cook 3 minutes more. Serve with hot rice.

Phyllis Whaley
Andrew Jackson Council

EASY MEAT LOAF

1 lb. ground beef
1 c. instant oatmeal
1 egg

1 small can tomato sauce with
  onions
1 Tbsp. A.1. steak sauce
1/2 c. grated American cheese

Mix all above ingredients together; form into your

favorite meat loaf design. Bake at 400° for about 45-50 minutes. Top with ketchup. (Microwave on High for 17 minutes covered with Saran Wrap.)

Cheryl V. Alderson
Columbia Council

HOLLYWOOD HAM

2 lb. cubed ham
1 medium head coarsely
  shredded cabbage
3 large cubed potatoes
3 large carrots, sliced

3/4 c. onion, diced
1/2 c. water
1 tsp. salt
1/4 tsp. pepper

Place all ingredients in 4 quart casserole. Cook, covered, in Radarange 35 minutes. Stir every 10 to 12 minutes. Let stand 15 minutes before serving.

Barbara Harris
Harpeth Council

JAMBALAYA

2 c. diced, cooked ham
1/2 c. chopped green
  pepper
1/2 c. chopped onion
1 garlic clove, minced
2 Tbsp. butter
1 (10 3/4 oz.) can con-
  densed tomato soup

1/2 c. shrimp or 1 (4 1/2
  oz.) can, drained
1 medium bay leaf, crushed
1/4 tsp. crushed oregano
1/3 c. water
1/8 tsp. salt
Dash of pepper
1 1/2 c. cooked rice

In 2 quart casserole, place ham, green pepper, onion, garlic and butter. Microwave at High 6 to 7 minutes or until vegetables are tender. Stir in soup, water, shrimp, bay leaf, oregano, salt and pepper; microwave at High 4 minutes. Stir in rice. Microwave at High 4 to 6 minutes more, or until bubbly. Total microwave time: 14-17 minutes. Makes 4 servings. Power Level: High (10).

Mrs. Harvey Cummings
Harpeth Council

PEPPER STEAK

4 (6 oz.) cube steaks	1/4 c. cold water
1/3 c. steak sauce	2 Tbsp. cornstarch
1 (10 oz.) can beef	1 medium green pepper, cut
consomme	into strips
1 tsp. seasoned salt	2 medium firm tomatoes, cut
	into chunks

In 12x8x2 inch dish, place cube steaks, overlapping if necessary. Brush with steak sauce; cover with waxed paper. Microwave at Medium High (7) 9 minutes, rotating dish 1/2 turn after 5 minutes. Transfer steaks to 2 quart casserole. Add consomme and seasoned salt; cover. Microwave at Medium (5) 18 to 20 minutes, rearranging steaks after 10 minutes. Remove steaks from sauce and keep warm. Mix together water and cornstarch; add to sauce. Cover; microwave at High (10) 3 to 4 minutes, until thickened. Stir well. Return meat to sauce and add green pepper and tomatoes. Microwave at Medium 5 to 7 minutes, until hot. Let stand a few minutes before serving. Vegetables will be crisp tender. Total microwave time: 35 to 40 minutes. Makes 4 servings.

Mrs. Harvey Cummings
Harpeth Council

SAUSAGE AND RICE CASSEROLE FOR MICROWAVE

1 lb. mild sausage	1 c. quick cooking rice or
1 chopped onion	Minute Rice
1 chopped green pepper	1 can cream of chicken soup
1/2 c. chopped celery	1 can cream of mushroom soup
4 oz. chopped pimento,	1 c. grated Cheddar cheese
drained	

Brown sausage on full power or normal for 4 minutes; drain well. Combine all ingredients; mix well. Microwave on full power for 14 minutes; do not cover.

Opal A. Jones
Harpeth Council

SALISBURY STEAK

1/2 c. onion, chopped	1/2 c. bread crumbs
1 tsp. vegetable oil	1 egg, slightly beaten
1 1/2 lb. ground beef	Dash of pepper
1 (10 3/4 oz.) can golden	1/4 c. water
cream of mushroom soup	

1. Place onion and oil in 1 quart casserole. Cook in microwave on High for 2 minutes, or until onion is tender.
2. Add ground beef, 1/4 cup soup, bread crumbs, egg and pepper; mix well. Shape into 6 patties. Arrange in 2 quart utility dish; cook in microwave on High for 8 minutes. Turn patties over halfway through cooking time; drain.
3. Blend remaining soup with water; pour over meat. Cook in microwave on High 2 to 4 minutes, or until meat is cooked as desired. Turn meat over and rearrange halfway through cooking time.

Cheryl Enoch
Harpeth Council

STEWED BEEF WITH VEGETABLES

2 lb. beef stew meat,	1/4 tsp. pepper
cut into 1 inch cubes	2 medium potatoes, cut into
2 c. water	1 inch cubes
2 (6 oz.) cans tomato paste	2 medium carrots, sliced
1 pkg. dry onion soup mix	1 (12 oz.) can yellow kernel
(half of 2 3/4 oz. box)	corn
1/4 tsp. garlic powder	

In 3 quart casserole, combine meat, water, tomato paste, onion soup mix, garlic powder and pepper; stir well. Cover; microwave at Medium (5) 60 minutes, stirring every 20 minutes. Add potatoes and carrots to stew. Microwave at Medium 15 to 20 minutes more, until meat is tender. Add corn, stirring well. Microwave at High (10) 5 to 10 minutes, until vegetables are tender. Stir well before serving. Total microwave time: 1 hour and 20 minutes to 1 hour and 30 minutes. Makes 8 to 10 servings.

Mrs. Harvey Cummings
Harpeth Council

STUFFED PORK ROAST

1/3 c. butter or margarine	1 tsp. salt
1/4 c. sesame seeds	3/4 tsp. poultry seasoning
3/4 c. finely chopped celery	1 tsp. Worcestershire sauce
1/4 c. finely chopped onion	1 (2 lb.) boneless pork loin
6 slices bread, cubed	roast

Combine butter, sesame seeds, celery and onion in glass bowl. Cook, uncovered, 4 to 4 1/2 minutes or until just about tender. Mix in remaining ingredients, except roast. Cut roast at 1/2 inch intervals, cutting almost through and forming about 8 slices. Place cut side up in 8x4 inch glass loaf pan. Spoon stuffing mixture between meat slices. Press between slices. Place inverted plate or larger baking dish over loaf dish. Invert plate and dish, leaving loaf dish over meat. Cook 10 minutes on Full Power; let stand 10 minutes. Drain excess juices; turn loaf dish and roast right side up. Remove plate; cover meat with waxed paper. Insert meat probe and cook 7 to 10 minutes or until thermometer registers about 170°.

Barbara Harris
Harpeth Council

SWISS STEAK

1 1/2 lb. round steak, 1/2 inch thick, tenderized or pounded with meat mallet	1 1/2 tsp. salt
	1/8 tsp. pepper
	1 medium onion, sliced thin
	1 (1 lb.) can tomatoes
1/4 c. flour	

Cut meat in 6 pieces, then coat with mixture of flour, salt and pepper. Place in 3 quart casserole. Cover with onion. Break up tomatoes with fork and pour over top. Cover; microwave at Medium (5) 60 to 70 minutes, rearranging meat after 30 minutes, until tender. Makes 6 servings. Total microwave time: 60 to 70 minutes.

Easy Swiss Steak: Substitute 1 (10 1/2 ounce) can condensed tomato soup or cream of mushroom soup, 1 cup water and 2 teaspoons beef bouillon granules for flour, salt, pepper, onion and tomato. Microwave as directed in above recipe.

Mrs. Harvey Cummings
Harpeth Council

TURKEY BREAST

Wash body cavity of poultry with water; pat dry with paper towels. Sprinkle body cavity with salt. Brush exterior with melted butter and sprinkle with paprika. Start poultry breast side down and cook on Full Power 6 to 7 minutes per pound. Change directions or turn 4 times during cooking. Let stand, covered, with aluminum foil at least 15 minutes.

Barbara Harris
Harpeth Council

TURKEY DIVAN

1 bunch broccoli, cooked
8-12 slices cooked turkey
   breast
2 c. white sauce

1/4 c. grated Parmesan
   cheese
1/4 c. grated Gruyere cheese

1. Place cooked broccoli in a baking dish with flower ends at ends of dish. Cover center of stalks with slices of cooked turkey. 2. Prepare white sauce and while it is still warm, add the cheeses. Stir until well blended. Pour over top of turkey; sprinkle with additional Parmesan cheese, if desired. 3. Cook, covered with plastic wrap or waxed paper, for 9 to 10 minutes or until turkey is piping hot. Yield: 4 to 6 servings.

Mrs. Bob Unkenholz
Harpeth Council

BARBECUE SAUCE

The traditional sauce to use when cooking ribs and chicken. Or, slice leftover beef or pork into barbecue sauce and serve warm as an entree or sandwich filling.

1 c. chili sauce
1/2 c. water
1/4 c. lemon juice
1 Tbsp. cooking oil
2 Tbsp. brown sugar,
   packed

1/4 tsp. paprika
1/4 tsp. liquid pepper
   seasoning (Tabasco sauce)
1 Tbsp. Worcestershire
   sauce
1/2 tsp. salt

In 1 quart casserole, thoroughly combine chili sauce, water, lemon juice, cooking oil, brown sugar, salt, paprika,

pepper seasoning and Worcestershire sauce. Cover; microwave at High (10) 5 to 7 minutes, stirring after 3 minutes,
until hot. Use as desired. Makes 2 cups.

Mrs. Harvey Cummings
Harpeth Council

TANGY BARBECUE SAUCE

3/4 c. chili sauce
1/3 c. tomato juice
3/4 c. chopped, peeled onion
2 Tbsp. Worcestershire
  sauce
1 Tbsp. cider vinegar

1 Tbsp. brown sugar,
  packed to measure
3/4 tsp. dry mustard
1/2 tsp. minced, peeled
  garlic
1/4 tsp. salt
1/4 tsp. pepper

Mix all ingredients in a heavy, medium sized saucepan
and bring to a boil over moderately high heat. Reduce heat
to moderately low; cover pan, leaving lid slightly ajar, and
simmer 45 minutes, stirring every 5 to 6 minutes, until flavors are blended and about 1 cup of sauce remains. Cool
completely before mixing with beef.

Marian Molteni
Harpeth Council

BASIC WHITE SAUCE

2 Tbsp. butter
2 Tbsp. flour

1/2 tsp. salt
1 c. milk

In a 1 quart glass measure, place butter, flour and
salt. Microwave on High for 2 minutes, stirring after 1
minute. Gradually stir in milk. Microwave on High for
3 1/2 - 4 1/2 minutes, stirring every minute until thick and
bubbly. Makes 1 cup. Variations -
    Cheese Sauce: To finished sauce, add 1 cup (4 ounces)
shredded sharp cheese and a dash of cayenne pepper.
Microwave on High for 1-2 minutes to melt cheese.
    Curry Sauce: Add 2-3 tablespoons curry powder along
with flour. Microwave as above.
    Thick White Sauce: Use 3 tablespoons flour instead of
2.

Mrs. Bob Unkenholz
Harpeth Council

SPAGHETTI SAUCE

If desired, you can omit sauteing the onion in butter by lengthening simmering time 2 hours.

2 c. chopped onion
2 Tbsp. butter
2 (1 lb. 14 oz.) cans
  tomatoes, cut up
2 (6 oz.) cans tomato paste
1/2 c. snipped parsley
1/4 c. brown sugar

2 tsp. salt
1 Tbsp. dried oregano,
  crushed
1/2 tsp. dried thyme,
  crushed
2 bay leaves

In 3 quart casserole, place onion and butter. Microwave at High (10) 4 to 5 minutes, until onion is slightly cooked. Add tomatoes, tomato paste, parsley, brown sugar, salt, oregano, thyme and bay leaves; mix together well. Insert temperature probe so tip is in liquid on bottom of dish. Cover tightly with plastic wrap, arranging loosely around probe to vent. Attach cable end at receptacle. Microwave at Automatic Simmer 3 to 4 hours. Makes 2 to 3 quarts.

Tip: Freeze in ice cube trays. When frozen hard, remove to plastic bags. Only amounts needed can be easily thawed and/or heated.

Mrs. Harvey Cummings
Harpeth Council

BUTTERMILK PRALINES

2 c. sugar
1 tsp. soda
1 c. buttermilk

3/4 c. butter or margarine
1 tsp. vanilla
2 c. pecan halves

1. Combine all ingredients, except vanilla and pecans, in buttered large glass mixing bowl. Cover with plastic wrap. 2. Microwave on Roast for 15 minutes; stir and continue cooking on Roast for 13 to 15 minutes or until a soft ball forms in cold water. Add vanilla and beat until mixture forms soft peaks. Stir in pecans. Pour into buttered 2 quart, 12x7 inch, glass baking dish; cool until firm. Cut into pieces. Makes 40 to 48 praline pieces.

Tip: Individual candies may be dropped from a teaspoon onto waxed paper.

Mrs. Bob Unkenholz
Harpeth Council

BUTTERSCOTCH CRUNCHIES

1 (6 oz.) pkg. butterscotch morsels

2 c. (3 oz.) chow mein noodles
1/2 c. salted peanuts

Melt butterscotch morsels in microwave for 2 1/2 minutes. Add noodles and nuts; stir until well coated. Drop by teaspoonfuls on waxed paper on a cookie sheet; chill. Makes 30.

Mrs. Bob Unkenholz
Harpeth Council

MICROWAVE PEANUT BRITTLE

1 c. sugar
1/2 c. white corn syrup
1 c. roasted, salted peanuts

1 tsp. butter
1 tsp. vanilla extract
1 tsp. baking soda

In 1 1/2 quart casserole, stir together sugar and syrup; microwave at High 4 minutes. Stir in peanuts. Microwave at High 3 to 5 minutes, until light brown. Add butter and vanilla to syrup, blending well. Microwave at High 1 to 2 minutes more. Peanuts will be lightly browned and syrup very hot. Add baking soda and gently stir until light and foamy. Pour mixture onto lightly greased cookie sheet or unbuttered nonstick coated cookie sheet. Let cool 1/2 to 1 hour. When cool, break into small pieces and store in airtight container. Makes about 1 pound.

Delma Orman
Memphis East Council

QUICKIE FUDGE

1 lb. powdered sugar
1/3 c. cocoa
1/4 c. evaporated milk

1 stick butter or margarine
1 Tbsp. vanilla
1/2 c. chopped nuts

Blend powdered sugar and cocoa in greased 8x8 inch square glass container. Add milk and butter; cook in microwave oven for 2 minutes. (Note: Do not mix these ingredients; merely place in bowl.) Remove bowl after cooking and stir just to mix ingredients. Add vanilla and nuts; stir.

Place in freezer for 20 minutes or in refrigerator for 1 hour. Cut and serve.

Mrs. Bob Unkenholz
Harpeth Council

BROWNIES

2 sq. or env. unsweetened
  chocolate
1/3 c. butter or margarine
1 c. sugar
2 eggs

1 c. unsifted all-purpose
  flour
1/4 tsp. baking powder
1/4 tsp. salt
1/2 tsp. vanilla
1/2 c. chopped nuts

1. Combine chocolate and butter in medium glass mixing bowl. 2. Microwave on Roast for 1 1/2 to 2 minutes or until melted. Stir in sugar; beat in eggs. Stir in remaining ingredients. Spread batter into 2 quart (8x8 inch) glass baking dish. 3. Microwave on Simmer for 7 minutes. 4. Microwave on High for 3 to 4 minutes or until puffed and dry on top. Cool until set; cut into bars. Makes 24 bars.

Tip: Top brownie squares with ice cream and chocolate sauce for a quick dessert.

Mrs. Bob Unkenholz
Harpeth Council

CHERRY NUT UPSIDE DOWN CAKE

2 Tbsp. margarine
1/2 c. nuts
1 can cherry pie filling

1 layer plain cake mix (2 c.
  batter), made by pkg.
  directions

To prepare dish (round 8 or 9 inch cake dish, 2 inches deep): 1. Coat sides with margarine. Pat on crushed nuts. Cut circle of waxed paper to fit bottom of dish. 2. Pour in pie filling. Top with cake mix batter. Cook on Medium or Slo Cook 7 minutes. Turn dish 1/4 turn every 2 minutes. Cook another 3 minutes on High. Let stand 10 minutes before turning out. Makes 8 servings.

Mrs. Bob Unkenholz
Harpeth Council

CINNAMON COFFEE CAKE

1/2 stick butter	1/4 c. chopped nuts
1/4 c. brown sugar	1/2 c. raisins
8 maraschino cherries, chopped	1 tsp. cinnamon
	1 pkg. canned biscuits

Melt butter in 1 1/2 quart round casserole dish. Invert a glass upside down to make a glass Bundt pan. Add brown sugar, cherries, nuts, raisins and cinnamon. Finally, add biscuits, turned in carousel fashion. Cook for 4 1/2 minutes in microwave oven.

Mrs. Bob Unkenholz
Harpeth Council

COCA-COLA CAKE

Cake:

2 c. all-purpose flour	3 Tbsp. cocoa
2 c. sugar	1/2 c. buttermilk
1 c. miniature marshmallows	1 tsp. soda
1/2 c. Crisco	2 eggs, beaten
3/4 c. Coke	

1. In a mixing bowl, sift flour and sugar together; stir in marshmallows. 2. Put Crisco, Coke and cocoa in a 2 cup glass measure. Heat in microwave until Crisco melts, 2 minutes; pour over flour mixture. 3. Stir in buttermilk, soda and eggs. Pour into greased glass dish, 11x7 inches. Cook on High for 11 minute; turn dish 1/4 turn every 3 minutes. (Begin to prepare icing.)

Icing:

6 Tbsp. margarine	2/3 box powdered sugar
3 Tbsp. cocoa	3/4 c. broken pecans
6 Tbsp. Coke	

1. Mix margarine, cocoa and Coke in 4 cup measure. Bring to boil in microwave, about 1 1/2 minutes. 2. Pour cocoa mixture over powdered sugar. Add pecans; mix well. Ice while cake is hot. Makes 18 squares.

Mrs. Bob Unkenholz
Harpeth Council

CRUMB PIE SHELL

A pretty scalloped pie shell can easily be made by lining the bottom of a pie plate with 1/2 of this recipe, then standing small whole cookies around the sides of the plate.

1/4 c. butter
2 Tbsp. sugar

1 1/4 c. fine cookie crumbs (vanilla wafer, graham cracker, chocolate wafer, gingersnaps, etc.)

In 9 inch pie plate, place butter. Microwave at High 1/2 minute, until melted. Blend in crumbs and sugar. If desired, reserve 2 tablespoons crumb mixture for garnish. Press firmly and evenly into 9 inch pie plate. Microwave at High 2 to 2 1/2 minutes, rotating dish 1/2 turn after 1 minute. Makes one 9 inch crumb shell.

Mrs. Harvey Cummings
Harpeth Council

DEEP DISH PINEAPPLE CRUMBLE

2 c. flour (all-purpose)
1 c. sugar
1/2 c. butter, softened
2 tsp. cinnamon

2 tsp. baking powder
2 eggs
3/4 c. unsweetened pineapple juice

1. Mix flour, sugar and butter together with a fork until crumbly. 2. For crumb topping, remove 1 cup of crumbly mixture; stir in cinnamon and reserve. 3. Stir baking powder into large crumbled mixture. 4. Whisk eggs with pineapple juice; mix lightly into crumb mixture. 5. Lightly grease a 2 quart round casserole or Bundt dish. Pour in mixture and sprinkle on crumb topping. Microwave on Medium 8 minutes, turning dish once. Cook on High 2 minutes. Makes 12 servings.

Mrs. Bob Unkenholz
Harpeth Council

FROZEN CHOCOLATE ALMOND PIE

1 Crumb Pie shell, made with vanilla wafers (above) or Chocolate Pastry Crust

4 (1.15 oz.) milk chocolate candy bars with almonds
1/2 (10 oz.) pkg. large marshmallows (about 20)

1489-81

1/2 c. milk   1 c. whipping cream, whipped

Microwave pie shell; cool. In 2 quart casserole, place candy, marshmallows and milk; microwave at High (10) 3 to 4 minutes, stirring after 2 minutes, until mixture can be stirred smooth. Chill in refrigerator about 30 to 40 minutes, or in pan of ice water until thickened, stirring occasionally. Fold whipped cream into cooled chocolate mixture. Pile into pie shell and freeze until firm. Makes one 9 inch pie. To serve, garnish pie wedges with whipped cream, chocolate curls and/or additional almonds, if desired. This pie cuts well straight from the freezer. No thawing is necessary. Use a wet knife for sharpest cut.

Mrs. Harvey Cummings
Harpeth Council

HOT AMBROSIA

1 (16 oz.) can pineapple chunks in unsweetened pineapple juice, undrained

2 (11 oz.) cans Mandarin orange sections, drained
1/4 c. sweetened flake coconut

Combine ingredients in a 3 quart casserole. Put in microwave oven; cook 5 minutes on high, stirring after 2 1/2 minutes, until hot. Serve over vanilla ice cream.

Leslie Stephens
Harpeth Council

LEMON FILLING FOR CAKE

1/2 c. sugar
2 Tbsp. cornstarch
1/8 tsp. salt
2/3 c. water

1 1/2 tsp. grated lemon peel
2 Tbsp. lemon juice
1 Tbsp. butter or margarine

1. Combine all ingredients in 2 cup glass measure; mix well. 2. Microwave on High for 2 minutes. Stir and continue cooking on High for 2 to 2 1/2 minutes or until thickened. Beat well. Cool and spread on cake. Makes 1 cup filling.

Tip: Yellow food coloring may be added, if desired.

Mrs. Bob Unkenholz
Harpeth Council

MARVELOUS MARBLE CHEESECAKE

Crust:

1/4 c. butter   1/4 c. sugar
1 c. vanilla wafer crumbs

Place butter in 9x2 inch glass pie plate. Cook in Radarange on Full Power 45-60 seconds or until melted. Add crumbs and sugar; blend well. Press crumb mixture firmly against sides and bottom of pie plate. Bake in Radarange on Full Power for 1 minute and 15 seconds, or until bubbling in center. Turn dish halfway through cooking time.

Cheesecake:

4 (3 oz.) pkg. cream cheese   1/3 c. semi-sweet chocolate
2 eggs   chips or butterscotch
1/2 c. sugar   morsels
1 tsp. vanilla   1 Tbsp. milk

Beat cream cheese until smooth. Beat in eggs, one at a time. Mix in sugar and vanilla until smooth and creamy. Pour over crust. Place chocolate or butterscotch chips in 1 cup measuring cup. Heat on Cookmatic Level 6 (Roast) for 2 - 2 1/2 minutes or until melted. Stir halfway through cooking time. Add milk; stir until well blended. Spoon mixture over cream cheese filling. Using fork, lightly swirl mixture through filling. Bake on Cookmatic Level 8 (Medium High) for 3 1/2 - 4 1/2 minutes or until outer edge is set. Turn dish halfway through cooking time. Chill before serving.

Barbara Harris
Harpeth Council

NUT CRUNCH PASTRY SHELL

1 c. flour   1/2 c. butter
1/2 c. light brown sugar,   1 c. finely chopped pecans
  packed   or walnuts

In small mixing bowl, place flour and brown sugar. With pastry blender, cut in butter until mixture is crumbly. Mix in nuts. Place mixture loosely in 9 inch pie plate. Microwave at High (10) 4 to 5 minutes, stirring every 1 or 2 minutes. Stir after cooking. If desired, reserve 2 table-spoons mixture to garnish top. Press remainder of hot crumbs into pie plate. Microwave at High 2 to 3 minutes, until set, rotating dish 1/4 turn every minute. Cool before filling. Makes one 9 inch shell.

Mrs. Harvey Cummings
Harpeth Council

PECAN PIE

3 Tbsp. butter or margarine
3 eggs, slightly beaten
1 c. dark corn syrup
1/4 c. packed brown sugar
1 1/2 tsp. all-purpose flour

1 tsp. vanilla
1 1/2 c. pecan halves
1 (9 inch) baked pastry shell
  in glass pie plate

1. Place butter in medium glass mixing bowl. 2. Microwave on Roast for about 1 to 1 1/2 minutes or until melted. Stir in remaining ingredients, except baked pastry shell; mix well. Pour filling in shell. 3. Microwave on Defrost for 25 to 30 minutes or until knife inserted near center comes out clean; cool. Makes 9 inch pie.

Mrs. Bob Unkenholz
Harpeth Council

PINEAPPLE UPSIDE DOWN CAKE

1/4 c. butter or margarine
1/2 c. packed brown sugar
6 slices canned pineapple,
  drained

6 maraschino cherries
1 (9 oz.) pkg. yellow cake
  mix

1. Place butter in 9 inch round glass baking dish. 2. Microwave on Roast for about 2 minutes or until melted. Stir in brown sugar; arrange pineapple on top. Place a cherry in center of each pineapple slice. Prepare cake mix as directed on package; pour over pineapple. 3. Microwave on Simmer for 7 minutes. 4. Microwave on High for 3 to 4 minutes or until toothpick inserted near center comes out clean. Let stand 1 minute. Turn out onto platter and serve warm or cool. Makes 4 to 6 servings.

Mrs. Bob Unkenholz
Harpeth Council

SWEET-TART LEMON SQUARES

1 (15 oz.) can sweetened
  condensed milk
1/2 c. lemon juice
1 tsp. grated lemon rind
  (optional)

1 1/2 c. graham cracker
  crumbs
1/3 c. brown sugar, packed
1/3 c. butter, melted

In small mixing bowl, stir together milk, lemon juice and rind until thick and smooth; set aside. Mix together crumbs, sugar and butter. Place about 2/3 of mixture in 8 inch square dish; press firmly into bottom of dish. Add milk mixture; spread evenly. Sprinkle remaining crumb mixture over top; pat down gently. Microwave on High for 8-10 minutes, rotating dish 1/4 turn after 4 minutes. Cut into small squares as cookies or in larger pieces as dessert. Makes 16-24 cookies or 9 desserts.

Mrs. Bob Unkenholz
Harpeth Council

** NOTES **

** NOTES **

FOOD PRESERVATION

SUGAR

Leslie Stephens

REFRIGERATION CHART

Food	Refrigerate	Freeze
Beef steaks	1-2 days	6-12 months
Beef roasts	1-2 days	6-12 months
Corned beef	7 days	2 weeks
Pork chops	1-2 days	3-4 months
Pork roasts	1-2 days	4-8 months
Fresh sausage	1-2 days	1-2 months
Smoked sausage	7 days	Not recommended
Cured ham	5-7 days	1-2 months
Canned ham	1 year	Not recommended
Ham slice	3 days	1-2 months
Bacon	7 days	2-4 months
Veal cutlets	1-2 days	6-9 months
Stew meat	1-2 days	3-4 months
Ground meat	1-2 days	3-4 months
Luncheon meats	3-5 days	Not recommended
Frankfurters	7 days	1 month
Whole chicken	1-2 days	12 months
Chicken pieces	1-2 days	9 months
Whole turkeys	1-2 days	6 months

NUTRITION

Everyone is very conscious today of the need for a diet balanced in nutrients. The nutritional information provided for each recipe will help you in determining the best choices for your needs. The key to the balance is variety. If every day your diet includes fruits and vegetables (4 servings), cereals, bread and grains (4 servings), milk or cheese (2 servings), and meat, poultry, seafood and eggs (2 servings), your body will get the nutrients it needs.

On the other hand, some of the nutrients of the foods we eat should be controlled. The danger of high cholesterol is well known, and too much salt can cause various health problems. Healthy eating is not difficult, but it does require a bit of planning and attention to making the plan work.

BEET   PICKLES

2 c. sugar	1 Tbsp. cinnamon
2 c. water	1 tsp. cloves
2 c. vinegar	1 thinly sliced lemon
1 tsp. allspice	Beets

Wash and clean beets; cook until tender. Dip in cold water; peel off skins. Cut into the size pieces you want or leave whole if small. Combine all other ingredients and bring to a boil to make a syrup. Pour syrup over beets; simmer 15 minutes. Pack into sterilized jars and seal. A little grated horseradish added to beets gives variety.

Joyce Mattice
Harpeth Council

PICKLED   BANANA   PEPPERS

Banana peppers	Pinch of salt
2 c. vinegar	1/2 tsp. pickling spices
1 c. water	1/2 tsp. mustard seed
1 1/2 c. sugar	1/2 tsp. celery seed

Wash banana peppers; make a slit in peppers and remove insides. Pour boiling water over peppers; let stand 1 hour. Put peppers in cold water for 4 minutes; pack in jars. Bring vinegar, water, sugar and salt to boiling; add spices. Pour mixture over peppers in jars and seal.

Judy Gibson
Harpeth Council

BANANA   PEPPER   PICKLES

8 c. vinegar	1/2 c. canning salt
1 c. sugar	Garlic cloves
3 c. water	Oil

Bring above ingredients to a boil. Pack cut peppers in clean quart jars. Put 2 garlic cloves in each jar; add 1 tablespoon oil to each jar. Cold pack for 5 minutes after mixture comes to a rolling boil.

Judy Gibson
Harpeth Council

MOM'S KETCHUP

7 qt. tomato puree (18 lb.
   tomatoes)
3 Tbsp. salt
2/3 c. sugar
1 Tbsp. paprika
1/4 tsp. cayenne pepper
1 Tbsp. dry mustard

1 Tbsp. whole black peppers
1 Tbsp. whole allspice
1 Tbsp. mustard seeds
1 Tbsp. dried basil
4 bay leaves
4 chili peppers
2 c. vinegar

Add all ingredients, except vinegar, to tomato puree. Spices should be tied loosely in a cloth bag and the dry mustard blended in a little tomato juice to prevent formation of lumps. Cook until thick, about 1 1/2 hours. Add vinegar the last 10 minutes of cooking. Remove spices. Pour into hot sterilized jars; seal at once. Process in boiling water bath, 212° F., for 10 minutes. Makes 4 pints.

To make tomato puree: Cook tomatoes until soft. Put through a sieve or a Foley food mill.

Nancy Bess Lord
Harpeth Council

GRANNIE'S RIPE TOMATO CATSUP

1 large can tomato juice
4 tsp. salt
1/2 tsp. red pepper
1 tsp. black pepper
1 1/2 Tbsp. dry mustard

1 Tbsp. cinnamon
1 Tbsp. allspice
1 pt. vinegar (apple cider)
1 1/2 c. sugar

Mix above ingredients and cook until thickened. Refrigerate. Makes 2 1/2 pints.

Claudia Davenport
Clarksville Council

RIPE TOMATO CATSUP

1 gal. ripe tomatoes,
   chopped
1 qt. onions, finely chopped
3 pods hot peppers, finely
   chopped

3 pods sweet peppers, finely
   chopped
3/4 c. salt
4 c. sugar
1 qt. vinegar
1 Tbsp. allspice

Combine tomatoes, onions, peppers and salt; let stand

2 hours. Put mixture in cloth sack or jelly bag; let drain overnight. Combine tomato mixture with sugar, vinegar and allspice; boil for 2 minutes. Pack into hot pint or quart jars.

Marie Barnett
Harpeth Council

MOTHER'S CUCUMBER APPLE RINGS

Peel 7 pounds cucumbers; slice and cut seeds out. Soak 24 hours in 1 cup of lime to the gallon of water; drain and rinse. Soak 3 hours in ice water; drain and rinse. Simmer 2 hours in:

1 c. vinegar	1 large bottle red food
1 Tbsp. alum	coloring
	Enough water to cover

Drain. Make syrup of:

3 c. vinegar	12 sticks cinnamon
3 c. water	2 pkg. red hot candy
11 c. sugar	

Bring to boil; pack rings in jars and pour syrup over rings and seal.

Brenda Coleman
Jackson Council

BREAD AND BUTTER PICKLES

4 qt. sliced medium cucumbers	1/3 c. coarse-medium salt
6 medium white onions, sliced	5 c. sugar
	3 c. cider vinegar
2 green peppers, chopped	1 1/2 tsp. turmeric
3 cloves garlic	1 1/2 tsp. celery seed
	2 Tbsp. mustard seed

Do not pare cucumbers; slice thin. Add onions, peppers and whole garlic cloves. Add salt; cover with cracked ice. Mix thoroughly. Let stand 3 hours; drain well. Combine remaining ingredients; pour over cucumber mixture. Heat just to boil. Seal in hot, sterilized jars. Makes 8 pints.

Judy Gibson
Harpeth Council

CUCUMBER PICKLES

Short Method: Select 50 cucumbers (2 1/2 inches long); wash and cover with hot brine, 1 cup coarse salt to 2 quarts water. Let stand until cold or overnight. Drain cucumbers. Cover with mixture of 3 quarts vinegar, 1 quart water, 4 tablespoons mixed pickling spice and 2 cups sugar. For sweeter pickles, increase sugar to 3 cups. Heat to boiling; pack cucumbers in hot, sterilized jars. Fill jars with hot syrup. Place piece of alum the size of a pea in each jar; seal.

Long Method:

150 (3-4 inch) cucumbers   1/2 tsp. celery seed
2 Tbsp. powdered alum   3/4 oz. stick cinnamon
4 c. sugar   1/2 c. horseradish
2 1/2 c. vinegar

Cover cucumbers with hot salt brine, 1 cup coarse salt to 2 quarts water; cool. Cover; let stand 7 days. Drain; cover with hot water. Let stand 24 hours; drain. Again cover with hot water; add alum and let stand 24 hours. Drain and split cucumbers. Combine remaining ingredients; heat to boiling and pour over cucumbers. Drain syrup from cucumbers each morning for 4 days; reheat and pour over cucumbers. Let cucumbers cool in syrup before covering. The last morning, tie cloth over jar; place weight on top. Pickles can be used in 2 weeks.

Judy Gibson
Harpeth Council

SOUR PICKLES

Slice small cucumbers; place in pint jars. Pour cold water over them; seal. Put in refrigerator overnight. Next morning, drain water off. Bring to boil:

1 gal. vinegar   2 c. salt (canning)
4 c. sugar

Pour over slices; seal again. Ready to eat in 3 weeks.
Linda Earp
Clarksville Council

CRISPY SWEET PICKLE

Slice 1 gallon sour pickles (whole) in 1/4 inch slices. Let stand in ice water 1 hour; drain.

1 box pickling spice   1 c. white vinegar
5 lb. white sugar   1 garlic clove

Layer pickles with sugar and spices until all are used. Add vinegar and sliced garlic on top of this in a crock or Tupperware container. Stir every day for 8 days. Pack into sterilized jars. Refrigerate before eating.

Mary Jane Bailey
Green Hills Council

SWEET CUCUMBER PICKLES

Put 1 gallon cucumbers in gallon jar and cover with vinegar and scant 1 tablespoon salt. Let stand 6 weeks in this. Take out and slice like bread and butter pickles. Put in pint jars with 1 cup sugar to each pint; seal.

Judy Gibson
Harpeth Council

YELLOW CUCUMBER SWEET PICKLES

Cucumbers   3 Tbsp. pickling spice
2 c. pickling lime   1/2 c. water
1 1/2 qt. vinegar   1 tsp. turmeric
9 c. sugar   4 tsp. salt

Peel and seed a grocery sack full of yellow cucumbers. Soak cucumbers for 24 hours in a solution of 2 gallons water and 2 cups pickling lime. At the end of 24 hours, wash the pickles 6 times in cool water, then soak for another 24 hours in a solution of vinegar, sugar, pickling spice, water, turmeric and salt. Boil about 15 minutes and pack into hot jars.

Doris Pursley
Harpeth Council

DILL PICKLES

3/4 c. sugar
1/2 c. salt
1 qt. vinegar
1 qt. water

3 Tbsp. mixed pickling spices
30-40 medium cucumbers, cut
   in halves lengthwise
Green or dry dill

Combine sugar, salt, vinegar and water. Tie spices in a cheesecloth bag; add to vinegar mixture. Simmer 15 minutes. Pack cucumbers into hot jars, leaving 1/4 inch head space. Put a head of dill in each jar. Heat brine to boiling. Pour boiling hot vinegar mixture over cucumbers, leaving 1/4 inch head space. Adjust caps. Process pints and quarts 15 minutes in boiling water bath. Yield: About 7 pints.

Judy Gibson
Harpeth Council

DILL PICKLES

1 gal. cucumbers
2 qt. water
1 qt. pure vinegar
1 c. plain salt

2 flowering sprigs of dill
2 buttons garlic
1 Tbsp. mixed spices per qt.

Pack washed cucumbers in sterilized jars. Place remaining ingredients in a pan and bring to a boil. Pour over cucumbers while boiling hot; seal.

Judy Gibson
Harpeth Council

DILL PICKLES

3/4 c. sugar
1/2 c. salt
1 qt. vinegar
2 1/2 qt. water
1/2 tsp. mustard seed
  (per jar)
1/2 tsp. celery seed (per
  jar)

1 pod hot pepper (per jar)
1 Tbsp. mixed pickling spice
1 dill head (fresh, per jar)
1 garlic clove (per jar)
1 onion slice (per jar)
30 to 40 cucumbers

Wash freshly picked cucumbers. Sterilize jars (quart size). Combine sugar, salt, vinegar and water. Tie mixed pickling spice in cheesecloth bag; add to vinegar mixture.

Bring to a boil for 5 minutes. Put a head of dill, onion, garlic, hot pepper, mustard seed and celery seed in each jar. Pack cucumbers in jar, leaving 1/4 inch head space. Pour boiling hot vinegar mixture over cucumbers; seal jars. Wait 1 week before serving.

Maxine Scott
East Memphis Council

ICE-WATER PICKLES

1 gal. cucumbers   1/2 c. salt
2 pt. crushed ice

Slice cucumbers thin, or in strips. Cover with ice and salt; let stand till ice is melted. Drain; drop cucumbers in following mixture:

4 c. sugar   1 Tbsp. turmeric
4 c. vinegar   1 Tbsp. mustard seed
1 Tbsp. ground cloves   2 Tbsp. celery seed

Let this come to a boil before dropping cucumbers. Let stand till color changes. Pack in hot jars and seal.

Judy Gibson
Harpeth Council

FREEZER PICKLES

Combine:
2 qt. cucumbers, sliced thin   2 Tbsp. salt
1 large onion, sliced thin

Let stand 2 hours; drain well. Pack in freezer containers, leaving 1 inch head space. Mix:

2/3 c. oil   2/3 c. sugar or 4 tsp. liquid
2/3 c. vinegar   sweetener
                1 tsp. dill (optional)

Pour into container to cover. Seal and freeze or refrigerate. Makes 2 quarts.

Betty J. Cowherd
Andrew Jackson Council

FROZEN CUCUMBER PICKLES
(Taste like bread and butter pickles.)

2 qt. unpeeled cucumbers,   2 Tbsp. salt
   thinly sliced   1 1/2 c. sugar
1 large onion, sliced   1/2 c. vinegar

Sprinkle salt over sliced cucumbers and onions; let stand 2 hours, then drain off water. Combine sugar and vinegar; pour over pickles. Let stand 10 minutes. Stir and place pickles into freezer containers. Keep frozen at least 2 days before eating. Thaw at room temperature, then keep refrigerated. Pickles will keep well in the freezer for a year.

Doris Pursley
Harpeth Council

FREEZER COLE SLAW

1 1/2 c. vinegar   2 c. sugar
1/2 c. water

Combine vinegar, water and sugar in saucepan; bring to boil. Boil 2 minutes; cool.

1 large head cabbage,   1 tsp. salt
   chopped   3 sweet peppers (red if
1 tsp. celery seed   possible), chopped
1 tsp. mustard seed   3 carrots, chopped
1/2 c. horseradish

Mix all of the ingredients together. Can be frozen or will keep in refrigerator 3 weeks. No need to seal.

Mrs. Dennis Rhea
Knoxville Council

FROZEN CUCUMBERS

2 qt. peeled and sliced   1 large onion, thinly sliced
   cucumbers   1 1/2 c. sugar
2 Tbsp. salt   1/2 c. white vinegar

Combine first 3 ingredients; refrigerate in covered container for 24 hours. Drain; add sugar and vinegar. Let stand in refrigerator 24 hours again. Put in freezer container and freeze.

Barbara S. Stanfill
Harpeth Council

GREEN TOMATO CHOW CHOW

1 gal. green tomatoes	1 c. onion
1 medium head cabbage	3 c. vinegar
6 pods bell peppers	2 c. sugar
6 small hot peppers (red and green)	2 Tbsp. plain salt

Bring vinegar and sugar to a boil. Combine other ingredients and add together. Simmer 20 minutes, stirring often. Pour into sterilized jars and seal.

Joyce Mattice
Harpeth Council

GREEN TOMATO PICKLE

7 lb. green tomatoes (real green and solid, average 4 medium tomatoes to 1 lb.)	5 lb. white sugar
	3 pt. apple cider vinegar
	1 tsp. cloves
	1 tsp. ginger
3 c. household lime (do not use pickling lime)	1 tsp. allspice
	1 tsp. celery flakes or seed
2 gal. water	1 tsp. cinnamon

Dissolve lime in water thoroughly. Slice tomatoes 1/4 inch thick; add to lime water. Soak for 24 hours. Remove tomatoes from lime water; drain, thoroughly removing all lime. Add tomatoes to 2 gallons fresh water; soak for 4 hours, changing water every hour. Lift tomatoes gently from last soaking and place in an enameled container (do not use an aluminum container). Dissolve sugar and spices in 3 pints of apple cider vinegar. Bring liquid to a boil; pour over tomatoes and let stand overnight. Next morning, boil for approximately 1 hour; syrup should not be allowed to thicken. Seal while hot. Yield: 8-11 pints.

Mrs. J.R. Minter
Nashville Council

MRS. HUFFMAN'S MUSTARD PICKLES

1 gal. vinegar   1 box dry mustard
1/2 c. salt

Mix all ingredients (do not heat). Put small cucumbers in mixture. They will be ready to eat in 3-4 days. Store in crock or jar. These pickles go good with cheese sandwiches.

Nancy Bess Lord
Harpeth Council

KRAUT

Wash cabbage; discard the core and shred. To each 5 pounds of shredded cabbage, use 2 ounces of pickling salt. Pack into a large crock container, mixing salt and cabbage together well with hands. Set a plate or saucer on top and weight it down. This keeps the cabbage packed down firmly so the liquid it makes stays above the top of the kraut. Lightly cover container with a cloth and leave undisturbed in an unairconditioned room for 10 days. A small amount of mold may form, but this doesn't hurt the kraut. Discard the top part of the kraut which has discolored. Package and freeze any that is not to be used soon.

Barbara Stanfill
Harpeth Council

OLD FASHION PEPPER JELLY

24 red sweet peppers   2 Tbsp. salt

Grind all together. Let stand 3 hours, then drain and wash.

4 lb. sugar   1 qt. vinegar

Mix sugar, vinegar and peppers together; let boil 1/2 hour. Seal in sterilized jars. (This is no trouble at all. It will thicken at once and it is really good.)

Lucille Britt
Clarksville Council

684

PEAR HONEY

Peel 6 pounds pears and cut up (28-30 pears). Grind pears, large cutter. Cook juice and pears together; add 4 pounds sugar. Cook until thick, 1 hour approximately, stirring frequently. Add 1 large can crushed pineapple; cook 20 minutes longer. Put into hot jars and seal. Makes 8 pints.

Mrs. Lucille Britt
Clarksville Council

PICKLED OKRA

1 clove garlic per pt.
1 pod hot pepper per pt.
1 tsp. dill seed per pt.
1 qt. vinegar

1 c. water
1/2 c. salt
Okra (try to use uniform
size pods)

Place garlic and pepper in bottom of hot jar. Wash and dry okra; remove part of stem of okra pod. Pack firmly in jars; add dill seed. Bring vinegar, water and salt to boiling, then simmer for 5 minutes. Pour over okra; seal jars. Makes about 6 pints. Ready to enjoy in 8 weeks.

Mary R. Veal
Chattanooga Council

PICKLED OKRA

Select small, firm pods of okra. Pack in jars, leaving part of the stem. Add to each jar:

1 tsp. dill seed
1 garlic button

1 small hot pepper

Bring to boil 1/2 gallon vinegar and 1 cup salt. Pour over okra and seal; let stand 6 weeks before using.

Judy Gibson
Harpeth Council

PICKLED OKRA

2 lb. fresh okra (about
  2 1/2 or 3 inches long)
5 pods hot red or green
  pepper
5 cloves garlic
1 qt. white vinegar

1/2 c. water
6 Tbsp. salt
1 Tbsp. celery or mustard
  seed
1/4 c. sugar

Wash okra and pack in 5 hot sterilized pint jars. Add 1 pepper and 1 clove of garlic to each jar. Bring rest of ingredients to boil; pour over okra. Seal. If you want to remove rings from jars, additional heat will have to be applied to get a stronger seal. Either place jars under pressure or in a pressure cooker for 1 minute or in boiling water bath for 2 minutes. If you do not wish to remove rings, the extra heating is not necessary. Pickles will be ready to eat in 6 to 8 weeks.

Joyce Mattice
Harpeth Council

SUMMER SAUSAGE

5 lb. hamburger
3 Tbsp. meat tenderizer
2 1/2 tsp. coarse black
  pepper

2 1/2 tsp. garlic powder
2 1/2 tsp. mustard seed
2 1/2 tsp. liquid smoke
1/4 tsp. red pepper

Mix all ingredients in large pan with hands. Seal in airtight container; refrigerate. Knead each day for 5 minutes for 4 days. On the fourth day, make into 6 sticks about as round as a half dollar. Place on broiler pan rack and bake at 225° for 5 to 6 hours. Sticks become red and shiny when done. May be eaten warm or cold. Can be wrapped in foil or plastic and frozen.

Betty Finchum
Morristown Council

SQUASH PICKLES

8 c. sliced squash
4 white onions, sliced

2 peppers (1 red, 1 green)
1/2 c. coarse salt

Combine above ingredients; mix and cover with ice. Let stand 3 hours. Make syrup of the following ingredients.

| 3 c. sugar | 1 Tbsp. mustard seed |
| 3 c. vinegar | 1 tsp. celery seed |

Bring syrup to boil; add previous mixture of vegetables. Boil 3 minutes; can and seal.

Judy Gibson
Harpeth Council

SQUASH PICKLES

8 c. thinly sliced squash	4 Tbsp. salt
2 c. thinly sliced onion	2 Tbsp. celery seeds
4 bell peppers, thinly sliced	2 Tbsp. mustard seeds
2 c. vinegar	3 c. sugar

Combine squash, onion and peppers; sprinkle with salt. Let stand 1 hour; drain off liquid. Mix in saucepan the remaining ingredients; bring to a hard boil. Add squash, onion and peppers; bring to another boil. Fill jars and seal. Makes 4 pints.

Maxine Scott
East Memphis Council

CUCUMBER RELISH

2 qt. chopped cucumbers	1 Tbsp. turmeric
(about 4 medium-large)	1/2 c. salt
2 c. chopped sweet red	1 Tbsp. mustard seed
peppers (about 4 medium)	2 tsp. whole cloves
2 c. chopped sweet green	2 tsp. whole allspice
peppers (about 4 medium)	2 sticks cinnamon
1 c. chopped onion	1 1/2 c. brown sugar, packed
	1 qt. vinegar

Combine cucumbers, peppers and onion; sprinkle with turmeric. Dissolve salt in 2 quarts cold water; pour over vegetables. Let stand 3 to 4 hours; drain. Cover vegetables with cold water; let stand 1 hour. Drain thoroughly. Tie spices in a cheesecloth bag; add to sugar and vinegar. Heat to boiling; pour over vegetables. Cover; let stand 12 to 18 hours in a cool place. Simmer until vegetables are hot; bring to boiling. Pack, boiling hot, into sterilized jars, leaving 1/8 inch head space. Adjust caps. Yield: About 6 pints.

Judy Gibson
Harpeth Council

CUCUMBER RELISH

12 cucumbers, peeled and chopped

5 onions, chopped

Mix together; sprinkle salt over and let stand 3 hours.

1 lb. sugar
2 2/3 c. vinegar

1 tsp. celery seed
1 tsp. turmeric

Combine and bring to boil. Add cucumbers and onions; bring to boil for about 8 minutes. Pour into sterilized jars and seal.

Joyce Mattice
Harpeth Council

HOT DOG RELISH

4 c. ground onions
1 medium head cabbage
(4 c. ground)
10 green tomatoes (4 c. ground)
12 green peppers
6 sweet red peppers

1/2 c. salt
6 c. sugar
1 Tbsp. celery seed
2 Tbsp. mustard seed
1 1/2 tsp. turmeric
4 c. cider vinegar
2 c. sugar

Grind vegetables, using coarse blade. Sprinkle with 1/2 cup salt; let stand overnight. Rinse and drain. Combine remaining ingredients; pour over vegetable mixture. Heat to boiling; simmer 3 minutes. Seal in hot, sterilized jars. Makes 8 pints.

Judy Gibson
Harpeth Council

FIG PRESERVES
(Excellent)

2 gal. (32 c.) figs
32 c. sugar

16 c. water
1 lemon

Sprinkle 1 cup baking soda over the figs. Cover with boiling water; let stand 15 minutes. Drain, then rinse in cold water. Cook sugar and water until sugar has dissolved and liquid is boiling. Gradually put in figs and cook until they are tender and transparent, about 1 1/2 hours. Lift figs out and cook syrup until consistency of honey. Return figs to syrup; let stand 12 hours before sealing.

Maxine Scott
East Memphis Council

FROZEN STRAWBERRY JAM

2 c. crushed strawberries
4 c. sugar

1 (1 3/4 oz.) box Sure-Jell

Stir sugar into fruit; let stand 10 minutes. Mix 3/4 cup water and 1 box Sure-Jell in saucepan. Bring to boil; boil 1 minute, stirring constantly. Remove from heat and stir into fruit mixture. Continue stirring 3 minutes. Pour into containers at once. Cover with lids; set at room temperature 24 hours. Freeze. Makes 5 to 6 cups jam. Very good as a topping for many dessert. One quart berries makes about 2 cups crushed berries.

Margaret McCafferty
Nashboro Council

Joyce Mattice
Harpeth Council
Nancy Bess Lord
Harpeth Council

WATERMELON PRESERVES

1 lb. watermelon rind cubes
2 qt. water
2 Tbsp. lime (calcium oxide)

2 c. sugar
1 qt. water
1/2 lemon

Trim off outer green skin and pink flesh, using only greenish white parts of rind. Cut rind into 1 inch cubes and weigh. Soak cubes for 3 1/2 hours in lime water (2 quarts water and 2 tablespoons lime). Drain and place cubes in clear water 1 hour. Again, drain off water and boil 1 1/2 hours in fresh water, then drain. Make a syrup of 2 cups sugar and 1 quart water. Add rind; boil 1 hour. As syrup thickens, add 1/2 lemon, thinly sliced, for each pound of fruit. When the syrup begins to thicken and the melon is clear, the preserves are ready. Pack preserves into hot, sterilized jars. Add enough syrup to cover and seal.

Jane York
Harpeth Council

** NOTES **

690

CRAFTS

&

MISCELLANEOUS

VIRGINIA KADERABEK

SUBSTITUTION CHART

	Instead of:	Use
Baking	1 teaspoon baking powder	$1/4$ teaspoon soda plus $1/2$ teaspoon cream of tartar
	1 tablespoon cornstarch (for thickening)	2 tablespoons flour or 1 tablespoon tapioca
	1 cup sifted all-purpose flour	1 cup plus 2 tablespoons sifted cake flour
	1 cup sifted cake flour	1 cup minus 2 tablespoons sifted all-purpose flour
	1 cup fine dry bread crumbs	$3/4$ cup fine cracker crumbs
Dairy	1 cup buttermilk	1 cup sour milk or 1 cup yogurt
	1 cup heavy cream	$3/4$ cup skim milk plus $1/3$ cup butter
	1 cup light cream	$7/8$ cup skim milk plus 3 tablespoons butter
	1 cup sour cream	$7/8$ cup sour milk plus 3 tablespoons butter
	1 cup sour milk	1 cup milk plus 1 tablespoon vinegar or lemon juice or 1 cup buttermilk
Seasoning	1 teaspoon allspice	$1/2$ teaspoon cinnamon plus $1/8$ teaspoon cloves
	1 cup catsup	1 cup tomato sauce plus $1/2$ cup sugar plus 2 tablespoons vinegar
	1 clove of garlic	$1/8$ teaspoon garlic powder or $1/8$ teaspoon instant minced garlic or $3/4$ teaspoon garlic salt or 5 drops of liquid garlic
	1 teaspoon Italian spice	$1/4$ teaspoon each oregano, basil, thyme, rosemary plus dash of cayenne
	1 tablespoon lemon juice	$1/2$ teaspoon vinegar
	1 tablespoon mustard	1 teaspoon dry mustard
	1 medium onion	1 tablespoon dried minced onion or 1 teaspoon onion powder
Sweet	1 1-ounce square chocolate	$1/4$ cup cocoa plus 1 teaspoon shortening
	$1 2/3$ ounces semisweet chocolate	1 ounce unsweetened chocolate plus 4 teaspoons granulated sugar
	1 cup honey	1 to $1 1/4$ cups sugar plus $1/4$ cup liquid or 1 cup corn syrup or molasses
	1 cup granulated sugar	1 cup packed brown sugar or 1 cup corn syrup, molasses or honey, reducing liquid by $1/4$ cup.

MAKING CANDLES

Preparing the wick: Soak a husky string the length you desire in the following solution -

1 Tbsp. salt	1 c. water
2 Tbsp. borax	

Dissolve and allow wicks to soak overnight; hang up to dry. When dry, dip the string in melted wax to stiffen. This will make it easier to insert in desired mold. Cottage cheese and milk cartons, cups, toilet paper and paper towel rolls make excellent molds for candles.

Quick Method: Melt old candles and paraffin together over hot water. Wax is highly inflammable and might catch on fire over direct heat. If a desired color is needed, melt crayons in with wax. Pour into mold around treated wick. Allow to harden in refrigerator overnight. Remove carton and your candle is ready.

Frosted Method: Wax may be allowed to cool until a film forms on top and then it can be whipped and poured in mold. Use a fork to put the fluffy wax around candle after it is molded to look like snow.

Dip Method: This is my favorite way. Just heat your wax in a deep juice can and start dipping the string in and out of the wax, allowing it to cool between dippings.

Mother used to keep us quiet and interested for hours on a cold, snowy night. We would place our candles out in the snow to chill. For a candle that dripped different colors, we would string our old crayons onto the wick by putting a hot ice pick through them and then dipping in melted paraffin.

Dinah Randolph
Harpeth Council

APPLE HEAD DOLLS

Use hard white apples. Peel the apple carefully, leaving a real smooth surface; do not bruise. A bit of peel left on the small end of the apple will make a wart for a witch's chin. Hollow out the blossom end of the apple to about half its depth and insert a wooden clothespin. This serves 3 purposes: It's a drying rack for the head; it makes a good

handle while carving the face; it's also the neck of the finished doll. Carve the face with a pocket knife. Shape the
nose by taking small pieces of apple between and below the
eye socket. This will form the bridge of the nose. Be
generous because the features will shrink as the face dries.
Cut off a flat piece below the nose to form the chin and
lower jaw line. Ears may be formed by making a thin slice
on each side of the head. Leave the bottom of the slice
attached so the ears will curl when drying. Stick the
clothespin in a glass and let apple dry for 3 weeks. Make
the framework for the doll out of twisted wire. Use bits of
cotton to pad the body. Wrap with string to hold cotton in
place, then cover with old hose or stretchy material. Dress
your doll to suit your fancy! Dye cotton to make hair.
Glue to head. Leave cotton white for old folks. Practice
will make you perfect!

Dinah Randolph
Harpeth Council

"CORN SHUCK DOLLS"
(America's First Dolls)

Steps in making: Use shucks that are a year old. 1.
Corn husks must first be cut from their woody bases. Braid
corn silk to be used for hair. 2. Soak husks in warm water
to make pliable. Tie in the middle to make waist. 3. Rolled
up husks are used to stuff body. 4. A second string com-
pletes the chest of body. 5. The arms are tied onto the
body. Later they will be tied to form hands. 6. A separate
piece of husk forms a shawl when crossed. Another piece
makes a belt. 7. Braided corn silk has been added to form
a wig and face features are drawn on the face. 8. In fin-
ishing the product, small pieces of husk may be used to
make hats, umbrellas, purses and other articles of dress.
Create your own dolls and decorate a pioneer Christmas tree.

Dinah Randolph
Harpeth Council

DRIED MOCK-ORANGE FLOWERS

Cut green mock-oranges in 1/8 inch slices and place in
a sunny, airy place. They dry nicely on a wire rack. Do
not leave outside at night or in the rain. In a week, they
will develop a woodlike texture and will be a bright gold
color. You can add color with spray paint or floral spray

692

color. Use a floral wire to run through center for stem.
Place a little Elmer's glue in the center and sprinkle wild
bird seeds in glue. These flowers can be attached to
branches for floral arrangements.

PATRIOTIC TABLE DECORATION

Elmer's glue
1 (2 inch) sq. styrofoam
1 (4 inch) sq. styrofoam
1 paper towel tube
4 flags
Tinsel
Floral wire

Ribbon (either red, white or
  blue)
Red, white, blue striped
  paper
8 toilet tissue tubes
Toothpicks
White lightweight cardboard

1. Cover towel and tissue tubes with striped paper.
2. Cut round circle the size of the end of the tubes from
white cardboard. Glue circle on one end of each tube. Cut
small piece of tinsel and glue on circle to give the appear-
ance of a lighted fuse. 3. Center the 2 inch square of
styrofoam on the 4 inch square of styrofoam and secure the
two squares together with toothpicks. 4. Mount tne covered towel tube on the center of the 2 inch square of stryo-
foam by pushing tube into styrofoam. 5. Mount 4 of the
tissue tubes on four corners of the 2 inch square of styrofoam at a 45° angle. 6. Mount remaining 4 tissue tubes
inside center of 4 inch square at 45° angle. 7. Tie small
ribbon bows and fill in spaces on base. 8. Add one flag
to each side of the arrangement at a 45° angle.

HELPFUL HINTS - BAKING CAKES

To make cakes bake level, wrap material (thickness of
pan) wet, not dripping, around pan and pin. An old
kitchen towel is suitable. Bake as normal and remove
material after cake is done.

If problems arise when cake crumbs rolling up on
icing, freeze cake for 30 to 40 minutes. Always good to
freeze chocolate cakes prior to icing.

Sylvia Kaffer
Clarksville Council

The following are a number of suggestions that have been helpful to many homemakers. Of course, circumstances differ in each home, so that what may be a timesaver to one may not help another. However, perhaps you can benefit from these practical suggestions.

Cleaning Apron: Buy or make an apron with large pockets (or use a clothespin apron) to carry some of your rags, sponges, etc., or to use for stray items you pick up as you clean.

Paintbrush "Duster": A small 1 to 2 inch (2-5 cm) soft paintbrush can be used for dusting delicate items and hard-to-reach places (knicknacks, lampshades, picture frames, even louvered doors).

Wax Windowsills and Sash: They will be easier to dust and keep clean if, after you wash them, you coat them with a hard finish wax.

Easier Oven Cleaning: Before it becomes dirty, line the bottom with aluminum foil (also line the trays under the gas burners) and coat the interior surface with a solution of 2 tablespoons baking soda in 1 cup of warm water. Though you may have pale gray streaks on your oven walls, the muck will come off easier when cleaning. Mix a little ammonia in a pan of water. Set this in the oven overnight for easier cleaning the next day.

Protect Floor When Moving Heavy Furniture: Slip an old sock or mitten over each of the legs (you may have to use string or a rubber band to hold them up) so that the legs will not damage the floor and the piece will be easier to move.

Washing Vinyl or Formica: Simply use a mild hand soap and warm water. Do not make the solution too sudsy. Dry with a soft towel or cloth. Often the leftover pieces from bars of soap can be saved and used in this manner.

Energy Saver: Alternate hard tasks with easy ones. Start with something strenuous, such as mopping and waxing the kitchen floor and then do an easier job, such as sorting dirty clothes or mending. If you have been on your feet ironing, try to make the next job one you can do while sitting down.

Bucket "Toolbox": If you carry all your rags, cleansers, brushes, waxes and polishes, window sprays, etc., in a small bucket, it will save you hundreds of extra steps.

Venetian-Blind "Gloves": To wash venetian blinds at the window, wear a cotton glove or an old sock dipped in a pail of thick suds. Squeeze out the excess moisture.

Efficient Dusting: Use a soft, damp cloth folded into a pad so that no loose corners will catch on things or leave loose threads on them. Start with the highest items and work down. Dust after you have made the beds but before you clean with water and cleanser. Otherwise, the dust may become light mud.

Scorched Pots and Pans: Soak these overnight in bleach, diluted about 4 to 1. They may require several days to come clean. When food sticks, making the pans very messy, boil a little water in the pan and squirt in some dishwashing liquid before you remove the pan from the stove.

"Dustless" Sweeping: To keep dust from frying when you sweep, dampen the broom bristles and the inside of the dustpan. Also, controlled strokes will keep the flying dust at a minimum.

Grease Spot on Rug: Rub corn meal into the spot and vacuum it the next day.

Bathtub "Mop": To avoid bending over to remove the dirty ring from the bathtub, go to the toy department and buy yourself a child's toy wet mop. It will be the perfect size to tackle that "ring" and yet you will not have to bend over and scrub.

Shaking Out a Dust Mop: This unpleasant task can be made simpler by placing the dirty end of the dust mop (while still attached to the handle) in a large paper sack. Close the paper sack around the handle of the mop, holding it firmly shut, and then shake it. If you shake it with the handle pointing up, the dirt will settle to the bottom of the sack and can then be discarded easily.

Janet Sexton
Harpeth Council

HINTS FOR MAKING BETTER ICE CREAM

Consistency of ice cream may vary from batch to batch. Several factors that affect the firmness or consistency of ice cream are recipe used, outside temperatures, size of ice, temperature of brine and temperature of mixture before it is churned.

Too Soft: If the motor continues to run freely after 30 minutes, the brine is not cold enough, therefore the cream is not hardening. You should now add another 1/3 cup of table salt or 1/2 cup of rock salt. This will begin to reduce the brine temperature and cause the cream to harden. As the ice cream melts, you may have to continue to add ice and salt as outlined in your instructions, until the motor goes into its intended stall.

Too Grainy, Icy or Hard: If the motor stalls in less than 20 minutes, resulting in coarse or an inconsistent texture of ice cream, the brine became too cold too fast. In this case, you used too much salt and the cream froze too fast on the edge of the can and/or you failed to use crushed ice.

Carolyn Mitchell
Memphis Council

KITCHEN HINTS

A pinch of salt added to hot chocolate enhances the flavor.

A small amount of sugar added to pimento cheese improves the flavor.

A small amount of lemon juice added to tuna salad cuts the fishy taste.

Kathy Pack
Harpeth Council

MEASURES

In case you buy firewood, stone or lumber -

*Cord of wood is a pile 8 feet long, 4 feet wide and 4 feet high.

*Perch of stone is 16 1/2 feet long, 1 1/2 feet thick and 1 foot high.

*Board foot is 1 foot long, 1 foot wide and 1 inch thick.

Dinah Randolph
Harpeth Council

FRAPP ROSE'S BIRD FOOD RECIPE

2 lb. plain lard   1 lb. peanut butter
2 lb. corn meal   2 lb. wild bird seed
2 lb. flour

Melt lard at low temperature; stir in peanut butter, then add other ingredients. Store in lard cans with lids or jars in a cool place. Will last 6-8 months. All wintering

birds will be attracted to this food. Apply food to holes
or cracks in bird feeder.

Bernice Curtis
Knoxville Council

CLEANING SOLUTION FOR WALLS AND TILE

1/2 gal. hot water	1 c. white vinegar
1 c. household ammonia	1/4 c. baking soda

Mix all ingredients in a 1 gallon jar. Work from bottom
up to clean walls. No rinsing necessary. Use as needed.

Dinah Randolph
Harpeth Council

HAND CREAM

1/4 lb. unsalted butter	1 Tbsp. honey
6 oz. rose water	1/2 c. finely ground oatmeal
2 egg yolks	

Whip together and refrigerate. Rub into hands before
retiring.

Dinah Randolph
Harpeth Council

HOMEMADE LYE SOAP

1 can pure lye	5 lb. old grease, strained
3 1/2 pt. warm water	

Dissolve 1 can lye in 3 1/2 pints warm water. Allow
this mixture to cool to about 80°. Heat 5 pounds old grease
to about 120°. Slowly pour the lye into the grease. Stir
until the mixture drips from stirrer like strained honey.
Do not stir too long; it will separate, 5 to 10 minutes is
about right. Pour mixture into molds or enamel pan*.
Cover with a heavy blanket and leave for 2 days. Now, cut
your snow white bars of soap the desired size.
   *Cut soap while warm if you desire uniform blocks.

Dinah Randolph
Harpeth Council

PLAY DOUGH (FOR CHILDREN)

1 c. flour
1 c. water
1/2 c. salt

1 Tbsp. cooking oil
2 tsp. cream of tartar
Few drops of food coloring

In a heavy aluminum saucepan, mix dry ingredients. Add oil, water and food coloring. Cook 3 minutes or until mixture pulls away from side of pan; knead slightly. Store in an airtight container.

Linda Earp
Clarksville Council

SILVER CLEANER

1 large enamelware pan
1 large piece aluminum foil
Water to cover silver to
  be cleaned

1 Tbsp. soda to each qt.
  water used
About 10 minutes of time
1 soft, dry cloth

Place foil in large pan; add silverware (do not overlap). Add water quart by quart and add 1 tablespoon soda to each quart of water. Heat to boiling; remove silver. Rinse and polish with soft cloth.

Dinah Randolph
Harpeth Council

WHITEWASH

2 oz. fresh slaked lime
2 qt. sweet milk

5 lb. whiting

Dissolve lime in milk. Gradually add whiting and beat well. Add a little bluing for a clear white and 1/4 pound of salt, if desired. This makes whitewash stick better.

Dinah Randolph
Harpeth Council

BILL SULLIVAN'S SUGAR CURING PROCESS FOR MEAT

Approx. 100 lb. fresh
  pork sides for bacon

4 lb. coarse meat curing salt
1 3/4 lb. sugar
5 oz. saltpetre

698

After meat is chilled and trimmed, mix salt, sugar and saltpetre. Using 2/3 of mixture, rub entire surface of meat. Stack sides of meat on top of each other on a board with a small amount of mixture between each piece. After 4 days, repeat procedure using remaining mixture. After 8-10 days from first application, wipe meat with a damp cloth and hang in smokehouse. Smoke, if desired.

The same procedure can be used for curing ham and shoulders, except entire curing time will be 3 to 4 weeks and mixture must be applied 3 or 4 times during curing time. More mixture will probably have to be made up as you use it.

Notes: Meat curing must be done in cold weather, with temperatures just above freezing best. Curing must be carried out in an unheated building, such as a smoke-house. Care must be taken that the meat does not get too warm or it will spoil before it cures.

Barbara Stanfill
Harpeth Council

** NOTES **

INDEX OF RECIPES

1489-81

CANDY AND COOKIES

DESSERTS

1489-81

1489-81

1489-81

1489-81

1489-81

This Cookbook is a perfect gift for Holidays, Weddings, Anniversaries and Birthdays.

You may order as many of our *Dining With Pioneers* cookbooks as you wish for the price of $10.00 each or order our other cookbooks: *Answering the Call of Those in Need* (Nutritional Cookbook) and *Just Kidding Around* (Children's Cookbook) at $5.00 each.

Save postage and handling charges by picking up your books at the Chapter Pioneer Office, 333 Commerce Street, Nashville, Tennessee, Telephone No. 615-214-6764.

Tennessee Chapter No. 21
Telephone Pioneers of America
333 Commerce Street, Suite 107
Nashville, Tennessee 37201-3300

Cookbooks	Qty.	Price	Total
Dining With Pioneers, Vol. I		$10.00	
Dining With Pioneers, Vol. II		$10.00	
Answering the Call of Those in Need		$5.00	
Just Kidding Around		$5.00	
Add $2.75 postage, handling and tax per book			
Grand Total			

Please Print:

Name

Address

Work Address

Floor or Room No.

City   State   Zip

Please make check payable to Telephone Pioneers Chapter No. 21.

** NOTES **

** NOTES **

** NOTES **

** NOTES **

** NOTES **

** NOTES **